THE WRITINGS OF ST. PAUL

A NORTON CRITICAL EDITION

THE WRITINGS OF ST. PAUL

A NORTON CRITICAL EDITION

ANNOTATED TEXT
CRITICISM

Edited by

WAYNE A. MEEKS

YALE UNIVERSITY

W·W·NORTON & COMPANY·INC· *New York*

HERBERT J. MULLER, General Editor

For Martha

Contents

Part VII. Paul and Religious Experience

Epilogue

Preface

This Norton Critical Edition contains the complete extant works attributed to the man who, next to Jesus, was the most important and the most enigmatic figure in the initial stages of Christianity. Because some of these works were probably written by disciples in Paul's name, I have divided them, following a common scholarly convention, into the seven letters undoubtedly authentic and the six whose authorship is questionable. As the notes will make plain, this does not mean that I personally regard all those in the second category as inauthentic. The Letter to the Hebrews was also commonly attributed to Paul between the third and the nineteenth centuries, but I have not included it because it does not in any sense represent the Pauline school. Within each group I have endeavored to place the letters in chronological order, though dates in several cases are impossible even to approximate. The reader will thus find the order here different from that in the New Testament, where the letters have been listed since antiquity in order of diminishing length. The introductions and notes are not designed to substitute for the standard reference works named in the Bibliography, but only to give the reader an entrée into the historical milieu of Pauline Christianity. In addition they point out particularly important elements of form and style that are frequently overlooked.

The text is from the Revised Standard Version. It was chosen from the several excellent contemporary English versions now available because its relatively conservative mode of translation enables the reader to recognize certain distinctive features of Paul's style. Certain of the alternate readings indicated in marginal notes by the RSV translators have been omitted here. As in every modern translation, paragraphing and sentence divisions follow the translators' understanding of sense units; often they do not coincide with *verse* divisions, which go back to printed Greek texts of the sixteenth century.

The anthology of secondary works has two purposes: (1) to suggest some of the major ways in which these writings and the reactions to them have contributed to the shape of Christianity and of Western thought and (2) to provide representative examples of modern critical studies. The selections could be multiplied endlessly. Any specialist will think of essays he would have wished included, even at the cost of some I have chosen. But choices had to be made.

Some readers may feel that German scholarship is overrepresented in the anthology. Two things are to be said in reply: First, it is a simple fact that the overwhelming majority of works which have had wide and lasting influence on international critical scholarship for the past century have been by German authors. Second, in some instances where limits of space forced me to choose between equally important essays on a given topic, I have unhesitatingly chosen one not readily available in English. Consequently several pivotal essays are here made available in English translation for the first time. (Translations are my own unless otherwise indicated.) In the excerpted materials, only those footnotes are reproduced that are essential for the reader's understanding. For the authors' complete references to other literature and to scholarly debate, the originals must be consulted.

I am grateful to Paul W. Meyer, Fred O. Francis, Paul S. Minear, and Herbert J. Muller for suggestions for the anthology. Hans W. Frei, Nils A. Dahl, David H. Kelsey, and my wife, Martha, have read portions of the manuscript and offered important criticisms. James L. Mairs of W. W. Norton & Company has been unfailingly helpful and encouraging at every stage of the book's conception and preparation. And I must not fail to thank, though it must be anonymously, the several dozens of students whose vigorous dialogue in seminars at Indiana and Yale universities has given this book both substance and purpose.

W. A. M.
HAMDEN, CONNECTICUT
MARCH 20, 1971

Introduction

Among the scores of religious sects that offered eternal hope or present ecstasy to the diverse peoples of the Roman Empire in the middle of the first century, Christianity was not conspicuous. An impartial observer, asked which of these cults might someday become the official religion of the empire, even a world religion, would perhaps have chosen Mithraism. He certainly would not have named the inconspicuous followers of a crucified Jew. The obscurity of the factors that would produce its incredible expansion makes the story of Christianity's first three centuries one of the most baffling and fascinating chapters in the history of human civilization. Since the impartial observers of its beginnings provide no solution to the puzzle, we are forced to turn to its partisans, who were certain from the beginning that their "gospel"—the "news" about the crucified and risen Christ—was the means by which God would "have mercy upon all men."

The best known of those partisans is the subject of this anthology, because he alone of first-century Christians left a substantial literary bequest. Letters attributed to him comprise a quarter of the New Testament, and another twelfth of its pages—most of the Book of Acts—is devoted to a description of his career. Closest attention has to be paid to the letters, for they are our most direct and earliest primary sources from the beginnings of Christianity. They were not intended as literature. Paul would have been doubly astonished that they should have a place in the "history of ideas," for he had no high opinion of philosophy, and he thought he was living at the end of history. On the other hand, they are not merely private letters. They are official correspondence, directed to a variety of immediate and urgent problems confronting the newly established Christian congregations in the cities of the eastern Mediterranean. For that reason they afford a most candid glimpse into the character of those congregations as well as of the man who founded them. And indirectly they provide precious hints about the form of Christianity which existed before his conversion and about the special school he shaped, which was destined to survive him.

Christianity was never a monolithic society, but a polymorphous movement, the vector constituted by tensions in many directions. Paul embodied many of those tensions. "A Hebrew of Hebrews," he called himself, trained in the Pharisaic tradition of oral law, whose techniques never ceased to show in his arguments. Yet when he quoted the Jewish scriptures, it was not in the Hebrew of his ancestors, but in the Greek translation heard in Hellenistic synagogues of the Diaspora. Born in Tarsus of Cilicia, he had early absorbed the language, the culture, the myths of Greek syncretism. According to the Book of Acts, he was even a Roman citizen, an extraordinary status for a Jew. He had done his utmost to destroy the new sect, the followers of the crucified Jesus, for he saw in them a dangerous threat to the central legal tradition of Judaism. Yet when he became a convert, in an event so dramatic that no biographer, even the earliest one, could refrain from romanticizing it (though his letters do not describe it at all!), he became an equally zealous opponent of those who wanted to continue that legal tradition in Christianity. No wonder the letters are often polemical and the history of Paulinism has been a history of controversy.

Though the Christian movement was born in the village culture of Palestine, its future lay in the cities. Paul was preeminently a man of the city—that is apparent whenever he tries to use an agricultural metaphor. His urgent crisscrossing of the eastern provinces of the empire followed the major roads and sea routes; his letters bear the names of the population centers and trading hubs. A passionate, perhaps quixotic determination to bring a token of unity to the Christians of Jerusalem, holy city of his past, brought the last of his many arrests. Fittingly, his life ended in Rome. The earliest documents do not describe his martyrdom, which later became the subject of legend. Even the Acts' account, though it hints strongly that his two years' imprisonment in Rome ended in death, says nothing definite. Probably he died around A.D. 64, just before Nero began his well-known general persecution of the Christians of the capital. Thirty years later the bishop of that city, after alluding to Paul's martyrdom in words more eloquent than informative, added: "He taught righteousness to all the world."

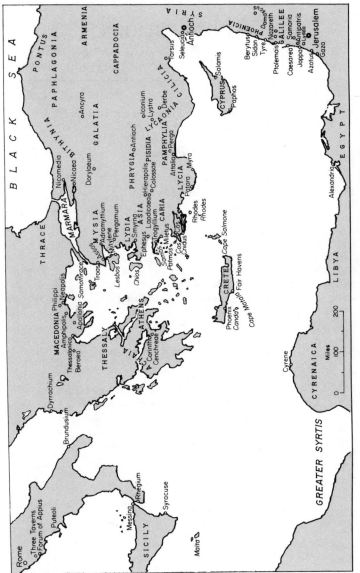

The Eastern Mediterranean in the Time of St. Paul

Abbreviations

b.	Babylonian Talmud (name of tractate follows)
1, 2 Chron.	First, Second Chronicles
Col.	Colossians
1, 2 Cor.	First, Second Corinthians
Dan.	Daniel
Deut.	Deuteronomy
Ecclus.	Ecclesiasticus (Jesus ben Sira)
Eph.	Ephesians
Ex.	Exodus
Ezek.	Ezekiel
Gal.	Galatians
Gen.	Genesis
Hab.	Habakkuk
Heb.	Hebrews, Hebrew
Hom.	Homily, Homilies (Pseudo-Clement)
Isa.	Isaiah
JB	*The Jerusalem Bible*
Jer.	Jeremiah
KJV	The King James Version (Authorized Version)
Lev.	Leviticus
lit.	literally
LXX	Septuagint (ancient Greek translation of OT)
1, 2, 3, 4 Macc.	The Books of the Maccabees
Matt.	Matthew
Mos.	Philo, *The Life of Moses*
NEB	*The New English Bible*
Neh.	Nehemiah
NT	New Testament
Num.	Numbers
OT	Old Testament
p.	Palestinian Talmud
1, 2 Pet.	First, Second Peter
Phil.	Philippians
Phlm.	Philemon
plur.	plural
Prov.	Proverbs
Ps.	Psalm, Psalms
1QS	The "Manual of Discipline" from Cave I, Qumran
4QPB	The "Patriarchal Blessings" scroll from Cave IV, Qumran

Recog.	Recognitions (Pseudo-Clement)
Rev.	Revelation (The Apocalypse)
Rom.	Romans
rp.	reprinted
RSV	The Revised Standard Version of the Bible
1, 2 Sam.	First, Second Samuel
Song	The Song of Songs (or, Song of Solomon)
1, 2 Thess.	First, Second Thessalonians
1, 2 Tim.	First, Second Timothy
Tit.	Titus
v., vv.	verse, verses
Wisd.	The Wisdom of Solomon
Zech.	Zechariah

PART I

The Undoubted Letters of St. Paul

The annotated text of the seven letters of Paul whose genuineness is beyond reasonable doubt.

THE FIRST LETTER TO THE THESSALONIANS (ca. 51)

This is the earliest of the extant letters of Paul. It was written from Corinth shortly before Paul was tried by Gallio (Acts 18:12 ff.), whose proconsulship can be dated, from an inscription found at Delphi, A.D. 51–52 (less likely, 52–53).

Thessalonica was an important port, the largest city of Macedonia. The Via Egnatia, linking Rome with the eastern provinces, ran through it, and the Romans made it the provincial capital but a free city. There, less than a year prior to the writing of this letter, Paul had established a small but vigorous Christian congregation. The letter suggests that it was composed basically of Gentiles, converted directly from paganism (1:9), although Acts pictures the mission as beginning with the synagogue (Acts 17:1–4).

Paul had been forced to leave Thessalonica abruptly (2:17), though probably after a longer stay than the three or four weeks suggested by Acts 17:2. Anxious over the fate of the new congregation, he sent Timothy from Athens (3:1–5). This return brought very good news about the church's general condition, although it had endured persecutions, and the death of some of its members had raised questions about the anticipated coming of Christ.

From the Acts' account we receive the impression that both the first Christians in Thessalonica and their opponents were Jews. In the letter itself, however, the Christians are addressed as former pagans, and their persecution by their "fellow countrymen" is clearly distinguished from the analogous persecution by the Jews experienced by Christians in Judea (2:14). The first part of Chap. 2 reads like an *apologia* by Paul, but there is no evidence that a personal attack on him had been made by anyone in Thessalonica; the defensive statements are rather typical of those by which Hellenistic missionaries, philosophers, and prophets sought to distinguish themselves from the numerous charlatans who claimed the same vocations.

The form of the letter is unusual. After the initial greeting (1:1) an extraordinarily large proportion of it is incorporated into the familiar epistolary thanksgiving (1:2–3:13), which rehearses the history of Paul's relationship with the readers: they are exemplary converts (1:2–10), as he has been an exemplary missionary (2:1–12), so that he can be thankful that they, as imitators of himself and of the Palestinian churches, have stood fast under persecution

(2:13–16). His personal concern led to the sending of Timothy, whose encouraging report occasions this letter, a temporary substitute for the apostle's own return to visit them, which he prays will be soon (2:17–3:13). The remainder of the content is subsumed under another familiar component of New Testament epistolary style, the admonitory or *parakalō*-section, so called by the verb that frequently introduces it, "I exhort you" (cf. 4:1; 5:14). This includes a traditional catechetical summary of the way of Christian "holiness" (4:2–8) and a mixture of ad hoc instructions and traditional phraseology under the headings "concerning love for the brethren (*philadelphia*)" (4:9–12), "concerning those who are asleep" (i.e., dead) (4:13–18), "Concerning the times and the seasons" (i.e., of the end of days and the return of Christ) (5:1–11), rounded off by an appeal to honor their leaders and to maintain an orderly but free and charismatic congregational life (5:12–22). Benedictions, greetings, and the adjuration that the letter be read to the assembled congregation bring it to a close (5:23–28).

---

1 Paul, Silvanus, and Timothy,[1]
To the church of the Thessalonians in God the Father and the Lord Jesus Christ:[2]
Grace to you and peace.

[2] We give thanks to God always for you all, constantly mentioning you in our prayers,[3] [3] remembering before our God and Father your work of faith and labor of love and steadfastness of hope in our Lord Jesus Christ.[4] [4] For we know, brethren beloved by God, that he has chosen you; [5] for our gospel came to you not only in word, but also in power and in the Holy Spirit and with full conviction. You know what kind of men we proved to be among you for your sake. [6] And you became imitators of us and of the Lord, for you received the word in much affliction, with joy

---

1. "Silvanus": like "Paul," a Greek name for a person known in Acts by a Hebrew name (Silas); see 2 Cor. 1:19; Acts 15:22, 32, 40; etc. The same as the writer of 1 Peter (1 Pet. 5:12)? "Timothy": see 2 Thess. 1:1; 1 Cor. 4:17; 16:10; 2 Cor. 1:1, 19; Rom. 16:21; Col. 1:1; 1 Tim. 1:2; 2 Tim. 1:2; Acts 16:1–3; 17:14 f.; 18:5; 19:22; 20:4.
2. Cf. 2 Thess. 1:1; cf. "saints in Christ Jesus," Phil. 1:1; Col. 1:2;

Eph. 1:1; hardly different in meaning from "the church of God," 1 Cor. 1:2; 2 Cor. 1:1.
3. A thanksgiving regularly began an ancient letter; Paul develops the form in an unusually free and expansive way.
4. Note the formula "faith, hope, love" as in 5:8; 1 Cor. 13:13; Col. 1:4 f.; cf. Rom. 5:1–5. "In our Lord ...": lit., "*of* our Lord . . ."

inspired by the Holy Spirit; [7] so that you became an example to all the believers in Macedonia and in Achaia:[5] [8] For not only has the word of the Lord sounded forth from you in Macedonia and Achaia, but your faith in God has gone forth everywhere, so that we need not say anything. [9] For they themselves report concerning us what a welcome we had among you, and how you turned to God from idols, to serve a living and true God, [10] and to wait for his Son from heaven, whom he raised from the dead, Jesus who delivers us from the wrath to come.[6]

2 For you yourselves know, brethren, that our visit[7] to you was not in vain; [2] but though we had already suffered and been shamefully treated at Philippi,[8] as you know, we had courage in our God to declare to you the gospel of God in the face of great opposition.[9] [3] For our appeal does not spring from error or uncleanness, nor is it made with guile; [4] but just as we have been approved by God to be entrusted with the gospel, so we speak, not to please men, but to please God who tests our hearts. [5] For we never used either words of flattery, as you know, or a cloak for greed, as God is witness; [6] nor did we seek glory from men, whether from you or from others, though we might have made demands as apostles of Christ.[1] [7] But we were gentle[2] among you, like a nurse taking care of her children. [8] So, being affectionately desirous of you, we were ready to share with you not only the gospel of God but also our own selves, because you had become very dear to us.

[9] For you remember our labor and toil, brethren; we worked night and day, that we might not burden any of you,[3] while we preached to you the gospel of God. [10] You are witnesses, and God also, how holy and righteous and blameless was our behavior to you believers; [11] for you know how, like a father with his children, we

---

5. As capital of Macedonia, Thessalonica was of strategic importance; the congregations there and at Philippi were the first we hear of on European soil (though that at Rome may have been founded a year or two earlier; see Suetonius, *Lives of the Caesars*, Claudius 25:3). Achaia was the neighboring province, of which Corinth now served as capital.

6. Vv. 9–10 provide a terse summary of the Gentile Christian preaching, perhaps a pre-Pauline formula.

7. Lit., "entrance," "arrival" as in 1:9, where the same word is translated "welcome." 2:1–12 elaborates 1:9.

8. See Acts 16:19–24.

9. Or, "with strenuous effort."

1. Vv. 3–6: cf. the defense in Gal. 1:10; 2 Cor. 2:17; 4:2–12; 12:16 f., where Paul's authority has been directly attacked. The sharp sarcasm of those passages is absent here, however;

the defense is stereotyped (see introductory note above, p. 3).

2. "Gentle" (*epioi*): several of the most ancient manuscripts read "babies" (*nepioi*), but that would produce a clash of metaphors extreme even for Paul. An early copyist evidently ·duplicated the *n* at the end of the previous word.

3. For Paul's pride in his self-support by handwork (according to Acts, tent-making) cf. 1 Cor. 9 and 2 Cor. 11:7–11. Propagandists for religious or philosophical cults were normally expected to live from the contributions of their audiences or converts. These passages show that this was the norm also in Christianity. Paul's contrasting practice agrees with that of Pharisaic teachers of Torah. He did accept money occasionally, however, especially from Philippi: Phil. 4:16; 2 Cor. 11:9.

exhorted each one of you and encouraged you and charged you [12] to lead a life worthy of God, who calls you into his own kingdom and glory.

[13] And we also thank God constantly for this, that when you received the word of God which you heard from us, you accepted it not as the word of men but as what it really is, the word of God, which is at work in you believers. [14] For you, brethren, became imitators of the churches of God in Christ Jesus which are in Judea; for you suffered the same things from your own countrymen[4] as they did from the Jews, [15] who killed both the Lord Jesus and the prophets,[5] and drove us out, and displease God and oppose all men[6] [16] by hindering us from speaking to the Gentiles that they may be saved—so as always to fill up the measure of their sins. But God's wrath has come upon them at last![7]

[17] But since we were bereft of you, brethren, for a short time, in person not in heart, we endeavored the more eagerly and with great desire to see you face to face; [18] because we wanted to come to you—I, Paul, again and again—but Satan[8] hindered us. [19] For what is our hope or joy or crown of boasting before our Lord Jesus at his coming?[9] Is it not you? [20] For you are our glory and joy.

3 Therefore when we could bear it no longer, we were willing to be left behind at Athens alone,[1] [2] and we sent Timothy, our

4. "Countrymen": the word suggests a common ethnic background, but here probably in a very loose, local sense. Contrasted with "the Jews" of Judea, it means the pagan population of Thessalonica.

5. The earliest instance of the tendency in Christian literature to put the entire blame for Jesus' execution on "the Jews"; cf. Acts 2:23, 36; 3:14 f.; Luke 23:25; Matt. 27:25; Mark 12:8. The martyrdom of the prophets (cf. 1 Kings 19:10, quoted by Paul, Rom. 11:3) became a prominent motif in Jewish legend; in the NT see Matt. 23:31 ff.; Mark 12:5; Luke 13:34. Evidently Christian apologetic very early connected Jesus' death with this tradition: cf. Acts 7:52.

6. Contempt for the gods and hatred of humanity were charges frequently made by anti-Semitic pamphleteers of Alexandria and Rome; from Paul the statement is astonishing. The whole of v. 15 is in solemn rhetorical style, produced by a series of rhyming words: *apokteinantōn, ekdioxantōn, mē areskontōn, enantiōn.* The basis for Paul's hostile statement, which contrasts so severely with his attitude elsewhere, is given in v. 16: the opposition by Jews (Judeans?) to his gentile mission.

7. Or, "completely." In Wisd. 16:5; 19:1, a similar phrase contrasts the punishment by God of Israel, "not to the end," with his destruction of the Egyptians, "to the end." "Forever" is also a possible translation, though that would make the contradiction of Rom. 9–11 absolute. On the revelation of "the wrath of God" against all men, "the Jew first and also the Greek," see Rom. 1:18–3:20.

8. "Satan": a Semitic word; Paul does not use the Greek equivalent *diabolos,* which appears however in Eph. and the Pastorals. Cf. 1 Cor. 5:5; 7:5; 2 Cor. 2:11; 11:14; 12:7; Rom. 16:20; 2 Thess. 2:9. What empirical circumstances "hindered" Paul cannot be determined.

9. The word *parousia,* "presence," had acquired in the Hellenistic period the technical usage "arrival," "visit," "appearance," particularly of divinities and kings. In the NT this technical sense is applied to the return of the exalted Christ, connected with the other events associated with the end of the age in Jewish eschatology, notably the final judgment.

1. Since the 1st person plur. is used ambiguously by Paul (often = "I"), it is debated whether Paul and Silvanus or Paul alone stayed in Athens. Cf. Acts 17:15; 18:1, 5.

brother and God's servant[2] in the gospel of Christ, to establish you in your faith and to exhort you, [3] that no one be moved by these afflictions. You yourselves know that this is to be our lot. [4] For when we were with you, we told you beforehand that we were to suffer affliction,[3] just as it has come to pass, and as you know. [5] For this reason, when I could bear it no longer, I sent that I might know your faith, for fear that somehow the tempter[4] had tempted you and that our labor would be in vain.

[6] But now that Timothy has come to us from you, and has brought us the good news of your faith and love and reported that you always remember us kindly and long to see us, as we long to see you—— [7] for this reason, brethren, in all our distress and affliction we have been comforted about you through your faith; [8] for now we live, if you stand fast in the Lord. [9] For what thanksgiving can we render to God for you, for all the joy which we feel for your sake before our God, [10] praying earnestly night and day that we may see you face to face and supply what is lacking in your faith?[5]

[11] Now may our God and Father himself, and our Lord Jesus, direct our way to you; [12] and may the Lord make you increase and abound in love to one another and to all men, as we do to you, [13] so that he may establish your hearts unblamable in holiness before our God and Father, at the coming[6] of our Lord Jesus with all his saints.[7]

4 Finally, brethren, we beseech and exhort you in the Lord Jesus, that as you learned from us[8] how you ought to live and to please God, just as you are doing, you do so more and more. [2] For

2. Some texts read "our brother and God's fellow worker," which is so unusual (but not un-Pauline: 1 Cor. 3:9) it may be the original reading; the several variant readings can all be explained as attempts to "correct" it.
3. That afflictions were *destined* for the Christians seems thus to have been a regular part of the instruction of new converts (cf. 1 Pet. *passim*). This may derive from the apocalyptic notion that a period of distress would precede the Messiah's coming (cf. 2 Thess. 2:3–12), but it was also soon connected with the suffering of Jesus (see 2 Cor. 4:7–12; Phil. 3:10 f.; 1 Pet. 2:19–24; 3:16–18; 4:1, 12–19).
4. "The tempter" = Satan (see on 2:18), so called also in Matt. 4:3.
5. This third recurrence of the basic thanksgiving formula (see 1:2; 2:13) sums up the whole first section of the letter and leads to the prayer in solemn, liturgical style that concludes this

portion (vv. 11–13). The rhetorical and liturgical style of the whole section (1:2–3:13) shows that the letter was dictated with the awareness it would be read in public worship (see 5:27); it is not just private "correspondence," though it is quite personal and connected with a specific occasion.
6. *Parousia*, as in 2:19 and 5:23. Eschatological notes in Pauline thanksgivings are common; the number of them here (1:10; 2:19; cf. 2:12, 16; 3:3 f.) points ahead to the questions dealt with in Chaps. 4 and 5.
7. "His saints": although the OT text lying behind this image, "The Lord my God will come, and all the *holy ones* with him" (Zech. 14:5, LXX), refers to the angels (cf. Mark 8:38; 13:27; 2 Thess. 1:7; Jude 14), Paul ordinarily uses the term to mean "Christians."
8. A technical term meaning "received as tradition."

you know what instructions we gave you through the Lord Jesus.[9]
[3] For this is the will of God, your sanctification: that you abstain
from immorality;[1] [4] that each one of you know how to take a wife
for himself[2] in holiness and honor, [5] not in the passion of lust like
heathen who do not know God; [6] that no man transgress, and
wrong his brother in this matter, because the Lord is an avenger in
all these things, as we solemnly forewarned you. [7] For God has not
called us for uncleanness, but in holiness. [8] Therefore whoever disregards this, disregards not man but God, who gives his Holy Spirit
to you.

[9] But concerning[3] love of the brethren you have no need to have
any one write to you, for you yourselves have been taught by God
to love one another; [10] and indeed you do love all the brethren
throughout Macedonia. But we exhort you, brethren, to do so
more and more, [11] to aspire to live quietly, to mind your own
affairs, and to work with your hands, as we charged you; [12] so that
you may command the respect of outsiders, and be dependent on
nobody.

[13] But we would not have you ignorant, brethren, concerning
those who are asleep, that you may not grieve as others do who
have no hope.[4] [14] For since we believe that Jesus died and rose
again, even so, through Jesus, God will bring with him those who
have fallen asleep. [15] For this we declare to you by the word of the
Lord,[5] that we who are alive, who are left until the coming of the
Lord, shall not precede those who have fallen asleep. [16] For the
Lord himself will descend from heaven with a cry of command,
with the archangel's call, and with the sound of the trumpet of
God. And the dead in Christ will rise first; [17] then we who are
alive, who are left, shall be caught up together with them in the

---

9. Vv. 3–9 are an example of such a
catechetical tradition, a pithy, hellenized summary of Lev. 18, whose key
word is "holiness." Perhaps it was
adapted by Christians from the diaspora synagogue (n.b. v. 5) for pre- or
post-baptismal instruction (cf. 1 Pet.
1:15 f.).
1. Cf. Acts 15:20, 29. *Porneia* is not
"immorality" in general, but specifically illicit sexual acts, "fornication."
2. Lit., "his own vessel, container, instrument." Interpretation of the metaphor is divided between "his body,"
which would fit common Greek usage,
and "his wife," which would accord
with the Hebrew equivalent in rabbinic
usage and better fit the traditional
context here.
3. As in 1 Cor. 7:1, 25; 8:1; 12:1, the
expression "but concerning . . ." (*peri
de*: 4:9, 13; 5:1) introduces a question
raised by the readers—though whether
in a letter, as in 1 Cor., or only by

Timothy's oral report, we cannot tell.
4. Presumably the death of some of
the Thessalonian Christians has raised
difficulties about the nature of the "deliverance" promised by the Son whom
they "await" (1:10); evidently Paul's
preaching, like that of the earliest
Christians in general, included Christ's
imminent *parousia* (compare 4:17 with
Mark 9:1). The explanation here is in
apocalyptic style. "To fall asleep" is a
common euphemism for "to die" and
says nothing about the specifically
Christian or Jewish belief in resurrection.
5. "Word of the Lord" may refer to a
saying of Jesus otherwise unknown (cf.
1 Cor. 7:10, 12, 25), but more likely
to an apocalypse received by a Christian prophet (cf. Rev. 1:1). Vv. 15–17
may be a direct quotation of this
"word"; the particle "that" is frequently equivalent to a quotation
mark.

cloud to meet the Lord in the air; and so we shall always be with the Lord. **18** Therefore comfort one another with these words.

5 But as to the times and the seasons, brethren, you have no need to have anything written to you. **2** For you yourselves know well that the day of the Lord will come like a thief in the night.[6] **3** When people say, "There is peace and security," then sudden destruction will come upon them as travail comes upon a woman with child, and there will be no escape. **4** But you are not in darkness, brethren, for that day to surprise you like a thief. **5** For you are all sons of light and sons of the day; we are not of the night or of darkness.[7] **6** So then let us not sleep, as others do, but let us keep awake and be sober. **7** For those who sleep sleep at night, and those who get drunk are drunk at night. **8** But, since we belong to the day, let us be sober, and put on the breastplate of faith and love, and for a helmet the hope of salvation. **9** For God has not destined us for wrath, but to obtain salvation through our Lord Jesus Christ, **10** who died for us so that whether we wake or sleep[8] we might live with him. **11** Therefore encourage one another and build one another up, just as you are doing.

12 But we beseech you, brethren, to respect those who labor among you and are over you in the Lord and admonish you,[9] **13** and to esteem them very highly in love because of their work. Be at peace among yourselves. **14** And we exhort you, brethren, admonish the idle, encourage the fainthearted, help the weak, be patient with them all. **15** See that none of you repays evil for evil, but always seek to do good to one another and to all. **16** Rejoice always, **17** pray constantly, **18** give thanks in all circumstances; for this is the will of God in Christ Jesus for you. **19** Do not quench the Spirit, **20** do not despise prophesying, **21** but test everything; hold fast what is good, **22** abstain from every form of evil.[1]

23 May the God of peace himself sanctify you wholly; and may

6. This traditional image is better attested: Matt. 24:43; Luke 12:39; 2 Pet. 3:10; Rev. 3:3; 16:15.
7. The dualism of Sons of Light *vs.* Sons of Darkness is essential to the apocalyptic world view, most clearly attested in the Dead Sea Scrolls; elsewhere in Pauline writings only in 2 Cor. 6:14–7:1 (an interpolation?) and Eph. 5:3–14; cf. Rom. 13:12; Col. 1:13. The metaphoric "armor" (v. 8) is closely associated with this dualism: the Qumran sect expected a literal "war of the sons of light with the sons of darkness."
8. "Wake or sleep": here and in 4:13–18, "live or die"; note the quite different meaning in the apocalyptic admonition of 5:2–9, where only those who "wake," i.e., are morally vigilant, are saved, while those who "sleep," i.e., are slothful, perish with the sons of darkness.
9. This sentence shows that at this early date there was *some* governing organization in the local congregation, but it offers no description. The three participles—"laboring, presiding, admonishing"—do not distinguish three offices, but three functions of the leadership.
1. Vv. 19–22 illustrate the prevalence of charismatic phenomena in early Christianity—and also Paul's ambivalence toward them (cf. in detail 1 Cor. 12–14). On "testing" claims made "in the Spirit," cf. 1 John 4:1.

your spirit and soul and body be kept sound and blameless at the coming of our Lord Jesus Christ. **24** He who calls you is faithful, and he will do it.

25 Brethren, pray for us.

26 Greet all the brethren with a holy kiss.[2]

27 I adjure you by the Lord that this letter be read to all the brethren.

28 The grace of our Lord Jesus Christ be with you.

THE LETTER TO THE GALATIANS (ca. 54)

Identification of "Galatia" hangs on the question whether Paul used the term properly, of the area comprised by the old Celtic (*galatai = keltai*) tribal kingdom in north central Asia Minor (capital, Ancyra), or more loosely of the Roman province which included that region but extended south to include also Lycaonia and other areas. Evidence favors the former, although in that case Paul's founding of the churches goes unmentioned in Acts.

Opinions about the date of Galatians vary widely; it has been called the earliest and the latest of Paul's letters. Thematic similarities with Romans suggest a relatively late date; 4:13 *can* be understood to imply two previous visits by Paul to Galatia, hence written after the journey of Acts 18:23; Ephesus (Acts 19:1 ff.) would be a convenient place from which to communicate with Galatia. Therefore, though none of these or of the other arguments commonly advanced is probative, most recent commentators have placed the writing between 53 and 55, from Ephesus.

Formally the most striking thing about the letter is the absence of the customary thanksgiving. After the normal salutation—which already hints at one of the principal themes—Paul explodes in a rebuke of the Galatian Christians (1:6). This angry tone persists throughout the letter. Anathemas are proclaimed freely, sarcasm abounds—about the "Pillars" in Jerusalem, about the Galatians, about those who "unsettle" them, even about Paul's own mission among them. At points this sarcasm becomes extremely bitter: "O foolish Galatians! Who has bewitched you?" (3:1); "I wish those who unsettle you would mutilate themselves!" (5:12); "If you bite and devour one another take heed that you are not consumed by one another" (5:15). There are a number of *anacolutha*—sentences

---

2. Cf. 1 Cor. 16:20; 2 Cor. 13:12; Rom. 16:16; also 1 Pet. 5:14. The "kiss of peace" soon received a fixed place in the liturgy of the Eucharist.

in which Paul pauses in mid-thought and continues with a different grammatical structure (e.g., 2:5–7).

Nevertheless, it would be a mistake to assume that the letter is a disordered outpouring of emotion. Chaps. 1–2 develop the theme stated in 1:1, 11 f. ("not from men nor through man") in the rhetorical sequence called *chiasm* (argument in the form of the Greek letter X, thus: a, b, b', a'). Smaller units also use chiasm (e.g., 4:4 f.), parallelism, and other rhetorical devices. The central example of the promise to Abraham, however obscure it may seem to modern readers, is rather tightly argued; perhaps Paul had worked it out previously. The same may be true of the Hagar–Sarah allegory (4:21–31), and of portions of the hortatory section (5:13–6:10).

The cause of Paul's anger is clear in general, though some details are baffling. There has been a direct challenge to Paul's apostolate in the Galatian region. In his absence another group of missionaries has visited the churches he founded there, preaching what both Paul and these other apostles regard as "a different gospel" from the one he proclaimed (1:6–9; 4:17; 5:10, 12; 6:12). Like Paul, these apostles believe that these two versions of the gospel are mutually exclusive. They accuse Paul of having watered down the requirements of Christian membership in order "to please men"; Paul in turn claims that they have "perverted" the gospel. At issue, then, are both the content of the Christian faith and the legitimacy of Paul's authority.

Some characteristics of the opponents can readily be deduced from the letter, but it has so far proved impossible to agree on their precise identity. The Jewish law stands at the forefront of the conflict; the opponents believe that pagan converts to Christianity must submit, in some general way, to being "under the law" (4:21; cf. 2:16 ff.; 3:2–4:7). They insist that all Christians be circumcised (5:2–12; 6:12–15. Cf. 2:3, 12). They observe a festival calendar (4:10). They hold Paul's apostolic credentials in contempt, accusing him of being the purveyor of merely human traditions, lacking independent authority but dependent upon the Jerusalem apostles (Chaps. 1–2). Perhaps they even accuse him of preaching circumcision himself, but not drawing their consequences from it (5:11). Perhaps also they emphasize the gift of the Spirit (3:2–5), calling themselves "the spirituals" (*pneumatikoi*, 6:1), though this interest in charisma may not go beyond what is common in Pauline congregations.

Closer identification of the opponents has been the subject of many divergent hypotheses. A century ago they were commonly identified with the "Jewish-Christian party" of Jerusalem, representing the kind of "converted Pharisees" of whom Acts speaks (Acts

15:1, 5), forerunners of the later Ebionites. But a Jerusalem-centered group would hardly have objected to Paul's alleged dependence upon Jerusalem, as this group clearly did (Chaps. 1–2), nor would Jewish-Christians of a Pharisaic type have suggested that one could be "under the law" and circumcised, without having to obey the *whole* law (5:3). Moreover, the connection between "being under the law" and being under "the elements of the universe," however the latter are understood, is difficult to explain if the Judaizers were of a Pharisaic persuasion. Suggestions early in this century that Paul was fighting on *two* fronts, against "Judaizers" on the one hand and "Libertines" on the other, fail to provide an adequate explanation for the unified character of the argument, and ignore the traditional and general character of the supposed "anti-libertine" exhortations. More recently, interpreters have focused attention upon the peculiar reference to the "elements of the universe," which in 4:3, 9 and in Col. 2:8, 20 seem to be personal, spiritual forces of some kind (see note below on 4:3). Assuming that the opponents themselves made the connection between circumcision, ritual calendar, and the "elemental spirits," some scholars have argued that the Galatian opponents were Gnostics who understood "circumcision" as "putting off the body" (cf. Col. 2:11). This hypothesis, however, fails to account for major emphases in Paul's argument. Other scholars have seen in the opponents Hellenistic Jewish-Christian missionaries, like the "superlative apostles" encountered in 2 Cor. 10–13, who wished to make Christianity, like their previous understanding of Judaism, into a kind of mystery religion in which one shared ritually in the worship of the "elements," understood as cosmic angels. That explanation is not impossible, though it remains highly speculative. It is possible that the opponents themselves did not make the connection between law and slavery to the "elements," but that this is only part of Paul's polemic against the law. In that case he would be more "Gnostic" than they. It is also possible that the opponents' understanding of the law was quite naïve and mixed with the kind of popular superstition, especially astrology, that is so frequently attested in inscriptions, amulets, and tomb and synagogue decorations of that period. Whatever their precise ideology, Paul regarded it as a kind of spiritual slavery, against which he spelled out for the first time his conviction that the essential mark of Christianity is freedom.

1 Paul an apostle—not from men nor through man,[1] but through Jesus Christ and God the Father, who raised him from the dead—[2] and all the brethren who are with me,

To the churches of Galatia:

[3] Grace to you and peace from God the Father and our Lord Jesus Christ, [4] who gave himself for our sins to deliver us from the present evil age, according to the will of our God and Father; [5] to whom be the glory for ever and ever. Amen.[2]

[6] I am astonished that you are so quickly deserting him[3] who called you in the grace of Christ and turning to a different gospel—[7] not that there is another gospel, but there are some who trouble you and want to pervert the gospel of Christ.[8] But even if we, or an angel from heaven, should preach to you a gospel contrary to that which we preached to you, let him be accursed. [9] As we have said before, so now I say again, If any one is preaching to you a gospel contrary to that which you received, let him be accursed.

[10] Am I now seeking the favor of men, or of God? Or am I trying to please men?[4] If I were still pleasing men, I should not be a servant[5] of Christ.

[11] For I would have you know, brethren, that the gospel which was preached by me is not man's[6] gospel. [12] For I did not receive it from man, nor was I taught it, but it came through a revelation of Jesus Christ.[7] [13] For you have heard of my former life in Judaism, how I persecuted the church of God violently and tried to destroy it; [14] and I advanced in Judaism beyond many of my own age among my people, so extremely zealous was I for the traditions

1. The issue of Paul's authority is thus joined in the first words of the salutation. With the following prepositional phrases, the word "apostle" retains something of its original verbal character, literally, "sent," in the technical sense of "commissioned as an agent." It had not yet become the title of a certain office, nor been limited to the circle of "the Twelve."
2. The opening formula, liturgical in style, is somewhat fuller than usual. Note that it contains a terse summary of the gospel, found in an epistolary introduction elsewhere only in Romans. While in Romans the summary defines the basis of his anticipated unity with the congregation, here it defines the gospel which he immediately accuses them of deserting.
3. God, not Paul or even Christ; cf. 1:15; 5:8; 1 Thess. 2:12; 5:24; 1 Cor. 1:9; Rom. 8:30; and elsewhere.
4. Probably this reflects one of the accusations made against Paul by the opponents; cf. 1 Thess. 2:4 and the note

there. When fundamental issues were not at stake, Paul did try "to please all men in everything," 1 Cor. 10:33.
5. "Servant": properly, "slave." Paul may have used the expression "slave of Christ" as a title analogous to the OT title "servant of the Lord," applied to Moses, David, and certain prophets.
6. "Man's": lit., "according to man," i.e., "[merely] human"; cf. v. 1.
7. This statement seems to contradict 1 Cor. 15:1, 3, where "the gospel" is identified with a formula that was "received" and "delivered"—technical terms for the transmission of tradition. But here Paul is concerned with the *authorization* of his message; Paul claims that legitimation did not come through any human agency. Naturally he learned much of the content of his preaching and teaching from those who were Christians before him, though apparently not from Jerusalem. (See the essay by Heitmüller below, pp. 308–19).

of my fathers.[8] [15] But when he who had set me apart before I was born,[9] and had called me through his grace, [16] was pleased to reveal his Son to[1] me, in order that I might preach him among the Gentiles, I did not confer with flesh and blood, [17] nor did I go up to Jerusalem to those who were apostles before me, but I went away into Arabia;[2] and again I returned to Damascus.

[18] Then after three years I went up to Jerusalem to visit Cephas,[3] and remained with him fifteen days. [19] But I saw none of the other apostles except James the Lord's brother. [20] (In what I am writing to you, before God, I do not lie!) [21] Then I went into the regions of Syria and Cilicia. [22] And I was still not known by sight to the churches of Christ in Judea; [23] they only heard it said, "He who once persecuted us is now preaching the faith he once tried to destroy." [24] And they glorified God because of me.

2 Then after fourteen years[4] I went up again to Jerusalem with Barnabas, taking Titus along with me. [2] I went up by revelation; and I laid before them (but privately before those who were of repute) the gospel which I preach among the Gentiles, lest somehow I should be running or had run in vain.[5] [3] But even Titus, who was with me, was not compelled to be circumcised, though he was a Greek. [4] But because of false brethren secretly brought in, who slipped in to spy out our freedom which we have in Christ Jesus, that they might bring us into bondage—[5] to them we did not yield submission even for a moment, that the truth of the

---

8. "Traditions of my fathers": particularly the "oral Torah" cultivated by the Pharisees.
9. A clear allusion to Isa. 49:1 and Jer. 1:5; Paul frequently hints that he thinks of himself as a prophet in the classical tradition, even a new Moses (see notes on 2 Cor. 3–4 and Rom. 9:3).
1. Greek, "in."
2. "Arabia" was vaguely defined, even including Sinai (4:25); here probably Paul means the northwest portion of the Nabatean kingdom, immediately southeast of Damascus. The romantic picture of Paul's meditation in the "desert" is improbable; the patristic commentators were more likely correct when they suggested that he was already preaching. Otherwise the hostility of the Nabatean ethnarch, who pursued him back to Damascus (2 Cor. 11:32 f.) is inexplicable. The Acts' account of this period is incomplete, resulting in a distorted picture of Paul's relationship to Jerusalem (Acts 9:19–30).
3. "Cephas": the Aramaic equivalent of Peter (cf. John 1:42).

4. The time periods are ambiguous; they could all be dated from the year of conversion, so that the fourteen-year period would include the three years. More likely they are successive, though the total might still be no more than fourteen full years, since it was common practice to count even a few days of the initial and final years as whole years.
5. The report of Paul's second visit to Jerusalem can hardly be harmonized with the account in Acts. The nature of the matters discussed parallels Acts 15, but that is the *third* visit mentioned by Acts; however, the second visit according to Acts (11:27–30) comes too early in Paul's career. Further, if the "apostolic council" actually produced the legislation quoted in Acts 15:20, 29; 21:25, then Paul's statement in Gal. 1:10 is less than candid. Various solutions have been proposed; probably the inadequacy of the sources used by the author of Acts and the requirements of his literary and theological outline have produced the disparity.

gospel might be preserved for you.[6] 6 And from those who were reputed to be something (what they were makes no difference to me; God shows no partiality)—those, I say, who were of repute added nothing to me; 7 but on the contrary, when they saw that I had been entrusted with the gospel to the uncircumcised, just as Peter had been entrusted with the gospel to the circumcised 8 (for he who worked through Peter for the mission to the circumcised worked through me also for the Gentiles), 9 and when they perceived the grace that was given to me, James and Cephas and John, who were reputed to be pillars, gave to me and Barnabas the right hand of fellowship, that we should go to the Gentiles and they to the circumcised; 10 only they would have us remember the poor,[7] which very thing I was eager to do.

11 But when Cephas came to Antioch I opposed him to his face, because he stood condemned. 12 For before certain men came from James,[8] he ate with the Gentiles; but when they came he drew back and separated himself, fearing the circumcision party. 13 And with him the rest of the Jews acted insincerely, so that even Barnabas was carried away by their insincerity. 14 But when I saw that they were not straightforward about the truth of the gospel, I said to Cephas before them all, "If you, though a Jew, live like a Gentile and not like a Jew, how can you compel the Gentiles to live like Jews?" 15 We ourselves, who are Jews by birth and not Gentile sinners, 16 yet who know that a man is not justified by works of the law but through faith in Jesus Christ, even we have believed in Christ Jesus, in order to be justified by faith in Christ, and not by works of the law, because by works of the law shall no one be justified. 17 But if, in our endeavor to be justified in Christ, we ourselves were found to be sinners, is Christ then an agent of sin? Certainly not! 18 But if I build up again those things which I

6. The sentence comprising vv. 3–5 is grammatically incomplete and logically confusing. What happened "because of false brethren"? Some commentators argue that because of them Titus after all was circumcised, but v. 5 seems to exclude that possibility. The circumcision of Timothy (if we are to believe Acts 16:3) forms a startling contrast, even though his case was different (by Jewish law, the child of a Jewish mother is a Jew). The identity of the "false brethren"—the term identifies them as members of the Christian movement—is obscure; they are not to be identified with the opponents in Galatia, and clearly not with the leaders of the Jerusalem church. The "spying" and attempted coercion may have taken place in Antioch.

7. "The poor": often thought to be a self-designation of the whole church in Jerusalem, in line with the usage of the Qumran Essenes and of the later Jewish-Christian "Ebionites." NT evidence suggests rather that Paul's collection was a one-time emergency fund for relief of those who were literally "poor among the saints in Jerusalem" (Rom. 15:26).

8. The first mention of James as the patron of a zealous Jewish-Christian party, a role that is emphasized in later Ebionite legend. The "men from James" are not to be identified with the opponents in Galatia, since the principal issue here, kosher food practices, is not mentioned elsewhere in the letter. Moreover, the Galatian opponents regard dependence on Jerusalem as a sign not of legitimacy, but of weakness.

tore down, then I prove myself a transgressor. **19** For I through the law died to the law,[9] that I might live to God. **20** I have been crucified with Christ; it is no longer I who live, but Christ who lives in me; and the life I now live in the flesh I live by faith in the Son of God, who loved me and gave himself for me. **21** I do not nullify the grace of God; for if justification[1] were through the law, then Christ died to no purpose.

3 O foolish Galatians! Who has bewitched you, before whose eyes Jesus Christ was publicly portrayed as crucified? **2** Let me ask you only this: Did you receive the Spirit by works of the law, or by hearing with faith? **3** Are you so foolish? Having begun with the Spirit, are you now ending with the flesh?[2] **4** Did you experience so many things in vain?—if it really is in vain. **5** Does he who supplies the Spirit to you and works miracles among you do so by works of the law, or by hearing with faith?

6 Thus Abraham "believed God, and it was reckoned to him as righteousness."[3] **7** So you see that it is men of faith who are the sons of Abraham. **8** And the scripture, foreseeing that God would justify the Gentiles by faith, preached the gospel beforehand to Abraham, saying, "In you shall all the nations be blessed."[4] **9** So then, those who are men of faith are blessed with Abraham who had faith.

10 For all who rely on works of the law are under a curse; for it is written, "Cursed be every one who does not abide by all things written in the book of the law, and do them."[5] **11** Now it is evi-

9. A puzzling phrase: how did Paul conceive of the law as the means by which the Christian dies to the law? The parallel in Rom. 7:4 is "through the body of Christ"; cf. Gal. 2:20, "crucified with Christ." Thus Paul evidently thinks of the law as the instrument of Jesus' execution (cf. John 19:7): "according to the law he ought to die"). The Christian is united with that event when he is baptized (Rom. 6:3).
1. Or, "righteousness."
2. "Flesh": perhaps a double entendre, alluding to circumcision, while placing it and all other "works of the law" within the sphere of "flesh," which for Paul is inalterably opposed to "spirit." "Ending with" may also be ironic, since the word implies "coming to perfection"; it could satirize the opponents' belief that the law is necessary to "complete" the faith of Gentile Christians.
3. Gen. 15:6. Here begins an argument articulated by the ingenious, sometimes obscure, connection of scriptural passages, in the fashion of *midrash aggadah*, the didactic exegesis practiced in the rabbinic academies.

4. Gen. 12:3: "the nations," originally in a quite general sense, here is taken in the common technical sense of "the Gentiles" as distinct from "the Jews."
5. Deut. 27:26. Vv. 9 and 10 are much more closely connected than the RSV translation suggests: v. 9, "those who belong to faith" (*hoi ek pisteōs*) "are blessed"; v. 10, "those who belong to works of law" (*hoi ex ergōn nomou*) are "cursed." The most baffling problem with the passage is that the citation from Deut. 27:26 says the exact opposite from what Paul wishes to prove by it; Deut. 28:1 f. in fact pronounces the "blessing" precisely on those who keep the commandments of the law. Possible solutions are: (1) The unstated assumption is that no one in fact can keep all the commandments, therefore in practice all are cursed. But Paul claimed himself to have kept the law "blamelessly" (Phil. 3:6); here and in Romans the opposite of faith is not failure to keep the law, but the "boasting" and self-righteousness that result in success in keeping it. (2) Paul is emphasizing the "all" of the Deut. text: "all things written in the book" include the pro-

dent that no man is justified before God by the law; for "He who through faith is righteous shall live";[6] [12] but the law does not rest on faith, for "He who does them shall live by them."[7] [13] Christ redeemed us from the curse of the law, having become a curse for us—for it is written, "Cursed be every one who hangs on a tree"[8]— [14] that in Christ Jesus the blessing of Abraham might come upon the Gentiles, that we might receive the promise of the Spirit through faith.

[15] To give a human example, brethren: no one annuls even a man's will,[9] or adds to it, once it has been ratified. [16] Now the promises were made to Abraham and to his offspring. It does not say, "And to offsprings," referring to many; but, referring to one, "And to your offspring,"[1] which is Christ. [17] This is what I mean: the law, which came four hundred and thirty years afterward, does not annul a covenant previously ratified by God, so as to make the promise void. [18] For if the inheritance is by the law, it is no longer by promise; but God gave it to Abraham by a promise.

[19] Why then the law? It was added because of[2] transgressions, till the offspring should come[3] to whom the promise had been made; and it was ordained by angels through an intermediary.[4] [20] Now an intermediary implies more than one; but God is one.[5]

---

phecies of the Christ and the testimonies to faith which Paul quotes here. (3) Paul is using a familiar technique of midrash in which two verses of scripture produce an impossible dilemma, to be solved by adducing a third. The dilemma is that, if one fails to "abide by . . . the law," one is cursed by God (Deut. 27:26), yet if one does abide by the law, he cannot obtain the righteousness that gives life, since that is promised only to faith (Hab. 2:4; Lev. 18:5). The escape from both law and curse is discovered in Deut. 21:23, interpreted by the Christian proclamation of the crucified Messiah.
6. Or, "the righteous shall live by faith," Hab. 2:4.
7. Lev. 18:5.
8. Deut. 21:23.
9. Paul plays on the ambiguity of the Greek word which ordinarily means "will, testament," but occasionally "contract," and in the latter sense was used to translate the Heb. *brit*, "covenant."
1. "Offspring": lit., "seed." Paul is of course aware that the word is a collective (see v. 29), but he probably depends here on a midrashic tradition that equates "the seed" (from 2 Sam. 7:12) with the Messiah.
2. "Because of": or "for the sake of"; cf. Rom. 5:20. The law precipitated transgressions, actualizing and exposing man's rebellion against the Creator.
3. "Until [x] should come" is a for-

mula found frequently in Jewish tradition indicating that temporary regulations will be superseded by the advent of some figure of the Endtime: e.g., Ezra 2:63; Neh. 7:65; 1 Macc. 4:46; 14:41; in the Dead Sea Scrolls, 1QS 9:11; 4QPB; in Talmud and Midrash, "until Elijah comes." Cf. Gen. 49:10, which the "Patriarchal Blessings" from the fourth cave of Qumran interprets: "until the Messiah of Righteousness comes, the Branch of David, for to him and to his *seed* has been given the covenant of kingship for his people for everlasting generations." Paul's radicality consists in regarding the whole legal aspect of the Torah as such a temporary ordinance, cancelled by the Messiah's advent.
4. That the angels were involved in transmitting the Torah on Sinai is a well-attested Jewish tradition; in the NT, cf. Acts 7:53; Heb. 2:2. If the opponents understood the "elements" as angels, this tradition may have played some role in their speculations, but that cannot be proved. The other "intermediary" mentioned here is, of course, Moses.
5. A puzzling sentence. Lit., "The mediator is not of one, but God is one." What Paul wishes to suggest, apparently, is that the promise, given directly by the one God to Abraham, is superior to the law, given through a multiplicity of mediators. Paul, of course, does not deny that the law came ultimately from God.

²¹ Is the law then against the promises of God? Certainly not; for if a law had been given which could make alive, then righteousness would indeed be by the law.⁶ ²² But the scripture consigned all things to sin, that what was promised to faith in Jesus Christ might be given to those who believe.

²³ Now before faith came, we were confined under the law, kept under restraint until faith should be revealed. ²⁴ So that the law was our custodian⁷ until Christ came, that we might be justified by faith. ²⁵ But now that faith has come, we are no longer under a custodian; ²⁶ for in Christ Jesus you are all sons of God, through faith. ²⁷ For as many of you as were baptized into Christ have put on Christ. ²⁸ There is neither Jew nor Greek, there is neither slave nor free, there is neither male nor female; for you are all one in Christ Jesus⁸ ²⁹ And if you are Christ's, then you are Abraham's offspring, heirs according to promise.

4 I mean that the heir, as long as he is a child, is no better than a slave, though he is the owner of all the estate; ² but he is under guardians and trustees until the date set by the father. ³ So with us; when we were children, we were slaves to the elemental spirits of the universe⁹ ⁴ But when the time had fully come, God sent forth his Son, born of woman, born under the law, ⁵ to redeem those who were under the law, so that we might receive adoption as sons. ⁶ And because you are sons, God has sent the Spirit of his Son into our hearts, crying, "Abba! Father!"¹ ⁷ So through God you are no longer a slave but a son, and if a son then an heir.

⁸ Formerly, when you did not know God, you were in bondage to beings that by nature are no gods; ⁹ but now that you have come to know God, or rather to be known by God, how can you turn back again to the weak and beggarly elemental spirits,² whose

6. This terse disclaimer is hardly intelligible by itself; see Rom. 7.
7. "Custodian": Greek *paidagogos*, a slave charged with the general custody, and especially the discipline, of children in a Greek or Roman family between the ages of six and sixteen. The translation "schoolmaster" (KJV) and even the recent "tutor" (NEB) are misleading.
8. Probably quoted from the baptismal liturgy (cf. 1 Cor. 12:13; Col. 3:11); the underlying notion is the restoration of the lost "image of God" (Gen. 1:26 f.), healing the fundamental divisions of mankind.
9. "The elements of the cosmos": evidently regarded, and not just metaphorically, as personal beings, both here and Col. 2:8, 20; hence the trans-

lation "elemental spirits." A number of critics identify the "elements" with angels, although no certain example exists of that use of the word. Another possibility is that stars and planets are so designated, naturally understood as living beings.
1. The Aramaic expression attests the antiquity of this acclamation, which perhaps belongs to baptism; the beginning of the "Lord's Prayer" could be meant, but not necessarily. Cf. Rom. 8:15.
2. Paul equates Christian adoption of the Jewish law with return to polytheism; whether the opponents themselves connected life under the law with proper relationship to the "elemental spirits" is not clear, although "you want to" might imply that.

slaves you want to be once more? **10** You observe days, and months, and seasons, and years!³ **11** I am afraid I have labored over you in vain.

12 Brethren, I beseech you, become as I am, for I also have become as you are. You did me no wrong; **13** you know it was because of a bodily ailment that I preached the gospel to you at first; **14** and though my condition was a trial to you, you did not scorn or despise⁴ me, but received me as an angel of God, as Christ Jesus. **15** What has become of the satisfaction you felt? For I bear you witness that, if possible, you would have plucked out your eyes and given them to me. **16** Have I then become your enemy by telling you the truth? **17** They make much of you, but for no good purpose; they want to shut you out, that you may make much of them. **18** For a good purpose it is always good to be made much of, and not only when I am present with you. **19** My little children, with whom I am again in travail until Christ be formed in you!⁵ **20** I could wish to be present with you now and to change my tone, for I am perplexed about you.

21 Tell me, you who desire to be under law, do you not hear the law?⁶ **22** For it is written that Abraham had two sons, one by a slave and one by a free woman. **23** But the son of the slave was born according to the flesh, the son of the free woman through promise. **24** Now this is an allegory: these women are two covenants. One is from Mount Sinai, bearing children for slavery; she is Hagar. **25** Now Hagar is Mount Sinai in Arabia;⁷ she corresponds to the present Jerusalem, for she is in slavery with her children. **26** But the Jerusalem above is free, and she is our mother. **27** For it is written,

"Rejoice, O barren one that dost not bear;

3. Concern with the festival calendar could indicate astrological interpretation of the law. There is evidence from Qumran that circumcision and meticulous keeping of the (solar) festival calendar permitted the worship of the community to unite with the liturgy conducted by the angels in heaven.
4. "Despise": lit., "to spit," a superstitious gesture to ward off the demonic influence thought to emanate from victims of certain diseases, especially epilepsy or insanity.
5. Paul uses the metaphor of his being the "father" or "mother" of his converts elsewhere (1 Cor. 4:15; 2 Cor. 6:13; 1 Thess. 2:7, 11; Phlm. 10); the metaphor is occasionally used of the relationship between a mystagogue and his initiates in the mystery religions.
6. Paul rejects the legal function of

the law (*halakah*), but upholds its revelatory or didactic function (*aggadah*). The allegory in vv. 21–31 is in the style of the Alexandrian exegesis rather than Pharisaic midrash.
7. The text is uncertain, another major group of manuscripts reading, "For Sinai is a mountain in Arabia"; copyists have evidently tried to help out Paul's limping allegory by adding notes. Some critics suggest that the whole sentence may be a gloss. "In Arabia" is perhaps suggested by traditional identification of Ishmael, Hagar's son, as forefather of the Arabs. Identification of Sinai with Jerusalem/Zion is frequent in Jewish tradition. Thus the basic allegory is: Hagar = Sinai = Jerusalem = the covenant of law; Sarah = the heavenly Jerusalem = the new covenant of grace.

break forth and shout, thou who art not in travail;
for the desolate hath more children
than she who hath a husband."
[28] Now we,[8] brethren, like Isaac, are children of promise. [29] But as at that time he who was born according to the flesh persecuted him who was born according to the Spirit, so it is now. [30] But what does the scripture say? "Cast out the slave and her son; for the son of the slave shall not inherit with the son of the free woman." [31] So, brethren, we are not children of the slave but of the free woman.

[5] For freedom Christ has set us free; stand fast therefore, and do not submit again to a yoke of slavery. [2] Now I, Paul, say to you that if you receive circumcision, Christ will be of no advantage to you. [3] I testify again to every man who receives circumcision that he is bound to keep the whole law.[9] [4] You are severed from Christ, you who would be justified by the law; you have fallen away from grace. [5] For through the Spirit, by faith, we wait for the hope of righteousness. [6] For in Christ Jesus neither circumcision nor uncircumcision is of any avail, but faith working through love.[1] [7] You were running well; who hindered you from obeying the truth? [8] This persuasion is not from him who called you. [9] A little leaven leavens the whole lump. [10] I have confidence in the Lord that you will take no other view than mine; and he who is troubling you will bear his judgment, whoever he is. [11] But if I, brethren, still preach circumcision, why am I still persecuted? In that case the stumbling block of the cross has been removed. [12] I wish those who unsettle you would mutilate themselves!

[13] For you were called to freedom, brethren; only do not use your freedom as an opportunity for the flesh,[2] but through love be servants of one another. [14] For the whole law is fulfilled in one word, "You shall love your neighbor as yourself."[3] [15] But if you bite and devour one another take heed that you are not consumed by one another.

[16] But I say, walk by the Spirit, and do not gratify the desires of

---

8. "You" is also well attested in the manuscripts.

9. Here speaks the ex-Pharisee, and of the strictest school; not all rabbis would agree with this principle, which is however attested in the Talmud. Paul insists on total antithesis: either obedience to *all* the commandments or life by faith.

1. Cf. 6:15; I Cor. 7:19.

2. The exhortations which follow are largely traditional and need not presuppose a "libertine" tendency among the Galatians. The use of freedom as license was a danger logically inherent in Paul's position, which he must defend against such a misinterpretation.

3. The use of this sentence from Lev. 19:18 to sum up the demands of the law (Rom. 13:9; Matt. 5:43; 22:39; Mark 12:31; Luke 10:27; James 2:8) was commonplace in Judaism as well as early Christianity.

the flesh. **17** For the desires of the flesh are against the Spirit, and the desires of the Spirit are against the flesh; for these are opposed to each other, to prevent you from doing what you would. **18** But if you are led by the Spirit you are not under the law. **19** Now the works of the flesh are plain: immorality, impurity, licentiousness, **20** idolatry, sorcery, enmity, strife, jealousy, anger, selfishness, dissension, party spirit, **21** envy, drunkenness, carousing, and the like.⁴ I warn you, as I warned you before, that those who do such things shall not inherit the kingdom of God. **22** But the fruit of the Spirit is love, joy, peace, patience, kindness, goodness, faithfulness, **23** gentleness, self-control; against such there is no law. **24** And those who belong to Christ Jesus have crucified the flesh with its passions and desires.

25 If we live by the Spirit, let us also walk by the Spirit. **26** Let us have no self-conceit, no provoking of one another, no envy of one another.

6 Brethren, if a man is overtaken in any trespass, you who are spiritual should restore him in a spirit of gentleness. Look to yourself, lest you too be tempted. **2** Bear one another's burdens, and so fulfil the law of Christ.⁵ **3** For if any one thinks he is something, when he is nothing, he deceives himself. **4** But let each one test his own work, and then his reason to boast will be in himself alone and not in his neighbor. **5** For each man will have to bear his own load.

6 Let him who is taught the word share all good things with him who teaches.

7 Do not be deceived; God is not mocked, for whatever a man sows, that he will also reap. **8** For he who sows to his own flesh will from the flesh reap corruption; but he who sows to the Spirit will from the Spirit reap eternal life. **9** And let us not grow weary in well-doing, for in due season we shall reap, if we do not lose heart. **10** So then, as we have opportunity, let us do good to all men, and especially to those who are of the household of faith.

11 See with what large letters I am writing to you with my own hand.⁶ **12** It is those who want to make a good showing in the

---

4. Catalogues of virtues (vv. 22 f.) and vices (vv. 19 f.) were the simplest of the standard forms of moral teaching in the Hellenistic world, including Judaism. They were sometimes placed into a dualistic framework, "the way of light" and "the way of darkness" (Qumran, the *Didache*); similarly, here Paul associates them with "flesh" and "Spirit." Some manuscripts add "murder" (*phonoi*) after "envy" (*phthonoi*) in v. 21.

5. "The law of Christ": a startling phrase after Paul's polemic against the law, but cf. Rom. 8:2; 1 Cor. 9:21. The notion occasionally attested in Judaism that the Messiah would bring a new, final interpretation of the law is a formal parallel, but "the law of Christ" for Paul does not consist of legislation at all.

6. Cf. 1 Cor. 16:21; Col. 4:18; and the note on 2 Thess. 3:17.

flesh that would compel you to be circumcised, and only in order that they may not be persecuted for the cross of Christ. [13] For even those who receive circumcision do not themselves keep the law, but they desire to have you circumcised that they may glory in your flesh. [14] But far be it from me to glory except in the cross of our Lord Jesus Christ, by which[7] the world has been crucified to me, and I to the world. [15] For neither circumcision counts for anything, nor uncircumcision, but a new creation. [16] Peace and mercy be upon all who walk by this rule, upon the Israel of God.[8]

[17] Henceforth let no man trouble me; for I bear on my body the marks of Jesus.[9]

[18] The grace of our Lord Jesus Christ be with your spirit, brethren. Amen.

THE FIRST LETTER TO THE CORINTHIANS (ca. 55)

Corinth was located on the isthmus between Attica and the Peloponnesus. Its site, with two harbors, one on the Saronian Gulf to the east, the other on the Gulf of Corinth to the north, assured commercial success. Refounded by Julius Caesar in 44 B.C., after having been destroyed in 146 B.C. by the Romans, it grew quickly to prominence again. In 27 B.C. it was made the capital of the province of Achaia, which in A.D. 44 became a senatorial province. The population, beginning with a colony of Roman freedmen, quickly became cosmopolitan and included a substantial community of Jews. The ancient city had been the butt of jokes, particularly in Athens, for the entertainments it offered, typical of what might be expected in a sailor's town; Aristophanes coined the term *korinthiazesthai*, "to practice fornication." Perhaps something of this atmosphere persisted in the new city; the Christians there, at least, seem to have suffered some confusion in sexual matters.

The church was founded by Paul, probably in A.D. 50 (Acts 18:1–11). After his initial stay there he carried on an extended correspondence with the Corinthian Christians, writing a total of at least four and possibly five or six letters to them (1 Cor. 5:9; 2 Cor.

---

7. Or, "through whom."
8. Designation of the whole church, Jew and Gentile alike, as "the Israel of God" is noteworthy, but quite characteristic of Paul's view.
9. "The marks of Jesus": not reproductions of the wounds of crucifixion, as in medieval legends of the stigmatization of St. Francis and others, but scars received in the rigors of his mission (cf. 2 Cor. 4:8–12; 11:24–28), perhaps regarded as the "brands" identifying him as "Christ's slave."

2:3 f.); visited them himself twice more; sent personal representatives more than once; and received delegations and informal reports from them. The first extant letter was written near the end of his stay in Ephesus (16:8, cf. Acts 19) in the spring probably of the year 55 or 56. It is a response to reports which have come to Paul by two means: (1) a letter, brought by an official delegation, Stephanus, Fortunatus, and Achaicus (16:17; cf. 7:1) and (2) gossip from "Chloe's people" (1:11), otherwise unknown. Although Timothy is already en route overland to Corinth (Paul expects the letter to arrive by sea before he does: 4:17; 16:10 f.; cf. Acts 19:22), and Paul himself expects to come soon, the problems are urgent enough to require immediate answer.

The problems are diverse, yet there seems to be an underlying connection between them. Paul has heard that there are "factions" or "quarrels" in the church, which stem from invidious comparisons among apostles: Paul, Apollos, Peter, and—Christ! (1:12). Basic to these divisions seems to be some peculiar understanding of baptism, in which the new Christian retains a special relationship to the person who baptized him or in whose name he was baptized (1:14–17). This baptismal ideology is also apparently connected with a special notion of "wisdom" which is imparted to "the spirituals" but not to ordinary men (1:17–3:4). Some Corinthian Christians challenge Paul's authority—apparently they think him lacking in this "wisdom"—and doubt that this unstable missionary will ever be seen again (4:18 f; cf. 16:5–7). There are also less subtle problems. A flagrant case of incest in the congregation (Chap. 5) produces "boasting" over this violation of ordinary taboos (5:2, 6). Some Christians are suing one another in pagan courts (6:1–8). Others defend their patronage of the famous Corinthian brothels with a slogan that sounds quite Pauline (6:9–20). Yet others reject sexuality altogether (Chap. 7). The "knowledge" (*gnōsis*) possessed by some leads to the conviction that they are free to participate in social occasions in pagan shrines or to eat meat technically "offered to idols"; others are scandalized by this practice (Chaps. 8–10). The dress and status of women in the assemblies for worship is a matter of contention (11:2–16; 14:34–36), and disorder infects the celebration of the Eucharist (11:23–34). Charismatic phenomena—especially ecstatic speech (*glossolalia*)—threaten to divide the community (Chaps. 12–14). And some do not believe in the resurrection of the dead (Chap. 15).

Unlike the Galatians, the Corinthian Christians needed no "outside agitators" to awaken this extraordinary array of difficulties, although they were soon to prove fertile soil for anti-Pauline missionaries (2 Cor.). Paul regards the work of Apollos in his absence entirely favorably (3:4–4:6), in stark contrast to his attitude toward the "troublers" in Galatia and the later "superlative apostles" of 2 Cor. 10–13. While recent commentators have pointed out impressive similarities between the Corinthians' ideology and certain forms of later Christian Gnosticism, it is unnecessary to postulate influence from some previous Gnostic movement. Rather, what we see happening in Corinth is more likely a splendid instance of the *birth* of a Gnostic movement, produced spontaneously by the confluence of notions common in Hellenistic syncretism with specific Jewish ideas and aspects of the Christian proclamation. Apparently certain of the Corinthian Christians regarded themselves as "spirituals" or *perfecti* because they had been initiated—in baptism by *their* apostle—into the sphere of heavenly, occult "wisdom." They did not believe in a future "resurrection of the dead" because they had been taught that "in Christ" they were already "raised . . . up with him and enthroned with him . . . in the heavenly places . . ." (Eph. 2:6; cf. 2 Tim. 2:18). Bodily and sexual life were no longer real—or no longer permitted, depending on the interpretation—because "there is neither male nor female . . . in Christ" (Gal. 3:28). Armed with the "knowledge" (*gnōsis*) of their heavenly status they were charmed against the influence of idols, demons, and the taboos that ordinary society finds necessary.

It is significant that the anathemas of Galatians are absent from 1 Corinthians. In their place are only particularly pointed examples of the sarcasm of which Paul was a master. His comparative gentleness is perhaps an indication that he himself acknowledges the parentage of their exotic ideas, however emphatically he may reject the conclusions they have drawn from his premises.

Formally the letter lacks the coherence of the shorter letters or of the more systematic letter to the Romans. Some scholars have questioned its integrity, suggesting that it may have been put together, as 2 Corinthians probably was, by a later editor from parts of two or more letters. These arguments, however, have not persuaded many commentators. The loose structure of the letter is occasioned by Paul's decision to answer one by one the problems reported by Chloe's group (Chaps. 1–6) and those contained in the official letter (Chaps. 7–14; the problem of the resurrection, Chap. 15, fundamental to the whole situation, may have been conveyed by either or both). It is framed by the salutation (1:1–3), thanksgiving (1:4–9), concluding greetings (16:19 f., including the personal greeting in Paul's own handwriting, 16:21) and benediction (16:24) in the normal Pauline style. The liturgical *anathema* and *maranatha* of 16:22 are an unusual element of the conclusion. The body of the letter contains a rich number of rhetorical figures, several pieces of quoted tradition (notably 15:3–5 and 11:23–25), and the famous prose-poem on love (Chap. 13).

---

1 Paul, called by the will of God to be an apostle of Christ Jesus, and our brother Sosthenes,[1]
2 To the church of God which is at Corinth, to those sanctified in Christ Jesus, /called to be saints/together with all those who in every place call on the name of our Lord Jesus Christ, both their Lord and ours:
3 Grace to you and peace from God our Father and the Lord Jesus Christ.

4 I give thanks to God[2] always for you because of the grace of God which was given you in Christ Jesus, **5** that in every way you were enriched in him with all speech and all knowledge— **6** even as the testimony to Christ was confirmed among you— **7** so that you are not lacking in any spiritual gift, as you wait for the revealing of our Lord Jesus Christ; **8** who will sustain you to the end, guiltless in the day of our Lord Jesus Christ. **9** God is faithful, by whom you were called into the fellowship of his Son, Jesus Christ our Lord.

10 I appeal to you, brethren, by the name of our Lord Jesus Christ, that all of you agree and that there be no dissensions among you, but that you be united in the same mind and the same judgment. **11** For it has been reported to me by Chloe's people[3] that there is quarreling among you, my brethren. **12** What I mean is that each one of you says, "I belong to Paul," or "I belong to Apollos," or "I belong to Cephas," or "I belong to Christ."[4] **13** Is

1. Acts 18:17 mentions a Sosthenes, president of the synagogue in Corinth, who, after opposing Paul before the proconsul, was beaten for his trouble. Identity of the two men, which has led to speculation about Sosthenes' conversion, cannot be shown; the name was common.
2. Many ancient authorities read "my God." The thanksgiving (vv. 4–9), brief as it is, nevertheless alludes to a number of the themes of the letter: "enriched" (v. 5) is used sarcastically in 4:7; *logos* and *gnōsis* (v. 5) are the subject of Chaps. 1–4; also 8:1, 7, 10, 11; cf. 12:8; 13:2; "spiritual gifts" (*charismata*, v. 7): Chaps. 12–14 cf.

7:7; the eschatological emphasis (vv. 7, 8) forms the underlying tension of the entire letter, explicitly 3:10–17; 4:1–5, reaching its climax in Chap. 15; "fellowship" (*koinōnia*, v. 9) suggests Paul's emphasis on the harmony and unity of the community.
3. Chloe's family? slaves? not further identifiable.
4. Some commentators think the phrase "I belong to Christ" a later gloss, but there is no manuscript evidence for this. Perhaps the "spirituals" regarded Christ as merely the ultimate mystagogue, initiating men into heavenly wisdom; for Paul he *is* "wisdom" (v. 30).

Christ divided? Was Paul crucified for you? Or were you baptized in the name of Paul? **14** I am thankful that I baptized none of you except Crispus and Gaius; **15** lest any one should say that you were baptized in my name[5] **16** (I did baptize also the household of Stephanas.[6] Beyond that, I do not know whether I baptized any one else.) **17** For Christ did not send me to baptize but to preach the gospel, and not with eloquent wisdom, lest the cross of Christ be emptied of its power.

18 For the word of the cross is folly to those who are perishing, but to us who are being saved it is the power of God. **19** For it is written,

> "I will destroy the wisdom of the wise,
> and the cleverness of the clever I will thwart."[7]

20 Where is the wise man? Where is the scribe? Where is the debater of this age? Has not God made foolish the wisdom of the world? **21** For since, in the wisdom of God, the world did not know God through wisdom, it pleased God through the folly of what we preach to save those who believe. **22** For Jews demand signs and Greeks seek wisdom, **23** but we preach Christ crucified, a stumbling block to Jews and folly to Gentiles, **24** but to those who are called, both Jews and Greeks, Christ the power of God and the wisdom of God. **25** For the foolishness of God is wiser than men, and the weakness of God is stronger than men.[8]

26 For consider your call, brethren; not many of you were wise according to worldly standards, not many were powerful, not many were of noble birth; **27** but God chose what is foolish in the world to shame the wise, God chose what is weak in the world to shame the strong, **28** God chose what is low and despised in the world, even things that are not, to bring to nothing things that are, **29** so that no human being might boast in the presence of God.[9] **30** He is the source of your life in Christ Jesus, whom God made our wisdom, our righteousness and sanctification and redemption; **31** therefore, as it is written, "Let him who boasts, boast of the Lord."[1]

2 When I came to you, brethren, I did not come proclaiming to you the testimony[2] of God in lofty words or wisdom. **2** For I

---

5. The Corinthian understanding of baptism as "initiation" apparently included a peculiarly intimate relationship with the baptizer; analogies are found in the mystery religions.

6. Stephanas, one of the delegates from Corinth, was present in Ephesus as Paul wrote (16:15–18); did he remind Paul of the omission while the latter was dictating?

7. Isa. 29:14.

8. Vv 18–25 are highly rhetorical; note the antithetic parallelism (18,

22–25); the climactic series of four questions (20). Similarities with Hellenistic Jewish homilies have often been noted.

9. Vv. 26–29 are a superb example of Paul's fondness of parallelism. Note the social status of the earliest Christians in Corinth implied here; that of the Thessalonians was similar.

1. Jer. 9:24.

2. "Testimony" (*martyrion*): "mystery" or "secret" (*mysterion*) is also very strongly attested; cf. v. 7.

decided to know nothing among you except Jesus Christ and him crucified. ³ And I was with you in weakness and in much fear and trembling; ⁴ and my speech and my message were not in plausible words of wisdom, but in demonstration of the Spirit and power,³ ⁵ that your faith might not rest in the wisdom of men but in the power of God.

⁶ Yet among the mature we do impart wisdom, although it is not a wisdom of this age or of the rulers of this age,⁵ who are doomed to pass away. ⁷ But we impart a secret and hidden wisdom of God, which God decreed before the ages for our glorification.⁶ ⁸ None of the rulers of this age understood this; for if they had, they would not have crucified the Lord of glory. ⁹ But, as it is written,

"What no eye has seen, nor ear heard,
nor the heart of man conceived,
what God has prepared for those who love him,"⁷

¹⁰ God has revealed to us through the Spirit. For the Spirit searches everything, even the depths of God. ¹¹ For what person knows a man's thoughts except the spirit of the man which is in him? So also no one comprehends the thoughts of God except the Spirit of God. ¹² Now we have received not the spirit of the world, but the Spirit which is from God, that we might understand the gifts bestowed on us by God. ¹³ And we impart this in words not taught by human wisdom but taught by the Spirit, interpreting spiritual truth to those who possess the Spirit.⁸

¹⁴ The unspiritual⁹ man does not receive the gifts of the Spirit

---

3. How God's Spirit and power were demonstrable is one of the points of contention between Paul and the "spirituals"; here, however, he speaks quite conventionally and may think of the miracles by which apostles and other "divine men" won attention (2 Cor. 12:12; Rom. 15:19; cf. 1 Thess. 1:5).
4. Or, "perfect." The word (*teleios*) could refer to one who had been "initiated" in the mysteries; also metaphorically for one who was "initiated" into the higher speculations of philosophy. For Philo, for example, the "sage" who had won virtue by self-discipline, mastered the rational means of acquiring truth, and gone on to ecstatic vision became *teleios*, "neither God nor man, but . . . on the borderline between" the two (*On Dreams*, ii. 234).
5. "Rulers of this age": commentators have disagreed whether these should be understood as political rulers or as demonic powers: the context speaks for the latter; cf. the "god of this age" (2 Cor. 4:4).

6. The pattern "formerly hidden/now revealed" was evidently a regular form of preaching in the Pauline school; cf. Rom. 16:25 f.; Col. 1:26 f.; Eph. 3:4 f., 9 f.: similarly 2 Tim. 1:9 f.; Tit. 1:2 f.; 1 Pet. 1:20 f.
7. Source of this quotation cannot be identified; Origen found it in an "Apocalypse of Elijah" which has not survived.
8. "Those who possess the Spirit" translates the adjective "spiritual" which, in the dative case, may be either masculine or neuter; hence it could mean, "comparing spiritual things with spiritual."
9. "Unspiritual": *psychikos*, i.e., having (only) "soul," *psyche*. Three classes of men are distinguished: the "spirituals" (*pneumatikoi*), the "souled" (*psychikoi*), and the "fleshly" (*sarkikoi, sarkinoi*). The "spirituals" are identical with the "perfect." The same division appears in some later Christian Gnostic systems; Paul uses it here sarcastically.

of God, for they are folly to him, and he is not able to understand them because they are spiritually discerned. 15 The spiritual man judges all things, but is himself to be judged by no one. 16 "For who has known the mind of the Lord so as to instruct him?"[1] But we have the mind of Christ.

3 But I, brethren, could not address you as spiritual men, but as men of the flesh, as babes in Christ. 2 I fed you with milk, not solid food; for you were not ready for it; and even yet you are not ready, 3 for you are still of the flesh. For while there is jealousy and strife among you, are you not of the flesh, and behaving like ordinary men? 4 For when one says, "I belong to Paul," and another "I belong to Apollos," are you not merely men?[2]

5 What then is Apollos?[3] What is Paul? Servants through whom you believed, as the Lord assigned to each. 6 I planted, Apollos watered, but God gave the growth. 7 So neither he who plants nor he who waters is anything, but only God who gives the growth. 8 He who plants and he who waters are equal, and each shall receive his wages according to his labor. 9 For we are fellow workers for God; you are God's field, God's building.

10 According to the commission of God given to me, like a skilled master builder I laid a foundation, and another man is building upon it. Let each man take care how he builds upon it. 11 For no other foundation can any one lay than that which is laid, which is Jesus Christ. 12 Now if any one builds on the foundation with gold, silver, precious stones, wood, hay, stubble— 13 each man's work will become manifest; for the Day[4] will disclose it, because it will be revealed with fire, and the fire will test what sort of work each one has done. 14 If the work which any man has built on the foundation survives, he will receive a reward. 15 If any man's work is burned up, he will suffer loss, though he himself will be saved, but only as through fire.

16 Do you not know that you are God's temple[5] and that God's

---

1. Isa. 40:13, LXX.

2. The simple word "men" (*anthrōpoi*) mocks the elitism expressed in the spiritual/souled/fleshly divisions. 3:1–4 forms a classic example of Paul's satire. In 2:6–16 Paul seems to accept the position of the "spirituals," that an apostle is one who imparts an esoteric "wisdom," accessible only to "the perfect." But for him that "hidden" wisdom is identical with the public proclamation, "Christ and him crucified." Therefore the mundane fact of their divisions and arguments shows that they are not "spirituals" but only "men of flesh," not "perfect" (i.e., "adults"), but only "babes."

3. On Apollos' mission to Corinth see Acts 18:24–28. Note that of the "factions" mentioned in 1:12 only that of Apollos is singled out here, and that not in a hostile fashion. It is doubtful whether Cephas=Peter ever actually visited Corinth.

4. I.e., "the day of the Lord," see note on 2 Thess. 2:2.

5. Spiritualization of the notion "temple" was common in Hellenism: God dwells in men. Here the temple is symbol of the community, however, not of individuals; a similar notion is found in apocalyptic Judaism, including the Dead Sea Scrolls.

Spirit dwells in you?⌉ 17 If any one destroys God's temple, God will destroy him.⁶ For God's temple is holy, and that temple you are.

18 Let no one deceive himself. If any one among you thinks that he is wise in this age, let him become a fool that he may become wise. 19 For the wisdom of this world is folly with God. For it is written, "He catches the wise in their craftiness,"⁷ 20 and again, "The Lord knows that the thoughts of the wise are futile."⁸ 21 So let no one boast of men. For all things are yours, 22 whether Paul or Apollos or Cephas or the world or life or death or the present or the future, all are yours; 23 and you are Christ's; and Christ is God's.⁹

4 This is how one should regard us, as servants of Christ and stewards¹ of the mysteries of God. 2 Moreover it is required of stewards that they be found trustworthy. 3 But with me it is a very small thing that I should be judged by you or by any human court. I do not even judge myself. 4 I am not aware of anything² against myself, but I am not thereby acquitted. It is the Lord who judges me. 5 Therefore do not pronounce judgment before the time, before the Lord comes, who will being to light the things now hidden in darkness and will disclose the purposes of the heart. Then every man will receive his commendation from God.

6 I have applied³ all this to myself and Apollos for your benefit, brethren, that you may learn by us to live according to scripture,⁴ that none of you may be puffed up in favor of one against another. 7 For who sees anything different in you? What have you that you did not receive? If then you received it, why do you boast as if it were not a gift?

8 Already⁵ you are filled! Already you have become rich! Without us you have become kings! And would that you did reign, so that we might share the rule with you! 9 For I think that God has exhibited us apostles as last of all, like men sentenced to death;

6. Sayings in this form ("if any one does *x*, *x* will be done to him") occur several places in early Christian literature (e.g., 1 Cor. 14:38; 2 Cor. 9:6; Rom. 2:12; Matt. 5:19; 6:14 f.; 10:32 f.; Mark 4:24 f.; 8:38; Rev. 22:18). The style is that of ancient sacral law (cf. Gen. 9:6; Deut. 28:1, 15; Aeschylus, *Choephoroe* 312 f.), with an eschatological setting.
7. Job 5:13.
8. Ps. 94:11.
9. Vv. 18–23 are a reprise of the themes introduced in 1:10–25; thus Chaps. 1–3 form a rhetorical "circle" or ring-composition. Note also the carefully stylized ending, vv. 21–23. Chap. 4, however, adds further comments on the same questions.

1. "Servants" and "stewards": common titles in civil, cultic, and business bureaucracies, less demeaning than Paul's usual "slave."
2. "I am ... aware of" translates a verb that is cognate with the noun "conscience."
3. The verb translated "applied" normally means "to transform," perhaps "to speak figuratively." The usage here is strange.
4. Most commentators despair of translating the first of these final clauses, which reads literally: "that you may learn, 'Not beyond what is written.'"
5. Paul satirizes the "realized eschatology" of the Corinthian "spirituals": see headnote above, p. 24.

because we have become a spectacle to the world, to angels and to men. **10** We are fools for Christ's sake, but you are wise in Christ. We are weak, but you are strong. You are held in honor, but we in disrepute. **11** To the present hour we hunger and thirst, we are ill-clad and buffeted and homeless, **12** and we labor, working with our own hands. When reviled, we bless; when persecuted, we endure; **13** when slandered, we try to conciliate; we have become, and are now, as the refuse of the world, the offscouring[6] of all things.

14 I do not write this to make you ashamed, but to admonish you as my beloved children. **15** For though you have countless guides in Christ, you do not have many fathers. For I became your father in Christ Jesus through the gospel. **16** I urge you, then, be imitators of me. **17** Therefore I sent to you Timothy, my beloved and faithful child in the Lord, to remind you of my ways in Christ, as I teach them everywhere in every church. **18** Some are arrogant, as though I were not coming to you. **19** But I will come to you soon, if the Lord wills, and I will find out not the talk of these arrogant people but their power. **20** For the kingdom of God does not consist in talk but in power. **21** What do you wish? Shall I come to you with a rod, or with love in a spirit of gentleness?

5 It is actually[7] reported that there is immorality among you, and of a kind that is not found even among pagans; for a man is living with his father's wife.[8] **2** And you are arrogant! Ought you not rather to mourn? Let him who has done this be removed from among you.

3 For though absent in body I am present in spirit, and as if present, I have already pronounced judgment **4** in the name of the Lord Jesus on the man who has done such a thing. When you are assembled, and my spirit is present, with the power of our Lord Jesus, **5** you are to deliver this man to Satan for the destruction of the flesh,[9] that his spirit may be saved in the day of the Lord Jesus.

6 Your boasting is not good. Do you not know that a little leaven leavens the whole lump? **7** Cleanse out the old leaven that you may be a new lump,[1] as you really are unleavened. For Christ, our paschal lamb, has been sacrificed. **8** Let us, therefore, celebrate the festival, not with the old leaven, the leaven of malice and evil, but with the unleavened bread of sincerity and truth.

6. "Refuse," "offscouring": common terms of contempt for the destitute, but also used of human victims in an ancient rite by which a city was "purified" of plague or some other disaster, hence "scapegoat." It is possible that Paul intends a double entendre here.
7. Possibly, "everywhere."
8. Apparently he has married his widowed stepmother, a relationship forbidden by both Roman and Jewish law (see Lev. 18:8).
9. The solemn excommunication is apparently accompanied by a curse that is expected to lead to death of the offender. It is not likely that he is the same man mentioned in 2 Cor. 2:5–11.
1. The metaphor is drawn from the Jewish custom that the household must be purged of every trace of leaven before Passover.

⁹ I wrote to you in my letter[2] not to associate with immoral men; ¹⁰ not at all meaning the immoral of this world, or the greedy and robbers, or idolaters, since then you would need to go out of the world. ¹¹ But rather I wrote to you not to associate with any one who bears the name of brother[3] if he is guilty of immorality or greed, or is an idolater, reviler, drunkard, or robber—not even to eat with such a one. ¹² For what have I to do with judging outsiders? Is it not those inside the church whom you are to judge? ¹³ God judges those outside. "Drive out the wicked person from among you."[4]

6 When one of you has a grievance against a brother, does he dare go to law before the unrighteous[5] instead of the saints? ² Do you not know that the saints will judge the world?[6] And if the world is to be judged by you, are you incompetent to try trivial cases? ³ Do you not know that we are to judge angels? How much more, matters pertaining to this life! ⁴ If then you have such cases, why do you lay them before those who are least esteemed by the church? ⁵ I say this to your shame. Can it be that there is no man among you wise enough to decide between members of the brotherhood, ⁶ but brother goes to law against brother, and that before unbelievers?

⁷ To have lawsuits at all with one another is defeat for you. Why not rather suffer wrong? Why not rather be defrauded? ⁸ But you yourselves wrong and defraud, and that even your own brethren.

⁹ Do you not know that the unrighteous will not inherit the kingdom of God? [Do not be deceived; neither the immoral, nor idolaters, nor adulterers, nor homosexuals, ¹⁰ nor thieves, nor the greedy, nor drunkards, nor revilers, nor robbers will inherit the kingdom of God.[7]] ¹¹ And such were some of you. But you were washed, you were sanctified, you were justified in the name of the Lord Jesus Christ and in the Spirit of our God.[8]

¹² "All things are lawful for me,"[9] but not all things are helpful. "All things are lawful for me," but I will not be enslaved by

---

2. This letter is lost; attempts to identify part of it with 2 Cor. 6:14–7:1 are not persuasive.
3. "Brother": the common designation of a Christian.
4. Deut. 17:7; 22:21, 24; 24:7; cf. 13:5.
5. I.e., in pagan courts; "unrighteous" here means no more than "unbelievers."
6. The notion comes from Jewish apocalyptic: cf. Dan. 7:22; Wisd. 3:8; Matt. 19:28; Luke 22:30.
7. On the "catalogue of vices" see note

on Gal. 5:20; cf. Eph. 5:5.
8. The "once/now" pattern was a regular form of early Christian preaching; cf. Gal. 4:3 f.; 4:8 f.; Rom. 6:17–22; 7:5 f.; 11:30; Col. 1:21 f.; 3:5–10; Eph. 2:1–10, 11–22; Tit. 3:3–7; 1 Pet. 2:10; 4:3 f.
9. Evidently a slogan of the Corinthian "spirituals"; they may well have learned it from Paul (cf. 3:21). The verb (*exestin*) is cognate with the noun *exousia*, "authority," important in Chaps. 8–10. Cf. 10:23.

anything.[1] **13** "Food is meant for the stomach and the stomach for food"—and God will destroy both one and the other. The body is not meant for immorality, but for the Lord, and the Lord for the body. **14** And God raised the Lord and will also raise us up by his power. **15** Do you not know that your bodies are members of Christ? Shall I therefore take the members of Christ and make them members of a prostitute? Never! **16** Do you not know that he who joins himself to a prostitute becomes one body with her? For, as it is written, "The two shall become one."[2] **17** But he who is united to the Lord becomes one spirit with him. **18** Shun immorality. Every other sin which a man commits is outside the body; but the immoral man sins against his own body. **19** Do you not know that your body is a temple of the Holy Spirit within you, which you have from God? You are not your own; **20** you were bought with a price. So glorify God in your body.

7 Now concerning the matters about which you wrote. It is well for a man not to touch a woman. **2** But because of the temptation to immorality, each man should have his own wife and each woman her own husband. **3** The husband should give to his wife her conjugal rights, and likewise the wife to her husband. **4** For the wife does not rule over her own body, but the husband does; likewise the husband does not rule over his own body, but the wife does. **5** Do not refuse one another except perhaps by agreement for a season, that you may devote yourselves to prayer; but then come together again, lest Satan tempt you through lack of self-control. **6** I say this by way of concession, not of command. **7** I wish that all were as I myself am. But each has his own special gift from God, one of one kind and one of another.

8 To the unmarried and the widows I say it is well for them to remain single as I do. **9** But if they cannot exercise self-control, they should marry. For it is better to marry than to be aflame with passion.

10 To the married I give charge, not I but the Lord,[3] that the wife should not separate from her husband **11** (but if she does, let her remain single or else be reconciled to her husband)—and that the husband should not divorce his wife.

12 To the rest I say, not the Lord, that if any brother has a wife who is an unbeliever, and she consents to live with him, he should not divorce her. **13** If any woman has a husband who is an unbeliever, and he consents to live with her, she should not divorce him. **14** For the unbelieving husband is consecrated through his wife,

---

1. Paul's pun, *exestin* / *exousiasthēsomai*, can hardly be imitated in English.
2. Lit., "one flesh," Gen. 2:24.

3. Cf. Matt. 5:32; 19:9; Mark 10:11 f.; Luke 16:18. One of Paul's very rare allusions to a saying of Jesus.

and the unbelieving wife is consecrated through her husband. Otherwise, your children would be unclean, but as it is they are holy. **15** But if the unbelieving partner desires to separate, let it be so; in such a case the brother or sister is not bound. For God has called us to peace. **16** Wife, how do you know whether you will save your husband? Husband, how do you know whether you will save your wife?

17 Only, let every one lead the life which the Lord has assigned to him, and in which God has called him. This is my rule in all the churches. **18** Was any one at the time of his call already circumcised? Let him not seek to remove the marks of circumcision. Was any one at the time of his call uncircumcised? Let him not seek circumcision. **19** For neither circumcision counts for anything nor uncircumcision, but keeping the commandments of God. **20** Every one should remain in the state in which he was called. **21** Were you a slave when called? Never mind. But if you can gain your freedom, avail yourself of the opportunity.[4] **22** For he who was called in the Lord as a slave is a freedman of the Lord. Likewise he who was free when called is a slave of Christ. **23** You were bought with a price; do not become slaves of men. **24** So, brethren, in whatever state each was called, there let him remain with God.[5]

25 Now concerning the unmarried,[6] I have no command of the Lord, but I give my opinion as one who by the Lord's mercy is trustworthy. **26** I think that in view of the impending[7] distress it is well for a person to remain as he is. **27** Are you bound to a wife? Do not seek to be free. Are you free from a wife? Do not seek marriage. **28** But if you marry, you do not sin, and if a girl marries she does not sin. Yet those who marry will have worldly troubles, and I would spare you that. **29** I mean, brethren, the appointed time has grown very short; from now on, let those who have wives live as though they had none, **30** and those who mourn as though they were not mourning, and those who rejoice as though they were not rejoicing, and those who buy as though they had no goods, **31** and those who deal with the world as though they had no dealings with it. For the form of this world is passing away.

32 I want you to be free from anxieties. The unmarried man is anxious about the affairs of the Lord, how to please the Lord; **33** but the married man is anxious about worldly affairs, how to please his wife, **34** and his interests are divided. And the unmarried woman or girl is anxious about the affairs of the Lord, how to be holy in body and spirit; but the married woman is anxious about

---

4. This translation is possible, but more likely is: "Even if you can gain your freedom, rather make use [of your slavery]."
5. Vv. 17–24 form a rhetorical "cir-

cle": n.b. repetition of the theme, vv. 17, 20, 24.
6. Lit., "virgins."
7. Or, "present."

worldly affairs, how to please her husband. **35** I say this for your own benefit, not to lay any restraint upon you, but to promote good order and to secure your undivided devotion to the Lord.

36 If any one thinks that he is not behaving properly toward his betrothed,[8] if his passions are strong, and it has to be, let him do as he wishes; let them marry—it is no sin. **37** But whoever is firmly established in his heart, being under no necessity but having his desire under control, and has determined this in his heart, to keep her as his betrothed, he will do well. **38** So that he who marries his betrothed does well; and he who refrains from marriage will do better.

39 A wife is bound to her husband as long as he lives. If the husband dies, she is free to be married to whom she wishes, only in the Lord. **40** But in my judgment she is happier if she remains as she is. And I think that I have the Spirit of God.

8 Now concerning food offered to idols:[9] we know that "all of us possess knowledge."[1] "Knowledge" puffs up, but love builds up. **2** If any one imagines that he knows something, he does not yet know as he ought to know.[2] **3** But if one loves God, one is known by him.

4 Hence, as to the eating of food offered to idols, we know that "an idol has no real existence," and that "there is no God but one." **5** For although there may be so-called gods in heaven or on earth—as indeed there are many "gods" and many "Lords"—**6** yet for us there is one God, the Father, from whom are all things and for whom we exist, and one Lord, Jesus Christ, through whom are all things and through whom we exist.

7 However, not all possess this knowledge. But some, through being hitherto accustomed to idols, eat food as really offered to an idol; and their conscience, being weak, is defiled. **8** Food will not commend us to God. We are no worse off if we do not eat, and no better off if we do. **9** Only take care lest this liberty of yours somehow become a stumbling block to the weak. **10** For if any one sees you, a man of knowledge, at table in an idol's temple,[3] might he

---

8. Lit., "his virgin," as also in v. 38. The traditional interpretation, which refers the passage to the question whether a father should marry off his daughter, is impossible. The case is either of engaged persons who, misunderstanding the basis of Paul's ascetic teachings, are afraid that marriage would be a sin, or of an early form of "spiritual marriage," i.e., without sexual relations, which is known from the third century on.
9. The topic of Chaps. 8–10; see the

essay by H. von Soden below, pp. 257–68.
1. Another slogan of the Corinthian spiritualists.
2. For the form of this maxim, cf. 3:18; 10:12.
3. Meals in the cult shrine were extremely important in the family, social, and civic life of Hellenistic culture; for many participants most such occasions had scarcely any religious significance except in the sense of civic religion.

not be encouraged,[4] if his conscience is weak, to eat food offered to idols? [11] And so by your knowledge this weak man is destroyed, the brother for whom Christ died. [12] Thus, sinning against your brethren and wounding their conscience when it is weak, you sin against Christ. [13] Therefore, if food is a cause of my brother's falling, I will never eat meat, lest I cause my brother to fall.

9 Am I not free?[5] Am I not an apostle? Have I not seen Jesus our Lord? Are not you my workmanship in the Lord? [2] If to others I am not an apostle, at least I am to you; for you are the seal of my apostleship in the Lord.

[3] This is my defense to those who would examine me. [4] Do we not have the right to our food and drink? [5] Do we not have the right to be accompanied by a wife,[6] as the other apostles and the brothers of the Lord and Cephas? [6] Or is it only Barnabas and I who have no right to refrain from working for a living? [7] Who serves as a soldier at his own expense? Who plants a vineyard without eating any of its fruit? Who tends a flock without getting some of the milk?

[8] Do I say this on human authority? Does not the law say the same? [9] For it is written in the law of Moses, "You shall not muzzle an ox when it is treading out the grain."[7] Is it for oxen that God is concerned? [10] Does he not speak entirely for our sake? It was written for our sake, because the plowman should plow in hope and the thresher thresh in hope of a share in the crop. [11] If we have sown spiritual good among you, is it too much if we reap your material benefits? [12] If others share this rightful claim upon you, do not we still more?

Nevertheless, we have not made use of this right, but we endure anything rather than put an obstacle in the way of the gospel of Christ. [13] Do you not know that those who are employed in the temple service get their food from the temple, and those who serve at the altar share in the sacrificial offerings? [14] In the same way, the Lord commanded that those who proclaim the gospel should get their living by the gospel.[8]

[15] But I have made no use of any of these rights,[9] nor am I

4. Lit., "built up," the sarcastic reverse of 8. 1b.
5. While Chap. 9 seems to interrupt the argument, actually it is a personal example of the principle being developed: Christian freedom includes the freedom to use or to renounce one's "right," depending on the communal situation. The theme word *exousia*, "authority," or "autonomy," is variously translated: "liberty" (8:9), "right" (9:4, 5, 6, 18), "rightful claim" (9:12); note the verbal form in 10:23 ("all things are lawful": *panta exestin*).
6. Lit., "a sister [i.e., a Christian] as wife."
7. Deut. 25:4.
8. Another allusion to a saying attributed to Jesus: cf. Luke 10:7; Matt. 10:10; Gal. 6:6; 1 Tim. 5:18.
9. Cf. 1 Thess. 2:9; 2 Cor. 11:7–11.

writing this to secure any such provision. For I would rather die than have any one deprive me of my ground for boasting. [16] For if I preach the gospel, that gives me no ground for boasting. For necessity is laid upon me. Woe to me if I do not preach the gospel! [17] For if I do this of my own will, I have a reward; but if not of my own will, I am entrusted with a commission. [18] What then is my reward? Just this: that in my preaching I may make the gospel free of charge, not making full use of my right in the gospel.

[19] For though I am free from all men, I have made myself a slave to all, that I might win the more. [20] To the Jews I became as a Jew, in order to win Jews; to those under the law I became as one under the law—though not being myself under the law—that I might win those under the law. [21] To those outside the law I became as one outside the law—not being without law toward God but under the law of Christ—that I might win those outside the law. [22] To the weak I became weak, that I might win the weak. I have become all things to all men, that I might by all means save some. [23] I do it all for the sake of the gospel, that I may share in its blessings.

[24] Do you not know that in a race all the runners compete, but only one receives the prize?[1] So run that you may obtain it. [25] Every athlete exercises self-control in all things. They do it to receive a perishable wreath, but we an imperishable. [26] Well, I do not run aimlessly, I do not box as one beating the air; [27] but I pommel my body and subdue it, lest after preaching to others I myself should be disqualified.

10 I want you to know, brethren,[2] that our fathers were all under the cloud, and all passed through the sea, [2] and all were baptized into Moses in the cloud and in the sea, [3] and all ate the same supernatural[3] food [4] and all drank the same supernatural[3] drink. For they drank from the supernatural[3] Rock which followed them,[4] and the Rock was Christ. [5] Nevertheless with most of them God was not pleased; for they were overthrown in the wilderness.

[6] Now these things are warnings to us, not to desire evil as they did.[5] [7] Do not be idolaters as some of them were; as it is written, "The people sat down to eat and drink and rose up to

---

1. Metaphors from athletics were favorites in popular Greek rhetoric of every school.
2. Vv 1–13 have the style of Hellenistic synagogue homilies.
3. Lit., "spiritual." The food is the manna (Ex. 16:4–35; Deut. 8:3; Ps. 78:23–25); the "spiritual drink," the water from the rock (Ex. 17:6; Num. 20:2–13).

4. The double account of the water miracle (Ex. 17; Num. 20) led to the legend of a rock that "went up with them to the hills and down to the valleys . . ." (Tosefta, *Sukkah* iii.11 and elsewhere).
5. Num. 11:4, 34; Ps. 78:29 f.; the Greek word translated "craving" in those passages is the same as that rendered "desire" here.

dance."[6] [8] We must not indulge in immorality as some of them did and twenty-three thousand fell in a single day.[7] [9] We must not put the Lord[8] to the test, as some of them did and were destroyed by serpents,[9] [10] nor grumble, as some of them did and were destroyed by the Destroyer.[1] [11] Now these things happened to them as a warning, but they were written down for our instruction, upon whom the end of the ages has come. [12] Therefore let any one who thinks that he stands take heed lest he fall. [13] No temptation has overtaken you that is not common to man. God is faithful, and he will not let you be tempted beyond your strength, but with the temptation will also provide the way of escape, that you may be able to endure it.

[14] Therefore, my beloved, shun the worship of idols. [15] I speak as to sensible men; judge for yourselves what I say. [16] The cup of blessing which we bless, is it not a participation in the blood of Christ? The bread which we break, is it not a participation[2] in the body of Christ? [17] Because there is one bread, we who are many are one body, for we all partake of the one bread. [18] Consider the practice of Israel;[3] are not those who eat the sacrifices partners in the altar? [19] What do I imply then? That food offered to idols is anything, or that an idol is anything? [20] No, I imply that what pagans sacrifice[4] they offer to demons and not to God. I do not want you to be partners with demons. [21] You cannot drink the cup of the Lord and the cup of demons. You cannot partake of the table of the Lord and the table of demons. [22] Shall we provoke the Lord to jealousy? Are we stronger than he?

[23] "All things are lawful,"[5] but not all things are helpful. "All things are lawful," but not all things build up. [24] Let no one seek his own good, but the good of his neighbor. [25] Eat whatever is sold in the meat market[6] without raising any question on the ground of conscience. [26] For "the earth is the Lord's, and everything in it."[7] [27] If one of the unbelievers invites you to dinner and you are disposed to go, eat whatever is set before you without raising any question on the ground of conscience. [28] (But if some one[8] says to you, "This has been offered in sacrifice," then out of

6. Ex. 32:6.
7. Num. 25.
8. Some texts read "Christ."
9. Num. 21:5 f.
1. Num. 14:2, 36; 16:41–49; Ps. 106:25–27.
2. Or, "communion."
3. Lit., "Israel according to the flesh."
4. Several important witnesses read "they [Israel] sacrifice." The clause is a quotation from Deut. 32:17, which refers to Israel's apostasy (cf. v. 7). In the Hebrew that apostasy is called a rejection of "the Rock," though the LXX translation is "God."

5. Cf. 6:12.
6. Much of the meat ordinarily sold had been involved in some form of sacrificial rite.
7. Ps. 24:1.
8. Who is this informant, a pagan or one of the "weak" Christians? Use of the pagan technical term for "sacrifice" here, rather than the Jewish and Christian parody of it found elsewhere in 1 Cor., suggests the former. The train of thought in vv. 28–30 is not clear; the parentheses inserted by RSV translators indicate the simplest solution.

consideration for the man who informed you, and for conscience' sake—**29** I mean his conscience, not yours—do not eat it.) For why should my liberty be determined by another man's scruples? **30** If I partake with thankfulness, why am I denounced because of that for which I give thanks?

31 So, whether you eat or drink, or whatever you do, do all to the glory of God. **32** Give no offense to Jews or to Greeks or to the church of God, **33** just as I try to please all men in everything I do, not seeking my own advantage, but that of many, that they may be saved. **11** Be imitators of me, as I am of Christ.

2 I commend you because you remember me in everything and maintain the traditions even as I have delivered them to you.[9] **3** But I want you to understand that the head of every man is Christ, the head of a woman is her husband, and the head of Christ is God. **4** Any man who prays or prophesies with his head covered[1] dishonors his head, **5** but any woman who prays or prophesies with her head unveiled dishonors her head[2]—it is the same as if her head were shaven. **6** For if a woman will not veil herself, then she should cut off her hair; but if it is disgraceful for a woman to be shorn or shaven, let her wear a veil. **7** For a man ought not to cover his head, since he is the image and glory of God;[3] but woman is the glory of man. **8** (For man was not made from woman, but woman from man. **9** Neither was man created for woman, but woman for man.) **10** That is why a woman ought to have a veil[4] on her head, because of the angels.[5] **11** (Nevertheless, in the Lord woman is not independent of man nor man of woman;

9. Vv. 2–16 are one of the most obscure passages in the Pauline letters. Only a few points are relatively clear: (1) The issue is raised by the prophetic movement that flourished briefly, practiced by both men and women, in the early church, and was regarded as a gift of the Spirit and a sign that Christians belonged already to the end of days. (2) It was already a "tradition" that "in Christ" there is "no 'male and female'" (Gal. 3:28); in Corinth there was an "enthusiastic" tendency to apply such statements quite realistically in the present life of the community (see above on Chap. 7). (3) Paul, though "praising" this fundamental position, wishes to limit the enthusiasm that threatens to lapse into fantasy. His rather awkward argument is based on Jewish custom (a woman with loose or uncovered hair dishonors her husband) and widespread speculations based on Gen. 1–2.
1. "With his head covered": the opposite "unveiled" in v. 5 seems to require this translation, but both grammar and Jewish custom speak against it. The Greek would normally mean, "having (something: long hair?) hanging down from the head."
2. "Head" in vv. 4, 5 must be a double entendre (v. 3), alluding to God and the husband respectively.
3. Gen. 1:26 f.
4. Most texts read "authority." The head covering ("veil" does not mean a covering for the face in this passage) is presumably a symbol of this, but in what sense? Under her husband's authority? To show that she has authority to prophesy?
5. No one knows what this means, though many guesses have been offered. To ward off the demonic powers (cf. Gen. 6:2 and note 2 Cor. 11:3, 14)? Because angels guard the created order? Because angels share in the community's worship (suggested by comparison with the Dead Sea Scrolls)? Because angels transmit prophecy? None of these is convincing.

¹² for as woman was made from man, so man is now born of woman. And all things are from God.) ¹³ Judge for yourselves; is it proper for a woman to pray to God with her head uncovered? ¹⁴ Does not nature itself teach you that for a man to wear long hair is degrading to him, ¹⁵ but if a woman has long hair, it is her pride?[6] For her hair is given to her for a covering. ¹⁶ If any one is disposed to be contentious, we recognize no other practice, nor do the churches of God.

¹⁷ But in the following instructions I do not commend you, because when you come together it is not for the better but for the worse. ¹⁸ For, in the first place, when you assemble as a church, I hear that there are divisions among you; and I partly believe it, ¹⁹ for there must be factions among you in order that those who are genuine among you may be recognized. ²⁰ When you meet together, it is not the Lord's supper that you eat. ²¹ For in eating, each one goes ahead with his own meal, and one is hungry and another is drunk. ²² What! Do you not have houses to eat and drink in? Or do you despise the church of God and humiliate those who have nothing? What shall I say to you? Shall I commend you in this? No, I will not.

²³ For I received from the Lord what I also delivered[7] to you, that the Lord Jesus on the night when he was betrayed took bread, ²⁴ and when he had given thanks, he broke it, and said, "This is my body which is for[8] you. Do this in remembrance of me." ²⁵ In the same way also the cup, after supper, saying, "This cup is the new covenant in my blood. Do this, as often as you drink it, in remembrance of me." ²⁶ For as often as you eat this bread and drink the cup, you proclaim the Lord's death until he comes.

²⁷ Whoever, therefore, eats the bread or drinks the cup of the Lord in an unworthy manner will be guilty of profaning the body and blood of the Lord. ²⁸ Let a man examine himself, and so eat of the bread and drink of the cup. ²⁹ For any one who eats and drinks without discerning[9] the body eats and drinks judgment upon himself. ³⁰ That is why many of you are weak and ill, and some have died. ³¹ But if we judged ourselves truly, we should not be judged. ³² But when we are judged by the Lord, we are chastened[1] so that we may not be condemned along with the world.

6. Similar statements are found in pagan and Jewish moralists of this period; e.g., Pseudo-Phocylides, 210–12.
7. "Received," "delivered" are technical terms for transmission of tradition; hence "from the Lord" here (contrast Gal. 1:11 f.) obviously includes, not excludes, human mediation. To the tradition itself, compare Matt. 26:26–28; Mark 14:22–24; Luke 22:17–19.
8. Some texts read "broken for," a few, "given for."
9. Or, "distinguishing," i.e., from profane meals (cf. vv. 20 f.).
1. Or, "when we are judged we are being chastened by the Lord."

³³ So then, my brethren, when you come together to eat, wait for one another—³⁴ if any one is hungry, let him eat at home—lest you come together to be condemned. About the other things I will give directions when I come.

12 Now concerning spiritual gifts,[2] brethren, I do not want you to be uninformed. ² You know that when you were heathen, you were led astray to dumb idols, however you may have been moved. ³ Therefore I want you to understand that no one speaking by the Spirit of God ever says "Jesus be cursed!"[3] and no one can say "Jesus is Lord" except by the Holy Spirit.

⁴ Now there are varieties of gifts, but the same Spirit; ⁵ and there are varieties of service, but the same Lord; ⁶ and there are varieties of working, but it is the same God who inspires them all in every one. ⁷ To each is given the manifestation of the Spirit for the common good. ⁸ To one is given through the Spirit the utterance of wisdom, and to another the utterance of knowledge according to the same Spirit, ⁹ to another faith by the same Spirit, to another gifts of healing by the one Spirit, ¹⁰ to another the working of miracles, to another prophecy, to another the ability to distinguish between spirits, to another various kinds of tongues, to another the interpretation of tongues. ¹¹ All these are inspired by one and the same Spirit, who apportions to each one individually as he wills.

¹² For just as the body is one and has many members, and all the members of the body, though many, are one body,[4] so it is with Christ. ¹³ For by one Spirit [we were all baptized into one body—]Jews or Greeks, slaves or free[5]—and all were made to drink of one Spirit.

¹⁴ For the body does not consist of one member but of many. ¹⁵ If the foot should say, "Because I am not a hand, I do not belong to the body," that would not make it any less a part of the body. ¹⁶ And if the ear should say, "Because I am not an eye, I do not belong to the body," that would not make it any less a part of the body. ¹⁷ If the whole body were an eye, where would be the

2. This theme, apparently answering another question of the Corinthians' letter, occupies Chaps. 12–14.
3. Various explanations are offered for this startling formula: (1) an allusion to requirement (attested from the second century) by Roman officers that recanting Christians curse Christ and acclaim Caesar as "Lord" to escape persecution—but nothing in 1 Cor. speaks of persecution; (2) an ecstatic cry by Corinthian "spirituals" or "Gnostics," assumed to distinguish between the physical "Jesus" and the spiritual "Christ"; (3) supposed Jewish curses of the crucified (Deut. 21:23)—but this would have no connection with the context; (4) merely Paul's hyperbole, formulated as a hypothetical opposite of the normal confession, "Jesus is Lord."
4. The metaphor of body and limbs to describe a society was ancient and very widespread. The more realistic, "sacramental" notion of "the body of Christ" may play some role in Paul's admonitions here (vv. 13, 27), though a very limited one compared with the later letters to Colossians and Ephesians.
5. Cf. Gal. 3:27 f.; Col. 3:11.

hearing? If the whole body were an ear, where would be the sense of smell? **18** But as it is, God arranged the organs in the body, each one of them, as he chose. **19** If all were a single organ, where would the body be? **20** As it is, there are many parts, yet one body. **21** The eye cannot say to the hand, "I have no need of you," nor again the head to the feet, "I have no need of you." **22** On the contrary, the parts of the body which seem to be weaker are indispensable, **23** and those parts of the body which we think less honorable we invest with the greater honor, and our unpresentable parts are treated with greater modesty, **24** which our more presentable parts do not require. But God has so adjusted the body, giving the greater honor to the inferior part, **25** that there may be no discord in the body, but that the members may have the same care for one another. **26** If one member suffers, all suffer together; if one member is honored, all rejoice together.

27 Now you are the body of Christ and individually members of it. **28** And God has appointed in the church first apostles, second prophets, third teachers, then workers of miracles, then healers, helpers, administrators, speakers in various kinds of tongues. **29** Are all apostles? Are all prophets? Are all teachers? Do all work miracles? **30** Do all possess gifts of healing? Do all speak with tongues? Do all interpret? **31** But earnestly desire the higher gifts.

And I will show you a still more excellent way.[6]

13 If I speak in the tongues of men and of angels, but have not love, I am a noisy gong or a clanging cymbal. **2** And if I have prophetic powers, and understand all mysteries and all knowledge, and if I have all faith, so as to remove mountains, but have not love, I am nothing. **3** If I give away all I have, and if I deliver my body to be burned,[7] but have not love, I gain nothing.

4 Love is patient and kind; love is not jealous or boastful; **5** it is not arrogant or rude. Love does not insist on its own way; it is not irritable or resentful; **6** it does not rejoice at wrong, but rejoices in the right. **7** Love bears all things, believes all things, hopes all things, endures all things.

6. The relation of 12:31b–13:13 to its present context is much disputed. It interrupts the train of thought; 14.1b would follow logically after 12:31a, while 14:1a repeats 12:31a almost verbatim—often the device of an editor who is making an insert. Moreover, Chap. 13 is a self-contained unit, composed in the style of an encomium on a virtue so familiar in Greek literature (the praises of Eros in Plato's *Symposium* are the most famous; for a Jewish example, see 3 Esdras [in Protestant editions of the Apocrypha, 1 Esd.] 4:34–40). On the other hand, vv. 1 f. connect directly with the problem of *charismata* in Corinth, while the depreciation of *gnōsis* in vv. 9 ff. is quite consonant with Paul's earlier admonitions (Chaps. 8–10). It is possible, therefore, that Paul himself inserted the previously composed rhetorical unit here, though transposition from another place (after Chap. 14?) or another letter or addition by a later editor are all possibilities. Only one aspect of the prose-poem seems un-Pauline: Jesus Christ is not once mentioned.

7. Ancient texts are divided between *kauthēsōmai*, "to be burned," and *kauchēsōmai*, "that I may boast." In either case the allusion is to martyrdom; cf. Dan. 3:28.

8 Love never ends; as for prophecies, they will pass away; as for tongues, they will cease; as for knowledge, it will pass away. **9** For our knowledge is imperfect and our prophecy is imperfect; **10** but when the perfect comes, the imperfect will pass away. **11** When I was a child, I spoke like a child, I thought like a child, I reasoned like a child; when I became a man, I gave up childish ways. **12** For now we see in a mirror dimly, but then face to face.[8] Now I know in part; then I shall understand fully, even as I have been fully understood. **13** So faith, hope, love abide, these three;[9] but the greatest of these is love.

14 Make love your aim, and earnestly desire the spiritual gifts, especially that you may prophesy. **2** For one who speaks in a tongue[1] speaks not to men but to God; for no one understands him, but he utters mysteries in the Spirit. **3** On the other hand, he who prophesies speaks to men for their upbuilding and encouragement and consolation. **4** He who speaks in a tongue edifies himself, but he who prophesies edifies the church. **5** Now I want you all to speak in tongues, but even more to prophesy. He who prophesies is greater than he who speaks in tongues, unless some one interprets, so that the church may be edified.

6 Now, brethren, if I come to you speaking in tongues, how shall I benefit you unless I bring you some revelation or knowledge or prophecy or teaching? **7** If even lifeless instruments, such as the flute or the harp, do not give distinct notes, how will any one know what is played? **8** And if the bugle gives an indistinct sound, who will get ready for battle? **9** So with yourselves; if you in a tongue utter speech that is not intelligible, how will any one know what is said? For you will be speaking into the air. **10** There are doubtless many different languages in the world, and none is without meaning; **11** but if I do not know the meaning of the language, I shall be a foreigner to the speaker and the speaker a foreigner to me. **12** So with yourselves; since you are eager for manifestations of the Spirit, strive to excel in building up[2] the church.

13 Therefore, he who speaks in a tongue should pray for the

---

8. The mirror metaphor is used in many ways by ancient authors; here it merely emphasizes the indirectness and incompleteness of knowledge in the present world; excessive claims of the Corinthian "spirituals" are thus quietly refuted.

9. The triad faith, hope, love was a cliché for Paul, perhaps already in pre-Pauline Christianity and even in Hellenistic Judaism. Cf. 1 Thess. 1:3; 5:8; Rom 5:1–5; Col. 1:4 f.

1. "Speaking in tongues" (*glossolalia*) was an ecstatic phenomenon, known in modern as well as ancient religious movements, consisting in involuntary utterance of rapid sequences of inarticulate sounds, perhaps in a chanting cadence. In the early church it was interpreted as a "gift of the Spirit," 12:10, 28, 30; 13:1, 8; Acts 2:4–13, where the author interprets the phenomenon in a more "rational," miraculous, and symbolic way; 10:46; 19:6; elsewhere in early Christian literature only in the spurious ending of Mark, 16:17.

2. "Building up": cf. vv. 3, 4, 5, 17, 26; a basic norm for Paul: 8:1; 10:23; 1 Thess. 5:11.

power to interpret. ¹⁴ For if I pray in a tongue, my spirit prays but my mind is unfruitful. ¹⁵ What am I to do? I will pray with the spirit and I will pray with the mind also; I will sing with the spirit and I will sing with the mind also. ¹⁶ Otherwise, if you bless³ with the spirit, how can any one in the position of an outsider⁴ say the "Amen" to your thanksgiving when he does not know what you are saying? ¹⁷ For you may give thanks well enough, but the other man is not edified. ¹⁸ I thank God that I speak in tongues more than you all; ¹⁹ nevertheless, in church I would rather speak five words with my mind, in order to instruct others, than ten thousand words in a tongue.

²⁰ Brethren, do not be children in your thinking; be babes in evil, but in thinking be mature.⁵ ²¹ In the law it is written, "By men of strange tongues and by the lips of foreigners will I speak to this people, and even then they will not listen to me, says the Lord."⁶ ²² Thus, tongues are a sign not for believers but for unbelievers, while prophecy is not for unbelievers but for believers. ²³ If, therefore, the whole church assembles and all speak in tongues, and outsiders or unbelievers enter, will they not say that you are mad? ²⁴ But if all prophesy, and an unbeliever or outsider enters, he is convicted by all, he is called to account by all, ²⁵ the secrets of his heart are disclosed; and so, falling on his face, he will worship God and declare that God is really among you.

²⁶ What then, brethren? When you come together,⁷ each one has a hymn, a lesson, a revelation, a tongue, or an interpretation. Let all things be done for edification. ²⁷ If any speak in a tongue, let there be only two or at most three, and each in turn; and let one interpret. ²⁸ But if there is no one to interpret, let each of them keep silence in church and speak to himself and to God. ²⁹ Let two or three prophets speak, and let the others weigh what is said. ³⁰ If a revelation is made to another sitting by, let the first be silent. ³¹ For you can all prophesy one by one, so that all may learn and all be encouraged; ³² and the spirits of prophets are subject to prophets. ³³ For God is not a God of confusion but of peace.

As in all the churches of the saints, ³⁴ the women should keep

3. "Bless": i.e., pronounce a blessing, a praise of God (in the form of the *berakah* of Jewish prayers).
4. "Outsider" here and in vv. 23 f. translates *idiōtēs*, "layman," "ordinary man." It may mean simply a Christian not endowed with glossolalia or, since the phrase here is literally "he who occupies the place of the *idiōtēs*," reference may be to "uninitiated" catechumens, who have a special place in the congregation and participate in the lit-

urgy (by pronouncing the "Amen").
5. See note on 2:6; Paul may be playing on the various connotations of the word to say that glossolalia is not a sure sign of spiritual "perfection" or "initiation," but may rather indicate immaturity.
6. Isa. 28:11–12.
7. Vv. 26–33 afford one of the rare glimpses we have into the typical phenomena of early Christian worship.

silence in the churches.[8] For they are not permitted to speak, but should be subordinate, as even the law says. [35] If there is anything they desire to know, let them ask their husbands at home. For it is shameful for a woman to speak in church. [36] What! Did the word of God originate with you, or are you the only ones it has reached?

[37] If any one thinks that he is a prophet, or spiritual, he should acknowledge that what I am writing to you is a command of the Lord. [38] If any one does not recognize this, he is not recognized.[9] [39] So, my brethren, earnestly desire to prophesy, and do not forbid speaking in tongues; [40] but all things should be done decently and in order.

15 Now I would remind you, brethren, in what terms I preached to you the gospel, which you received, in which you stand, [2] by which you are saved, if you hold it fast—unless you believed in vain.

[3] For I delivered to you as of first importance what I also received,[1] that Christ died for our sins in accordance with the scriptures, [4] that he was buried, that he was raised on the third day in accordance with the scriptures, [5] and that he appeared to Cephas, then to the twelve. [6] Then he appeared to more than five hundred brethren at one time, most of whom are still alive, though some have fallen asleep. [7] Then he appeared to James, then to all the apostles. [8] Last of all, as to one untimely born,[2] he appeared also to me. [9] For I am the least of the apostles, unfit to be called an apostle, because I persecuted the church of God. [10] But by the grace of God I am what I am, and his grace toward me was not in vain. On the contrary, I worked harder than any of them, though it was not I, but the grace of God which is with me. [11] Whether then it was I or they, so we preached and so you believed.

8. This statement seems flatly to contradict 11:2–16, which presupposes that women are free to prophesy in the church. If 14.33b–35 is taken to refer only to non-ecstatic discussion in the assembly, as v. 35 suggests, then it is not clear why the passage stands in the context of a chapter dealing with ecstasy. Some manuscripts place it after v. 10. Some modern commentators regard it as an interpolation by some later, conservative Paulinist; cf. 1 Tim. 2:11 f. The place of women was evidently an important issue between Paul and the Corinthian spiritualists, however, for the latter probably took the abolition of distinctions ("no 'male and female'") as evidence of their resurrected status.
9. On the form of v. 38, see note on 3:17. The issue is conflict between charismatics; Paul's assertion of authority is a step toward institutionaliza-

tion.
1. On the technical designation of tradition, see notes on 11.23 and Gal. 1.12. The tradition is carefully formulated:

> that Christ died for our sins
> > in accordance with the scriptures
> and that he was buried
> that he was raised on the third day
> > in accordance with the scriptures
> and that he appeared
> > to Cephas, then to
> > the twelve.

Where it ends is not certain, since Paul adds other reports that are also, in a looser sense, "tradition."
2. "One untimely born": an "abortion" or "miscarriage," perhaps a term of abuse used by Paul's opponents; v. 9 can be regarded as interpreting the term.

12 Now if Christ is preached as raised from the dead, how can some of you say that there is no resurrection of the dead?[3] **13** But if there is no resurrection of the dead, then Christ has not been raised; **14** if Christ has not been raised, then our preaching is in vain and your faith is in vain. **15** We are even found to be misrepresenting God, because we testified of God that he raised Christ, whom he did not raise if it is true that the dead are not raised. **16** For if the dead are not raised, then Christ has not been raised. **17** If Christ has not been raised, your faith is futile and you are still in your sins. **18** Then those also who have fallen asleep in Christ have perished. **19** If for this life only we have hoped in Christ,[4] we are of all men most to be pitied.

20 But in fact Christ has been raised from the dead, the first fruits of those who have fallen asleep. **21** For as by a man came death, by a man has come also the resurrection of the dead. **22** For as in Adam all die, so also in Christ shall all be made alive. **23** But each in his own order: Christ the first fruits, then at his coming those who belong to Christ. **24** Then comes the end, when he delivers the kingdom to God the Father after destroying every rule and every authority and power. **25** For he must reign until he has put all his enemies under his feet. **26** The last enemy to be destroyed is death. **27** "For God has put all things in subjection under his feet."[5] But when it says, "All things are put in subjection under him," it is plain that he is excepted who put all things under him. **28** When all things are subjected to him, then the Son himself will also be subjected to him who put all things under him, that God may be everything to every one.

29 Otherwise, what do people mean by being baptized on behalf of the dead?[6] If the dead are not raised at all, why are people baptized on their behalf? **30** Why am I in peril every hour? **31** I protest, brethren, by my pride in you which I have in Christ Jesus our Lord, I die every day! **32** What do I gain if, humanly speaking, I fought with beasts[7] at Ephesus? If the dead are not raised, "Let us eat and drink, for tomorrow we die."[8] **33** Do not be deceived:

---

3. The Corinthian spirituals do not deny Christ's resurrection—or their own. Rather, since they regard themselves as already raised with Christ spiritually, by their baptismal initiation (see note on 4.8), they see no sense in a *future* resurrection "from the dead."

4. Or, "If in this life we who are in Christ have only hope." Grammatically, this translation is more likely. The problem with it is that it seems to express the opponents' position, not Paul's, for whom "hope" is a positive term.

5. Ps. 110:1 (the OT text cited more often than any other in the NT).

6. Nothing further is known about the practice of vicarious baptism, though church fathers report similar practices later by Marcionites, Montanists, and Cerinthians (schismatic groups of the second to the fourth centuries).

7. Probably to be taken figuratively, as frequently in Cynic-Stoic diatribes, the style of which permeates this passage. Note the modifier, "humanly speaking," lit., "according to man."

8. Isa. 22:13.

"Bad company ruins good morals."[9] 34 Come to your right mind, and sin no more. For some have no knowledge of God. I say this to your shame.

35 But some one will ask, "How are the dead raised? With what kind of body do they come?" 36 You foolish man! What you sow does not come to life unless it dies. 37 And what you sow is not the body which is to be, but a bare kernel, perhaps of wheat or of some other grain. 38 But God gives it a body as he has chosen, and to each kind of seed its own body. 39 For not all flesh is alike, but there is one kind for men, another for animals, another for birds, and another for fish. 40 There are celestial bodies and there are terrestrial bodies; but the glory of the celestial is one, and the glory of the terrestrial is another. 41 There is one glory of the sun, and another glory of the moon, and another glory of the stars; for star differs from star in glory.

42 So is it with the resurrection of the dead. What is sown is perishable, what is raised is imperishable. 43 It is sown in dishonor, it is raised in glory. It is sown in weakness, it is raised in power. 44 It is sown a physical body, it is raised a spiritual body. If there is a physical body, there is also a spiritual body. 45 Thus it is written, "The first man Adam became a living being";[1] the last Adam became a life-giving spirit. 46 But it is not the spiritual which is first but the physical, and then the spiritual. 47 The first man was from the earth, a man of dust; the second man is from heaven. 48 As was the man of dust, so are those who are of the dust; and as is the man of heaven, so are those who are of heaven. 49 Just as we have borne the image of the man of dust, we shall also bear the image of the man of heaven. 50 I tell you this, brethren: flesh and blood cannot inherit the kingdom of God, nor does the perishable inherit the imperishable.

51 Lo! I tell you a mystery.[2] We shall not all sleep, but we shall all be changed, 52 in a moment, in the twinkling of an eye, at the last trumpet. For the trumpet will sound, and the dead will be raised imperishable, and we shall be changed. 53 For this perishable nature must put on the imperishable, and this mortal nature must put on immortality. 54 When the perishable puts on the imperishable, and the mortal puts on immortality, then shall come to pass the saying that is written:

"Death is swallowed up in victory."

55 "O death, where is thy victory?
"O death, where is thy sting?"[3]

9. Menander, *Thais*, frag. 218.
1. Gen. 2:7. Paul is apparently alluding to and rejecting (v. 46) a tradition, attested by Philo and certain Gnostic texts, that distinguished the "heavenly man" of Gen. 1:26 ff. from the "earthly man" of Gen. 2.
2. Cf. 1 Thess. 4:13–18.
3. The quotation is composite: Isa. 25:8; Hos. 13:14.

⁵⁶ The sting of death is sin, and the power of sin is the law. ⁵⁷ But thanks be to God, who gives us the victory through our Lord Jesus Christ.

⁵⁸ Therefore, my beloved brethren, be steadfast, immovable, always abounding in the work of the Lord, knowing that in the Lord your labor is not in vain.

16 Now concerning the contribution for the saints:[4] as I directed the churches of Galatia, so you also are to do. ² On the first day of every week, each of you is to put something aside and store it up, as he may prosper, so that contributions need not be made when I come. ³ And when I arrive, I will send those whom you accredit by letter to carry your gift to Jerusalem. ⁴ If it seems advisable that I should go also, they will accompany me.

⁵ I will visit you after passing through Macedonia, for I intend to pass through Macedonia, ⁶ and perhaps I will stay with you or even spend the winter, so that you may speed me on my journey wherever I go. ⁷ For I do not want to see you now just in passing; I hope to spend some time with you, if the Lord permits. ⁸ But I will stay in Ephesus until Pentecost,[5] ⁹ for a wide door for effective work has opened to me, and there are many adversaries.

¹⁰ When Timothy comes, see that you put him at ease among you, for he is doing the work of the Lord, as I am. ¹¹ So let no one despise him. Speed him on his way in peace, that he may return to me; for I am expecting him with the brethren.

¹² As for our brother Apollos, I strongly urged him to visit you with the other brethren, but it was not at all his will[6] to come now. He will come when he has opportunity.

¹³ Be watchful, stand firm in your faith, be courageous, be strong. ¹⁴ Let all that you do be done in love.

¹⁵ Now, brethren, you know that the household of Stephanas were the first converts in Achaia, and they have devoted themselves to the service of the saints; ¹⁶ I urge you to be subject to such men and to every fellow worker and laborer. ¹⁷ I rejoice at the coming of Stephanas and Fortunatus and Achaicus, because they have made up for your absence; ¹⁸ for they refreshed my spirit as well as yours. Give recognition to such men.

¹⁹ The churches of Asia send greetings. Aquila and Prisca,[7] together with the church in their house, send you hearty greetings in the Lord. ²⁰ All the brethren send greetings. Greet one another with a holy kiss.[8]

---

4. Cf. 2 Cor. 8, 9; Rom. 15:25–31; Gal. 2:10.
5. Note that Paul can write to the predominantly Gentile-Christian congregation off-handedly of the Jewish festival Pentecost-Shavuot cf. 5:7 f.
6. Or, "God's will for him."
7. See Acts 18:2, 18, 26; Rom. 16:3.
8. Cf. 1 Thess. 5:26; 2 Cor. 13:12; Rom. 16:16.

21 I, Paul, write this greeting with my own hand. **22** If any one has no love for the Lord, let him be accursed. Our Lord, come![9] **23** The grace of the Lord Jesus be with you. **24** My love be with you all in Christ Jesus. Amen.

THE SECOND LETTER TO THE CORINTHIANS (ca. 56)

Two issues have preoccupied the scholarly discussion of 2 Corinthians for a century: (1) Do we have the letter as it was written, or is it really a composite of several fragments? (2) Who were the opponents whom Paul so vigorously attacks, particularly in the last four chapters? No consensus has been attained on either question.

The primary reason for doubting the unity of the letter is the stark contrast between the last four chapters and the previous ones. The early chapters are irenic; they speak of a conflict between Paul and the Corinthians which has been happily resolved. Chapters 10–13, on the other hand, portray a congregation in open rebellion against Paul's authority, evidently incited by a group of rival apostles who have come to Corinth from outside. Even in the first part of the letter there are abrupt transitions. The long self-defense, 2:14–7:4, not only carries quite a different tone from 1:1–2:13 and 7:5 ff., it also interrupts Paul's report of his trip from Troas to Macedonia (2:13; 7:5). Similarly the appeal of 6:13, "Widen your hearts," is interrupted in mid-sentence, to resume again in 7:2. The intervening admonition not only seems out of context, it is so different from Paul's usual writing in style, vocabulary, and content that most scholars think he can hardly have written it. Finally, both Chaps. 8 and 9 speak of the collection that Paul was arranging to be sent to Jerusalem, but the two admonitions seem quite independent of each other and make their appeals on different grounds.

Hence many scholars think that the present work is a composite, assembled by some ancient editor from fragments of as many as four or five original letters. One plausible reconstruction of the sequence of events and letters is: (1) A visit by Titus and an unnamed "brother" to supervise the collection for Jerusalem, soon after the writing of 1 Corinthians. (2) Arrival in Corinth of the new missionaries whom Paul was to call "superlative apostles." (3) A letter from Paul warning against these interlopers, perhaps partly preserved in 2 Cor. 2:14–7:4 (omitting 6:14–7:1, a later interpola-

9. The Greek transliterates the Aramaic *marana tha*; possibly both this and the preceding anathema belong to the early eucharistic liturgy.

tion). (4) A quick visit by Paul, only to be publicly humiliated by someone in the congregation (cf. 12:21; 2:5–11; 7:12). (5) A furious letter (2:4), including the present Chaps. 10–13. (6) Trouble, possibly imprisonment, in Asia (Ephesus?) (cf. 1:3–11). Escaping that danger, Paul hurries to Macedonia to meet Titus, who had been sent off to learn what was happening in Corinth (1:23–2:4; 7:5). (7) Titus' report of repentance in the Corinthian church and censure of the person who had insulted Paul. (8) A conciliatory letter, containing at least 1:1–2:4; 7:5–16, and perhaps one of the notes about the collection (Chap. 8 or 9). The other may have belonged to a still later letter.

The identity of Paul's opponents remains a matter for speculation, but a number of their characteristics can be inferred rather directly from the letter(s). From Paul's parodies it is apparent that they used the titles "apostle," "worker," and "servant (*diakonos*) of Christ" (11:13–15, 23). That they were Jewish Christians is clear from their pride in being "Hebrews," "Israelites," and "Seed of Abraham" (11:22). At issue were the authority and power of the apostle, both the form in which authority was exercised and the means by which it could be authenticated. The group opposing Paul evidently tended, at least in Paul's eyes, to equate authority with power; their demands on the Corinthian congregation were direct and assertive (11:20); they scoffed at Paul's "weakness" (11:30; cf. Chaps. 3–4 *passim*). They made Paul's refusal to accept money from the Corinthians a ground for suspecting his legitimacy and his motives (11:7–11; 12:13–18). Moreover, it seems that their right to exert this authority was vindicated by visible manifestations of power, that is, of the possession of the spirit: by performance of miracles (12:12), by the experience of "visions and revelations of the Lord" (12:1), by the skill of their extemporaneous speaking (11:6) and the impressiveness of their appearance (10:1–11). It is interesting to observe that Paul, too, can make similar claims—to an outsider he, like these "apostles," would resemble a typical Hellenistic "pneumatic," the itinerant, charismatic propagandist for a new religious cult or philosophical school. Only Paul, at least at this point in his career, regards such a means of self-authentication as "speaking as a fool" (11:21; Chaps. 11–12 *passim*).

Not surprisingly, there is a certain competitiveness and pride inherent in the style of mission sketched here. The "superlative apostles" are wont to "measure" or "compare themselves with one another," and to "commend themselves" (10:12, 18); they have "letters of recommendation" (3:1). They recognize no limits to their territory, but are eager to test themselves in "other men's (fields of) labors" (10:13–18). Finally, we may perhaps surmise from Chaps. 3–4 that the opposing apostles pride themselves in their allegorical interpretation of scripture, by which they follow in Moses' footsteps (and Christ's?) to a mystic vision of God through the mirror of the Torah. Perhaps they have a special Christology connected with this notion of Moses and scripture (11:4: "another Jesus . . . a different spirit . . . a different gospel").

The superlative apostles thus had many characteristics in common both with the Hellenistic "prophets," mendicant priests, and "philosophers" who proliferated in the Greco-Roman world, and with the apologetic theology developed by diaspora Jews in the same period. Some scholars have conjectured that Hellenistic Judaism had already produced such missionaries—wandering, charismatic, miracle-workers—before Christianity began. Certainly the type is often met in early Christianity. The portraits of the apostles in the Book of Acts (including Paul!) conform to the type, and in the later apocryphal "Acts" the resemblance is even closer.

Since the time of F. C. Baur (see below, pp. 277–88) connections have frequently been drawn between the superlative apostles of Corinth and the Jerusalem original apostles, or the "Judaizers" of Galatia. Neither is likely, however. Neither Jerusalem nor requirements of the law figure in Paul's counterarguments. The title "Hebrews" can no more prove a Palestinian origin of the opponents than it can for Paul, and Paul's opposition to the Law of Moses in Chaps. 3–4 presupposes a completely different issue from that under debate in Galatians. Thus we can no more be sure where the rival missionaries originated than we can know who signed their "letters of recommendation." Paul's conflict with them, however, does shed light on important aspects of his own understanding of his mission and of divergent tendencies in early Christianity.

---

1 Paul, an apostle to Christ Jesus by the will of God, and Timothy our brother.

To the church of God which is at Corinth, with all the saints who are in the whole of Achaia:

2 Grace to you and peace from God our Father and the Lord Jesus Christ.

3 Blessed be the God[1] and Father of our Lord Jesus Christ, the

---

1. The blessing is a variant of the usual epistolary thanksgiving (cf. Eph. 1:3; 1 Pet. 1:3). A Christianized version of the ancient Jewish formula *barukh adonay*, it doubtless reflects liturgical usage.

Father of mercies and God of all comfort,[2] [4] who comforts us in all our affliction, so that we may be able to comfort those who are in any affliction, with the comfort with which we ourselves are comforted by God. [5] For as we share abundantly in Christ's sufferings, so through Christ we share abundantly in comfort too.[3] [6] If we are afflicted, it is for your comfort and salvation; and if we are comforted, it is for your comfort, which you experience when you patiently endure the same sufferings that we suffer. [7] Our hope for you is unshaken; for we know that as you share in our sufferings, you will also share in our comfort.

[8] For we do not want you to be ignorant, brethren, of the affliction we experienced in Asia;[4] for we were so utterly, unbearably crushed that we despaired of life itself. [9] Why, we felt that we had received the sentence of death; but that was to make us rely not on ourselves but on God who raises the dead; [10] he delivered us from so deadly a peril,[5] and he will deliver us; on him we have set our hope that he will deliver us again. [11] You also must help us by prayer, so that many will give thanks on our behalf for the blessing granted us in answer to many prayers.[6]

[12] For our boast is this, the testimony of our conscience that we have behaved in the world, and still more toward you, with holiness and godly sincerity, not by earthly wisdom but by the grace of God. [13] For we write you nothing but what you can read and understand; I hope you will understand fully, [14] as you have understood in part, that you can be proud of us as we can be of you, on the day of the Lord Jesus.

[15] Because I was sure of this, I wanted to come to you first, so that you might have a double pleasure;[7] [16] I wanted to visit you on my way to Macedonia, and to come back to you from Macedonia and have you send me on my way to Judea.[8] [17] Was I vacillating when I wanted to do this? Do I make my plans like a worldly man, ready to say Yes and No at once? [18] As surely as God is faithful, our word to you has not been Yes and No. [19] For the Son of

---

2. Stylistically the repetition of the words "comfort" (both the noun *paraklēsis* and the verb *parakaleō*) and "affliction"/"afflict" in vv. 3–7 is extraordinary. A similar cluster occurs in 7:4–13. "Affliction" is the key word that connects vv. 8–11 to the first half of the blessing. The effect in Greek is slightly less monotonous than in English; nevertheless the style is more oral than literary.

3. Or, "For as the sufferings of Christ abound for us, so also our comfort abounds through Christ."

4. Despite countless guesses, the event referred to remains unknown, but cf. Acts 19:23–41.

5. Lit., "so great a death"; some texts have the plural.

6. This sentence, which continues v. 10, is clumsy because Paul has inverted his usual "I give thanks" clause, putting the verb in the passive voice, and has added redundant expressions to provide a climax. Omitting the redundancies, one could translate: ". . . will deliver us again, since you are helping us by prayer, so that thanks may be given by many persons for the gift granted me."

7. "Pleasure" (*chara*); some witnesses read "favor" (*charis*).

8. Contrast 1 Cor. 16:5–7.

God, Jesus Christ, whom we preached among you, Silvanus and Timothy and I, was not Yes and No; but in him it is always Yes. 20 For all the promises of God find their Yes in him. That is why we utter the Amen through him, to the glory of God. 21 But it is God who establishes us with you in Christ, and has commissioned us;[9] 22 he has put his seal upon us and given us his Spirit in our hearts as a guarantee.

23 But I call God to witness against me—it was to spare you that I refrained from coming to Corinth.[1] 24 Not that we lord it over your faith; we work with you for your joy, for you stand firm in your faith.

2 For I made up my mind not to make you another painful visit.[2] 2 For if I cause you pain, who is there to make me glad but the one whom I have pained? 3 And I wrote as I did, so that when I came I might not be pained by those who should have made me rejoice,[3] for I felt sure of all of you, that my joy would be the joy of you all. 4 For I wrote you out of much affliction and anguish of heart and with many tears, not to cause you pain but to let you know the abundant love that I have for you.

5 But if any one has caused pain,[4] he has caused it not to me, but in some measure—not to put it too severely—to you all. 6 For such a one this punishment by the majority is enough; 7 so you should rather turn to forgive and comfort him, or he may be overwhelmed by excessive sorrow. 8 So I beg you to reaffirm your love for him. 9 For this is why I wrote, that I might test you and know whether you are obedient in everything. 10 Any one whom you forgive, I also forgive. What I have forgiven, if I have forgiven anything, has been for your sake in the presence of Christ, 11 to keep Satan from gaining the advantage over us; for we are not ignorant of his designs.

12 When I came to Troas to preach the gospel of Christ, a door was opened for me in the Lord; 13 but my mind could not rest because I did not find my brother Titus[5] there. So I took leave of them and went on to Macedonia.[6]

---

9. Lit., "anointed us"; "anointed," "sealed," "gave the Spirit" all refer to baptism.

1. If 2 Cor. is a unity, this must refer to the *second* visit promised in 1 Cor. 16:5; a different translation of 2:1 would be required (see following note). Otherwise, the reference is to the third visit threatened in 2 Cor. 13:1 f.; cf. 12:14. This seems to create fewer difficulties.

2. Those who deny that Paul had already made a second, "painful" visit (see above, pp. 48f.) have to translate: "... not to make you another visit, which would be painful," which is possible, but less natural. Note that in 1:23–2:11 "pain" and "joy" take up the themes "affliction" and "comfort" of 1:3–11.

3. Cf. 13:1–10.

4. Paul alludes so delicately to the painful event that we cannot be sure what happened. We may surmise that on his second visit some individual in the congregation took the side of the rival apostles, inciting the Corinthian Christians to rebuff Paul. Cf. 12:21.

5. Titus was the bearer of the letter mentioned in the previous verses.

6. The itinerary is not resumed until 7:5.

14 But thanks be to God, who in Christ always leads us in triumph, and through us spreads the fragrance of the knowledge of him everywhere. **15** For we are the aroma[7] of Christ to God among those who are being saved and among those who are perishing, **16** to one a fragrance from death to death, to the other a fragrance from life to life. Who is sufficient for these things?[8] **17** For we are not, like so many, peddlers of God's word; but as men of sincerity, as commissioned by God, in the sight of God we speak in Christ.

3 Are we beginning to commend ourselves again? Or do we need, as some do, letters of recommendation to you, or from you? **2** You yourselves are our letter of recommendation, written on your[9] hearts, to be known and read by all men; **3** and you show that you are a letter from Christ delivered by us, written not with ink but with the Spirit of the living God, not on tablets of stone[1] but on tablets of human hearts.

4 Such is the confidence that we have through Christ toward God. **5** Not that we are sufficient of ourselves to claim anything as coming from us; our sufficiency is from God, **6** who has qualified[2] us to be ministers of a new covenant, not in a written code but in the Spirit; for the written code kills, but the Spirit gives life.

7 Now if the dispensation[3] of death, carved in letters on stone, came with such splendor that the Israelites could not look at Moses' face because of its brightness,[4] fading as this was, **8** will not dispensation of the Spirit be attended with greater splendor? **9** For if there was splendor in the dispensation of condemnation, the dispensation of righteousness must far exceed it in splendor. **10** Indeed, in this case, what once had splendor has come to have no splendor at all, because of the splendor that surpasses it. **11** For

7. While the metaphor might have been suggested by the incense carried in triumphal processions (v. 14), and could suggest the OT technical term for a burnt offering (e.g., Lev. 1:9, 13; 2:9; cf. Phil. 4:18; Eph. 5:2), the figure was fairly common.
8. This abrupt question is the theme for the rambling self-defense that occupies 2:17–7:4. It is the first hint in the letter that someone in Corinth has challenged Paul's apostolic credentials.
9. Most ancient authorities read "our," which is also presupposed by 7:3.
1. Thinking of Jer. 31:31–33 (source of the "new covenant" notion which follows) Paul abruptly shifts the metaphor.
2. "Sufficient," "sufficiency," "qualified" are all cognates in Greek.
3. The nouns *diakonos* and *diakonia* are translated variously in this section: "minister" (3:6), "servant" (6:4); "dispensation" (3:7, 8, 9), "ministry" (4:1; 5:18; 6:3). For both Paul and

the rival apostles, *diakonos*, like *apostolos*, designates the function or office of the missionary as Christ's personal representative. The issue is how one demonstrates his "sufficiency" for that function; Paul introduces a contrast with the office of Moses, i.e., the function (as Paul sees it) of the law. For the notion of the law as agent of death, see Rom. Chap. 7.
4. Ex. 34:30. The following discussion (3:7–4:6) alludes constantly to Ex. 34:29–35, in the manner of some forms of *midrash aggadah*. In Jewish and Samaritan legend the "glory" of Moses' face was commonly identified with the "image of God" lost by Adam when he sinned, but restored at Sinai to those who received the law. Paul insists that that "glory" was only temporary, since the true glory-image could only be restored in Jesus Christ (3:18; 4:4, 6). Note that a single Greek word has been translated variously as "brightness," "splendor," and "glory."

if what faded away came with splendor, what is permanent must have much more splendor.

[12] Since we have such a hope, we are very bold, [13] not like Moses, who put a veil over his face[5] so that the Israelites might not see the end of the fading splendor. [14] But their minds were hardened; for to this day, when they read the old covenant, that same veil remains unlifted, because only through Christ is it taken away. [15] Yes, to this day whenever Moses is read a veil lies over their minds; [16] but when a man turns to the Lord the veil is removed.[6] [17] Now the Lord is the Spirit,[7] and where the Spirit of the Lord is, there is freedom. [18] And we all, with unveiled face, beholding[8] the glory of the Lord, are being changed into his likeness from one degree of glory to another; for this comes from the Lord who is the Spirit.

4 Therefore, having this ministry by the mercy of God,[9] we do not lose heart. [2] We have renounced disgraceful, underhanded ways; we refuse to practice cunning or to tamper with God's word, but by the open statement of the truth we would commend ourselves to every man's conscience in the sight of God.[1] [3] And even if our gospel is veiled, it is veiled only to those who are perishing. [4] In their case the god of this world[2] has blinded the minds of the unbelievers, to keep them from seeing the light of the gospel of the glory of Christ, who is the likeness[3] of God. [5] For what we preach is not ourselves, but Jesus Christ as Lord, with ourselves as your servants[4] for Jesus' sake. [6] For it is the God who said, "Let light shine out of darkness,"[5] who has shone in our hearts to give the light of the knowledge of the glory of God in the face of Christ.

[7] But we have this treasure in earthen vessels, to show that the transcendent power belongs to God and not to us.[6] [8] We are

---

5. Ex. 34:33, 35. By suggesting that the veil was to conceal the loss of Moses' "glory," Paul departs from the biblical text and contradicts the prevailing Jewish interpretation, that Moses' face shone until his death. For Paul's allegory, Moses' glory had to be "fading," because it symbolized the "ministry of the law," which was temporary.

6. Ex. 34:34.

7. Probably "the Lord" should be in quotation marks, understood as an exegetical remark: " 'the Lord' (in Ex. 34:34) means 'the Spirit.' "

8. "Beholding": the word usually refers to looking in a mirror; it could be translated "reflecting." The notion is that by looking at the image of God revealed in Christ, man sees, as in a magic mirror, his true self, destined from creation (Gen. 1:26 f.), and is miraculously transformed into that pattern. The language may have originated in a procedure in mystery initia-

tions; it became a stock notion in Gnosticism.

9. Lit., "as we have received mercy."

1. An accusation against the "superlative apostles" may be implied here (cf. 2:17; 11:1–5, 12–15, 19 f.), or only a defense against their accusations (10:1–5; 12:16).

2. A surprisingly sharp expression of the limited dualism which Paul shared with Jewish apocalyptic groups, including the Qumran community. Cf. 1 Cor. 2:6, 8; Eph. 2:2; John 12:31; 14:30; 16:11.

3. Or, "image," as in 3:18; cf. Col. 1:15; 3:10; also 1 Cor. 15:49.

4. Lit., "slaves."

5. Cf. Gen. 1:3.

6. This may be an indirect polemic against the "superlative apostles," who evidently think that the "glory" of an apostle should be visible in his credentials, his rhetoric, and his charismatic powers. The contrary is a fundamental theme for Paul.

afflicted in every way, but not crushed; perplexed, but not driven to despair; 9 persecuted, but not forsaken; struck down, but not destroyed; 10 always carrying in the body the death of Jesus, so that the life of Jesus may also be manifested in our bodies.7 11 For while we live we are always being given up to death for Jesus' sake so that the life of Jesus may be manifested in our mortal flesh. 12 So death is at work in us, but life in you.

13 Since we have the same spirit of faith as he had who wrote, "I believed, and so I spoke,"8 we too believe, and so we speak, 14 knowing that he who raised the Lord Jesus will raise us also with Jesus and bring us with you into his presence. 15 For it is all for your sake, so that as grace extends to more and more people it may increase thanksgiving, to the glory of God.

16 So we do not lose heart. Though our outer nature9 is wasting away, our inner nature is being renewed every day. 17 For this slight momentary affliction is preparing for us an eternal weight of glory beyond all comparison, 18 because we look not to the things that are seen but to the things that are unseen; for the things that are seen are transient, but the things that are unseen are eternal.

5 For we know that if the earthly tent we live in is destroyed, we have a building from God, a house not made with hands, eternal in the heavens. 2 Here indeed we groan, and long to put on our heavenly dwelling, 3 so that by putting it on1 we may not be found naked. 4 For while we are still in this tent, we sigh with anxiety; not that we would be unclothed, but that we would be further clothed, so that what is mortal may be swallowed up by life. 5 He who has prepared us for this very thing is God, who has given us the Spirit as a guarantee.2

6 So we are always of good courage; we know that while we are at home in the body we are away from the Lord, 7 for we walk by faith, not by sight. 8 We are of good courage, and we would rather

7. In the Greek, rhythm and internal rhyme heighten the rhetorical effect of vv. 8–10.
8. Greek version of Ps. 116:10 (i.e., LXX Ps. 115:1).
9. "Nature": lit., "man" (*anthropos*). In the section 4:16–5:10 the language of popular Hellenistic anthropology—inner/outer man, visible-transient/unseen-eternal, the body as a "tent"—alternates with images belonging to apocalyptic—present affliction/eternal glory, a house stored up in heaven, final judgment. Apocalyptic contributes the main lines of thought. Differences from Paul's other statements about the *parousia* and resurrection (1 Thess. 4:13–18; 1 Cor. 15:35–57; Rom. 8:18–25; Phil. 1:20–24) are less significant than has sometimes been urged; they are occasioned by the polemic context.
1. Some witnesses read "even if we take it off." The notion that the soul must strip off the body before it could ascend to the heavenly world was a mythical commonplace; it became particularly important in Gnosticism, along with the concept of the heavenly garment which, as the Gnostic's true self, was to replace the earthly body. Paul accepts the latter imagery, but not the former. Note, however, that he does not use the word "soul" here; he is less dualistic than his opponents. The heavenly house/garment is the same as the "spiritual body" of 1 Cor. 15:44.
2. Or, "down payment"; cf. 1:22; Eph. 1:14; Rom. 8:23.

be away from the body and at home with the Lord. [9] So whether we are at home or away, we make it our aim to please him. [10] For we must all appear before the judgment seat of Christ, so that each one may receive good or evil, according to what he has done in the body.[3]

[11] Therefore, knowing the fear of the Lord, we persuade men; but what we are is known to God, and I hope it is known also to your conscience. [12] We are not commending ourselves to you again but giving you cause to be proud of us, so that you may be able to answer those who pride themselves on a man's position[4] and not on his heart. [13] For if we are beside ourselves,[5] it is for God; if we are in our right mind, it is for you. [14] For the love of Christ[6] controls us, because we are convinced that one has died for all; therefore all have died. [15] And he died for all, that those who live might live no longer for themselves but for him who for their sake died and was raised.

[16] From now on, therefore, we regard no one from a human point of view;[7] even though we once regarded Christ from a human point of view, we regard him thus no longer. [17] Therefore, if any one is in Christ, he is a new creation;[8] the old has passed away, behold, the new has come. [18] All this is from God, who through Christ reconciled us to himself and gave us the ministry of reconciliation; [19] that is, God was in Christ reconciling[9] the world to himself, not counting their trespasses against them, and entrusting to us the message of reconciliation. [20] So we are ambassadors for Christ, God making his appeal through us. We beseech you on behalf of Christ, be reconciled to God. [21] For our sake he made him to be sin who knew no sin, so that in him we might become the righteousness of God.

6 Working together with him, then, we entreat you not to accept the grace of God in vain. [2] For he says,

"At the acceptable time I have listened to you,
    and helped you on the day of salvation."[1]

Behold, now is the acceptable time; behold, now is the day of salvation. [3] We put no obstacle in any one's way, so that no fault may be found with our ministry, [4] but as servants of God we commend

---

3. Cf. 1 Cor. 3:12–15; 4:5; Rom. 2:16; 14:10.

4. "Position": lit., "face." Cf. Chap. 10.

5. "Beside ourselves": "ecstasy" in the technical sense (the verb used here is a cognate of the English "ecstasy") is meant; mystical experiences are not, Paul insists, a means for legitimating apostleship, but are essentially private. Cf. 12:1–6; and the similar statement about glossolalia in 1 Cor. 14:2.

6. I.e., "Christ's love for us," as the following clause makes plain.

7. Lit., "according to flesh." Some see in these words a hint that the opponents prided themselves on having known Jesus during his lifetime, but that is very dubious. "Flesh" for Paul connotes not just the physical, but humanity in rebellion against God.

8. Lit., "If any one is in Christ—a new creation!" Perhaps this should be understood as, "he perceives that there is a new creation"; note the following two clauses, which allude to Isa. 43: 18 f. Cf. Gal. 6:15.

9. Or, "in Christ God was reconciling . . ."

1. Isa. 49:8.

ourselves in every way:[2] through great endurance, in afflictions, hardships, calamities, [5] beatings, imprisonments, tumults, labors, watching, hunger; [6] by purity, knowledge, forbearance, kindness, the Holy Spirit, genuine love, [7] truthful speech, and the power of God; with the weapons of righteousness for the right hand and for the left; [8] in honor and dishonor, in ill repute and good repute. We are treated as impostors, and yet are true; [9] as unknown, and yet well known; as dying, and behold we live; as punished, and yet not killed; [10] as sorrowful, yet always rejoicing; as poor, yet making many rich; as having nothing, and yet possessing everything.

[11] Our mouth is open to you, Corinthians; our heart is wide. [12] You are not restricted by us, but you are restricted in your own affections. [13] In return—I speak as to children—widen your hearts also.[3]

[14] Do not be mismated with unbelievers. For what partnership have righteousness and iniquity? Or what fellowship has light with darkness? [15] What accord has Christ with Belial?[4] Or what has a believer in common with an unbeliever? [16] What agreement has the temple of God with idols? For we are the temple[5] of the living God; as God said,

"I will live in them and move among them,
and I will be their God,
and they shall be my people.
[17] Therefore come out from them,
and be separate from them, says the Lord,
and touch nothing unclean;
then I will welcome you,
[18] and I will be a father to you,
and you shall be my sons and daughters,
says the Lord Almighty."[6]

2. Vv. 4–10 comprise a "catalogue of difficulties" (peristasis catalogue) such as are found often in the Cynic-Stoic diatribe; cf. 1 Cor. 4:11–13; 2 Cor. 11:23–29. "It is difficulties that show what men are" (Epictetus, I:24.1). The list of virtues (vv. 6 f.) varies the content. The form is simple but dramatic: a series of eighteen nouns, each with the preposition "in," the last four embellished by modifers (vv. 4b–7a); three phrases with the preposition "through" (vv. 7b–8a); seven antitheses of increasing length (8b–10). 3. See 7:2. The following admonition was certainly not composed for this context. Since the discovery of the Dead Sea Scrolls, much of the terminology of 6:14–7:1 has been recognized as very close to the technical language of the Qumran sect, i.e., Essene. The insistence on radical separation of the "sons of light" from the "sons of darkness" was fundamental to the Qumran community's life; it is strange to Paul (note 1 Cor. 5:9 ff.). How the fragment came to be placed here—whether by Paul or some later editor—cannot be determined. Perhaps it was inserted to suggest that rejection of the apostle was tantamount to "being mismated with unbelievers." 4. Greek, "Beliar." A semitic word meaning "worthless," *Belial* became one of the names of the prince of evil spirits, found in the Dead Sea Scrolls, the Testaments of the Twelve Patriarchs, and other Jewish and early Christian literature. 5. The concept of the community as God's temple is important at Qumran, but also for Paul: 1 Cor. 3:16; individualized 1 Cor. 6:19. 6. The quotation is composite, paraphrased in part: Lev. 26:11 f.; Isa. 52:11; Ezek. 20:34; 37:27; 2 Sam. 7:14.

7 Since we have these promises, beloved, let us cleanse ourselves from every defilement of body and spirit, and make holiness perfect in the fear of God.

2 Open your hearts to us; we have wronged no one, we have corrupted no one, we have taken advantage of no one. **3** I do not say this to condemn you, for I said before that you are in our hearts, to die together and to live together. **4** I have great confidence in you; I have great pride in you; I am filled with comfort. With all our affliction, I am overjoyed.[7]

5 For even when we came into Macedonia, our bodies had no rest but we were afflicted at every turn—fighting without and fear within. **6** But God, who comforts the downcast, comforted us by the coming of Titus, **7** and not only by his coming but also by the comfort with which he was comforted in you, as he told us of your longing, your mourning, your zeal for me, so that I rejoiced still more. **8** For even if I made you sorry with my letter,[8] I do not regret it (though I did regret it), for I see that that letter grieved you, though only for a while. **9** As it is, I rejoice, not because you were grieved, but because you were grieved into repenting; for you felt a godly grief, so that you suffered no loss through us. **10** For godly grief produces a repentance that leads to salvation and brings no regret, but worldly grief produces death. **11** For see what earnestness this godly grief has produced in you, what eagerness to clear yourselves, what indignation, what alarm, what longing, what zeal, what punishment! At every point you have proved yourselves guiltless in the matter. **12** So although I wrote to you, it was not on account of the one who did the wrong,[9] nor on account of the one who suffered the wrong, but in order that your zeal for us might be revealed to you in the sight of God. **13** Therefore we are comforted.

And besides our own comfort we rejoiced still more at the joy of Titus, because his mind has been set at rest by you all. **14** For if I have expressed to him some pride in you, I was not put to shame; but just as everything we said to you was true, so our boasting before Titus has proved true. **15** And his heart goes out all the more to you, as he remembers the obedience of you all, and the

---

7. The break between vv. 4 and 5, together with the fact that v. 5 continues 2:13, is often taken as an indication that 2:14–7.4 are part of an earlier letter (see introduction). Against this is the fact that v. 4 takes up the themes—comfort and joy despite affliction—that dominated the opening eulogy and which again fill 7:5–16 (see notes on 1:2; 2:1).

8. Cf. 2:3. The letter in question cannot be the present 1 Cor.; if part of it is not to be identified with the present 2 Cor. 10–13, it is entirely lost. The specific incident referred to in 2:5 ff. and 7:12 is not mentioned in Chaps. 10–13, so presumably *part* of the "severe letter" is lost in any case.

9. The wrongdoer is certainly not the incestuous man of 1 Cor. 5, for this is a case of personal injury, and "the one who suffered the wrong" is obviously Paul.

fear and trembling with which you received him. 16 I rejoice, because I have perfect confidence in you.

8 We want you to know, brethren, about the grace of God which has been shown in the churches of Macedonia, 2 for in a severe test of affliction, their abundance of joy and their extreme poverty have overflowed in a wealth of liberality on their part. 3 For they gave according to their means, as I can testify, and beyond their means, of their own free will, 4 begging us earnestly for the favor of taking part in the relief of the saints—5 and this, not as we expected, but first they gave themselves to the Lord and to us by the will of God. 6 Accordingly we have urged Titus that as he had already made a beginning,¹ he should also complete among you this gracious work. 7 Now as you excel in everything—in faith, in utterance, in knowledge, in all earnestness, and in your love for us—see that you excel in this gracious work also.

8 I say this not as a command, but to prove by the earnestness of others that your love also is genuine. 9 For you know the grace of our Lord Jesus Christ, that though he was rich, yet for your sake he became poor, so that by his poverty you might become rich.² 10 And in this matter I give my advice: it is best for you now to complete what a year ago³ you began not only to do but to desire, 11 so that your readiness in desiring it may be matched by your completing it out of what you have. 12 For if the readiness is there, it is acceptable according to what a man has, not according to what he has not. 13 I do not mean that others should be eased and you burdened, 14 but that as a matter of equality your abundance at the present time should supply their want, so that their abundance may supply your want, that there may be equality. 15 As it is written, "He who gathered much had nothing over, and he who gathered little had no lack."⁴

16 But thanks be to God who puts the same earnest care for you into the heart of Titus. 17 For he not only accepted our appeal, but being himself very earnest he is going to you of his own accord.

1. Cf. v. 10. The visits of Titus are a puzzle. Assuming the hypothetical reconstruction of the correspondence we adopted above, there must have been three, in this order: (1) a visit soon after 1 Cor. (perhaps as bearer of that letter), accompanied by one anonymous "brother," to begin the collection (8:6; 12:18); (2) the mission with the "severe letter," which succeeded in reconciling the church with Paul (2:13; 7:6–16); (3) the trip to "complete" the collection, accompanied by the famous (but anonymous) delegate-at-large and another unnamed brother (8:6, 16–19, 22). Those who defend the unity of 2 Cor., or who think

Chaps. 10–13 were written later than Chaps. 1–9, naturally offer different solutions. On the collection, see 1 Cor. 16:1–4; Rom. 15:25–31; and the note on Gal. 2:10.
2. A typically Pauline, terse summary of the gospel. For the form, cf. 5:21 and, slightly different, Rom. 4:25; for the content, cf. Phil. 2:6–11.
3. "A year ago": rather, "last year"; the expression does not indicate that twelve months have elapsed, but only that a New Year's Day has intervened. The beginning of the collection was evidently shortly after 1 Cor. was received; see 1 Cor. 16:1–4.
4. Ex. 16:18.

[18] With him we are sending the brother who is famous among all the churches for his preaching of the gospel;[5] [19] and not only that, but he has been appointed by the churches to travel with us in this gracious work which we are carrying on, for the glory of the Lord and to show our good will. [20] We intend that no one should blame us about this liberal gift which we are administering, [21] for we aim at what is honorable not only in the Lord's sight but also in the sight of men.[6] [22] And with them we are sending our brother whom we have often tested and found earnest in many matters, but who is now more earnest than ever because of his great confidence in you. [23] As for Titus, he is my partner and fellow worker in your service; and as for our brethren, they are messengers[7] of the churches, the glory of Christ. [24] So give proof, before churches, of your love and of our boasting about you to these men.

9 Now it is superfluous for me to write to you about the offering for the saints,[8] [2] for I know your readiness, of which I boast about you to the people of Macedonia, saying that Achaia has been ready since last year; and your zeal has stirred up most of them. [3] But I am sending the brethren so that our boasting about you may not prove vain in this case, so that you may be ready, as I said you would be; [4] lest if some Macedonians come with me and find that you are not ready, we be humiliated—to say nothing of you—for being so confident. [5] So I thought it necessary to urge the brethren to go on to you before me, and arrange in advance for this gift you have promised, so that it may be ready not as an exaction but as a willing gift.

[6] The point is this: he who sows sparingly will also reap sparingly, and he who sows bountifully will also reap bountifully.[9] [7] Each one must do as he has made up his mind, not reluctantly or under compulsion, for God loves a cheerful giver.[1] [8] And God is able to provide you with every blessing in abundance, so that you may always have enough of everything and may provide in abundance for every good work. [9] As it is written,

"He scatters abroad, he gives to the poor;
his righteousness endures for ever."[2]

[10] He who supplies seed to the sower and bread for food[3] will supply and multiply your resources[4] and increase the harvest of

---

5. The identity of this messenger is unknown, despite many guesses; why Titus' companions are not named, contrary to Paul's usual practice, remains unexplained. "Brother," of course, means simply "fellow Christian."
6. Prov. 3:4 LXX.
7. Greek "apostles"; the term means "commissioned agent."
8. This new introduction of the topic of the collection can hardly have stood originally in the same letter with Chap.

8. It could have been sent either before or after the letter containing Chap. 8; the latter poses fewer difficulties. Some conjecture that it may have gone not to Corinth, but to another congregation in Achaia—Cenchreae?
9. For the form, see the note on 1 Cor. 3:17.
1. Prov. 22:8 LXX.
2. Ps. 112:9.
3. Isa. 55:10.
4. Lit., "sowing" or "seed."

your righteousness.⁵ **11** You will be enriched in every way for great generosity, which through us will produce thanksgiving to God; **12** for the rendering of this service not only supplies the wants of the saints but also overflows in many thanksgivings to God. **13** Under the test of this service, you will glorify God by⁶ your obedience in acknowledging the gospel of Christ, and by the generosity of your contribution for them and for all others; **14** while they long for you and pray for you, because of the surpassing grace of God in you. **15** Thanks be to God for his inexpressible gift!

10 I, Paul, myself entreat you, by the meekness and gentleness of Christ—I who am humble when face to face with you, but bold to you when I am away!⁷—**2** I beg of you that when I am present I may not have to show boldness with such confidence as I count on showing against some who suspect us of acting in worldly⁸ fashion. **3** For though we live in the world we are not carrying on a worldly war, **4** for the weapons of our warfare are not worldly but have divine power to destroy strongholds. **5** We destroy arguments and every proud obstacle to the knowledge of God, and take every thought captive to obey Christ, **6** being ready to punish every disobedience, when your obedience is complete.⁹

7 Look¹ at what is before your eyes.² If any one is confident that he is Christ's, let him remind himself that as he is Christ's, so are we. **8** For even if I boast a little too much of our authority, which the Lord gave for building you up and not for destroying you, I shall not be put to shame. **9** I would not seem to be frightening you with letters. **10** For they say, "His letters are weighty and strong, but his bodily presence is weak, and his speech of no account."³ **11** Let such people understand that what we say by letter when absent, we do when present. **12** Not that we venture to class or compare ourselves with some of those who commend themselves. But when they measure themselves by one another, and compare themselves with one another, they are without understanding.⁴

13 But we will not boast beyond limit, but will keep to the limits God has apportioned us, to reach even to you. **14** For we are not

---

5. The term may also mean "benevolence" or "charity."
6. Or, "they will glorify God for ..."
7. In diatribe style Paul ironically repeats an accusation made by his opponents; cf. v. 10.
8. The expressions translated "world" and "worldly" here all contain the word "flesh," in Paul's technical usage: human powers used in rebellious denial of God's authority.
9. Cf. 2.9.
1. Or, "You are looking," or "are you [only] looking ...?"
2. Lit., "according to the face"; cf.

5:12, and recall the discussion of the "glory" of Moses'/Christ's face, Chaps. 3–4.
3. The rival charismatics evidently regarded an apostle's "glory" as something which must be visibly manifested in extemporary rhetorical skill and impressive "presence."
4. Several manuscripts lack the words "they are ... but we," giving a totally different sense: "But we, measuring ourselves by ourselves and comparing ourselves with ourselves, will not boast ..." This reading may very well be the original one.

overextending ourselves, as though we did not reach you; we were the first to come all the way to you with the gospel of Christ. [15] We do not boast beyond limit, in other men's labors; but our hope is that as your faith increases, our field among you may be greatly enlarged, [16] so that we may preach the gospel in lands beyond you, without boasting of work already done in another's field.[5] [17] "Let him who boasts, boast of the Lord."[6] [18] For it is not the man who commends himself that is accepted, but the man whom the Lord commends.

11 I wish you would bear with me in a little foolishness. Do bear with me! [2] I feel a divine jealousy for you, for I betrothed you to Christ to present you as a pure bride to her one husband.[7] [3] But I am afraid that as the serpent deceived Eve by his cunning,[8] your thoughts will be led astray from a sincere and pure devotion to Christ. [4] For if some one comes and preaches another Jesus than the one we preached, or if you receive a different spirit from the one you received, or if you accept a different gospel[9] from the one you accepted, you submit to it readily enough. [5] I think that I am not in the least inferior to these superlative apostles. [6] Even if I am unskilled in speaking,[1] I am not in knowledge; in every way we have made this plain to you in all things.

[7] Did I commit a sin in abasing myself so that you might be exalted, because I preached God's gospel without cost to you?[2] [8] I robbed other churches by accepting support from them in order to serve you. [9] And when I was with you and was in want, I did not burden any one, for my needs were supplied by the brethren who came from Macedonia, So I refrained and will refrain from burdening you in any way. [10] As the truth of Christ is in me, this boast of mine shall not be silenced in the regions of Achaia. [11] And why? Because I do not love you? God knows I do!

[12] And what I do I will continue to do, in order to undermine

---

5. Cf. Rom. 15:20.
6. Jer. 9:24; cf. 1 Cor. 1:31.
7. The imagery of the Messiah as the bridegroom of a renewed and purified Israel is known from apocalyptic writings, both Jewish and Christian (cf. Rev. 21:2, 9; Matt. 9:15=Mark 2:19 f.=Luke 5:34 f.; Matt. 25:1–13); behind that usage is the OT metaphor of Israel's union with God (Hos. 1–3; Ezek. 16; Isa. 50:1; 54.5 ff.). Cf. also Eph. 5:22–32. In certain late rabbinic traditions Moses is the matchmaker who betrothed Israel to God at Sinai; perhaps Paul, who elsewhere compares himself with Moses, knows that tradition and puts himself in the same role here.
8. Cf. v. 14. A legend based on the puzzling text of Gen. 4:1b said that the serpent (Satan) seduced Eve by

pretending to be God's angel, so that he was Cain's father (cf. 1 John 3:12).
9. Paul does not discuss the differences in doctrine apparently implied by this verse. That the "other Jesus" whom the rivals proclaimed was the earthly Jesus, as a miracle-working "divine man," has been suggested, but cannot be proved. Perhaps Paul only means that their missionary claims and methods *imply* a different Christology from his own.
1. See note on 10:10.
2. On Paul's departure from the normal missionary practice of living from contributions of converts, for which he is here under suspicion, see 1 Cor. 9; 1 Thess. 2:9 (and note); 2 Thess. 3:7–9. Cf. below, 12:14–18.

the claim of those who would like to claim that in their boasted mission they work on the same terms as we do. **13** For such men are false apostles, deceitful workmen, disguising themselves as apostles of Christ. **14** And no wonder, for even Satan disguises himself as an angel of light.³ **15** So it is not strange if his servants also disguise themselves as servants of righteousness. Their end will correspond to their deeds.

16 I repeat, let no one think me foolish; but even if you do, accept me as a fool, so that I too may boast a little. **17** (What I am saying I say not with the Lord's authority but as a fool, in this boastful confidence; **18** since many boast of worldly⁴ things I too will boast.) **19** For you gladly bear with fools, being wise yourselves! **20** For you bear it if a man makes slaves of you, or preys upon you, or takes advantage of you, or puts on airs, or strikes you in the face. **21** To my shame, I must say, we were too weak for that!

But whatever any one dares to boast of—I am speaking as a fool—I also dare to boast of that. **22** Are they Hebrews? So am I. Are they Israelites? So am I. Are they descendants of Abraham?⁵ So am I. **23** Are they servants of Christ? I am a better one—I am talking like a madman—with far greater labors,⁶ far more imprisonments, with countless beatings, and often near death. **24** Five times I have received at the hands of the Jews the forty lashes less one. **25** Three times I have been beaten with rods; once I was stoned. Three times I have been shipwrecked; a night and a day I have been adrift at sea; **26** on frequent journeys, in danger from rivers, danger from robbers, danger from my own people, danger from Gentiles, danger in the city, danger in the wilderness, danger at sea, danger from false brethren; **27** in toil and hardship, through many a sleepless night, in hunger and thirst, often without food, in cold and exposure. **28** And, apart from other things, there is the daily pressure upon me of my anxiety for all the churches. **29** Who is weak, and I am not weak? Who is made to fall, and I am not indignant?

30 If I must boast, I will boast of the things that show my weakness. **31** The God and Father of the Lord Jesus, he who is blessed for ever, knows that I do not lie. **32** At Damascus, the governor under King Aretas guarded the city of Damascus in order to seize me, **33** but I was let down in a basket through a window in the wall, and escaped his hands.⁷

12 I must boast; there is nothing to be gained by it, but I will

3. See note on v. 3.
4. "Worldly": see note on 10:2.
5. "Hebrews," "Israelites," and "descendants of Abraham" show that the rival apostles were of Jewish background, but do not prove that they came from Palestine.
6. This "peristasis catalogue" (see note on 6:4), vv. 23–33, has the style of royal inscriptions that celebrated victorious expeditions (like the Roman imperial *res gestae*), which heightens Paul's irony.
7. Cf. Acts 9:23–25, where the plot is mistakenly blamed on "the Jews."

go on to visions and revelations of the Lord.[8] **2** I know a man in Christ[9] who fourteen years ago was caught up to the third heaven—whether in the body or out of the body[1] I do not know, God knows. **3** And I know that this man was caught up into Paradise—whether in the body or out of the body I do not know, God knows—**4** and he heard things that cannot be told, which man may not utter. **5** On behalf of this man I will boast, but on my own behalf I will not boast, except of my weaknesses. **6** Though if I wish to boast, I shall not be a fool, for I shall be speaking the truth. But I refrain from it, so that no one may think more of me than he sees in me or hears from me. **7** And to keep me from being too elated by the abundance of revelations, a thorn was given me in the flesh,[2] a messenger of Satan, to harass me to keep me from being too elated. **8** Three times I besought the Lord about this, that it should leave me; **9** but he said to me, "My grace is sufficient for you, for my power is made perfect in weakness."[3] I will all the more gladly boast of my weaknesses, that the power of Christ may rest upon me. **10** For the sake of Christ, then, I am content with weaknesses, insults, hardships, persecutions, and calamities; for when I am weak, then I am strong.

11 I have been a fool! You forced me to it, for I ought to have been commended by you.[4] For I am not at all inferior to these superlative apostles, even though I am nothing. **12** The signs of a true apostle were performed among you in all patience, with signs and wonders and mighty works. **13** For in what were you less favored than the rest of the churches, except that I myself did not burden you? Forgive me this wrong!

14 Here for the third time I am ready to come to you. And I will not be a burden, for I seek not what is yours but you; for children

8. Evidently, therefore, ecstatic experiences were one of the evidences upon which the "superlative apostles" based their authority. "Heavenly journeys" were claimed as authentication of a wide variety of esoteric lore in apocalyptic books and in Gnosticism, while actual mystical experiences were cultivated in several circles of Judaism, as well as in pagan Hellenism, in Paul's time.

9. The peculiar, stilted way in which Paul speaks of himself in the third person serves to distance himself, in his role as authoritative apostle, from that singular personal experience.

1. This repeated and strangely emphatic aside may be intended to satirize the claim of many mystics and shamans to leave the body on their "trips."

2. "Thorn": or, "stake"; even "cross" is possible. Most ancient and modern

commentators have taken this expression and the quite different one that follows, "a messenger of Satan to harass [or, "beat"] me," to refer to some kind of illness, but there is no agreement about the diagnosis. Since Paul gives metaphors rather than describing symptoms, the puzzle is not likely to be solved.

3. The style may be a parody on the inscriptions erected in praise of healing gods (such as Asclepius) by grateful beneficiaries of miraculous healing. The inscriptions reported reassuring oracles; Paul's oracle was negative. To the content of the oracle, compare Philo's allegory in which the burning bush (Ex. 3) becomes a voice proclaiming to Israel, "Do not lose heart; your weakness is your strength" (*Mos.* i.69).

4. Cf. 3:1–3.

ought not to lay up for their parents, but parents for their children. 15 I will most gladly spend and be spent for your souls. If I love you the more, am I to be loved the less? 16 But granting that I myself did not burden you. I was crafty, you say, and got the better of you by guile.[5] 17 Did I take advantage of you through any of those whom I sent to you? 18 I urged Titus to go, and sent the brother with him.[6] Did Titus take advantage of you? Did we not act in the same spirit? Did we not take the same steps?

19 Have you been thinking all along that we have been defending ourselves before you? It is in the sight of God that we have been speaking in Christ, and all for your upbuilding, beloved. 20 For I fear that perhaps I may come and find you not what I wish, and that you may find me not what you wish; that perhaps there may be quarreling, jealousy, anger, selfishness, slander, gossip, conceit, and disorder. 21 I fear that when I come again my God may humble me[7] before you, and I may have to mourn over many of those who sinned before and have not repented of the impurity, immorality, and licentiousness which they have practiced.

13 This is the third time I am coming to you. Any charge must be sustained by the evidence of two or three witnesses.[8] 2 I warned those who sinned before and all the others, and I warn them now while absent, as I did when present on my second visit, that if I come again I will not spare them—3 since you desire proof[9] that Christ is speaking in me. He is not weak in dealing with you, but is powerful in you. 4 For he was crucified in weakness, but lives by the power of God. For we are weak in him, but in dealing with you we shall live with him by the power of God.

5 Examine yourselves, to see whether you are holding to your faith. Test yourselves. Do you not realize that Jesus Christ is in you?—unless indeed you fail to meet the test! 6 I hope you will find out that we have not failed. 7 But we pray God that you may not do wrong—not that we may appear to have met the test, but that you may do what is right, though we may seem to have failed. 8 For we cannot do anything against the truth, but only for the truth. 9 For we are glad when we are weak and you are strong. What we pray for is your improvement. 10 I write this while I am away from you, in order that when I come I may not have to be severe in my use of the authority which the Lord has given me for building up and not for tearing down.

11 Finally, brethren, farewell. Mend your ways, heed my appeal,

---

5. The collection for Jerusalem may have provided the occasion for this accusation.
6. See the note on 8:6.
7. Possibly this should be translated, "when I come my God may humble me again . . ." In that case the former "humiliation" would presumably be the incident alluded to in 2:5; 7:12.
8. Deut. 19:15.
9. This is the underlying issue throughout 2:14–7:4; 10–13.

agree with one another, live in peace, and the God of love and peace will be with you. ¹² Greet one another with a holy kiss. ¹³ All the saints greet you.

¹⁴ The grace of the Lord Jesus Christ and the love of God and the fellowship of¹ the Holy Spirit be with you all.

THE LETTER TO THE ROMANS (ca. 57)

Paul wrote this, the longest of his extant letters, from Corinth, during his final, three-month stay there (Acts 20:2 f.). Given the obvious importance of the imperial capital, it is not surprising that Paul should want to preach in Rome (1:15), or that he should send a letter in advance of his visit, since he had not founded the church and hence exercised no direct authority over it (note the careful choice of words in 1:8–15). He intended his visit to be only in passing, however, for he hoped to go on to begin a new mission in Spain (15:24–28). Before that he would complete the collection for Jerusalem, a project with which he had been busy for several years. The Jerusalem trip obviously evoked some anxiety (15:31)— amply justified by subsequent events, for Paul was destined to make his journey from Jerusalem to Rome in chains, there, according to firm early tradition, to die at the hands of an imperial executioner. The premonition of danger, however, is a very faint note in the letter, which is dominated by a mood of confidence, even triumph. Clearly the trip to Jerusalem and then to the West represents for Paul a decisive turning point in his career. He speaks of his mission in the East as "completed" (15:19); he no longer has "any room for work in these regions" (15:23). He looks to Rome, therefore, as the center of the known world, and his visit there becomes a symbol for the universality of his mission "among all the Gentiles" (1:5, cf. v. 14; 15:16 ff.).

But why did Paul write *this* kind of letter in order to introduce himself to the Roman Christians? Clearly it resembles more a theological treatise than an ordinary letter of self-commendation. One might suppose that Paul's reputation as a controversial figure had preceded him to Rome, requiring a defense rather than an introduction to pave the way for his coming. And Paul's preoccupation with his mission was so total that in his case a self-defense would have to take the form of a defense of his proclamation (1:16 f.). Yet the letter is certainly not a systematic summary of Pauline theology— his Christology, for example, is presupposed, not described. The thematic exposition in Chaps. 1–11 turns about the single question of

1. Or, "and participation in . . ."

the relationship between Jew and Gentile, with the necessary corollary, the place of the law in Christianity. From his other correspondence we would not suspect that this was *the* central concern of Paul's proclamation, for elsewhere only in Galatians does it become the dominant issue. On the other hand, the admonitions in the ethical portion of the letter, particularly in Chaps. 14 f., recall some of the issues dealt with in the Corinthian correspondence. Thus the Letter to Romans presents no retrospective survey of Paul's thought, but takes up only some of those issues which have been uppermost in his mind during the past two or three years. It contains the fruit of his reflection on the controversies of Galatia and Corinth. Remarkably the Galatian issue of law and gospel overshadows the more recent debate with the Corinthian "spirituals." Evidently the former had come for Paul to have such fundamental significance that it should be expounded to the church at large and particularly the church at Rome.

Perhaps there were also factors in the Roman church itself that influenced Paul's choice of themes. There is, to be sure, no indication in the letter of any particular crisis in Rome to which Paul is responding, nor was Paul, as a stranger to that church, in any position to speak directly to local problems as he would in one of the churches he had founded. Furthermore, it is uncertain how much Paul would have known about the Roman congregations. Nevertheless certain general facts would certainly have been well known and would call for attention. The Roman church evidently originated within the Jewish community, which was quite large. It is known that the emperor Claudius expelled the Jews from the city, probably in the year A.D. 49; the historian Suetonius, writing three-quarters of a century later, said that Claudius had done so because of "disturbances at the instigation of Chrestus." Assuming a natural confusion between *Christus* and *Chrestus*, this probably means that the disturbances arose from the first missionary activity of Christians among the Roman Jews. After the accession of Nero in 54, the Claudian decree was annulled, and Jews, very likely including Jewish-Christians, drifted back to Rome. (If Romans 16 is original, Aquila and Prisca were among the returning exiles.) In the meantime the church had become preponderantly Gentile—it is evident throughout Paul's letter that he addresses a group principally Gentile but with some former Jews among them. Considering the circumstances of the Claudian expulsion, one can readily imagine that the relationships must have been very sensitive both between church and synagogue and between former Jew and former Gentile within the church. Paul's emphasis both on the unity of Jew and Gentile and on the abiding validity of God's promises to Israel would certainly have had immediate relevance to those relationships.

On the other hand, it is very doubtful whether it is possible to deduce from Paul's admonitions the actual problems existing in Rome. For example, the warning against heresy in 16:17–20 is quite general and stereotyped; it by no means indicates that a particular kind of heresy was rampant in Rome at that moment—indeed v. 19 would seem to indicate the contrary. The same is true of the admonitions of Chaps. 12 and 13, which show signs of having been assembled for catechetical purposes. Even the issue dealt with at length in Chaps. 14 f.—the mutual responsibilities of "weak" and "strong" Christians in questions of dietary rules and similar regulations—may well be a generalized paradigm based on experiences in Corinth (1 Cor. 8–10), rather than response to a present issue in Rome.

The question of the letter's purpose is further complicated by uncertainties about its original form. There is manuscript evidence that the letter circulated in three forms of varying lengths: one a text of sixteen chapters as commonly printed today; one equivalent to only the first fourteen chapters; and another to the first fifteen. There also was one version that omitted all reference to Rome (1:7, 15). Some scholars, believing the greetings of 16:3–16 to be more appropriate to Ephesus than Rome, have suggested that Paul composed a circular letter, two copies of which were later collated. Recent studies of the style of epistolary conclusions, however, have added strong support to the view that the longest version, with the Roman address, is the original. Probably either liturgical use or the letter's position at the head of the Pauline collection (in most ancient editions) prompted the abbreviations that made it more like a universal treatise.

The form of the letter is both more orderly and more complex than that of the earlier letters. The basic division is between Chaps. 1–11, which are didactic, elaborating the theme of 1:16 f., and Chaps. 12–15, which are admonitory. Systematic outlines of the letter are misleading, for the argument proceeds by stating certain themes which are then elaborated from various sides in turn, returning each time to the theme. Questions are raised along the way which have to be deferred for later discussion. The resultant interlocking structure is pointed out by our notes on key verses.

---

1 Paul, a servant[1] of Jesus Christ, called to be an apostle, set apart for the gospel of God **2** which he promised beforehand

1. Or, "slave."

through his prophets in the holy scriptures, **3** the gospel concerning his Son,[2] who was descended from David according to the flesh **4** and designated Son of God in power according to the Spirit of holiness by[3] his resurrection from the dead, Jesus Christ our Lord, **5** through whom we have received grace and apostleship to bring about the obedience of faith[4] for the sake of his name among all the nations, **6** including yourselves who are called to belong to Jesus Christ;

7 To all God's beloved in Rome, who are called to be saints:

Grace to you and peace from God our Father and the Lord Jesus Christ.

8 First, I thank[5] my God through Jesus Christ for all of you, because your faith is proclaimed in all the world. **9** For God is my witness, whom I serve with my spirit in the gospel of his Son, that without ceasing I mention you always in my prayers, **10** asking that somehow by God's will I may now at last succeed in coming to you. **11** For I long to see you, that I may impart to you some spiritual gift to strengthen you, **12** that is, that we may be mutually encouraged by each other's faith, both yours and mine. **13** I want you to know, brethren, that I have often intended to come to you (but thus far have been prevented), in order that I may reap some harvest among you as well as among the rest of the Gentiles. **14** I am under obligation both to Greeks and to barbarians, both to the wise and to the foolish:[6] **15** so I am eager to preach the gospel to you also who are in Rome.

16 For I am not ashamed of the gospel: it is the power of God for salvation to every one who has faith, to the Jew first and also to the Greek.[7] **17** For in it the righteousness of God is revealed through faith for faith,[8] as it is written, "He who through faith is righteous shall live."[9]

2. Vv. 3b–4 probably are an early Christian creedal summary (like 1 Cor. 15:3–5) which Paul quotes. Note the antithetic form, "... according to the flesh," "... according to the Spirit ..." The Jewish tradition that the Messiah, as "seed of David," would be called Son of God, based on 2 Sam. 7:12–14, does not appear elsewhere in Paul, but see note on Gal. 3:16.

3. Or, "since."

4. This may mean "obedience that consists of faith," or "faithful obedience."

5. This thanksgiving (vv. 8–17) is somewhat less fluid and well integrated than those of the other letters. The reason for the halting style lies in the necessity for exercising great tact in expressing Paul's extraordinary sense of mission and authority to a church unrelated to him.

6. "Greeks and barbarians," "wise and foolish" are Greek clichés, here a peri-

phrastic way of saying "everyone." Notably Jews as such are not mentioned; contrast the quite different implications of the formula in v. 16 and elsewhere, "Jew and Greek."

7. Cf. 1 Cor. 1:18–24.

8. Lit., "from faith to faith," perhaps only a rhetorical emphasis, "faith and nothing but faith," or perhaps, as in 3:22, expressing the relational character of faith in the Pauline sense, "from [God's or Christ's] faithfulness to [man's] faith." "The righteousness of God" is the fundamental concept in Romans. Its precise meaning for Paul has been debated for centuries (see Part IV below). Originating in the OT and Judaism, the term includes both "the justice of God" (JB) and "God's way of righting wrong" (NEB). See also note on 3.26.

9. Or, "The righteous shall live by faith." Hab. 2:4. Cf. Gal. 3:11.

18 For the wrath of God is revealed[1] from heaven against all ungodliness and wickedness of men who by their wickedness suppress the truth. **19** For what can be known about God is plain to them, because God has shown it to them. **20** Ever since the creation of the world his invisible nature, namely, his eternal power and deity, has been clearly perceived in the things that have been made. So they are without excuse; **21** for although they knew God they did not honor him as God or give thanks to him, but they became futile in their thinking and their senseless minds were darkened. **22** Claiming to be wise, they became fools, **23** and exchanged the glory of the immortal God for images resembling mortal man or birds or animals or reptiles.

24 Therefore God gave them up[2] in the lusts of their hearts to impurity, to the dishonoring of their bodies among themselves, **25** because they exchanged the truth about God for a lie and worshiped and served the creature rather than the Creator, who is blessed for ever! Amen.

26 For this reason God gave them up to dishonorable passions. Their women exchanged natural relations for unnatural, **27** and the men likewise gave up natural relations with women and were consumed with passion for one another, men committing shameless acts with men and receiving in their own persons the due penalty for their error.

28 And since they did not see fit to acknowledge God, God gave them up to a base mind and to improper conduct. **29** They were filled with all manner of wickedness, evil, covetousness, malice. Full of envy, murder, strife, deceit, malignity, they are gossips, **30** slanderers, haters of God, insolent, haughty, boastful, inventors of evil, disobedient of parents, **31** foolish, faithless, heartless, ruthless.[3] **32** Though they know God's decree that those who do such things deserve to die, they not only do them but approve those who practice them.

2 Therefore you have no excuse,[4] O man, whoever you are, when you judge another; for in passing judgment upon him you condemn yourself, because you, the judge, are doing the very same

1. First of two variations of the theme 1:17a which subdivide Chaps. 1–3: see 3:21, and note the change of tense as well as subject. "The wrath of God" was virtually a technical term for punishment at the last judgment; cf. 2:5; 1 Thess. 1:10. Connection of this eschatological term with the present tense, "is revealed" (parallelism with v. 17 requires us to understand "in the gospel"), sets up a characteristic Pauline paradox. Otherwise, vv. 18–32 read like a typical Hellenistic-Jewish polemic against paganism; Wisd. Chaps. 13 f. are a very close parallel both in theme and language.
2. This phrase is solemnly repeated in vv. 26, 28.
3. The "vice catalogue" by repetition of similar sounds in Greek achieves a certain rhetorical luxuriance that climaxes the first part of the homily, in which Paul has doubtless followed familiar conventions. V. 32 provides the transition to his deliberately abrupt irony in Chap. 2.
4. This picks up and universalizes the statement of 1:20b, preparing the way for 3:9, 19 f., 23.

things. **2** We know that the judgment of God rightly falls upon those who do such things. **3** Do you suppose, O man, that when you judge those who do such things and yet do them yourself, you will escape the judgment of God? **4** Or do you presume upon the riches of his kindness and forbearance and patience? Do you not know that God's kindness is meant to lead you to repentance?[5] **5** But by your hard and impenitent heart you are storing up wrath for yourself on the day of wrath when God's righteous judgment will be revealed. **6** For he will render to every man according to his works:[6] **7** to those who by patience in well-doing seek for glory and honor and immortality, he will give eternal life; **8** but for those who are factious[7] and do not obey the truth, but obey wickedness, there will be wrath and fury. **9** There will be tribulation and distress for every human being who does evil, the Jew first and also the Greek, **10** but glory and honor and peace for every one who does good, the Jew first and also the Greek. **11** For God shows no partiality.[8]

12 All who have sinned without the law will also perish without the law, and all who have sinned under the law will be judged by the law. **13** For it is not the hearers of the law who are righteous before God, but the doers of the law who will be justified. **14** When Gentiles who have not the law do by nature what the law requires, they are a law to themselves, even though they do not have the law. **15** They show that what the law requires is written on their hearts, while their conscience also bears witness and their conflicting thoughts acccuse or perhaps excuse them **16** on that day when, according to my gospel, God judges the secrets of men by Christ Jesus.[9]

17 But if you call yourself a Jew and rely upon the law and boast of your relation to God **18** and know his will and approve what is excellent, because you are instructed in the law, **19** and if you are sure that you are a guide to the blind, a light to those who are in darkness, **20** a corrector of the foolish, a teacher of children, having in the law the embodiment of knowledge and truth—**21** you then who teach others, will you not teach yourself? While you preach against stealing, do you steal? **22** You who say that one must not commit adultery, do you commit adultery? You who abhor idols, do you rob temples? **23** You who boast in the law, do you dishonor

5. One of the very rare occurrences of the term "repentance" in Paul's letters; the statement here is typical of Judaism, for which repentance is the way prescribed by God to overcome failure to achieve the righteousness demanded by the Torah.
6. Prov. 24:12; cf. Ps. 62:12. Note the use of parallelism to add solemnity to the following lines, and the *chiasm* (for definition, see p. 11) of vv. 7–10 (good/bad//bad/good).
7. Or, "selfishly ambitious."
8. A fundamental principle in Judaism: Deut. 10:17; 2 Chron. 19:7; see the Mishnah tractate *Aboth*, 4:22. However, Paul's use of the principle to deny any distinction between Jew and Gentile is radical.
9. The first specifically Christian statement in the argument.

God by breaking the law? ²⁴ For, as it is written, "The name of God is blasphemed among the Gentiles because of you."¹

²⁵ Circumcision indeed is of value if you obey the law,² but if you break the law, your circumcision becomes uncircumcision. ²⁶ So, if a man who is uncircumcised keeps the precepts of the law, will not his uncircumcision be regarded as circumcision? ²⁷ Then those who are physically uncircumcised but keep the law will condemn you who have the written code and circumcision but break the law. ²⁸ For he is not a real Jew who is one outwardly, nor is true circumcision something external and physical. ²⁹ He is a Jew who is one inwardly, and real circumcision is a matter of the heart, spiritual and not literal. His praise is not from men but from God.³
3 Then what advantage has the Jew? Or what is the value of circumcision? ² Much in every way. To begin with, the Jews are entrusted with the oracles of God. ³ What if some were unfaithful? Does their faithlessness nullify the faithfulness of God?⁴ ⁴ By no means! Let God be true though every man be false,⁵ as it is written,

"That thou mayest be justified in thy words,
and prevail when thou art judged."⁶

⁵ But if our wickedness serves to show the justice of God, what shall we say? That God is unjust to inflict wrath on us? (I speak in a human way.) ⁶ By no means! For then how could God judge the world? ⁷ But if through my falsehood God's truthfulness abounds to his glory, why am I still being condemned as a sinner? ⁸ And

1. Isa. 52:5 LXX.
2. This admission may seem astonishing in the light of the antithesis in Gal. 5:2, but this is only a preliminary stage of Paul's argument; his basic conviction is that summarized in Gal. 5:6; 6:15.
3. Apart from the passing mention of "the gospel" and "Christ Jesus" in 2:16, there is nothing in 1:18–2:29 which cannot be found in Jewish sources contemporary with Paul—only the conclusion to which he drives the logic of these statements is un-Jewish. Paul has one essential point to make: there is now in God's eyes no more distinction between Jew and Gentile. Therefore details of the argument are not to be pressed. If he speaks for the moment as if the final judgment were based entirely on man's works—flatly contradicting the main point he is leading up to in Chap. 3—that is only a concession in order to make the point that, even within the terms of common Jewish interpretation of God's judgment, there is finally no distinction be-

tween the status of those who have and those who do not have the Torah. Further, the accusations made against the Jews in Chap. 2 by no means imply that the average Jew is guilty of the crimes enumerated in vv. 21–23, any more than 1:18–31 can mean that the average pagan is guilty of all the vices listed there. The point is not that empirically one group is more or less moral than the other, but that God judges all men by their works and their "heart," not by prior status. Chap. 3 will take the further step to argue that, on that basis, all are found guilty.
4. The style of Chap. 3 is typical of Paul's adaptation of the Cynic-Stoic diatribe. The objections voiced by rhetorical questions here are only rejected by quick retorts; they receive longer answers later in the letter. Thus the question of v. 3 becomes the topic of Chaps. 9–11.
5. The last phrase is biblical: Ps. 116:11 LXX (115:2).
6. Ps. 51:4.

why not do evil that good may come?[7]—as some people slander-ously charge us with saying. Their condemnation is just.

[9] What then? Are we Jews any better off? No, not at all;[8] for I have already charged[9] that all men, both Jews and Greeks, are under the power of sin, [10] as it is written:

> "None is righteous, no, not one;
> [11] no one understands, no one seeks for God.
> [12] All have turned aside, together they have gone wrong;
> no one does good, not even one."
> [13] "Their throat is an open grave,
> they use their tongues to deceive."
> "The venom of asps is under their lips."
> [14] "Their mouth is full of curses and bitterness."
> [15] "Their feet are swift to shed blood,
> [16] in their paths are ruin and misery,
> [17] and the way of peace they do not know."
> [18] There is no fear of God before their eyes."[1]

[19] Now we know that whatever the law says[2] it speaks to those who are under the law, so that every mouth may be stopped, and the whole world may be held accountable to God. [20] For no human being will be justified in his sight by works of the law, since through the law comes knowledge of sin.[3]

[21] But now the righteousness of God has been manifested apart from law,[4] although the law and the prophets bear witness to it, [22] the righteousness of God through faith in Jesus Christ for all who believe. For there is no distinction; [23] since all have sinned and fall short of the glory of God, [24] they are justified by his grace as a gift, through the redemption which is in Christ Jesus, [25] whom God put forward as an expiation by his blood, to be received by faith. This was to show God's righteousness, because in

---

7. This question is dealt with in Chap. 6.

8. The translation and the meaning have been disputed since ancient times. Other possibilities are: "Are we ["Jews" is not in the text, but has to be supplied from the context] any better off? Not altogether." "Are we any worse off? Not at all [or, "Not altogether]." The principal objection to the translation in the text above is that it makes Paul contradict what he said in v. 1—but such paradoxes are a familiar aspect of his style.

9. I.e., in Chaps. 1–2. "I" translates Greek "we"; Paul frequently uses the plural of authorship.

1. The chain of quotations includes Ps. 14:1–3 (or 53:1–3); 5:9; 140:3; 10:7; Isa. 59:7 f. (cf. Prov. 1:16);

Ps. 36:1.

2. "The law" here means "Torah" in the broad sense, "scripture," i.e., as exemplified in the catena of Psalm and prophetic texts just before.

3. The first clause is from Ps. 143:2; Paul adds "by works of the law" and the epigrammatic statement of the law's function as he now sees it—the statement will be elaborated in 7:7–25. "Knowledge of sin" means concrete experience of sin, actualizing sin; the statement thus differs from the Epicurean aphorism often quoted by commentators: "The beginning of salvation is the knowledge of sin."

4. Cf. 1:17, 18. This restatement of the theme is the major turning point in the argument of the first part of the letter.

his divine forbearance he had passed over former sin;[5] **26** it was to prove at the present time that he himself is righteous and that he justifies[6] him who has faith in Jesus.

27 Then what becomes of our boasting? It is excluded. On what principle?[7] On the principle of works? No, but on the principle of faith. **28** For we hold that a man is justified by faith apart from works of law. **29** Or is God the God of Jews only? Is he not the God of Gentiles also? Yes, of Gentiles also, **30** since God is one; and he will justify the circumcised on the ground of their faith and the uncircumcised through their faith. **31** Do we then overthrow the law by this faith?[8] By no means! On the contrary, we uphold the law.

4 What then shall we say about[9] Abraham, our forefather according to the flesh? **2** For if Abraham was justified by works, he has something to boast about,[1] but not before God. **3** For what does the scripture say? "Abraham believed God, and it was reckoned to him as righteousness."[2] **4** Now to one who works, his wages are not reckoned as a gift but as his due. **5** And to one who does not work but trusts him who justifies the ungodly,[3] his faith is reckoned as righteousness. **6** So also David pronounces a blessing upon the man to whom God reckons righteousness apart from works:

> **7** "Blessed are those whose iniquities are forgiven, and whose sins are covered;
> **8** blessed is the man against whom the Lord will not reckon his sin."[4]

9 Is this blessing pronounced only upon the circumcised, or also

5. Vv. 24 f. are probably a formula which Paul quotes and then comments on to reinforce his argument. The first phrase of v. 26 repeats almost exactly the phrase from v. 25 which Paul wishes to expound (the duplication is obscured by the translation; lit., the phrase is "for the demonstration of his righteousness"). The phrases "by his grace" (v. 24) and "by faith" (v. 25, "to be received," is not in the Greek) are probably also added by Paul to the formula.

6. The cognate relation of "righteous" (*dikaios*) and "justifies" (*dikaiounta*) can hardly be preserved in English. The double expression conveys with utmost brevity Paul's understanding of God's righteousness as both an inherent quality of God and God's characteristic action toward man. The verb is drawn from the field of law, where it may mean "to pass sentence," but also "to acquit," "to declare righteous." For Paul it clearly means this and more: "to put into a right relationship" with God.

7. The word translated "principle" is the same elsewhere translated "law."

8. The answer to this question has to wait until 7:7–25.

9. Many manuscripts add "was gained by," probably an early attempt to clarify the elliptical expression.

1. Cf. 3:27; Chap. 4 can be regarded as a footnote on that statement: "All boasting is excluded—even Abraham's."

2. Gen. 15:6. Chap. 4 is a midrash on this passage, like Gal. 3:6–29.

3. Contrast Ex. 23:7; the unthinkable notion that God would "justify the ungodly" (the Greek phrase is identical in Ex. 23:7; in Isa. 5:23 it is used of corrupt judges) is stated deliberately by Paul; cf. Rom. 5:6–8.

4. Ps. 32:1 f. Note that the key-word "reckon" provides Paul the springboard of his argument, by a common rule of midrash. The Ps. passage permits the inference that "reckoning" may take place even where works have failed, while the Gen. passage connects "reckoning" with "believing." Contrast the opposite conclusion arrived at in James 2:21–24, a midrash on the same Gen. text.

upon the uncircumcised? We say that faith was reckoned to Abraham as righteousness. 10 How then was it reckoned to him? Was it before or after he had been circumcised? It was not after, but before he was circumcised. 11 He received circumcision as a sign or seal of the righteousness which he had by faith while he was still uncircumcised. The purpose was to make him the father of all who believe without being circumcised and who thus have righteousness reckoned to them, 12 and likewise the father of the circumcised who are not merely circumcised but also follow the example of the faith which our father Abraham had before he was circumcised.

13 The promise to Abraham and his descendants, that they should inherit the world, did not come through the law but through the righteousness of faith. 14 If it is the adherents of the law who are to be the heirs, faith is null and the promise is void. 15 For the law brings wrath, but where there is no law there is no transgression.

16 That is why it depends on faith, in order that the promise may rest on grace and be guaranteed to all his descendants—not only to the adherents of the law but also to those who share the faith of Abraham, for he is the father of us all, 17 as it is written, "I have made you the father of many nations"⁵—in the presence of the God in whom he believed, who gives life to the dead⁶ and calls into existence the things that do not exist. 18 In hope he believed against hope, that he should become the father of many nations; as he had been told, "So shall your descendants be."⁷ 19 He did not weaken in faith when he considered his own body, which was as good as dead because he was about a hundred years old, or when he considered the barrenness⁸ of Sarah's womb. 20 No distrust made him waver concerning the promise of God, but he grew strong in his faith as he gave glory to God, 21 fully convinced that God was able to do what he had promised. 22 That is why his faith was "reckoned to him as righteousness." 23 But the words, "it was reckoned to him," were written not for his sake alone, 24 but for ours also. It will be reckoned to us who believe in him that raised from the dead Jesus our Lord,⁹ 25 who was put to death for our trespasses and raised for our justification.¹

5 Therefore, since we are justified by faith, we² have peace with

---

5. Gen. 17:5.
6. The phrase recalls the second blessing of the Jewish daily prayer, which was frequently associated with Abraham on the basis of a legend that Isaac was actually sacrificed (Gen. 22) and restored to his father only by resurrection (cf. Heb. 11:17–19).
7. Gen. 15:5; cf. 22:16 f.
8. Lit., "deadness"; the choice of words describing both Abraham and Sarah emphasizes that Abraham's faith is in the God "who raises the dead,"

and thus the prototype of Christian faith (v. 24).
9. See previous note.
1. Perhaps another quoted formula, though the terse antithesis is also typical of Paul's style.
2. Many ancient authorities read, "let us" (the difference in Greek is a single letter), but the context demands the indicative. The themes of vv. 1–11 are elaborated in Chap. 8; Chaps. 5–8 are therefore to be understood as a unit.

God through our Lord Jesus Christ. [2] Through him we have obtained access[3] to this grace in which we stand, and we[4] rejoice in our hope of sharing the glory of God. [3] More than that, we rejoice in our sufferings, knowing that suffering produces endurance, [4] and endurance produces character, and character produces hope, [5] and hope does not disappoint us, because God's love has been poured into our hearts through the Holy Spirit which has been given to us.

[6] While we were yet helpless, at the right time Christ died for the ungodly. [7] Why, one will hardly die for a righteous man—though perhaps for a good man one will dare even to die. [8] But God shows his love for us in that while we were yet sinners Christ died for us. [9] Since, therefore, we are now justified by his blood, much more shall we be saved by him from the wrath of God. [10] For if while we were enemies we were reconciled to God by the death of his Son, much more, now that we are reconciled, shall we be saved by his life.[5] [11] Not only so, but we also rejoice in God through our Lord Jesus Christ, through whom we have now received our reconciliation.

[12] Therefore as sin came into the world through one man and death through sin,[6] and so death spread to all men because all men sinned[7]—[13] sin indeed was in the world before the law was given, but sin is not counted where there is no law. [14] Yet death reigned from Adam to Moses, even over those whose sins were not like the transgression of Adam, who was a type[8] of the one who was to come.

[15] But the free gift is not like the trespass. For if many died through one man's trespass, much more have the grace of God and the free gift in the grace of that one man Jesus Christ abounded for many. [16] And the free gift is not like the effect of that one man's sin. For the judgment following one trespass brought condemnation, but the free gift following many trespasses brings justification. [17] If, because of one man's trespass, death reigned

3. Other ancient authorities add, "by faith."
4. Or, "let us"; so also in the following verse.
5. Note that v. 10 simply restates v. 9 with slightly different language; "justified" and "reconciled" thus function as synonyms.
6. Gen. 2:17; 3:19.
7. The sentence is incomplete; cf. v. 18, where the correlation is filled out. It can, however, be read as a complete sentence if "and so" is understood as "so also" (Greek, *houtōs kai* instead of *kai houtōs*). That would yield a *chiasm*: sin, therefore death; death, be-

cause of sin. How Paul (and some Jewish authors contemporary with him) conceived of the connection between Adam's sin and death and those of following generations, he does not explain.
8. The notion of "type" and "anti-type" was one way of interpreting present or anticipated events by scriptural patterns; cf. 1 Cor. 10:6, 11 (where the word "type" is rendered "warning"). The analogy between the beginning and the end of human history was particularly cultivated. For the comparison between Adam and Christ, cf. 1 Cor. 15:45 ff.

through that one man, much more will those who receive the abundance of grace and the free gift of righteousness reign in life through the one man Jesus Christ.

18 Then as one man's trespass led to condemnation for all men, so one man's act of righteousness leads to acquittal and life for all men. **19** For as by one man's disobedience many were made sinners, so by one man's obedience many will be made righteous. **20** Law came in, to increase the trespass; but where sin increased, grace abounded all the more, **21** so that, as sin reigned in death, grace also might reign through righteousness to eternal life through Jesus Christ our Lord.[9]

6 What shall we say then? Are we to continue in sin that grace may abound?[1] **2** By no means! How can we who died to sin still live in it? **3** Do you not know that all of us who have been baptized into Christ Jesus were baptized into his death? **4** We were buried therefore with him by baptism into death, so that as Christ was raised from the dead by the glory of the Father, we too might walk in newness of life.[2]

5 For if we have been united with him in a death like his, we shall certainly be united with him in a resurrection like his. **6** We know that our old self was crucified with him so that the sinful body[3] might be destroyed, and we might no longer be enslaved to sin. **7** For he who has died is freed from sin.[4] **8** But if we have died with Christ, we believe that we shall also live with him. **9** For we know that Christ being raised from the dead will never die again;

9. The logic of this section is difficult. The basic pattern is an argument *a minori* (rabbis would say, "light and heavy"): If Adam's sin brought death to many, it is all the more certain that Christ's obedience brought life to many. What is stressed, however, is the counterpoint: "But the free gift is not like the trespass." Paul thus upsets his own analogy, so that the act of grace does not simply undo the transgression of Adam—the result in that case would be a kind of magic in which man's automatic fall in Adam would be reversed by automatic salvation in Christ. What breaks the analogy is the law, whose purpose, Paul claims, was to *increase* transgression! (v. 20, cf. Gal. 3:19). Confronted with the law's commandments, man's potential rebellion against God becomes actual (cf. 7:5, 7–10); every man disobeys as Adam did. The "superabundance" of grace (v. 20b) is its justification of the multiplicity of human sin and its giving life which overwhelms the death wrought by human rebellion against the Creator.
1. The question follows logically, in diatribe style, as a possible objection

to 5:20 f.; it has been raised previously: 3:8.
2. Paul presupposes tradition familiar to the Roman Christians; he is probably alluding to portions of the common Hellenistic Christian baptismal liturgy. That liturgy undoubtedly contained from the beginning a strong ethical emphasis (cf. Col. Chap. 3; 1 Pet. *passim*), which here Paul tries to relate logically to his doctrine of grace. Probably the liturgy spoke of resurrection with Christ as something already accomplished in baptism (Col. 3:1; Eph. 2:1, 5 f.; see note on 1 Cor. 15:12); here Paul carefully stresses its futurity.
3. Lit., "body of sin," i.e., the self "enslaved to sin." Paul does not mean that the physical nature is the source of sin, as in Gnosticism; the opposite of the "body of sin" is not the soul, but the "body of Christ," "the new man."
4. In the Talmud a similar saying is attributed to R. Johanan (third century A.D.): "As soon as a man dies he is free from the commandments" (b. Niddah 61b; Shabbat 30a, 151b). The word translated "is freed" is the one elsewhere translated "is justified."

death no longer has dominion over him. **10** The death he died he died to sin, once for all, but the life he lives he lives to God. **11** So you also must consider yourselves dead to sin and alive to God in Christ Jesus.

12 Let not sin therefore reign in your mortal bodies, to make you obey their passions. **13** Do not yield your members to sin as instruments of wickedness, but yield yourselves to God as men who have been brought from death to life, and your members to God as instruments of righteousness. **14** For sin will have no dominion over you, since you are not under law but under grace.[5]

15 What then? Are we to sin because we are not under law but under grace?[6] By no means! **16** Do you not know that if you yield yourselves to any one as obedient slaves, you are slaves of the one whom you obey, either of sin, which leads to death, or of obedience, which leads to righteousness? **17** But thanks be to God, that you who were once slaves of sin have become obedient from the heart to the standard of teaching to which you were committed,[7] **18** and, having been set free from sin, have become slaves of righteousness. **19** I am speaking in human terms, because of your natural limitations. For just as you once yielded your members to impurity and to greater and greater iniquity,[8] so now yield your members to righteousness for sanctification.

20 When you were slaves of sin, you were free in regard to righteousness. **21** But then what return did you get from the things of which you are now ashamed? The end of those things is death. **22** But now that you have been set free from sin and have become slaves of God, the return you get is sanctification and its end, eternal life. **23** For the wages of sin is death, but the free gift of God is eternal life in Christ Jesus our Lord.[9]

7 Do you not know, brethren—for I am speaking to those who know the law—that the law is binding on[1] a person only during his life? **2** Thus a married woman is bound by law to her husband as long as he lives; but if her husband dies she is discharged from the

5. Note that the law is presumed here to be the instrument by which "sin" exercises "dominion" over man; cf. 7:7–20; Gal. 3:19–4:10.

6. The question reformulates the beginning point (v. 1) in terms of the argument so far, dividing the chapter into two parts. In the first the contrast death/life dominates; in the latter, slavery/freedom.

7. "Obedient ... to the standard of teaching" interrupts the train of thought, which would proceed smoothly if this whole clause were omitted. Since, moreover, Paul ordinarily uses the word translated "standard" with a quite different sense, the clause could

be a gloss. However, there is no manuscript evidence to support this conjecture.

8. Lit., "to iniquity for iniquity [i.e., with iniquity as the only outcome]," precisely parallel with the following antithesis.

9. That the "return" (lit., "fruit") of ethical conduct is not a reward is now stressed by the characteristic Pauline contrast between "wages" and "free gift": cf. 4:4 f.

1. Lit., "has dominion over," cf. 6:14. The discussion of freedom from the law in 7:1–6 runs parallel to the exposition of freedom from sin in 6:12–23.

law concerning the husband.[2] [3] Accordingly, she will be called an adulteress if she lives with another man while her husband is alive. But if her husband dies she is free from that law, and if she married another man she is not an adulteress.

[4] Likewise, my brethren, you have died to the law through the body of Christ, so that you may belong to another, to him who has been raised from the dead in order that we may bear fruit for God.[3] [5] While we were living in the flesh, our sinful passions, aroused by the law, were at work in our members to bear fruit for death. [6] But now we are discharged from the law, dead to that which held us captive, so that we serve not under the old written code but in the new life of the Spirit.[4]

[7] What then shall we say? That the law is sin?[5] By no means! Yet, if it had not been for the law, I should not have known sin.[6] I should not have known what it is to covet if the law had not said "You shall not covet."[7] [8] But sin, finding opportunity in the commandment, wrought in me all kinds of covetousness. Apart from the law sin lies dead. [9] I was once alive apart from the law,[8] but when the commandment came, sin revived[9] and I died; [10] the very commandment which promised life proved to be death to me. [11] For sin, finding opportunity in the commandment, deceived me and by it killed me.[1] [12] So the law is holy, and the commandment is holy and just and good.

[13] Did that which is good, then, bring death to me? By no means! It was sin, working death in me through what is good, in order that sin might be shown to be sin, and through the commandment might become sinful beyond measure.[2] [14] We know that the law is spiritual; but I am carnal, sold under sin. [15] I do not understand my own actions.[3] For I do not do what I want, but I do the very thing I hate. [16] Now if I do what I do not want, I agree that the law is good. [17] So then it is no longer I that do it, but sin which dwells within me. [18] For I know that nothing good

2. By introducing this illustration, which does not quite fit either the principle just enunciated or the analogy to be drawn in vv. 4 ff., Paul produces a crippled metaphor. But since the point he is trying to make presupposes a resurrection, it is a little hard to find an analogy in ordinary jurisprudence.
3. "Bearing fruit" of course still belongs to the marriage metaphor, though it links also with common Christian moral discourse: 6:21, 22; Gal. 5:22; Eph. 5:9.
4. Cf. Gal. 5:1; 2 Cor. 3:7 f.
5. Again Paul takes up an objection (cf. 6:1, 15), one raised at 3:31 and made more urgent by the subsequent argument (4:15; 5:13, 20; 6:14; 7:5

f.!). The section 7:7–25 has been one of the most controversial in the Pauline letters; see the essay by Stendahl below, pp. 422–34.
6. See 3:20.
7. Ex. 20:17; Deut. 5:21. The Greek translation quoted by Paul reads lit., "You shall not desire."
8. Some interpreters see here an allusion to the freedom of the Jewish boy before he becomes *bar mitsvah*; others find a reference to the paradise story of Gen. 2–3.
9. Or, "came to life."
1. Cf. Gen. 3:1–5.
2. Cf. 5:20.
3. Or, "I do not know what I am bringing about."

dwells within me, that is, in my flesh. I can will what is right,[4] but I cannot do it. [19] For I do not do the good I want, but the evil I do not want is what I do. [20] Now if I do what I do not want, it is no longer I that do it, but sin which dwells within me.

[21] So I find it to be a law that when I want to do right, evil lies close at hand. [22] For I delight in the law of God, in my inmost self, [23] but I see in my members another law at war with the law of my mind and making me captive to the law of sin which dwells in my members. [24] Wretched man that I am! Who will deliver me from this body of death? [25] Thanks be to God through Jesus Christ our Lord! So then, I of myself serve the law of God with my mind, but with my flesh I serve the law of sin.[5]

8 There is therefore[6] now no condemnation for those who are in Christ Jesus. [2] For the law of the Spirit of life in Christ Jesus has set me[7] free from the law of sin and death. [3] For God has done what the law, weakened by the flesh, could not do: sending his own Son in the likeness of sinful flesh and for sin,[8] he condemned sin in the flesh, [4] in order that the just requirement of the law might be fulfilled in us, who walk not according to the flesh but according to the Spirit. [5] For those who live according to the flesh set their minds on the things of the flesh, but those who live according to the Spirit set their minds on the things of the Spirit. [6] To set the mind on the flesh is death, but to set the mind on the Spirit is life and peace. [7] For the mind that is set on the flesh is hostile to God; it does not submit to God's law, indeed it cannot; [8] and those who are in the flesh cannot please God.

[9] But you are not in the flesh,[9] you are in the Spirit, if the Spirit

4. "What is right" is perhaps a misleading translation of *to kalon*, which to the Greek ear would have had a broader connotation: "what is excellent, beautiful." So also in v. 21. *To agathon*, translated "the good" in v. 19, is a synonym.

5. A number of commentators think v. 25b is a later gloss, or that it belongs before v. 24. There is no manuscript evidence for a different text, however, and other interpreters regard it as a summary of the whole chapter.

6. The "therefore" does not link with what immediately precedes, but with 7:6. As 7:7–25 elaborated the negative side of that statement, so 8:1–17 elaborates the positive side.

7. Other witnesses read "you" (singular) or "us." There is no difference in meaning, since all have a universal sense in the dialogue style, like the "I" of Chap. 7. The surprising phrase "law of the Spirit of life" is chosen to contrast with "the law of sin and death" which he has discussed in Chap. 7. The personification of law ("in Christ Jesus") was a familiar thought in the Hellenistic world: for Stoics the ideal king was "living law," and Philo applies this notion to Moses.

8. Or, "as a sin-offering." The pattern of vv. 3b–4 had apparently become stereotyped in early Christian preaching and liturgy: "Christ . . . for us, in order that we . . ." Cf. 1 Thess. 5:9 f.; Gal. 3:13 f.; 4:4 f.; 2 Cor. 5:14 f., 21; also Phil. 2:6–11.

9. Here (and 7:5) "in the flesh" means "in the power of the flesh," although elsewhere it means only "living a physical existence," theologically neutral as distinguished from "according to the flesh" (see Gal. 2:20; Phil. 1:22; especially 2 Cor. 10:3). Paul obviously had not developed a consistent, technical vocabulary.

of God really dwells in you.[1] Any one who does not have the Spirit of Christ does not belong to him. [10] But if Christ is in you, although your bodies are dead because of sin, your spirits are alive because of righteousness. [11] If the Spirit of him who raised Jesus from the dead dwells in you, he who raised Christ Jesus from the dead will give life to your mortal bodies also through his Spirit which dwells in you.

[12] So then, brethren, we are debtors, not to the flesh, to live according to the flesh—[13] for if you live according to the flesh you will die, but if by the Spirit you put to death the deeds of the body[2] you will live. [14] For all who are led by the Spirit of God are sons of God. [15] For you did not receive the spirit of slavery to fall back into fear, but you have received the spirit of sonship. When we cry, "Abba! Father!" [16] it is the Spirit himself bearing witness with our spirit that we are children of God, [17] and if children, then heirs, heirs of God and fellow heirs with Christ,[3] provided[4] we suffer with him in order that we may also be glorified with him.

[18] I consider that the sufferings of this present time are not worth comparing with the glory that is to be revealed to us. [19] For the creation waits with eager longing for the revealing of the sons of God; [20] for the creation was subjected to futility,[5] not of its own will but by the will of him who subjected it in hope; [21] because the creation itself will be set free from its bondage to decay and obtain the glorious liberty of the children of God. [22] We know that the whole creation has been groaning in travail together until now; [23] and not only the creation, but we ourselves, who have the first fruits of the Spirit, groan inwardly as we wait for adoption as sons, the redemption of our bodies. [24] For in this hope we were saved. Now hope that is seen is not hope. For who hopes for what he sees? [25] But if we hope for what we do not see, we wait for it with patience.[6]

[26] Likewise the Spirit helps us in our weakness; for we do not know how to pray as we ought, but the Spirit himself intercedes for us with sighs too deep for words. [27] And he who searches the hearts of men knows what is the mind of the Spirit, because[7] the

---

1. Contrast the notion of "sin dwelling in me" in 7:17–25.
2. Paul would usually say, "deeds of the flesh," since ordinarily "body" is for him a neutral term. Some manuscripts have corrected "body" to "flesh" here, indicating that copyists were sometimes more consistent than Paul.
3. Cf. Gal. 3:26–4:7.
4. Or, "since." The two compound verbs in *sun-* (suffer *with*, be glorified *with*) recall 6:1–11. V. 17 announces the theme of vv. 18–39.

5. In common with many people of the Hellenistic age, Paul thinks of the world as captive to hostile powers, but he immediately limits this dualistic notion by mentioning the will of the one God. The total picture is therefore that common in Jewish and Christian apocalyptic.
6. Paul's emphasis on hope rather than sight here should be compared with his polemic against the "realized eschatology" of the Corinthian spirituals. See esp. notes on 1 Cor. 15.
7. Or, "that."

Spirit intercedes for the saints according to the will of God.[8]

28 We know that in everything God works for good[9] with those who love him, who are called according to his purpose. **29** For those whom he foreknew he also predestined to be conformed to the image of his Son, in order that he might be the first-born among many brethren. **30** And those whom he predestined he also called; and those whom he called he also justified; and those whom he justified he also glorified.

31 What then shall we say to this? If God is for us, who is against us? **32** He who did not spare his own Son[1] but gave him up for us all, will he not also give us all things with him? **33** Who shall bring any charge against God's elect? It is God who justifies; **34** who is to condemn? Is it Christ Jesus, who died, yes, who was raised from the dead, who is at the right hand of God, who indeed intercedes for us?[2] **35** Who shall separate us from the love of Christ? Shall tribulation, or distress, or persecution, or famine, or nakedness, or peril, or sword? **36** As it is written,

"For thy sake we are being killed all day long;
we are regarded as sheep to be slaughtered."[3]

37 No, in all these things we are more than conquerors through him who loved us. **38** For I am sure that neither death, nor life, nor angels, nor principalities, nor things present, nor things to come, nor powers, **39** nor height, nor depth, nor anything else in all creation, will be able to separate us from the love of God in Christ Jesus our Lord.

9 I am speaking the truth in Christ, I am not lying; my conscience bears me witness in the Holy Spirit, **2** that I have great sorrow and unceasing anguish in my heart.[4] **3** For I could wish that

---

8. Compare the mystical notion of "infused prayer."

9. Another reading, very well attested, omits "God"; it can be translated either "in everything he works for good" or "everything works for good." For Paul the meaning would be the same in all three instances.

1. An allusion to Abraham's "binding of Isaac," Gen. 22:16.

2. Some commentators punctuate this as a statement, but rhetorical form would be destroyed unless all clauses in vv. 31–35 are taken as questions. Note also the so-called "law of expanding members" in this unit, which provides an impressive close to the whole section, Chaps. 5–8.

3. Ps. 44:22.

4. This solemn oath (cf. 2 Cor. 11:31; Gal. 1:20) opens a new section (Chaps. 9–11), which however returns to the theme of Chaps. 1–3: both Jew and Gentile are saved by grace, not works prescribed by law. At the same time, these chapters answer the specific question raised in 3:1–4, whether Paul's doctrine of grace does not invalidate God's promises to Israel. The style of the Cynic-Stoic diatribe and the Pharisaic method of midrash both characterize the section, which can be summarized thus: (1) The history of Israel shows God's utter freedom in selecting whomever he will; the Gentile mission is only the latest example of that freedom (9:6–29). Except for a small remnant (the Jewish-Christians) Israel has erred by pursuing righteousness as if it were based on works (9:30–10:21). Nevertheless, God has not *rejected* Israel, since even their disobedience fits his purpose to save all men. Only now Israel stands in the same relationship to God as the Gentiles once did, until they learn to receive God's righteousness as a gift (11:1–32). The discussion is bracketed by the opening oath (9:1–5) and a concluding doxology (11:33–36).

I myself were accursed and cut off from Christ for the sake of my brethren, my kinsmen by race.[5] 4 They are Israelites, and to them belong the sonship, the glory, the covenants, the giving of the law, the worship, and the promises; 5 to them belong the patriarchs, and of their race, according to the flesh, is the Christ. God who is over all be blessed for ever.[6] Amen.

6 But it is not as though the word of God had failed.[7] For not all who are descended from Israel belong to Israel, 7 and not all are children of Abraham because they are his descendants; but "Through Isaac shall your descendants be named."[8] 8 This means that it is not the children of the flesh who are the children of God, but the children of the promise are reckoned as descendants. 9 For this is what the promise said, "About this time I will return and Sarah shall have a son."[9] 10 And not only so, but also when Rebecca had conceived children by one man, our forefather Isaac, 11 though they were not yet born and had done nothing either good or bad, in order that God's purpose of election might continue, not because of works but because of his call, 12 she was told, "The elder will serve the younger."[1] 13 As it is written, "Jacob I loved, but Esau I hated."[2]

14 What shall we say then? Is there injustice on God's part?[3] By no means! 15 For he says to Moses, "I will have mercy on whom I have mercy, and I will have compassion on whom I have compassion."[4] 16 So it depends not upon man's will or exertion, but upon God's mercy. 17 For the scripture says to Pharaoh, "I have raised you up for the very purpose of showing my power in you, so that my name may be proclaimed in all the earth."[5] 18 So then he has mercy upon whomever he wills, and he hardens the heart of whomever he wills.

19 You will say to me then, "Why does he still find fault? For who can resist his will?" 20 But who are you, a man, to answer back to God? Will what is molded say to its molder, "Why have you made me thus?" 21 Has the potter no right over the clay, to make out of the same lump one vessel for beauty and another for menial use? 22 What if God, desiring to show his wrath and to

---

5. A Jewish reader would recognize that here Paul compares himself with Moses, the great intercessor for Israel (Ex. 32:32). In Jewish tradition this was part of the role of every prophet.
6. The grammatical construction suggests rather, "Christ, who is God over all, blessed forever," but Paul nowhere else calls Christ "God."
7. Cf. 3:3. Note that the problem is not just Paul's sentimental attachment to the Jews, but that God's veracity is tied up with the fate of Israel.
8. Gen. 21:12; not only Paul's midrash on Abraham and Isaac (Chap. 4;

Gal. 3:6 ff.) but also the Sarah/Hagar allegory (Gal. 3:21 ff.) are in his mind here.
9. Gen. 18:10, 14.
1. Gen. 25:23.
2. Mal. 1:2 f.
3. Cf. 3:5.
4. Ex. 33:19.
5. Ex. 9:16. The midrashic link between this passage and the preceding is found in the phrase "to proclaim my name." The combination then gives Paul the warrant for his negative restatement of the former passage in v. 18.

make known his power, has endured with much patience the vessels of wrath made for destruction, **23** in order to make known the riches of his glory for the vessels of mercy, which he has prepared beforehand for glory,[6] **24** even us whom he has called, not from the Jews only but also from the Gentiles? **25** As indeed he says in Hosea,

"Those who were not my people
I will call 'my people,'
and her who was not beloved
I will call 'my beloved.' "
26 "And in the very place where it was said to them, 'You are
not my people,'
they will be called 'sons of the living God.' "[7]

27 And Isaiah cries out concerning Israel: "Though the number of the sons of Israel be as the sand of the sea, only a remnant of them will be saved; **28** for the Lord will execute his sentence upon the earth with vigor and dispatch."[8] **29** And as Isaiah predicted,

"If the Lord of hosts had not left us children,
we would have fared like Sodom and been made like
Gomorrah."[9]

30 What shall we say, then? That Gentiles who did not pursue righteousness have attained it, that is, righteousness through faith; **31** but that Israel who pursued the righteousness which is based on law did not succeed in fulfilling that law. **32** Why? Because they did not pursue it through faith, but as if it were based on works. They have stumbled over the stumbling stone, **33** as it is written,

"Behold, I am laying in Zion a stone that will make men
stumble,
a rock that will make them fall;
and he who believes in him will not be put to shame."[1]

10 Brethren, my heart's desire and prayer to God for them is that they may be saved.[2] **2** I bear them witness that they have a zeal for God, but it is not enlightened. **3** For, being ignorant of the righteousness that comes from God, and seeking to establish their own, they did not submit to God's righteousness.[3] **4** For Christ is the end of the law,[4] that every one who has faith may be justified.

5 Moses writes that the man who practices the righteousness

---

6. There are several allusions to OT passages in these verses: Isa. 29:16; 45:9; Jer. 18:6; 50:25 (LXX 27:25); Isa. 54:16 f. (LXX). See also Wisd. 12:12; 15:7.
7. Hos. 2:23; 1:10.
8. Isa. 10:22 f.
9. Isa. 1:9.
1. A combination of Isa. 8:14 and 28:16.
2. See the note on 9:3.
3. Failure to "submit to God's right-

eousness" means for Paul simply failure to acknowledge Jesus as the Messiah, since the Christian preaching of the crucified Messiah disrupted the Jewish understanding of fulfillment of the covenant.
4. There has been much fruitless debate over the question whether "end" here means "termination" or "goal." For Paul both were true, though the immediate context here stresses the latter.

which is based on the law shall live by it.[5] [6] But the righteousness based on faith says, Do not say in your heart, "Who will ascend into heaven?" (that is, to bring Christ down) [7] or "Who will descend into the abyss?" (that is, to bring Christ up from the dead). [8] But what does it say? The word is near you, on your lips and in your heart (that is, the word of faith which we preach)[6]; [9] because if you confess with your lips that Jesus is Lord[7] and believe in your heart that God raised him from the dead, you will be saved. [10] For man believes with his heart and so is justified, and he confesses with his lips and so is saved. [11] The scripture says, "No one who believes in him will be put to shame."[8] [12] For there is no distinction between Jew and Greek;[9] the same Lord is Lord of all and bestows his riches upon all who call upon him. [13] For, "every one who calls upon the name of the Lord will be saved."[1]

[14] But how are men to call upon him in whom they have not believed? And how are they to believe in him of whom they have never heard? And how are they to hear without a preacher? [15] And how can men preach unless they are sent? As it is written, "How beautiful are the feet of those who preach good news!"[2] [16] But they have not all heeded the gospel; for Isaiah says, "Lord, who has believed what he has heard from us?"[3] [17] So faith comes from what is heard, and what is heard comes by the preaching of Christ.[4]

[18] But I ask, have they not heard? Indeed they have; for

"Their voice has gone out to all the earth,
and their words to the ends of the world."[5]

[19] Again I ask, did Israel not understand? First Moses says,

"I will make you jealous of those who are not a nation;
with a foolish nation I will make you angry."[6]

[20] Then Isaiah is so bold as to say,

"I have been found by those who did not seek me;
I have shown myself to those who did not ask for me."

[21] But of Israel he says, "All day long I have held out my hands to a disobedient and contrary people."[7]

11 I ask, then, has God rejected his people?[8] By no means! I myself am an Israelite, a descendant of Abraham, a member of the tribe of Benjamin.[9] [2] God has not rejected his people whom he foreknew. Do you not know what the scripture says of Elijah, how

---

5. Lev. 18:5; cf. Gal. 3:12.
6. Deut. 30:11–14, originally speaking of the Torah! Paul, by midrash, substitutes "Christ" for Torah.
7. One of the earliest Christian confessions, and the most important in most Greek-speaking areas.
8. Isa. 28:16.
9. Cf. 3:22.
1. Joel 2:32.

2. Isa. 52:7.
3. Isa. 53:1.
4. I.e., "preaching about Christ," not "Christ's preaching."
5. Ps. 19:4.
6. Deut. 32:21.
7. Isa. 65:1, 2.
8. Cf. Ps. 94:14; 1 Sam. 12:22; Jer. 31:37; contrast Isa. 2:6.
9. Cf. Phil. 3:5.

he pleads with God against Israel? [3] "Lord they have killed thy prophets, they have demolished thy altars, and I alone am left, and they seek my life." [4] But what is God's reply to him? "I have kept for myself seven thousand men who have not bowed the knee to Baal."[1] [5] So too at the present time there is a remnant, chosen by grace. [6] But if it is by grace, it is no longer on the basis of works; otherwise grace would no longer be grace.

[7] What then? Israel failed to obtain what it sought. The elect obtained it, but the rest were hardened, [8] as it is written,

"God gave them a spirit of stupor,
eyes that should not see and ears that should not hear,
down to this very day."[2]

[9] And David says,

"Let their feast become a snare and a trap,
a pitfall and a retribution for them;
[10] let their eyes be darkened so that they cannot see,
and bend their backs for ever."[3]

[11] So I ask, have they stumbled so as to fall? By no means! But through their trespass salvation has come to the Gentiles, so as to make Israel jealous. [12] Now if their trespass means riches for the world, and if their failure means riches for the Gentiles, how much more will their full inclusion mean!

[13] Now I am speaking to you Gentiles. Inasmuch then as I am an apostle to the Gentiles, I magnify my ministry [14] in order to make my fellow Jews jealous, and thus save some of them. [15] For if their rejection means the reconciliation of the world, what will their acceptance mean but life from the dead? [16] If the dough offered as first fruits is holy, so is the whole lump;[4] and if the root is holy, so are the branches.

[17] But if some of the branches were broken off, and you, a wild olive shoot, were grafted in their place to share the richness[5] of the olive tree, [18] do not boast over the branches. If you do boast, remember it is not you that support the root, but the root that supports you. [19] You will say, "Branches were broken off so that I might be grafted in." [20] That is true. They were broken off because of their unbelief, but you stand fast only through faith. So do not become proud, but stand in awe. [21] For if God did not spare the natural branches, neither will he spare you. [22] Note then the kindness and the severity of God: severity toward those who have fallen, but God's kindness to you, provided you continue in his kindness; otherwise you too will be cut off. [23] And even the others, if they do not persist in their unbelief, will be grafted in, for God has the power to graft them in again. [24] For if you have been

1. 1 Kings 19:10, 14, 18.
2. Deut. 29:4; cf. Isa. 29:10.
3. Ps. 69:22 f.
4. Cf. Num. 15:17–21.
5. Other ancient authorities read, "rich root."

cut from what is by nature a wild olive tree, and grafted, contrary to nature, into a cultivated olive tree, how much more will these natural branches be grafted back into their own olive tree.[6]

25 Lest you be wise in your own conceits, I want you to understand this mystery;[7] brethren: a hardening has come upon part of Israel, until the full number of the Gentiles come in, **26** and so all Israel will be saved; as it is written,

"The Deliverer will come from Zion,
he will banish ungodliness from Jacob";
27 "and this will be my covenant with them
when I take away their sins."[8]

28 As regards the gospel they are enemies of God, for your sake; but as regards election they are beloved for the sake of their forefathers.[9] **29** For the gifts and the call of God are irrevocable. **30** Just as you were once disobedient to God but now have received mercy because of their disobedience, **31** so they have now been disobedient in order that by the mercy shown to you they also may[1] receive mercy. **32** For God has consigned all men to disobedience, that he may have mercy upon all.[2]

33 O the depth of the riches and wisdom and knowledge of God! How unsearchable are his judgments and how inscrutable his ways!

34 "For who has known the mind of the Lord,
or who has been his counselor?"
35 "Or who has given a gift to him
that he might be repaid?"[3]

36 For from him and through him and to him are all things. To him be glory for ever. Amen.

12 I appeal to you[4] therefore, brethren, by the mercies of God, to present your bodies as a living sacrifice,[5] holy and acceptable to God, which is your spiritual worship. **2** Do not be conformed to

6. Paul's allegory limps, but the point is rather clear.
7. Paul uses the term elsewhere in an apocalyptic sense: the secret to be revealed at the end of days. Cf. 1 Cor. 15:51.
8. A composite quotation: Isa. 59:20, 27:9.
9. Probably Paul alludes to the well-known Pharisaic notion of the *zakut avot*—the "merit of the fathers." The next verse shows, however, that he is no longer thinking of the fathers' *merit*, but of God's fidelity to the promises he made to the fathers.
1. Some texts add "now."
2. Cf. 3:19–26.
3. Isa. 40:13; Job 41:11. Note that this doxology brings a formal conclusion not only to Chaps. 9–11, but to the whole didactic portion of the letter,

1:18–11:32.
4. As in 1 Thess. 4:1; Eph. 4:1 (cf. 1 Pet. 2:11), this "appeal" or admonition introduces a collection of ethical injunctions, 12:3–15:13. Many of these are traditional, some adapted from the Hellenistic synagogue, all shaped by use in the oral instruction of converts in the churches. The individual maxims or brief groups of sayings follow one another without systematic order, occasionally linked together by mnemonic key-words.
5. Both in Judaism and in pagan authors of the Hellenistic era "living sacrifice" or "spiritual [or, rational] worship" was often opposed to the "bloody sacrifices" of traditional cults. "Bodies" here means the whole man, as mention of the "mind" in the following verse shows.

this world[6] but be transformed by the renewal of your mind, that you may prove[7] what is the will of God, what is good and acceptable and perfect.[8]

3 For by the grace given to me I bid every one among you not to think of himself more highly than he ought to think, but to think with sober judgment, each according to the measure of faith which God has assigned him. 4 For as in one body we have many members, and all the members do not have the same function, 5 so we, though many, are one body in Christ, and individually members one of another.[9] 6 Having gifts that differ according to the grace given to us, let us use them: if prophecy, in proportion to our faith; 7 if service, in our serving; he who teaches, in his teaching; 8 he who exhorts, in his exhortation; he who contributes, in liberality; he who gives aid,[1] with zeal; he who does acts of mercy, with cheerfulness.

9 Let love be genuine; hate what is evil, hold fast to what is good; 10 love one another with brotherly affection; outdo one another in showing honor. 11 Never flag in zeal, be aglow with the Spirit, serve the Lord. 12 Rejoice in your hope, be patient in tribulation, be constant in prayer. 13 Contribute to the needs of saints, practice hospitality.[2]

14 Bless those who persecute you; bless and do not curse them.[3] 15 Rejoice with those who rejoice, weep with those who weep. 16 Live in harmony with one another; do not be haughty, but associate with the lowly;[4] never be conceited.[5] Repay no one evil for evil, but take thought for what is noble in the sight of all.[6] 18 If possible, so far as it depends upon you, live peaceably with all. 19 Beloved, never avenge yourselves, but leave it[7] to the wrath

6. Or, "age" (*aiōn*). The contrast between "this age" and "the age to come" is an apocalyptic notion fundamental to Paul's world view—as to virtually all early Christianity. In Chaps. 1–11 he has argued that the Christians are in the paradoxical situation of having already received the eschatological righteousness of God as a gift, even though they must still live in "this age." The Spirit, as "down payment" of the age to come, enables them to live the life of the new age in the old. Here they are admonished to manifest the new life they have received in concrete ethical acts. Chaps. 6 and 8 in particular show how Paul makes the connection between his understanding of salvation and the traditional ethical requirements.
7. "Prove" here in the older sense of "test," "determine by trying." In Paul's ethics this becomes very important, since the commandments of the law no longer provide, for the Christian, the direct guides of moral behavior.
8. Or, "what is the good and acceptable and perfect will of God."
9. Cf. 1 Cor. 12.
1. Or, "he who presides."
2. The style of vv. 9–13 is remarkably compact; there are no finite verbs, but only adjectives and participles describing the recommended mode of life. The same form for rules of behavior is found in 1 Pet. 2:18; 3:7 ff.; 4:7 ff.; there are parallels also in rabbinic rules.
3. Cf. Matt. 5:44; Luke 6:28. Note that Paul does not designate this as a saying of Jesus.
4. Or, "give yourselves to humble tasks."
5. Prov. 3:7.
6. Prov. 20:22; 3:4 (LXX).
7. Lit., "give place."

of God; for it is written, "Vengeance is mine, I will repay, says the Lord."[8] **20** No, "if your enemy is hungry, feed him; if he is thirsty, give him drink; for by so doing you will heap burning coals upon his head."[9] **21** Do not be overcome by evil, but overcome evil with good.

13 Let every person be subject to the governing authorities.[1] For there is no authority except from God, and those that exist have been instituted by God. **2** Therefore he who resists the authorities resists what God has appointed, and those who resist will incur judgment. **3** For rulers are not a terror to good conduct, but to bad. Would you have no fear of him who is in authority? Then do what is good, and you will receive his approval, **4** for he is God's servant for your good. But if you do wrong, be afraid, for he does not bear the sword in vain; he is the servant of God to execute his wrath on the wrongdoer. **5** Therefore one must be subject, not only to avoid God's wrath but also for the sake of conscience. **6** For the same reason you also pay taxes, for the authorities are ministers of God, attending to this very thing. **7** Pay all of them their dues, taxes to whom taxes are due, revenue to whom revenue is due, respect to whom respect is due, honor to whom honor is due.

8 Owe[2] no one anything, except to love one another; for he who loves his neighbor has fulfilled the law. **9** The commandments, "You shall not commit adultery, You shall not kill, You shall not steal, you shall not covet,"[3] and any other commandment, are summed up in this sentence, "You shall love your neighbor as yourself."[4] **10** Love does no wrong to a neighbor; therefore love is the fulfilling of the law.

11 Besides this you know what hour it is, how it is full time now for you to wake from sleep. For salvation is nearer to us now than when we first believed; **12** the night is far gone, the day is at hand. Let us then cast off the works of darkness and put on the armor of light; **13** let us conduct ourselves becomingly as in the day, not in reveling and drunkenness, not in debauchery and licentiousness, not in quarreling and jealousy. **14** But put on the Lord

---

8. Deut. 32:35.
9. Prov. 25:21 f.
1. Vv. 1–7 have been important in the development of Western political thought, receiving usually a conservative but occasionally a revolutionary interpretation. This section was probably adapted by the church from the Hellenistic synagogue.
2. "Owe" (*opheilete*) is cognate with "dues" (*opheilas*) in v. 7; this shows how disparate material was linked together by mnemonics for oral instruction.
3. Paul quotes the commandments in the order found in the LXX of Deut. 5:17 ff.; some manuscripts complete the list by adding "you shall not bear false witness."
4. Lev. 19:18. The summing up of the law by this commandment is found frequently in Judaism as well as in early Christianity: Mark 12:28–34; Matt. 22:34–40; Luke 10:27; James 2:8; Gal. 5:14. For the rabbis, the specific commandments were expressions of the law of love; for Hellenistic Christianity, and above all for Paul, love *replaced* the commandments.

Jesus Christ, and make no provision for the flesh, to gratify its desires.[5]

14 As for the man who is weak[6] in faith, welcome him, but not for disputes over opinions. [2] One believes he may eat anything, while the weak man eats only vegetables. [3] Let not him who eats despise him who abstains, and let not him who abstains pass judgment on him who eats; for God has welcomed him. [4] Who are you to pass judgment on the servant of another? It is before his own master that he stands or falls. And he will be upheld, for the Master is able to make him stand.

[5] One man esteems one day as better than another, while another man esteems all days alike. Let every one be fully convinced in his own mind. [6] He who observes the day, observes it in honor of the Lord. He also who eats, eats in honor of the Lord, since he gives thanks to God; while he who abstains, abstains in honor of the Lord and gives thanks to God. [7] None of us lives to himself, and none of us dies to himself. [8] If we live, we live to the Lord, and if we die, we die to the Lord; so then, whether we live or whether we die, we are the Lord's. [9] For to this end Christ died and lived again, that he might be Lord both of the dead and of the living.[7]

[10] Why do you pass judgment on your brother?[8] Or you, why do you despise your brother? For we shall all stand before the judgment seat of God; [11] for it is written,

"As I live, says the Lord, every knee shall bow to me,
and every tongue shall give praise[9] to God."

[12] So each of us shall give account of himself to God.[1]

[13] Then let us no more pass judgment on one another, but rather decide never to put a stumbling block or hindrance in the way of a brother. [14] I know and am persuaded in the Lord Jesus that nothing is unclean in itself; but it is unclean for any one who thinks it unclean. [15] If your brother is being injured by what you eat, you are no longer walking in love. Do not let what you eat cause the ruin of one for whom Christ died. [16] So do not let what is good to you be spoken of as evil. [17] For the kingdom of God does not mean food and drink but righteousness and peace and joy in the Holy Spirit; [18] he who thus serves Christ is acceptable to God and approved by men. [19] Let us then pursue what makes for

---

5. This section, vv. 11–14, reads like a formal conclusion to the preceding admonitions; what follows is less stereotyped, probably formulated directly on the basis of the Corinthian experience. The eschatological framework is common in early Christian exhortation: cf. especially 1 Thess. 5:2–8; Eph. 5:3 ff.

6. For the problem of the "weak" and the "strong," cf. 1 Cor. 8–10. In Rom. Paul has generalized the problem; the question of "meat offered to idols" is not mentioned.

7. Cf. 1 Thess. 5:10.

8. Note that this repeats, with a significant variation ("brother" for "the servant of another"), the question of v. 4. Vv. 3–12 thus comprise a kind of "ring-composition."

9. Or, "confess."

1. Isa. 45:23 (plus a phrase from 49:18).

peace and for mutual upbuilding. **20** Do not, for the sake of food, destroy the work of God. Everything is indeed clean, but it is wrong for any one to make others fall by what he eats; **21** it is right not to eat meat or drink wine or do anything that makes your brother stumble.[2] **22** The faith that you have, keep between yourself and God; happy is he who has no reason to judge himself for what he approves. **23** But he who has doubts is condemned, if he eats, because he does not act from faith; for whatever does not proceed from faith is sin.[3]

15 We who are strong ought to bear with the failings of· the weak, and not to please ourselves; **2** let each of us please his neighbor for his good, to edify him. **3** For Christ did not please himself; but, as it is written, "The reproaches of those who reproached thee fell on me."[4] **4** For whatever was written in former days was written for our instruction,[5] that by steadfastness and by the encouragement of the scriptures we might have hope. **5** May the God of steadfastness and encouragement grant you to live in such harmony with one another, in accord with Christ Jesus, **6** that together you may with one voice glorify the God and Father of our Lord Jesus Christ.

7 Welcome one another,[6] therefore, as Christ has welcomed you, for the glory of God. **8** For I tell you that Christ became a servant to the circumcised to show God's truthfulness, in order to confirm the promises given to the patriarchs, **9** and in order that the Gentiles might glorify God for his mercy. As it is written,

"Therefore I will praise thee among the Gentiles,
and sing to thy name";[7]

10 and again it is said,

"Rejoice, O Gentiles, with his people";[8]

11 and again,

"Praise the Lord, all Gentiles,
and let all the people praise him";[9]

12 and further Isaiah says,

"The root of Jesse shall come,
he who rises to rule the Gentiles;
in him shall the Gentiles hope."[1]

13 May the God of hope fill you with all joy and peace in believing, so that by the power of the Holy Spirit you may abound in hope.

---

2. Other texts add, "or be upset or be weakened."
3. Some texts insert here the doxology found at 16:25—27; it was probably formulated to serve as a conclusion for the shortened version of the letter (see above, p. 68).
4. Ps. 69:9.
5. Cf. 1 Cor. 10:11.
6. Cf. 14:1. The pattern, "Do [x], as

Christ did [x]," is evidently one of the standard forms of early Christian exhortation: cf. Eph. 4:32; 5:2, 25, 29; Col. 3:12 f.; similarly Rom. 15:2 f.; Mark 10:44 f.; 1 Pet. 2:21 ff.
7. Ps. 18:49=2 Sam. 22:50.
8. Deut. 32:43 LXX.
9. Ps. 117:1.
1. Isa. 11:1, 10.

14 I myself am satisfied about you, my brethren, that you yourselves are full of goodness, filled with all knowledge, and able to instruct one another. **15** But on some points I have written to you very boldly by way of reminder[2] because of the grace given me by God **16** to be a minister of Christ Jesus to the Gentiles in the priestly service of the gospel of God, so that the offering of the Gentiles may be acceptable, sanctified by the Holy Spirit.[3] **17** In Christ Jesus, then, I have reason to be proud of my work for God. **18** For I will not venture to speak of anything except what Christ has wrought through me to win obedience from the Gentiles, by word and deed, **19** by the power of signs and wonders, by the power of the Holy Spirit, so that from Jerusalem and as far round as Illyricum I have fully preached the gospel of Christ, **20** thus making it my ambition to preach the gospel, not where Christ has already been named, lest I build on another man's foundation,[4] **21** but as it is written,

"They shall see who have never been told of him,
and they shall understand who have never heard of him."[5]

22 This is the reason why I have so often been hindered from coming to you. **23** But now, since I no longer have any room for work in these regions, and since I have longed for many years to come to you, **24** I hope to see you in passing as I go to Spain, and to be sped on my journey there by you, once I have enjoyed your company for a little. **25** At present, however, I am going to Jerusalem with aid for the saints.[6] **26** For Macedonia and Achaia have been pleased to make some contribution for the poor among the saints at Jerusalem; **27** they were pleased to do it, and indeed they are in debt to them, for if the Gentiles have come to share in their spiritual blessings, they ought also to be of service to them in material blessings. **28** When therefore I have completed this, and have delivered to them what has been raised,[7] I shall go on by way of you to Spain; **29** and I know that when I come to you I shall come in the fulness of the blessing[8] of Christ.

30 I appeal to you, brethren, by our Lord Jesus Christ and by the love of the Spirit, to strive together with me in your prayers to God on my behalf, **31** that I may be delivered from the unbelievers in Judea, and that my service for Jerusalem may be acceptable to the saints,[9] **32** so that by God's will I may come to you with joy and

---

2. Note how tactfully Paul hedges his expressions of apostolic authority at the beginning and end of the letter; cf. 1:11 f.
3. The sacrificial imagery is reminiscent of 12:1–3.
4. Cf. 1 Cor. 3:10; 2 Cor. 10:13 ff.
5. Isa. 52:15.
6. Cf. Gal. 2:10; 1 Cor. 16:1–4; 2 Cor. 8; 9.

7. Lit., "sealed to them this fruit." This rather obscure metaphor evidently comes from the commercial practice of sealing sacks of produce to protect the contents.
8. Some texts insert "of the gospel."
9. The account in Acts 21:17 ff. shows that Paul's fears were well founded. Unfortunately Acts does not mention the collection.

be refreshed in your company. **33** The God of peace be with you all. Amen.[1]

16 I commend to you our sister Phoebe, a deaconess of the church at Cenchreae,[2] **2** that you may receive her in the Lord as befits the saints, and help her in whatever she may require from you, for she has been a helper of many and of myself as well.

3 Greet Prisca and Aquila,[3] my fellow workers in Christ Jesus, **4** who risked their necks for my life, to whom not only I but also all the churches of the Gentiles give thanks; **5** greet also the church in their house. Greet my beloved Epaenetus, who was the first convert[4] in Asia for Christ. **6** Greet Mary, who has worked hard among you, **7** Greet Andronicus and Junias, my kinsmen and my fellow prisoners; they are men of note among the apostles, and they were in Christ before me. **8** Greet Ampliatus, my beloved in the Lord. **9** Greet Urbanus, our fellow worker in Christ, and my beloved Stachys. **10** Greet Apelles, who is approved in Christ. Greet those who belong to the family of Aristobulus. **11** Greet my kinsman Herodion. Greet those in the Lord who belong to the family of Narcissus. **12** Greet those workers in the Lord, Tryphaena and Tryphosa. Greet the beloved Persis, who has worked hard in the Lord. **13** Greet Rufus, eminent in the Lord, also his mother and mine. **14** Greet Asyncritus, Phlegon, Hermes, Patrobas, Hermas, and the brethren who are with them. **15** Greet Philologus, Julia, Nereus and his sister, and Olympas, and all the saints who are with them. **16** Greet one another with a holy kiss.[5] All the churches of Christ greet you.

17 I appeal to you, brethren, to take note of those who create dissensions and difficulties, in opposition to the doctrine which you have been taught; avoid them. **18** For such persons do not serve our Lord Christ, but their own appetites,[6] and by fair and flattering words they deceive the hearts of the simple-minded. **19** For while your obedience is known to all, so that I rejoice over you, I would have you wise as to what is good and guileless as to what is evil; **20** then the God of peace will soon crush Satan under your feet. The grace of our Lord Jesus Christ be with you.[7]

21 Timothy,[8] my fellow worker, greets you; so do Lucius and Jason and Sosipater, my kinsmen.

22 I Tertius, the writer of this letter, greet you in the Lord.

1. One very early manuscript has the doxology (16:25–27) at this point.
2. The eastern port of Corinth.
3. Aquila and Prisca had been among the Jews expelled from Rome by Claudius; they had settled first in Corinth, then in Ephesus: Acts 18:2 ff.; 1 Cor. 16:19.
4. Lit., "first fruits."

5. Cf. 1 Thess. 5:26; 1 Cor. 16:20; 2 Cor. 13:12; also 1 Pet. 5:14.
6. Lit., "their own belly"; cf. Phil. 3:19.
7. Some texts have this benediction (with the addition of the word "all") as v. 24; a few place it after v. 27.

8. See note on 1 Thess. 1:1.

23 Gaius, who is host to me and to the whole church, greets you. Erastus, the city treasurer, and our brother Quartus, greet you.[9]

25 Now to him who is able to strengthen you according to my gospel and the preaching of Jesus Christ, according to the revelation of the mystery which was kept secret for long ages **26** but is now disclosed and through the prophetic writings is made known to all nations, according to the command of the eternal God, to bring about the obedience of faith—**27** to the only wise God be glory for evermore through Jesus Christ! Amen.[1]

THE LETTER TO THE PHILIPPIANS
(ca. 62? ca. 56?)

The story of Paul's founding of the church at Philippi is told in Acts 16, replete with miraculous details which appropriately underscore the significance of his first work on European soil. While Philippi was not actually "the leading city of the district of Macedonia" (Acts 16:12: Thessalonica was capital of the province, and Amphipolis capital of the first district in which Philippi lay), it was an important one. It bore the name of its founder, Philip of Macedon. It had been made a Roman military colony by Octavian, with the legal prerogatives and the largely Latin population that implied. Although the apostle's initial preaching there, according to Acts, was tumultuous and brief, the church evidently flourished and its relationship with Paul was extraordinarily cordial. Only in the case of Philippi, as the letter itself tells us, did Paul break his customary rule of not accepting money from his converts. Such a gift was the occasion, in fact, for at least part of the present letter to the Philippians (4:10–20).

One must say "at least part," because it is not at all clear that the letter as we have it is a unity. A number of scholars in recent years, several quite independently, have come to the conclusion that it has been pieced together from parts of three letters. The principal reason is the polemical warning of Chap. 3, which breaks abruptly into material that sounds like the typical concluding portions of a Pauline letter. The question is also raised whether Paul would really wait until the very end of the letter (4:10 ff.) before mentioning the Philippian gift which is presumably the occasion for his writing. It would also be somewhat surprising that he waited so long—until Epaphroditus has recovered from a major illness and is ready to

---

9. Some texts add as v. 24, the benediction given here as v. 20b.
1. The doxology is generally regarded as a late addition; cf. Eph. 3:20 f.; 1 Tim. 1:17; Jude 24 f. For the pattern "once hidden/now revealed," see note on 1 Cor. 2:7.

return—before thanking them, since there has obviously been communication back and forth in the meantime (they have heard Epaphroditus was ill, and he has heard that they are worried: 2:26). The difficulties with the text are somewhat similar to those of 2 Corinthians, and the solution offered is analogous. Among the scholars who adopt this solution, there is agreement on the general extent of the three letters, but differences in detail.

It is impossible to determine the place of writing. Paul was in prison at the time of writing—at least of 1:1–3.1a. In the ancient church it was universally supposed that the imprisonment was in Rome (Acts 28). Paul was in prison many times, however, and modern scholars have proposed either Caesarea (Acts 25–26) or Ephesus. Of the two Ephesus is far the more plausible. Although no imprisonment in Ephesus is mentioned anywhere in the New Testament, 2 Cor. 1:8 f. may very well allude to one (1 Cor. 15:32 is often cited as further evidence, but it is almost certain that "I fought with beasts" is to be taken figuratively). Of the several objections raised against Rome as the place of origin, the one substantial one is that the distance between Rome and Philippi (about 800 miles, a trip of five to seven weeks each way) would have made the several communications between Paul and the congregation implied by the letter very difficult. However, since Paul was in prison in Rome at least two years, that is not an insuperable difficulty. On the other hand, a number of elements in the letter, such as mention of the *praetorium*, "Caesar's household," and Paul's conviction that his case is about to be settled, would be more natural in Rome, though none of them is impossible in Ephesus (or even Caesarea). One solution, for those who accept a theory of multiple letters, would be to regard 3:1a–4.1 as part of a letter written from Ephesus ca. 56, while the other two were written during the Roman imprisonment, ca. 62.

Whatever its history, the letter stands as an example of the finest elements in Paul's thought and style, addressed to a community for whom he had the deepest affection.

---

1 Paul and Timothy, servants[1] of Christ Jesus,

To all the saints in Christ Jesus who are at Philippi, with the bishops and deacons:[2]

1. Or, "slaves."
2. The first mention in Christian literature of "bishops" (i.e., "overseers," "administrators") and "deacons" (i.e., "ministers,") as distinct offices or functions. The two terms were often used interchangeably, along with a third equivalent, "presbyters" ("elders"); "deacon" could also be used as a title of an "apostle" (2 Cor. 12:23). Perhaps in Philippi the development toward a more highly structured organization was taking place more rapidly than elsewhere.

[2] Grace to you and peace from God our Father and the Lord Jesus Christ.

[3] I thank my God in all my remembrance of you, [4] always in every prayer of mine for you all making my prayer with joy, [5] thankful for your partnership[3] in the gospel from the first day until now. [6] And I am sure that he who began a good work in you will bring it to completion at the day of Jesus Christ. [7] It is right for me to feel thus about you all, because I hold you in my heart, for you are all partakers with me of grace, both in my imprisonment and in the defense and confirmation of the gospel. [8] For God is my witness, how I yearn for you all with the affection of Christ Jesus. [9] And it is my prayer that your love may abound more and more, with knowledge and all discernment, [10] so that you may approve what is excellent, and may be pure and blameless for the day of Christ, [11] filled with the fruits of righteousness[4] which come through Jesus Christ, to the glory and praise of God.

[12] I want you to know, brethren, that what has happened to me has really served to advance the gospel, [13] so that it has become known throughout the whole praetorian guard[5] and to all the rest that my imprisonment is for Christ;[6] [14] and most of the brethren have been made confident in the Lord because of my imprisonment, and are much more bold to speak the word of God without fear.

[15] Some indeed preach Christ from envy and rivalry, but others from good will. [16] The latter do it out of love, knowing that I am put here[7] for the defense of the gospel; [17] the former proclaim Christ out of partisanship,[8] not sincerely but thinking to afflict me in my imprisonment. [18] What then? Only that in every way, whether in pretense or in truth, Christ is proclaimed; and in that I rejoice.

[19] Yes, and I shall rejoice. For I know that through your prayers and help of the Spirit of Jesus Christ this will turn out for my deliverance,[9] [20] as it is my eager expectation and hope that I shall not be at all ashamed, but that with full courage now as always Christ will be honored in my body, whether by life or by death. [21] For to me to live is Christ, and to die is gain. [22] If it is to be life in the flesh, that means fruitful labor for me. Yet which I shall choose I cannot tell. [23] I am hard pressed between the two. My

---

3. This could be an allusion to the concrete expression of their "partnership" in the gift they had sent him (4:10 ff.); Paul could use the same term (*koinōnia*) to refer to the collection for Jerusalem (2 Cor. 8:4; 9:13). The referent is also much broader, however, as v. 7 shows (where "partakers with me" translates *sunkoinōnous*).
4. The phrase is biblical: e.g., Prov.

11:30; Amos 6:12; cf. James 3:18. See also Gal. 5:22; Rom. 7:4.
5. Lit., "in the whole praetorium." The term was used both of the official residence of a governor and of the imperial bodyguard.
6. Lit., "my bonds have become manifest in Christ."
7. Or, "I am destined."
8. Or, "ambition," as in Rom. 2:8.
9. Job 13:16 LXX.

desire is to depart and be with Christ,[1] for that is far better. [24] But to remain in the flesh is more necessary on your account. [25] Convinced of this, I know[2] that I shall remain and continue with you all, for your progress and joy in the faith, [26] so that in me you may have ample cause to glory in Christ Jesus, because of my coming to you again.

[27] Only let your manner of life be worthy of the gospel of Christ, so that whether I come and see you or am absent, I may hear of you that you stand firm in one spirit, with one mind striving side by side for the faith of the gospel, [28] and not frightened in anything by your opponents. This is a clear omen to them of their destruction, but of your salvation, and that from God.[3] [29] For it has been granted to you that for the sake of Christ you should not only believe in him but also suffer for his sake, [30] engaged in the same conflict which you saw and now hear to be mine.

[2] So if there is any encouragement in Christ, any incentive of love, any participation in the Spirit, any affection and sympathy, [2] complete my joy by being of the same mind, having the same love, being in full accord and of one mind. [3] Do nothing from self-ishness or conceit, but in humility count others better than your-selves. [4] Let each of you look not only to his own interests, but also to the interests of others. [5] Have this mind among yourselves, which you have in Christ Jesus,[4]

> [6] who, though he was in the form of God,[5]
> did not count equality with God
> a thing to be grasped,[6]

1. Being "with Christ" seems here to be anticipated immediately upon death, in 1 Thess. 4:14 only at the Parousia. If Paul had a clear and consistent picture of what the believer would experience after death, it is not apparent from his letters: cf. 1 Cor. 15; 2 Cor. 5:1–5; Rom. 8:18–23.

2. Paul "knows" only in the sense of personal conviction; contrast 2:23 f.

3. Cf. 2 Thess. 1:5 ff.

4. This introductory clause requires the reader to supply some verb (lit., "Think this, which —— in Christ Jesus"). The way the translator completes the sentence depends upon his understanding of the way the following hymn (vv. 6–11) is being used: Is the "humility" of Christ as depicted in the poem an example to be imitated? So most older commentators, but this view is rejected by almost all recent inter-preters. Is the redemptive act of Christ depicted in mythical form, as the basis (rather than model) of ethical re-sponse? In the latter view, "in Christ Jesus" is seen as Paul's usual technical formula, meaning "in the domain of Christ's lordship," i.e., in the church.

There have been wide disagreements about the background of the hymn's religious language—Palestinian Ju-daism, Hellenistic folk religion, Gnosti-cism—its function in Christian wor-ship—eucharist or baptism—and its precise literary structure. Recently some of these alternatives have been seen to be not so mutually exclusive as was formerly believed.

5. Three synonyms are used in vv. 6–8: *morphē* (vv. 6, 7), *schēma* (v. 8), both translated "form," and *hom-oiōma* (v. 7), translated "likeness." An allusion to the "image" and "likeness" of God borne by the first man (Gen. 1:26 f.) is likely; this notion was very important in early Christian baptism (see e.g., Col. 1:15; 3:10), but also in Gnostic circles.

6. The rare word translated by this phrase has been much discussed. It could mean "act of robbery" (cf. KJV), or "booty," either to be seized or already possessed and to be clung to. But the whole phrase "count . . . a thing to be grasped" has been found to be a proverbial expression for "treat something as a stroke of luck." Some commentators have seen in the phrase an allusion to the Lucifer myth, others, more plausibly, to the Adam myth.

[7] but emptied himself,
taking the form of a servant,[7]
being born in the likeness of men.
[8] And being found in human form
he humbled himself
and became obedient unto death,
        even death on a cross.[8]
[9] Therefore God has highly exalted him
and bestowed on him the name
which is above every name,
[10] that at the name of Jesus
every knee should bow,
in heaven and on earth and under the earth,[9]
[11] and every tongue confess
that Jesus Christ is Lord,
to the glory of God the Father.[1]

[12] Therefore, my beloved, as you have always obeyed,[2] so now, not only as in my presence but much more in my absence, work out your own salvation with fear and trembling; [13] for God is at work in you, both to will and to work for his good pleasure.

[14] Do all things without grumbling or questioning, [15] that you may be blameless and innocent, children of God without blemish in the midst of a crooked and perverse generation, among whom you shine as lights in the world, [16] holding fast the word of life, so that in the day of Christ I may be proud that I did not run in vain or labor in vain. [17] Even if I am to be poured as a libation upon the sacrificial offering of your faith, I am glad and rejoice with you all. [18] Likewise you also should be glad and rejoice with me.

[19] I hope in the Lord Jesus to send Timothy to you soon, so that I may be cheered by news of you. [20] I have no one like him, who will be genuinely anxious for your welfare. [21] They all look after their own interests, not those of Jesus Christ. [22] But Timothy's worth you know, how as a son with a father he has served with me in the gospel. [23] I hope therefore to send him just as soon as I see how it will go with me; [24] and I trust in the Lord that shortly I myself shall come also.[3]

---

7. Or, "slave." In the Greco-Roman world human life was frequently regarded as enslaved to demonic forces. Cf. Gal. 4:1–9.
8. The appositive phrase, which interrupts the rhythm, was undoubtedly added by Paul.
9. The three-fold division of the world was common in Hellenism; the reference is most likely to superhuman powers, here envisioned as making forced obeisance to the new cosmic ruler.
1. The final strophe is a Christian expansion of Isa. 45:23.
2. The following passage (vv. 12–18) has the style of a farewell address or "testament"; it has been compared with the testament of Moses in Deut. 32, a phrase from which (32:5) is quoted in v. 15.
3. If Phil. is written from Rome, this statement would mean that Paul has abandoned his plan for a Spanish mission (Rom. 15:24, 28). We do not know whether either hope was fulfilled.

25 I have thought it necessary to send to you Epaphroditus my brother and fellow worker and fellow soldier, and your messenger and minister to my need,[4] **26** for he has been longing for you all, and has been distressed because you heard that he was ill. **27** Indeed he was ill, near to death. But God had mercy on him, and not only on him but on me also, lest I should have sorrow upon sorrow. **28** I am the more eager to send him, therefore, that you may rejoice at seeing him again, and that I may be less anxious. **29** So receive him in the Lord with all joy; and honor such men, **30** for he nearly died for the work of Christ, risking his life to complete your service to me.

3 Finally, my brethren, rejoice[5] in the Lord. To write the same things to you is not irksome to me, and is safe for you.[6]

2 Look out for the dogs,[7] look out for the evil-workers,[8] look out for those who mutilate the flesh.[9] **3**For we are the true circumcision, who worship God in spirit,[1] and glory in Christ Jesus, and put no confidence in the flesh. **4** Though I myself have reason for confidence in the flesh also.[2] If any other man thinks he has reason for confidence in the flesh, I have more: **5** circumcised on the eighth day, of the people of Israel, of the tribe of Benjamin, a Hebrew born of Hebrews; as to the law a Pharisee, **6** as to zeal a persecutor of the church, as to righteousness under the law blameless. **7** But whatever gain I had, I counted as loss for the sake of[3] Christ. **8** Indeed I count everything as loss because of the surpassing worth of knowing Christ Jesus my Lord. For his sake I have suffered the loss of all things, and count them as refuse, in order that I may gain Christ **9** and be found in him, not having a righteousness of my own, based on law, but that which is through faith in Christ, the righteousness from God that depends on faith; **10** that I may know him and the power of his resurrection, and may share his sufferings, becoming like him in his death, **11** that if possible I may attain the resurrection from the dead.

12 Not that I have already obtained this[4] or am already perfect;

4. Cf. 4:10–20.

5. The word could be translated "farewell," but see 4:4.

6. There is no agreement about the place of v. 1b, nor the referent of "the same things." Since what follows is probably a fragment of another letter (see introduction), the verse may have served to connect it with its original context.

7. The phrase is harsh, but also humorous (*cave canem,* "beware the dog"). Some think the epithet would be especially offensive to Jewish ears, but that is doubtful. The most famous man of antiquity to be called a dog was Diogenes, whose followers turned the jest into a proudly ironic nickname: "Cynics."

8. Cf. 2 Cor. 11:13.

9. *Katatomē,* "incision" or "mutilation," a pun on *peritomē,* "circumcision" (following verse). Cf. Gal. 5:12.

1. The vast majority of witnesses read, "worship [or, more likely, "serve"] by the spirit of God." As in Rom. 1:9 the verb "serve [cultically]" refers to missionary work.

2. For the following, cf. 2 Cor. 11:21 ff.

3. Or, "because of." The metaphors here are commercial; Paul says, in effect, that he was, despite his religious affluence, bankrupted by Christ.

4. Or, possibly, "him," and also in the following clause (cf. vv. 8 f.). The verbs have no object in Greek.

but I press on to make it my own, because Christ Jesus has made me his own. [13] Brethren, I do not consider that I have made it my own; but one thing I do, forgetting what lies behind and straining forward to what lies ahead, [14] I press on toward the goal for the prize of the upward call of God in Christ Jesus. [15] Let those of us who are mature[5] be thus minded; and if in anything you are otherwise minded, God will reveal that also to you. [16] Only let us hold true to what we have attained.

[17] Brethren, join in imitating me, and mark those who so live as you have an example in us. [18] For many, of whom I have often told you and now tell you even with tears, live as enemies of the cross of Christ. [19] Their end is destruction, their god is the belly,[6] and they glory in their shame, with minds set on earthly things. [20] But our commonwealth is in heaven, and from it we await a Savior, the Lord Jesus Christ, [21] who will change our lowly body to be like his glorious body, by the power which enables him even to subject all things to himself.[7]

4 Therefore, my brethren, whom I love and long for, my joy and crown, stand firm thus in the Lord, my beloved.

[2] I entreat Euodia and I entreat Syntyche to agree in the Lord. [3] And I ask you also, true yokefellow[8], help these women, for they have labored side by side with me in the gospel together with Clement and the rest of my fellow workers, whose names are in the book of life.

[4] Rejoice in the Lord[9] always; again I will say, Rejoice. [5] Let all men know your forbearance. The Lord is at hand. [6] Have no anxiety about anything, but in everything by prayer and supplication with thanksgiving let your requests be made known to God. [7] And the peace of God, which passes all understanding, will keep your hearts and your minds in Christ Jesus.

[8] Finally, brethren, whatever is true, whatever is honorable, whatever is just, whatever is pure, whatever is lovely, whatever is gracious, if there is any excellence, if there is anything worthy of praise, think about these things. [9] What you have learned and

---

5. See the note on 1 Cor. 2:6. As in 1 Cor., Paul is warning against a spiritual perfectionism which regards "resurrection" as a state already attained.
6. Cf. Rom. 16:18. This and the following phrase do not necessarily refer to sensuality or immoral behavior in a narrow sense, but may only imply that Paul regards the motives of the rival missionaries as selfish.
7. Some commentators find in v. 21 clear allusions to the hymn 2:6–11, but in fact the themes are found elsewhere in Paul (e.g., 1 Cor. 15:51 ff.;

2 Cor. 3:18; Rom. 8:29) and are probably part of the baptismal ideology of early Hellenistic Christianity (cf. Col. 1:15–20; 3:1–11).
8. Like other anonymous persons mentioned by Paul, the identity of the "true yokefellow" has aroused the wildest ingenuity of generations of commentators. Clement of Alexandria and others even thought Paul's wife was meant (though the adjective "true" is masculine).
9. Cf. 3:1a.

received and heard and seen in me, do; and the God of peace will be with you.

¹⁰ I rejoice in the Lord greatly that now at length you have revived your concern for me;¹ you were indeed concerned for me, but you had no opportunity. ¹¹ Not that I complain of want; for I have learned, in whatever state I am, to be content. ¹² I know how to be abased, and I know how to abound; in any and all circumstances I have learned the secret² of facing plenty and hunger, abundance and want. ¹³ I can do all things in him who strengthens me.

¹⁴ Yet it was kind of you to share my trouble. ¹⁵ And you Philippians yourselves know that in the beginning of the gospel, when I left Macedonia, no church entered into partnership with me in giving and receiving except you only³; ¹⁶ for even in Thessalonica you sent me help⁴ once and again. ¹⁷ Not that I seek the gift; but I seek the fruit which increases to your credit. ¹⁸ I have received full payment, and more; I am filled, having received from Epaphroditus the gifts you sent, a fragrant offering, a sacrifice acceptable and pleasing to God. ¹⁹ And my God will supply every need of yours according to his riches in glory in Christ Jesus. ²⁰ To our God and Father be glory for ever and ever. Amen.

²¹ Greet every saint in Christ Jesus. The brethren who are with me greet you. ²² All the saints greet you, especially those of Caesar's household.⁵

²³ The grace of the Lord Jesus Christ be with your spirit.

THE LETTER TO PHILEMON
(ca. 62? ca. 56?)

Both ancient and modern writers have wondered why this letter, written to an individual about a private matter, should have been preserved and canonized alongside the "official" letters of Paul. Yet the letter is not entirely private. Although the body of the letter is all in the first and second person singular ("I" and "you"), in the salutation Timothy is associated with Paul as a sender, and besides

---

1. Vv. 10–20 may comprise (part of?) a note of thanks sent earlier than Chaps. 1–2 (see the introduction).
2. Lit., "I have been initiated."
3. See 2 Cor. 11:8 f.
4. Most witnesses read "[money] for my needs."

5. "Caesar's household" comprised all who were employed in the imperial administration, mostly slaves and freedmen. While this establishment was particularly large in Rome, "those of Caesar's household" would also be found throughout the empire.

Philemon not only Apphia and Archippus but the whole "church in [Philemon's] house" are addressed. Moreover, the request which Paul makes of Philemon may not be quite so private a matter as it appears at first glance.

Most commentators assume that Paul merely wants Philemon to receive back his runaway slave without the severe punishment that, legally, he could exact. The letter would thus stand as a fairly exact parallel to a famous second-century letter by the pagan writer Pliny the younger, appealing to a friend for clemency toward a freedman who had offended him.[1] A few scholars have argued, however, that Paul wished Onesimus to be set free, while John Knox and Théo Preiss, apparently independently, have argued very persuasively that Paul's real desire was that Onesimus should be sent back to him to serve as a fellow evangelist. The notes in the text will show that Paul's puns and double entendres actually make this intent almost unmistakable. Knox's further suggestion, that the actual owner of the slave is Archippus, and his yielding to Paul's request is precisely the "ministry" urged in Col. 4:17, is less persuasive. Knox and others have speculated that the Bishop Onesimus of Ephesus to whom Ignatius wrote four or five decades later was the same man, indicating the success of Paul's plea and vindicating his judgment of character. That is an interesting possibility, but no more.

Paul was in prison when he wrote the letter, but again the place of his imprisonment is uncertain. Rome, Caesarea, and Ephesus have been advocated; of these Caesarea is least likely. Since Ephesus was much closer to Colossae, it would be easier for a runaway slave from Colossae (Col. 4:9) to meet Paul there than in Rome, and more understandable that Paul writes Philemon to prepare a guest room for him (Phlm. 22). On the other hand, most scholars think Colossians must have been written very late in Paul's career, and, if that letter is authentic, it must have been written at about the same time as Philemon (compare the greetings at the end of the two letters.)

The Roman laws governing fugitive slaves were strict, and Paul observes the legal necessities punctiliously. Anyone aiding a fugitive was liable for all damages due the master; Paul gives Philemon his personal note for those damages (18 f.). Above all, the fugitive had to be returned; and Paul is sending Onesimus back. At the same time, Paul's half-stated request, the subtle pleas, the almost bantering tone of his several puns, render the legal situation so incongruous as to shatter it. Paul's manipulation of Philemon is perfectly transparent, and carried out so adroitly that the latter could hardly

---

1. A translation of Pliny's letter is conveniently available in Morton S. Enslin, *The Literature of the Christian Movement* (New York, 1956), p. 287. The Latin text is printed by Martin Dibelius, *An die Kolosser, Epheser, an Philemon* (3d ed., ed. H. Greeven, Tübingen, 1953), appendix 7.

be offended; his freedom of decision is preserved, even though Paul is "confident of [his] obedience."

---

1 Paul, a prisoner for Christ Jesus, and Timothy our brother,
To Philemon our beloved fellow worker [2] and Apphia our sister and Archippus our fellow soldier, and the church in your house:[1]

[3] Grace to you and peace from God our Father and the Lord Jesus Christ.

[4] I thank my God always when I remember you[2] in my prayers, [5] because I hear[3] of your love and of the faith which you have toward the Lord Jesus and all the saints, [6] and I pray that the sharing of your faith may promote the knowledge of all the good that is ours in Christ.[4] [7] For I have derived much joy and comfort from your love, my brother, because the hearts of the saints have been refreshed through you.

[8] Accordingly, though I am bold enough in Christ to command you to do what is required,[5] [9] yet for love's sake I prefer to appeal to you—I, Paul, an ambassador[6] and now a prisoner also for Christ Jesus— [10] I appeal to you for my child, Onesimus, whose father I have become[7] in my imprisonment. [11] (Formerly he was useless to you, but now he is indeed useful[8] to you and to me.) [12] I am sending him back to you, sending my very heart. [13] I would have been glad to keep him with me, in order that he might serve me on your behalf during my imprisonment for the gospel; [14] but I preferred to do nothing without your consent in order that your goodness might not be by compulsion but of your own free will.

[15] Perhaps this is why he was parted from you for a while, that you might have him back for ever, [16] no longer as a slave but more

---

1. Naturally in the earliest period the Christian congregations had no special buildings erected for their assemblies. For the "house church," see also 1 Cor. 16:19; Rom. 16:5; Col. 4:15.
2. "You" here and in the following lines is singular; that in v. 3 is plural.
3. Elsewhere Paul uses this kind of expression only in the case of those with whom he is unacquainted directly (Rom. 1:8; Col. 1:4; Eph. 1:15). Yet the rest of the letter, especially v. 19b, suggests that Paul knows Philemon rather well.
4. This content of Paul's prayer is undoubtedly related to the concrete request he wishes to make of Philemon.

Does he hope that the latter's "sharing of ... faith" will take the form of sending back Onesimus as his agent in Paul's work (Preiss)? The translation here, which is tendentious ("may promote" renders lit., "may become active in"), supports this view.
5. Or, "what is proper," "your duty." Paul deliberately does not state what that "duty" is, but only makes it plain by indirection.
6. Or, "old man."
7. That is, by converting him to Christianity; see note on Gal. 4:19.
8. A pun on the name "Onesimus," which meant "useful."

than a slave, as a beloved brother, especially to me but how much more to you, both in the flesh and in the Lord. **17** So if you consider me your partner, receive him as you would receive me. **18** If he has wronged you at all, or owes you anything, charge that to my account. **19** I, Paul, write this with my own hand, I will repay it—to say nothing of your owing me even your own self.[9] **20** Yes, brother, I want some benefit[1] from you in the Lord. Refresh my heart in Christ.[2]

21 Confident of your obedience, I write to you, knowing that you will do even more than I say.[3] **22** At the same time, prepare a guest room for me, for I am hoping through your prayers to be granted to you.

23 Epaphras, my fellow prisoner in Christ Jesus, sends greetings to you, **24** and so do Mark, Aristarchus, Demas, and Luke, my fellow workers.[4]

25 The grace of the Lord Jesus Christ be with your spirit.

9. This is most readily explained as an allusion to Philemon's conversion, though that is of course denied by commentators who insist that Paul did not know him (see above, v. 5). Since Paul regarded Epaphras as his representative (Col. 1:7), Paul could perhaps speak this way of any Colossian Christian.

1. "want . . . benefit": *onaimēn*, a second pun on "Onesimus."

2. A third word play? In v. 7 Paul gives thanks that Philemon has previously "refreshed the hearts" of the saints; in v. 12 he says that Onesimus is Paul's "very heart"; now he asks that Philemon "refresh my heart."

3. In the light of the puns and double entendres throughout the letter, the phrase "even more than I say" is significant.

4. Cf. Col. 4:10 ff.; of the companions that send greetings in that letter, only Jesus Justus is not named here (his name could easily have been omitted by an early copyist, if it originally followed "Christ Jesus").

PART II

Works of
the Pauline School

The annotated text of six letters bearing Paul's name, the authenticity of which is disputed among modern scholars.

THE SECOND LETTER TO THE
THESSALONIANS (ca. 51?)

If authentic, 2 Thessalonians was written within a few months after 1 Thessalonians. The scholars who think that it was not written by Paul, but by a disciple or even an opponent, offer a discouraging variety of possible dates, mostly around 70, some as late as 100. It was quoted by Polycarp, bishop of Smyrna, in his letter to the Philippians, ca. 110.

The letter's authenticity has been questioned principally on two grounds: the unusually close similarity in phrase and order of large parts of 1 and 2 Thessalonians, and the apparent contradictions between the theologies expressed in the two letters. The latter problem was first raised by J. E. Christian Schmidt in 1798, who found it impossible to harmonize the eschatology of 2 Thess. 2:1–12 with that of 1 Thess. 5:1–11. If "the day of the Lord will come like a thief in the night," how can it be heralded by visible, predictable events? Attempts were made to connect 2 Thess. 2:1–12 to specific historical occasions, such as the death of Nero and the legend of his expected resurrection, or with the Jewish revolt of 66–70. These attempts were eventually abandoned, and it was recognized that both the suddenness of the Lord's coming and the signs beforehand were found side by side in many apocalypses, including Mark 13, and its parallels, and the Apocalypse of John. Nevertheless, many readers have continued to find the two documents ideologically incompatible. Some have felt that the theology of 2 Thessalonians simply could not be harmonized logically with that of, say, the Letter to the Romans; hence Paul could not have written it. More common is the opinion that Paul could, indeed, have written 2 Thessalonians, but only if the situation in the Thessalonian church had changed radically. That would require a long time lapse between the two letters, but then the literary similarity between them could only be explained by direct copying, rather than by copying from memory. Such copying would seem more likely if done by a forger than if by Paul himself.

Advocates of Pauline authorship point out that none of the arguments for inauthenticity has succeeded in offering a satisfactory explanation for the existing form of the letter. To have produced a document so similar to 1 Thessalonians in parts yet so different in others, the forger would have had to master the Pauline vocabulary and style so thoroughly that he could use it as freely as Paul himself. Furthermore, if one recognizes that traditional, formulaic, and idiomatic elements, including Pauline clichés, account for most of the parallels, then the copying hypothesis becomes unnecessary. The simplest and most comprehensive explanation of the *literary* factors remains the assumption that Paul wrote both letters, to be sure within a rather short space of time, though perhaps as much as several months.

The question of theological incompatibility is more important, and more difficult to decide objectively. There has been a growing recognition that the eschatology of 2 Thessalonians is not incompatible with that of 1 Thessalonians. Each speaks of one aspect of the typical apocalyptic scenario of the world's end, and does so in traditional language. The question really comes down to this: to what extent can Paul plausibly be thought to have availed himself of traditional apocalyptic imagery? That question, however, must not be confused with the question whether Paul, to be logically consistent, *ought* to have used such imagery. That Paul did use such imagery, and to counter a local situation not unlike that presupposed in 2 Thessalonians, is demonstrated by 1 Cor. 15. Many of the criticisms of the theology of 2 Thessalonians have presupposed a consistency in Paul's thought—by modern standards of theological discourse— that is difficult to demonstrate in the undoubted letters.

The situation in the church as perceived by the author of 2 Thessalonians is certainly different from that of 1 Thessalonians. It is not necessary, however, to postulate a change so great that years or even a generation must have intervened. Identification of the problem attacked by 2 Thessalonians as "Gnostic" should be done only with great caution. If the Thessalonian Christians thought that "the day of the Lord has come" (2:2), then they may have spiritualized the apocalyptic concept, as Gnostics sometimes spiritualized the notion of the resurrection, to mean a present liberation of the soul from all bodily cares and the affairs of the world. That happened, a very short time later, in the church at Corinth. But it would be possible for enthusiastic, immature converts to reach that conclusion directly from Paul's own teachings (see, e.g., 2 Cor. 6:2) and from the liturgy of baptism in the Hellenistic Christian churches (see, e.g., Eph. 2:4–6). And that is exactly what the author of 2 Thess. 2:2 suggests has happened.

Formally 2 Thessalonians is similar to 1 Thessalonians, though somewhat simpler. It begins with a salutation almost identical with that of the first letter (1:1–2). In the place of the very long thanksgiving of the first, it has two thanksgiving periods, the first (1:3–12) developing the theme of God's "just judgment," rewarding the oppressed and punishing the oppressors. It is followed by a hortatory section introduced by the typical "we beg you" (2:1–12), whose theme is the necessity that the "lawless man" be revealed before the Parousia (the most controversial section of the letter). The second thanksgiving is extremely brief (2:13–17), interrupted by an exhortation (v. 15), but concluding with a benediction exactly in the style of 1 Thess. 3:11–13. Appeal for mutual prayers (3:1–5) is followed by a second hortatory section (3:6–15) dealing with the "idle." The usual benedictions (3:16, 18) bracket an extraordinary authentication in Paul's handwriting (v. 17), which, ironically, many critics have regarded as the overclever ruse of the forger.

---

1 Paul, Silvanus, and Timothy,

To the church of the Thessalonians in God our Father and the Lord Jesus Christ:

2 Grace to you and peace from God the Father and the Lord Jesus Christ.[1]

3 We are bound to give thanks to God always for you, brethren, as is fitting, because your faith is growing abundantly, and the love of every one of you for one another is increasing. **4** Therefore we ourselves boast of you in the churches of God for your steadfastness and faith[2] in all your persecutions and in the afflictions which you are enduring.

5 This is evidence[3] of the righteous judgment of God, that you may be made worthy of the kingdom of God, for which you are suffering— **6** since indeed God deems it just to repay with affliction those who afflict you, **7** and to grant rest with us to you who are afflicted,[4] when the Lord Jesus is revealed from heaven with his mighty angels in flaming fire, **8** inflicting vengeance upon those who do not know God and upon those who do not obey the gospel

1. The salutation differs from that of 1 Thess. only in the addition of "our" in v. 1 and the phrase "from God . . . and . . . Christ" in v. 2. Both are standard Pauline phrases, but the result is a repetitiveness in vv. 1 and 2 that is not normal for Paul.
2. The triad "faith, love, hope" of 1 Thess. 1:3 is varied here into: "faith, love; steadfastness and faith."
3. Both the construction and the meaning of v. 5 are difficult. In Greek vv. 3–12 are one sentence, and the grammatical function of "evidence" is ambiguous. The RSV translators add "this is," in agreement with most commentators, for clarity, but what "this" refers back to remains uncertain. Is the mere fact of persecution evidence of the righteous judgment that is coming, or is it the fact that the Christians "endure"? V. 6 and the apocalyptic context speak in favor of the former. For language and thought, compare Phil. 1:28.
4. Assonance of the words (*tois thlibousin . . . thlipsin, . . . tois thlibomenois anesin . . .*) emphasizes the fittingness of reward and punishment. This understanding of the "just judgment" is typically but not exclusively apocalyptic. It is often felt to be un-Pauline, despite such passages as Rom. 2:5–10.

of our Lord Jesus. **9** They shall suffer the punishment of eternal destruction and exclusion from the presence of the Lord and from the glory of his might,[5] **10** when he comes on that day to be glorified in his saints,[6] and to be marveled at in all who have believed, because our testimony to you was believed. **11** To this end we always pray for you, that our God may make you worthy of his call, and may fulfil every good resolve and work of faith by his power, **12** so that the name of our Lord Jesus may be glorified in you, and you in him, according to the grace of our God and the Lord Jesus Christ.

2 Now concerning the coming[7] of our Lord Jesus Christ and our assembling to meet him, we beg you, brethren, **2** not to be quickly shaken in mind[8] or excited, either by spirit or by word, or by letter[9] purporting to be from us, to the effect that the day of the Lord[1] has come. **3** Let no one deceive you in any way; for that day will not come[2] unless the rebellion[3] comes first, and the man of lawlessness[4] is revealed, the son of perdition,[5] **4** who opposes and exalts himself against every so-called god or object of worship, so that he takes his seat in the temple of God, proclaiming himself to be God.[6] **5** Do you not remember that when I was still with you

5. V. 9 is a quotation from Isa. 2:10. Vv. 6–10 are in fact saturated with the language of the Greek OT, particularly language which speaks of the theophanies of "the Lord" (Yahweh), here transferred to "the Lord Jesus" Cf. Ex. 3:2; Isa. 66:4, 15; Jer. 10:25; 4 Macc. 10:15; Isa. 2:10, 19, 21; Ps. 67:36 LXX (English 68:35); 88:8 LXX (English 89:8); Isa. 2:11, 17; 66:5, 18.
6. "Saints": "holy ones" may be angels: see note on 1 Thess. 3:13.
7. "Coming": *parousia*; see note on 1 Thess. 2:19.
8. Lit., "shaken out of [your] mind"; the second phrase, "to be excited," occurs in a similar context in the synoptic apocalypse: Mark 13:7=Matt. 24:6.
9. Cf. 2:15, where Paul refers to previous teachings "by word or by letter." "By spirit" denotes a prophecy; cf. 1 Thess. 5:19 f. "Purporting to be from us" may be an overtranslation; the Greek particle *hōs*, "as," does not necessarily imply that the alleged means of information was not really from Paul. This phrase, moreover, exactly parallel in construction to the three preceding phrases, should perhaps be connected with all three: "assuming I had said, whether by prophecy, by declaration, or by letter."
1. An OT notion (e.g., Amos 5:18–20) transferred by the Christians to Jesus; cf. 1 Thess. 5:2; also 1 Cor.

1:8; 5:5; 2 Cor. 1:14; 2 Pet. 3:10.
2. "That day will not come": necessary for sense; the Greek sentence lacks this obvious main clause.
3. Use of the definite article marks this as a known quantity, like "the man of lawlessness"; these are familiar elements in the apocalyptic scenario. "Rebellion" can mean either political revolt or religious "apostasy" (the Greek word is *apostasia*). The latter is probaby meant here (cf. Matt. 24:10–12), but in the sense of pagan opposition (n.b. v. 4) rather than Christian lapses.
4. Many manuscripts and ancient quotations read "the man of sin"; the meaning is the same: the legendary Antichrist—more correctly, the false prophet whose activity was expected to set in motion the last success of the powers of evil before the day of the Lord. Cf. Rev. 13.
5. A Semitic form of expression like "sons of light"; one who belongs essentially to destruction, and is destined for destruction. John 17:12 uses the same term for Judas.
6. The picture of the tyrant who put himself in the place of God in the temple entered apocalyptic imagery from the desecration of the Jerusalem temple by the Syrian king Antiochus IV (168 B.C.) and was reinforced by the attempt of the Roman emperor Gaius Caligula to install his own statue there in A.D. 40; cf. also Ezek. 28:2.

I told you this? 6 And you know what is restraining[7] him now so that he may be revealed in his time. 7 For the mystery of lawlessness is already at work; only he who now restrains it will do so until he is out of the way. 8 And then the lawless one will be revealed, and the Lord Jesus will slay him with the breath of his mouth[8] and destroy him by his appearing and his coming.[9] 9 The coming of the lawless one by the activity of Satan will be with all power and with pretended signs and wonders, 10 and with all wicked deception for those who are to perish, because they refused to love the truth and so be saved. 11 Therefore God sends[1] upon them a strong delusion, to make them believe what is false, 12 so that all may be condemned who did not believe the truth but had pleasure in unrighteousness.

13 But we are bound to give thanks to God always for you, brethren beloved by the Lord, because God chose you from the beginning[2] to be saved, through sanctification by the Spirit and belief in the truth.[3] 14 To this he called you through our gospel, so that you may obtain the glory of our Lord Jesus Christ. 15 So then, brethren, stand firm and hold to the traditions which you were taught by us, either by word of mouth or by letter.

16 Now may our Lord Jesus Christ himself, and God our Father, who loved us and gave us eternal comfort and good hope through grace, 17 comfort your hearts and establish them in every good work and word.

3 Finally, brethren, pray for us, that the word of the Lord may speed on and triumph, as it did among you, 2 and that we may be delivered from wicked and evil men; for not all have faith. 3 But the Lord is faithful; he will strengthen you and guard you from evil.[4] 4 And we have confidence in the Lord about you, that you

7. "What is restraining" (neuter); in v. 7, "he who restrains" (masc.); neither participle has a complement ("him" and "it" are added by the translators). If the original readers "know," as Paul says, the puzzling force or person who holds back the events of the end, the secret died with them, for subsequent commentators have conjectured every possible identification, from Paul's own mission to the Roman Empire to Satan. The notion as such perhaps stems from the myth of a monster bound at creation, to be released at the end of the world: cf. Rev. 20:1–3 for one apocalyptic variation.
8. The image is from Isa. 11:4, cf. Job 4:9; Rev. 19:15.
9. Lit., "by the appearance of his coming," a pleonasm, since "epiphany" and "parousia" are synonyms.
1. As always in Jewish apocalyptic, the dualism of the myth is circumscribed by the monotheistic insistence that God ultimately controls the whole sequence of events. For the God-sent "power of error," cf. 1 Kings 22:22 f.
2. The manuscripts are divided between "from the beginning" (*ap' archēs*) and "first fruits" (*aparchēn*). The former expression is not used elsewhere by Paul; he uses the latter figuratively in Rom. 16:5; 1 Cor. 16:15 for "first converts" in an area, but the Philippian, not the Thessalonian church was the first in Macedonia and Europe. Perhaps the meaning is that Christians in general are the "first fruits" of mankind, as in James 1:18.
3. V. 13 is formulated in contrast to the preceding threats against the unbelieving. It recapulates the thanksgiving of 1:3–12.
4. "Evil": or, "the evil one."

are doing and will do the things which we command. [5] May the Lord direct your hearts to the love of God and to the steadfastness of Christ.

[6] Now we command you, brethren, in the name of our Lord Jesus Christ, that you keep away from any brother who is living in idleness[5] and not in accord with the tradition that you received from us. [7] For you yourselves know how you ought to imitate us; we were not idle when we were with you, [8] we did not eat any one's bread without paying, but with toil and labor we worked night and day, that we might not burden any of you. [9] It was not because we have not that right, but to give you in our conduct an example to imitate.[6] [10] For even when we were with you, we gave you this command: If any one will not work, let him not eat.[7] [11] For we hear that some of you are living in idleness, mere busybodies, not doing any work. [12] Now such persons we command and exhort in the Lord Jesus Christ to do their work in quietness and to earn their own living. [13] Brethren, do not be weary in well-doing.

[14] If any one refuses to obey what we say in this letter, note that man, and have nothing to do with him, that he may be ashamed. [15] Do not look on him as an enemy, but warn him as a brother.

[16] Now may the Lord of peace himself give you peace at all times in all ways. The Lord be with you all.

[17] I, Paul, write this greeting with my own hand.[8] This is the mark in every letter of mine; it is the way I write. [18] The grace of our Lord Jesus Christ be with you all.

THE LETTER TO THE COLOSSIANS (ca. 62?)

Colossae, located on the Lycus River in Phrygia and on the main highway from Ephesus to Tarsus, had once been a very important mercantile city. By the first century, however, competition with

5. Adverbial form of the same word that appears in 1 Thess. 5:14. The ordinary meaning is "disorderly," but here in the specific sense, also attested outside the NT, of "not doing any work" (v. 11). In the second and third centuries ascetic Christian movements, especially in Eastern Syria, showed how "realized eschatology" could lead to a contempt for a settled life, including ordinary trade; cf. Gosp. of Thomas, 64: "Tradesmen and merchants shall not enter the places of my Father."
6. For Paul's "example" of earning his own living, see 1 Cor. 9; 2 Cor. 11:7–11, and the note on 1 Thess.

2:9.
7. An example of the "tradition" mentioned in v. 6. Whether Paul coined or quoted this "golden rule of work," he certainly assured its place in Western proverbial wisdom. It is quoted, for example (without attribution), in art. XII of the 1936 Constitution of the U.S.S.R.
8. Letters and legal documents in antiquity, dictated to a scribe, were frequently signed in the author's own hand; cf. 1 Cor. 16:21; Gal. 6:11; Col. 4:18. The emphatic way in which attention is called to his handwriting here, however, is unusual.

nearby Laodicea and Hierapolis had reduced it to a minor market town. Paul never visited it, but Epaphras, who had evidently been trained by Paul, founded a vigorous church there. Little is heard of Colossae in later years; the town may have been destroyed by an earthquake which, according to several ancient authors, struck the Lycus valley during the reign of Nero. We would be greatly helped in deciding on the letter's date and authenticity if more precise information about the earthquake were available, but the ancient reports do not agree on either its extent or its date. Since the site of Colossae has unfortunately never been excavated, archaeological confirmation is lacking.

While the letter seems at first glance to have only a general, pastoral character, rehearsing doctrines familiar to the recipients from their liturgy and adding stereotyped ethical instructions, yet Chap. 2 reveals that its central purpose is to combat a deviant form of Christianity. The polemic is much more restrained than in the comparable passages of Galatians and 2 Cor. 10–13. The style is more didactic and admonitory; elements of the diatribe, so typical of Paul elsewhere, are almost entirely missing, except for 2:20–23. There are only a few instances of Paul's well-known sarcasm. Perhaps, therefore, the opposing doctrine had not yet made much headway in Colossae; perhaps also the fact that Paul had no direct connection with the congregation inhibited the vigor of his attack. In any case, the subtlety of the polemic makes the task of reconstructing the opposing position excruciatingly difficult. And without at least a general picture of that position a satisfactory understanding of the letter itself is impossible.

The opponents' teaching is called "philosophy" (2:8); the word does not refer in this case to rational inquiry but, as often in the Hellenistic age, to occult speculations and practices, depending on a body of "tradition" (*ibid.*). Thus it was concerned with "the elemental spirits of the universe" (*ibid.*), or "the worship of angels" (2:18). It set forth "regulations" (*dogmata*) requiring adherence to a festival calendar (2:16) and ascetic practices (2:16, 18, 20–23). The key to understanding how these strange elements fit together is probably hidden in 2:18, a verse so difficult that many commentators have despaired of either understanding or translating it. A generation ago Martin Dibelius proposed an interpretation that has won wide assent. On the basis of similar language in inscriptions found on the wall of an Apollo shrine in Claros, not far from Colossae, he argued that the Colossian version of Christianity took the form of a mystery initiation, in which worship of occult forces filled the adepts with spiritual power. More recently, however, a young American scholar, Fred O. Francis, has shown that the linguistic evidence employed by Dibelius was incorrectly interpreted. His alternative explanation, based on parallels in Jewish mysticism, sees in the ascetic discipline at Colossae a means of obtaining mystical experiences in which the adepts shared in "the angels' worship"[1] in heaven, rather than "worshiping angels."

Many contemporary scholars believe that Colossians was not written by Paul, but by a disciple using his name. The reasons for doubting its authenticity are the obvious divergences of style and content from the accepted letters, but the significance of those divergences has proved very difficult to measure. There is hardly one of the special stylistic features in Colossians which is totally absent from the undoubted letters; only the quantity of them is unusual. Moreover, recognition in recent years that many peculiarities of style and vocabulary are the result of liturgical influence and of allusions to the "heresy" combatted by the author has invalidated any stylistic studies which do not allow for quoted and stereotyped phrases. Similar questions may be raised about most of the unique ideas in the letter—such as the cosmic dimensions of Christ's work of redemption and the metaphor of "head" and "body."

Perhaps the most important question, however, is whether the relation between sacraments and eschatology in Colossians is one that Paul could have agreed with. Here it is stated, for example, that the believer has already been resurrected (presumably, in baptism) with Christ (3:1). Some scholars say categorically that Paul could never have made such a statement, which seems to express precisely the position he combatted in 1 Corinthians. They call attention to the careful way in which he breaks up the obvious parallelism of his statements about baptism into Christ in Rom. 6 by using only the future tense to speak of sharing in Christ's resurrection. Others, however, point out that the future dimension of the Christian life is guarded with equal care in Colossians (3:3 f., and the whole of the ethical admonitions), only in different language. It seems likely that the baptismal liturgy in the Pauline (and other Hellenistic) churches spoke of dying *and* rising with Christ in baptism. The author of Colossians is perhaps closer to the language of the liturgy than Paul is in 1 Corinthians and Romans, but the difference of emphasis may be dictated by the different situation. The future element, for example, receives hardly any mention in Galatians, where Paul opposes a movement that had some things in common with the Colossian opponents.

The question of authenticity thus remains moot. Perhaps it is not so important a question as it once seemed, for once we recognize Paul's indirect relationship with the church addressed, and the extent to which this letter is filled with materials which were common traditions cultivated in the Pauline churches, then it has

1. "Humility and Angelic Worship in Col. 2:18, *Studia Theologica* 16 (1963): 109–34; *A Re-examination of* the Colossian Controversy (Ph.D. Dissertation, Yale University; microfilm; Ann Arbor, 1965).

to be understood as representative of the Pauline *school*, whoever was its immediate author.

So long as we are unsure about authenticity, the place and date of origin cannot be determined. If it was written by Paul, then the traditional locus, his imprisonment in Rome at the time of Nero, is perfectly plausible. Other suggestions have been Caesarea and Ephesus, which would require an earlier date, but are otherwise quite possible.

Formally, the letter exhibits the usual Pauline thanksgiving, 1:3–23, which contains two inlays: vv. 5–8, reflecting on the church's origin, not at all unusual in such a context, and vv. 15–20, a carefully formed christological creed, perhaps a quoted hymn. A statement of the apostle's present situation, the nature of his office, and his relationship to the Lycus valley congregations (1:24–2:5) lays the foundation for his authoritative warnings against heresy (2:6–23). The parenesis (3:1–4:6) contains mostly stereotyped elements, some of which very likely belonged to baptismal catechesis. Here we meet for the first time in Christian literature a form that was very common in Hellenistic moral philosophy, the "household table" (3:18–4:1). A commendation of the bearers of the letter, Tychicus and Onesimus (!), and the usual greetings, followed by Paul's autograph (4:7–18), conclude the letter.

---

1 Paul, an apostle of Christ Jesus by the will of God, and Timothy our brother,

2 To the saints and faithful brethren[1] in Christ at Colossae: Grace to you and peace from God our Father.

3 We always thank God,[2] the Father of our Lord Jesus Christ, when we pray for you, **4** because we have heard of your faith in Christ Jesus and of the love which you have for all the saints, **5** because of the hope[3] laid up for you in heaven. Of this you have heard before in the word of the truth,[4] the gospel **6** which has come to you, as indeed in the whole world it is bearing fruit and

---

1. The two expressions are synonymous for Paul.
2. In Greek the first sentence of the thanksgiving includes vv. 3–8; the structure is rambling.
3. Note the common early Christian triad, "faith, love, hope"; see the note on 1 Thess. 1:3. Usually in Pauline usage "hope" means the act of hoping; here it is the object of hope. For the

notion of a reward "stored up" in heaven, an image found also in Jewish apocalypses of the same period, see 1 Pet. 1:4.
4. "Word of truth" was one of the standard synonyms for "gospel"; see Eph. 1:13; 2 Tim. 2:15; James 1:18; cf. 2 Cor. 6:7. The phrase was biblical: e.g., Ps. 119:43.

growing—so among yourselves, from the day you heard and understood the grace of God in truth, [7] as you learned it from Epaphras[5] our beloved fellow servant. He is a faithful minister of Christ on our[6] behalf [8] and has made known to us your love in the Spirit.

[9] And so, from the day we heard of it, we have not ceased to pray for you, asking that you may be filled with the knowledge of his will in all spiritual wisdom and understanding, [10] to lead a life worthy of the Lord, fully pleasing to him, bearing fruit in every good work and increasing in the knowledge of God. [11] May you be strengthened with all power, according to his glorious might,[7] for all endurance and patience with joy, [12] giving thanks to the Father, who has qualified us[8] to share in the inheritance of the saints[9] in light. [13] He has delivered us from the dominion of darkness and transferred us to the kingdom of his beloved Son, [14] in whom we have redemption, the forgiveness of sins.

[15] He is the image of the invisible God,[1] the first-born of all creation; [16] for in him all things were created, in heaven and on earth, visible and invisible, whether thrones or dominions or principalities or authorities[2]—all things were created through him and for him.[3] [17] He is before all things, and in him all things hold together. [18] He is the head of the body, the church,[4] he is the beginning, the first-born from the dead, that in everything he might be pre-eminent. [19] For in him all the fulness of God was pleased to dwell, [20] and through him to reconcile to himself all

5. According to Phlm. 23, in prison with Paul. Epaphras is otherwise unknown.
6. Though some manuscripts read "your," the reading in the text is almost certainly correct. Thus Epaphras' authority is backed by that of the apostle; presumably Paul thought of the whole territory as his missionary responsibility.
7. The accumulation of synonymous expressions, both verbs and nouns, is typical of the style of Col. and Eph.
8. "You" is also well attested in the manuscripts; there is confusion between the first and second person pronouns (HMEIC was easily mistaken for YMEIC) in the text tradition throughout the letter.
9. Some commentators take the word translated "saints" to refer to angels (cf. note on 1 Thess. 3:13), in which case this verse would already allude to the "worship of angels" practiced by the opponents. But note Paul's normal use of the word in v. 2. The language of vv. 12 f. has parallels in the Dead Sea Scrolls, where speculations about the angels were also important.
1. Vv. 15–20 are probably a liturgical poem (some commentators speak of a "hymn," others, a "creed"), of two strophes: (1) "He [lit., who] is the image . . ., the first-born of all creation . . ."; (2) "He [who] is the beginning, the first-born from the dead. . . ." If a hymn, an introductory phrase (something like "Praise the Lord," or "Praised be Christ") would have stood originally at the beginning. The language of the first strophe has many parallels in the Jewish wisdom tradition, especially in Philo, who could speak of the Logos as the image and "first-born" of God. The same stock of images was prominent in the development of Gnosticism. The beginning of the second strophe, however, shows that the poem itself is Christian.
2. These are spiritual beings: angels or demons.
3. Stoics used a similar formula of God (for them = nature); in the NT, it is used of both God and Christ (Rom. 11:36; 1 Cor. 8:6; Eph. 4:6). This statement of Christ's role in creation goes beyond anything in the earlier Pauline letters (though 1 Cor. 8:6 indicates the beginning of such a notion); the closest NT parallel is the prologue to the Fourth Gospel.
4. "The church" is regarded by many commentators as an addition to the hymn by the author of the letter. In the hymn, the "body" would refer to the cosmos, cf. 2:10.

things, whether on earth or in heaven,[5] making peace by the blood of his cross.

[21] And you,[6] who once were estranged and hostile in mind, doing evil deeds, [22] he has now reconciled in his body of flesh by his death, in order to present you holy and blameless and irreproachable before him, [23] provided that you continue in the faith, stable and steadfast, not shifting from the hope of the gospel which you heard, which has been preached to every creature[7] under heaven, and of which I, Paul, became a minister.

[24] Now I rejoice in my sufferings for your sake, and in my flesh I complete what is lacking in Christ's afflictions[8] for the sake of his body, that is, the church, [25] of which I became a minister according to the divine office which was given to me for you, to make the word of God fully known, [26] the mystery hidden for ages and generations but now made manifest to his saints.[9] [27] To them God chose to make known how great among the Gentiles are the riches of the glory of this mystery, which is Christ in you, the hope of glory. [28] Him we proclaim, warning every man and teaching every man in all wisdom, that we may present every man mature[1] in Christ. [29] For this I toil, striving with all the energy which he mightily inspires within me.

[2] For I want you to know how greatly I strive for you, and for those at Laodicea, and for all who have not seen my face, [2] that their hearts may be encouraged as they are knit together in love, to have all the riches of assured understanding and the knowledge of God's mystery, of Christ, [3] in whom are hid all the treasures of wisdom and knowledge. [4] I say this in order that no one may delude you with beguiling speech. [5] For though I am absent in body, yet I am with you in spirit, rejoicing to see your good order and the firmness of your faith in Christ.

[6] As therefore you received Christ Jesus the Lord, so live in him, [7] rooted and built up in him and established in the faith, just as you were taught, abounding in thanksgiving.

[8] See to it that no one makes a prey of you by philosophy and empty deceit, according to human tradition, according to the ele-

5. For the cosmic dimensions of the activity of Christ, cf. Phil. 2:10 f. The phrase "by the blood of his cross" may be an addition to the hymn by the letter's author.
6. It is quite characteristic of Paul that the cosmic imagery of the hymn should now be connected directly with the human congregation.
7. Or, "in the whole creation"; for the hyperbole, cf. 1 Thess. 1:8; Rom. 15:18–23.
8. The meaning of this expression is obscure. Since the author wishes to emphasize to the Colossians the *complete-*

ness of the victory won by Christ (2:8–15), he certainly does not mean to imply here that Christ's sufferings did not accomplish all that was needed. Some commentators point to the Jewish notion of the "woes of the Messiah," shared by the community of the end of days, as a possible source for the notion, but there is nothing in the context to suggest that.
9. For the form of this verse, see note on 1 Cor. 2:7.
1. On the word "mature," see note on 1 Cor. 2:6.

mental spirits of the universe,[2] and not according to Christ. [9] For in him the whole fulness of deity dwells bodily,[3] [10] and you have come to fulness of life in him, who is the head of all rule and authority. [11] In him also you were circumcised with a circumcision made without hands, by putting off the body of flesh[4] in the circumcision of Christ; [12] and you were buried with him in baptism, in which you were also raised with him through faith in the working of God, who raised him from the dead. [13] And you, who were dead in trespasses and the uncircumcision of your flesh, God made alive together with him, having forgiven us all our trespasses, [14] having canceled the bond which stood against us with its legal demands[5]; this he set aside, nailing it to the cross. [15] He disarmed[6] the principalities and powers and made a public example of them, triumphing over them in him.[7]

[16] Therefore let no one pass judgment on you in questions of food and drink or with regard to a festival or a new moon or a sabbath.[8] [17] These are only a shadow of what is to come; but the substance belongs to Christ.[9] [18] Let no one disqualify you, insisting on self-abasement and worship of angels, taking his stand on visions,[1] puffed up without reason by his sensuous mind, [19] and not holding fast to the Head, from whom the whole body, nourished and knit together through its joints and ligaments, grows with a growth that is from God.

[20] If with Christ you died to the elemental spirits of the uni-

2. See note on Gal. 4:3.
3. This picks up a statement from the poem, 1:19. In second-century Gnosticism, "fullness" (*plērōma*) became a technical term for the whole heavenly world composed of emanations from the highest god.
4. The connection of "putting off the body of flesh" with circumcision is unusual, but the association of this idea with baptism is found elsewhere. The use of a change of clothing to symbolize a change of life is found in many forms of initiation rite. For Christians, removal of clothing before baptism represented removal of "the old man," reclothing after immersion (from a later period, the use of white robes, "robes of light," is attested) depicted "putting on Christ"="the new man." See 3:9 f and cf. Gal. 3:27.
5. The "bond" is a personal note of indebtedness, a common metaphor for sin in Judaism. "Legal demands" is an allusion to the law, but also to the "regulations" imposed by the "angel worshippers" (see v. 20).
6. Lit., "stripped"; the same verb as in v. 11b. The picture is that of a triumphal procession in which a returning conqueror exhibits his captives.

7. Grammatically, "in it" (i.e., the cross) is possible, but the context supports the translation above.
8. "Festival, new moon, sabbath": a stereotyped formula found in biblical and post-biblical Jewish literature to refer to the whole sacrificial cultus.
9. The contrast shadow/substance (lit., "body") is found frequently in Hellenistic literature, including Josephus and Philo; note also the equivalent pair, "shadow/image" in Heb. 10:1. Possibly the opponents themselves called their cultus a "shadow," implying that it was an earthly copy of heavenly worship.
1. This sentence is fraught with difficulties. The word translated "taking his stand," is found associated with mystery and oracle cults, but it meant simply "entering"; its most frequent use is "to enter into possession" (of property). Possibly entrance *into heaven* (mystically) is meant. "Worship of angels" may equally well mean "angels' worship." Francis offers this translation of the whole: "Let no one disqualify you, being bent upon humility and religion of angels, which he has seen upon entering. . . ."

verse, why do you live as if you still belonged to the world? Why do you submit to regulations,[2] [21] "Do not handle, Do not taste, Do not touch" [22] (referring to things which all perish as they are used),[3] according to human precepts and doctrines? [23] These have indeed an appearance of wisdom in promoting rigor of devotion and self-abasement and severity to the body, but they are of no value in checking the indulgence of the flesh.[4]

3 If then you have been raised with Christ, seek the things that are above, where Christ is, seated at the right hand of God.[5] [2] Set your minds on things that are above, not on things that are on earth. [3] For you have died, and your life is hid with Christ in God. [4] When Christ who is our life appears, then you also will appear with him in glory.

[5] Put to death therefore what is earthly in you:[6] immorality, impurity, passion, evil desire, and covetousness, which is idolatry. [6] On account of these the wrath of God is coming.[7] [7] In these you once walked, when you lived in them. [8] But now put them all away: anger, wrath, malice, slander, and foul talk from your mouth. [9] Do not lie to one another, seeing that you have put off the old nature[8] with its practices [10] and have put on the new nature, which is being renewed in knowledge after the image of its creator. [11] Here there cannot be Greek and Jew, circumcised and uncircumcised, barbarian, Scythian, slave, free man, but Christ is all, and in all.[9]

[12] Put on then, as God's chosen ones, holy and beloved, compassion, kindness, lowliness, meekness, and patience, [13] forbearing one another and, if one has a complaint against another, forgiving each other; as the Lord has forgiven you, so you also must forgive. [14] And above all these put on love, which binds everything together in perfect harmony. [15] And let the peace of Christ rule in your hearts, to which indeed you were called in the one body. And be thankful. [16] Let the word of Christ dwell in you richly, as you teach and admonish one another in all wisdom, and as you sing psalms and hymns and spiritual songs with thankfulness in your

2. "Submit to regulations" (*dogmatizesthe*) is cognate with "legal demands" (*dogmata*), v. 14. The regulations are clearly ascetic; the first, translated "Do not handle," probably means "Do not engage in sexual acts." The third could mean "Do not approach" (the heavenly mysteries), as in Ex. 19:12 LXX.
3. Or, "Which [i.e., the "regulations"] all tend to corruption because of misuse" (Francis).
4. Or, "are of no value, serving only to indulge the flesh."
5. Ps. 110:1.

6. Lit., "the limbs that are on earth"; the myth of the cosmic body is here moralized. There is reason to believe that the admonitions in this section follow a pattern which developed in the baptismal instruction for new Christians. Hence the allusions to "dying," "rising," "putting off," "putting on," "putting to death."
7. Some texts add, "upon the sons of disobedience."
8. Lit., "man," and also in the following verse.
9. Cf. Gal. 3:28; 1 Cor. 12:13.

hearts to God. **17** And whatever you do, in word or deed, do everything in the name of the Lord Jesus, giving thanks to God the Father through him.

18 Wives,[1] be subject to your husbands, as is fitting in the Lord. **19** Husbands, love your wives, and do not be harsh with them. **20** Children, obey your parents in everything, for this pleases the Lord. **21** Fathers, do not provoke your children, lest they become discouraged. **22** Slaves, obey in everything those who are your earthly masters, not with eyeservice, as men-pleasers, but in singleness of heart, fearing the Lord. **23** Whatever your task, work heartily, as serving the Lord and not men, **24** knowing that from the Lord you will receive the inheritance as your reward; you are serving the Lord Christ. **25** For the wrongdoer will be paid back for the wrong he has done, and there is no partiality.

4 Masters, treat your slaves justly and fairly, knowing that you also have a Master in heaven.

2 Continue steadfastly in prayer, being watchful in it with thanksgiving; **3** and pray for us also, that God may open to us a door for the word, to declare the mystery of Christ, on account of which I am in prison, **4** that I may make it clear, as I ought to speak.

5 Conduct yourselves wisely toward outsiders, making the most of the time.[2] **6** Let your speech always be gracious, seasoned with salt, so that you may know how you ought to answer every one.

7 Tychicus[3] will tell you all about my affairs; he is a beloved brother and faithful minister and fellow servant in the Lord. **8** I have sent him to you for this very purpose, that you may know how we are and that he may encourage your hearts, **9** and with him Onesimus,[4] the faithful and beloved brother, who is one of yourselves. They will tell you of everything that has taken place here.

10 Aristarchus my fellow prisoner greets you, and Mark the cousin of Barnabas (concerning whom you have received instructions—if he comes to you, receive him), **11** and Jesus who is called Justus. These are the only men of the circumcision among my fellow workers for the kingdom of God, and they have been a comfort to me. **12** Epaphras, who is one of yourselves, a servant of Christ Jesus, greets you, always remembering you earnestly in his prayers, that you may stand mature and fully assured in all the will

1. The following admonitions, 3:18–4:1, are in the form of a "household table," in which each stratum of a community was assigned its "proper" duties. The form is said to have originated with Zeno, founder of the Stoa; it became the common property of all schools of Hellenistic moral philosophy, including Hellenistic Judaism. It is Christianized here by only minor features: "in the Lord" and the like.

2. Lit., "buying up the time [or, "the opportunity"]."

3. Both Tychicus and Aristarchus (v. 10) are mentioned among Paul's companions in Acts 20:4; otherwise they are unknown.

4. See Phlm., *passim.*

of God. **13** For I bear him witness that he has worked hard for you and for those in Laodicea and in Hierapolis. **14** Luke the beloved physician and Demas greet you.[5] **15** Give my greetings to the brethren at Laodicea, and to Nympha and the church in her house. **16** And when this letter has been read among you, have it read also in the church of the Laodiceans; and see that you read also the letter from Laodicea.[6] **17** And say to Archippus,[7] "See that you fulfil the ministry which you have received in the Lord."

18 I, Paul, write this greeting with my own hand. Remember my fetters. Grace be with you.

THE LETTER TO THE EPHESIANS (ca. 62?)

Despite the antiquity of its traditional title, the Letter to the Ephesians was certainly not written to Ephesus. Several of the oldest and best manuscripts, including the famous Chester Beatty papyrus, omit the words "in Ephesus" usually found in 1:1. The third-century church fathers Tertullian and Origen and the heretic Marcion also used texts that lacked these words, and Marcion identified the letter with the lost Letter to the Laodiceans (see note on Col. 4:16). More important, this letter was written for people who did not know Paul personally (3:2 ff.; cf. 1:15); it could hardly have been intended for Christians in Ephesus, where Paul worked for two years.

In fact there is nothing in the letter which would suggest that it was addressed to any particular congregation. There are no references to any local situation, no greetings to or from individuals— the contrast with Colossians, a letter also addressed to a congregation which Paul had not seen personally, is instructive. If one were to remove the salutation (1:1–2), the normal Pauline thanksgiving (1:15–23), the description of Paul's personal mission (3:1–13), the phrase "a prisoner for the Lord" (4:1), and the reference to Tychicus—which virtually duplicates Col. 4:7 f.—then every trace of a *letter* would disappear. What would remain would be something like part of a liturgy, including a brief address to newly baptized Christians. In this respect Ephesians is very much like the so-called

5. Compare the list of companions with that in Phlm. 23.
6. The letter in question, obviously one Paul had sent to the neighboring city, was lost before the Pauline letters were collected. It can hardly be identified with Phlm., as some have suggested. A spurious Letter to the Laodiceans is

extant in some Latin Bible manuscripts; it was obviously forged, perhaps as early as the second century, to supply the missing letter. Marcion gave the title "to the Laodiceans" to our Letter to Ephesians.
7. Phlm. 2.

First Letter of Peter, which is specifically designated (1:1) as a cyclical letter, and which is regarded by many modern scholars as an adaptation of a baptismal liturgy or homily. There is good reason, then, to believe that Ephesians was intended to be read to new converts in a group of churches in the southwestern part of the province of Asia (modern Turkey), as a written substitute for a personal address by the apostle to the newly baptized.

Whether it could have been written by Paul himself, however, is a question that continues to provoke vigorous disagreement. The doubts directed against the authenticity of this letter are much stronger than in the case of Colossians, and in part because of the relationship between these two letters. Verbal parallels between them are so close in many passages that a number of scholars have been convinced that Ephesians is the work of a forger who used Colossians as a literary model. Most surprisingly, some words and phrases that occur in both letters seem to have quite a different meaning in Ephesians. Yet the order in which these agreements occur, and the specific differences that are present in every case, are extremely difficult to explain on the hypothesis of copying. Moreover, there are also striking parallels of language and style with 1 Peter, but no grounds whatever to suppose a literary relationship. Consequently most of these parallels are best explained by assuming that all three letters are filled with allusions to the baptismal liturgy used in the areas of the Pauline mission. This liturgy is not to be understood as a fixed prayerbook, but as a set general pattern within which free variation was possible, certain phrases and certain styles of speech becoming quickly stereotyped. Naturally the liturgy of the Greek-speaking synagogue contributed extensively to the formation of these early Christian patterns.

Supporters of authenticity point out that there is hardly any single element of the Ephesians' style that, taken individually, cannot be found somewhere among the undoubted letters, and hardly one of the theological ideas which can be called categorically un-Pauline. But it is precisely the accumulation of such individual features that marks off Ephesians as significantly different from the other letters, even Colossians.

If we can assume that Paul himself would have written a letter adapted almost entirely from liturgical elements, then the peculiarities of Ephesians need not count against Pauline authorship—but precisely that assumption seems precarious in the light of the strong personal stamp that Paul made upon each of the other letters. Hence many scholars would prefer to attribute the letter to a disciple of Paul—the use of the founder's name by a member of a given school was regarded in Hellenistic literature as praiseworthy. If this is the case, then the disciple was a worthy representative of the school; he understood the distinctively Pauline form of Christianity better than any other author in the postapostolic period whose work has survived.

The letter consists of two main parts, which are quite clearly defined by formal elements. The first, like 2 Corinthians and 1 Peter, begins with a blessing in hymnic style, rather than the conventional Pauline thanksgiving (1:3–14). Curiously, however, a perfectly normal thanksgiving follows immediately (1:15–23). A meditation on the new status of Gentiles who have become Christians and on the great "mystery" of the unification of Jew and Gentile (Chap. 2) forms the only didactic portion of the letter; it is followed by an encomium on Paul's own ministry to the Gentiles (3:1–13). The prayer style is resumed by an intercession (3:14–19), and a doxology concludes the whole part (3:20 f.).

The second part, which consists of admonitions in traditional patterns, begins with the conventional, "I appeal to you. . ." (4:1). The basic exhortation (4:1–16) is to realize and maintain the unity and harmony which, according to Chap. 2, were the gift of God accomplished in Christ's death. There follow admonitions based on the motifs of the old man and the new ("put off" "put on": 4:17–24); on a special form of the virtue and vice catalogues, in which a vice is paired with its opposite virtue (4:24–5:5), continued by the opposition between the "children of light" and of darkness (5:6–14), and between the "wise" and the "foolish" (5:15–20); on the "household table" (5:21–6:9); and on arming for the moral battle against spiritual powers of evil (6:10–20). A word about Tychicus, almost identical with Col. 4:7 f., followed by a benediction, brings the letter to a close.

If Paul did not write the letter, its date cannot be fixed. If he did, then it must have been written at very nearly the same time as Colossians and Philemon, and Paul's imprisonment in Rome near the end of his life is the most plausible occasion.

---

1 Paul, an apostle of Christ Jesus by the will of God,

To the saints who are also faithful[1] in Christ Jesus:

2 Grace to you and peace from God our Father and the Lord Jesus Christ.

3 Blessed be the God and Father of our Lord Jesus Christ, who has blessed us in Christ with every spiritual blessing in the heavenly

---

1. Most manuscripts read, "who are at Ephesus and faithful," but the oldest witnesses read as translated above (see above, p. 121). Yet this text cannot be original either (the participle translated "who are" is always followed in Pauline letters by a place name). The encyclical letter may have had a blank space here, to be filled in by Tychicus. Or someone at Ephesus may have seen the letter intended for other churches and made a copy, omitting the name.

places,[2] [4] even as he chose us in him before the foundation of the world, that we should be holy and blameless before him. [5] He destined us in love[3] to be his sons through Jesus Christ, according to the purpose of his will, [6] to the praise of his glorious grace which he freely bestowed on us in the Beloved. [7] In him we have redemption through his blood, the forgiveness[4] of our trespasses, according to the riches of his grace [8] which he lavished upon us. [9] For he has made known to us in all wisdom and insight the mystery of his will, according to his purpose which he set forth in Christ [10] as a plan for the fulness of time, to unite all things[5] in him, things in heaven and things on earth.

[11] In him, according to the purpose of him who accomplishes all things according to the counsel of his will, [12] we who first hoped in Christ have been destined and appointed to live for the praise of his glory. [13] In him you[6] also, who have heard the word of truth, the gospel of your salvation, and have believed in him, were sealed with the promised Holy Spirit, [14] which is the guarantee[7] of our inheritance until we acquire possession of it,[8] to the praise of his glory.

[15] For this reason, because I have heard of your faith in the Lord Jesus and your love[9] toward all the saints, [16] I do not cease to give thanks[1] for you, remembering you in my prayers, [17] that

2. A peculiar phrase occurring only in Eph. (1:20; 2:6; 3:10; 6:12). The blessing (vv. 3–14; cf. 2 Cor. 1:3–7; 1 Pet. 1:3–9) is a single sentence, linked together by relative clauses and prepositions. It is enriched by word plays ("blessed," "has blessed us," "blessing"; "in love," "the Beloved"), parallelism ("redemption through his blood"//"forgiveness of our trespasses" "guarantee of our inheritance"//(lit.) "redemption of the possession"); chains of synonyms ("purpose of his will"; "will . . . purpose . . . plan"); repetition of the phrase "in him" or "in whom." For a close approximation of the Greek style, see the KJV—though even the seventeenth-century translators felt obliged to divide the passage into three sentences! The repeated phrase "to the praise of his glory" (v. 6a, "to the praise of the glory of his grace") provides a natural division: vv. 3–6a, 6b–12, 13–14.
3. Or, "before him in love, having destined us."
4. In the Pauline letters the word "forgiveness" occurs only here and in the almost identical clause in Col. 1:14. Cf. the connection of "redemption," "blood," "passing over of sins" in the early formula quoted in Rom. 3:24 f.
5. Cf. Col. 1:20; Phil. 2:10. The special theme of Eph. is that this ultimate cosmic reunification is foreshadowed on earth in the unity of the church, parti-

cularly in the reconciliation of Jew and Gentile. In some respects Rom. 8:18–25 provides a parallel.
6. The shift to the second person from the hymnic first person applies the general statements of the benediction to the readers and provides the transition to what follows in the letter.
7. Cf. 2 Cor. 1:22; 5:5; Rom. 8:23. The word is used commonly of a down-payment.
8. Lit., "until the redemption of the possession." The word translated "possession" or its equivalent is often used of Israel as God's elect people (Ex. 19:5; 23:22 LXX; Deut. 7:6; 14:2; Isa. 43:21; Tit. 2:14; 1 Pet. 2:9).
9. A number of ancient witnesses omit "and your love," most likely because of a copyist's error.
1. Vv. 15–23, a complete epistolary thanksgiving of the normal Pauline type, seems formally redundant after the opening "blessing." Some scholars see in this redundance a sign of pseudonymity, the work of an overzealous imitator. However, it is not unusual for Paul to resume a long introduction by repeating the basic thanksgiving formula: 1 Thess. 2:13; cf. 2 Thess. 2:13; Col. 1:9. The style of the present thanksgiving is consistent with the rest of Eph. (see note on 1:3); the themes are reminiscent of Col., Phil., and 1 Cor. thanksgivings.

the God of our Lord Jèsus Christ, the Father of glory, may give you a spirit of wisdom and of revelation in the knowledge of him, [18] having the eyes of your hearts enlightened, that you may know what is the hope to which he has called you, what are the riches of his glorious inheritance in the saints, [19] and what is the immeasurable greatness of his power in us who believe, according to the working of his great might [20] which he accomplished in Christ when he raised him from the dead and made him sit at his right hand in the heavenly places, [21] far above all rule and authority and power and dominion, and above every name that is named, not only in this age but also in that which is to come;[2] [22] and he has put all things under his feet[3] and has made him the head over all things for the church, [23] which is his body, the fulness of him who fills all in all.[4]

2 And you he made alive,[5] when you were dead through the trespasses and sins [2] in which you once walked, following the course[6] of this world, following the prince of the power of the air, the spirit that is now at work in the sons of disobedience. [3] Among these we all once lived in the passions of our flesh, following the desires of body and mind, and so we were by nature children of wrath, like the rest of mankind. [4] But God, who is rich in mercy, out of the great love with which he loved us, [5] even when we were dead through our trespasses, made us alive together with Christ (by grace you have been saved), [6] and raised us up with him, and made us sit with him in the heavenly places in Christ Jesus,[7] [7] that in the coming ages he might show the immeasurable riches of his grace in kindness toward us in Christ Jesus. [8] For by grace you have been saved through faith; and this is not your own doing, it is the gift of God—[9] not because of works, lest any man should boast.[8] [10] For we are his workmanship, created in Christ Jesus for good works, which God prepared beforehand, that we should walk in them.

2. Cf. Phil. 2:10 f.
3. Ps. 110:1, the basic text used in early Christian exposition to support the notion of Christ's exaltation.
4. Cf. Col. 2:9 f.; 1:18. Two notions are combined here: (1) Christ is the head of the cosmos (represented by angelic or demonic forces), (2) he is head of the church, as his body. Perhaps the myth of the cosmic man, his body composed of the elements, has played a role in the imagery. "Fullness" is used in a somewhat different sense here from that in Col. 1:19 (see note there).
5. In the Greek this verb does not appear until v. 5, for the sentence structure has broken down under the weight of the loosely connected clauses of vv. 2–4. The thought is resumed in v. 5

by repetition.
6. Lit., "the aeon"; since the style of Eph. suggests that "prince" and "spirit" are synonyms, this is to be taken as a personal designation: "the Aeon." The name Aeon for a god of endless time, probably derived from the Persian *Zurvan*, is found in several Hellenistic religious and magical contexts. In Mithraic inscriptions and magical amulets he was depicted as a lion-headed man surrounded by snakes. Here, however, he appears as the prince of evil forces, like the Essene Belial. Cf. 2 Cor. 4:4.
7. Cf. Col. 3:1, and compare and contrast Rom. 6.
8. A distinctively Pauline summary, like the parenthesis in v. 5.

11 Therefore remember that at one time you Gentiles in the flesh, called the uncircumcision by what is called the circumcision, which is made in the flesh by hands—**12** remember that you were at that time separated from Christ, alienated from the commonwealth of Israel, and strangers to the covenants of promise, having no hope and without God in the world.[9] **13** But now in Christ Jesus you who once were far off have been brought near[1] in the blood of Christ. **14** For he is our[2] peace, who has made us both one, and has broken down the dividing wall[3] of hostility, **15** by abolishing[4] in his flesh the law of commandments and ordinances, that he might create in himself one new man[5] in place of the two, so making peace, **16** and might reconcile us both to God in one body[6] through the cross, thereby bringing the hostility to an end. **17** And he came and preached peace to you who were far off and peace to those who were near; **18** for through him we both have access in one Spirit to the Father. **19** So then you are no longer strangers and sojourners, but you are fellow citizens with the saints and members of the household of God, **20** built upon the foundation of the apostles and prophets,[7] Christ Jesus himself being the cornerstone,[8] **21** in whom the whole structure is joined together and grows into a holy temple[9] in the Lord; **22** in whom you also are built into it for a dwelling place of God in the Spirit.

3 For this reason I, Paul, a prisoner for Christ Jesus on behalf

9. To this list of Israel's prerogatives, cf. Rom. 9:4 f.

1. The "far" and the "near" were terms used in Judaism for Gentiles and faithful Jews respectively. They are drawn from Isa. 57:18 f., which serves as the basis for the meditation in vv. 14–18 (combined with Isa. 52:7, as in Acts 10:36 f.).

2. Note the shift of person; the style of vv. 14–18 is hymnic or creedal, and some commentators think it might even quote an early Christian canticle.

3. The image may have been suggested by the wall that separated the court of the Gentiles from the sacred areas of the temple in Jerusalem. Another possible allusion is to a barrier separating heaven and earth, a notion that plays a role in certain later Gnostic texts, though in them the savior's function is sometimes to break, sometimes to restore the wall. In the present passage the wall is identified with the Jewish law—insofar as it consists of "commandments and ordinances." Compare the pejorative sense of "ordinances" (*dogmata*) in Col. 2:14, 20.

4. Elsewhere Paul is careful not to go so far as to speak of "abolishing" the law: cf. Rom. 3:31; 7:12; but see Col. 2:14.

5. A baptismal motif, connected with the idea of restoring the lost "image of God" according to which the first man was created. Cf. Gal. 3:28; 1 Cor. 12:13; Col. 3:11.

6. "Body" here has a double meaning: the physical body of Jesus which was crucified and the metaphorical "body of Christ," the church.

7. A surprising metaphor on two counts: In 1 Cor. 3:10 ff. Paul speaks of the apostles as builders, working on the foundation which is Christ. Nowhere else in Paul are the apostles the foundation (but cf. Rev. 21:14). And the pairing of apostles with "prophets" (Christian charismatics are meant, not OT prophets: see 3:5) is unparalleled in the other letters, though found in later Christian literature.

8. Some would translate "keystone" or "capstone," but there is probably an allusion to Isa. 28:16, the only occurrence of the rare Greek word in the LXX, where it clearly means "cornerstone." The imagery of the whole passage is not entirely transparent, because the metaphor of the building is mixed with that of the body.

9. On the community as the new temple, cf. 1 Cor. 3:16; 2 Cor. 6:16. A motif prominent in the Dead Sea Scrolls as well as in early Christianity; see also 1 Pet. 2:4–10.

of you Gentiles[1]—[2] assuming that you have heard of the stewardship of God's grace that was given to me for you, [3] how the mystery was made known to me by revelation, as I have written
briefly.[2] [4] When you read this you can perceive my insight into
the mystery of Christ, [5] which was not made known to the sons of
men in other generations as it has now been revealed to his holy
apostles and prophets[3] by the Spirit; [6] that is, how the Gentiles are
fellow heirs, members of the same body, and partakers of the promise in Christ Jesus through the gospel.

[7] Of this gospel I was made a minister according to the gift of
God's grace which was given me by the working of his power. [8] To
me, though I am the very least of all the saints,[4] this grace was
given, to preach to the Gentiles the unsearchable riches of Christ,
[9] and to make all men see what is the plan of the mystery hidden
for ages in God who created all things; [10] that through the church
the manifold wisdom of God might now be made known to the
principalities and powers in the heavenly places.[5] [11] This was
according to the eternal purpose which he has realized in Christ
Jesus our Lord, [12] in whom we have boldness and confidence of
access through our faith in him. [13] So I ask you not to[6] lose heart
over what I am suffering for you, which is your glory.

[14] For this reason I bow my knees before the Father, [15] from
whom every family in heaven and on earth is named,[7] [16] that
according to the riches of his glory he may grant you to be
strengthened with might through his Spirit in the inner man,[8]
[17] and that Christ may dwell in your hearts through faith; that
you, being rooted and grounded in love, [18] may have power to
comprehend with all the saints what is the breadth and length and
height and depth, [19] and to know the love of Christ which sur-

---

1. The sentence is interrupted here, to
resume in v. 14. The digression explains
the phrase "a prisoner . . . on behalf of
you Gentiles."
2. Presumably the reference is to the
previous chapters of Eph., though some
(notably Goodspeed) have argued that
the collected letters of Paul are meant,
assuming Eph. to be an "introduction"
to the collection.
3. This verse has the "hidden for
ages/now revealed" pattern frequent in
early Christian preaching (see note on
1 Cor. 2:7), with two surprising elements: (1) elsewhere Paul speaks of
the "mystery" being revealed to all
Christians ("the saints": Col. 1:26);
here it is to "his holy apostles and
prophets" (see note on 2:20; the word
"holy" is the same as the word
"saints"; a few early manuscripts omit
"apostles" here); (2) the content of the
mystery is here specified as the unifica-

tion of Jew and Gentile (v. 6).
4. Cf. 1 Cor. 15:9, where Paul refers
to himself as "the least of the apostles." "Least of all the saints" is surprising; would it be easier to understand a disciple having written this
phrase? See 1 Tim. 1:15 f.!
5. Again the "hidden/revealed" pattern,
now expanded to include the striking
thought that *through the church* the
occult powers from whom the mystery
was hidden are now enlightened.
6. Or, "I ask that I may not."
7. English cannot imitate the word
play between "family" (*patria*) and
"father" (*patēr*) which explains "is
named." Again the allusion is to a
cosmic unity—not only of all human
clans, but of all classes of angels—of
which the unity of Jew and Gentile in
the church is, in the author's view, the
first crystallization point.
8. Cf. Rom. 7:22; 2 Cor. 4:16.

passes knowledge,[9] that you may be filled with all the fulness of God.

20 Now to him who by the power at work within us is able to do far more abundantly than all that we ask or think, **21** to him be glory in the church and in Christ Jesus to all generations, for ever and ever. Amen.

4 I therefore, a prisoner for the Lord, beg you to lead a life worthy of the calling[1] to which you have been called, **2** with all lowliness and meekness, with patience, forbearing one another in love, **3** eager to maintain the unity of the Spirit in the bond of peace. **4** There is one body and one Spirit, just as you were called to the one hope that belongs to your call, **5** one Lord, one faith, one baptism, **6** one God and Father of us all, who is above all and through all and in all. **7** But grace was given to each of us according to the measure of Christ's gift. **8** Therefore it is said,

"When he ascended on high he led a host of captives,
    and he gave gifts to men."[2]

9 (In saying, "He ascended," what does it mean but that he had also descended into the lower parts of the earth?[3] **10** He who descended is he who also ascended far above all the heavens, that he might fill all things.) **11** And his gifts were that some should be apostles, some prophets, some evangelists, some pastors and teachers, **12** for the equipment of the saints,[4] for the work of ministry, for building up the body of Christ, **13** until we all attain to the unity of the faith and of the knowledge of the Son of God, to mature manhood, to the measure of the stature of the fulness of Christ; **14** so that we may no longer be children, tossed to and fro and carried about with every wind of doctrine, by the cunning of men, by their craftiness in deceitful wiles. **15** Rather, speaking the truth in love, we are to grow up in every way into him who is the head, into Christ, **16** from whom the whole body, joined and knit together by every joint with which it is supplied, when each part is working properly, makes bodily growth and upbuilds itself in love.[5]

9. In view of the "Gnostic" language that fills this chapter, this final mention of "love . . . which surpasses knowledge" (*gnosis*) is significant, and typically Pauline: 1 Cor. 8:1; 12–14 *passim*.

1. Cf. 1 Thess. 2:12. The specific aspect of the "calling" which is here made central, in keeping with the theme of the first three chapters, is "unity."

2. Ps. 68:18, quoted in a form that differs from the standard OT texts. Jewish tradition applied the verse to Moses, who brought the "gift" of the Torah from heaven; the Christians (and Gnostics) insisted that only one who had descended from heaven could ascend to heaven (cf. John 3:13).

3. Or, "into the lower regions, viz., the earth." The reference is not likely to the "descent to Hades" that appears in later Christian literature (cf. 1 Pet. 3:19) but to the incarnation.

4. Probably the comma should be omitted after "saints": "the work of ministry" belongs to the whole congregation.

5. Note the close parallel in Col. 2:19.

17 Now this I affirm and testify in the Lord, that you must no longer live as the Gentiles[6] do, in the futility of their minds; **18** they are darkened in their understanding, alienated from the life of God because of the ignorance that is in them, due to their hardness of heart; **19** they have become callous and have given themselves up to licentiousness, greedy to practice every kind of uncleanness. **20** You did not so learn Christ!—**21** assuming that you have heard about him and were taught in him, as the truth is in Jesus. **22** Put off your old nature[7] which belongs to your former manner of life and is corrupt through deceitful lusts, **23** and be renewed in the spirit of your minds, **24** and put on the new nature, created after the likeness of God[8] in true righteousness and holiness.

25 Therefore, putting away falsehood, let every one speak the truth with his neighbor,[9] for we are members one of another. **26** Be angry but do not sin,[1] do not let the sun go down on your anger, **27** and give no opportunity to the devil. **28** Let the thief no longer steal, but rather let him labor, doing honest work with his hands, so that he may be able to give to those in need. **29** Let no evil talk come out of your mouths, but only such as is good for edifying, as fits the occasion, that it may impart grace to those who hear. **30** And do not grieve the Holy Spirit of God, in whom you were sealed for the day of redemption. **31** Let all bitterness and wrath and anger and clamor and slander be put away from you, with all malice, **32** and be kind to one another, tenderhearted, forgiving one another, as God in Christ forgave you.

5 Therefore be imitators of God,[2] as beloved children. **2** And walk in love, as Christ loved us and gave himself up for us, a fragrant offering and sacrifice to God.

3 But immorality and all impurity or covetousness must not even be named among you, as is fitting among saints. **4** Let there be no filthiness, nor silly talk, nor levity, which are not fitting; but instead let there be thanksgiving. **5** Be sure of this, that no immoral or impure man, or one who is covetous (that is, an idolater), has any inheritance in the kingdom of Christ and of God. **6** Let no one deceive you with empty words, for it is because of these things

6. The Gentiles are described here in language common in Jewish apologetic literature; cf. Rom. 1:18–31. Naturally those "Gentile Christians" addressed in the letter are no longer regarded as Gentiles—and no longer expected to behave as such.
7. "Putting off" and "putting on" the old and new natures (lit., "man") is a baptismal motif basic to the exposition in Chap. 2 (2:15: "one new man") and to the exhortations here; cf. Col. 3:1–17.

8. Cf. Gen. 1:26 f. and Col. 3:10.
9. Zech. 8:16.
1. Ps. 4:4.
2. The notion of 'imitating God" was known to the Platonic and Stoic traditions, but in quite a different sense; also rabbinic Judaism could speak of imitating God, and that usage comes closer to what is said here. Elsewhere Paul speaks of imitating Christ and himself (1 Thess. 1:6; 1 Cor. 11:1; 4:16; 2 Thess. 3:7–9) but not God.
3. Cf. Gal. 5:19–21; 1 Cor. 6:9 f.

that the wrath of God comes upon the sons of disobedience.
7 Therefore do not associate with them,[4] **8** for once you were darkness, but now you are light in the Lord; walk as children of light
9 (for the fruit of light is found in all that is good and right and true), **10** and try to learn what is pleasing to the Lord. **11** Take no part in the unfruitful works of darkness, but instead expose them.
12 For it is a shame even to speak of the things that they do in secret; **13** but when anything is exposed by the light it becomes visible, for anything that becomes visible is light. **14** Therefore it is said,

"Awake, O sleeper, and arise from the dead,
and Christ shall give you light."[5]

15 Look carefully then how you walk, not as unwise men but as wise, **16** making the most of the time, because the days are evil.
17 Therefore do not be foolish, but understand what the will of the Lord is. **18** And do not get drunk with wine, for that is debauchery; but be filled with the Spirit,[6] **19** addressing one another in psalms and hymns and spiritual songs, singing and making melody to the Lord with all your heart, **20** always and for everything giving thanks in the name of our Lord Jesus Christ to God the Father.
21 Be subject[7] to one another out of reverence for Christ.
22 Wives, be subject to your husbands, as to the Lord. **23** For the husband is the head of the wife as Christ is the head[8] of the church, his body, and is himself its Savior. **24** As the church is subject to Christ, so let wives also be subject in everything to their husbands. **25** Husbands, love your wives, as Christ loved the church and gave himself up for her, **26** that he might sanctify her, having cleansed her by the washing of water with the word, **27** that he might present the church to himself in splendor, without spot or wrinkle or any such thing, that she might be holy and without blemish.[9] **28** Even so husbands should love their wives as their own bodies. He who loves his wife loves himself. **29** For no man ever hates his own flesh, but nourishes and cherishes it, as Christ does

4. This admonition and the following use of the metaphors "light" and "darkness" have close parallels in the sectarian language of the Dead Sea Scrolls. Note the limits set to such a sect-consciousness in 1 Cor. 5:9–13.
5. The origin of the quotation is unknown; perhaps it comes from an apocryphal book now lost, more likely from an early Christian hymn used at baptism. Similar strophes occur in the liturgy of the Mandaean Gnostics, in the "Hymn of the Pearl" found in the apocryphal Acts of Thomas, and elsewhere, all later in their extant forms than Eph.
6. The notion of "sober intoxication"

is frequent in the language of Hellenistic mysticism, but here it is applied to the communal worship rather than individual experience.
7. In Greek this verb is a participle connected with the previous sentence; the verse is transitional, introducing the "household table" (5:22–6:9). On the form of the latter, see note at Col. 3:18. The remarkable thing about this example of the household table is the christological reinterpretation of the husband/wife paragraph; cf. 2 Cor. 11:2.
8. Cf. 1 Cor. 11:3.
9. Cf. Song 4:7.

Paul christ
church models for intersexuality(?)
models or not

the church, 30 because we are members of his body. 31 "For this
reason a man shall leave his father and mother and be joined to his
wife, and the two shall become one."[1] 32 This is a great mystery,
and I take it to mean Christ and the church; 33 however, let each
one of you love his wife as himself, and let the wife see that she
respects her husband.

6 Children, obey your parents in the Lord, for this is right.
2 "Honor your father and mother"[2] (this is the first commandment with a promise), 3 "that it may be well with you and that
you may live long on the earth." 4 Fathers, do not provoke your
children to anger, but bring them up in the discipline and instruction of the Lord.

5 Slaves, be obedient to those who are your earthly masters, with
fear and trembling, in singleness of heart, as to Christ; 6 not in the
way of eye-service, as men-pleasers, but as servants[3] of Christ,
doing the will of God from the heart, 7 rendering service with a
good will as to the Lord and not to men, 8 knowing that whatever
good any one does, he will receive the same again from the Lord,
whether he is a slave or free. 9 Masters, do the same to them, and
forbear threatening, knowing that he who is both their Master and
yours is in heaven, and that there is no partiality with him.

10 Finally, be strong in the Lord and in the strength of his
might. 11 Put on the whole armor of God, that you may be able to
stand against the wiles of the devil.[4] 12 For we are not contending
against flesh and blood, but against the principalities, against the
powers, against the world rulers of this present darkness, against the
spiritual hosts of wickedness in the heavenly places. 13 Therefore
take the whole armor of God, that you may be able to withstand in
the evil day, and having done all, to stand. 14 Stand therefore,
having girded your loins with truth, and having put on the breastplate of righteousness, 15 and having shod your feet with the equipment of the gospel of peace; 16 above all taking the shield of faith,
with which you can quench all the flaming darts of the evil one.
17 And take the helmet of salvation, and the sword of the Spirit,
which is the word of God. 18 Pray at all times in the Spirit,

1. Gen. 2:24.
2. Ex. 20:12=Deut. 5:16. This is the
only place in the Pauline letters where
one of the Ten Commandments is used
to support a rule for the church.
3. "Slaves."
4. "Put on" recalls the "put off" of
4:25; cf. 4:22–24. The idea of a
cosmic struggle against evil powers reminds one of the eschatological battle
envisioned in the "Rule for the War of
the Sons of Light against the Sons of
Darkness" found among the Dead Sea
Scrolls. In the present passage, how-

ever, the warfare is metaphorical. The
notion that the moral struggle is ultimately part of a cosmic war also has
many parallels in other religions, notably in Mithraism, Christianity's strongest rival in the Roman Empire. The
donning of armor as a metaphor for
practicing virtues was, however, a commonplace in Hellenistic moral discourse, including Hellenistic Judaism as
well as early Christianity. Cf. 1 Thess.
5:8. Several of the specific images here
are drawn from Isa. 11:5; 52:7;
59:17.

with all prayer and supplication. To that end keep alert with all perseverance, making supplication for all the saints, **19** and also for me, that utterance may be given me in opening my mouth boldly to proclaim the mystery of the gospel, **20** for which I am an ambassador in chains; that I may declare it boldly, as I ought to speak.

21 Now that you also may know how I am and what I am doing, Tychicus the beloved brother and faithful minister in the Lord will tell you everything. **22** I have sent him to you for this very purpose, that you may know how we are, and that he may encourage your hearts.[5]

23 Peace be to the brethren, and love with faith, from God the Father and the Lord Jesus Christ. **24** Grace be with all who love our Lord Jesus Christ with love undying.

THE PASTORAL LETTERS (ca. 125?)

The closely related group of documents which purport to be Paul's letters of instruction to Timothy and Titus (they received the label "pastoral" in 1753) are almost certainly pseudonymous. Of course, the evidence is not conclusive, and there are important scholars who still support Pauline authorship. But the evidence to the contrary is so extensive that it is doubtful whether anyone would continue to defend the traditional position apart from reluctance to admit that a deliberate fiction could have been accepted into the New Testament canon. Yet the practice of pseudonymous publication was so common in antiquity that it would be astonishing if no pseudonymous work (among the dozens that we know of in early Christian literature) made it into the canon. Moreover, this is "fiction" of a very special kind, since its nucleus is a collection of traditions which with good reason were thought to go back to the apostle or to stand in some sense under his aegis.

The only strong argument for authenticity is the tradition of the ancient church, yet that tradition gives no certain evidence for the existence of the Pastorals before the third quarter of the second century. Marcion (fl. 150) did not include the Pastoral Letters in his canon, and, since later Marcionites did use them, it is not likely that he excluded them on dogmatic grounds. The earliest extant manuscript of Paul's letters, the Chester Beatty papyrus (early third century) also lacks the Pastorals; its seven missing pages would not

5. Cf. Col. 4:7 f.

have afforded room for them. There are certain passages in the letters of Ignatius of Antioch and Polycarp of Smyrna which are strikingly similar to passages in the Pastorals, but these occur primarily in material that is clearly traditional. Far from being "quotations" from the Pastorals, as is sometimes asserted, these parallels tend to establish a common milieu and date for the Pastorals with Ignatius (d. 110) and Polycarp (d. 155/6).

The Pastorals are essentially manuals for church officers. This genre of literature became very important in the second- and third-century church, as the solidification of catholic organization became an important bulwark against multiplying schismatic movements. The earliest example of the genre is the so-called *Didache*, the "Teaching of the Twelve Apostles," which probably dates from the first decade of the second century. First Timothy and Titus receive their form from a combination of the topics of a church manual (directives for prayer and worship, duties of bishops and deacons) with the old hortatory form, the "household table," which is now transformed to speak not of the members of an ordinary family, but of the "household of God." The only parallel for this combination is in the letter of Polycarp, a fact which led one scholar to suggest that Polycarp wrote the Pastorals. More likely both belonged to a similar situation and period and used similar traditional materials.

The vocabulary and style of the Pastorals is quite different from that of the other Pauline letters. Of particular importance is the meager use of the particles and other short words so frequent in Paul; these tend to be unconscious aspects of speech not readily changed and not ordinarily variable with subject matter. Also impressive is the difference in technical theological vocabulary. Some of Paul's most distinctive terms are missing altogether, and in their place are words and phrases that are commonplaces in Greek popular religion and the emperor cult. Some phrases, moreover, are used in a different sense from that which they have in the undoubted letters.

The Pastorals seem to presuppose a much more elaborate church organization than in Paul's time: not only are there "elders" and "bishops" (though apparently these are still different names for the same office, as in Philippians), but "deacons," now a separate office, and "widows" as an official designation. Biographically, too, it is difficult to fit the epistles into what we know of the final years of Paul's life. To be sure, there is an early tradition, albeit not very well attested, that Paul was released at the end of his first imprisonment in Rome to travel to Spain on a mission. But that "tradition" is probably merely a guess based on Rom. 15:28. The silence of Acts on Paul's death cannot be used to support this tradition, because the style of the final chapters of Acts is that of a martyrology, paralleling Luke's account of Jesus' trials. The author would hardly have written in this fashion unless he knew that Paul's imprisonment ended in death. Particularly the "farewell address" of Acts 20 predicts Paul's death (and "prophecies" in the literary structure of Acts are always fulfilled!), or at the very least that he would never return to the *eastern* regions of the empire. And it is precisely another eastern journey, not a journey to the West, that is presupposed by the Pastorals. In fact the itinerary they assume seems an artificial construction by an author familiar with Acts.

Finally, there are striking differences between the theology of the Pastorals and that of any of the earlier Pauline letters. Particularly important is the shift of focus in the christological formulations: it is not the death and resurrection that are central here, but "epiphany." Like "savior," which is prominent also in the Pastorals, "epiphany" is a technical term of popular Hellenistic religion, particularly of the emperor cult in the eastern parts of the empire. While there are summary statements about salvation as God's gift which sound thoroughly Pauline (e.g., Tit. 3:4 f.), they stand alongside statements about the law and good works which would have satisfied Paul's Galatian opponents (1 Tim. 1:9; Tit. 2:11–14). The notion of tradition in the Pastorals is also a mark of their lateness. While for Paul tradition (*paradosis*) played an important role, it was used very freely and evidently construed quite dynamically (see the notes on Gal. 1:12 and 1 Cor. 15:3–5). In the Pastorals, however, tradition is described as a "deposit" (*parathēkē*, a commercial term), which is only to be "kept" or "guarded," not developed or interpreted. This is a typical mark of the defensive use of tradition; it contrasts not only with Paul's usage, but also with the later Catholic notion of a "living tradition."

The eschatological tension of Paul's authentic letters is almost dissolved here. We see a "bourgeois Christianity" (Dibelius) making itself at home in the world, equating "faith" with "sound teaching," which is expected to produce a rather conservative and commonplace morality as the mark of "piety" or "religiosity." If this is the work of Paul, then it is of an aging Paul with the fire gone out. Most likely the Pastorals must be regarded as a pious work, which erects a fitting memorial to the apostle whose name was already surrounded with a sacred aura, and makes use of that aura to guarantee the integrity of the collected traditions ("the deposit") which are set down against the variety of heresies (including the "falsely so-called *gnosis*," 1 Tim. 6:20) that beset the church in the areas of Paul's mission. Fittingly enough, 2 Timothy has the form of a "last will and testament" from Paul to the succeeding generation.

The First Letter to Timothy

1 Paul, an apostle of Christ Jesus by command of God our Savior and of Christ Jesus our hope,

2 To Timothy, my true child in the faith:
Grace, mercy, and peace from God the Father and Christ Jesus our Lord.

3 As I urged you when I was going to Macedonia, remain at Ephesus[1] that you may charge certain persons not to teach any different doctrine, **4** nor to occupy themselves with myths and endless genealogies[2] which promote speculations rather than the divine training[3] that is in faith; **5** whereas the aim of our charge is love that issues from a pure heart and a good conscience[4] and sincere faith. **6** Certain persons by swerving from these have wandered away into vain discussion, **7** desiring to be teachers of the law,[5] without understanding either what they are saying or the things about which they make assertions.

8 Now we know that the law is good,[6] if any one uses it lawfully, **9** understanding this, that the law is not laid down for the just but for the lawless and disobedient, for the ungodly and sinners, for the unholy and profane, for murderers of fathers and murderers of mothers, for manslayers, **10** immoral persons, sodomites, kidnapers, liars, perjurers, and whatever else is contrary to sound doctrine,[7] **11** in accordance with the glorious gospel of the blessed God with which I have been entrusted.

1. The situation implied here cannot be fitted into Paul's travels as described in Acts, but it could have been suggested by Acts 20:1 if 19:22 were overlooked.

2. This would be an apt description of Gnostic teaching, whose "myths" often describe the origins of the world by "genealogies" of pairs of gods that emanate from the highest deity. On the other hand, the phrase "myths and genealogies" seems to have been a cliché, as old as Plato.

3. Or "order" or "plan," as in Eph. 1:10; 3:9; in the undoubted letters of Paul the word refers to his apostolic "stewardship."

4. "Good" or "pure conscience" (3:9; 2 Tim. 1:3) and its opposite, "seared" (4:2) or "soiled" (Tit. 1:15) is a usage from popular speech, found in later Latin Stoics, but not in Paul, for whom conscience could be rather "strong" or "weak," but not "good" or "bad."

5. The heresy opposed evidently has some Jewish or OT connections; perhaps in view of v. 8 allegorical interpretations ("myths and genealogies" based on the creation story, for example) are meant.

6. A verbal parallel to Rom. 7:16, but the following clause is hardly Pauline.

7. The phrase "sound [i.e., "healthy"] doctrine [or "words"]," while common in Greek philosophical writings, is not found elsewhere in the NT. It is very important in the Pastorals (6:3; 2 Tim. 1:13; 4:3; Tit. 1:9; 13; 2:1, 2, 8). Note the close connection between "healthy teaching" and morality.

12 I thank him[8] who has given me strength for this, Christ Jesus our Lord, because he judged me faithful by appointing me to his service, **13** though I formerly blasphemed and persecuted and insulted him; but I received mercy because I had acted ignorantly in unbelief, **14** and the grace of our Lord overflowed for me with the faith and love that are in Christ Jesus. **15** The saying is sure and worthy of full acceptance,[9] that Christ Jesus came into the world to save sinners. And I am the foremost of sinners,[1] **16** but I received mercy for this reason, that in me, as the foremost, Jesus Christ might display his perfect patience for an example to those who were to believe in him for eternal life. **17** To the King of ages, immortal, invisible, the only God, be honor and glory for ever and ever. Amen.

18 This charge I commit to you, Timothy, my son, in accordance with the prophetic utterance which pointed to you,[2] that inspired by them you may wage the good warfare, **19** holding faith and a good conscience. By rejecting conscience, certain persons have made shipwreck of their faith, **20** among them Hymenaeus and Alexander, whom I have delivered to Satan[3] that they may learn not to blaspheme.

2 First of all, then, I urge that supplications, prayers, intercessions, and thanksgivings be made for all men, **2** for kings and all who are in high positions, that we may lead a quiet and peaceable life, godly and respectful in every way. **3** This is good, and it is acceptable in the sight of God our Savior, **4** who desires all men to be saved and to come to the knowledge of the truth. **5** For there is one God, and there is one mediator between God and men, the man Christ Jesus, **6** who gave himself as a ransom for all, the testimony to which was borne at the proper time.[4] **7** For this I was appointed a preacher and apostle (I am telling the truth, I am not lying), a teacher of the Gentiles in faith and truth.

8 I desire then that in every place the men[5] should pray, lifting holy hands without anger or quarreling; **9** also that women should

---

8. Here begins the epistolary thanksgiving, which however differs in both position and form from those in the authentic letters. Cf. 2 Tim. 1:3–7; Tit. lacks a thanksgiving.

9. This phrase or a shorter form occurs five times: 3:1; 4:9; 2 Tim. 2:11; Tit. 3:8.

1. Cf. Gal. 1:13; 1 Cor. 15:8 f.; but especially Eph. 3:8.

2. Cf. 4:14. For participation of prophets in the commissioning of a missionary, cf. Acts 13:1–3.

3. Cf. 1 Cor. 5:5. Hymenaeus is mentioned again, in different company, in 2 Tim. 2:17; an Alexander, in 2 Tim.

4:14.

4. Vv. 5–6 are probably part of a liturgical formula. The last clause is puzzling, but should probably be translated, "as the testimony in [God's] own time." "The Man" as a christological title occurs elsewhere, notably in John 19:5, also in Gnostic texts; it could be related to the title "Son of Man" found in the gospels.

5. Here begins the first variation of the "household table" (note the subscription in 3:15), in which "men," "women" (vv. 9–15), "bishops" (3:1–7), and "deacons" (3:8–13) receive general instructions.

adorn themselves modestly and sensibily in seemly apparel, not with braided hair or gold or pearls or costly attire [10] but by good deeds, as befits women who profess religion. [11] Let a woman learn in silence with all submissiveness. [12] I permit no woman to teach or to have authority over men; she is to keep silent.[6] [13] For Adam was formed first, then Eve; [14] and Adam was not deceived, but the woman was deceived and became a transgressor. [15] Yet woman will be saved through bearing children,[7] if she continues[8] in faith and love and holiness, with modesty.

3 The saying is sure: If any one aspires to the office of bishop, he desires a noble task. [2] Now a bishop must be above reproach, the husband of one wife,[9] temperate, sensible, dignified, hospitable, an apt teacher, [3] no drunkard, not violent but gentle, not quarrelsome, and no lover of money. [4] He must manage his own household well, keeping his children submissive and respectful in every way; [5] for if a man does not know how to manage his own household, how can he care for God's church? [6] He must not be a recent convert, or he may be puffed up with conceit and fall into the condemnation of the devil;[1] [7] moreover he must be well thought of by outsiders, or he may fall into reproach and the snare of the devil.

[8] Deacons likewise must be serious, not double-tongued, not addicted to much wine, not greedy for gain; [9] they must hold the mystery of the faith with a clear conscience. [10] And let them also be tested first; then if they prove themselves blameless let them serve as deacons. [11] The women[2] likewise must be serious, no slanderers, but temperate, faithful in all things. [12] Let deacons be the husband of one wife, and let them manage their children and their households well; [13] for those who serve well as deacons gain a good standing for themselves and also great confidence in the faith which is in Christ Jesus.

[14] I hope to come to you soon, but I am writing these instructions to you so that, [15] if I am delayed, you may know how one ought to behave in the household of God, which is the church of the living God, the pillar and bulwark of the truth. [16] Great indeed, we confess,[3] is the mystery of our religion:

---

6. Cf. 1 Cor. 14:34 f.
7. An obscure clause. Some would translate "by the birth of the child" (RSV margin), thinking of an allusion to Gen. 3:15, understood as a prediction of Christ's birth, but the Greek will hardly bear such a translation.
8. Lit., "they continue."
9. I.e., married only once; the meaning is made clear by the corresponding phrase used of widows, 5:9.
1. Though the word *diabolos* means

"slanderer" and is so used in the plural in the Pastorals (3:11; 2 Tim. 3:3; Tit. 2:3), in the singular it certainly refers to "the devil." It is not so used in the undoubted letters of Paul, but see Eph. 4:27; 6:11.
2. This could refer to the deacons' wives, but more likely to female deacons; that there were such is shown by Rom. 16:1.
3. Or, "confessedly," "undeniably."

> He[4] was manifested in the flesh,
>   vindicated[5] in the Spirit,
> seen by angels,
>   preached among the nations,
> believed on in the world,
>   taken up in glory.

4 Now the Spirit expressly says[6] that in later times some will depart from the faith by giving heed to deceitful spirits and doctrines of demons, **2** through the pretensions of liars whose consciences are seared, **3** who forbid marriage[7] and enjoin abstinence from foods which God created to be received with thanksgiving by those who believe and know the truth. **4** For everything created by God is good, and nothing is to be rejected if it is received with thanksgiving; **5** for then it is consecrated by the word of God and prayer.

6 If you put these instructions before the brethren, you will be a good minister[8] of Christ Jesus, nourished on the words of the faith and of the good doctrine which you have followed. **7** Have nothing to do with godless and silly myths. Train yourself in godliness; **8** for while bodily training is of some value, godliness is of value in every way, as it holds promise for the present life and also for the life to come. **9** The saying is sure and worthy of full acceptance. **10** For to this end we toil and strive,[9] because we have our hope set on the living God, who is the Savior of all men, especially of those who believe.

11 Command and teach these things. **12** Let no one despise your youth, but set the believers an example in speech and conduct, in love, in faith, in purity. **13** Till I come, attend to the public reading of scripture, to preaching, to teaching.[1] **14** Do not neglect the gift you have, which was given you by prophetic utterance when the elders laid their hands upon you.[2] **15** Practice these duties, devote yourself to them, so that all may see your progress. **16** Take

---

4. Greek "Who"; cf. the beginning of the hymns in Phil. 2:6; Col. 1:15. The relative pronoun has no grammatical connection here; some manuscripts therefore substitute "God" or "which." The six lines have only a rough meter; they are best construed as three strophes of two lines each in the pattern ab/ba/ab.
5. Or, "justified."
6. We cannot know whether the allusion is to a specific prophecy. Many apocalyptic texts speak of apostasy as a sign of the "last days."
7. There were a number of movements in the early church that opposed marriage, including Marcion and the Encratites (see below, pp. 193–207). Cf.

also the errors combatted in Col.
8. The word translated "minister" is the same as that translated "deacon." Here the older usage, referring to a missionary (e.g., 1 Cor. 3:5; 2 Cor. 11:23) persists alongside the new technical usage for a local office.
9. Some texts read, "suffer reproach."
1. These are apparently three cardinal elements in public worship. The word translated "preaching" means "admonition" or "exhortation"; homilies to the congregation, not missionary proclamation, are meant.
2. One of the earliest testimonies to the ritual of "laying on of hands" for ordination; cf. 5:22; 2 Tim. 1:6; Acts 6:6; 13:3.

heed to yourself and to your teaching; hold to that, for by so doing you will save both yourself and your hearers.

5 Do not rebuke an older man[3] but exhort him as you would a father; treat younger men like brothers, 2 older women like mothers, younger women like sisters, in all purity.

3 Honor widows[4] who are real widows. 4 If a widow has children or grandchildren, let them first learn their religious duty to their own family and make some return to their parents; for this is acceptable in the sight of God. 5 She who is a real widow, and is left all alone, has set her hope on God and continues in supplications and prayers night and day; 6 whereas she who is self-indulgent is dead even while she lives. 7 Command this, so that they may be without reproach. 8 If any one does not provide for his relatives, and especially for his own family, he has disowned the faith and is worse than an unbeliever.

9 Let a widow be enrolled if she is not less than sixty years of age, having been the wife of one husband; 10 and she must be well attested for her good deeds, as one who has brought up children, shown hospitality, washed the feet of the saints, relieved the afflicted, and devoted herself to doing good in every way. 11 But refuse to enrol younger widows; for when they grow wanton against Christ they desire to marry, 12 and so they incur condemnation for having violated their first pledge. 13 Besides that, they learn to be idlers, gadding about from house to house, and not only idlers but gossips and busybodies, saying what they should not. 14 So I would have younger widows marry, bear children, rule their households, and give the enemy no occasion to revile us. 15 For some have already strayed after Satan. 16 If any believing woman has relatives who are widows,[5] let her assist them; let the church not be burdened, so that it may assist those who are real widows.

17 Let the elders[6] who rule well be considered worthy of double honor,[7] especially those who labor in preaching and teaching; 18 for the scripture says, "You shall not muzzle an ox when it is

3. Here in the ordinary sense; elsewhere (e.g., v. 17) the same word refers to the office of "elder." Vv. 1 f. reflect an ancient Greek ideal for behavior of a person in authority; Plato already used very similar language to describe relationships among the "guardians" of his ideal republic (*Repub.* V, 463c).
4. Vv. 3–16 are a surprisingly elaborate set of regulations for the enrollment of widows eligible for church support. The special concern for widows (and orphans) had long been characteristic of Judaism. A similar set of rules, but much shorter, is found in the Letter of Polycarp (d. 155/6) 4:3, and later books of church order deal with the

same problem.
5. The words "relatives who are" are not in the Greek text, though that is perhaps the simplest explanation—but why would only a "believing woman" and not also believing men have this responsibility? Some manuscripts therefore add "or believing man."
6. "Elders" here has the official sense, identical with "bishops" (see Tit. 1:5–7).
7. Or, "double pay"—as clearly implied by v. 18. But does this mean that one group of elders, as executives, are distinguished from others who receive lesser pay? Possibly the elders receive twice the stipend of widows.

treading out the grain,"[8] and, "The laborer deserves his wages."[9]
[19] Never admit any charge against an elder except on the evidence
of two or three witnesses.[1] [20] As for those who persist in sin,
rebuke them in the presence of all, so that the rest may stand in
fear. [21] In the presence of God and of Christ Jesus and of the elect
angels I charge you to keep these rules without favor, doing nothing from partiality. [22] Do not be hasty in the laying on of hands,
nor participate in another man's sins; keep yourself pure.

[23] No longer drink only water, but use a little wine for the sake
of your stomach and your frequent ailments.[2]

[24]The sins of some men are conspicuous, pointing to judgment,
but the sins of others appear later. [25] So also good deeds are conspicuous; and even when they are not, they cannot remain hidden.
6 Let all who are under the yoke of slavery[3] regard their masters as worthy of all honor, so that the name of God and the teaching may not be defamed. [2] Those who have believing masters must
not be disrespectful on the ground that they are brethren; rather
they must serve all the better since those who benefit by their service are believers and beloved.

Teach and urge these duties. [3] If any one teaches otherwise and
does not agree with the sound words of our Lord Jesus Christ and
the teaching which accords with godliness,[4] [4] he is puffed up with
conceit, he knows nothing; he has a morbid craving for controversy
and for disputes about words, which produce envy, dissension, slander, base suspicions, [5] and wrangling among men who are depraved
in mind and bereft of the truth, imagining that godliness is a
means of gain.[5] [6] There is great gain in godliness with contentment,[6] [7] for we brought nothing into the world, and[7] we cannot
take anything out of the world;[8] [8] but if we have food and cloth-

8. Deut. 25:4; cf. 1 Cor. 9:9.
9. Quoted as a saying of Jesus in Luke
10:7 (cf. Matt. 10:10), and alluded to
by Paul in 1 Cor. 9:14. If "scripture
says" is to be taken strictly as referring to both quotations, then this
would be the earliest instance of one of
the gospels (or a prior collection of
Jesus' sayings: "Q") being placed on a
par with what Christians would later
call "the Old Testament."
1. Deut. 19:15.
2. Vv. 24 f. are more closely connected
with v. 22 than this verse; typical of
the loose topical arrangement of much
hortatory literature. V. 23 sets a limit
to the last clause of v. 22: "keep yourself pure," a necessary limit in view of
ascetic tendencies combatted elsewhere
in the Pastorals (e.g., 4:3).
3. A fragment of the more conventional type of "household table"; note
the concern with the church's reputation in the larger society.
4. The term translated "godliness"
throughout the Pastorals is a very

common word in Hellenistic literature
(never, however, used in the authentic
letters of Paul), which could be translated "piety," or "religion" (like the
synonym in 2:10). This religion is not
precisely defined, nor are the doctrines
of those who "teach otherwise"; clearly
the primary defense against "heresy" is
becoming institutional rather than
Paul's method of direct arguments with
opposing viewpoints.
5. The accusation that the teaching of
new doctrines was motivated by desire
for profit is very common in polemical
literature of the philosophical schools,
of the satirists, and of Christian antiheretical literature from this point on.
6. "Contentment" was a fundamental
virtue in the Stoic tradition, from
which it became a cliché in popular
moral philosophy. Note Paul's use of
the term in Phil. 4:11.
7. Some manuscripts insert, 'it is certain that."
8. A commonplace in both Greek and
Jewish sources; cf. Job 1:21.

ing, with these we shall be content. **9** But those who desire to be rich fall into temptation, into a snare, into many senseless and hurtful desires that plunge men into ruin and destruction. **10** For the love of money is the root of all evils;[9] it is through this craving that some have wandered away from the faith and pierced their hearts with many pangs.

11 But as for you, man of God,[1] shun all this; aim at righteousness, godliness, faith, love, steadfastness, gentleness. **12** Fight the good fight of the faith; take hold of the eternal life to which you were called when you made the good confession in the presence of many witnesses. **13** In the presence of God who gives life to all things, and of Christ Jesus who in his testimony before Pontius Pilate made the good confession,[2] **14** I charge you to keep the commandment unstained and free from reproach until the appearing of our Lord Jesus Christ; **15** and this will be made manifest at the proper time by the blessed and only Sovereign, the King of kings and Lord of lords, **16** who alone has immortality and dwells in unapproachable light, whom no man has ever seen or can see. To him be honor and eternal dominion. Amen.

17 As for the rich in this world, charge them not to be haughty, nor to set their hopes on uncertain riches but on God who richly furnishes us with everything to enjoy. **18** They are to do good, to be rich in good deeds, liberal and generous, **19** thus laying up for themselves a good foundation for the future, so that they may take hold of the life which is life indeed.

20 Timothy, guard what has been entrusted you.[3] Avoid the godless chatter and contradictions of what is falsely called knowledge,[4] **21** for by professing it some have missed the mark as regards the faith.

Grace be with you.

The Second Letter to Timothy

1 Paul, an apostle of Christ Jesus by the will of God according to the promise of the life which is in Christ Jesus,

2 To Timothy, my beloved child:

9. Another cliché of popular moralizing.

1. An OT title, used there of exceptional charmismatics (Deut. 33:1; Josh. 14:6; 1 Sam. 9:6 f.; 1 Kings 17:18; 2 Kings 4:7; Neh. 12:24). Vv. 11–16 seem a self-contained unit, perhaps drawn from an exhortation used at baptism or ordination.

2. The description of Jesus as the model martyr who, by his fortitude, encourages followers to "keep the faith" is foreign to Paul but increasingly important in subapostolic Christianity. A similar theology of martyr-

dom developed in Jewish literature around the figures of the Maccabees.

3. Lit., "the deposit," a commercial term here applied to the authoritative tradition; cf. 2 Tim. 1:12, 14.

4. The first attestation for the use of the word *gnosis* as a technical designation for an esoteric movement. But cf. 1 Cor. 8:1, 7, 10; 13:2; 14:6. Some have found in the word "contradictions" (*antitheseis*) a specific reference to Marcion's work, "The Antitheses" (see below, pp. 188–90), but that is hardly likely.

Grace, mercy, and peace from God the Father and Christ Jesus our Lord.

[3] I thank God whom I serve with a clear conscience, as did my fathers,[1] when I remember you constantly in my prayers. [4] As I remember your tears, I long night and day to see you, that I may be filled with joy. [5] I am reminded of your sincere faith, a faith that dwelt first in your grandmother Lois and your mother Eunice[2] and now, I am sure, dwells in you. [6] Hence I remind you to rekindle the gift of God that is within you through the laying on of my hands;[3] [7] for God did not give us a spirit of timidity but a spirit of power and love and self-control.

[8] Do not be ashamed then of testifying to our Lord, nor of me his prisoner, but take your share of suffering[4] for the gospel in the power of God, [9] who saved us and called us with a holy calling, not in virtue of our works but in virtue of his own purpose and the grace which he gave us in Christ Jesus ages ago, [10] and now has manifested through the appearing of our Savior Christ Jesus, who abolished death and brought life and immortality to light through the gospel.[5] [11] For this gospel I was appointed a preacher[6] and apostle and teacher, [12] and therefore I suffer as I do. But I am not ashamed,[7] for I know whom I have believed, and I am sure that he is able to guard until that Day what has been entrusted to me.[8] [13] Follow the pattern of the sound words which you have heard from me, in the faith and love which are in Christ Jesus; [14] guard the truth that has been entrusted to you[9] by the Holy Spirit who dwells within us.

[15] You are aware that all who are in Asia[1] turned away from me, and among them Phygelus and Hermogenes, [16] May the Lord grant mercy to the household of Onesiphorus, for he often refreshed me; he was not ashamed of my chains, [17] but when he

---

1. Lit., "from my ancestors." The notion that in Judaism Paul served the same God and "with a clear conscience" is certainly in harmony with the authentic letters, even though the paradoxical relationship between Judaism and Christianity is no longer so clear in the Pastorals.
2. Cf. Acts 16:1.
3. See note on 1 Tim. 4:14.
4. Or, "share with me in suffering."
5. Vv. 9 f. are a carefully formulated summary, following a pattern frequently found in early Christian preaching: "hidden for ages/now revealed" (cf. note on 1 Cor. 2:7 ff). The typically Pauline terms "mystery" and "hidden" are wanting here, and the terms "appearing" ("epiphany")

and "savior," so important in the Pastorals, are central. The latter were stock expressions in many forms of Hellenistic religion, including healing cults and the cult of the emperors. (One inscription describes Caesar as "the son of Ares and Aphrodite, god manifest [*epiphanē*] and universal savior of mankind.")
6. Lit., "herald."
7. Cf. Rom. 1:16.
8. Or, "what I have entrusted to him," lit., "my deposit."
9. Lit., "guard the excellent deposit"; the same word is used in v. 12.
1. The Roman province, roughly the western half of Asia Minor, of which Ephesus was the capital.

arrived in Rome he searched for me eagerly and found me—[18] may the Lord grant him to find mercy from the Lord on that Day—and you well know all the service he rendered at Ephesus.[2]

2 You then, my son, be strong in the grace that is in Christ Jesus, [2] and what you have heard from me before many witnesses entrust to faithful men who will be able to teach others also. [3] Take your share of suffering as a good soldier of Christ Jesus. [4] No soldier on service gets entangled in civilian pursuits, since his aim is to satisfy the one who enlisted him. [5] An athlete is not crowned unless he competes according to the rules. [6] It is the hard-working farmer who ought to have the first share of the crops. [7] Think over what I say, for the Lord will grant you understanding in everything.

[8] Remember Jesus Christ, risen from the dead, descended from David,[3] as preached in my gospel, [9] the gospel for which I am suffering and wearing fetters like a criminal. But the word of God is not fettered. [10] Therefore I endure everything for the sake of the elect, that they also may obtain the salvation which in Christ Jesus goes with eternal glory. [11] The saying is sure:

If we have died with him, we shall also live with him;

[12] if we endure, we shall also reign with him;

if we deny him, he also will deny us;

[13] if we are faithless, he remains faithful—

for he cannot deny himself.[4]

[14] Remind them of this, and charge them before the Lord[5] to avoid disputing about words, which does no good, but only ruins the hearers. [15] Do your best to present yourself to God as one approved, a workman who has no need to be ashamed, rightly handling the word of truth.[6] [16] Avoid such godless chatter, for it will lead people into more and more ungodliness, [17] and their talk will eat its way like gangrene. Among them are Hymenaeus and Philetus, [18] who have swerved from the truth by holding that the resurrection is past already.[7] They are upsetting the faith of some. [19] But God's firm foundation stands, bearing this seal: "The Lord

2. Such personal notes, with those of Chap. 4 are taken by many commentators as signs of authenticity. Some suggest that fragments of an authentic letter have been used by the pseudonymous author. The persons mentioned here are not otherwise known, until the late apocryphal book The Acts of Paul, which mentions Hermogenes and gives a few more details about Onesiphorus. 3. A very brief summary, evidently fragmentary; cf. Rom. 1:3 f. 4. The style of this quotation is striking; it may be part of a baptismal hymn: note fragmentary parallels in Rom. 6:5, 8; Col. 3:1. Polycarp quotes similar lines (Polycarp 5:2). The *style* is found in the concluding hymn of the Qumran "Manual of Discipline." 5. Other authorities read "God." 6. The unusual word translated "rightly handling" is found elsewhere only in Prov. 3:6; 11:5; where it refers to clearing a straight road. For "word of truth," a common expression for the gospel, see note on Col. 1:5. 7. On the possibility of an earlier appearance of this notion, see notes on 1 Cor. 15.

knows those who are his,"[8] and "Let every one who names the name of the Lord depart from iniquity."[9]

20 In a great house there are not only vessels of gold and silver but also of wood and earthenware, and some for noble use, some for ignoble. **21** If any one purifies himself from what is ignoble, then he will be a vessel for noble use, consecrated and useful to the master of the house, ready for any good work. **22** So shun youthful passions and aim at righteousness, faith, love, and peace, along with those who call upon the Lord from a pure heart. **23** Have nothing to do with stupid, senseless controversies; you know that they breed quarrels. **24** And the Lord's servant must not be quarrelsome but kindly to every one, an apt teacher, forbearing, **25** correcting his opponents with gentleness. God may perhaps grant that they will repent and come to know the truth, **26** and they may escape from the snare of the devil, after being captured by him to do his will.[1]
3 But understand this, that in the last days there will come times of stress.[2] **2** For men will be lovers of self, lovers of money, proud, arrogant, abusive, disobedient to their parents, ungrateful, unholy, **3** inhuman, implacable, slanderers, profligates, fierce, haters of good, **4** treacherous, reckless, swollen with conceit, lovers of pleasure rather than lovers of God, **5** holding the form of religion but denying the power of it. Avoid such people. **6** For among them are those who make their way into households and capture weak women, burdened with sins and swayed by various impulses, **7** who will listen to anybody[3] and can never arrive at a knowledge of the truth. **8** As Jannes and Jambres opposed Moses,[4] so these men also oppose the truth, men of corrupt mind and counterfeit faith; **9** but they will not get very far, for their folly will be plain to all, as was that of those two men.

10 Now you have observed my teaching, my conduct, my aim in life, my faith, my patience, my love, my steadfastness, **11** my persecutions, my sufferings, what befell me at Antioch, at Iconium, and at Lystra, what persecutions I endured; yet from them all the Lord rescued me.[5] **12** Indeed all who desire to live a godly life in Christ Jesus will be persecuted, **13** while evil men and impostors will go

8. Num. 16:5 LXX.
9. This quotation is not found in the OT, though cf. Num. 16:26.
1. By strict rules of Greek grammar, the word translated "his" ought to refer to a different antecedent from that of "him," so some would translate "by him, to do his [God's] will," but the result is even more awkward grammatically.
2. A typical formulation in the genre "Testament" or "Farewell Discourse." In the NT, cf. 2 Pet. 3:3; Mark 13:3 ff. and parallels; in the OT, the testaments of Jacob (Gen. 49) and Moses

(Deut. 33; 34); in the Pseudepigrapha, the "Testaments of the Twelve Patriarchs," etc.
3. Lit., "always learning," i.e., fascinated by any novel teaching.
4. Legend gave these names to the "magicians of Egypt" who, according to Ex. 7, contended with Moses in Pharaoh's presence. They are prototypes for opponents of the truth "at the end of days" also in the Dead Sea Scrolls.
5. Cf. 2 Cor. 11:23–29, and the note on 2 Cor. 6:4.

on from bad to worse, deceivers and deceived. 14 But as for you, continue in what you have learned and have firmly believed, knowing from whom you learned it 15 and how from childhood you have been acquainted with the sacred writings which are able to instruct you for salvation through faith in Christ Jesus. 16 All scripture is inspired by God and profitable[6] for teaching, for reproof, for correction, and for training in righteousness, 17 that the man of God may be complete, equipped for every good work.

4 I charge you in the presence of God and of Christ Jesus who is to judge the living and the dead, and by his appearing and his kingdom: 2 preach the word, be urgent[7] in season and out of season, convince, rebuke, and exhort, be unfailing in patience and in teaching. 3 For the time is coming when people will not endure sound teaching, but having itching ears they will accumulate for themselves teachers to suit their own likings, 4 and will turn away from listening to the truth and wander into myths. 5 As for you, always be steady, endure suffering, do the work of an evangelist, fulfil your ministry.

6 For I am already on the point of being sacrificed;[8] the time of my departure has come. 7 I have fought the good fight, I have finished the race, I have kept the faith. 8 Henceforth there is laid up for me the crown of righteousness, which the Lord, the righteous judge, will award to me on that Day, and not only to me but also to all who have loved his appearing.

9 Do your best to come to me soon.[9] 10 For Demas, in love with this present world, has deserted me and gone to Thessalonica; Crescens has gone to Galatia, Titus to Dalmatia. 11 Luke alone is with me. Get Mark and bring him with you; for he is very useful in serving me. 12 Tychicus I have sent to Ephesus. 13 When you come, bring the cloak that I left with Carpus at Troas, also the books, and above all the parchments. 14 Alexander the coppersmith did me great harm; the Lord will requite him for his deeds. 15 Beware of him yourself, for he strongly opposed our message. 16 At my first defense[1] no one took my part; all deserted me. May it not be charged against them! 17 But the Lord stood by me and gave me strength to proclaim the word fully, that all the Gentiles might hear it. So I was rescued from the lion's mouth.[2] 18 The Lord will rescue me from every evil and save me for his heavenly kingdom.

6. More likely, "Every God-inspired scripture is profitable."
7. Or, "be alert," "be on duty."
8. Lit., "I am already being poured out [as a libation]"; cf. Phil. 2:17.
9. The sudden shift of mood has lent color to the hypothesis that fragments of a genuine letter have been used; see note on 1:18.
1. Traditionally this has been taken to refer to Paul's first Roman imprisonment, on the assumption that, after a brief period of freedom, he now writes during a second imprisonment. More likely, however, "first defense" refers to a preliminary hearing; the Pastorals throughout seem to presuppose only *one* imprisonment.
2. To be understood figuratively (cf. 1 Cor. 15:32 and note); "the lion" is the power of the empire.

To him be the glory for ever and ever. Amen.

19 Greet Prisca and Aquila,[3] and the household of Onesiphorus. **20** Erastus remained at Corinth; Trophimus I left ill at Miletus. **21** Do your best to come before winter. Eubulus sends greetings to you, as do Pudens and Linus and Claudia and all the brethren.

22 The Lord be with your spirit. Grace be with you.

The Letter to Titus

1 Paul, a servant[1] of God and an apostle of Jesus Christ, to further the faith of God's elect and their knowledge of the truth which accords with godliness, **2** in hope of eternal life which God, who never lies, promised ages ago **3** and at the proper time manifested in his word through the preaching with which I have been entrusted by command of God our Savior;

4 To Titus, my true child in a common faith:

Grace and peace from God the Father and Christ Jesus our Savior.

5 This is why I left you in Crete,[2] that you might amend what was defective, and appoint elders[3] in every town as I directed you, **6** if any man is blameless, the husband of one wife, and his children are believers and not open to the charge of being profligate or insubordinate. **7** For a bishop, as God's steward, must be blameless; he must not be arrogant or quick-tempered or a drunkard or violent or greedy for gain, **8** but hospitable, a lover of goodness, master of himself, upright, holy, and self-controlled; **9** he must hold firm to the sure word as taught, so that he may be able to give instruction in sound doctrine and also to confute those who contradict it. **10** For there are many insubordinate men, empty talkers and deceivers, especially the circumcision party[4]; **11** they must be silenced, since they are upsetting whole families by teaching for base gain what they have no right to teach. **12** One of themselves, a prophet of their own,[5] said, "Cretans are always liars, evil beasts, lazy gluttons." **13** This testimony is true. Therefore rebuke them sharply, that they may be sound in the faith, **14** instead of giving

---

3. Cf. 1 Cor. 16:19; Rom 16:3; Acts 18:2 ff.

1. "Slave," as elsewhere.

2. The only other mention of Crete in the NT is Acts 27:7 ff., where the ship bearing Paul as prisoner to Rome is said to have touched briefly at a Cretan harbor. The foundation of a church there is unrecorded.

3. "Elders" and "bishops" are used interchangeably. The form of the rule for the officers' qualifications is the same as in 1 Tim. 3:2–7 (simply parallel lists of virtues and vices), though there are a number of variations in detail. In many respects Tit. reads like an abbreviated version of 1 Tim.

4. Or simply "Jewish converts" (NEB); lit., "those from the circumcision."

5. The verse is said by Clement of Alexandria to come from a book by Epimenides, a teacher and miracle worker of Crete (fl. 500 B.C.). The line had become proverbial.

heed to Jewish myths or to commands of men who reject the truth. 15 To the pure all things are pure, but to the corrupt and unbelieving nothing is pure; their very minds and consciences are corrupted. 16 They profess to know God, but they deny him by their deeds; they are detestable, disobedient, unfit for any good deed.

2 But as for you, teach what befits sound doctrine. 2 Bid the older men[6] be temperate, serious, sensible, sound in faith, in love, and in steadfastness. 3 Bid the older women likewise to be reverent in behavior, not to be slanderers or slaves to drink; they are to teach what is good, 4 and so train the young women to love their husbands and children, 5 to be sensible, chaste, domestic, kind, and submissive to their husbands, that the word of God may not be discredited. 6 Likewise urge the younger men to control themselves. 7 Show yourself in all respects a model of good deeds, and in your teaching show integrity, gravity, 8 and sound speech that cannot be censured, so that an opponent may be put to shame, having nothing evil to say of us. 9 Bid slaves to be submissive to their masters and to give satisfaction in every respect; they are not to be refractory, 10 nor to pilfer, but to show entire and true fidelity, so that in everything they may adorn the doctrine of God our Savior.[7]

11 For the grace of God has appeared[8] for the salvation of all men, 12 training us to renounce irreligion and worldly passions, and to live sober, upright, and godly lives in this world, 13 awaiting our blessed hope, the appearing of the glory of our great God and Savior[9] Jesus Christ, 14 who gave himself for us to redeem us from all iniquity and to purify for himself a people of his own who are zealous for good deeds.

15 Declare these things; exhort and reprove with all authority. Let no one disregard you.[1]

3 Remind them to be submissive to rulers and authorities,[2] to be obedient, to be ready for any honest work, 2 to speak evil of no one, to avoid quarreling, to be gentle, and to show perfect courtesy toward all men. 3 For we ourselves were once foolish, disobedient, led astray, slaves to various passions and pleasures, passing our days

---

6. 2:1–10 is a "household table," for older men, older women, young women, young men, and slaves.

7. Note that both here and in 1 Tim. 6:1–2 (also 1 Pet. 2:18 ff.) there is no corresponding admonition to the masters; contrast Col. 4:1; Eph. 6:9.

8. Vv. 11–15 provide the theological basis for the style of morality urged in the "household table." The language, which has elements of liturgical style, is paralleled in many statements of Hellenistic Jewish apologetics, in which God's saving act (primarily the Exodus and Sinai revelation) procured for him "a special people" (cf. Ex. 19:5), to be "trained" by his commandments and thus marked out by its superior morality. The terms used here to describe this morality belong to the classic Greek tradition.

9. Or, "of the great God and our Savior."

1. Cf. 1 Tim. 4:12.

2. Cf. Rom. 13:1–7; 1 Pet. 2:13–17.

in malice and envy, hated by men and hating one another; **4** but when the goodness and loving kindness of God our Savior appeared, **5** he saved us, not because of deeds done by us in righteousness, but in virtue of his own mercy,³ by the washing of regeneration⁴ and renewal in the Holy Spirit, **6** which he poured out upon us richly through Jesus Christ our Savior, **7** so that we might be justified by his grace and become heirs in hope of eternal life. **8** The saying is sure.

I desire you to insist on these things, so that those who have believed in God may be careful to apply themselves to good deeds;⁵ these are excellent and profitable to men. **9** But avoid stupid controversies, genealogies, dissensions, and quarrels over the law, for they are unprofitable and futile. **10** As for a man who is factious, after admonishing him once or twice, have nothing more to do with him, **11** knowing that such a person is perverted and sinful; he is self-condemned.

12 When I send Artemas or Tychicus⁶ to you, do your best to come to me at Nicopolis,⁷ for I have decided to spend the winter there. **13** Do your best to speed Zenas the lawyer and Apollos⁸ on their way; see that they lack nothing. **14** And let our people learn to apply themselves to good deeds, so as to help cases of urgent need, and not to be unfruitful.

15 All who are with me send greetings to you. Greet those who love us in the faith.

Grace be with you all.

---

3. That this summary is consciously Pauline is unmistakable.

4. Or, "rebirth." The notion of death and rebirth in a rite of initiation is common in the mystery religions. While the term is not used in the authentic letters of Paul, it is a natural expression of the common understanding of baptism which he presupposed; later it becomes more common in Christian writings.

5. It is possible to translate "enter honorable occupations" (so RSV margin; NEB), and so also in v. 14, but the translation above is more natural in the context.

6. Cf. Col. 4:7; Eph. 6:21; 2 Tim. 4:12; Acts 20:4.

7. A number of cities bearing the name Nicopolis could be meant; perhaps the most likely is in Epirus, on the western coast of the Greek mainland.

8. 1 Cor. 1:12; 3:4 ff.; 4:6; Acts 18:24; 19:1.

PART III

Views of Paul
in the Ancient Church

The ambivalent history of Paulinism began within the pages of the New Testament. If the consensus of critical scholars is correct, several of the letters attributed to Paul were written by followers some time after his death. That suggests that Paul founded a "school" that continued to develop a distinctly Pauline tradition. His method of missionary activity, in close association with Timothy, Titus, Silvanus, Apollos, and others, points in the same direction.[1] Especially in the Pastoral Letters there is clearly visible an effort to make Paul into the *founder* of reliable tradition, the guarantor of the "deposit" of correct church organization, morality, and "sound doctrine," as well as the model of Christian conversion (1 Tim. 1:12–16).

On the other hand, some wariness about Paulinism is also expressed in certain passages. The author of 2 Peter, perhaps the latest work in the canon, could already apply the term "scriptures" (though perhaps not in the full technical sense) to Paul's letters, yet in the same breath he warned that "there are some things in them hard to understand, which the ignorant and unstable twist to their own destruction . . ." (2 Pet. 3:16). And the warnings in the Epistle of James against those who say that faith suffices without works can hardly be understood in any other way than an attack upon a caricatured or poorly understood Paulinism.

Most important of all is the direct biographical account of Paul's career that comprises fully two-thirds of the Acts of the Apostles. The ordinary picture of the apostle's career owes more to Acts than to data which can be extracted from the letters. The vivid descriptions of the Damascus road Christophany and Paul's subsequent conversion are found only in Acts. The "three missionary journeys" are part of Luke's systematic plan; we could never reconstruct them from the letters alone. The dramatic speech on the Areopagus in Athens, the confrontation between Paul and his fellow Jews in synagogue after synagogue, the poignant farewell speech,

1. Cf. Hans Conzelmann, "Luke's Place in the Development of Early Christianity," in *Studies in Luke–Acts*, ed. Leander E. Keck and J. Louis Martyn (Nashville, 1966), pp. 307 f.

Paul's continuing dedication to the Jewish law and piety, the tumult in Jerusalem, the series of trials leading to Rome—all these would be missing from the standard biography of Paul but for the art of the unknown first-century historian.

But is the detailed account of Paul's career in Acts factually reliable? Not by far, in the opinion of some scholars, beginning with F. C. Baur in the last century (see his essay in Part V below). Significant aspects of the portrait, they argue, derive not from historical reminiscence, but from conventions of Hellenistic literary style and, more important, from the author's, rather than Paul's, theological perspective. A growing number of detailed investigations of the Lukan style have given weight to this position. Among them the essay by Vielhauer, excerpted below, has become a classic, though by no means without opposition.[2]

In the postapostolic period, polar views of Paul continued to be expressed. At one extreme were the Jewish-Christian groups such as the Ebionites who, because of their own continued devotion to the Law of Moses, were more concerned than the "catholics" with Paul's rejection of the law as a way of salvation, and who therefore rejected Paul. At the opposite extreme was the perplexing and fascinating figure of Marcion, who became convinced that Paul was the *only* true apostle of Christ, all the rest having been victims or perpetrators of a conspiracy against the truth. Since both Marcion and the Ebionites were pushed out of the main stream of the church, their writings have not survived. They have to be represented by fragments picked out of more orthodox documents, in most cases written by their opponents.

Paul's influence upon ascetic movements in Western Christianity, and the influence in turn of ascetic Christianity upon the common picture of Paul, are important enough to merit special attention. The apocryphal Acts of Paul and Thecla shows clearly how Encratite Christians pictured Paul's mission; it is prefaced by a historical sketch of Paul's place in the development of early asceticism.

Alongside these rather exotic portraits of Paul must be set the picture of the apostle that appears in the writings of the major catholic fathers. Maurice Wiles' judicious survey of the patristic commentaries on Paul's letters, from the earliest to Augustine, provides an excellent sketch of that image.

2. For a contrary point of view, defending the reliability of the Acts' portrait, see for example Alfred Wikenhauser, *Die Apostelgeschichte und ihr Geschichtswert* (1921; his position is summarized in his *New Testament Introduction* [1958], pp. 329–41); F. F. Bruce, *The Acts of the Apostles* (London, 1951), pp. 34–40; Johannes Munck, *The Acts of the Apostles* (The Anchor Bible, Garden City, N.Y., 1967), pp. LV–LXI.

"LUKE"

The Chosen Instrument (ca. 95) †

* * *

6 ⁷ And the word of God increased; and the number of the disciples multiplied greatly in Jerusalem, and a great many of the priests were obedient to the faith.

⁸ And Stephen, full of grace and power, did great wonders and signs among the people. ⁹ Then some of those who belonged to the synagogue of the Freedmen (as it was called), and of the Cyrenians, and of the Alexandrians, and of those from Cilicia and Asia, arose and disputed with Stephen. ¹⁰ But they could not withstand the wisdom and the Spirit with which he spoke. ¹¹ Then they secretly instigated men, who said, "We have heard him speak blasphemous words against Moses and God." ¹² And they stirred up the people and the elders and the scribes, and they came upon him and seized him and brought him before the council, ¹³ and set up false witnesses who said, "This man never ceases to speak words against this holy place and the law; ¹⁴ for we have heard him say that this Jesus of Nazareth will destroy this place, and will change the customs which Moses delivered to us." ¹⁵ And gazing at him, all who sat in the council saw that his face was like the face of an angel.

7 And the high priest said, "Is this so?" ² And Stephen said: "Brethren and fathers, hear me.

* * *

⁵¹ "You stiff-necked people, uncircumcised in heart and ears, you always resist the Holy Spirit. As your fathers did, so do you. ⁵² Which of the prophets did not your fathers persecute? And they killed those who announced beforehand the coming of the Righteous One, whom you have now betrayed and murdered, ⁵³ you who received the law as delivered by angels and did not keep it."

⁵⁴ Now when they heard these things they were enraged, and they ground their teeth against him. ⁵⁵ But he, full of the Holy

† From The Acts of the Apostles 6:7– 7:2; 7:51–8:3; 9:1–31; 11:19–30; 12:25–28:31; Revised Standard Version. The author of this work, the first volume of which is the Gospel According to Luke, has traditionally been iden-tified with the Luke who is mentioned occasionally in Pauline and deutero-Pauline letters as "the physician" and a companion of Paul (Phlm. 24; Col. 4:14; 2 Tim. 4:11).

Spirit, gazed into heaven and saw the glory of God, and Jesus standing at the right hand of God; 56 and he said, "Behold, I see the heavens opened, and the Son of man standing at the right hand of God." 57 But they cried out with a loud voice and stopped their ears and rushed together upon him. 58 Then they cast him out of the city and stoned him; and the witnesses laid down their garments at the feet of a young man named Saul. 59 And as they were stoning Stephen, he prayed, "Lord Jesus, receive my spirit." 60 And he knelt down and cried with a loud voice, "Lord, do not hold this sin against them." And when he had said this, he fell asleep. 8 And Saul was consenting to his death.

And on that day a great persecution arose against the church in Jerusalem; and they were all scattered throughout the region of Judea and Samaria, except the apostles. 2 Devout men buried Stephen, and made great lamentation over him. 3 But Saul laid waste the church, and entering house after house, he dragged off men and women and committed them to prison.

* * *

9 But Saul, still breathing threats and murder against the disciples of the Lord, went to the high priest 2 and asked him for letters to the synagogues at Damascus, so that if he found any belonging to the Way, men or women, he might bring them bound to Jerusalem. 3 Now as he journeyed he approached Damascus, and suddenly a light from heaven flashed about him. 4 And he fell to the ground and heard a voice saying to him, "Saul, Saul, why do you persecute me?" 5 And he said, "Who are you, Lord?" And he said, "I am Jesus, whom you are persecuting; 6 but rise and enter the city, and you will be told what you are to do." 7 The men who were traveling with him stood speechless, hearing the voice but seeing no one. 8 Saul arose from the ground; and when his eyes were opened, he could see nothing; so they led him by the hand and brought him into Damascus. 9 And for three days he was without sight, and neither ate nor drank.

10 Now there was a disciple at Damascus named Ananias. The Lord said to him in a vision, "Ananias." And he said, "Here I am, Lord." 11 And the Lord said to him, "Rise and go to the street called Straight, and inquire in the house of Judas for a man of Tarsus named Saul; for behold, he is praying, 12 and he has seen a man named Ananias come in and lay his hands on him so that he might regain his sight." 13 But Ananias answered, "Lord, I have heard from many about this man, how much evil he has done to thy saints at Jerusalem; 14 and here he has authority from the chief priests to bind all who call upon thy name." 15 But the Lord said

to him, "Go, for he is a chosen instrument of mine to carry my name before the Gentiles and kings and the sons of Israel; **16** for I will show him how much he must suffer for the sake of my name." **17** So Ananias departed and entered the house. And laying his hands on him he said, "Brother Saul, the Lord Jesus, who appeared to you on the road by which you came, has sent me that you may regain your sight and be filled with the Holy Spirit." **18** And immediately something like scales fell from his eyes and he regained his sight. Then he rose and was baptized, **19** and took food and was strengthened.

For several days he was with the disciples at Damascus. **20** And in the synagogues immediately he proclaimed Jesus, saying, "He is the Son of God." **21** And all who heard him were amazed, and said, "Is not this the man who made havoc in Jerusalem of those who called on this name? And he has come here for this purpose, to bring them bound before the chief priests." **22** But Saul increased all the more in strength, and confounded the Jews who lived in Damascus by proving that Jesus was the Christ.

23 When many days had passed, the Jews plotted to kill him, **24** but their plot became known to Saul. They were watching the gates day and night, to kill him; **25** but his disciples took him by night and let him down over the wall, lowering him in a basket.

26 And when he had come to Jerusalem he attempted to join the disciples; and they were all afraid of him, for they did not believe that he was a disciple. **27** But Barnabas took him, and brought him to the apostles, and declared to them how on the road he had seen the Lord, who spoke to him, and how at Damascus he had preached boldly in the name of Jesus. **28** So he went in and out among them at Jerusalem, **29** preaching boldly in the name of the Lord. And he spoke and disputed against the Hellenists; but they were seeking to kill him. **30** And when the brethren knew it, they brought him down to Caesarea, and sent him off to Tarsus.

31 So the church throughout all Judea and Galilee and Samaria had peace and was built up; and walking in the fear of the Lord and in the comfort of the Holy Spirit it was multiplied.

* * *

11 **19** Now those who were scattered because of the persecution that arose over Stephen traveled as far as Phoenicia and Cyprus and Antioch, speaking the word to none except Jews. **20** But there were some of them, men of Cyprus and Cyrene, who on coming to Antioch spoke to the Greeks[1] also, preaching the Lord Jesus. **21** And the hand of the Lord was with them, and a great number

1. Other ancient authorities read "Hellenists."

that believed turned to the Lord. 22 News of this came to the ears of the church in Jerusalem, and they sent Barnabas to Antioch. 23 When he came and saw the grace of God, he was glad; and he exhorted them all to remain faithful to the Lord with steadfast purpose; 24 for he was a good man, full of the Holy Spirit and of faith. And a large company was added to the Lord. 25 So Barnabas went to Tarsus to look for Saul; 26 and when he had found him, he brought him to Antioch. For a whole year they met with[2] the church, and taught a large company of people; and in Antioch the disciples were for the first time called Christians.

* * *

[A *trip to Jerusalem with famine relief for the church there sets the stage for Paul's "first missionary journey," which is described in Chaps.* 13–14. *It takes him and Barnabas as far as Pisidia, in Asia Minor.*]

14 24 Then they passed through Pisidia, and came to Pamphylia. 25 And when they had spoken the word in Perga, they went down to Attalia; 26 and from there they sailed to Antioch, where they had been commended to the grace of God for the work which they had fulfilled. 27 And when they arrived, they gathered the church together and declared all that God had done with them, and how he had opened a door of faith to the Gentiles. 28 And they remained no little time with the disciples.

15 But some men came down from Judea and were teaching the brethren, "Unless you are circumcised according to the custom of Moses, you cannot be saved." 2 And when Paul and Barnabas had no small dissension and debate with them, Paul and Barnabas and some of the others were appointed to go up to Jerusalem to the apostles and the elders about this question. 3 So, being sent on their way by the church, they passed through both Phoenicia and Samaria, reporting the conversion of the Gentiles, and they gave great joy to all the brethren. 4 When they came to Jerusalem, they were welcomed by the church and the apostles and the elders, and they declared all that God had done with them. 5 But some believers who belonged to the party of the Pharisees rose up, and said, "It is necessary to circumcise them, and to charge them to keep the law of Moses."

6 The apostles and the elders were gathered together to consider this matter. 7 And after there had been much debate, Peter rose and said to them, "Brethren, you know that in the early days God made choice among you, that by my mouth the Gentiles should

2. Or, "were guests of."

hear the word of the gospel and believe. **8** And God who knows the heart bore witness to them, giving them the Holy Spirit just as he did to us; **9** and he made no distinction between us and them, but cleansed their hearts by faith. **10** Now therefore why do you make trial of God by putting a yoke upon the neck of the disciples which neither our fathers nor we have been able to bear? **11** But we believe that we shall be saved through the grace of the Lord Jesus, just as they will."

12 And all the assembly kept silence; and they listened to Barnabas and Paul as they related what signs and wonders God had done through them among the Gentiles. **13** After they finished speaking, James replied, "Brethren, listen to me. **14** Symeon has related how God first visited the Gentiles, to take out of them a people for his name. **15** And with this the words of the prophets agree, as it is written,

> **16** 'After this I will return,
> and I will rebuild the dwelling of David, which has fallen;
> I will rebuild its ruins,
> and I will set it up,
> **17** that the rest of men may seek the Lord,
> and all the Gentiles who are called by my name,
> **18** says the Lord, who has made these things known from of old.'

19 Therefore my judgment is that we should not trouble those of the Gentiles who turn to God, **20** but should write to them to abstain from the pollutions of idols and from unchastity and from what is strangled[3] and from blood. **21** For from early generations Moses has had in every city those who preach him, for he is read every sabbath in the synagogues."

22 Then it seemed good to the apostles and the elders, with the whole church, to choose men from among them and send them to Antioch with Paul and Barnabas. They sent Judas called Barsabbas, and Silas, leading men among the brethren, **23** with the following letter: "The brethren, both the apostles and the elders, to the brethren who are of the Gentiles in Antioch and Syria and Cilicia, greeting. **24** Since we have heard that some persons from us have troubled you with words, unsettling your minds, although we gave them no instructions, **25** it has seemed good to us in assembly to choose men and send them to you with our beloved Barnabas and Paul, **26** men who have risked their lives for the sake of our Lord Jesus Christ. **27** We have therefore sent Judas and Silas, who themselves will tell you the same things by word of mouth. **28** For it has seemed good to the Holy Spirit and to us to lay upon you no greater burden than these necessary things: **29** that you abstain

---

3. Other early authorities omit "and from what is strangled."

from what has been sacrificed to idols and from blood and from what is strangled[4] and from unchastity. If you keep yourselves from these, you will do well. Farewell."

30 So when they were sent off, they went down to Antioch; and having gathered the congregation together, they delivered the letter. 31 And when they read it, they rejoiced at the exhortation. 32 And Judas and Silas, who were themselves prophets, exhorted the brethren with many words and strengthened them. 33 And after they had spent some time, they were sent off in peace by the brethren to those who had sent them.[5] 35 But Paul and Barnabas remained in Antioch, teaching and preaching the word of the Lord, with many others also.

36 And after some days Paul said to Barnabas, "Come, let us return and visit the brethren in every city where we proclaimed the word of the Lord, and see how they are." 37 And Barnabas wanted to take with them John called Mark. 38 But Paul thought best not to take with them one who had withdrawn from them in Pamphylia, and had not gone with them to the work. 39 And there arose a sharp contention, so that they separated from each other; Barnabas took Mark with him and sailed away to Cyprus, 40 but Paul chose Silas and departed, being commended by the brethren to the grace of the Lord. 41 And he went through Syria and Cilicia, strengthening the churches.

16 And he came also to Derbe and to Lystra. A disciple was there, named Timothy, the son of a Jewish woman who was a believer; but his father was a Greek. 2 He was well spoken of by the brethren at Lystra and Iconium. 3 Paul wanted Timothy to accompany him; and he took him and circumcised him because of the Jews that were in those places, for they all knew that his father was a Greek. 4 As they went on their way through the cities, they delivered to them for observance the decisions which had been reached by the apostles and elders who were at Jerusalem. 5 So the churches were strengthened in the faith, and they increased in numbers daily.

* * *

[*Directed by a vision, Paul enters Macedonia, where, in Philippi, he soon wins converts. The cure of a demoniac prophetess, however, leads to arrest for disturbing the peace. After miraculous signs and the conversion of the jailer, Paul and Silas are released, but forced to leave town.*]

4. Other early authorities omit "and from what is strangled."
5. Other ancient authorities insert v.

34, "But it seemed good to Silas to remain there."

17 Now when they had passed through Amphipolis and Apollonia, they came to Thessalonica, where there was a synagogue of the Jews. **2** And Paul went in, as was his custom, and for three weeks[6] he argued with them from the scriptures, **3** explaining and proving that it was necessary for the Christ to suffer and to rise from the dead, and saying, "This Jesus, whom I proclaim to you, is the Christ." **4** And some of them were persuaded, and joined Paul and Silas; as did a great many of the devout Greeks and not a few of the leading women. **5** But the Jews were jealous, and taking some wicked fellows of the rabble, they gathered a crowd, set the city in an uproar, and attacked the house of Jason, seeking to bring them out to the people. **6** And when they could not find them, they dragged Jason and some of the brethren before the city authorities, crying, "These men who have turned the world upside down have come here also, **7** and Jason has received them; and they are all acting against the decrees of Caesar, saying that there is another king, Jesus." **8** And the people and the city authorities were disturbed when they heard this. **9** And when they had taken security from Jason and the rest, they let them go.

10 The brethren immediately sent Paul and Silas away by night to Beroea; and when they arrived they went into the Jewish synagogue. **11** Now these Jews were more noble than those in Thessalonica, for they received the word with all eagerness, examining the scriptures daily to see if these things were so. **12** Many of them therefore believed, with not a few Greek women of high standing as well as men. **13** But when the Jews of Thessalonica learned that the word of God was proclaimed by Paul at Boroea also, they came there too, stirring up and inciting the crowds. **14** Then the brethren immediately sent Paul off on his way to the sea, but Silas and Timothy remained there. **15** Those who conducted Paul brought him as far as Athens; and receiving a command for Silas and Timothy to come to him as soon as possible, they departed.

16 Now while Paul was waiting for them at Athens, his spirit was provoked within him as he saw that the city was full of idols. **17** So he argued in the synagogue with the Jews and the devout persons, and in the market place every day with those who chanced to be there. **18** Some also of the Epicurean and Stoic philosophers met him. And some said, "What would this babbler say?" Others said, "He seems to be a preacher of foreign divinities"—because he preached Jesus and the resurrection. **19** And they took hold of him and brought him to the Areopagus, saying, "May we know what this new teaching is which you present? **20** For you bring some strange things to our ears; we wish to know therefore what these things mean." **21** Now all the Athenians and the foreigners who

6. Or, "sabbaths."

lived there spent their time in nothing except telling or hearing something new.

22 So Paul, standing in the middle of the Areopagus, said: "Men of Athens, I perceive that in every way you are very religious. 23 For as I passed along and observed the objects of your worship, I found also an altar with this inscription, 'To an unknown god.' What therefore you worship as unknown, this I proclaim to you. 24 The God who made the world and everything in it, being Lord of heaven and earth, does not live in shrines made by man, 25 nor is he served by human hands, as though he needed anything, since he himself gives to all men life and breath and everything. 26 And he made from one every nation of men to live on all the face of the earth, having determined allotted periods and the boundaries of their habitation, 27 that they should seek God, in the hope that they might feel after him and find him. Yet he is not far from each one of us, 28 for

'In him we live and move and have our being';
as even some of your poets have said,
'For we are indeed his offspring.'

29 Being then God's offspring, we ought not to think that the Deity is like gold, or silver, or stone, a representation by the art and imagination of man. 30 The times of ignorance God overlooked, but now he commands all men everywhere to repent, 31 because he has fixed a day on which he will judge the world in righteousness by a man whom he has appointed, and of this he has given assurance to all men by raising him from the dead."

32 Now when they heard of the resurrection of the dead, some mocked; but others said, "We will hear you again about this." 33 So Paul went out from among them. 34 But some men joined him and believed, among them Dionysius the Areopagite and a woman named Damaris and others with them.

* * *

[*The following chapters tell of Paul's work in Corinth, Ephesus, and elsewhere, and a brief visit to Jerusalem (18:22). His trial before Gallio, proconsul of Achaia (18:12–17) provides the one occasion in Paul's life that can be rather precisely dated by modern scholarship.*]

19 21 Now after these events Paul resolved in the Spirit to pass through Macedonia and Achaia and go to Jerusalem, saying, "After I have been there, I must also see Rome."

* * *

[*The artisans and worshipers of Artemis, disturbed by Paul's success, provoke a near riot in Ephesus. Paul departs for Macedonia. After working there until after Passover, he begins his final journey to Jerusalem, pausing en route in Miletus.*]

20 ¹⁷ And from Miletus he sent to Ephesus and called to him the elders of the church. ¹⁸ And when they came to him, he said to them:

"You yourselves know how I lived among you all the time from the first day that I set foot in Asia, ¹⁹ serving the Lord with all humility and with tears and with trials which befell me through the plots of the Jews; ²⁰ how I did not shrink from declaring to you anything that was profitable, and teaching you in public and from house to house, ²¹ testifying both to Jews and to Greeks of repentance to God and of faith in our Lord Jesus Christ. ²² And now, behold, I am going to Jerusalem, bound in the Spirit, not knowing what shall befall me there; ²³ except that the Holy Spirit testifies to me in every city that imprisonment and afflictions await me. ²⁴ But I do not account my life of any value nor as precious to myself, if only I may accomplish my course and the ministry which I received from the Lord Jesus, to testify to the gospel of the grace of God. ²⁵ And now, behold, I know that all you among whom I have gone about preaching the kingdom will see my face no more. ²⁶ Therefore I testify to you this day that I am innocent of the blood of all of you, ²⁷ for I did not shrink from declaring to you the whole counsel of God. ²⁸ Take heed to yourselves and to all the flock, in which the Holy Spirit has made you guardians, to feed the church of the Lord[7] which he obtained with his own blood.[8] ²⁹ I know that after my departure fierce wolves will come in among you, not sparing the flock; ³⁰ and from among your own selves will arise men speaking perverse things, to draw away the disciples after them. ³¹ Therefore be alert, remembering that for three years I did not cease night or day to admonish every one with tears. ³² And now I commend you to God and to the word of his grace, which is able to build you up and to give you the inheritance among all those who are sanctified. ³³ I coveted no one's silver or gold or apparel. ³⁴ You yourselves know that these hands ministered to my necessities, and to those who were with me. ³⁵ In all things I have shown you that by so toiling one must help the weak, remembering the words of the Lord Jesus, how he said, 'It is more blessed to give than to receive.' "

7. Other ancient authorities read, "of God." 8. Or, "with the blood of his Own."

36 And when he had spoken thus, he knelt down and prayed with them all. **37** And they all wept and embraced Paul and kissed him, **38** sorrowing most of all because of the word he had spoken, that they should see his face no more. And they brought him to the ship.

* * *

21 **7** When we had finished the voyage from Tyre, we arrived at Ptolemais; and we greeted the brethren and stayed with them for one day. **8** On the morrow we departed and came to Caesarea; and we entered the house of Philip the evangelist, who was one of the seven, and stayed with him. **9** And he had four unmarried daughters, who prophesied. **10** While we were staying for some days, a prophet named Agabus came down from Judea. **11** And coming to us he took Paul's girdle and bound his own feet and hands, and said, "Thus says the Holy Spirit, 'So shall the Jews at Jerusalem bind the man who owns this girdle and deliver him into the hands of the Gentiles.' " **12** When we heard this, we and the people there begged him not to go up to Jerusalem. **13** Then Paul answered, "What are you doing, weeping and breaking my heart? For I am ready not only to be imprisoned but even to die at Jerusalem for the name of the Lord Jesus." **14** And when he would not be persuaded, we ceased and said, "The will of the Lord be done."

15 After these days we made ready and went up to Jerusalem. **16** And some of the disciples from Caesarea went with us, bringing us to the house of Mnason of Cyprus, an early disciple, with whom we should lodge.

17 When we had come to Jerusalem, the brethren received us gladly. **18** On the following day Paul went in with us to James; and all the elders were present. **19** After greeting them, he related one by one the things that God had done among the Gentiles through his ministry. **20** And when they heard it, they glorified God. And they said to him, "You see, brother, how many thousands there are among the Jews of those who have believed; they are all zealous for the law, **21** and they have been told about you that you teach all the Jews who are among the Gentiles to forsake Moses, telling them not to circumcise their children or observe the customs. **22** What then is to be done? They will certainly hear that you have come. **23** Do therefore what we tell you. We have four men who are under a vow; **24** take these men and purify yourself along with them and pay their expenses, so that they may shave their heads. Thus all will know that there is nothing in what they have been told about you but that you yourself live in observance of the law. **25** But as for the Gentiles who have believed, we have sent a letter with our judgment that they should abstain from what has been sacrificed to idols and from blood and from what is strangled[9] and from unchastity." 26 Then Paul took the men, and the next day he purified himself with them and went into the temple, to give notice when the days of purification would be fulfilled and the offering presented for every one of them.

27 When the seven days were almost completed, the Jews from Asia, who had seen him in the temple, stirred up all the crowd, and laid hands on him, 28 crying out, "Men of Israel, help! This is the man who is teaching men everywhere against the people and the law and this place; moreover he also brought Greeks into the temple and he has defiled this holy place." 29 For they had previously seen Trophimus the Ephesian with him in the city, and they supposed that Paul had brought him into the temple. 30 Then all the city was aroused, and the people ran together; they seized Paul and dragged him out of the temple, and at once the gates were shut. 31 And as they were trying to kill him, word came to the tribune of the cohort that all Jerusalem was in confusion. 32 He at once took soldiers and centurions, and ran down to them; and when they saw the tribune and the soldiers, they stopped beating Paul. 33 Then the tribune came up and arrested him, and ordered him to be bound with two chains. He inquired who he was and what he had done. 34 Some in the crowd shouted one thing, some another; and as he could not learn the facts because of the uproar, he ordered him to be brought into the barracks. 35 And when he came to the steps, he was actually carried by the soldiers because of the violence of the crowd; 36 for the mob of the people followed, crying, "Away with him!"

*　*　*

[*Paul makes a speech to the mob, recounting the story of his conversion. His defense before the council and chief priests the next day cleverly exploits the division between Pharisees and Sadducees on belief in resurrection. Transferred to Caesarea to avoid a plot to lynch him, Paul is next tried before the procurator Felix, who delays Paul's case for two years, until Porcius Festus succeeds to the governorship.*]

25 Now when Festus had come into his province, after three days he went up to Jerusalem from Caesarea. 2 And the chief priests and the principal men of the Jews informed him against Paul; and they urged him, 3 asking as a favor to have the man sent to Jerusalem, planning an ambush to kill him on the way. 4 Festus

---

9. Other early authorities omit "and from what has been strangled."

replied that Paul was being kept at Caesarea, and that he himself intended to go there shortly. 5 "So," said he, "let the men of authority among you go down with me, and if there is anything wrong about the man, let them accuse him."

6 When he had stayed among them not more than eight or ten days, he went down to Caesarea; and the next day he took his seat on the tribunal and ordered Paul to be brought. 7 And when he had come, the Jews who had gone down from Jerusalem stood about him, bringing against him many serious charges which they could not prove. 8 Paul said in his defense, "Neither against the law of the Jews, nor against the temple, nor against Caesar have I offended at all." 9 But Festus, wishing to do the Jews a favor, said to Paul, "Do you wish to go up to Jerusalem, and there be tried on these charges before me?" 10 But Paul said, "I am standing before Caesar's tribunal, where I ought to be tried; to the Jews I have done no wrong, as you know very well. 11 If then I am a wrong-doer, and have committed anything for which I deserve to die, I do not seek to escape death; but if there is nothing in their charges against me, no one can give me up to them. I appeal to Caesar." 12 Then Festus, when he had conferred with his council, answered, "You have appealed to Caesar; to Caesar you shall go."

13 Now when some days had passed, Agrippa the king and Bernice arrived at Caesarea to welcome Festus. 14 And as they stayed there many days, Festus laid Paul's case before the king, saying, "There is a man left prisoner by Felix; 15 and when I was at Jerusalem, the chief priests and the elders of the Jews gave information about him, asking for sentence against him. 16 I answered them that it was not the custom of the Romans to give up any one before the accused met the accusers face to face, and had opportunity to make his defense concerning the charge laid against him. 17 When therefore they came together here, I made no delay, but on the next day took my seat on the tribunal and ordered the man to be brought in. 18 When the accusers stood up, they brought no charge in his case of such evils as I supposed; 19 but they had certain points of dispute with him about their own superstition and about one Jesus, who was dead, but whom Paul asserted to be alive. 20 Being at a loss how to investigate these questions, I asked whether he wished to go to Jerusalem and be tried there regarding them. 21 But when Paul had appealed to be kept in custody for the decision of the emperor, I commanded him to be held until I could send him to Caesar." 22 And Agrippa said to Festus, "I should like to hear the man myself." "Tomorrow," said he, "you shall hear him."

23 So on the morrow Agrippa and Bernice came with great pomp, and they entered the audience hall with the military tribunes and

the prominent men of the city. Then by command of Festus Paul was brought in. 24 And Festus said, "King Agrippa and all who are present with us, you see this man about whom the whole Jewish people petitioned me, both at Jerusalem and here, shouting that he ought not to live any longer. 25 But I found that he had done nothing deserving death; and as he himself appealed to the emperor, I decided to send him. 26 But I have nothing definite to write to my lord about him. Therefore I have brought him before you, and, especially before you, King Agrippa, that, after we have examined him, I may have something to write. 27 For it seems' to me unreasonable, in sending a prisoner, not to indicate the charges against him."

26 Agrippa said to Paul, "You have permission to speak for yourself." Then Paul stretched out his hand and made his defense:

2 "I think myself fortunate that it is before you, King Agrippa, I am to make my defense today against all the accusations of the Jews, 3 because you are especially familiar with all customs and controversies of the Jews; therefore I beg you to listen to me patiently.

4 "My manner of life from my youth, spent from the beginning among my own nation and at Jerusalem, is known by all the Jews. 5 They have known for a long time, if they are willing to testify, that according to the strictest party of our religion I have lived as a Pharisee. 6 And now I stand here on trial for hope in the promise made by God to our fathers, 7 to which our twelve tribes hope to attain, as they earnestly worship night and day. And for this hope I am accused by Jews, O king! 8 Why is it thought incredible by any of you that God raises the dead?

9 "I myself was convinced that I ought to do many things in opposing the name of Jesus of Nazareth. 10 And I did so in Jerusalem; I not only shut up many of the saints in prison, by authority from the chief priests, but when they were put to death I cast my vote against them. 11 And I punished them often in all the synagogues and tried to make them blaspheme; and in raging fury against them, I persecuted them even to foreign cities.

12 "Thus I journeyed to Damascus with the authority and commission of the chief priests. 13 At midday, O king, I saw on the way a light from heaven, brighter than the sun, shining round me and those who journeyed with me. 14 And when we had all fallen to the ground, I heard a voice saying to me in the Hebrew language, 'Saul, Saul, why do you persecute me? It hurts you to kick against the goads.' 15 And I said, 'Who are you, Lord?' And the Lord said, 'I am Jesus whom you are persecuting. 16 But rise and stand upon your feet; for I have appeared to you for this purpose, to appoint you to serve and bear witness to the things in which you

have seen me and to those in which I will appear to you,
17 delivering you from the people and from the Gentiles—to
whom I send you **18** to open their eyes, that they may turn from
darkness to light and from the power of Satan to God, that they
may receive forgiveness of sins and a place among those who are
sanctified by faith in me.'

19 "Wherefore, O King Agrippa, I was not disobedient to the
heavenly vision, **20** but declared first to those at Damascus, then at
Jerusalem and throughout all the country of Judea, and also to the
Gentiles, that they should repent and turn to God and perform
deeds worthy of their repentance. **21** For this reason the Jews
seized me in the temple and tried to kill me. **22** To this day I have
had the help that comes from God, and so I stand here testifying
both to small and great, saying nothing but what the prophets and
Moses said would come to pass: **23** that the Christ must suffer, and
that, by being the first to rise from the dead, he would proclaim
light both to the people and to the Gentiles."

24 And as he thus made his defense, Festus said with a loud
voice, "Paul, you are mad; your great learning is turning you mad."
25 But Paul said, "I am not mad, most excellent Festus, but I am
speaking the sober truth. **26** For the king knows about these things
and to him I speak freely; for I am persuaded that none of these
things has escaped his notice, for this was not done in a corner.
27 King Agrippa, do you believe the prophets? I know that you
believe." **28** And Agrippa said to Paul, "In a short time you think
to make me a Christian!" **29** And Paul said, "Whether short or
long, I would to God that not only you but also all who hear me
this day might become such as I am—except for these chains."

30 Then the king rose, and the governor and Bernice and those
who were sitting with them; **31** and when they had withdrawn,
they said to one another, "This man is doing nothing to deserve
death or imprisonment." **32** And Agrippa said to Festus, "This
man could have been set free if he had not appealed to Caesar."

27 And when it was decided that we should sail for Italy, they
delivered Paul and some other prisoners to a centurion of the
Augustan Cohort, named Julius. **2** And embarking in a ship of
Adramyttium, which was about to sail to the ports along the coast
of Asia, we put to sea, accompanied by Aristarchus, a Macedonian
from Thessalonica. **3** The next day we put in at Sidon; and Julius
treated Paul kindly, and gave him leave to go to his friends and be
cared for. **4** And putting to sea from there we sailed under the lee
of Cyprus, because the winds were against us. **5** And when we had
sailed across the sea which is off Cilicia and Pamphylia, we came to
Myra in Lycia. **6** There the centurion found a ship of Alexandria
sailing for Italy, and put us on board.

* * *

[*The omitted portions describe the voyage, including a shipwreck on Malta. Paul's prescience and his miraculous recovery from the bite of a viper, as well as other miracles, are important aspects of the Acts' portrait.*]

28 ¹¹ After three months we set sail in a ship which had wintered in the island, a ship of Alexandria, with the Twin Brothers as figurehead. ¹² Putting in at Syracuse, we stayed there for three days. ¹³ And from there we made a circuit and arrived at Rhegium; and after one day a south wind sprang up, and on the second day we came to Puteoli. ¹⁴ There we found brethren, and were invited to stay with them for seven days. And so we came to Rome. ¹⁵ And the brethren there, when they heard of us, came as far as the Forum of Appius and Three Taverns to meet us. On seeing them Paul thanked God and took courage. ¹⁶ And when we came into Rome, Paul was allowed to stay by himself, with the soldier that guarded him.

¹⁷ After three days he called together the local leaders of the Jews; and when they had gathered, he said to them, "Brethren, though I had done nothing against the people or the customs of our fathers, yet I was delivered prisoner from Jerusalem into the hands of the Romans. ¹⁸ When they had examined me, they wished to set me at liberty, because there was no reason for the death penalty in my case. ¹⁹ But when the Jews objected, I was compelled to appeal to Caesar—though I had no charge to bring against my nation. ²⁰ For this reason therefore I have asked to see you and speak with you, since it is because of the hope of Israel that I am bound with this chain." ²¹ And they said to him, "We have received no letters from Judea about you, and none of the brethren coming here has reported or spoken any evil about you. ²² But we desire to hear from you what your views are; for with regard to this sect we know that everywhere it is spoken against."

²³ When they had appointed a day for him, they came to him at his lodging in great numbers. And he expounded the matter to them from morning till evening, testifying to the kingdom of God and trying to convince them about Jesus both from the law of Moses and from the prophets. ²⁴ And some were convinced by what he said, while others disbelieved. ²⁵ So, as they disagreed among themselves, they departed, after Paul had made one statement: "The Holy Spirit was right in saying to your fathers through Isaiah the prophet:

²⁶ 'Go to this people, and say,
You shall indeed hear but never understand,

and you shall indeed see but never perceive.
27 For this people's heart has grown dull,
and their ears are heavy of hearing,
and their eyes they have closed;
lest they should perceive with their eyes,
and hear with their ears,
and understand with their heart,
and turn for me to heal them.'

28 Let it be known to you then that this salvation of God has been sent to the Gentiles; they will listen."[1]

30 And he lived there two whole years at his own expense,[2] and welcomed all who came to him, **31** preaching the kingdom of God and teaching about the Lord Jesus Christ quite openly and unhindered.

PHILIPP VIELHAUER

On the "Paulinism" of Acts (1950) †

The following discussion poses the question whether and to what extent the author of Acts took over and passed on theological ideas of Paul, whether and to what extent he modified them. (I refer to the author of Acts as Luke, for the sake of brevity and in order to identify him with the author of the Third Gospel. I do not thereby equate him with the physician and companion of Paul whom tradition has identified as the author of the two-volume work, Luke and Acts.) Although one would hardly expect from Acts a compendium of Pauline theology, the question which we put is nonetheless justified, for the author portrays Paul as a missionary and thereby also as a theologian, at least in his speeches, which are generally acknowledged to be compositions of the author and which, according to ancient literary custom, had deliberate and paradigmatic significance.[1] The way in which the author presents Paul's theology

1. Other ancient authorities add v. 29, "And when he had said these words, the Jews departed, holding much dispute among themselves."
2. Or, "in his own hired dwelling."
† From an essay first published in *Evangelische Theologie* 10 (1950-51): 1-15; tr. by Wm. C. Robinson, Jr., and Victor P. Furnish, in *Perkins School of Theology Journal* 17 (1963) and *Studies in Luke–Acts*, ed. Leander E. Keck and J. Louis Martyn

(Nashville, 1966), pp. 33-50. Vielhauer (b. 1914) is Professor of New Testament at Bonn University.
1. See M. Dibelius, "The Speeches in Acts and Ancient Historiography" (1949) in *Studies in the Acts of the Apostles* (New York, 1956). Unless otherwise designated, all subsequent references to Dibelius will be to this volume of collected essays, although in each case the original publication date will be indicated.

will not only disclose his own understanding of Paul, but will also indicate whether or not he and Paul belong together theologically.

*   *   *

Since this discussion is focused upon the theology involved, we leave aside the question whether Acts gives an accurate portrayal of the person and history of Paul and of his relationship to the earliest congregation, and also the question (which dominated the work of the Tübingen School) as to the party conflicts within the church which lay behind the discrepancy between the Pauline and Lucan accounts of the same historical events and conditions. We restrict ourselves to the elements of the Lucan portrayal of Paul which characterize him as a theologian; that is, we limit ourselves primarily if not exclusively to his speeches and group the theological statements of the Paul of Acts under four headings: natural theology, law, Christology, and eschatology, and compare them with statements on these themes from the letters of Paul.

I

At the high point of his book Luke lets Paul make a speech at the Areopagus in Athens before Stoic and Epicurean philosophers, the only sermon to Gentiles by the missionary to the Gentiles to be found in Acts. In the formal opening of his address the speaker takes his point of departure from an altar inscription, "To an unknown God," and says to his hearers: "What therefore you worship as unknown, this I proclaim to you." (Acts 17:22–23). Then he speaks of God, the creator and Lord of the world, who needs no temple to honor him because he is without need (vv. 24 f.), of the divine providence which so determines men that they should seek God (vv. 26 f.), and their kinship to God which excludes the veneration of images (vv. 28 f.). At the conclusion he gives a call to repentance in view of the impending day of judgment "on which God will judge the world in righteousness by a man whom he has appointed, and of this he has given assurance to all men by raising him from the dead" (vv. 30 f.).

In his study "Paul on the Areopagus"[2] Martin Dibelius has carefully analyzed the Areopagus speech as a whole and in its individual motifs, and has come to the convincing conclusions (1) that the speech was conceived as an example of a sermon to Gentiles, (2) that it comes from Luke and not from Paul, and (3) that the speech, looked at from the viewpoint of the comparative study of religion, is a "Hellenistic speech about the true knowledge of

2. *Op. cit.*, pp. 26–77.

God,"[3] which becomes a Christian speech only at its conclusion.[4]

The speech presupposes on the part of its Gentile hearers a presentiment of the true God and seeks by enlightenment to advance this presentiment to a monotheistic idea of God and to a worship of God without images. It describes God as the creator and Lord of the world (vv. 24 f.); yet the Old Testament idea is hellenized both by the concept "cosmos" and by the motif of God's having no needs, both of which are foreign to the Old Testament and are of Hellenistic, specifically Stoic, origin.[5]

* * *

The conclusion of the speech presents judgment as the motivation to repentance, mentions Jesus (without naming him) and his resurrection as proof of his election (vv. 30 f.), but does not mention the saving significance of his death. Indeed, due to the natural kinship to God and the fact that the knowledge of God is vitiated only through ignorance, this is not necessary. The repentance which is called for consists entirely in the self-consciousness of one's natural kinship to God.[6]

Paul also speaks of the pagan's natural knowledge of God: "for what can be known about God is plain to them, because God has shown it to them. Ever since the creation of the world his invisible nature, namely, his eternal power and deity, has been clearly perceived in the things that have been made" (Rom. 1:19 f.). It has long been recognized and acknowledged that this terminology and viewpoint came from Stoic natural theology. Both for Stoicism and for Paul to know God from nature as creator is at the same time to know oneself, insofar as in this knowledge man understands himself in his relationship to God and in his orientation within the cosmos which is ordered and determined by the divine logos.[7] However in Paul the assertion of the natural knowledge of God is surrounded by statements about God's wrath and human guilt; this knowledge of God has led neither to honoring nor to thanking God (v. 21), but to "ungodliness" and "wickedness" in "suppressing the truth" (v. 18) and therefore has called forth the "wrath of God" (v. 18). Paul states the result of this natural knowledge of God unequivocally: "they are without excuse" (v. 20).

In the Areopagus speech the worship of images was an indication of "ignorance," but was by no means inexcusable; "you worship as unknown," says Paul on the Areopagus (Acts 17:23), "although

3. *Ibid.*, p. 57.
4. *Ibid.*, pp. 27, 56.
5. *Ibid.*, pp. 38–46.
6. *Ibid.*, p. 58.

7. Bultmann, "Anknüpfung und Widerspruch," *Theologische Zeitschrift* II (1946), 401 f.; see also his *Primitive Christianity* (1955), pp. 135 ff.

they knew God they did not honor him as God," says Paul in Romans (1:21), and that is "ungodliness" and "wickedness." But this means that the natural theology has an utterly different function in Rom. 1 and in Acts 17; in the former passage it functions as an aid to the demonstration of human responsibility and is thereafter immediately dropped; in the latter passage it is evaluated positively and employed in missionary pedagogy as a forerunner of faith: the natural knowledge of God needs only to be purified, corrected, and enlarged, but its basic significance is not questioned. "Grace does not destroy nature but presupposes and completes it."

In Paul there is no parallel to the motif of man's kinship to God. Dibelius rightly points out that the Pauline analogue to this is man's nearness to Christ; Paul speaks of fellowship with Christ, not of fellowship with God, and the man who participates in this fellowship is not the natural man but rather the redeemed man.[8] By sin the natural man is essentially separated from God and hostile to God. The connection with God is only established through Christ, through his death on the cross, whereby God judges and pardons the world (II Cor. 5:20 f.; Rom. 3:25 f.). Only "in Christ" is man united with God. It is no accident that in the Areopagus speech the concepts "sin" and "grace" are lacking, not only the words, but also the ideas. Due to its kinship to God the human race is capable of a natural knowledge of God and of ethics (Acts 10:35) and has immediate access to God. The "word of the cross" has no place in the Areopagus speech because it would make no sense there; it would be "folly." The author of this speech has eliminated Christology from Paul's sermon to the Gentiles.

To be sure this speech functions only as preliminary instruction, but at this place in Acts and in the function which the author intends it to fulfill it is a self-contained whole. The basic difference from the Pauline view of Christian and pre-Christian existence cannot be ignored. When the Areopagus speaker refers to the unity of the human race in its natural kinship to God and to its natural knowledge of God, and when he refers to the altar inscription and to the statements of pagan poets to make this point, he thereby lays claim to pagan history, culture, and religion as the prehistory of Christianity. His distance from Paul is just as clear as his nearness to the apologists. Justin, for example, counted the Greek philosophers and the righteous men among the barbarians just as much the forefathers of Christianity as were the patriarchs; however he gave this thesis a christological basis, in that he maintained that these men partook of the logos which is identical with Christ.[9]

8. Dibelius, p. 60.
9. *Apology* I, 5.4; II, 10; 13.4. Cf. B. Seeberg, *Zeitschrift für Kirchenge-* *schichte*, LVIII (1939), 1–81, esp. 53–69; 76–81.

II

Acts depicts Paul's attitude toward the ancient religion of the Jews just as positively as the Areopagus speech presents his attitude toward the ancient religion of the Greeks. His attitude toward the law is reflected in Acts less in basic discussions in his speeches than in his practical attitude toward Judaism and Jewish Christianity. This attitude is characterized by the following aspects (of which only those of basic significance will be discussed here):

1. By his missionary method: beginning at the synagogue; only after a formal rejection by the Jews does he turn directly to the Gentiles;

2. By his submission to the Jerusalem authorities;

3. By the circumcision of Timothy (16:3);

4. By spreading the apostolic decree (16:4) (nonhistorical);

5. By assuming a vow (18:18);

6. By trips to Jerusalem to participate in Jewish religious festivals (18:21; 20:16). In Rom. 15:25 Paul gives as the reason for his last trip to Jerusalem the collection for the congregation, whereas Acts 24:17 combines both reasons: "to bring my nation alms and offerings." But the account in Acts, having said nothing previously about the collection, thus places the major emphasis upon participation in Jewish worship;

7. By participating, on the advice of James, in a Nazirite vow with four members of the Jerusalem congregation (21:18–28);

8. By stressing when on trial that he is a Pharisee (23:6; 26:5) and that he stands for nothing other than the "hope" of the Jews in the resurrection of the dead.

Acts portrays the Gentile missionary Paul as a Jewish Christian who is utterly loyal to the law. Or more precisely said, it pictures him as a true Jew, since he believes in Jesus as the Messiah in contrast to the Jews who have been hardened, who do not share this faith. This portrayal of Paul in Acts is vigorously challenged as well as untiringly defended. According to Paul's letters, however, the Acts' portrayal of his attitude seems to be quite possible with one or two exceptions; whether it is also historical is another question.

*　*　*

In view of Paul's understanding of freedom one must consider as possible not only his participation in the worship of the synagogue, but also his participation in temple worship, in the observation of Jewish festivals, his assumption of private vows, and his participation in the vows of others as portrayed in Acts 21.

To be sure the motivation of this last episode is highly suspect. This ostentatious participation was intended to disprove the accusations of Jews and Jewish Christians, who charged that Paul was teaching apostasy from Moses to all the Jews of the diaspora, that is, that he was teaching them that they should not circumcise their children and that they should not live according to Jewish customs; on the contrary, Paul's participation in the vow was intended to show "that you yourself live in observance of the law" (21:24). True enough, the Jewish accusations are formulated as biased distortions of Paul's teachings; but it was Pauline doctrine that the Mosaic law was not the way of salvation, that circumcision was not a condition of salvation, and that Jewish "customs" were without significance with regard to salvation. To this extent the charge of "apostasy from Moses" was entirely appropriate. To convince the Jew that the charge was unjust would have been extremely difficult for the pioneer of the Gentile church and the author of Galatians and II Corinthians. For Paul, Moses was not a prototype but an antitype of the Messiah and a personification of "the dispensation of death" and "of condemnation" (II Cor. 3:4–18); for him the acknowledgment of circumcision meant a nullification of the redemptive act of Christ on the cross (Gal. 5:1–12). Had Paul undertaken to show that such a charge was unjust, he would hardly have succeeded by performing a cultic work of supererogation. Had Paul followed the advice of James, he would not only have been hiding in ambiguity, but he would have been unambiguously denying his actual practice and his gospel; that is, this would have been a denial that the cross of Christ alone was of saving significance for Gentiles and Jews. It is extremely unlikely that Paul participated in this episode for the reasons given in Acts. It is also difficult to assume that James, who knew Paul, his gospel, and his mission, could have suggested such a deception to Paul.

Now it is clear, on the one hand, that Acts wishes to portray James' advice and Paul's conduct as subjectively honorable and objectively correct and, on the other hand, that Acts looks upon the Jewish charges as slander. This last corresponds with the fact that Acts ascribes the motivation for the Jews' hostility toward Paul primarily to their jealous rivalry or to their disbelief in the messiahship of Jesus, but never to Paul's doctrine of the freedom from law (and thereby also from circumcision). But it was precisely this doctrine which was the reason for the Jewish hostility, because it nullified the absolute significance of the Jewish people.[1] If the portrayal in Acts is not a biased distortion of the facts, then it represents the author's own theory of the circumstances, which he sets forth in good faith. Whether or not the action here attributed to Paul is his-

1. F. Chr. Baur, *Paul* (German: 1866; English: 1876), I, 197.

torical, the motivation to which Acts ascribes it is due to the author of Acts and "simply shows that the author wished to represent matters in such a way as if in all his preaching on the subject of the law the Apostle had never said anything affecting Judaism in the very least."[2]

* * *

Luke did know that Paul proclaimed justification by faith, but he did not know its central significance and absolute importance; he thought it was valid primarily for the Gentiles. This understanding of justification is a product of his understanding of the law. In Acts the law, together with the prophets, is sometimes the sacred book of divine prophecies of the Messiah and in this capacity is common possession of Jews and Christians. Sometimes, however, it is a collection of cultic and ritual commands and as such is property of the Jewish people and of the Christians who stemmed from them, but is not obligatory for Gentile Christians, who indeed possess an analogue to the law and the prophets in their natural knowledge of God, and because of their immediacy to God do not need to make the detour by way of Judaism. As a Greek and Gentile Christian, Luke had never experienced the law as a way to salvation and therefore did not understand the Pauline antithesis law—Christ. Paul's question regarding the law as a way of salvation, regarding good works as the condition of salvation—the whole problem of the law —was entirely foreign to Luke. Paul's biographer was no longer troubled by a question which of necessity confronted Paul: "Is the law sin?" Either Luke no longer knew the basic nature of the battle over the law, or else he did not wish to acknowledge it because this battle had long ago been fought out. Luke speaks of the inadequacy of the law, whereas Paul speaks of the end of the law, which is Christ (Rom. 10:4). In the doctrine of the law which is in Acts, the "word of the cross" has no place because in Acts it would make no sense. The distinction between Luke and Paul was in Christology.

III

In Acts the contents of Paul's message was in general terms first of all the "kingdom" or "the kingdom of God" (19:8; 20:25; 28:23, 31); then Jesus (19:13; 22:18), "Jesus, whom Paul asserted to be alive" (25:19), "the things concerning me" (23:11), "Jesus and the resurrection" (17:18). In Acts Paul describes the content of the preaching as "the whole counsel of God" (20:27), the

2. *Ibid.*, p. 199.

gospel of God's grace (20:24), repentance and conversion (26:20; cf. 20:21), and, when on trial, as has already been mentioned, the prediction of the law and the prophets and the hope of the fathers in a resurrection of the dead (23:6; 24:14 f., 26:6 ff.; 28:20).

In Acts the only Pauline statements on Christology of any length are made before Jews, in the synagogue in Antioch (13:13–43) and before Agrippa (26:22 f.). They consist primarily in the assertion that Jesus is the Messiah who was promised in the Old Testament and expected by the Jews, and in the scriptural proof that his suffering and resurrection were according to the scripture: " ... saying nothing but what the prophets and Moses said would come to pass: that the Christ must suffer, and that, by being the first to rise from the dead, he would proclaim light both to the people and to the Gentiles" (26:22 f.). Thus both the Messiah's suffering and resurrection and the justification of the world mission are shown to be according to scripture. The same motifs occur in Acts 13: the suffering and resurrection of Jesus are the fulfillment of "all that was written of him" (v. 29). The resurrection receives a detailed scripture proof in vv. 34–37 (Ps. 16:10 is the main proof text, and the mode of argument is the same as that in Acts 2:27–31); the Christian mission is also connected to the resurrection (v. 32). In addition to these parallels Jesus is referred to by name, is designated a descendant of David, is called "Savior" and, according to Ps. 2:7, Son of God (vv. 23, 33).

In Paul's letters there are parallels to these passages at Rom. 1:3 f. and I Cor. 15:3 f.: Jesus is descended from David and installed as Son of God (Rom. 1:3 f.), his appearing is in fulfillment of prophetic writings (v. 2). In I Cor. 15:3 f. both death and resurrection are described as according to the Scriptures, and also the burial is mentioned. But according to Paul's own statement this passage is an element of tradition from the earliest congregation, and Rom. 1:3 f. is also acknowledged as a pre-Pauline formulation which Paul inserted. Thus it appears that the christological statements of Paul in Acts 13:16–37 and 26:22 f. are neither specifically Pauline nor Lucan but are property of the earliest congregation.

* * *

Luke himself is closer to the Christology of the earliest congregation, which is set forth in the speeches of Peter, than he is to the Christology of Paul, which is indicated only in hints. To what extent his own viewpoint accords with the concepts of "the servant of God" and "the author of life/leader" (Acts 3:13, 26; 4:27, 30; 3:15; 5:31) cannot be determined with certainty. He reproduces them but does not expound them.

IV

After what has already been said about the speeches of Paul the question as to the eschatology of the Paul of Acts has in a large measure been answered. The eschatology disappears. It leads a modest existence on the periphery of his speeches as a hope in the resurrection and as faith in the return of Christ as the judge of the world (17:30 f.), and in this aspect as a motivation of the exhortation to repentance. Eschatology has been removed from the center of Pauline faith to the end and has become a "section on the last things."

But that is Lucan theology. He distinguishes himself thereby not only from Paul but also from the earliest congregation which expected the return of Christ, the resurrection of the dead, and the end of the world in the immediate future, and understood the parousia as the beginning of the new aeon. Paul also lived in the expectation of the imminent parousia—it motivated his mission and determined his relationship to the world as that of the "as if not" (I Cor. 7:29 ff.)—but the turning point of the world's history has already occurred, the new aeon is already there with the saving act of God in Christ (Gal. 4:4). Paul still awaits the conversion of Israel (Rom. 9–11), the redemption of the "creation" (Rom. 8:19 ff.), and a final cosmic drama with the conquest of hell and of death (I Cor. 15), and speaks of "this present evil age" (Gal. 1:4); but he never speaks of the "age to come," because the "fullness of time" is already fulfilled. Characteristically, the Pauline "already" and "not yet" are not thought of quantitatively, and their relationship is not understood as a temporal process of gradual realization. It is a question of the paradoxical contemporaneity of the presence and the futurity of salvation, not a question of a temporal but of an ontological dualism. Instructive for this eschatological understanding of history which is Paul's are his statements in I Cor. 15:20, 23 f., which define the present as the time of the resurrection of the dead, which began with the resurrection of Christ: "Christ the first fruits, then at his coming those who belong to Christ, then the end." With this "then" all of world history between Easter and the parousia is majestically ignored; during this interval nothing more of significance can happen, especially no redemptive *history*; the time between resurrection and return is simply a parenthesis in the life of Christ. With Paul eschatology has become a structural element of Christology.

Luke also held that the new aeon had broken in (Acts 2:16–35; cf. Luke 16:16); that joins Luke to Paul and separates him from the earliest congregation. But the essential has not yet occurred and will take place only at the parousia, which brings the "restoration" (Acts 3:19 ff.); that joins Luke with the earliest congregation and separates him from Paul. The Lucan "already" and "not yet" are understood quantitatively and are conceived in the categories of a temporal dualism which finds its resolution in a temporal process. The time between Pentecost and the parousia is the time of the Spirit and of the progressive evangelization of the world, which is thus an ascending redemptive history.

* * *

To summarize: the author of Acts is in his Christology pre-Pauline, in his natural theology, concept of the law, and eschatology, post-Pauline. He presents no specifically Pauline idea. His "Paulinism" consists in his zeal for the worldwide Gentile mission and in his veneration for the greatest missionary to the Gentiles. The obvious material distance from Paul raises the question whether this distance is not also temporal distance, and whether one may really consider Luke, the physician and travel companion of Paul, as the author of Acts. But of greater importance than the question of authorship is that of the author's distinctive theological viewpoint and his place in the history of theology.

* * *

Paul as Satan's Apostle:
Jewish-Christian Opponents

EDITOR'S NOTE

Paul's letter to Galatians attests to a vigorous conflict between the apostle and certain rival missionaries who insisted that Gentile Christians must be circumcised and must adhere to the Law of Moses. While Paul's vehement self-defense was apparently successful at that time in Galatia, the opposition was not silenced. Again and again in the writings of the church fathers, we hear of Jewish-Christian groups who were incensed by Paul's strictures against circumcision and the law and who refused to acknowledge the authority of his writings. The precise nature of the Jewish-Christian groups is as difficult to determine as is the precise character of those earlier opponents in Galatia. The most important of them are called Ebionites, from the Semitic word for "poor," and on the basis of passages such as Rom. 15:26 and Gal. 2:10 they have been identified as descendants of the original disciples in Jerusalem.[1] That is improbable, although it is clear that some of the Ebionites themselves labored to establish such a connection in the second and third centuries.[2] The orthodox heresiologists classified the Ebionites with the Gnostics. While that guilt-by-association is to be taken with a grain of salt, it is true that the groups we know most about were quite syncretistic. The Jewishness of the group that produced the *Kerygmata Petrou* excerpted below, for instance, would seem bizarre from the perspective of rabbinic Judaism; it could more readily be compared with such esoteric movements as the Essenes.[3]

Not surprisingly, the picture of Paul represented by these sources is a very flat caricature. The originators of these traditions seem to have had no substantial information about Paul. The main points are drawn from the letters and Acts. Stories are concocted, appar-

1. An important element in F. C. Baur's scheme of early Christian development (see below pp. 277–88) revived in this century by H. J. Schoeps, *Theologie und Geschichte des Judenchristentums* (Tübingen, 1949); *Jewish Christianity: Factional Disputes in the Early Church* (Philadelphia, 1949); S. G. F. Brandon, *The Fall of Jerusalem and the Christian Church* (London, 1951), and others.

2. See Leander E. Keck, "The Poor Among the Saints in Jewish Christianity," *Zeitschr. f. d. Neutestamentliche Wissenschaft*, 57 (1966): 54–78.
3. On the history of Jewish-Christianity, see, besides the works cited above, Jean Daniélou, *Theology of Jewish-Christianity* (Chicago, 1964) and M. Simon, *Recherches d'histoire judéo-chrétienne* (Paris, 1962)

ently, out of thin air (as in "The Ascents of James") or adapted from existing legends (as in the curious story of Paul's attack on James, which has some connection with the legend of James' martyrdom recounted by Hegesippus[4]). Even on the central point of contention, Paul's rejection of the law, there is no clarity. The Jewish-Christian groups had, of course, no interest in repeating the subtleties of Paul's argument; Paul's supporters had trouble enough with those. In fact there is little indication that specifically Pauline attitudes toward the law were under discussion. They attacked the Paul depicted by the slowly solidifying main stream of catholic Christianity, all now practically more or less free of the law, at least in its ceremonial aspects. The intricately nuanced argument of the Letter to the Romans was hardly understood by either side, nor was there much incentive to try.

ANONYMOUS

A False Proselyte (Third Century?) †

They [sc. the Ebionites] invoke other acts of apostles, in which are many things full of impiety, which they use primarily to arm themselves against the truth. They also produce certain pilgrimages[1] and expositions, namely in "The Ascents of James," pretending that James spoke against the Temple and the sacrifices and against the fire of the altar, and many other things full of empty talk. So also, in the same place, they are not ashamed to slander Paul, using certain charges trumped up by the malice and error of their pseudo-apostles. They say that he was not only a citizen of Tarsus, as he himself admits and does not deny, but also of Greek origin, basing this on the passage in which Paul candidly says, "I am a Tarsan, citizen of no mean city" [Acts 21:39]. Then they declare that he was a Greek, child of a Greek mother and a Greek father. He went up to Jerusalem, they say, and when he had spent some time there, he was seized with a passion to marry a daughter of the priest. For

4. See below, and compare Eusebius, *Ecclesiastical History* II, 23, 4–18; cf. Josephus, *Antiquities* xx, 200.
† From "The Ascents of James" (*anabathmoi Iakobou*), of uncertain date, here as paraphrased by Epiphanius (ca. 315–403, bishop of Salamis), *Panarion, haer.* 30.16.6–9. I translate the critical edition by Karl Holl (Leipzig, 1915).
1. The word *anabathmos* ordinarily means staircase or the like; hence it was once wrongly suggested that the

book was the same as the "Ladder of Jacob" extant in Slavonic. The context shows that not the patriarch but the "brother of the Lord" Jacob (="James") is meant. *Anabathmos* is evidently used here as a synonym of *anabasis*, "ascent," referring to James' ascents or pilgrimages to Jerusalem. (See Holl's note *ad loc.* in his edition of Epiphanius and G. Strecker, *Das Judenchristentum in den Pseudoklementinen* [Berlin, 1958], p. 252.)

this reason he became a proselyte and was circumcised. Then, when he failed to get the girl, he flew into a rage and wrote against circumcision and against Sabbath and Law.

EPIPHANIUS

The Cerinthians (ca. 375) †

For they use the Gospel according to Matthew—in part, because of the human genealogy, but not all of it—and they adduce this proof-text from the Gospel: "It is enough for the disciple to be like his teacher" [Matt. 10:25]. What then, they say—Jesus was circumcised; be circumcised yourself. Christ lived according to the Law, they say, and you must do the same. Hence some of these, like men seized by poisonous drugs, are convinced by the specious arguments based on Christ's having been circumcised. They break with Paul because he does not accept circumcision, but they also reject him because he said, "You who would be justified by the law have fallen away from grace" [Gal. 5:4] and "If you receive circumcision, Christ will be of no advantage to you" [Gal. 5:2].

* * *

ANONYMOUS

Messenger of Satan (ca. 200?) ‡

The Letter of Peter to James

1 ¹ Peter to James the lord and bishop of the holy church. By the Father of all things through Jesus Christ (may you be) in peace always.

† From *Panarion, haer.* 28.5.1–3. Epiphanius says he is describing the beliefs of followers of the Gnostic Cerinthus, but there is some evidence that he has confused them with the Ebionites.

‡ From "The Preachings of Peter" (*Kerygmata Petrou*), introduced by a cover letter from Peter to James. The Jewish-Christian group that produced the original form of this fiction were concerned to demonstrate that their tradition came straight from Peter via James the brother of Jesus, who is described as the first bishop of Jerusalem. Since Paul's interpretation of Christianity depended upon a mere vision, it could not stand against this authentic tradition. Moreover, the document inserts Paul into a dualistic framework to show that he belonged to a long series of false prophets. "The Preachings of Peter" was incorporated, with much later material, into a novel that has survived in two major versions, both falsely ascribed to Pope Clement I. (For the problems involved in isolating the different constituents of this literature, see the introduction by G. Strecker in Hennecke's *New Testament Apocrypha*, ed. W. Schneemelcher, trans. by R. McL. Wilson, II [Philadelphia, 1965], pp. 102–11; a different viewpoint in notes by J. Irmscher, *ibid.*, pp. 532–35.) In the novel, which has undergone catholic editing, Peter's enemy is the rival religious founder Simon Magus, but it was clearly Paul who played that role in the original. I translate the critical Greek text of the *Homilies*, ed. by Bernhard Rehm (Berlin, 1969).

2 Knowing that you, my brother, eagerly pursue what is of common benefit to us all, I request and implore you not to impart the books of my preachings which I am sending you to any of the Gentiles, nor even to a fellow Jew before he is tested. But if someone, upon examination, is found worthy, then to him you may hand them over, in the same way as Moses handed on (the tradition) to the seventy who succeeded to his chair. 3 Because of this, the fruit of his precaution is apparent until the present. For his fellow nationals everywhere hold to the same rule of monotheism and the same moral constitution, since they cannot be led by the ambiguities of scripture to adopt any other viewpoint. 4 Rather they try to correct the disagreements of the scriptures according to the norm handed down to them, in case anyone who chances not to know the traditions should be shocked by the ambiguous statements of the prophets. 5 For this reason they permit no one to teach until he has learned how the scriptures ought to be used. Thus among them there is one God, one Law, one Hope.

2 1 In order then that the same situation may obtain among us, hand over the books of my preachings to our seventy brothers with similar secrecy, that they may prepare those who want to take up the office of teacher. 2 Otherwise, if this is not done, our word of truth will be divided into many opinions. It is not as a prophet that I know this; rather I already see the beginning of this evil. 3 For some of those of Gentile origin have rejected my lawful proclamation, accepting rather a lawless and silly teaching of "the enemy."[1] 4 And even while I am still alive some have undertaken to distort my words, by certain intricate interpretations, into an abolition of the law, as if I myself thought such a thing, but did not preach it openly—God forbid! 5 For to take such a position is to act against the Law of God which was spoken through Moses and whose eternal endurance was attested by our Lord. For he said: "Heaven and earth will pass away; not an iota, not a dot, will pass from the law." 6 And he said this, "that everything might come to pass."[2] But these people who have my mind at their disposal, I know not how, undertake to interpret the words which they heard from me more intelligently than I who spoke them. They tell those who are taking instruction from them that this is my opinion—something I never dreamed of. 7 If they dare to fabricate this kind of lies while I am still alive, how much more will they dare to do who come after me?

*   *   *

1. "The enemy." lit., "the hostile man"; the phrase is probably suggested by Matt. 13:25, 28. As *Recog.* I, 71:3 (below) makes plain, Paul was meant in the original version of "The Preach-ings."

2. Cf. Matt. 5:18, where however the last clause reads "until everything comes to pass."

(Homily II, 16–17)

16 ¹ As in the beginning God, who is one, created first the heaven, then the earth, like a right and left hand, so he also arranged all the pairs in sequence. In the case of men, however, he no longer does this, but reverses all the pairs. ² For while from him the first things are better, the second inferior, in the case of men we find the opposite: the first things are worse, the second better. ³ Thus from Adam, who was made in the image of God, came first the unjust Cain, second the just Abel. ⁴ Again, from the one whom you call Deucalion symbols of two spirits were sent forth, an impure and a pure, that is the black raven and the white dove second. ⁵ And from the founder of our nation, Abraham, two different ones³ were born, first Ishmael, then Isaac who was blessed by God. ⁶ In the same way again two issued from Isaac, Esau the impious and Jacob the pious. ⁷ Thus in order came first, as first-born in the world, the High Priest [sc. Aaron], then the Lawgiver [sc. Moses].

17 ¹ In the same way—for the pair pertaining to Elijah, which ought to come (next), was deliberately postponed until another time, to take it up according to plan at another, appropriate moment—² therefore he who is "among those born of women"⁴ came first, then he who is among the sons of men appeared second. ³ By following this sequence anyone can understand to whom "Simon" [i.e., Paul] belongs, who first went to the Gentiles, before me, and to whom I [sc. Peter] belong, who came after him, appearing as light after darkness, as knowledge after ignorance, as healing after sickness. ⁴ Thus, as the True Prophet told us, first a false gospel must come through a certain deceiver, and then, after the destruction of the holy place, a true gospel must be propagated secretly in order to rectify the existing heresies.

*　*　*

(Homily XI, 35, 3–6)

35 * * * ³ Our Lord and Prophet who commissioned us explained to us how the evil one, having disputed with him without success for forty days, promised to send apostles from his retinue for the purpose of deception. ⁴ Therefore remember above all not to receive any apostle or prophet or teacher who has not first presented his gospel to James—who is called the brother of the Lord and to whom the direction of the church of the Hebrews in Jerusalem was

---

3. Accepting Wieseler's emendation; the text reads "two first."　　4. Cf. Matt. 11.11 = Luke 7.28.

entrusted—and comes to you with witnesses.[5] [5] Otherwise the wickedness that disputed with the Lord for forty days and could do nothing, and which later "fell like lightning from heaven" to earth[6], would send against you a herald, as now he has sent "Simon" against us, preaching, under pretext of the truth, in the name of our Lord[7], but actually sowing error. [6] For this reason the one who commissioned us said, "Many shall come to you in sheep's clothing, but inwardly they are ravenous wolves; by their fruits you shall know them."[8]

(Homily XVII, 13–19)

* * *

13 [1] When "Simon" heard this, he interrupted [Peter] to say, "* * * You assert that you thoroughly understand your teacher's concerns because, in his physical presence, you saw and heard him directly, but no one else could gain such understanding by means of a dream or a vision. [2] But I shall show that this is false. One who hears something directly cannot be quite certain about what was said, for the mind must consider whether, being merely human, he has been deceived by the sense impression. But the vision, by the very act of appearing, presents its own proof to the seer that it is divine. First give me an answer to this."

14 [1] And Peter said, "* * * [3] The prophet, once he has proved that he is a prophet, is infallibly believed in the matters which are directly spoken by him. Also, when his truthfulness has been previously recognized, he can give answers to the disciple, however the latter may wish to examine and interrogate him. But one who puts his trust in a vision or an apparition or dream is in a precarious position, for he does not know what it is he is trusting. [4] For it is possible that it is an evil demon or a deceitful spirit, pretending in the speeches to be what he is not. [5] Then if anyone should wish to inquire who it was who spoke, he could say of himself whatever he chose. Thus, like an evil flash of lightning[9], he stays as long as he chooses and then vanishes, not remaining with the inquirer long enough to answer his questions. * * *

5. So the Greek; the parallel passage in the *Recognitions* reads "testimonials." The *Recognitions* passage adds, in a sentence that may well go back to the original *Kerygmata*, a comparison of the twelve apostles with the twelve months of the year, thus tacitly declaring any "thirteenth" claimant to apostolicity, such as Paul, to be inauthentic.
6. Luke 10:18; probably understood here as an allusion to Paul's Damascus

vision: see Acts 9:3 and below, Hom. XVII, 14,5.
7. This phrase shows that Simon Magus could not have been meant by the original *Kerygmata*, for Simon, who regarded himself as a manifestation of the Supreme Power, did not preach "in the name of (the) Lord."
8. Matt. 7:15 f.
9. This may be another allusion to Acts 9:3; see above, Hom. XI, 35,5.

16 ¹ And Peter said, "* * * We know * * * ² that many idolaters and adulterers and all kinds of sinners have seen visions and true dreams, while others have seen appearances of demons. For I assert that it is not possible to see the incorporeal form of Father or Son, because mortal eyes are dazzled by the great light. ³ Therefore it is not because God is jealous, but because he is merciful that he remains invisible to flesh-oriented man. For no one who sees can survive¹. ⁴ For the extraordinary light would dissolve the flesh of the beholder, unless the flesh were changed by the ineffable power of God into the nature of light, so that it could see the light—or unless the light-substance were changed into flesh, so that it could be seen by flesh. For the Son alone is able to see the Father without being transformed. The case of the righteous is different: in the resurrection of the dead, when their bodies, changed into light, become like angels, then they will be able to see. Finally, even if an angel is sent to appear to a man, he is changed into flesh, that he can be seen by flesh. For no one can see the incorporeal power of the Son or even of an angel. But if someone *sees a vision*, let him understand this to be an evil demon. **17** ¹ But it is obvious that impious people also see true visions and dreams, and I can prove it from scripture [The cases of Abimelech (Gen. 20:3 ff.), the Egyptian Pharaoh (Gen. 41), and Nebuchadnezzar (Dan. 2) are adduced.] * * * ⁵ Thus the fact that one sees visions and dreams and apparitions by no means assures that he is a religious person. Rather, to the pure and innate religious mind the truth gushes up, not eagerly courted by a dream, but granted to the good by intelligence. **18** ¹ It was in this way that the Son was revealed to me by the Father. Therefore I know what the nature of revelation is, since I learned it myself. [The following passage discusses Peter's Confession, as recounted in Matt. 16:13–16, then cites Num. 2:6–8.] * * * ⁶ You see how revelations of anger are through visions and dreams, while those to a friend are "mouth to mouth,"² by sight and not by puzzles and visions and dreams, as they are to an enemy. **19** ¹ So even if our Jesus did appear in a dream to you, making himself known and conversing with you, he did so in anger, speaking to an opponent. That is why he spoke to you through visions and dreams—through revelations which are external. ² But can anyone be qualified by a vision to become a teacher? And if you say it is possible, then why did the Teacher remain for a whole year conversing with those who were awake? ³ How can we believe even your statement that he appeared to you? How could he have

---

1. Cf. Ex. 33:20.   2. Ex. 33:11; Num. 12:8; Deut. 34:10.

appeared to you, when your opinions are opposed to his teaching? **4** No, if you were visited and taught by him for a single hour and thus became an apostle, proclaim his utterances, interpret his teachings, love his apostles—and do not strive against me, who was his companion. For you have "opposed" me[3], the firm Rock, foundation of the church.[4] **5** If you were not an enemy, you would not slander me and disparage what is preached by me, as if I were obviously "condemned"[5] and you were approved. **6** If you call me "condemned," you are accusing God who revealed the Christ to me, and are opposing the one who blessed me because of the revelation. **7** Rather, if you really want to work together for the truth, first learn from us what we learned from him. Then, having become a disciple of the truth, become our fellow-worker.

ANONYMOUS

Persecutor of the Faith (date unknown) †

[The preceding chapters describe a debate in Jerusalem between the apostles and the leaders of each of the Jewish sects.] * * * And when matters were at that point that they should come and be baptized, some one of our enemies,[1] entering the temple with a few men, began to cry out, and to say, 'What mean ye, O men of Israel? Why are you so easily hurried on? Why are ye led headlong by most miserable men, who are deceived by a magician? While he was thus speaking, and adding more to the same effect, and while James the bishop was refuting him, he began to excite the people and to raise a tumult, so that the people might not be able to hear what was said. Therefore he began to drive all into confusion with shouting, and to undo what had been arranged with much labour, and at the same time to reproach the priests, and to enrage them with revilings and abuse, and like a madman, to excite every one to murder, saying, 'What do ye? Why do ye hesitate? Oh, sluggish and inert, why do we not lay hands upon them, and pull all these fellows to pieces?' When he had said this, he first, seizing a strong brand from the altar, set the example of smiting. Then others also, seeing him, were carried away with like madness. Then ensued a tumult on either side, of the beating and the beaten. Much blood is

---

3. Cf. Gal. 2:11.
4. Cf. Matt. 16:18.
5. Gal. 2:11.
† From the *Recognitions of Clement*, Bk. I, Chaps. 70–71, tr. by Thomas Smith, in *The Ante-Nicene Fathers*, Vol. VIII (New York, 1899; rp. Grand Rapids, 1951). The Pseudo-Clementine

novelist has here used a different source, stemming from the Jewish-Christian community that fled from Jerusalem to Pella at the time of the Jewish revolt in A.D. 68.
1. This "enemy" is Paul. The same phrase is applied to him in the Letter of Peter to James (above).

shed; there is a confused flight, in the midst of which that enemy attacked James, and threw him headlong from the top of the steps; and supposing him to be dead, he cared not to inflict further violence upon him.

But our friends lifted him up, for they were both more numerous and more powerful than the others; but, from their fear of God, they rather suffered themselves to be killed by an inferior force, than they would kill others. But when the evening came the priests shut up the temple, and we returned to the house of James, and spent the night there in prayer. Then before daylight we went down to Jericho, to the number of 5000 men. Then after three days one of the brethren came to us from Gamaliel, whom we mentioned before, bringing us secret tidings that that enemy had received a commission from Caiaphas, the chief priest, that he should arrest all who believed in Jesus, and should go to Damascus with his letters, and that there also, employing the help of the unbelievers, he should make havoc among the faithful; and that he was hastening to Damascus chiefly on this account, because he believed that Peter had fled thither. And about thirty days thereafter he stopped on his way while passing through Jericho going to Damascus. At that time we were absent, having gone out to the sepulchres of two brethren which were whitened of themselves every year, by which miracle the fury of many against us was restrained, because they saw that our brethren were had in remembrance before God. * * *

The Only True Apostle:
Marcion's Radical Paul

EDITOR'S NOTE

The enemies of Paul were much less of a problem for the emerging catholic consensus than were some of his friends. In the second century and even later several of the movements that claimed most enthusiastically to be Paul's true interpreters were very far out of that stream of Christianity which would succeed in the contest for dominance and therefore gain the crown of "orthodoxy." The distinction between heresy and orthodoxy, always relative, was very fluid in the first four centuries of Christianity. Many differing groups appealed to "apostolic" origins, to special oral traditions allegedly stemming from the apostles, to true interpretation of the scriptures. If for nothing else than the bulk of his writings and the notoriety of his missionary efforts, Paul was named *the* apostle in groups that differed radically from one another in their interpretation of his teachings.

The very same things that made Paul abhorrent for the Jewish Christians may have evoked the special sympathy for Paul that existed among certain of the Christian Gnostic groups. For Gnosticism exhibits an almost schizophrenic relationship to Judaism. Frequently engaged, sometimes obsessed, with the Jewish scriptures and traditions, yet it despises the Jewish God and his world.[1] Paul, the ex-Pharisee who uses the law against legalism, naturally held a peculiar fascination for them. His understanding of the Christian gospel, like that of all Gnostics, concentrated on the question of man's redemption. His sharp dichotomies between works and faith, flesh and spirit, his emphasis on freedom, his use of traditional myths to depict a heavenly Christ who comes down to take the "form of man," his talk of "inexpressible mysteries," his asceticism —all these points, if taken out of Paul's basically Jewish context and placed into an anticosmic dualism, were fertile soil for Gnostic mythmaking.[2] Valentinus, perhaps the most creative of the individual Gnostic teachers known to us by name, claimed, according to Clement of Alexandria,[3] that his teacher Theodas had been a personal disciple of Paul. Passages from the Pauline letters are frequently employed in Gnostic allegory, not least in the documents of the Nag Hammadi Gnostic library discovered in 1945 in Egypt and only now being systematically published.[4]

There was no one in the ancient church, however, either "heretic" or "orthodox," who made such serious and exclusive

1. On the "metaphysical anti-Semitism" of Gnosticism, see Hans Jonas, "Response to G. Quispel's 'Gnosticism and the New Testament,'" in *The Bible in Modern Scholarship*, ed. J. Philip Hyatt (Nashville, 1965), pp. 286–93, and "Delimitation of the Gnostic Phenomenon—Typological and Historical," in *The Origins of Gnosticism*, ed. Ugo Bianchi (Leiden, 1967), pp. 100–103.
2. Eva Aleith, *Paulusverständnis in der alten Kirche* (Berlin, 1937) pp. 39–49. This is not the place to pursue the question of influence in the opposite direction, i.e., whether there were predecessors or early forms of the Gnostic movements older than Christianity, which may have influenced Paul himself, as well as the Hellenistic Christianity before and alongside him. An affirmative answer to this question is a major working hypothesis of Rudolf Bultmann and of all the continental and American scholars who have been

heavily influenced by him: see below, pp. 409–22. Serious objections have been raised, especially to a tendency to perceive "the Gnostic religion" as a unitary movement: see e.g., Carsten Colpe, *Die religionsgeschichtliche Schule* (Göttingen, 1961); A. D. Nock, "Gnosticism," *Harv. Theol. Rev.* 57 (1964): 255–79. Still, while important qualifications are necessary, the hypothesis of a "pre-Christian gnosis" is regarded by a growing number of specialists as a necessary one. See the attempts at definition of "gnosis" and "Gnosticism" by the Messina Colloquy on *The Origins of Gnosticism* (n. 1 above).
3. *Stromateis* VII, 17, 106 f.
4. See e.g., R. McL. Wilson, *Gnosis and the New Testament* (Oxford, 1968), pp. 119 f., and the reports by James M. Robinson in *New Testament Studies* 14 (1968): 356–401 and 16 (1970): 185–91.

claims on Paul and Paul alone as did Marcion. Born some twenty or
thirty years after Paul's death, Marcion became convinced that salvation by grace alone was the purest essence of the Christian gospel.
But carried to its logical conclusion, he believed this would mean
that the God of grace manifested in Jesus Christ was distinct from
the God of the Old Testament. The creation and the law were the
products of the God of justice, but man's hope lay in the God of
pure love, unknown before Christ and totally unrelated to this
world. Catholic Christianity's insistence on the identity of the two
Gods was in Marcion's eyes a devilish mixture of opposites, the
result of a Judaizing conspiracy in which all the apostles except Paul
had engaged. They had even dared to corrupt the text of Paul's letters, which must therefore be expurgated of references to the Creator and his prophets. Marcion produced his own "critical" New
Testament, which several scholars believe to have been the first
strictly defined Christian canon of scripture. To it he added his
single original writing, "The Antitheses," portions of which are
quoted below.

When Marcion's teaching of the two rival gods got him expelled
from the church in Rome—reportedly he had been excommuni-
cated years earlier from his home church in Sinope, Pontus, of
which his own father was bishop—he set about to reform the
church from without, establishing independent parishes and
dioceses, tightly disciplined and organized on lines parallel to the
catholics. His reformer's zeal was prodigious—for good reason Harnack has seen in him a second-century Luther—and his success was
so great that his churches were serious contenders for dominance
over the catholics in many parts of the empire for two centuries.
"Tracts 'Against Marcion' were still being written," notes Bardenhewer, "when the name of Valentinus had long since faded away.[5]

Marcion was not a Gnostic. True, his hatred of the world resembles the Gnostic's existential nausea,[6] but his doctrine of grace is
fundamentally anti-Gnostic. For the Gnostic, salvation of the spiritual part of man is possible only because that part is consubstantial
with the saving deity. For Marcion the essence of grace is that the
good God is totally other; he has no relationships with man before
his absolutely free decision to save him. In this radical notion of
grace, Marcion is not Gnostic, but ultimately Pauline. Yet it is a
perversely one-sided (one might say with Harnack, perversely consistent) Paulinism which, in its very zeal to be truly Pauline, has
demolished the dialectic that is most characteristic of Paul's genius.
Marcion was the only one in the second century who understood

5. Otto Bardenhewer, *Geschichte der altchristlichen Literatur* (Freiburg i. Br., 1912, rp. Darmstadt, 1962) I, 371.

6. Jonas, "Delimitation . . .," p. 104.

Paul, said Harnack, and he misunderstood him.[7]

Since no connected work by Marcion survived the final suppression of his schism, he must be represented here only by a few hostile but revealing words from two of his orthodox opponents, by conjectured fragments of his "Antitheses," and by excerpts from a modern description of his thought which has become a scholar's classic.

IRENAEUS

Marcion (182–188) [†]

Marcion of Pontus . . . increased the [Gnostic] school through his unblushing blasphemy against Him who was proclaimed as God by the law and the prophets, declaring that He was the cause of evils, desirous of war, changeable in opinion and the author of inconsistent statements. He says that Jesus came from the Father, who is above the Creator, to Judaea in the time of Pontius Pilate the governor, who was the procurator of Tiberius Caesar, and in the form of a man was manifested to the people who were then in Judaea. He says that he rendered null and void the prophets and the law and all the works of the Creator God, whom they call Cosmocrator. He used an expurgated edition of the Gospel of Luke, removing all the passages that referred to the birth of our Lord, and many things from his teaching in which he very plainly referred to the creator of this universe as his Father. In the same way he mutilated the Epistles of Paul, cutting out all that the Apostle said about the God who made the world, and which went to show that he was the Father of our Lord Jesus Christ, and also passages bearing on the advent of our Lord, which that Apostle had quoted from the prophets.

TERTULLIAN

Marcion's Special Work (207) [‡]

* * * Marcion's special and principal work is the separation of the law and the gospel; and his disciples will not deny that in this point

---

7. This witticism, made famous by Harnack, was coined by Franz Overbeck, as he says in *Christentum und Kultur* (Basel, 1919), pp. 218 f.

† From *The Treatise of Irenaeus of Lugdunum Against the Heresies*, tr. by F. R. Montgomery Hitchcock (London, 1916), I. 41 f. (= I.25.1 in Harvey's ed. of Irenaeus, I.27.2 in Massuet's)

Irenaeus (ca.130–ca.200), a native of Asia Minor, was bishop of Lyons.

‡ From *Against Marcion*, I.19, tr. by Peter Holmes in the *Ante-Nicene Christian Library* (Edinburgh, 1868), VII, 34. Tertullian (ca.160–ca.220), a native of Carthage, was the first important Christian theologian to write in Latin.

they have their very best pretext for initiating and confirming themselves in his heresy. These are Marcion's "Antitheses," or contradictory propositions, which aim at committing the gospel to a variance with the law, in order that from the diversity of the two documents which contain them, they may contend for a diversity of gods also. * * *

MARCION

The Antitheses (ca. 140?) †

1. The Creator was known to Adam and to the following generations, but the Father of Christ is unknown, as Christ himself said of him in these words: "No one has known the Father except the Son" [Luke 10:22].

2. The Creator did not even know where Adam was, so he cried, "Where are you?" But Christ knew even the thoughts of men [cf. Luke 5:22; 6:8; 9:47].

3. Joshua conquered the land with violence and terror; but Christ forbade all violence and preached mercy and peace.

4. The God of Creation did not restore the sight of the blinded Isaac, but our Lord, because he is good, opened the eyes of many blind men [Luke 7:21].

5. Moses intervened unbidden in the brothers' quarrel, chiding the offender, "Why do you strike your neighbor?" But he was rejected by him with the words, "Who made you master or judge over us?" Christ, on the contrary, when someone asked him to settle a question of inheritance between him and his brother, refused his assistance even in so honest a cause—because he is the Christ of the Good, not of the Just God—and said, "Who made me a judge over you?" [Luke 12:13 f.]

6. At the time of the Exodus from Egypt, the God of Creation commanded Moses, "Be ready, your loins girded, your feet shod, staffs in your hands, knapsacks on your shoulders, and carry off gold and silver and everything that belongs to the Egyptians" [cf. Exod. 3:22; 11:2; 12:35]. But our Lord, the good, said to his disciples as he sent them into the world: "Have no sandals on your feet, nor knapsack, nor two tunics, nor coppers in your belts" [cf. Luke 9:3].

† The epigrammatic antithesis reproduced here are those which Adolf von Harnack reconstructed (*Marcion: Das Evangelium vom fremden Gott* [Leipzig: J. C. Hinrichs, 1924; rp. 1960], pp. 89–92; sources, pp. 266*–296*). It is not certain that all go back to Marcion; several are quoted in a form attributed to Marcion's disciple Megethius in the fourth-century Dialogues of Adamantius. As Harnack showed, "The Antitheses" contained, besides such epigrams, a more systematic theological part, which is impossible to reconstruct.

7. The prophet of the God of Creation, when the people was engaged in battle, climbed to the mountain peak and extended his hands to God, imploring that he kill as many as possible in the battle. [cf. Exod. 17:8 ff.]. But our Lord, the good, extended his hands [on the cross] not to kill men, but to save them.

8. In the Law it is said, "An eye for an eye, a tooth for a tooth" [Exod. 21:24; Deut. 19:21]. But the Lord, being good, says in the Gospel: "If anyone strikes you on the cheek, offer him the other as well" [cf. Luke 6:29].

9. In the Law it is said, "A coat for a coat." [Where?] But the good Lord says, "If anyone takes your coat, give him your tunic as well" [Luke 6:29].

10. The prophet of the God of Creation, in order to kill as many as possible in battle, kept the sun from going down until he finished annihilating those who made war on the people [Josh. 10:12 ff.]. But the Lord, being good, says: "Let not the sun go down on your anger" [Eph. 4:26].

11. David, when he besieged Zion, was opposed by the blind who sought to prevent his entry, and he had them killed. But Christ came freely to help the blind.

12. The Creator, at the request of Elijah, sent the plague of fire [2 Kings 1:9–12]; Christ however forbids the disciples to beseech fire from heaven [Luke 9:51 ff.].

13. The prophet of the God of Creation commanded bears to come from the thicket and devour the children who had opposed him [2 Kings 2:14]; the good Lord, however, says, "Let the children come to me and do not forbid them, for of such is the Kingdom of Heaven" [Luke 18:16].

14. Elisha, prophet of the Creator, healed only one of the many Israelite lepers, and that a Syrian, Naaman. But Christ, though himself "the alien," healed an Israelite, whose own Lord did not want him healed. Elisha used material for the healing, namely water, and seven times; but Christ healed through a single, bare word. Elisha healed only one leper; Christ healed ten, and this contrary to the Law. . . .

15. The prophet of the Creator says: "My bow is strung and my arrows are sharp against them" [Isa. 5:28], the Apostle says: "Put on the armor of God, that you may quench the fiery arrows of the Evil One" [Eph. 6:11, 16].

16. The Creator says, "Hear and hear, but do not understand" [Isa. 6:9]; Christ on the contrary says, "He who has ears to hear, let him hear" [Luke 8.8, etc.].

17. The Creator says, "Cursed is everyone who hangs on the tree" [Deut. 21:23,] but Christ suffered the death of the cross [cf. Gal. 3:13 f.].

18. The Jewish Christ was designated by the Creator solely to restore the Jewish people from the Diaspora; but our Christ was commissioned by the good God to liberate all mankind.

19. The Good is good toward all men; the Creator, however, promises salvation only to those who are obedient to him. The Good redeems those who believe in him, but he does not judge those who are disobedient to him; the Creator, however, redeems his faithful and judges and punishes the sinners.

20. Cursing characterizes the Law; blessing, the faith.

21. The Creator commands to give to one's brothers; Christ, however, to all who ask [Luke 6:30].

22. In the Law the Creator said, "I make rich and poor [cf. Prov. 22:2]; Jesus calls the poor blessed [Luke 6:20].

23. In the Law of the Just [God] fortune is given to the rich and misfortune to the poor; but Christ calls [only] the poor blessed.

24. In the Law God says, "Love him who loves you and hate your enemy [cf. Lv. 19:18 and Matt. 5:43]; our Lord, the good, says: "Love your enemies and pray for those who persecute you" [cf. Luke 6:1 ff.].

25. The Creator established the Sabbath; Christ abolishes it [cf. Luke 6:1 ff.].

26. The Creator rejects the tax collectors as non-Jews and profane men; Christ accepts the tax collectors [Luke 5:27 ff.]

27. The Law forbids touching a woman with a flow of blood; Christ not only touches her, but heals her [Luke 8:45].

28. Moses permits divorce [Deut. 24:1], Christ forbids it [Luke 16:18; 1 Cor. 7:10].

29. The Christ [of the Old Testament] promises to the Jews the restoration of their former condition by return of their land and, after death, a refuge in Abraham's bosom in the underworld. Our Christ will establish the Kingdom of God, an eternal and heavenly possession.

30. Both the place of punishment and that of refuge of the Creator are placed in the underworld for those who obey the Law and the Prophets. But Christ and the God who belongs to him have a heavenly place of rest and a haven, of which the Creator never spoke.

ADOLF VON HARNACK

Marcion's Starting Point (1924) †

* * * The starting point for Marcion's criticism of the tradition is unmistakable. It lay in the Pauline opposition of Law and

† From *Marcion: Das Evangelium vom fremden Gott* (Leipzig, 1924; rp. Darmstadt, 1960), pp. 30–35. Adolf von Harnack (1851–1930) was a distinguished church historian who taught in Leipzig, Giessen, Marburg, and Berlin. His study of Marcion remains unequalled.

Gospel—on the one side malicious, narrow, and vindictive justice; on the other, merciful love. Marcion immersed himself in the basic thought of the Letters to Galatians and Romans, and in them he discovered the full explanation of the nature of Christianity, the Old Testament, and the world. It must have been for him a day of brilliant light, but also a day of trembling over the darkness that had eclipsed this light in Christianity, when he recognized that Christ presented and proclaimed a quite new God. Moreover, he saw that religion itself is nothing else than the faith that abandons itself to this Redeemer-God who transforms man, while the whole of previous world history is the evil and repulsive drama of a deity who possesses no higher value than the dull and nauseating world itself, of which he is the creator and governor.

All of Paul's religious antitheses were brought to the sharpest possible expression through this discovery—though this exaggeration moves very far from the apostle's intentions. Marcion remained true to those intentions only in his enthusiastic certainty of *gratia gratis data* (grace freely given) in contrast to the *justitia ex operibus* (righteousness based on works), as well as in the consciousness of a liberation, surpassing all reason, from a terrifying state of perdition. This conviction included the universality of redemption, in contrast to its restriction to a single people. The religious principle that summed up all higher truth in the opposition between Law and Gospel is also the principle which for Marcion explains the whole of nature and history.

In Marcion's new awareness, the religion of redemption and subjectivity is incomparably heightened to an ethical metaphysics that determines everything. The inexorable result was the abandonment of the Old Testament. * * *

* * *

The Old Testament was abandoned—in that moment, however, the new religion stood naked, uprooted and defenseless. One must renounce all proof from antiquity, indeed every historical and literary proof. Yet a deeper speculation taught Marcion that this defenselessness and lack of proof was demanded by the Gospel itself, which therefore they actually supported. Grace is *gratis data* —so taught both Christ and Paul—and that is the entire content of the religion. But how could grace be *gratis data* if he who gave it had also the least obligation to prove it? Yet if he were the creator of mankind, and their tutor and lawgiver from the beginning, then he would be *obliged* to accept them. Only a miserable and groveling sophistry could save the deity from this obligation! Hence God must have no natural or historical connection with the men whom he loved and redeemed—that is, he cannot be the Creator and

Lawgiver. * * * The Redeemer-God—the only true God—has never encountered man in any revelation of any kind before his appearance in Christ: that is the necessary consequence of the nature of his act of redemption. He could be understood only as the absolutely alien. Thence it follows also that the Enemy, from which one is redeemed through Christ, can be nothing less than the world itself, together with its Creator. Now since Marcion remained true to the Jewish-Christian tradition insofar as he identified the Creator with the Jewish God, and in the Old Testament saw not a false book, but the true depiction of actual history (a remarkable limitation to his religious anti-Judaism!), he had to regard the Jewish God together with his charter, the Old Testament, as the real Enemy.

* * *

But only after Marcion achieved clarity about the basic principle and basic antinomy did his new task begin. He must now expound for faith and life the true content, so drastically misunderstood, of Jesus' and Paul's proclamation. * * * Marcion must begin his great task for Christianity as critic and restorer, for the Gospel and the testimonies were deeply obscured. In fact, no Christian critic has ever had such a difficult task: to prove from the New Testament scriptures that mankind must be redeemed and had been redeemed from their God and Father. Marcion was not daunted; over against the old books, the Law and the Prophets, he placed new books: the book of the Gospel and the letters of Paul.

To Marcion, certain that the authentic Pauline faith was his own, all seemed lost in the inner constitution of the mainline Christianity around him. While he was convinced that Christ had abolished the Old Testament and its God and had proclaimed an alien God, the Church more and more identified the two Gods and founded itself upon the Old Testament. It became, that is, thoroughly "Jewish." Moreover, books which bore the celebrated names of the first apostles obviously helped and undergirded this error by their narratives. Finally and worst, even in the letters of Paul there were many passages that unambiguously supported the heresy that Christ was the Son of the Creator and that he had advanced the will of this Father.

How had that happened, and how could it happen, when the truth in some major passages in the Pauline letters was so unambiguous and clear? A massive conspiracy against the truth must have begun immediately after Christ left the world and have achieved its goals with decisive success. * * * Marcion seized on this explanation. But he had no means of proving it other than the rec-

ollection of the struggle that Paul had had with his Judaizing opponents. Moreover, he knew nothing of this struggle but what he read
in the Apostle's letters. * * *

The Model Ascetic

EDITOR'S NOTE

One aspect of Marcion's version of Paulinism has not been mentioned: his asceticism. In order to be baptized into the Marcionite
church, one had to take a vow of celibacy. If already married, one
was not permitted divorce (Marcion retained Luke 16:18 and perhaps 1 Cor. 7:10 in his canon; see Antithesis 28 above), but must
abstain from intercourse after baptism. That Marcion thought he
was following the intention of his master is indicated by his "restoration" of the text of Eph. 5:21–33, the famous allegory on marriage. He altered vv. 28 f. to read: "He loves his flesh who loves his
wife as Christ (loved) the church [i.e., asexually]"; while v. 31 is
made to say, "For the sake of her [sc. the church] a man shall
leave his father and mother, and the two [sc. man and the church]
shall be one flesh."[1]
Marcion was by no means alone in his belief that Pauline Christianity was ascetic Christianity. That was the conclusion drawn by
some of Paul's own converts during his lifetime,[2] and he has been
praised and blamed ever since for having introduced the ideal of celibacy into the Christian ethic. It is significant, however, that Marcion and other ascetics who appealed to Paul had to alter or ignore
some passages from the Pauline letters in order to make their tutor
speak unequivocally on the subject. Paul's teaching was in fact quite
complex, as a glance even at the single chapter 1 Cor. 7 makes
plain. Paul obviously did regard sexual continence as desirable—yet
not because sex was immoral or marriage a metaphysical trap in an
evil world, but only because "the form of the world is passing
away" and "the appointed time has grown very short" (1 Cor. 7:29,
31). Paul's heightened eschatology, which he shared with most of
early Christianity, made marriage seem a distraction from the
intensely urgent task at hand (1 Cor. 7:32–35), but not evil.
Indeed, while the Old Testament commandment "Be fruitful and

1. Harnack, *op. cit.*, pp. 119* f., cf. p.   2. See notes on 1 Cor. 7.
50.

multiply" had in Paul's eyes been superseded (like all commandments!) by the coming of Christ, yet in practice the implicit mutual obligations between husband and wife were still valid so long as the world endured (1 Cor. 7:1–6). It is not surprising that not only the advocates of a thoroughgoing asceticism but also their opponents were able to appeal to Paul for support.

Apart from Marcion, there were a number of groups in early Christianity who insisted upon rigorous asceticism; wealth, food and drink, and sex were the principal areas of concern.[3] 1 Tim. 4:1–5 combats those "who forbid marriage and enjoin abstinence from foods," and the "self-abasement" insisted on by some Colossian Christians (Col. 2:18, 21 f.) doubtless referred to similar requirements.[4] The heresiologists of the second, third, and fourth centuries applied to such movements the label "Encratites," from the Greek word meaning "self-control." Irenaeus of Lyons (ca. A.D. 185) typically traces the heresy back to one teacher, "a certain Tatian," who had been a disciple of Justin Martyr (d. ca. 165 in Rome). Rejected by the churches of the West, Tatian migrated to Eastern Syria, where the extent of his influence is suggested by the fact that his composite version of the four gospels, the Diatessaron, became *the* gospel in the Syriac New Testament until the fifth century. Whether directly as a result of Tatian's influence or, more likely, because of underlying social factors affecting the origins of Christianity in Mesopotamia, the dominant tendencies of the Eastern Syrian churches were toward an extreme asceticism. Some scholars have argued that a vow of celibacy was actually a requirement for baptism in the earliest Syrian Christianity,[5] since "the fundamental conception around which the Christian belief centered was the doctrine that the Christian life is unthinkable outside the bounds of virginity."[6] Others have vigorously disputed both the early date and the extent of this severe discipline.[7] In any case, numerous documents from the Syriac-speaking church exalt virginity as the proper state for Christians, and occasionally these documents represent Paul as preaching this doctrine. We have to face the question, therefore, to what extent Encratism may have been an outgrowth of Paulinism.

Tatian's own use of the Pauline letters affords one test, which can be applied because Tatian's "Oration to the Greeks" and fragments of other writings have survived. From these it is "plain that

3. See the survey by Hans von Campenhausen, "Early Christian Asceticism," in *Tradition and Life* (Philadelphia, 1968), pp. 90–122.
4. See above, p. 119, n. 2.
5. Karl Müller, *Die Forderung der Ehelosigkeit für alle Getauften in der alten Kirche (Tübingen, 1927)*; Arthur Vööbus, *Celibacy, a Requirement for*

Admission to Baptism in the Early Syrian Church (Stockholm, 1951), and *History of Asceticism in the Syrian Orient* I, II (CSCO 184, 197; Louvain, 1958, 1960).
6. Vööbus, *History*, I, 69.
7. E.g., A. F. J. Klijn, *The Acts of Thomas*, p. 50, n. 2, and further references there.

Tatian knows Paul well and that in part, at least, his theology is based on the Pauline epistles, including Hebrews."[8] Two examples will demonstrate the way in which Tatian used Paul: First, Paul's advice that husband and wife should "not refuse one another except perhaps by agreement for a season, that you may devote yourselves to prayer ..." (1 Cor. 7:5) is thus interpreted by Tatian:

> While agreement to be continent makes prayer possible, intercourse of corruption destroys it. By the very disparaging way in which he [Paul] allows it, he forbids it. For although he allowed them to come together again because of Satan and the temptation to incontinence, he indicated that the man who takes advantage of this permission will be serving two masters, God if there is "agreement," but, if there is no such agreement, incontinence, fornication, and the devil.[9]

Second, we are told by St. Jerome that Tatian took Paul's statement, "He who sows to his own flesh will from the flesh reap corruption," to refer to sexual intercourse.[1] There is no way to be sure how important these arguments were for Tatian, but they appear rather isolated in his extant works. The style of his argument, moreover, is not that of a man who has discovered a new and compelling idea in the text itself; Tatian would hardly have found these implications in these two texts had he not brought them to the texts from elsewhere. The whole tradition about Tatian suggests rather than he was preoccupied with the gospels and with the picture of Jesus as the paradigmatic ascetic that he found there. The Pauline letters he used quite selectively and freely only to the extent that they could support his major concerns. This judgment is confirmed by the fact that Tatian rejected 1 Timothy altogether because of its antiascetic statement (4:1-5, quoted above), but accepted the letter to Titus, presumably because it contained the word "continent" (*enkratē* 1:8).[2] In only one respect the Encratite's doctrine seems related essentially to Paul's: "Tatian felt strongly that the concept of the Christian life is adequately depicted only by the term 'cross.'"[3] But while Paul draws analogies from the Crucifixion and Resurrection to the apostle's joyful acceptance of suffering encountered in the rigors of his missionary task, Tatian refers to self-chosen and self-inflicted suffering. A fundamentally different atmosphere is present in the writings of the two men. Tatian was not a Paulinist, however much he may have depicted Paul as an Encratite.

As a matter of fact, some of the strongest arguments by oppo-

8. Robert M. Grant, "Tatian and the Bible," in *Studia Patristica*, I (Berlin, 1957), 303.
9. From "On Perfection According to the Savior," quoted by Clement of Alexandria, *Strom.* III, 81, tr. Henry Chadwick in *Alexandrian Christianity* (Philadelphia, 1968), pp. 77 f.
1. *Comm. in Ep. ad Gal.*, col. 640; cited by Vööbus, *History*, I, 36; cf. Grant, *op. cit.*, p. 302.
2. Jerome, *In ep. ad. Tit.*, *praef.*, cited by Grant, *op. cit.*, p. 301.
3. Vööbus, *History*, I, 44.

nents of Encratism were based on Paul. Hippolytus of Rome (ca. 170–ca. 236), for example, quotes 1 Tim. 4:1–5 *in extenso* against those "who call themselves Encratites," and concludes, "Thus this voice of the blessed Paul is sufficient to refute those who live this way and who pride themselves in their righteousness, and to show that this, too, is a heresy."[4] His older and more learned contemporary, Clement of Alexandria, derives his refutation of the ascetics very largely from 1 Cor. 7. On the whole, he is an accurate interpreter of Paul's doctrine of freedom in the realm of sexuality—the "as if not" of 1 Cor. 7:29-31 appears several times—even though Clement has a much more positive place for the law and a much more schematic position.[5] While Clement is more "liberal" towards sex than most of his contemporaries even in the catholic mainstream, his view would still seem ascetic in ordinary Hellenistic society: sexual relations were to be permitted only in monogamous marriage, and then only for procreation.[6] Moreover, Clement is representative of the emerging catholic position in his approval of celibacy *for those given the special grace for this state*, while regarding it as not at all superior to "chaste marriage."[7] This double standard, which is clearly derived directly from 1 Cor. 7, was destined for extensive development and significant influence in the moral teachings of Western Christianity. It could be applied, as Clement interpreted it and as Paul doubtless intended, to enhance the freedom of individual Christians to undertake different forms of discipline without disparaging others. But it was a very short step to the conclusion that, while both married and celibate were Christian, the celibate were more so. When Chrysostom (ca. 347–407) distinguished between "that which is good and far more excellent" and that which is merely "safe and suited to assist your weakness," he could still appeal to the same passage of Paul's Corinthian letter. The medieval limitation of the Pauline word *vocatio* to the calling to monastic discipline as the only perfect Christian life was the ultimate outgrowth of this development, in which Paul's distinction between command and concession (1 Cor. 7:6) played a fateful role.[8]

If we are to believe the antiheretical writers of the early church, many of the Gnostics were not ascetics, but libertines. It is tempting to suppose that Paul's "antinomian" passages may have contributed to such a view, just as his proclamation of freedom in the

4. *Refutatio* VIII, 20,2 (my trans.).
5. *Strom.* III, *passim.* Clement must have had some success in reclaiming Paul for his "liberal" view of sex, for his pupil Origen reported that the Encratites in his time refused to accept the letters of Paul as scripture (*c.Cels.*, V, 65).
6. *Strom.* III, 96 and elsewhere. It is interesting that Paul himself, in his discussion of the sexual rights and obligations of husband and wife to each other (1 Cor. 7:1–7), never mentions procreation.
7. See especially *Strom.* III, 105.
8. On the early development see Maurice F. Wiles, *The Divine Apostle* (Cambridge, 1967), pp. 128–30.

spirit at Corinth may have contributed to the excesses he had later to combat in 1 Cor. 6. There is a certain Pauline resonance, for example, to the statement by which Carpocrates, according to Irenaeus, defended his insistence that "souls ought to experience every kind of life and action":

> For through faith and love we are saved; all else is indifferent after the opinion of men, and is sometimes considered good, sometimes bad. Nothing is evil by nature.[9]

If Irenaeus describes the Carpocrateans correctly, however, the real basis for their program was an anthropological dualism in which actions of body and soul were radically antithetical—just the kind of dualism that Paul rejects in 1 Cor. 6:12-20. Here again, as in the case of Tatian, Pauline slogans have been used selectively to gain "apostolic" support for positions arrived at independently of any authentic Pauline tradition.

One could more readily make a case for the Pauline origins of another very curious tradition, that equates salvation with the restoration of the lost unity of male and female. This very widespread belief, especially but not only in Gnostic circles, presupposes that the separation of male from female constitutes the most fundamental instance of man's self-alienation: "When Eve was in Adam, there was no death; but when she was separated from him death came into being."[1] Ultimately, that separation would be overcome in heaven, but already in the church it is overcome sacramentally, either in baptism or, in certain Gnostic groups of the Valentinian school, in a special "Sacrament of the bridal chamber."[2] The earliest witness to such sacramental reunification is Paul, who says to those who have "put on Christ" in baptism, "There is neither Jew nor Greek, there is neither slave nor free, there is no 'male and female'; for you are all one in Christ Jesus" (Gal. 3:28).[3] This does not mean, however, that Paul introduced this notion; he is probably quoting here an element of an early baptismal liturgy. There is no evidence that the later writers who elaborate on the reunification of

9. Irenaeus, *Adv. haer.* I, 25, 5 (=Harvey's ed. I, 20, 3), tr. Robert M. Grant in *Gnosticism: A Source Book of Heretical Writings from the Early Christian Period* (New York, 1961), p. 38. For other instances of Gnostic appeals to Paul, see above, p. 185.

1. *The Gospel of Philip*, tr. R. McL. Wilson (London, 1962), 116, 22–24; p. 44.

2. The sacrament or "mystery" of the bridal chamber, mentioned in Irenaeus' description of the Marcosian Gnostics (*Adv. haer.* I, 13, 3 = Harvey I, 7, 2; also Epiphanius, *haer.* 34, 2, 6–11), is now coming to be better known

through documents of the Chenoboskion Gnostic library: the Gospel of Philip, the yet-unpublished Exegesis of the Soul, and also, though less explicitly, the Gospel of Thomas shed light on the sacramental reunification of male and female. Early Syrian baptismal liturgy apparently described the newly baptized Christian as a bridegroom; the notion was also present outside Christianity, e.g., in late forms of the Gnostic movement that stemmed from Simon Magus.

3. I have modified the RSV translation to bring out the Greek's clear allusion to Gen. 1:27; see note *in loc.*

male and female are citing Paul; they represent rather a tradition with which Paul was acquainted, but which developed further quite independently of his influence. Paul, in fact, seems not to have been particularly interested in the male/female aspect of baptismal reunification, for in the other places where he alludes to the baptismal formula, that aspect is omitted (1 Cor. 12:13; Col. 3:11; cf. Eph. 2:14-16; 6:8). It is the reunification of Jew and Gentile that occupies Paul's primary attention.

Despite the polar tendencies of the interpreters of Paul's teachings on marriage, perhaps the dominant impression of Paul in the ancient church was that of the celibate who by "treading down and subjugating the body" made himself "a beautiful example and pattern to believers."[4] That is certainly the way he is depicted in the apocryphal Acts—those miracle-filled novels of apostolic exploits that were written in the second and third centuries. One of those, the Acts of Paul, contains our only physical description of Paul, one which strongly influenced the depiction of the apostle in painting and sculpture. The whole Acts of Paul has not survived except in fragments of varying extent, but the portion reprinted here, which circulated separately, has come down in numerous manuscripts and translations. The story principally of Thecla, a virgin saved by Paul from the terrible fate of marriage, it gives a clear picture of the way the apostle's mission was conceived in Encratite circles. Whether the Acts of Paul was itself written by an Encratite is doubtful; Encratite ideology appears in fact only in the Thecla cycle, suggesting that these stories originated in such circles, but were adapted into a more "orthodox" novel about Paul by the compiler of the Acts. Tertullian (ca. 200) attributes the compilation to "a presbyter in Asia," who lost his position when he confessed his forgery.[5] It is commonly argued that Tertullian must have meant the compiler of the whole Acts of Paul, but that is by no means certain, since he mentions Thecla, and his language suggests that the book was issued under the pseudonym of Paul. Eric Peterson has proposed that the Acts of Paul was a mediating work, modelled after the Acts of Peter, of Thomas, of Andrew, and of John, which are rather clearly of Encratite or related origins. The new work was intended to commend Paul to the ascetics.[6] That is plausible, despite objections which have been raised,[7] but the precise situation that produced these Acts is far from being clarified.

4. From "The First Epistle Concerning Virginity" of pseudo-Clement, Ch. 9, tr. M. B. Riddle in The Ante-Nicene Fathers (Grand Rapids, 1951), VIII, 58.
5. De baptismo, 17.
6. "Einige Beobachtungen zu den Anfangen der christlichen Askese," and "Einige Bemerkungen zum Hamburger Papyrusfragment der Acta Pauli," both reprinted in Frühkirche, Judentum and Gnosis (Rome, Freiburg, Vienna, 1959), pp. 183–220.
7. P. Devos, "Actes de Thomas et Actes de Paul," in Analecta Bollandiana 69 (1951); 119–30; W. Schneemelcher in New Testament Apocrypha II (London and Philadelphia, 1965), pp. 349–51.

ANONYMOUS

The Acts of Paul and Thecla (ca. 190?) †

1 As Paul went up to Iconium after his flight from Antioch, his travelling companions were Demas and Hermogenes the coppersmith, who were full of hyprocisy and flattered Paul as if they loved him. But Paul, who had eyes only for the goodness of Christ, did them no evil, but loved them greatly, so that he sought to make sweet to them all the words of the Lord, of the doctrine and of the interpretation of the Gospel, both of the birth and the resurrection of the Beloved, and he related to them word for word the great acts of Christ as they had been revealed to him.

2 And a man named Onesiphorus, who had heard that Paul was come to Iconium, went out with his children Simmias and Zeno and his wife Lectra to meet Paul, that he might receive him to his house. For Titus had told him what Paul looked like. For (hitherto) he had not seen him in the flesh, but only in the spirit. 3 And he went along the royal road which leads to Lystra, and stood there waiting for him, and looked at (all) who came, according to Titus' description. And he saw Paul coming, a man small of stature, with a bald head and crooked legs, in a good state of body, with eyebrows meeting and nose somewhat hooked, full of friendliness; for now he appeared like a man, and now he had the face of an angel.

4 And when Paul saw Onesiphorus he smiled; and Onesiphorus said: "Greeting, thou servant of the blessed God!" And he replied: "Grace be with thee and thy house!" But Demas and Hermogenes grew jealous, and went even further in their hypocrisy; so that Demas said: "Are we then not (servants) of the Blessed, that thou didst not greet us thus?" And Onesiphorus said: "I do not see in you any fruit of righteousness; but if ye are anything, come ye also into my house and rest yourselves!" 5 And when Paul was entered into the house of Onesiphorus there was great joy, and bowing of knees and breaking of bread, and the word of God concerning continence and the resurrection, as Paul said:

"Blessed are the pure in heart, for they shall see God.
Blessed are they who have kept the flesh pure, for they shall become a temple of God.
Blessed are the continent, for to them will God speak.
Blessed are they who have renounced this world, for they shall

† Tr. by Wilhelm Schneemelcher in Edgar Hennecke's *New Testament Apocrypha*, ed. Wilhelm Schnee- melcher; ET ed. R. McL. Wilson, vol. II (London and Philadelphia, 1965), pp. 353–64.

be well pleasing unto God.

Blessed are they who have wives as if they had them not, for they shall inherit God.

Blessed are they who have fear of God, for they shall become angels of God.

6 Blessed are they who tremble at the words of God, for they shall be comforted.

Blessed are they who have received (the) wisdom of Jesus Christ, for they shall be called sons of the Most High.

Blessed are they who have kept their baptism secure, for they shall rest with the Father and the Son.

Blessed are they who have laid hold upon the understanding of Jesus Christ, for they shall be in light.

Blessed are they who through love of God have departed from the form of this world, for they shall judge angels and at the right hand of the Father they shall be blessed.

Blessed are the merciful, for they shall obtain mercy, and shall not see the bitter day of judgment.

Blessed are the bodies of the virgins, for they shall be well pleasing to God, and shall not lose the reward of their purity.

For the word of the Father shall be for them a work of salvation in the day of his Son, and they shall have rest for ever and ever."

7 And while Paul was thus speaking in the midst of the assembly in the house of Onesiphorus, a virgin (named) Thecla—her mother was Theocleia—who was betrothed to a man (named) Thamyris, sat at a nearby window and listened night and day to the word of the virgin life as it was spoken by Paul; and she did not turn away from the window, but pressed on in the faith rejoicing exceedingly. Moreover, when she saw many women and virgins going in to Paul she desired to be counted worthy herself to stand in Paul's presence and hear the word of Christ; for she had not yet seen Paul in person, but only heard his word. 8 Since however she did not move from the window, her mother sent to Thamyris. He came in great joy as if he were already taking her in marriage. So Thamyris said to Theocleia "Where is my Thecla, that I may see her?" And Theocleia said: "I have a new tale to tell thee, Thamyris. For indeed for three days and three nights Thecla has not risen from the window either to eat or to drink, but gazing steadily as if on some joyful spectacle she so devotes herself to a strange man who teaches deceptive and subtle words that I wonder how a maiden of such modesty as she is can be so sorely troubled. 9 Thamyris, this man is upsetting the city of the Iconians, and thy Thecla in addition; for all the women and young people go in to

him, and are taught by him. 'You must' he says, 'fear one single God only, and live chastely.' And my daughter also, like a spider at the window bound by his words, is dominated by a new desire and a fearful passion; for the maiden hangs upon the things he says, and is taken captive. But go thou to her and speak to her, for she is betrothed to thee." 10 And Thamyris went to her, at one and the same time loving her and yet afraid of her distraction, and said: "Thecla, my betrothed, why dost thou sit thus? And what is this passion that holds thee distracted? Turn to thy Thamyris and be ashamed." And her mother also said the same: "Child, why dost thou sit thus looking down and making no answer, but like one stricken?" And those who were in the house wept bitterly, Thamyris for the loss of a wife, Theocleia for that of a daughter, the maidservants for that of a mistress. So there was a great confusion of mourning in the house. And while this was going on (all around her) Thecla did not turn away, but gave her whole attention to Paul's word.

11 But Thamyris sprang up and went out into the street, and closely watched all who went in to Paul and came out. And he saw two men quarrelling bitterly with one another, and said to them: "You men, who are you, tell me, and who is he that is inside with you, the false teacher who deceives the souls of young men and maidens, that they should not marry but remain as they are? I promise now to give you much money if you will tell me about him; for I am the first man of this city." 12 And Demas and Hermogenes said to him: "Who this man is, we do not know. But he deprives young men of wives and maidens of husbands, saying: 'Otherwise there is no resurrection for you, except ye remain chaste and do not defile the flesh, but keep it pure'." 13 And Thamyris said to them: "Come into my house, you men, and rest with me." And they went off to a sumptuous banquet, with much wine, great wealth and a splendid table. And Thamyris gave them to drink, for he loved Thecla and wished to have her for his wife. And during the dinner Thamyris said: "Tell me, you men, what is his teaching, that I also may know it; for I am greatly distressed about Thecla because she so loves the stranger, and I am deprived of my marriage." 14 But Demas and Hermogenes said:"Bring him before the governor Castellius, on the ground that he is seducing the crowds to the new doctrine of the Christians, and so he will have him executed and thou shalt have thy wife Thecla. And we shall teach three concerning the resurrection which he says is to come, that it has already taken place in the children whom we have, and that we are risen again in that we have come to know the true God."

15 When Thamyris had heard this from them, he rose up early in the morning full of jealousy and wrath and went to the house of

Onesiphorus with the rulers and officers and a great crowd with cudgels, and said to Paul: "Thou hast destroyed the city of the Iconians, and my betrothed, so that she will not have me. Let us go to the governor Castellius!" And the whole crowd shouted: "Away with the sorcerer! For he has corrupted all our wives." And the multitude let themselves be persuaded. **16** And Thamyris stood before the judgement-seat and cried aloud: "Proconsul, this man—we know not whence he is—who does not allow maidens to marry, let him declare before thee for what cause he teaches these things." And Demas and Hermogenes said to Thamyris: "Say that he is a Christian, and so thou wilt destroy him." But the governor was not easily to be swayed, and he called Paul, saying to him: "Who art thou, and what dost thou teach? For it is no light accusation that they bring against thee." **17** And Paul lifted up his voice and said: "If I today am examined as to what I teach, then listen, Proconsul. The living God, the God of vengeance, the jealous God, the God who has need of nothing, has sent me since he desires the salvation of men, that I may draw them away from corruption and impurity, all pleasure and death, and they may sin no more. For this cause God sent His own Son, whom I preach and teach that in him men have hope, who alone had compassion upon a world in error; that men may no longer be under judgment but have faith, and fear of God, and knowledge of propriety, and love of truth. If then I teach the things revealed to me by God, what wrong do I do, Proconsul?" When the governor heard this, he commanded Paul to be bound and led off to prison until he should find leisure to give him a more attentive hearing. **18** But Thecla in the night took off her bracelets and gave them to the door-keeper, and when the door was opened for her she went off to the prison. To the gaoler she gave a silver mirror, and so went in to Paul and sat at his feet and heard (him proclaim) the mighty acts of God. And Paul feared nothing, but comported himself with full confidence in God; and her faith also was increased, as she kissed his fetters. **19** But when Thecla was sought for by her own people and by Thamyris, they hunted her through the streets as one lost; and one of the door-keeper's fellow slaves betrayed that she had gone out by night. And they questioned the door-keeper, and he told them: "She has gone to the stranger in the prison." And they went as he had told them and found her, so to speak, bound with him in affection. And they went out thence, rallied the crowd about them, and disclosed to the governor what had happened.

20 He commanded Paul to be brought to the judgment-seat; but Thecla rolled herself upon the place where Paul taught as he sat in the prison. The governor commanded her also to be brought to the judgment-seat, and she went off with joy exulting. But when Paul was brought forward again, the crowd shouted out even louder: "He is a sorcerer! Away with him!" But the governor heard Paul gladly concerning the holy works of Christ; and when he had taken counsel he called Thecla and said: "Why dost thou not marry Thamyris according to the law of the Iconians?" But she stood there looking steadily at Paul. And when she did not answer, Theocleia her mother cried out, saying: "Burn the lawless one! Burn her that is no bride in the midst of the theatre, that all the women who have been taught by this man may be afraid!" **21** And the governor was greatly affected. He had Paul scourged and drove him out of the city, but Thecla he condemned to be burned. And forthwith the governor arose and went off to the theatre, and all the crowd went out to the unavoidable spectacle. But Thecla sought for Paul, as a lamb in the wilderness looks about for the shepherd. And when she looked upon the crowd, she saw the Lord sitting in the form of Paul and said: "As if I were not able to endure, Paul has come to look after me." And she looked steadily at him; but he departed into the heavens. **22** Now the young men and maidens brought wood and straw that Thecla might be burned. And as she was brought in naked, the governor wept and marvelled at the power that was in her. The executioners laid out the wood and bade her mount the pyre; and making the sign of the Cross (i.e., stretching out her arms) she climbed up on the wood. They kindled it, and although a great fire blazed up the fire did not touch her. For God in compassion caused a noise beneath the earth and a cloud above, full of rain and hail, overshadowed (the theatre) and its whole content poured out, so that many were in danger and died, and the fire was quenched and Thecla saved. **23** But Paul was fasting with Onesiphorus and his wife and the children in an open tomb on the way by which they go from Iconium to Daphne. And when many days were past, as they were fasting the boys said to Paul: "We are hungry." And they had nothing with which to buy bread, for Onesiphorus had left the things of the world and followed Paul with all his house. But Paul took off his outer garment and said: "Go, my child, ⟨sell this and⟩ buy several loaves and bring them here." But while the boy was buying he saw his neighbour Thecla, and was astonished and said: "Thecla, where art thou going?" And she said: "I am seeking after Paul, for I was saved from the fire." And the boy said: "Come, I will take thee to him, for he has been mourning for thee and praying and fasting six days already." **24** But when she came to the tomb Paul had bent his knees and was praying and saying: "Father of Christ, let not the fire touch Thecla, but be merciful to her, for she is thine!" But she standing behind him cried out: "Father, who didst make heaven and earth, the Father of thy beloved Son ⟨Jesus Christ⟩, I praise thee that thou didst save me from the fire, that I might see Paul!" And as Paul arose he saw her and said: "O God the knower of hearts, Father of our Lord Jesus Christ, I praise thee that thou hast so speedily (accomplished) what I asked, and hast hearkened unto me." **25** And within in the tomb there was much love, Paul rejoicing, and Onesiphorus and all of them. But they had five loaves, and vegetables, and water, and they were joyful over the holy works of Christ. And Thecla said to Paul: "I will cut my hair short and follow thee wherever thou goest." But he said: "The season is unfavourable, and thou are comely. May no other temptation come upon thee, worse than the first, and thou endure not and play the coward!" And Thecla said: "Only give me the seal in Christ, and the temptation shall not touch me." And Paul said: "Have patience, Thecla, and thou shalt receive the water."

26 And Paul sent away Onesiphorus with all his family to Iconium, and so taking Thecla came into Antioch. But immediately as they entered a Syrian by the name of Alexander, one of the first of the Antiochenes, seeing Thecla fell in love with her, and sought to win over Paul with money and gifts. But Paul said: "I do not know the woman of whom thou dost speak, nor is she mine." But he, being a powerful man, embraced her on the open street; she however would not endure it, but looked about for Paul and cried out bitterly, saying: "Force not the stranger, force not the handmaid of God! Among the Iconians I am one of the first, and because I did not wish to marry Thamyris I have been cast out of the city." And taking hold of Alexander she ripped his cloak, took off the crown from his head, and made him a laughing-stock. **27** But he, partly out of love for her and partly in shame at what had befallen him, brought her before the governor; and when she confessed that she had done these things, he condemned her to the beasts, ⟨since Alexander was arranging games⟩. But the women were panic-stricken, and cried out before the judgment-seat: "An evil judgment! A godless judgment!" But Thecla asked of the governor that she might remain pure until she was to fight with the beasts. And a rich woman named Tryphaena, whose daughter had died, took her under her protection and found comfort in her. **28** When the beasts were led in procession, they bound her to a fierce lioness, and the queen Tryphaena followed her. And as Thecla sat upon her back, the lioness licked her feet, and all the crowd was amazed. Now the charge upon her superscription was: Guilty of Sacrilege. But the women with their children cried out from above, saying: "O God, an impious judgment is come to pass in this city!" And after the procession Tryphaena took her again; for her daughter who was dead had spoken to her in a dream: "Mother, thou shalt have in my place the stranger, the desolate Thecla, that she may pray for me and I be translated to the place of the just." **29** So

when Tryphaena received her back from the procession she was at
once sorrowful, because she was to fight with the beasts on the following day, but at the same time loved her dearly like her own
daughter Falconilla; and she said: "Thecla, my second child, come
and pray for my child, that she may live; for this I saw in my
dream." And she without delay lifted up her voice and said: "Thou
God of heaven, Son of the Most High, grant to her according to
her wish, that her daughter Falconilla may live for ever!" And
when Thecla said this, Tryphaena mourned, considering that such
beauty was to be thrown to the beasts. **30** And when it was dawn,
Alexander came to take her away—for he himself was arranging the
games—and he said: "The governor has taken his place, and the
crowd is clamouring for us. Give me her that is to fight the beasts,
that I may take her away." But Tryphaena cried out so that he
fled, saying: "A second mourning for my Falconilla is come upon
my house, and there is none to help; neither child, for she is dead,
nor kinsman, for I am a widow. O God of Thecla my child, help
thou Thecla." **31** And the governor sent soldiers to fetch Thecla.
Tryphaena however did not stand aloof, but taking her hand herself led her up, saying: "My daughter Falconilla I brought to the
tomb; but thee, Thecla, I bring to fight the beasts." And Thecla
wept bitterly and sighed to the Lord, saying: "Lord God, in whom
I trust, with whom I have taken refuge, who didst deliver me from
the fire, reward thou Tryphaena, who had compassion upon thy
handmaid, and because she preserved me pure." **32** Then there was
a tumult, and roaring of the beasts, and a shouting of the people
and of the women who sat together, some saying: "Bring in the
sacrilegious one!" but the women saying: "May the city perish for
this lawlessness! Slay us all, Proconsul! A bitter sight, an evil judgment!" **33** But Thecla was taken out of Tryphaena's hands and
stripped, and was given a girdle and flung into the stadium. And
lions and bears were set upon her, and a fierce lioness ran to her and
lay down at her feet. And the crowd of the women raised a great
shout. And a bear ran upon her, but the lioness ran and met it, and
tore the bear asunder. And again a lion trained against men, which
belonged to Alexander, ran upon her; and the lioness grappled with
the lion, and perished with it. And the women mourned the more,
since the lioness which helped her was dead. **34** Then they sent in
many beasts, while she stood and stretched out her hands and
prayed. And when she had finished her prayer, she turned and saw a
great pit full of water, and said: "Now is the time for me to wash."
And she threw herself in, saying: "In the name of Jesus Christ I
baptize myself on the last day!" And when they saw it, the women
and all the people wept, saying: "Cast not thyself into the water!";
so that even the governor wept that such beauty should be
devoured by seals. So then, she threw herself into the water in the

name of Jesus Christ; but the seals, seeing the light of a lightning-flash, floated dead on the surface. And there was about her a cloud of fire, so that neither could the beasts touch her nor could she be seen naked. **35** But as other more terrible beasts were let loose, the women cried aloud, and some threw petals, others nard, others cassia, others amomum, so that there was an abundance of perfumes. And all the beasts let loose were overpowerd as if by sleep, and did not touch her. So Alexander said to the governor: "I have some very fearsome bulls—let us tie her to them." The governor frowning gave his consent, saying: "Do what thou wilt." And they bound her by the feet between the bulls, and set red-hot irons beneath their bellies that being the more enraged they might kill her. The bulls indeed leaped forward, but the flame that blazed around her burned through the ropes, and she was as if she were not bound. **36** But Tryphaena fainted as she stood beside the arena, so that her handmaids said: "The Queen Tryphaena is dead!" And the governor took note of it, and the whole city was alarmed. And Alexander fell down at the governor's feet and said: "Have mercy upon me, and on the city, and set the prisoner free, lest the city also perish with her. For if Caesar should hear this he will probably destroy both us and the city as well, because his kinswoman Tryphaena has died at the circus gates."

37 And the governor summoned Thecla from among the beasts, and said to her: "Who art thou? And what hast thou about thee, that not one of the beasts touched thee?" She answered: "I am a handmaid of the living God. As to what I have about me, I have believed in him in whom God is well pleased, His Son. For his sake not one of the beasts touched me. For he alone is the goal of salvation and the foundation of immortal life. To the storm-tossed he is a refuge, to the oppressed relief, to the despairing shelter; in a word, whoever does not believe in him shall not live, but die for ever." **38** When the governor heard this, he commanded garments to be brought, and said: "Put on these garments." But she said: "He who clothed me when I was naked among the beasts shall clothe me with salvation in the day of judgment." And taking the garments she put them on.

And straightway the governor issued a decree, saying: "I release to you Thecla, the pious handmaid of God." But all the women cried out with a loud voice, and as with one mouth gave praise to God, saying: "One is God, who has delivered Thecla!", so that all the city was shaken by the sound. **39** And Tryphaena when she was told the good news came to meet her with a crowd, and embraced Thecla and said: "Now I believe that the dead are raised up! Now I believe that my child lives! Come inside, and I will assign to thee all that is mine." So Thecla went in with her and rested in her house for eight days, instructing her in the word of God, so that the majority of the maidservants also believed; and there was great joy in the house.

40 But Thecla yearned for Paul and sought after him, sending in every direction. And it was reported to her that he was in Myra. So she took young men and maidservants and girded herself, and sewed her mantel into a cloak after the fashion of men, and went off to Myra, and found Paul speaking the word of God and went to him. But he was astonished when he saw her and the crowd that was with her, pondering whether another temptation was not upon her. But observing this she said to him: "I have taken the bath, Paul; for he who worked with thee for the Gospel has also worked with me for my baptism." **41** And taking her by the hand Paul led her into the house of Hermias, and heard from her everything (that had happened), so that Paul marvelled greatly and the hearers were confirmed and prayed for Tryphaena. And Thecla arose and said to Paul: "I am going to Iconium." But Paul said: "Go and teach the word of God!" Now Tryphaena sent her much clothing and gold, so that she could leave (some of it) for the service of the poor. **42** But she herself went away to Iconium and went into the house of Onesiphorus, and threw herself down on the floor where Paul had sat and taught the oracles of God, and wept, saying: "My God, and God of this house where the light shone upon me, Christ Jesus the Son of God, my helper in prison, my helper before governors, my helper in the fire, my helper among the beasts, thou art God, and to thee be the glory for ever. Amen." **43** And she found Thamyris dead, but her mother still alive; and calling her mother to her said to her: "Theocleia my mother, canst thou believe that the Lord lives in heaven? For whether thou dost desire money, the Lord will give it thee through me; or thy child, see, I stand beside thee."

And when she had borne this witness she went away to Seleucia; and after enlightening many with the word of God she slept with a noble sleep.

MAURICE F. WILES

The Domesticated Apostle (1967) †

We have come to the end of our study and the question that immediately arises in our minds is the question "How far then did the early commentators give a true interpretation of Paul's meaning?" Yet the very form in which the question arises is not without

† From the Epilogue to *The Divine Apostle: The Interpretation of St. Paul's Epistles in the Early Church* (Cambridge, 1967), a study of the commentaries on Paul's letters by the Church Fathers, from the earliest to Augustine. Maurice Wiles was formerly Dean of Clare College in the University of Cambridge, now professor of Christian Doctrine at King's College, London.

danger. It implies the assumption that we have a true interpretation of Paul's meaning—or at least a truer one than that of those whom we have studied—in the light of which theirs may be tested and judged. It may be so; but we as much as they are children of our own times and there may well be aspects of Pauline thought to which we are blinded by the particular presuppositions and patterns of theological thinking in our own day. If therefore we seek to pass judgement on other interpreters it can only be in the recognition that we also stand in need of judgement, even and perhaps especially when we are least conscious of that need.

Certainly the early commentators were much influenced by the tendencies of their times. In Pauline thought about the flesh and about the law there appears to be an element of unresolved tension. Gnostic thought, especially in its most Christian form in the teaching of Marcion, had stressed exclusively the element of Paul's hostility in both cases to a degree that was certainly false and equally certainly dangerous. It was inevitable that in orthodox exegesis the pendulum should swing strongly in the opposite direction. As a result, although for the most part they show a sound understanding of these aspects of Paul's thought, the orthodox commentaors are apt to be unbalanced and one-sided in their judgements. Thus on the subject of the flesh they are in general right to insist on the moral rather than the physical meaning of the word *sarx* [flesh] in many Pauline contexts. But in their determination not to deviate an inch from this basic understanding they are inclined to oversimplify the pattern of Paul's thought at the cost of complicating the exegesis of his words. It is somewhat ironic that Origen should have been most bitterly condemned for his teaching on the resurrection body, a point on which he was probably nearer to Paul's thought than his calumniators. So it was also with the concept of the law. The early commentators were right in seeing that Marcion had misunderstood Paul's view of the matter; Paul did see his teaching as a confirmation of the law. But on this issue also they were determined to make Paul entirely self-consistent and thus overemphasized the positive nature of his attitude to the law. But it was not only with himself that Paul had to be shown to be wholly consistent. Their view of inspiration involved the belief that all Scripture was self-consistent in the same thoroughgoing way. Augustine indeed declares that the thing which held him back from accepting and appreciating the value of Paul's writings in the time before his conversion was the way in which they appeared to him to be both self-contradictory and inconsistent with the Old Testament. Thus any exegetical device, however far-fetched, which could remove all trace of apparent internal inconsistency or conflict with the Old Testament was to be welcomed. Two main approaches to the problem predominate in their writings. In the first instance they give great prominence to the educative function of the law as a schoolmaster preparing men for the coming of Christ. In so doing a genuinely Pauline concept is given a proportionately greater emphasis than it holds in the writings of Paul himself, but no serious distortion of his thought would seem to be involved. Secondly, a clear distinction is drawn between the moral and the ceremonial laws. In this case they would seem to be introducing a wholly new line of thought not grounded at all in the writings of Paul himself. Such changes of emphasis and importation of new ideas were the more easily made because the commentators were thinking all the time primarily in terms of their own situation. In the closing years of the fourth century, when most of the commentaries were being written, the problem of the Jewish law was not a pressing issue. They could safely speak in positive terms of its confirmation in Christ without any fear that the Christians who heard them would even for a moment consider that they might be expected to follow it out in every detail. If Jewish critics did press the point, emphasis could always be laid upon the fact that the fulfilment of the law in Christ was of a spiritual nature. It is only very rarely that they make any attempt to enter into the very different conditions of Paul's own day and seek to understand his attitude to the law in the light of his own real situation. For them, living in the midst of a rapidly decaying civilization, the maintenance of law was an issue of the utmost importance. Too often it was in the light of this context that they reflected upon Paul's teaching on the law.

In the realm of Christology also it is the situation of the commentators' day rather than that of Paul's day which dominates the scene. This does not seem to have resulted in any serious distortion of the general substance of Paul's teaching, but it did lead to the introduction of an entirely alien element of precision into their interpretation of Paul's language about the person of Christ. In other words they were right in seeing that Paul's conception of Christ was better understood in terms of Nicene orthodoxy and of that developing line of thought which led ultimately to Chalcedon than in terms of any other rival definition of his person; they were altogether unjustified in seeing the details of those later beliefs explicitly indicated by the specific wording of the Pauline statements.

When we turn on to the great issues of grace, faith, and works, we turn to a field in which the early commentators were not so dominated by the exigencies of contemporary debate. It is true that Gnostic determinism was something to be denounced at every opportunity, but the great debate about grace within the Christian Church lay still just in the future. The commentaries of Augustine and of Pelagius both date from before the outbreak of the Pelagian controversy. In this respect it is the modern interpreter who is the more likely to be unduly influenced by the theological situation in which he stands. If the early commentators could only see Paul's teaching about the law through anti-Marcionite spectacles, the majority of Protestant critics of the Fathers have only been able to see their teaching through Reformed and Lutheran spectacles. 'In toto Origene non est verbum unum de Christo', wrote Luther; what no doubt he really meant was that Origen did not teach the same doctrine of justification by faith alone which he found in the writings of Paul. That is what many later Protestant writers have really meant when they have complained of the unpauline character of Origen and other patristic writers. In so far as that is what they really wanted to assert, they are undoubtedly correct; but it does not warrant the utter dismissal of the early commentators as totally insensitive to Paul's teaching. The Eastern writers were by no means unconcerned with the concept of divine grace. They fully recognized its prominent position in the teaching of Paul. But they also recognized (and here their fear of any form of Gnostic determinism certainly played its part) that the idea of divine grace must be linked closely with the correlative idea of the freedom of human response. Paul, they argued, was not a systematic theologian, and it was the religious purpose of his writing which led to the apparently one-sided stress on divine grace in his teaching. Once again therefore they endeavoured, however tortuous the detail of the exegesis might prove to be, to present Paul's thought as uniform throughout and as revealing a proper balance between divine grace and human freedom. Yet, while insisting in this way that any systematic exposition of Paul's thought must allow for the free human response of faith, they did not even so regard that faith as being itself a purely human matter. It too was in some important way the gift of God. Yet it could not, they argued, be simply and solely the gift of God, or else there would be nothing to prevent the immediate salvation of all. In the initial act of faith the element of human freedom must be retained. If it be objected that thereby they do make man in the last analysis determinative of his own salvation, two comments may be made. In the first place this type of approach was, with important differences of detailed application, characteristic of all the early commentators, even of Augustine in his early days. As long as the discussion is kept in the terms in which it was then conceived, it is difficult to find any alternative pattern of interpretation short of an unqualified predestinarianism, as the development of Augustine's thought bears witness. If Augustine's later thought seems to do better justice to some aspects of Paul's teaching, there are other aspects which it reduces to meaninglessness. Secondly, the early writers kept a firm hold on the conception of man as created by God's grace in his image. That which makes the initial response of faith in man is after all not man as over against God but the image of God in man. By that stress they sought to alleviate the apparently irreconcilable conflict between the ideas of divine grace and human freedom.

It would appear to be more in their understanding of the nature of faith than in their accounts of its relation to divine grace that the commentators are apt to misrepresent the substance of Paul's thought. If the Epistle of James was intended as a corrective to certain misunderstandings of Paul's teaching in an antinomian direction, then it certainly performed its task effectively. The great majority of the Fathers see the Pauline conception of faith through the eyes of the author of the Epistle of James. Faith is primarily intellectual assent to certain dogmatic truths; and once that definition of faith has been given it is inevitable that any genuinely religious mind will add on works also as being necessary to salvation. This occurs frequently in the commentaries. Two exceptions to this understanding of the idea of faith are to be found in the earliest of the Greek and of the Latin commentators. Origen puts forward a profound resolution of the whole issue of faith and works in his insistence upon Christ not merely possessing but being his attributes of truth, righteousness, wisdom, peace and so forth. Victorinus in a different way lays a notable emphasis on faith as full personal fellowship and identification with Christ. But the determinative pattern of interpretation in the great majority of the commentaries is closer to that of the Epistle of James than to that of Paul himself.

Two other characteristics of the interpretation of this aspect of Paul's teaching are deserving of note. The concept of merit plays its part in the thought of all the interpreters, even of Augustine in the later stages of his career. Romans ii was felt to show its fully Pauline character as a category for understanding God's dealings with men. It was claimed, not only by Augustine but also by the Eastern writers, to be fully consonant with the Pauline teaching about grace if applied only to good works subsequent to faith. The second feature to be noted is the eschatological emphasis in Theodore of Mopsuestia's understanding of Paul's theology. It may be objected that Theodore is false to Paul in stressing death rather than sin as the root of man's problem. But at least it enables him in his presentation of the positive aspects of Paul's thought to declare Paul's message with striking effect as a message of resurrection life experienced in anticipation now and soon to be realized in all its fullness. Theodore has always been noted for the shrewd and careful nature of his comments on the grammatical form and contextual structure of the Epistles. There are certainly times when he forces his own theological system out of the text, but there are also times when his eschatological emphasis leads to a unique insight into Paul's meaning. For example it enables him to appreciate the radical nature of Paul's approach to the question of the law with an unusual degree of penetration. All in all there is a dynamic quality about the commentaries of Theodore which is lacking in the work of many of the other commentators.

The traditional Protestant complaint that the early commentators as a whole present a falsely moralistic understanding of Paul's thought is not without foundation. This moralistic emphasis had already come to characterize Christian thought and writing long before the task of Pauline exegesis had been begun. The experience of Christian missions in different parts of the world has consistently revealed the moralistic tendency of second- and third-generation Christian churches. When the first flush of the preaching of the gospel is over, the predominant task of the Church appears as the bringing up of a new generation in distinctively Christian ways over against the non-Christian traditions of their environment. New converts too need to be taught the agreed patterns of conduct expected of members of the Christian community. These tasks are essential and they are not easily performed without the development of required codes of behaviour of a moralistic, and even of a legalitic, kind. The practice develops first; the rationalizing thelogical explanation comes later. Processes of this kind were clearly at work in the Church of the second century. Paul had differentiated the Christian way of the obedience of faith from the Jewish way of observance of the law. The *Didache* is equally anxious to differentiate between the ways of Christianity and of Judaism, but does so in a manner which is far more superficial but which is also easier both to inculcate and to practise; the Christian is to fast on the fourth and sixth days of the week in contrast to the Jewish fasts on the second and the fifth. Moreover, if a set pattern of conduct throughout a long period of catechumenate is required before admission to baptism is granted, it is no long step to regarding that conduct as contributing to the attainment of salvation. In their very different ways both the persecutions of the third century and the influx of nominal Christians in the fourth served to enhance this emphasis upon the observance of a set pattern of behavior. It is hardly surprising if in such a situation the commentators on Paul's epistles should emphasize both the positive aspect of Paul's attitude to the law and the necessity of works. The pattern of church life within which they lived and worked could not but affect their exegesis of Paul's thought in this way. Yet it never made them wholly blind to his message. The priority of divine grace was more widely and more strongly upheld than has often been recognized. Moreover, as we have just seen, an understanding of faith in terms of personal communion with Christ is a prominent feature in the thought both of Origen and of Victorinus. It is perhaps not without significance that both writers were men much influenced by the spiritual character of Middle Platonist and Neoplatonist teaching. It is common to speak of Platonism in relation to the early Church's understanding of the faith of the Bible as being the siren voice which drew men away from the dynamic patterns of biblical thought. But that is certainly not the whole story of the influence it exerted. Neoplatonism was never a popular movement in the sense in which Christianity was. It was therefore in less danger of losing its spiritual quality in a merely moralistic interpretation of man's need. It may have helped to keep alive amongst Christian thinkers a more spiritual approach to the message of Paul, and it would appear at least to have been one important factor in opening the eyes of Augustine to the truth and profundity of that message.

No brief or simple answer can be given to the question how far the early commentators truly understood the mind of Paul. The early exegetical tradition is often forced in its detailed outworking, but there is more in it which reveals than which distorts the text which it expounds. Nevertheless, the total impression which it leaves upon the reader is that Paul has been tamed in the process. In part that is inevitable. A work of commentary can never have the same dynamic vitality as the original which it sets out to interpret. In this instance this general tendency was exaggerated by two main causes. In the first place Paul's interpreters were writing for the everyday needs of a Church whose nature as an established community and whose situation within the Roman Empire were totally different from what they had been in Paul's day. In the second place their understanding of Scripture required that Paul's vigorous affirmations be reduced to a wholly self-consistent system. For all their recognition of the pragmatic, religious intention of his letters, they still felt the need to show that all his words were true as general philosophical statements about the precise nature of God and man. Thus pedagogic utility and philosophical systematization were always important aspects of their aim in the work of commentary. Such aims are likely to tame the writings of the most vigorous prophet.

There is no single commentator of whom we may assert that he catches and reflects the fullness of Paul's thought. If Chrysostom's commentaries are the most consistently sound and reliable in their judgements, they yet lack conspicuously that penetration of sympathetic insight which alone could fully justify the panegyrics which some later writers have heaped upon them. On the other hand, there is no commentator whose work has come down to us in any quantity in whose writings there are not to be found comments of real and lasting worth. For all their very real shortcomings, at least the theory that the thought of Paul was totally lost in the obscurity of a dark Pelagian world until the shining of the great Augustinian light is one deserving to be dismissed to that very limbo of outworn ideas in which it would itself seek to place the early patristic commentaries on the writings of the divine apostle.

PART IV

Law Versus Grace
and the Problem of Ethics

Since the beginning of the fifth century, Paul has been understood in Western Christianity primarily as the theologian of grace, whose most central doctrine could be indicated by the phrase "justification by grace." By being linked with the word "justification," grace was given a certain legal cast. The human problem was defined by the question, How could one be found innocent before the bar of God's final judgment? Paul's influence was not needed to produce this juridical concept of salvation, but from Augustine on, the discussion of salvation in the West was shaped by a distinctly Pauline paradox: the very God who by his nature requires of his creatures "righteousness" and gives his law to define that righteousness, is the God who in Jesus Christ "justifies" man "apart from the law."

Before Augustine the sharpness of the Pauline paradox was grasped only by certain Christians who stood outside the emerging catholic consensus. It was seized by Marcion and made into the center and essence of Christianity in so radical a way that everything else—the Old Testament as a whole, all gospels but one, and all apostles but Paul—had to be rejected. At the opposite pole those Jewish-Christian groups who recognized Paul as the teacher of grace against the law rejected Paul. Most of the ecclesiastical writers who hailed Paul as "the divine apostle," however, either ignored or banalized his troublesome statements about the law. In the second and third centuries the church was preoccupied with survival, unity, and internal moral discipline. Correspondingly, Paul was treated by and large as an authority behind the church's teachings, as the author of moral advice, and as an example of the moral and spiritual life to be emulated by believers.[1] In the Eastern churches, Paul's justification doctrine never had great

1. A preface to Paul's letters, probably composed near the end of the fourth century and so popular in the Eastern churches that it was incorporated into scores of medieval manuscripts of the NT, describes the letters as "exhorta-tions to a virtuous life" and "advice concerning what men ought to do." See Louis Charles Willard, "A Critical Study of the Euthalian Apparatus" (Unpub. Ph.D. Diss., Yale University, 1970), p. 198.

impact. The Letter to the Romans, in which that doctrine is most fully and systematically developed, was frequently passed over or sketchily treated in the commentaries of the Greek-speaking churches, which devoted attention rather to Paul's "mysticism," his doctrine of the church as Christ's body, his statements about Christ as the image of God, and his sacramental teaching.[2]

There were a number of reasons why the church may have been reluctant to give any central place to Paul's doctrine of grace. The Greek fathers consciously felt that there was a danger of overemphasizing divine grace at the cost of man's rational freedom of choice—which had been a precious part of the Greek classical heritage.[3] In the Latin West, law was an equally sacred cultural tradition, which took on added significance under the political dangers of the late fourth century, by which time Paul's peculiar problem with advocates of the Jewish law had ceased to be an issue at all.[4] Perhaps the most important factor, however, was simply the controversial character of the justification doctrine because of its association with heretical groups. Tertullian even referred to Paul as "the apostle of the heretics."

It was a doctrine born in controversy, and it is precisely in the storm centers of controversy that it has reappeared in the history of Western Christianity. Paul first stated the radical disjunction between grace and law in his letter to the Galatians, which was a counterattack upon Jewish-Christian groups who were seeking to overturn his authority there. It was in response to attack also that Augustine began his preoccupation with this doctrine. A British monk, Pelagius, who had come to Rome around 400 and thence, when Rome fell to Alaric in 410, to North Africa, had accused Augustine of undermining the moral law by preaching grace. The long series of counterattacks which Augustine wrote are all basically expositions of Paul's letters.

For Martin Luther, Paul's attack on the law became the warrant for his own attack upon the dogmas and structures of the medieval church. The selection below, from his "Lectures on Galatians," shows clearly the way in which Luther found Paul a comrade in arms, identifying his own struggles and his own enemies with those of the apostle.

In the present century, the young Karl Barth brought Paul once again into the center of controversy, calling him to arms against the prevailing Protestant liberalism. Liberalism had come to terms with Paul as the missionary who founded a Christian civilization, as a thinker who released Christianity from the historically limited chrysalis of Judaism to develop into a universal religion of humanity, and especially as a *homo religiosus*, the model of deep religious experience. In this framework, "justification" was understood primarily as forgiveness, the expression of God's eternal quality of fatherly mercy and his will to unite himself with man's upward-striving spirit. Paul's doctrines of sin, judgment, and justification were often treated as mere relics of his Jewish heritage, implicitly broken by his universalism and therefore to be ignored. But Barth read in the signs of his

2. See Ernst Benz, "Das Paulus-Verständnis in der morgenländischen und abendländischen Kirche," *Zeitschr. für Religions- und Geistesgeschichte* 3 (1951): 289–309.
3. Wiles, *op. cit.*, pp. 94–109.
4. See Wiles, above, pp. 208 f.

times, in the collapse of Europe in World War I, the fatal weakness of that benign "culture-Protestantism," with its naïve optimism and its helplessness before the unanticipated demonism of "modern" institutions. And he began a massive assault upon it by writing—not an ordinary tract, but—a commentary on Paul's letter to the Romans.

If the Pauline doctrine of grace has maintained its explosive potential within Western Christendom, the objections raised against it in the ancient church have also reasserted themselves repeatedly. First, it is frequently objected that if salvation is understood as entirely God's work, then the ultimate sanction for human morality is removed. If all men are sinners and God's choice among them depends, not on their attempts to be good, but only on *his* goodness, then there is hardly any reason left to try to be good. There were people in Paul's lifetime already who thought that was the implication of his teaching; his replies are found in Rom. 3:8; 6:1–7:6; Gal. 5; 1 Cor. 10, and elsewhere. It was the underlying concern voiced by Pelagius, and it has been raised anew whenever and wherever the Pauline attack on "the law" has been recalled. Does not the categorical rejection of law imply the elimination of any rules for ethical behavior? This concern has frequently led to attempts to limit the force of Paul's strictures against the law. For example, in the ancient church it was regularly assumed that he meant to disparage only the "ceremonial," not the moral commandments, although Augustine demonstrated once and for all that Paul did not make that distinction. Luther taught that the law remained valid in the kingdom of the world, being radically displaced only within the church. Calvinists believed that Christians still needed the law for governing both church and society, although they agreed with Paul that *salvation* could not be accomplished by law. Others, however, have found Paul's doctrine attractive just because its ethical implications seemed radical. It would surely not be a mistake to see here the basis for Kierkegaard's opposition between the ethical stage and the religious stage of life, as well as the framework for the present-day controversy over "contextual" or "situational" ethics as opposed to ethics of rules or principles.

Second, does not the expression of the gospel in forensic terms have fateful consequences for the understanding of God? Some have blamed Paul for the retention in Christianity of the "Jewish" picture of God as arbitrary, omnipotent, and judgmental (see the selection from Nietzsche in Part V). The most extreme forms of this attack came from the prophets of Aryan racial purity, from Paul de Lagarde in the nineteenth century to Alfred Rosenberg and the "German Christians" in the 1930's. But milder statements in the same direction have been heard rather frequently both within and without Christian circles. Even so devoted a student of Paul as John Knox asks whether Paul did not introduce a fatal split into the conception of God's character, setting his justice at odds with his mercy.[5] Yet the opposite complaint has also been made: that Paul has, by attacking the law, severed Christianity's roots in Judaism. By cutting away the historic center of Jewish commitment, Paul, these opponents argue, de-historicized Christianity, leaving it subject to unchecked mythmaking and prey to all kinds of romanticism (see the essays in Part VI).

5. *Chapters in a Life of Paul* (Nashville, 1950), pp. 141–55.

Third, both kinds of anti-Paulinists have tended to agree that Paul's concept of God as utterly transcendent and holy (either because this concept is "too Jewish" or not Jewish enough, depending on the point of view) results in a perverse view of man. Paul seems, it is frequently asserted, preoccupied with sin, with human nothingness, with man's "total depravity," (Nietzsche's aphorisms in Part V, and Kierkegaard's homily, in Part VII, represent opposite but not entirely unrelated perspectives on this question.) Does not this doctrine of grace reduce human beings to passive lumps in the hand of an arbitrary God? Does not the pernicious doctrine of predestination follow? Is it not true that the most ardent Paulinists in the history of the West have been the advocates of predestinarianism in its most fatalistic form, with its eternally unalterable registers of the Elect and the Damned? The discussion by Karl Barth of "the new man" presents a novel way of responding to some of these questions, in the belief that Paul's doctrine of grace lays the foundation for a new humanism and a new universalism. Also relevant to this topic, besides what is said about it by Augustine and Luther, are the essays by Rudolf Bultmann and Krister Stendahl in Part VII below.

This glimpse of the vehement and polar reactions that have been evoked again and again by the Pauline doctrine of grace suggests that there are two further broad questions that have to be kept in mind. First, was this really the central or unique teaching of Paul? As we have already seen, the church in the second and third centuries, while praising Paul, largely ignored this doctrine, and the Eastern churches have always shown minimal concern for it. Even within the Augustinian-Lutheran tradition there have been frequent demurrers, and Wilhelm Wrede and Albert Schweitzer in this century (see Part VII) insist that Paul's concern with the "righteousness of God" was only a "subsidiary crater" on the periphery of his religion. Even Karl Barth, who appears here as a modern advocate of that concern, points to the necessity of keeping it in balance with other concerns: "The problem of justification does not need artificially to be absolutized and given a monopoly. It has its own dignity and necessity to which we do more and not less justice if we do not ascribe to it a totalitarian claim which is not proper to it, or allow all other questions to culminate or merge into it . . ."[6] There certainly are other concerns in Paul's letters, and some of them seem to exist in a certain tension with the concept of justification by grace. Whether that tension is creative or destructive is perhaps the primary question under discussion here. In 1872 Hermann Lüdemann published a book on Paul's anthropology[7] that distinguished two notions of salvation in Paul: the one, justification by faith, a Jewish notion; the other, a sacramental, quasi-magical salvation by means of baptism, a Hellenistic idea. For half a century there ensued a debate over the relation between the "juridical" and the "sacramental," or between the "ethical" and the "mystical" sides of Paul. The essay by Hans von Soden below was addressed specifically to this group of questions; the essays by Deissmann, Schweitzer, and Dibelius excerpted in Part VII were also involved to a certain extent in the same debate.[8]

6. *Church Dogmatics*, IV/1, §61 (Edinburgh, 1956), p. 528.
7. *Die Anthropologie des Apostels Paulus and ihre Stellung innerhalb seiner Heilslehre* (Kiel, 1872).

8. For more recent and comprehensive work on Paul's ethics, see the works by Enslin, Furnish, and Schnackenburg named in the Bibliography (p. 446).

The second general question, and a sobering one, is this: Do we really understand what Paul meant by justification? In an important series of lectures on "The Role of the Apostle Paul in the Theological Development of the Early Church,"[9] the Catholic New Testament scholar Otto Kuss warns that any study of Paul must take account of his "strangeness." He means Paul's difference from ourselves, the difference of his culture and situation, of his problems, of his opponents, of his personal status. And in a similar vein Krister Stendahl, in the essay reprinted below, speaks of the "peril of modernizing Paul." These warnings stir up questions which are haunting sensitive historians today: Can we truly know the past? Can we truly understand it? We have come to see that solemn vows of objectivity are not enough to assure that we shall. What is required is a profound openness to the "strangeness" of the past, perhaps not separable from an openness to "strange" points of view in our present. The possibility of nurturing that kind of openness is obviously one of the reasons for the existence of the *Norton Critical Editions in the History of Ideas.* And it may be that that possibility is not unrelated to the freedom borne by faith of which Paul speaks.

9. *Münchener Theo. Zeitschr.* 14 (1963); 1–59, 109–87; see esp. pp. 39–51.

AURELIUS AUGUSTINE

On Grace and Free Will (427) †

Chapter XIX

HOW IS ETERNAL LIFE BOTH A REWARD FOR SERVICE AND A FREE
GIFT OF GRACE?

* * * If eternal life is rendered to good works, as the Scripture
most openly declares: "Then He shall reward every man according
to his works:"[1] how can eternal life be a matter of grace, seeing
that grace is not rendered to works, but is given gratuitously, as the
apostle himself tells us: "To him that worketh is the reward not
reckoned of grace, but of debt;"[2] and again: "There is a remnant
saved according to the election of grace;" with these words immediately subjoined: "And if of grace, then is it no more of works; otherwise grace is no more grace"?[3] How, then, is eternal life by grace,
when it is received from works? Does the apostle perchance not say
that eternal life is a grace? Nay, he has so called it, with a clearness
which none can possibly gainsay. It requires no acute intellect, but
only an attentive reader, to discover this. For after saying, "The
wages of sin is death," he at once added, "The grace of God is eternal life through Jesus Christ our Lord."[4]

Chapter XX

THE QUESTION ANSWERED. JUSTIFICATION IS GRACE SIMPLY AND
ENTIRELY. ETERNAL LIFE IS REWARD AND GRACE

This question, then, seems to me to be by no means capable of
solution, unless we understand that even those good works of ours,

† St. Augustine (354–430) was bishop
of Hippo Regius in North Africa and,
because of his extensive writings, without doubt the most important of the
early Western "Doctors of the
Church." This treatise from his last
years was less directly involved in the
polemic against Pelagius than such earlier works as "On the Spirit and the
Letter" and "On Nature and Grace,"
but it does present in brief compass
the mature fruit of Augustine's involve-
ment in that controversy. The immediate occasion was a debate among certain monks at Adrumetum, which had
been provoked by Augustine's anti-
Pelagian writings. The first few chapters of the treatise, omitted here, reject
both poles of the logical dichotomy
that had divided the monks: either the
denial of man's free will, in order to
preserve the Pauline concept of grace,
or the reduction of grace to God's mere
cooperation with man's natural good,
in order to preserve free will. Scripture, says Augustine with heavy use of
Pauline texts, clearly teaches *both*
God's free grace *and* man's free responsibility. Chapter 19 begins with the
paradox thus stated. The translation is
by P. Holmes in *Basic Writings of
Saint Augustine*, ed. Whitney J. Oates
(New York, 1948) I, 748–74.
1. Matt. 16:27.
2. Rom. 4:4.
3. Rom. 11:5, 6.
4. Rom. 6:23.

which are recompensed with eternal life, belong to the grace of God, because of what is said by the Lord Jesus: "Without me ye can do nothing."[5] And the apostle himself, after saying, "By grace are ye saved through faith; and that not of yourselves, it is the gift of God: not of works, lest any man should boast;"[6] saw, of course, the possibility that men would think from this statement that good works are not necessary to those who believe, but that faith alone suffices for them; and again, the possibility of men's boasting of their good works, as if they were of themselves capable of performing them. To meet, therefore, these opinions on both sides, he immediately added, "For we are His workmanship, created in Christ Jesus unto good works, which God hath before ordained that we should walk in them."[7] What is the purport of his saying, "Not of works, lest any man should boast," while commending the grace of God? And then why does he afterwards, when giving a reason for using such words, say, "For we are His workmanship, created in Christ Jesus unto good works"? Why, therefore, does it run, "Not of works, lest any man should boast"? Now, hear and understand. "Not of works" is spoken of the works which you suppose have their origin in yourself alone; but you have to think of works for which God has moulded (that is, has formed and created) you. For of these he says, "We are His workmanship, created in Christ Jesus unto good works." Now he does not here speak of that creation which made us human beings, but of that in reference to which one said who was already in full manhood, "Create in me a clean heart, O God;"[8] concerning which also the apostle says, "Therefore, if any man be in Christ, he is a new creature: old things are passed away; behold, all things are become new. And all things are of God."[9] We are framed, therefore, that is, formed and created, "in the good works which" we have not ourselves prepared, but "God hath before ordained that we should walk in them." It follows, then, dearly beloved, beyond all doubt, that as your good life is nothing else than God's grace, so also the eternal life which is the recompense of a good life is the grace of God; moreover it is given gratuitously, even as that is given gratuitously to which it is given. But that to which it is given is solely and simply grace; this therefore is also that which is given to it, because it is its reward—grace is for grace, as if remuneration for righteousness; in order that it may be true, because it is true, that God "shall reward every man according to his works."[1]

5. John 15:5.
6. Eph. 2:8, 9.
7. Eph. 2:10.
8. Ps. 51:12.

9. 2 Cor. 5:17, 18.
1. Matt. 16:27; Ps. 62:12; Rev. 22:12.

* * *

Chapter XXII

WHO IS THE TRANSGRESSOR OF THE LAW? THE OLDNESS OF ITS LETTER. THE NEWNESS OF ITS SPIRIT

Therefore, brethren, you ought by free will not do evil but do good; this, indeed, is the lesson taught us in the law of God, in the Holy Scriptures—both Old and New. Let us, however, read, and by the Lord's help understand, what the apostle tells us: "Because by the deeds of the law there shall no flesh be justified in His sight; for by the law is the knowledge of sin."[2] Observe, he says "*the knowledge,*" not "the destruction," of sin. But when a man knows sin, and grace does not help him to avoid what he knows, undoubtedly the law works wrath. And this the apostle explicitly says in another passage. His words are: "The law worketh wrath."[3] The reason of this statement lies in the fact that God's wrath is greater in the case of the transgressor who by the law knows sin, and yet commits it; such a man is thus a transgressor of the law, even as the apostle says in another sentence, "For where no law is, there is no transgression."[4] It is in accordance with this principle that he elsewhere says, "That we may serve in newness of spirit, and not in the oldness of the letter;"[5] wishing *the law* to be here understood by "the oldness of the letter," and what else by "newness of spirit" than *grace?* Then, that it might not be thought that he had brought any accusation, or suggested any blame, against the law, he immediately takes himself to task with this inquiry: "What shall we say, then? Is the law sin? God forbid." He then adds the statement: "Nay, I had not known sin but by the law;"[6] which is of the same import as the passage above quoted: "By the law is the knowledge of sin."[7] Then: "For I had not known lust," he says, "except the law had said, 'Thou shalt not covet.'[8] But sin, taking occasion by the commandment, wrought in me all manner of concupiscence, For without the law sin was dead. For I was alive without the law once; but when the commandment came, sin revived, and I died. And the commandment, which was ordained to life, I found to be unto death. For sin, taking occasion by the commandment, deceived me, and by it slew me. Wherefore the law is holy; and the commandment holy, just, and good. Was, then, that which is good made death unto me? God forbid. But sin, that it might appear sin,

2. Rom. 3:20.
3. Rom. 4:15.
4. *Ibid.*
5. Rom. 7:6.

6. Rom. 7:6, 7.
7. Rom. 3:20.
8. Ex. 20:17.

worked death in me by that which is good—in order that the sinner, or the sin, might by the commandment become beyond measure."[9] And to the Galatians he writes: "Knowing that a man is not justified by the works of the law, except through faith in Jesus Christ, even we have believed in Jesus Christ, that we might be justified by the faith of Christ, and not by the works of the law; for by the works of the law shall no flesh be justified."[1]

Chapter XXIII

THE PELAGIANS MAINTAIN THAT THE LAW IS THE GRACE OF GOD WHICH HELPS US NOT TO SIN

Why, therefore, do those very vain and perverse Pelagians say that the law is the grace of God by which we are helped not to sin? Do they not, by making such an allegation, unhappily and beyond all doubt contradict the great apostle? He, indeed, says, that by the law sin received strength against man; and that man, by the commandment, although it be holy, and just, and good, nevertheless dies, and that death works in him through that which is good, from which death there is no deliverance unless the Spirit quickens him, whom the letter had killed—as he says in another passage, "The letter killeth, but the Spirit giveth life."[2] And yet these obstinate persons, blind to God's light, and deaf to His voice, maintain that the letter which kills gives life, and thus gainsay the quickening Spirit. "Therefore, brethren" (that I may warn you with better effect in the words of the apostle himself), "we are debtors not to the flesh, to live after the flesh; for if ye live after the flesh ye shall die; but if ye through the Spirit do mortify the deeds of the body, ye shall live."[3] I have said this to deter your free will from evil, and to exhort it to good by apostolic words; but yet you must not therefore glory in man—that is to say, in your own selves—and not in the Lord, when you live not after the flesh, but through the Spirit mortify the deeds of the flesh. For in order that they to whom the apostle addressed this language might not exalt themselves, thinking that they were themselves able of their own spirit to do such good works as these, and not by the Spirit of God, after saying to them, "If ye through the Spirit do mortify the deeds of the flesh, ye shall live," he at once added, "For as many as are led by the Spirit of God, they are the sons of God."[4] When, therefore, you by the Spirit mortify the deeds of the flesh, that you may have life, glorify Him, praise Him, give thanks to Him by whose Spirit you are so led

9. Rom. 7:7–13.
1. Gal. 2:16.
2. 2 Cor. 3:6.

3. Rom. 8:12–13.
4. Rom. 8:14.

as to be able to do such things as show you to be the children of God; "for as many as are led by the Spirit of God, they are the sons of God."

Chapter XXIV

WHO MAY BE SAID TO WISH TO ESTABLISH THEIR OWN RIGHTEOUSNESS. "GOD'S RIGHTEOUSNESS," SO CALLED, WHICH MAN HAS FROM GOD

As many, therefore, as are led by their own spirit, trusting in their own virtue, with the addition merely of the law's assistance, without the help of grace, are not the sons of God. Such are they of whom the same apostle speaks as "being ignorant of God's righteousness, and wishing to establish their own righteousness, who have not submitted themselves to the righteousness of God."[5] He said this of the Jews, who in their self-assumption rejected grace, and therefore did not believe in Christ. Their own righteousness, indeed, he says, they wish to establish; and this righteousness is of the law—not that the law was established by themselves, but that they had constituted their righteousness in the law which is of God, when they supposed themselves able to fulfil that law by their own strength, ignorant of God's righteousness—not indeed that by which God is Himself righteous, but that which man has from God. And that you may know that he designated as *theirs* the righteousness which is of the law, and as *God's* that which man receives from God, hear what he says in another passage, when speaking of Christ: "For whose sake I counted all things not only as loss, but I deemed them to be dung, that I might win Christ, and be found in Him—not having my own righteousness, which is of the law, but that which is through the faith of Christ, which is of God."[6] Now what does he mean by "not having my own righteousness, which is of the law," when the law is really not his at all, but God's—except this, that he called it his own righteousness, although it was of the law, because he thought he could fulfil the law by his own will, without the aid of grace which is through faith in Christ? Wherefore, after saying, "Not having my own righteousness, which is of the law," he immediately subjoined, "But that which is through the faith of Christ, which is of God." This is what they were ignorant of, of whom he says, "Being ignorant of God's righteousness"—that is, the righteousness which is of God (for it is given not by the letter, which kills, but by the life-giving Spirit), "and wishing to establish their own righteousness," which he expressly described as the righteousness of the law, when he said, "Not having my own righteousness, which is of the law;" they were not subject to the

5. Rom. 10:3.   6. Phil. 3:8, 9.

righteousness of God—in other words, they submitted not themselves to the grace of God. For they were under the law, not under grace, and therefore sin had dominion over them, from which a man is not freed by the law, but by grace. On which account he elsewhere says, "For sin shall not have dominion over you; because ye are not under the law, but under grace."⁷ Not that the law is evil; but because they are under its power, whom it makes guilty by imposing commandments, not by aiding. It is by grace that any one is a doer of the law; and without this grace, he who is placed under the law will be only a hearer of the law. To such persons he addresses these words: "Ye who are justified by the law are fallen from grace."⁸

Chapter XXV

AS THE LAW IS NOT, SO NEITHER IS OUR NATURE ITSELF THAT GRACE BY WHICH WE ARE CHRISTIANS

Now who can be so insensible to the words of the apostle, who so foolishly, nay, so insanely ignorant of the purport of his statement, as to venture to affirm that the law is grace, when he who knew very well what he was saying emphatically declares, "Ye who are justified by the law are fallen from grace"? Well, but if the law is not grace, seeing that in order that the law itself may be kept, it is not the law, but only grace which can give help, will not nature at any rate be grace? For this, too, the Pelagians have been bold enough to aver, that grace is the nature in which we were created, so as to possess a rational mind, by which we are enabled to understand—formed as we are in the image of God, so as to have dominion over the fish of the sea, and over the fowl of the air, and over every living thing that creepeth upon the earth. This, however, is not the grace which the apostle commends to us through the faith of Jesus Christ. For it is certain that we possess this nature in common with ungodly men and unbelievers; whereas the grace which comes through the faith of Jesus Christ belongs only to them to whom the faith itself appertains. "For all men have not faith."⁹ Now, as the apostle, with perfect truth, says to those who by wishing to be justified by the law have fallen from grace, "If righteousness come by the law, then Christ is dead in vain;"¹ so likewise, to those who think that the grace which he commends and faith in Christ receives, is nature, the same language is with the same degree of truth applicable: if righteousness come from nature, then Christ is dead in vain. But the law was in existence up to that time, and it did not justify; and nature existed too, but it did not justify. It was

7. Rom. 6:14.
8. Gal. 5:4.

9. 2 Thess. 3:2.
1. Gal. 2:21.

not, then, in vain that Christ died, in order that the law might be fulfilled through Him who said, "I am come not to destroy the law, but to fulfil it;"[2] and that our nature, which was lost through Adam, might through Him be recovered, who said that "He was come to seek and to save that which was lost;"[3] in whose coming the old fathers likewise who loved God believed.

* * *

Chapter XXVIII

FAITH IS THE GIFT OF GOD

I have already discussed the point concerning faith, that is, concerning the will of him who believes, even so far as to show that it appertains to grace—so that the apostle did not tell us, "I have obtained mercy because I was faithful;" but he said, "I have obtained mercy in order to be faithful."[4] And there are many other passages of similar import—among them that in which he bids us "think soberly, according as God hath dealt out to every man the proportion of faith;"[5] and that which I have already quoted: "By grace are ye saved through faith; and that not of yourselves; it is the gift of God;"[6] and again another in the same *Epistle to the Ephesians*: "Peace be to the brethren, and love with faith, from God the Father, and the Lord Jesus Christ;"[7] and to the same effect that passage in which he says, "For unto you it is given in the behalf of Christ not only to believe on Him, but also to suffer for His sake."[8] Both alike are therefore due to the grace of God—the faith of those who believe, and the patience of whose who suffer, because the apostle spoke of both as *given*. Then, again, there is the passage, especially noticeable, in which he says, "We, having the same spirit of faith,"[9] for his phrase is not *"the knowledge of faith,"* but *"the spirit of faith;"* and he expressed himself thus in order that we might understand how that faith is given to us, even when it is not sought, so that other blessings may be granted to it at its request. For "how," says he, "shall they call upon Him in whom they have not believed?"[1] The spirit of grace, therefore, causes us to have faith, in order that through faith we may, on praying for it, obtain the ability to do what we are commanded. On this account the apostle himself constantly puts faith before the law; since we are not able to do what the law commands unless we obtain the strength to do it by the prayer of faith.

2. Matt. 5:17.
3. Matt. 18:11; Luke 19:10.
4. 1 Cor. 7:25.
5. Rom. 12:3.
6. Eph. 2:8.

7. Eph. 6:23.
8. Phil. 1:29.
9. 1 Cor. 4:13.
1. Rom. 10:14.

Chapter XXIX

GOD IS ABLE TO CONVERT OPPOSING WILLS, AND TO TAKE AWAY FROM THE HEART ITS HARDNESS

Now if faith is simply of free will, and is not given by God, why do we pray for those who will not believe, that they may believe? This it would be absolutely useless to do, unless we believe, with perfect propriety, that Almighty God is able to turn to belief wills that are perverse and opposed to faith. Man's free will is addressed when it is said, "To-day, if ye will hear His voice, harden not your hearts."[2] But if God were not able to remove from the human heart even its obstinacy and hardness, He would not say, through the prophet, "I will take from them their heart of stone, and will give them a heart of flesh."[3] That all this was foretold in reference to the New Testament is shown clearly enough by the apostle when he says, "Ye are our epistle, . . . written not with ink, but with the Spirit of the living God; not in tables of stone, but in fleshly tables of the heart."[4] * * * Nor can we possibly, without extreme absurdity, maintain that there previously existed in any man the good merit of a good will, to entitle him to the removal of his stony heart, when all the while this very heart of stone signifies nothing else than a will of the hardest kind and such as is absolutely inflexible against God? For where a good will precedes, there is, of course, no longer a heart of stone.

* * *

Chapter XXXI

FREE WILL HAS ITS FUNCTION IN THE HEART'S CONVERSION; BUT GRACE TOO HAS ITS

Lest, however, it should be thought that men themselves in this matter do nothing by free will, it is said in the Psalm, "Harden not your hearts;"[5] and in Ezekiel himself, "Cast away from you all your transgressions, which ye have impiously committed against me; and make you a new heart and a new spirit; and keep all my commandments. For why will ye die, O house of Israel, saith the Lord? For I have no pleasure in the death of him that dieth, saith the Lord God: and turn ye, and live."[6] We should remember that it is He

2. Ps. 95:7, 8.
3. Ezek. 11:19.
4. 2 Cor. 3:2, 3.

5. Ps. 95:8.
6. Ezek. 18:31, 32.

who says, "Turn ye and live," to whom it is said in prayer, "Turn us again, O God."[7] We should remember that He says, "Cast away from you all your transgressions," when it is even He who justifies the ungodly. We should remember that He says, "Make you a new heart and a new spirit," who also promises, "I will give you a new heart, and a new spirit will I put within you."[8] How is it, then, that He who says, "Make you," also says, "I will give you"? Why does He command, if He is to give? Why does He give if man is to make, except it be that He gives what He commands when He helps him to obey whom He commands? There is, however, always within us a free will—but it is not always good; for it is either free from righteousness when it serves sin—and then it is evil—or else it is free from sin when it serves righteousness—and then it is good. But the grace of God is always good; and by it it comes to pass that a man is of a good will, though he was before of an evil one. By it also it comes to pass that the very good will, which has now begun to be, is enlarged, and made so great that it is able to fulfil the divine commandments which it shall wish, when it shall once firmly and perfectly wish. This is the purport of what the Scripture says: "If thou wilt, thou shalt keep the commandments;"[9] so that the man who wills but is not able knows that he does not yet fully will, and prays that he may have so great a will that it may suffice for keeping the commandments. And thus, indeed, he receives assistance to perform what he is commanded. Then is the will of use when we have ability; just as ability is also then of use when we have the will. For what does it profit us if we will what we are unable to do, or else do not will what we are able to do?

Chapter XXXII

IN WHAT SENSE IT IS RIGHTLY SAID THAT, IF WE LIKE, WE MAY KEEP GOD'S COMMANDMENTS

The Pelagians think that they know something great when they assert that "God would not command what He knew could not be done by man." Who can be ignorant of this? But God commands some things which we cannot do, in order that we may know what we ought to ask of Him. For this is faith itself, which obtains by prayer what the law commands.

* * *

7. Ps. 80:3.   9. Ecclus. 15:15.
8. Ezek. 36:26.

Chapter XXXIII

A GOOD WILL MAY BE SMALL AND WEAK; AN AMPLE WILL,
GREAT LOVE. OPERATING AND CO-OPERATING GRACE

He, therefore, who wishes to do God's commandment, but is unable, already possesses a good will, but as yet a small and weak one; he will, however, become able when he shall have acquired a great and robust will. When the martyrs did the great commandments which they obeyed, they acted by a great will—that is, with great love. Of this love the Lord Himself thus speaks: "Greater love hath no man than this, that a man lay down his life for his friends."[1] In accordance with this, the apostle also says, "He that loveth his neighbor hath fulfilled the law. For this: Thou shalt not commit adultery, Thou shalt not kill, Thou shalt not steal, Thou shalt not covet; and if there be any other commandment, it is briefly comprehended in this saying, namely, Thou shalt love thy neighbor as thyself.[2] Love worketh no ill to his neighbor: therefore love is the fulfilling of the law."[3] This love the Apostle Peter did not yet possess, when he for fear thrice denied the Lord.[4] "There is no fear in love," says the Evangelist John in his first *Epistle*, "but perfect love casteth out fear."[5] But yet, however small and imperfect his love was, it was not wholly wanting when he said to the Lord, "I will lay down my life for Thy sake;"[6] for he supposed himself able to effect what he felt himself willing to do. And who was it that had begun to give him his love, however small, but He who prepares the will, and perfects by His co-operation what He initiates by His operation? Forasmuch as in beginning He works in us that we may have the will, and in perfecting works with us when we have the will. On which account the apostle says, "I am confident of this very thing, that He which hath begun a good work in you will perform it until the day of Jesus Christ."[7] He operates, therefore, without us, in order that we may will; but when we will, and so will that we may act, He co-operates with us. We can, however, ourselves do nothing to effect good works of piety without Him either working that we may will, or co-working when we will. Now, concerning His working that we may will, it is said: "It is God which worketh in you, even to will."[8] While of His co-working with us, when we will and act by willing, the apostle says, "We know that in all things there is co-working for good to them that

1. John 15:13.
2. Lev. 19:18.
3. Rom. 13:8–10.
4. Matt. 26:69–75.

5. 1 John 4:18.
6. John 13:37.
7. Phil. 1:6.
8. Phil. 2:13.

love God."[9] What does this phrase, "all things," mean, but the terrible and cruel sufferings which affect our condition? That burden, indeed, of Christ, which is heavy for our infirmity, becomes light to love. For to such did the Lord say that His burden was light,[1] as Peter was when he suffered for Christ, not as he was when he denied Him.

* * *

Chapter XXXVII

THE LOVE WHICH FULFILS THE COMMANDMENTS IS NOT OF OURSELVES, BUT OF GOD

All these commandments, however, respecting love or charity (which are so great, and such that whatever action a man may think he does well is by no means well done if done without love) would be given to men in vain if they had not free choice of will. But forasmuch as these precepts are given in the law, both old and new (although in the new came the grace which was promised in the old, but the law without grace is the letter which killeth, but in grace the Spirit which giveth life) from what source is there in men the love of God and of one's neighbor but from God Himself? For indeed, if it be not of God but of men, the Pelagians have gained the victory; but if it come from God, then we have vanquished the Pelagians. Let, then, the Apostle John sit in judgment between us; and let him say to us "Beloved, let us love one another." Now, when they begin to extol themselves on these words of John, and to ask why this precept is addressed to us at all if we have not of our own selves to love one another, the same apostle proceeds at once, to their confusion, to add, "For love is of God."[2] It is not of ourselves, therefore, but it is of God. Wherefore, then, is it said, "Let us love one another, for love is of God," unless it be as a precept to our free will, admonishing it to seek the gift of God? Now, this would be indeed a thoroughly fruitless admonition if the will did not previously receive some donation of love, which might seek to be enlarged so as to fulfil whatever command was laid upon it. When it is said, "Let us love one another," it is law; when it is said, "For love is of God," it is grace. For God's "wisdom carries law and mercy upon her tongue."[3] Accordingly, it is written in the *Psalm*, "For He who gave the law will give blessings."[4]

* * *

9. Rom. 8:28.   3. Prov. 3:16.
1. Matt. 11:30.   4. Ps. 84:6.
2. 1 John 4:7.

Chapter XLI

THE WILLS OF MEN ARE SO MUCH IN THE POWER OF GOD, THAT HE CAN TURN THEM WHITHERSOEVER IT PLEASES HIM

I think I have now discussed the point fully enough in opposition to those who vehemently oppose the grace of God, by which, however, the human will is not taken away, but changed from bad to good, and assisted when it is good. I think, too, that I have so discussed the subject that it is not so much I myself as the inspired Scripture which has spoken to you, in the clearest testimonies of truth; and if this divine record be looked into carefully, it shows us that not only men's good wills, which God Himself converts from bad ones, and, when converted by Him, directs to good actions and to eternal life, but also those which follow the world are so entirely at the disposal of God, that He turns them whithersoever He wills, and whensoever He wills—to bestow kindness on some, and to heap punishment on others, as He Himself judges right by a counsel most secret to Himself, indeed, but beyond all doubt most righteous. For we find that some sins are even the punishment of other sins, as are those "vessels of wrath" which the apostle describes as "fitted to destruction,"[5] as is also that hardening of Pharaoh, the purpose of which is said to be to set forth in him the power of God,[6] as, again, is the flight of the Israelites from the face of the enemy before the city of Ai, for fear arose in their heart so that they fled, and this was done that their sin might be punished in the way it was right that it should be; by reason of which the Lord said to Joshua the son of Nun, "The children of Israel shall not be able to stand before the face of their enemies."[7] What is the meaning of, "They shall not be able to stand"? Now, why did they not stand by free will, but, with a will perplexed by fear, took to flight, were it not that God has the lordship even over men's wills, and when He is angry turns to fear whomsoever He pleases? Was it not of their own will that the enemies of the children of Israel fought against the people of God, as led by Joshua, the son of Nun? And yet the Scripture says, "It was of the Lord to harden their hearts, that they should come against Israel in battle, that they might be exterminated."[8] And was it not likewise of his own will that the wicked son of Gera cursed King David? And yet what says David, full of true, and deep, and pious wisdom? What did he say to him who wanted to smite the reviler? "What," said he, "have I to do with you, ye sons of Zeruiah? Let him alone and let him curse, because

5. Rom. 9:22.
6. Ex. 7:3, and 10:1.
7. Josh. 7:4, 12.
8. Josh. 11:20.

the Lord hath said unto him, Curse David. Who, then, shall say, Wherefore hast thou done so?"[9] And then the inspired Scripture, as if it would confirm the king's profound utterance by repeating it once more, tells us: "And David said to Abishai, and to all his servants, Behold, my son, which came forth from my bowels, seeketh my life: how much more may this Benjamite do it! Let him alone, and let him curse; for the Lord hath bidden him. It may be that the Lord will look on my humiliation, and will requite me good for his cursing this day."[1] Now what prudent reader will fail to understand in what way the Lord bade this profane man to curse David? It was not by a command that He bade him, in which case his obedience would be praiseworthy; but He inclined the man's will, which had become debased by his own perverseness, to commit this sin, by His own just and secret judgment. Therefore it is said, "The Lord said unto him." No if this person had obeyed a command of God, he would have deserved to be praised rather than punished, as we know he was afterwards punished for this sin. Nor is the reason an obscure one why the Lord told him after this manner to curse David. "It may be," said the humbled king, "that the Lord will look on my humiliation, and will requite me good for his cursing this day." See, then, what proof we have here that God uses the hearts of even wicked men for the praise and assistance of the good. Thus did He make use of Judas when betraying Christ; thus did He make use of the Jews when they crucified Christ. And how vast the blessings which from these instances He has bestowed upon the nations that should believe in Him! He also uses our worst enemy, the devil himself, but in the best way, to exercise and try the faith and piety of good men—not for Himself indeed, who knows all things before they come to pass, but for our sakes, for whom it was necessary that such a discipline should be gone through with us. Did not Absalom choose by his own will the counsel which was detrimental to him? And yet the reason of his doing so was that the Lord had heard his father's prayer that it might be so. Wherefore the Scripture says that "the Lord appointed to defeat the good counsel of Ahithophel, to the intent that the Lord might bring all evils upon Absalom."[2] It called Ahithophel's counsel "*good*," because it was for the moment of advantage to his purpose. It was in favor of the son against his father, against whom he had rebelled; and it might have crushed him, had not the Lord defeated the counsel which Ahithophel had given, by acting on the heart of Absalom so that he rejected this counsel, and chose another which was not expedient for him.

9. 2 Sam. 16:9, 10.
1. 2 Sam. 16:11, 12.

2. 2 Sam. 17:14.

* * *

Chapter XLIII

GOD OPERATES ON MEN'S HEARTS TO INCLINE THEIR WILLS WHITHERSOEVER HE PLEASES

From these statements of the inspired word, and from similar passages which it would take too long to quote in full, [it is] I think, sufficiently clear that God works in the hearts of men to incline their wills whithersoever He wills, whether to good deeds according to His mercy, or to evil after their own deserts; His own judgment being sometimes manifest, sometimes secret, but always righteous. This ought to be the fixed and immovable conviction of your heart, that there is no unrighteousness with God. Therefore, whenever you read in the Scriptures of Truth, that men are led aside, or that their hearts are blunted and hardened by God, never doubt that some ill deserts of their own have first occurred, so that they justly suffer these things. Thus you will not run counter to that proverb of Solomon: "The foolishness of a man perverteth his ways, yet he blameth God in his heart."[3] Grace, however, is not bestowed according to men's deserts; otherwise grace would no longer be grace.[4] For grace is so designated because it is given gratuitously. Now if God is able, either through the agency of angels (whether good ones or evil), or in any other way whatever, to operate in the hearts even of the wicked, in return for their deserts—whose wickedness was not made by Him, but was either derived originally from Adam, or increased by their own will—what is there to wonder at if, through the Holy Spirit, He works good in the hearts of the elect, who has wrought it that their hearts become good instead of evil?

Chapter XLIV

GRATUITOUS GRACE EXEMPLIFIED IN INFANTS

Men, however, may suppose that there are certain good deserts which they think are precedent to justification through God's grace; all the while failing to see, when they express such an opinion, that they do nothing else than deny grace. But, as I have already remarked, let them suppose what they like respecting the case of adults, in the case of infants, at any rate, the Pelagians find no means of answering the difficulty. For these in receiving grace have

3. Prov. 19:3.   4. Rom. 11:6.

no will, from the influence of which they can pretend to any precedent merit. We see, moreover, how they cry and struggle when they are baptized, and feel the divine sacraments. Such conduct would, of course, be charged against them as a great impiety, if they already had free will in use; and notwithstanding this, grace cleaves to them even in their resisting struggles. But most certainly there is no prevenient merit, otherwise the grace would be no longer grace. Sometimes, too, this grace is bestowed upon the children of unbelievers, when they happen by some means or other to fall, by reason of God's secret providence, into the hands of pious persons; but, on the other hand, the children of believers fail to obtain grace, some hindrance occurring to prevent the approach of help to rescue them in their danger. These things, no doubt, happen through the secret providence of God, whose judgments are unsearchable, and His ways past finding out. These are the words of the apostle; and you should observe what he had previously said, to lead him to add such a remark. He was discoursing about the Jews and Gentiles, when he wrote to the Romans—themselves Gentiles—to this effect: "For as ye, in times past, have not believed God, yet have now obtained mercy, through their unbelief; even so have these also now not believed, that through your mercy they also may obtain mercy; for God hath concluded them all in unbelief, that He might have mercy upon all."[5] Now, after he had thought upon what he said, full of wonder at the certain truth of his own assertion, indeed, but astonished at its great depth, how God concluded all in unbelief that He might have mercy upon all—as if doing evil that good might come—he at once exclaimed, and said, "O the depth of the riches both of the wisdom and knowledge of God! how unsearchable are His judgments, and His ways past finding out;"[6] Perverse men, who do not reflect upon these unsearchable judgments and untraceable ways, indeed, but are ever prone to censure, being unable to understand, have supposed the apostle to say, and censoriously gloried over him for saying, "Let us do evil, that good may come!" God forbid that the apostle should say so! But men, without understanding, have thought that this was in fact said, when they heard these words of the apostle: "Moreover, the law entered, that the offence might abound; but where sin abounded, grace did much more abound."[7] But grace, indeed, effects this purpose—that good works should now be wrought by those who previously did evil; not that they should persevere in evil courses and suppose that they are recompensed with good. Their language, therefore, ought

5. Rom. 11:30–32.
6. Rom. 11:33.

7. Rom. 5:20.

not to be: "Let us do evil, that good may come;" but: "We have done evil, and good has come; let us henceforth do good, that in the future world we may receive good for good, who in the present life are receiving good for evil." Wherefore it is written in the *Psalm*, "I will sing of mercy and judgment unto Thee, O Lord."[8] When the Son of man, therefore, first came into the world, it was not to judge the world, but that the world through Him might be saved.[9] And this dispensation was for mercy; by and by, however, He will come for judgment—to judge the quick and the dead. And yet even in this present time salvation itself does not eventuate without judgment—although it be a hidden one; therefore He says, "For judgment I am come into this world, that they which see not may see, and that they which see may be made blind."[1]

Chapter XLV

THE REASON WHY ONE PERSON IS ASSISTED BY GRACE, AND ANOTHER IS NOT HELPED, MUST BE REFERRED TO THE SECRET JUDGMENTS OF GOD

You must refer the matter, then, to the hidden determinations of God, when you see, in one and the same condition, such as all infants unquestionably have—who derive their hereditary evil from Adam—that one is assisted so as to be baptized, and another is not assisted, so that he dies in his very bondage; and again, that one baptized person is left and forsaken in his present life, who God foreknew would be ungodly, while another baptized person is taken away from this life, "lest that wickedness should alter his understanding;"[2] and be sure that you do not in such cases ascribe unrighteousness or unwisdom to God, in whom is the very fountain of righteousness and wisdom, but, as I have exhorted you from the commencement of this treatise, "whereto you have already attained, walk therein,"[3] and "even this shall God reveal unto you"[4]—if not in this life, yet certainly in the next, "for there is nothing covered that shall not be revealed."[5] When, therefore, you hear the Lord say, "I the Lord have deceived that prophet,"[6] and likewise what the apostle says: "He hath mercy on whom He will have mercy, and whom He will He hardeneth,"[7] believe that, in the case of him whom He permits to be deceived and hardened, his evil deeds have deserved the judgment; whilst in the case of him to whom He

8. Ps. 101:1.
9. John 3:17.
1. John 9:39.
2. Wisd. 4:11.
3. Phil. 3:16.

4. Phil. 3:15.
5. Matt. 10:26.
6. Ezek. 14:9.
7. Rom. 9:18.

shows mercy, you should loyally and unhesitatingly recognize the grace of the God who "rendereth not evil for evil; but contrariwise blessing."[8] Nor should you take away from Pharaoh free will, because in several passages God says, "I have hardened Pharaoh;" or, "I have hardened or I will harden Pharaoh's heart;"[9] for it does not by any means follow that Pharaoh did not, on this account, harden his own heart. For this, too, is said of him, after the removal of the fly-plague from the Egyptians, in these words of the Scripture: "And Pharaoh hardened his heart at this time also; neither would he let the people go."[1] Thus it was that both God hardened him by His just judgment, and Pharaoh by his own free will. Be ye then well assured that your labor will never be in vain, if, setting before you a good purpose, you persevere in it to the last. For God, who fails to render, according to their deeds, only to those whom He liberates, will then "recompense everyman according to his works."[2] God will, therefore, certainly recompense both evil for evil, because He is just; and good for evil, because He is good; and good for good, because He is good and just; only, evil for good He will never recompense, because He is not unjust. He will, therefore, recompense evil for evil—punishment for unrighteousness; and He will recompense good for evil—grace for unrighteousness; and He will recompense good for good—grace for grace.

* * *

MARTIN LUTHER

Death to the Law (1535) †

* * *

I have referred earlier in this epistle to the occasion for St. Paul's discussion of Christian righteousness, namely, that right after he had gone away false teachers among the Galatians had destroyed what he had built up so painstakingly. These false apostles, adherents of

---

8. 1 Pet. 3:9.
9. Ex. 4:21; 7:3; 14:4.
1. Ex. 8:32.
2. Matt. 16:27.
† Martin Luther (1483–1546) was the initiator of the German Reformation. These comments on Galatians, which he once called "my epistle, to which I am betrothed," are drawn from his "Lectures on Galatians," delivered in 1531, first published in 1535. The translation is by Jaroslav Pelikan in *Luther's Works*, ed. Jaroslav Pelikan and Walter A. Hansen (St. Louis, 1963), vols. 26, 27.

Judaism and of Pharisaism at that, were men of great prestige and authority. Among the people they boasted that they belonged to the holy and elect race of the Jews, that they were Israelites of the seed of Abraham, that the promises and the patriarchs belonged to them, finally that they were ministers of Christ and pupils of the apostles, whom they had known personally and whose miracles they had witnessed. They may even have performed some signs or miracles themselves, for Christ declares (Matt. 7:22) that the wicked also perform miracles. When men with such authority come into any country or city, the people immediately develop great admiration for them; and they fool even those who are educated and quite steadfast in the faith. They subvert the Galatians by saying: "Who is Paul anyway? After all, was he not the very last of those who were converted to Christ? But we are the pupils of the apostles, and we knew them intimately. We saw Christ perform miracles, and we heard Him preach. But Paul is a latecomer and is our inferior. It is impossible that God should permit us to fall into error, us who are His holy people, who are the ministers of Christ, and who have received the Holy Spirit. Besides, we are many, while Paul is only one. He did not know the apostles, nor has he seen Christ. In fact, he persecuted the church of Christ. Do you imagine that on account of Paul alone God would permit so many churches to be deceived?"

In our time, whenever the pope does not have the authority of the Scriptures on his side, he always uses this same single argument against us: "The church, the church! Do you suppose that God is so offended that for the sake of a few heretical Lutherans He will reject His whole church? Do you suppose that He would leave His church in error for so many centuries?" With might and main he insists that the church can never be destroyed or overthrown. This argument persuades many people. With these and similar arguments these false apostles impressed the Galatians, so that Paul lost his authority among them and his doctrine came under suspicion.

In opposition to this boasting of the false apostles Paul boldly and with great *parrhēsia* pits his apostolic authority, commends his calling, and defends his ministry. Although he does not do this anywhere else, he refuses to yield to anyone, even to the apostles themselves, much less to any of their pupils. To counteract their pharisaical pride and insolence, he refers to the events that took place in Antioch, where he withstood Peter himself. In addition, he pays no attention to the possible offense but says plainly in the text that he took it upon himself to reprove Peter himself, the prince of the apostles, who had seen Christ and had known Him intimately. "I am an apostle," he says, "and one who does not care what others are. Indeed, I did not shrink from reproving the very pillar of the other apostles."

* * *

[Comment on Gal. 1:11]

* * *

Peter, the prince of the apostles, lived and taught contrary to the Word of God. Therefore he was in error. And because he was at fault, Paul "opposed him to the face" (Gal. 2:11), attacking him because he was not in conformity with the truth of the Gospel. Here you see that Peter, the most holy apostle, erred. Thus I will not listen to the church or the fathers or the apostles unless they bring and teach the pure Word of God.

Today, too, this argument makes quite a telling point against us. For if we are to believe neither the pope nor the fathers nor Luther nor anyone else unless they teach us the pure Word of God, whom are we to believe? Who will give our consciences sure information about which party is teaching the pure Word of God, we or our opponents? For they, too, claim to have and to teach the pure Word of God. On the other hand, we do not believe the papists, because they neither teach nor can teach the Word of God. They again hate us bitterly and persecute us as the vilest heretics and seducers of the people. What is to be done here? Is every fanatic to have the right to teach whatever he pleases, since the world refuses to listen to or tolerate our teaching? With Paul we boast that we teach the pure Gospel of Christ. Not only should the pope, the sectarians, the fathers, and the church submit to this Gospel; they should receive it with open arms, accept it gratefully, embrace it, and propagate it to others. But if anyone teaches otherwise, whether the pope or St. Augustine or an apostle or an angel from heaven, let him and his gospel be accursed. Still we do not make any progress but are forced to hear that our boasting is not only vain, brazen, and arrogant but blasphemous and demonic. And yet, if we lower ourselves and yield to the ravings of our opponents, both the papists and the sectarians will become proud. The sectarians will brag that they are bringing some strange new doctrine never before heard of by the world, and the papists will reestablish their old abominations. Therefore let everyone take care to be most certain of his calling and doctrine, so that he may boldly and surely say with Paul (Gal. 1:8): "Even if we, or an angel from heaven, etc."

* * *

[Comment on Gal. 2:4 f.]

* * *

The truth of the Gospel is this, that our righteousness comes by faith alone, without the works of the Law. The falsification or corruption of the Gospel is this, that we are justified by faith but not without the works of the Law. The false apostles preached the Gospel, but they did so with this condition attached to it. The scholastics do the same thing in our day. They say that we must believe in Christ and that faith is the foundation of salvation, but they say that this faith does not justify unless it is "formed by love."[1] This is not the truth of the Gospel; it is falsehood and pretense. The true Gospel, however, is this: Works or love are not the ornament or perfection of faith; but faith itself is a gift of God, a work of God in our hearts, which justifies us because it takes hold of Christ as the Savior. Human reason has the Law as its object. It says to itself: "This I have done; this I have not done." But faith in its proper function has no other object than Jesus Christ, the Son of God, who was put to death for the sins of the world. It does not look at its love and say: "What have I done? Where have I sinned? What have I deserved?" But it says: "What has Christ done? What has He deserved?" And here the truth of the Gospel gives you the answer: "He has redeemed you from sin, from the devil, and from eternal death." Therefore faith acknowledges that in this one Person, Jesus Christ, it has the forgiveness of sins and eternal life. Whoever diverts his gaze from this object does not have true faith; he has a phantasy and a vain opinion. He looks away from the promise and at the Law, which terrifies him and drives him to despair.

Therefore what the scholastics have taught about justifying faith "formed by love" is an empty dream. For the faith that takes hold of Christ, the Son of God, and is adorned by Him is the faith that justifies, not a faith that includes love. For if faith is to be sure and firm, it must take hold of nothing but Christ alone; and in the agony and terror of conscience it has nothing else to lean on than this pearl of great value (Matt. 13:45–46). Therefore whoever takes hold of Christ by faith, no matter how terrified by the Law and oppressed by the burden of his sins he may be, has the right to boast that he is righteous. How has he this right? By that jewel, Christ, whom he possesses by faith. Our opponents fail to understand this.

1. On the meaning of *fides charitate formata* cf. Thomas Aquinas, *Summa Theologica*, II—II, Qu. 4, Art. 3.

Therefore they reject Christ, this jewel; and in His place they put their love, which they say is a jewel. But if they do not know what faith is, it is impossible for them to have faith, much less to teach it to others. And as for what they claim to have, this is nothing but a dream, an opinion, and natural reason, but not faith.

* * *

[Comment on Gal. 2:16]

* * *

Now the true meaning of Christianity is this: that a man first acknowledge, through the Law, that he is a sinner, for whom it is impossible to perform any good work. For the Law says: "You are an evil tree. Therefore everything you think, speak, or do is opposed to God. Hence you cannot deserve grace by your works. But if you try to do so, you make the bad even worse; for since you are an evil tree, you cannot produce anything except evil fruits, that is, sins. 'For whatever does not proceed from faith is sin' (Rom. 14:23)." Trying to merit grace by preceding works, therefore, is trying to placate God with sins, which is nothing but heaping sins upon sins, making fun of God, and provoking His wrath. When a man is taught this way by the Law, he is frightened and humbled. Then he really sees the greatness of his sin and finds in himself not one spark of the love of God; thus he justifies God in His Word and confesses that he deserves death and eternal damnation. Thus the first step in Christianity is the preaching of repentance and the knowledge of oneself.

The second step is this: If you want to be saved, your salvation does not come by works; but God has sent His only Son into the world that we might live through Him. He was crucified and died for you and bore your sins in His own body (1 Pet. 2:24). Here there is no "congruity" or work performed before grace, but only wrath, sin, terror, and death. Therefore the Law only shows sin, terrifies, and humbles; thus it prepares us for justification and drives us to Christ. For by His Word God has revealed to us that He wants to be a merciful Father to us. Without our merit—since, after all, we cannot merit anything—He wants to give us forgiveness of sins, righteousness, and eternal life for the sake of Christ. For God is He who dispenses His gifts freely to all, and this is the praise of His deity. But He cannot defend this deity of His against the self-righteous people who are unwilling to accept grace and eternal life from Him freely but want to earn it by their own works. They simply want to rob Him of the glory of His deity. In order to retain it, He is compelled to send forth His Law, to terrify and crush those very hard rocks as though it were thunder and lightning.

This, in summary, is our theology about Christian righteousness, in opposition to the abominations and monstrosities of the sophists about "merit of congruity and of condignity" or about works before grace and after grace. Smug people, who have never struggled with any temptations or true terrors of sin and death, were the ones who made up these empty dreams out of their own heads; therefore they do not understand what they are saying or what they are talking about, for they cannot supply any examples of such works done either before grace or after grace. Therefore these are useless fables, with which the papists delude both themselves and others.

* * *

[2:] 19. *For I through the Law died to the Law, that I might live to God.*

This is amazing language and unheard-of speech which human reason simply cannot understand. It is spoken briefly but very emphatically. Paul seems to be speaking from a fervent and ardent spirit, with great zeal, as though he were indignant. It is as though he were saying: "Why do you boast so much about the Law, about which I do not want to know anything? Why do you din this into me so often? But if there must be a Law, I have a Law of my own." As though he were speaking by the indignation of the Holy Spirit, he calls grace itself "Law." He stamps the content of grace with a new name, as an expression of contempt for the Law of Moses and for the false apostles, who claimed that it was necessary for justification. Thus he opposes the Law to the Law. This is most delicious language. In Scripture, especially in Paul, Law is often opposed to Law, sin to sin, death to death, captivity to captivity, the devil to the devil, hell to hell, altar to altar, lamb to lamb, Passover to Passover.

Rom. 8:3: "For sin He condemned sin"; Ps. 68:18 and Eph. 4:8: "He led captivity captive"; Hos. 14:14; "O death, I will be your death. O hell, I will be your destruction." Thus he says here that through the Law he has died to the Law. It is as though he were saying: "The Law of Moses accuses and damns me. But against that accusing and damning Law I have another Law, which is grace and freedom. This Law accuses the accusing Law and damns the damning Law." Thus death killed death, but this death which kills death is life itself. But it is called the death of death, by an exuberant indignation of the spirit against death. So also righteousness takes the name "sin," because it damns sin; and this damning sin is true righteousness.

Here Paul is the most heretical of heretics; and his heresy is unheard-of, because he says that, having died to the Law, he lives to God. The false apostles taught: "Unless you live to the Law, you do not live to God. That is, unless you live according to the Law, you are dead in the sight of God." But Paul teaches the opposite: "Unless you are dead to the Law, you do not live to God." The doctrine of the fanatics today is the same as that of the false apostles at that time. "If you want to live to God," they say, "that is, to be alive in the sight of God, then live to the Law, or according to the Law." But we say in opposition: "If you want to live to God, you must completely die to the Law." Human reason and wisdom do not understand this doctrine. Therefore they always teach the opposite: "If you want to live to God, you must observe the Law; for it is written (Matt. 19:17): 'If you would enter life, keep the Commandments.' " This is a principle and maxim of all the theologians: "He who lives according to the Law lives to God." Paul says the exact opposite, namely, that we cannot live to God unless we have died to the Law. Therefore we must climb up to this heavenly altitude, in order that we may establish for certain that we are far above the Law, in fact, that we are completely dead to the Law. Now if we are dead to the Law, then the Law has no jurisdiction over us, just as it has no jurisdiction over Christ, who has liberated us from the Law in order that in this way we may live to God. This supports the declaration that the Law does not justify, but that only faith in Christ justifies.

Paul is not speaking about the Ceremonial Law here. He sacrificed in the temple, circumcised Timothy and cut his hair at Cenchreae. He would not have done these things if he had died to the Ceremonial Law. But he is speaking about the entire Law. For the Christian, therefore, the entire Law has been completely abrogated —whether it be the Ceremonial Law or the Decalog—because he has died to it. This does not mean that the Law is destroyed; for it remains, lives, and rules in the wicked. But the godly man is dead to the Law as he is dead to sin, the devil, death, and hell, all of which still remain, and all of which the world and the wicked will inherit. Therefore when the sophist takes Paul to mean that only the Ceremonial Law is abrogated, you understand that for Paul and for every Christian the entire Law is abrogated, and yet that the Law still remains.

For example, when Christ arises from the dead, He is free from the grave; and yet the grave remains. Peter is liberated from prison, the paralytic from his bed, the young man from his coffin, the girl from her couch; nevertheless, the prison, the bed, the coffin, and the couch remain. So also the Law is abrogated when I am freed from it, and the Law dies when I have died to it; and yet the Law still remains. But because I die to it, it also dies to me. Thus Christ's grave, Peter's prison, the girl's couch—all remain. But by His resurrection Christ dies to the grave; by his deliverance Peter is freed from the prison; by her restoration to life the girl is delivered from the couch.

* * *

[Comment on Gal. 2:20]

* * *

Nevertheless, I live; yet not I, but Christ lives in me.

When he says: "Nevertheless, I live," this sounds rather personal, as though Paul were speaking of his own person. Therefore he quickly corrects it and says: "Yet not I." That is, "I do not live in my own person now, but Christ lives in me." The person does indeed live, but not in itself or for its own person. But who is this "I" of whom he says: "Yet not I"? It is the one that has the Law and is obliged to do works, the one that is a person separate from Christ. This "I" Paul rejects; for "I," as a person distinct from Christ, belongs to death and hell. This is why he says: "Not I, but Christ lives in me." Christ is my "form,"[2] which adorns my faith as color or light adorns a wall. (This fact has to be expounded in this crude way, for there is no spiritual way for us to grasp the idea that Christ clings and dwells in us as closely and intimately as light or whiteness clings to a wall.) "Christ," he says, "is fixed and cemented to me and abides in me. The life that I now live, He lives in me. Indeed, Christ Himself is the life that I now live. In this way, therefore, Christ and I are one."

Living in me as He does, Christ abolishes the Law, damns sin, and kills death; for at His presence all these cannot help disappearing. Christ is eternal Peace, Comfort, Righteousness, and Life, to which the terror of the Law, sadness of mind, sin, hell, and death have to yield. Abiding and living in me, Christ removes and absorbs all the evils that torment and afflict me. This attachment to Him causes me to be liberated from the terror of the Law and of sin, pulled out of my own skin, and transferred into Christ and into His kingdom, which is a kingdom of grace, righteousness, peace, joy, life, salvation, and eternal glory. Since I am in Him, no evil can harm me.

Meanwhile my old man (Eph. 4:22) remains outside and is sub-

---

2. That is, Christ, not charity, is the *forma* of faith.

ject to the Law. But so far as justification is concerned, Christ and I must be so closely attached that He lives in me and I in Him. What a marvelous way of speaking! Because He lives in me, what-ever grace, righteousness, life, peace, and salvation there is in me is all Christ's; nevertheless, it is mine as well, by the cementing and attachment that are through faith, by which we become as one body in the Spirit. Since Christ lives in me, grace, righteousness, life, and eternal salvation must be present with Him; and the Law, sin, and death must be absent. Indeed, the Law must be crucified, devoured, and abolished by the Law—and sin by sin, death by death, the devil by the devil. In this way Paul seeks to withdraw us completely from ourselves, from the Law, and from works, and to transplant us into Christ and faith in Christ, so that in the area of justification we look only at grace, and separate it far from the Law and from works, which belong far away.

Paul has a peculiar phraseology—not human, but divine and heavenly. The evangelists and the other apostles do not use it, except for John, who speaks this way from time to time. If Paul had not used this way of speaking first and prescribed it for us in explicit terms, no one even among the saints would have dared[3] use it. It is unprecedented and insolent to say: "I live, I do not live; I am dead, I am not dead; I am a sinner, I am not a sinner; I have the Law, I do not have the Law." But this phraseology is true in Christ and through Christ. When it comes to justification, there-fore, if you divide Christ's Person from your own, you are in the Law; you remain in it and live in yourself, which means that you are dead in the sight of God and damned by the Law. For you have a faith that is, as the sophists imagine, "formed by love." I am speaking this way for the sake of illustration. For there is no one who has such a faith; therefore what the sophists have taught about "faith formed by love" is merely a trick of Satan. But let us concede that a man could be found who had such a faith. Even if he had it, he would actually be dead, because he would have only a historical faith about Christ, something that even the devil and all the wicked have (James 2:19).

But faith must be taught correctly, namely, that by it you are so cemented to Christ that He and you are as one person, which cannot be separated but remains attached to Him forever and declares: "I am as Christ." And Christ, in turn, says: "I am as that sinner who is attached to Me, and I to him. For by faith we are joined together into one flesh and one bone." Thus Eph. 5:30 says: "We are members of the body of Christ, of His flesh and of His bones," in such a way that this faith couples Christ and me more

3. The Weimar text has *fuisses* here, but we have read *fuisset*.

intimately than a husband is coupled to his wife. Therefore this faith is no idle quality; but it is a thing of such magnitude that it obscures and completely removes those foolish dreams of the sophists' doctrine—the fiction of a "formed faith" and of love, of merits, our worthiness, our quality, etc. I would like to treat this at greater length if I could.

*   *   *

[3:] 24. *So that the Law was our custodian until Christ came.*

When Paul says that "the Law was our custodian until Christ came," he once more joins Law and Gospel together in feeling, even though in themselves they are as far apart as possible. This analogy of the custodian is truly outstanding; therefore it must be considered carefully. Although a schoolmaster is very useful and really necessary for the education and training of boys, show me one boy or pupil who loves his schoolmaster! For example, did the Jews love Moses warmly and willingly do what he commanded? Their love and obedience toward Moses was such, as the history shows, that at times they would have been willing to stone him. Therefore it is impossible for a pupil to love his schoolmaster. For how could he love the one by whom he is being detained in prison, that is, by whom he is being forbidden to do what he would like to do? If he commits something that is against his schoolmaster's orders, he is denounced and scolded by him; what is more, he is forced to embrace and kiss his whip.[4] How wonderful the pupil's righteousness is, that he obeys a threatening and harsh schoolmaster and even kisses his whip! Does he do this willingly and joyfully? When the schoolmaster is absent, he will break the whip or throw it into the fire. And if he had authority over the schoolmaster, he would not let himself be beaten by the schoolmaster's whips but would order that the schoolmaster be whipped. Nevertheless, a schoolmaster is extremely necessary for a boy, to instruct and chastise him; for otherwise, without this instruction, good training, and discipline, the boy would come to ruin.

Therefore the schoolmaster gives the boy the impression of being his taskmaster and executioner and of holding him captive in prison. To what end and for how long? So that this severe, hateful authority of the schoolmaster and the slavery of the boy will last forever? No, but for a predetermined time, so that this obedience, prison, and discipline may work for the boy's good and so that in due time he may become the heir and the king. For it is not the

4. From other references in Luther it seems that it was customary for a child to have to kiss the whip after he had been punished.

father's intention that the son be subject to the schoolmaster forever and be whipped by him, but that through the instruction and discipline of the schoolmaster the son may be made fit for accession to his inheritance.

* * *

By means of this fine illustration, therefore, Paul shows the true use of the Law: that it does not justify hypocrites, because they remain outside Christ in their presumptuousness and smugness; on the other hand, if those who have been frightened use the Law as Paul teaches, it does not leave them in death and damnation but drives them to Christ. Those who continue in these terrors and in their faintheartedness and do not take hold of Christ by faith despair utterly. With his allegory of the custodian, therefore, Paul clearly portrays the true use of the Law. For just as the custodian scolds, drives, and troubles his pupils, not with the intention that this custody should last forever, but that it should come to an end when the pupils have been properly educated and trained and that they should then eagerly and freely enjoy their liberty and their inheritance without the constraint of their custodian, so those who are frightened and crushed by the Law should know that these terrors and blows will not be permanent, but that by them they are being prepared for the coming of Christ and the freedom of the Spirit.

* * *

[Comments on Gal. 5:1]

* * *

Every word is emphatic. "Stand fast," he says, "in freedom." In what freedom? Not in the freedom for which the Roman emperor has set us free but in the freedom for which Christ has set us free. The Roman emperor gave—indeed, was forced to give—the Roman pontiff a free city and other lands, as well as certain immunities, privileges, and concessions. This, too, is freedom; but it is a political freedom, according to which the Roman pontiff with all his clergy is free of all public burdens. In addition, there is the freedom of the flesh, which is chiefly prevalent in the world. Those who have this obey neither God nor the laws but do what they please. This is the freedom which the rabble pursues today; so do the fanatical spirits, who want to be free in their opinions and actions, in order that they may teach and do with impunity what they imagine to be right. This is a demonic freedom, by which the devil sets the wicked free to sin against God and men. We are not dealing with this here although it is the most widespread and is the only goal and objective of the entire world. Nor are we dealing with political freedom. No, we are dealing with another kind, which the devil hates and attacks most bitterly.

This is the freedom with which Christ has set us free, not from some human slavery or tyrannical authority but from the eternal wrath of God. Where? In the conscience. This is where our freedom comes to a halt; it goes no further. For Christ has set us free, not for a political freedom or a freedom of the flesh but for a theological or spiritual freedom, that is, to make our conscience free and joyful, unafraid of the wrath to come (Matt. 3:7). This is the most genuine freedom; it is immeasurable. When the other kinds of freedom—political freedom and the freedom of the flesh—are compared with the greatness and the glory of this kind of freedom, they hardly amount to one little drop. For who can express what a great gift it is for someone to be able to declare for certain that God neither is nor ever will be wrathful but will forever be a gracious and merciful Father for the sake of Christ? It is surely a great and incomprehensible freedom to have this Supreme Majesty kindly disposed toward us, protecting and helping us, and finally even setting us free physically in such a way that our body, which is sown in perishability, in dishonor, and in weakness, is raised in imperishability, in honor, and in power (1 Cor. 15:42–43). Therefore the freedom by which we are free of the wrath of God forever is greater than heaven and earth and all creation.

From this there follows the other freedom, by which we are made safe and free through Christ from the Law, from sin, death, the power of the devil, hell, etc. For just as the wrath of God cannot terrify us—since Christ has set us free from it—so the Law, sin, etc., cannot accuse and condemn us. Even though the Law denounces us and sin terrifies us, they still cannot plunge us into despair. For faith, which is the victor over the world (1 John 5:4), quickly declares: "Those things have nothing to do with me, for Christ has set me free from them." So it is that death, which is the most powerful and horrible thing in the world, lies conquered in our conscience through this freedom of the Spirit. Therefore the greatness of Christian freedom should be carefully measured and pondered. The words "freedom from the wrath of God, from the Law, sin, death, etc.," are easy to say; but to feel the greatness of this freedom and to apply its results to oneself in a struggle, in the agony of conscience, and in practice—this is more difficult than anyone can say.

*   *   *

[Comment on Gal. 5: 3]

*   *   *

What I am saying here on the basis of the words of Paul I learned from my own experience in the monastery about myself and about others. I saw many who tried with great effort and the best of intentions to do everything possible to appease their conscience. They wore hair shirts; they fasted; they prayed; they tormented and wore out their bodies with various exercises so severely that if they had been made of iron, they would have been crushed. And yet the more they labored, the greater their terrors became. Especially when the hour of death was imminent, they became so fearful that I have seen many murderers facing execution die more confidently than these men who had lived such saintly lives.

Thus it is certainly true that those who keep the Law do not keep it. The more men try to satisfy the Law, the more they transgress it. The more someone tries to bring peace to his conscience through his own righteousness, the more disquieted he makes it. When I was a monk, I made a great effort to live according to the requirements of the monastic rule. I made a practice of confessing and reciting all my sins, but always with prior contrition; I went to confession frequently, and I performed the assigned penances faithfully. Nevertheless, my conscience could never achieve certainty but was always in doubt and said: "You have not done this correctly. You were not contrite enough. You omitted this in your confession." Therefore the longer I tried to heal my uncertain, weak, and troubled conscience with human traditions, the more uncertain, weak, and troubled I continually made it. In this way, by observing human traditions, I transgressed them even more; and by following the righteousness of the monastic order, I was never able to reach it. For, as Paul says, it is impossible for the conscience to find peace through the works of the Law, much less through human traditions, without the promise and the Gospel about Christ.

*   *   *

[Comment on Gal. 5:13]

*   *   *

This evil is very widespread, and it is the worst of all the evils that Satan arouses against the teaching of faith: that in many people he soon transforms the freedom for which Christ has set us free into an opportunity for the flesh. Jude complains of this same thing in his epistle (ch. 4): "Admission has been secretly gained by some ungodly persons who pervert the grace of our God into licentiousness.' For the flesh simply does not understand the teaching of grace, namely, that we are not justified by works but by faith alone, and that the Law has no jurisdiction over us. Therefore when it hears this teaching, it transforms it into licentiousness and immediately draws the inference: "If we are without the Law, then let us live as we please. Let us not do good, let us not give to the needy; much less do we have to endure anything evil. For there is no Law to compel or bind us."

Thus there is a danger on both sides, although the one is more tolerable than the other. If grace or faith is not preached, no one is saved; for faith alone justifies and saves. On the other hand, if faith is preached, as it must be preached, the majority of men understand the teaching about faith in a fleshly way and transform the freedom of the spirit into the freedom of the flesh. This can be discerned today in all classes of society, both high and low. They all boast of being evangelicals and boast of Christian freedom. Meanwhile, however, they give in to their desires and turn to greed, sexual desire, pride, envy, etc. No one performs his duty faithfully; no one serves another by love. This misbehavior often makes me so impatient that I would want such "swine that trample pearls underfoot" (Matt. 7:6) still to be under the tyranny of the pope. For it is impossible for this people of Gomorrah to be ruled by the Gospel of peace.

What is more, we ourselves, who teach the Word, do not perform our own duty with as much care and zeal here in the light of truth as we used to in the darkness of ignorance. The more certain we are about the freedom granted to us by Christ, the more unresponsive and slothful we are in presenting the Word, praying, doing good works, enduring evil, and the like. And if Satan were not troubling us inwardly with spiritual trials and outwardly with persecution by our enemies and with the contempt and ingratitude of our own followers, we would become utterly smug, lazy, and useless for anything good; thus in time we would lose the knowledge of Christ and faith in Him, would forsake the ministry of the Word, and would look for some more comfortable way of life, more suitable to our flesh. This is what many of our followers are beginning to do, motivated by the fact that those who labor in the Word not only do not get their support from this but are even treated shamefully by those whom their preaching of the Gospel has set free from the miserable slavery of the pope. Forsaking the poor and offensive figure of Christ, they involve themselves in the business of this present life; and they serve, not Christ but their own appetites (Rom.

16:18), with results that they will experience in due time.

We know that the devil lies in wait especially for us who have the Word—he already holds the others captive to his will—and that he is intent upon taking the freedom of the Spirit away from us or at least making us change it into license. Therefore we teach and exhort our followers with great care and diligence, on the basis of Paul's example, not to think that this freedom of the Spirit, achieved by the death of Christ, was given[5] to them as an opportunity for the flesh or, as Peter says, "to use as a pretext for evil" (1 Pet. 2:16), but for them to be servants of one another through love.

As we have said, therefore, the apostle imposes an obligation on Christians through this law about mutual love in order to keep them from abusing their freedom. Therefore the godly should remember that for the sake of Christ they are free in their conscience before God from the curse of the Law, from sin, and from death, but that according to the body they are bound; here each must serve the other through love, in accordance with this commandment of Paul. Therefore let everyone strive to do his duty in his calling and to help his neighbor in whatever way he can. This is what Paul requires of us with the words "through love be servants of one another," which do not permit the saints to run free according to the flesh but subject them to an obligation.

* * *

KARL BARTH

The End of Religion (1919, 1921) †

Paul, as a child of his age, addressed his contemporaries. It is, however, far more important that, as Prophet and Apostle of the Kingdom of God, he veritably speaks to all men of every age. The differences between then and now, there and here, no doubt require careful investigation and consideration. But the purpose of such investigation can only be to demonstrate that these differences are, in fact, purely trivial. The historical-critical method of Biblical investigation

5. For the reading *donatum* in the Weimar text we have substituted *donatam*.
† From *The Epistle to the Romans*, tr. by Edwyn C. Hoskyns (London, 1933), pp. 1, 35–40, 238 f. The German original, first published in 1919, was completely rewritten in 1921; the English version is from the sixth edition, 1928. Barth (1886–1969), a village pastor when he wrote the Romans commentary, became soon thereafter a professor of theology in Göttingen, then in Bonn. When he was dismissed in 1935 because of his opposition to National Socialism, he returned to his native Basel, where he taught for the rest of his career. His influence on Protestant and ecumenical thought in the twentieth century has been inestimable.

has its rightful place: it is concerned with the preparation of the intelligence—and this can never be superfluous. But, were I driven to choose between it and the venerable doctrine of Inspiration, I should without hesitation adopt the latter, which has a broader, deeper, more important justification. The doctrine of Inspiration is concerned with the labour of apprehending, without which no technical equipment, however complete, is of any use whatever. Fortunately, I am not compelled to choose between the two. Nevertheless, my whole energy of interpreting has been expended in an endeavour to see through and beyond history into the spirit of the Bible, which is the Eternal Spirit. What was once of grave importance, is so still. What is to-day of grave importance—and not merely crotchety and incidental—stands in direct connexion with that ancient gravity. If we rightly understand ourselves, our problems are the problems of Paul; and if we be enlightened by the brightness of his answers, those answers must be ours.

* * *

The Theme of the Epistle

I. 16, 17

For I am not ashamed of the gospel: for it is the power of God unto salvation to every one that believeth; to the Jew first, and also to the Greek. For therein is revealed the righteousness of God from faithfulness unto faith: as it is written, But the righteous shall live from my faithfulness.

I am not ashamed. The gospel neither requires men to engage in the conflict of religions or the conflict of philosophies, nor does it compel them to hold themselves aloof from these controversies. In announcing the limitation of the known world by another that is unknown, the Gospel does not enter into competition with the many attempts to disclose within the known world some more or less unknown and higher form of existence and to make it accessible to men. The Gospel is not a truth among other truths. Rather, it sets a question-mark against all truths. The Gospel is not the door but the hinge. The man who apprehends its meaning is removed from all strife, because he is engaged in a strife with the whole, even with existence itself. Anxiety concerning the victory of the Gospel—that is, Christian Apologetics—is meaningless, because the Gospel is the victory by which the world is overcome. By the Gospel the whole concrete world is dissolved and established. It does not require representatives with a sense of responsibility, for it is as responsible for those who proclaim it as it is for those to whom it is proclaimed. It is the advocate of both. Nor is it necessary for the Gospel that Paul should take his stand in the midst of the spiritual cosmopolitanism of Rome; though he can, of course, enter the city without shame, and will enter it as a man who has been consoled by the Gospel. God does not need us. Indeed, if He were not God, He would be ashamed of us. We, at any rate, cannot be ashamed of Him.

The Gospel of the Resurrection is the—power of God, His *virtus* (Vulgate), the disclosing and apprehending of His meaning, His effective pre-eminence over all gods. The Gospel of the Resurrection is the action, the supreme miracle, by which God, the unknown God dwelling in light unapproachable, the Holy One, Creator, and Redeemer, makes Himself known: *What therefore ye worship in ignorance, this set I forth unto you* (Acts xvii. 23). No divinity remaining on this side the line of resurrection; no divinity which dwells in temples made with hands or which is served by the hand of man; no divinity which NEEDS ANYTHING, any human propaganda (Acts xvii. 24, 25),—can be God. God is the unknown God, and, precisely because He is unknown, He bestows life and breath and all things. Therefore the power of God can be detected neither in the world of nature nor in the souls of men. It must not be confounded with any high, exalted force, known or knowable. The power of God is not the most exalted of observable forces, nor is it either their sum or their fount. Being completely different, it is the KRISIS of all power, that by which all power is measured, and by which it is pronounced to be both something and—nothing, nothing and—something. It is that which sets all these powers in motion and fashions their eternal rest. It is the Primal Origin by which they all are dissolved, the consummation by which they all are established. The power of God stands neither at the side of nor above—supernatural!—these limited and limiting powers. It is pure and pre-eminent and—beyond them all. It can neither be substituted for them nor ranged with them, and, save with the greatest caution, it cannot even be compared with them. The assumption that Jesus is the Christ (i. 4) is, in the strictest sense of the word, an assumption, void of any content that can be comprehended by us. The appointment of Jesus to be the Christ takes place in the Spirit and must be apprehended in the Spirit. It is self-sufficient, unlimited, and in itself true. And moreover, it is what is altogether new, the decisive factor and turning-point in man's consideration of God. This it is which is communicated between Paul and his hearers. To the proclamation and receiving of this Gospel the whole activity of the Christian community—its teaching, ethics, and worship—is strictly related. But the activity of the community is related to the Gospel only in so far as it is no more than a crater formed by the explosion of a shell and seeks to be no more than a void in which the Gospel reveals itself. The people of Christ, His community, know that no sacred word or work or thing exists in its own right: they know only those words and works and things which by their negation are sign-posts to the Holy One. If anything Christian(!) be unrelated to the Gospel, it is a human by-product, a dangerous religious survival, a regrettable misunderstanding. For in this case content would be substituted for a void, convex for concave, positive for negative, and the characteristic marks of Christianity would be possession and self-sufficiency rather than deprivation and hope. If this be persisted in, there emerges, instead of the community of Christ, Christendom, an ineffective peace-pact or compromise with that existence which, moving with its own momentum, lies on this side resurrection. Christianity would then have lost all relation to the power of God. Now, whenever this occurs, the Gospel, so far from being removed from all rivalry, stands hard pressed in the midst of other religions and philosophies of this world. Hard pressed, because, if men must have their religious needs satisfied, if they must surround themselves with comfortable illusions about their knowledge of God and particularly about their union with Him,—well, the world penetrates far deeper into such matters than does a Christianity which misunderstands itself, and of such a 'gospel' we have good cause to be ashamed. Paul, however, is speaking of the power of the UNKNOWN God, of —*Things which eye saw not and ear heard not, and which entered not into the heart of man.* Of such a Gospel he has no cause to be ashamed.

The power of God is power—unto salvation. In this world men find themselves to be imprisoned. In fact the more profoundly we become aware of the limited character of the possibilities which are open to us here and now, the more clear it is that we are farther from God, that our desertion of Him is more complete (i. 18, v. 12), and the consequences of that desertion more vast (i. 24, v. 12), than we had ever dreamed. Men are their own masters. Their union with God is shattered so completely that they cannot even conceive of its restoration. Their sin is their guilt; their death is their destiny; their world is formless and tumultuous chaos, a chaos of the forces of nature and of the human soul; their life is illusion. This is the situation in which we find ourselves. The question 'Is there then a God?' is therefore entirely relevant and indeed inevitable! But the answer to this question, that is to say, our desire to comprehend the world in its relation to God, must proceed either from the criminal arrogance of religion or from that final apprehension of truth which lies beyond birth and death—the perception, in other words, which proceeds from God outwards. When the problem is formulated thus, it is evident that, just as genuine coins are open to suspicion so long as false coins are in circulation, so the perception which proceeds outwards from God cannot have free course until the arrogance of religion be done away. Now, it is the Gospel that opens up the possibility of this final perception, and, if this possibility is to be realized, all penultimate perceptions must be withdrawn from circulation. The Gospel speaks of God as He is: it is concerned with Him Himself and with Him only. It speaks of the Creator who shall be our Redeemer and of the Redeemer who is our Creator. It is pregnant with our complete conversion; for it announces the transformation of our creatureliness into freedom. It proclaims the forgiveness of our sins, the victory of life over death, in fact, the restoration of everything that has been lost. It is the signal, the fire-alarm of a coming, new world. But what does all this mean? Bound to the world as it is, we cannot here and now apprehend. We can only receive the Gospel, for it is the recollection of God which is created by the Gospel that comprehends its meaning. The world remains the world and men remain men even whilst the Gospel is being received. The whole burden of sin and the whole curse of death still press heavily upon us. We must be under no illusion: the reality of our present existence continues as it is! The Resurrection, which is the place of exit, also bars us in, for it is both barrier and exit. Nevertheless, the 'No' which we encounter is the 'No'—of God. And therefore our veritable deprivation is our veritable comfort in distress. The barrier marks the frontier of a new country, and what dissolves the whole wisdom of the world also establishes it. Precisely because the 'No' of God is all-embracing, it is also His 'Yes'. We have therefore, in the power of God, a look-out, a door, a hope; and even in this world we have the possibility of following the narrow path and of taking each simple little step with a 'despair which has its own consolation' (Luther). The prisoner becomes a watchman. Bound to his post as firmly as a prisoner in his cell, he watches for the dawning of the day: *I will stand upon my watch, and set me upon the tower, and will look forth to see what he will speak with me, and what he will answer concerning my complaint. And the Lord answered me, and said, Write the vision, and make it plain upon tables, that he may run that readeth it. For the vision is yet for the appointed time, and it hasteth toward the end, and shall not lie; though it tarry, wait for it; because it will surely come, it will not delay* (Hab. ii. 1–3).

The Gospel requires—*faith*. Only for those who believe is it the *power of God unto salvation*. It can therefore be neither directly communicated nor directly apprehended. Christ hath been appointed to be the Son of God—*according to the Spirit* (i. 4). 'Now, Spirit is the denial of direct immediacy. If Christ be very God, He must be unknown, for to be known directly is the characteristic mark of an idol' (Kierkegaard). So new, so unheard of, so unexpected in this world is the power of God unto salvation, that it can appear among us, be received and understood by us, only as contradiction. The Gospel does not expound or recommend itself. It does not negotiate or plead, threaten, or make promises. It withdraws itself always when it is not listened to for its own sake. 'Faith directs itself towards the things that are invisible. Indeed, only when that which is believed on is hidden, can it provide an opportunity for faith. And moreover, those things are most deeply hidden which most clearly contradict the obvious experience of the senses. Therefore, when God makes alive, He kills; when He justifies, He imposes guilt; when He leads us to heaven, He thrusts us down into hell' (Luther). The Gospel of salvation can only be believed in; it is a matter for faith only. It demands choice. This is its seriousness. To him that is not sufficiently mature to accept a contradiction and to rest in it, it becomes a scandal—to him that is unable to escape the necessity of contradiction, it becomes a matter for faith. Faith is awe in the presence of the divine incognito; it is the love of God that is aware of the qualitative distinction between God and man and God and the world; it is the affirmation of resurrection as the turning-point of the world; and therefore it is the affirmation of the divine 'No' in Christ, of the shattering halt in the presence of God. He who knows the world to be bounded by a will that contradicts it; he who knows himself to be bounded by a will that contradicts him; he who, knowing too well that he must be satisfied to live with this contradiction and not attempt to escape from it, finds it hard to kick against the pricks (Overbeck); he who finally makes open confession of the contradiction and determines to base his life upon it—he it is that believes. The believer is the man who puts his trust in God, in God Himself, and in God alone; that is to say, the man who, perceiving the faithfulness of God in the very fact that He has set us within the realm of that which contradicts the course of this world, meets the faithfulness of God with a corresponding fidelity, and with God says 'Nevertheless' and 'In spite of this'. The believer discovers in the Gospel the power of God unto salvation, the rays which mark the coming of eternal blessedness, and the courage to stand and watch. This discovery is, however, a free choice between scandal and faith, a choice presented to him always and everywhere and at every moment. Depth of feeling, strength of conviction, advance in perception and in moral behaviour, are no more than things which accompany the birth of faith. Being of this world, they are in themselves no more than unimportant signs of the occurrence of faith. And moreover, as signs of the occurrence of faith they are not positive factors, but negations of other positive factors, stages in the work of clearance by which room is made in this world for that which is beyond it. Faith, therefore, is never identical with 'piety', however pure and however delicate. In so far as 'piety' is a sign of the occurrence of faith, it is so as the dissolution of all other concrete things and supremely as the dissolution of itself. Faith lives of its own, because it lives of God. This is the *Centrum Paulinum* (Bengel).

There is no man who ought not to believe or who cannot believe. Neither the Jew nor the Greek is disenfranchised from the Gospel. By setting a question-mark against the whole course of this world and its inevitability, the Gospel directly concerns every man. As surely as no one is removed from the universal questionableness of human life, so surely is no one excluded from the divine contradiction that is in Christ, by which this questionableness seeks to make itself known to men. The Jew, the religious and ecclesiastical man, is, it is true, FIRST summoned to make the choice; this is because he stands quite normally on the frontier of this world and at the point where the line of intersection by the new dimensional plane (i. 4) must be veritably seen (ii. 17–20; iii. 1, 2; ix. 4, 5; x. 14, 15). But the advantage of the Jew provides him with no precedence. The problem 'Religion or Irreligion'—not to speak of the problem 'Church or World'—is no longer a fundamental problem. The possibility of hearing the Gospel is as universal as is the responsibility to hear it, and as is the promise vouchsafed to them who do hear it.

* * *

Having died to that wherein we were held prisoners. The frontier of religion is the line of death which separates flesh from spirit, time from eternity, human possibility from the possibility of God. In so far as this sharp sword has cleft its way through; in so far, that is, as the power and significance of the Cross, which is the token of judgement and of grace, has cast upon us its shadow—we are *discharged from the law*. We supposed that we could escape the all-embracing *Memento mori*, and we were thereby imprisoned. What seemed to us pure and upright and unbroken was shown to be for that very reason impure and crooked and crippled. Engaged in earnest and vigorous acts of piety, we thought ourselves in possession of that which could never be frozen into stark death. And so religion blossomed forth as the supreme possibility; and who can rid himself of this humanity? Is it not demonstrably clear that expectation of life is the most characteristic feature of religious piety; and that men cling to religion with a bourgeois tenacity, supposing it to be that final thing of soul and sense which is deathless and unshattered. But religion must die. In God we are rid of it. We must apprehend this last concrete thing bounded—aye, radically bounded and placed in question. We, like all clear-sighted men from Job to Dostoevsky, are compelled to recognize, whether we acknowledge it or not, that our concrete status in the world of time and of men and of things lies under the shadow of death. Living under the shadow of the Cross, we acknowledge our relatedness to Christ (vi. 5); and, when we say that we are discharged from the law, we know what we are doing—as men who do not know! It is permitted to us to say that under law we are more exceedingly under grace; for we are 'devout'—as though we were not so; we live—ignoring our experiences, or rather, transcending them. We are, then, competent to look, it may be but a little way, beyond ourselves, beyond what is in us and through us and of us, to smile and to weep at what we are. Perhaps even our religion retains some vestige of its own insignificance; perhaps it also knows its lack of solemnity and efficacy, and is conscious of its limitations. Perhaps, however, our piety lacks this perception. Whether we perceive it or not, whenever men are *under the law*, there emerges a piety which celebrates no final triumph and boasts no final justification, but which, nevertheless, refuses to regard its failure as the final tragedy, because it is a piety which continually bears witness to a significance lying beyond itself. The road of religion passes through prophecy, through speaking with tongues, through the knowledge of mysteries, through the giving-of-the-body-to-be-burned, through the giving-of-goods to feed the poor, through all such things—and it passes onwards still. The road is most strangely defined almost entirely in negatives: but it is named the 'incomprehensible way of love' (1 Cor. xii. 31). Can this be rightly named a road? It is no road—which we can observe or investigate or even enter upon. We can only pass along it. It is the road —which is the shadow cast by the Cross upon all 'healthy' human life: which is the place where the tenacity of men is invisibly, yet most effectually, disturbed and shattered and dissolved; the place where the competence of God, of the Spirit, of Eternity, can enter within our horizon.

* * *

HANS FREIHERR VON SODEN

Sacrament and Ethics in Paul (1931) †

The real difficulty of Pauline theology lies in its antinomies, because these create constant uncertainty for the expositor. Marcion, who perceived them most intensely, tried to solve the problem by the

† The essay excerpted here first appeared in *Marburger Theologische Studien* (Rudolf Otto-Festgruss) I (Gotha, 1931), pp. 1–40; rp. in *Urchristentum und Geschichte* (Tübingen, 1951), pp. 239–75, and in *Das Paulusbild in der neueren deutschen Forschung,* ed. K. H. Rengstorf (Darmstadt, 1964), pp. 338–79. Freiherr von Soden (1881–1945) taught at Berlin and Breslau before becoming Professor of New Testament and Early Church History at Marburg in 1924, a post he held until 1933, when he became leader of the Confessing Church of Kurhessen-Waldeck.

violent expedient of a grandiose theory of interpolations. That theory, as his patristic opponents already observed, did not succeed in eliminating the inner dualism of the apostle's teaching. It is possible to explain this dualism, in terms of the history of religions, on the basis of the double roots of Paul's proclamation: Judaism and Hellenism; or the rabbinic, perhaps also Stoic, legalism and Hellenistic spiritualism; the doctrine of justification and the doctrine of redemption. And insofar as historical explanation can or wants to answer only the question of sources, then in fact that would be accomplished by such an explanation. However, the essential question arises, how the combination of the two elements is to be evaluated in interpreting the content of Paul's theological statements. * * * The history of exegesis of Paul since the beginning of historical criticism has not produced a decision for [the priority of] either of the two sides, but rather has again and again led to the conclusion that their combination itself forms the essence and peculiarity of Paul. It is not a question of two sides of the historical, personal conditioning of Paul (the understanding of which would be neither more nor less important than understanding his language), but of the two sides of the subject matter itself which he wanted to make known. But how are they to be joined, and what is the relation between the antinomy of the subject matter and the duality of origin? * * *

* * *

The course of the argument in 1 Cor. 8 and 10 could be summarized briefly as follows. So far as pagan sacrificial meat is concerned, we may indeed eat so-called sacrificial meat without qualms, for there are no idols, and eating or not eating means nothing before God's judgment. Nevertheless we are bound by consideration for the conscience of the weak brother, whom we must not bring into the danger of (supposed) idolatry. Insofar as we endanger him, we make ourselves guilty of Christ who died for him, and thereby we endanger ourselves as much as him. This danger is by no means simply imaginary; whoever falls into it is lost, as the example of the Israelites shows. For behind the non-existent idols lurk the really existing demons, and the statement that the communion with Christ—in his blood and body—excludes communion with demons does not mean that the demons can no longer touch us in any case, but that we have to avoid them carefully. But how should we act, since no one is safe from the possibility of eating sacrificial meat, either at the meatmarket or when invited to dinner? We should have no fear whatever of unknowing and unintentional eating—the earth is the Lord's and everything in it, and the conscientiousness demanded here requires no investigation. But conscious and public eating we should avoid for the sake of the injury to conscience that would ensue. In that case we would sin, not in exercising our freedom, but in affronting God's honor.

The difficulty of this train of thought for modern readers and the problem of its inner unity lies exclusively in 10:14 ff., which introduces the *koinōnia tōn daimoniōn* [communion of demons[1]]. J. Weiss gives a very characteristic expression to that difficulty when he thinks he can criticize the apostle with the declaration, "Paul has done away with the materialistic *deisidaimonia* [superstition], but not yet with the spiritual" (*Der erste Korintherbrief*, p. 264). Indeed, if we ignore 10:14 ff., we obtain a thought as fine as it is simple, that would immediately appeal to a modern man, in which even 10:1-13 would fit smoothly: The danger of idolatrous sacrificial meat lies not in any quality of the meat, but in the act of eating, insofar as this in some circumstances becomes loveless and therefore sacrilegious. The meat that is eaten harms no one, but God, whom we offend by our eating, punishes us. The *opus operatum* is of no consequence, but the *opus operantis* carries responsibility. Is this ethical line of thought in fact broken by the discourse on the communion of demons which Paul introduces as a critically prudent argument "to sensible men"? For him it is the mandatory exegesis of 10:1-13; hence it cannot be separated from it, for instance by literary criticism. Is a second, divergent and inferior motif introduced here, namely that "spiritual superstition"? Does that mean that the nerve of the ethical appeal for consideration of the other person is broken by the superstitious, magical reminder of one's own danger? Is the demand of love propped up by a questionable fear of spirits?

Yet these critical questions may fit the history of religions situation as little as they do Paul's religious thought. They proceed from a conception that in many ways limits or misleads the theological understanding of 1 Corinthians, a conception of the Corinthian Gnostics as enlightened libertines. Rather, they are unrestrained enthusiasts of spiritualist faith. They put their trust not in the rationalistic judgment that there are no idols—for they also probably did not deny the existence and activity of demons—but in the belief that those initiated by Christ's sacraments are charmed against all powers and therefore possess a limitless *exousia* [authority]. *Exousia* is obviously a major slogan of the Corinthian Gnostics. For them the Christ-sacrament is absolute security, because in itself it is the realization of salvation—somewhat in the manner of the faith characterized by Cynic invective in these terms: "Pattaicion the thief will receive a better fate when he dies than Epaminondas, because

1. [RSV, "to be partners with demons."]

he has been initiated."[2] Here as elsewhere Paul is in no position to attack the sacramental beliefs from a modern understanding of spirit and thereby at the same time to ward off its fanaticism. He is in a much more difficult situation, having to oppose the (inauthentic) sacrament on the basis of the (authentic) sacrament, to refute the sacramental superstition on the basis of the sacramental faith. For that reason he adduces in Chap. 10 the biblical proof that the sacraments do not provide a charm, that they do not provide security insofar as they do not bind God, that the sacramental gift in the present does not eliminate the eschatological reservation and its future. The sacraments are not talismans or magic cloaks that license intercourse with the demons and enjoyment of their gifts with impunity. For Paul the sacrament is a sign of obligation, to use Zwingli's term, though to be sure not in the sense of a symbol, but of a dynamic reality. It is effective, but critically not mechanically. If it pledges God's certain promise, on the other hand it lays an obligation on man and punishes every misuse of itself. It binds man to God, but not God to man. It derives its effectiveness from God's power, but it does not put this power at man's disposal. * * * It is no accident and not without reason that Paul proves this meaning of the sacrament from the Old Testament, for it is the Old Testament and Jewish idea of God's free act of power which Paul sets in opposition to the Hellenistic idea of God. In the former, all the acts of God remain in his control; in the latter a spiritual substance, bound up with the quality in question, can be grasped and therefore fixed. [For Paul] the Christ-sacraments as such are effective in a quite specific context of meaning and history, which is defined by the blood and body of Christ, and may not be separated from this context. They cannot be actualized and individualized for any use one chooses to make of them, as if they were potencies carrying a certain quantity of power. "It is impossible" (*ou dynasthe*)—it is historically excluded—that one could sit at the table of Christ and at the table of demons. The union with the one can be accomplished only in separation from the other. The Corinthians, however, thought participation at both tables possible because they regarded the power of the demons as broken, neutral-

2. Plutarch, *Quomodo adulescens poetas audire debeat* 4, pp. 21 f. In the same way, in my opinion, the question in 1 Cor. 15 is not a denial of the resurrection—Paul formulates it that way from his eschatological understanding of the resurrection—but the declaration that the resurrection had already occurred (in *gnosis*, in the spirit). What was denied in Corinth was the bodily and eschatological character (both belong essentially together) of the resurrection. Karl Barth's interpretation (*Die Auferstehung der Toten*, p. 144; ET, *The Resurrection of the Dead*, p. 201) of the Corinthians as representatives of the belief in the immortality of the soul is also false. They are not idealists but gnostics. On the contrary, I am afraid I see in Barth's own dialectical understanding of Paul's resurrection proclamation (p. 116; ET pp. 202 f.) a modern revival of the enthusiastic, uneschatological belief of the Corinthians.

ized, in the power of Christ. Moreover, the meaning of the Christian forgiveness of sins is not (as they thought) that concrete sin is permitted, but rather that man can sin no more. The covenant with God, the possession of his Spirit, is therefore secure only for those who are conscious of the great danger of this covenant, this possession, who are conscious at the same time of a *possessio passiva* [i.e., being possessed by God]. Indeed, no misfortune befalls the person who is joined to the Lord by the sacrament, yet precisely this person faces the punitive judgment of disorder. The word of the forgiveness of all transgressions is valid only together with the threat of blasphemy against the Spirit, and one who has faith to move mountains does not put this to the test. Thus we cannot speak of an unassimilated relic of spiritual superstition that impedes the full power and clarity of the faith in Christ and God. Rather it is a question of that fear of the devil without which one cannot speak of any serious fear of God. It is the living possession at the same time of the *Deus iratus* and the *Deus placatus*, the *Deus revelatus* and the *Deus absconditus* and thus the only real "possession," namely being possessed by God. This fear of the devil still stands even with the recognition that there is no devil, no anti-God in the world. We are not talking about a relic of the suspicion that God might after all not be all-powerful, that one might after all not be able to risk everything with him alone. On the contrary, we are saying of that reservation of all God-given, otherwise unlimited *exousia* [authority], that God himself is its limit, that there is no *exousia* against God, no right to him or against him: "But when it says, 'All things are put in subjection under him,' it is plain that he is excepted who put all things under him" (1 Cor. 15:27).

If it is acknowledged that the understanding presented here fits the meaning of the "sacramental" passages in our text, then the discussion of the communion of the demons is not in any way contradictory to that which we read before it and find taken up again in the concluding paragraph. Rather, it is its explication and probably, in Paul's mind, its climax, the ultimate thing he could say on the subject. The basic thought of the whole is not broken here, but is entirely unfolded for the first time; indeed the essential and decisive motif of the position Paul's critique attacks is here for the first time clearly picked up and effectively invalidated. For all those involved think sacramentally: "The strong," the enthusiasts or "exusiasts," as one could call them from their own slogan, who believe that in the body of Christ (for them that is the same thing as, with Christ in their body) nothing can harm them. The weak, who are terrified of every defilement, like modern men with a germ phobia (for today human superstition is frequently found in medical rather than religious garb). But also Paul himself, who rises above both groups, yet is convinced with both that there is a spiritual, blessed eating and drinking, that koinōnia [communion] is effected and dissolved therein, and that God's secret, numinous presence is effective everywhere. There is no direct reference in 1 Cor. 10:1-22 to suneidēsis [conscience], yet what the Israelites did was done with suneidēsis, and—in notable distinction from modern thought—eating and drinking for Paul was qualified, not neutralized, by the suneidēsis. Certainly, as we see, the stamp of the sacramental thought which is erected by each on the common ground of self-evident recognition and use of the sacraments is very notably different. These differences must be specified all the more clearly, as the participants seem not to be aware of them; each of them reads his own sacramental thought into that of the others.

The specifically Hellenistic sacramental thought, the more or less sublimated, animistic naturalism, is obviously not that of Paul—in his real intention. Yet it is not rejected by him but reinterpreted. "Spiritual food" and "spiritual drink" in 1 Cor. 10:4 do not mean actually that spirit is eaten and drunk, and the "participation in the blood and body of Christ" by the blessed cup and broken bread does not mean that the blood of Christ is drunk as wine and his body (flesh) eaten as bread. Food and drink are "spiritual" in 10:4 in the same sense as "the Rock" mentioned immediately thereafter. In this way the things named are designated as phenomena that point to and depend upon pneuma [spirit]. They are miraculous phenomena, revelatory phenomena, promissory phenomena, intended to convey an event effected by God.

That is proven by the usage elsewhere of pneumatikos [spiritual], which is always pregnant with history and means the pneuma theou [spirit of God]. In the same way koinōnia tou haimatos means participation in death, in the dying of Christ. Haima designates "blood" spilled in death, not the substance of blood as life-substance (cf. Rom. 3:25; 5:9 f.). And koinōnia tou sōmatos means participation in the body, the spiritual body of Christ—the same (spiritual) body of Christ that is mentioned in 1 Cor. 6:12 ff.; 12:13 ff.; Rom. 7:4; 12:5. The unity of the loaf means the unity of the body; the bread is not compared as a substance with the substance of flesh, and there is no thought of any transubstantiation or consubstantiation, but only of communion. It is incontestable that, from 10:20, the koinōnia tou kuriou [communion with the Lord] is to be interpreted exactly analogously to koinōnia tōn daimoniōn [communion with the demons]. But in the latter case there is no question of absorbing the demons into one's own body by eating and drinking, thus not of eating and drinking demons (for in that case what would correspond to the "body and blood" of Christ?), but of union with the demons (which is obligation to them) by means of table fellowship. Decisive support is found in 10:18, where eating of the sacrifice effects *koinōnia* with the altar (the altar stands for the God of the altar, as said before); therefore that which is eaten is not of the same substance as that with which it joins the eater. Also 10:4 reinforces this view: Christ is the Rock that gives the miraculous water; he gives the drink, he is not the drink. Finally, the parallels from other religions which have been adduced to this passage also prove the same thing. This interpretation of 1 Cor. 10:16 ff. is further reinforced by the fact that it eliminates the much discussed tension between this passage and the second treatment of the Eucharist by Paul in 1 Cor. 11. * * * [In the latter passage, Jesus'] death and his coming are to be proclaimed in the Eucharist. Hence the eating and drinking as such do not accomplish it, as the individualists or particularists upbraided by Paul believe—their sacramental thought is again really animistic, and therefore they think each may eat and drink his own for himself alone—rather, they are by waiting upon one another and sharing with one another to become one (one loaf). We must not understand Paul in the sense of the Johannine and Ignatian "eating of flesh," but must take as the norm of interpretation the unity of his own thought in his disparate statements. Only we must not attempt to interpret his sacramental concept in idealistic, symbolic terms. We are not contesting his unmistakable realism, but seeking to recognize what is for him the *res sacramenti*: the *koinōnia tou kuriou*, the self-communication of the Lord.

If one means by sacramental thinking something opposed to ethical thinking, which makes material things into mechanical, magical vehicles of the spiritual, thereby defined naturalistically and individualistically * * *, then in that sense there is no sacramental thinking whatever in Paul, and to that extent no contradiction either between sacramental and ethical thinking. Besides, one can ask whether the "weak" persons addressed by Paul think sacramentally in the animistic sense. Their attitude could also be interpreted as not sacramental, but legalistic anxiety. In favor of this interpretation would be the analogy of Jewish discussions of the problem of participation in idolatrous worship. * * * Whether the "weak" thought more legalistically or more sacramentally we cannot determine, for Paul is not the least bit interested in such a differentiation here or elsewhere—a sign indeed that one should not press the differentiation when speaking of Paul's understanding and his time, for at that time the law itself was a sacrament. His own decision seems indeed to remain in the line of Jewish legal discussions to the extent that he seems to distinguish the different cases according to the question whether each has idolatry as its outcome or not. But the way he carries out his argument is totally different from what we find in the Jewish tradition.[3] It does not make any determination of the source and use of the things in question into the criterion for *exousia* [right, authority], but rather the intentional character of the action, as determined by the conscience. In this way Paul dissolves and transcends every formal law in the mental law of conscience.

For this reason it seems questionable whether one can understand Paul as forbidding altogether in 10:1–22 participation in pagan festival meals, to which "the strong" seem according to Chaps. 8, 9 to want to go, while in 10:23–33 the regulation we have discussed above applies only to private purchase of meat and participation in private meals in pagan houses. The most important element in such an interpretation, the ban on festival meals (meals *en eidōleiō*, "in the idol shrine"), is only inferred, while the text yields no indication that the "If one of the unbelievers invites you to dinner and you are disposed to go" (10:27) applies to a more limited set of cir- cumstances than Chap. 8. Also archaeological findings do not sup- port this implicitly assumed differentiation. The formula *kalein* [invite] is used of temple meals as well as meals in private houses.[4] Most of the Corinthian Christians and many of their pagan rela- tives or associates will not likely have been able to hold banquets in their private dwellings. And in itself the act of eating in a room which contained the image of a deity, if this were ignored, would probably be no more problematic than attending the public bath.[5] The cultic character of such meals was as attentuated as was later the Christian "love feast"; in that time it would not have been pos- sible to delineate a sharp difference between cultic and purely hos- pitable or fraternal festivals. Precisely for that reason, the problems discussed in our text arose in the intercourse of Christians with the world, and even Paul gives no clues for making such a distinction. It is of course self-evident that Christian participation was forbid- den in any meal whose circumstances or form stamped its essential meaning without doubt as that of idolatry (*koinōnia tōn daimon- iōn*), so that no "informer" was needed to point out the sacrificial meat. But it seems to me that one would limit the freedom, and at the same time destroy the sharpness of the Pauline directive, if one were to introduce any kind of external criterion before, or alongside of, conscience, that is, the conscious and confessional character of the act. That would mean to bend Paul's directives in the direction

3. Von Soden is talking about the Talmudic tradition, particularly trac- tate *Aboda Zara.* This tradition has al- ways seemed more "legalistic" and "ca- suistic" to Christian scholars than to Talmudists. [*Editor*]
4. The oft quoted invitations "to a dinner of the Lord Serapis" (*eis klei-* *nēn tou kuriou Sarapidos*) found in pa- pyri [e.g., *Oxyrhynchus Papyri,* ed. Grenfell and Hunt, I, 110] * * * could in my opinion be entirely of the type meant in 1 Cor. 10:27.
5. On the bath, see Babylonian Tal- mud, Aboda Zara 44b * * * .

of the talmudic, and while that cannot be rejected a priori, in view of the given historical situation. (Paul's presuppositions and the problems of his congregations are indeed the same as those of Judaism), still it is simply a fact, as we have tried to show, that his stand is no less opposed to a casuistic nomism than to a spiritual "exusiasm." That is proved again with full certainty by the analogy of Rom. 14–15. Here the viewpoint of idolatry is not even considered; it is a question rather of ritualistic asceticism. In this passage also Paul rejects explicitly any legal regulation and proclaims as a matter of principle individual freedom in the style of life. With clearest precision he says, "I know and am persuaded in the Lord Jesus that nothing is unclean in itself; but it is unclean for any one who thinks it unclean" (Rom. 14:14). Just because the latter clause as well as the former is true, mutual incrimination should be replaced by mutual heed and concern. The "strong" has the obligation, precisely in his freedom, not by giving offense to endanger the brother for whom Christ died (Rom. 14:15, cf. 1 Cor. 8:11). There is absolutely nothing said here about a minimal degree of asceticism valid independently of personal responsibility. The church was not able to retain the Pauline decision, but fell back, in Jewish fashion, on casuistic rules and the determination of minimal requirements. It gave up the enthusiasm which Paul, by reflection and modification, sought to perfect. It dissolved the tension of sacrament and ethic in a legal code that joins both but breaks both. It had to do that, for Paul's decision is spirit and not law; it leads out beyond the law that was recognized in his sphere and does not admit to any adjudication (cf. 1 Cor. 6:7 ff., contra 6:1 ff.). Hence it can only be carried out in a community that possesses the Spirit and proclaims the coming of the Lord, not in a community that possesses ecclesiastical office and would use this to instruct the coming Christ, in the manner of Dostoievski's Grand Inquisitor. But the history of the catholicizing of Paulinism in the church cannot be pursued here nor its theological problematic discussed. It suffices to have shown something about the Pauline sacramental teaching in 1 Corinthians which, in my opinion, is proved by the investigation of the Pauline theology at every important point: that Paul holds a thoroughly critical attitude toward the Hellenization of Christianity. His concept of spirit and sacrament is critically opposed to the spirit and sacrament concept of his time, and he knew how to distinguish his faith as decisively against the "exusiasm" of a Hellenistic divinizing gnosis as against a Jewish legalism. An analysis of the Pauline baptismal teaching in Romans (Chap. 6; cf. Gal. 3:26 f.; 1 Cor. 6:11; 12:13; Col. 2:11 f.) would have exactly the same results. Here also the underlying hylozoic understanding is only the metaphysic of the age, which is reduced to a mere form filled with a historical, christological, and eschatological content. The death of Christ is the sacrament; baptism is the sacramental confession of it, in which participation in it is acquired, the incorporation into the body of Christ.

* * *

The foregoing does not imply that ethics is the only content of this Pauline text that has theological value. The sacrament is not merely the cultural wrapping of that content. We must rather recognize that Paul's ethic is itself sacramental (in his sense), i.e., that it is historically, christologically, and eschatologically tied down, a specifically theological ethic and an ethical theology. * * *

Popular philosophical ethics frequently criticize Christian morality and moral teachings by saying that they break up the pure morality and objectivity of decisions on questions of action by introducing the "eudaemonistic" motif of fear of God and the perspective of eternal life, or by saying that they cripple the moral will with the notion that a divine predestination determines our will and capacity. Furthermore, since the belief in God itself admittedly is not a universal and necessary truth, it is said that the universality and necessity that belong to the essence of ethical demands cannot be achieved in connection with faith. To be sure, Christian ethics can receive these reproaches with equanimity so long as the philosophers have not settled their endless controversy over the choice between, or the combination of, a subjective-formal ethic of intention and an objective-empirical ethic of value. * * * Yet theological ethics, as the system of Christian morals and morality, has allowed itself to be pushed by these attacks into an unfortunate defensive posture, instead of seizing the offensive. One does not outline a theological ethic simply by teaching that our duties should be seen as God's commandments, or by labelling the natural and cultural values which are to be cultivated and developed in ethical behavior "values of creation"—thus placing God himself at the pinnacle of the value pyramid. In this way theology fulfills only a demand pressed upon it by a mistaken concept of science, which it ought rather to reject, namely that it develop its content while ignoring the faith in God which cannot be scientifically confirmed. Thus it develops the content of this faith either not at all or only indirectly and in fragments, at the cost of the logic of the system. Thus it makes a peace of appeasement with the deism that has ever and again fatefully dominated the Western development of theology. Deism makes the knowledge of God into a rational knowledge, which robs it of all present, historical meaning. But to found a theological ethic it also does not suffice to say that faith in God is the personal condition for ethical activity, and to declare that an actualized morality without faith is impossible, or to devalue such morality as imperfect. Rather the theologian must proceed as Paul does vis à vis the Corinthians: by making of every concrete question about relation to others (Chaps. 8, 9) a question about the relation to God (Chap. 10), and from the question of decision between two given possibilities to expose the question of obedience to God as the really decisive one. Thus the solution of the ethical conflict is to be achieved in a strictly theological judgment (*krinein*, 1 Cor. 10:15).

The ethical question on a given occasion, seen from this theological perspective, asks neither about the inner form of an action in terms of universal motivation by the idea of the good nor about the value of good toward which it is intentionally and teleologically directed (because it is not in either sense a question about an ideal or a law). Rather, it asks about the particular temporal occasion (1 Cor. 10:11, cf. 7:29) and its historical demand. This occasion is seen as one that determines a historical future, and the required decision is sought on the basis of the past history which for its part has determined this occasion. From this perspective an ethical decision is not a decision for a definite, eternal, formal principle or a timeless, objective value (both are concepts in which reality is not grasped), but rather in a specific historical situation the decision for a specific comprehension of history as such, which appears always as at the same time already given (according to Paul: in the death of Christ) and still to be demonstrated (according to Paul: at the end of the age). If this is recognized, it completely excludes the attempt, antinomian in a highly unfortunate sense, to find the correct decision in such a way that it would be appropriate with or without the presupposition of faith in God, by virtue of the validity of its formal attitude or its material definition. The correctness of faith in God cannot be proved by showing that it coincides with truth that is known independently of itself (in that case God would become in truth not the sanctioning but the sanctioned, not establishing value, but himself established as a value). Rather it is established when one acknowledges God as the truth—acknowledges in the full, sacramental sense of Paul, i.e., that one must take seriously God's action as present and free. The matter can also be expressed in this way: in genuine ethical decision man does not decide as one who disposes, but grasps the decision which God has made about him. The *krisis* [judgment] of this decision is passive. Man does not possess the *exousia* about which the ethical systems want to give him advice or prescription. He is not lord, but can only share lordship insofar as he obeys. In this sense Paul refers back to the sacrament in both 1 Cor. 10 and Rom. 6: in what has happened to us in it, we are already pre-obligated and pre-authorized. We cannot do, we are not able to do anything we want, but only one thing. And only an ethic that is in this sense sacramental, an ethic of obligation established and authorized through history, is a Christian ethic and can be carried out as a theological science. The task of theological ethics is to unfold ethics historically out of the logic of faith in God, on the basis of the Christ revelation. Such an ethic would truly not be an abstract one, as the whole of 1 Corinthians shows, but would grasp the practical conflicts in their full complexity and would solve them, where formalism and value theory fail. Such an ethic would no longer neutralize dogmatic theology, but would be strictly and inwardly united with it. * * *

* * *

KARL BARTH

The New Man (1952) †

* * *

Jesus Christ is the secret truth about the essential nature of man, and even sinful man is essentially related to Him. That is what we have learned from Rom. 5:12–21.

Now we shall try to summarize our conclusions: We have seen how, according to vv. 1–11, Jesus Christ is a sharply-defined individual, and how, as such, He is clearly the representative of an undetermined multitude of other men. In His life and destiny He represents and anticipates their life and their destiny so that they, without ceasing to be distinct individuals, must make their life an image and reflection of His life and must work out the destiny that overtook them in Him. They have to identify themselves with Him, because He has already identified Himself with them. There is no question of any merging or any confusion between Him and them, but neither can there be any question of any abstraction or separation. He in His individuality is theirs, and so they in their individuality can only be His. The ineffaceable distinction between Him and them is the guarantee of their indissoluble unity with Him. They as receivers are subordinated and yet indissolubly related to Him as Giver; they as members are subordinated and yet indissolubly united to Him as Head.

But vv. 1–11 only speak of Jesus Christ and those who *believe* in

† This selection is Barth's own summary of his book *Christ and Adam*, a discussion of Romans 5 published in German in 1952, translated into English by T. A. Smail (New York, 1956), pp. 107–17.

Him. If we read that first part of the chapter by itself, we might quite easily come to the conclusion that for Paul Christ's manhood is significant only for those who are united to Him in faith. We would then have no right to draw any conclusion about the relationship between Christ and *man as such*, from what Paul says about the "religious" relationship between Christ and Christians. We could not then expect to find in the manhood of Christ the key to the essential nature of man.

But in vv. 12–21 Paul does not limit his context to Christ's relationship to believers but gives fundamentally the same account of His relationship to all men. The context is widened from Church history to world history, from Christ's relationship to Christians to His relationship to all men. It should be noted that in these verses there is no further mention of faith or even of the gift of the Holy Spirit, and that the first person plural which is continually used in vv. 1–11 is here (with the exception of the last phrase of v. 21) replaced by a quite general third person plural. What is said here applies generally and universally, and not merely to one limited group of men. Here "religious" presuppositions are not once hinted at. The fact of Christ is here presented as something that dominates and includes all men. The nature of Christ objectively conditions human nature and the work of Christ makes an objective difference to the life and destiny of all men. Through Christ grace overflows upon them, bringing them pardon and justification and opening before them a prospect of life with God. In short, "grace rules," as it is put in v. 21. And all that is an exact correspondence to what happens to human nature in its objective relationship to Adam. There sin rules, in exactly the same way, and all men become sinners and unrighteous in Adam, and as such must die. The question about what is the special mark of the *Christian* is just not raised at all. What we are told is what it means for man as such that his objective relationship to Adam is subordinate to and dependent upon and included in his objective relationship to Christ. The question raised here—as distinct from vv. 1–11—concerns the relationship between Christ and all men.

Paul had obviously no intention of fathering an idle and arbitrary speculation when in this passage he passed on to this further account of the same subject. If we have understood the *dia touto* (therefore) of v. 12 rightly, his intention was rather to consolidate the special account he had already given of the relationship between Christ and faith, by placing it in this wider and more general context. Our standing as believers is as vv. 1–11 have described it, because our standing as men is as vv. 12–21 describe it. Our relationship to Christ as believers is based upon our prior relationship to Him as Adam's children and heirs. For even when we were, in the words of vv. 1–11, weak, sinners, godless, and enemies, Christ died for us and so brought us into His Kingdom and under His power.

We have come *to* Christ as believers and Christians, because we had already come *from* Christ, so that there was nothing else for us to do but believe in Him. What is said in vv. 1–11 is not just "religious" truth that only applies to specially talented, specially qualified, or specially guided men; it is truth for *all* men, whether they know it or not, as surely as they are all Adam's children and heirs. The assurance of Christians, as it is described in vv. 1–11, has as its basis the fact that the Christian sphere is not limited to the "religious" sphere. What is *Christian* is secretly but fundamentally identical with what is *universally human*. Nothing in true human nature can ever be alien or irrelevant to the Christian; nothing in true human nature can ever attack or surpass or annul the objective reality of the Christian's union with Christ. Much in true human nature is unrelated to "religion," but nothing in true human nature is unrelated to the Christian faith. That means that we can understand true human nature only in the light of the Christian gospel that we believe. For Christ stands above and is first, and Adam stands below and is second. So it is Christ that reveals the true nature of man. Man's nature in Adam is not, as is usually assumed, his true and original nature; it is only truly human at all in so far as it reflects and corresponds to essential human nature as it is found in Christ. True human nature, therefore, can only be understood by Christians who look to Christ to discover the essential nature of man. Vv. 12–21 are revolutionary in their insistence that what is true of Christians must also be true of all men. That is a principle that has an incalculable significance for all our action and thought. To reject this passage as empty speculation is tantamount to denying that the human nature of Christ is the final revelation of the true nature of man.

What Rom. 5:12–21 is specially concerned to make clear is that man as we know him, man in Adam who sins and dies, has his life so ordered that he is both a distinct individual and, at the same time, the responsible representative of humanity and of all other men. In the same way there are no other responsible representatives of humanity than individual men. We are what Adam was and so are all our fellow men. And the one Adam is what we and all men are. Man is at once an individual and only an individual, and, at the same time, without in any way losing his individuality, he is the responsible representative of all men. He is always for himself and always for all men. That being so, can we build on this foundation? Is it true that essential human nature must always be the existence of the man in humanity and of humanity in the man? We recognize that, first, only in relation to Adam and the many who are like him, and so only in relation to sinful and dying men like ourselves. But have we understood man correctly when we understand him in that way? Could not all that be quite wrong? Might not humanity be a corporate personality of which individuals are only insignificant manifestations or fragmentary parts? Or might not the whole notion of humanity be a fiction, and the reality consist only of a collection of individuals each essentially unrelated to the others and each responsible only for himself? Rom. 5:12–21 points in neither of these directions. If we base our thinking on this passage, we can have nothing to do with either collectivism on the one hand or individualism on the other. It understands the true man in neither of these ways.

But how does this passage come to be so definite about its own interpretation of the true man? For it is dealing expressly with Adam and so with corrupt man, and it might seem questionable to base such definite statements about the true nature of man upon our knowledge of him. What is Paul's authority for basing a categorical conclusion about the structure of human nature upon nothing sounder than his knowledge of fallen man? We have seen that Paul dares to draw this conclusion because he sees Adam not in isolation but in his relationship to Christ. And for him Christ and Adam do not represent two conflicting interpretations of human nature. For in that case the doubt as to which was ultimately valid would still arise—and the tone of vv. 1–11 shows that Paul has no doubts at all. The answer is in vv. 13–14 and 20, where it is shown that the formal correspondence and identity between Adam and Christ is based upon their material disparity. In the encounter between them Christ has more right and power, and Adam less. It is only in this disparity of status and in this disproportion that they can be compared. Adam is subordinate to Christ, and not Christ to Adam. And if Adam is subordinate to Christ, then Adam represents true and genuine human nature in so far as he shows us the man in humanity and humanity in the man. Whatever else in his representation of human nature may have to be accounted for by its later corruption and ruin, this ordering principle at least belongs to its condition and character as created and untouched by sin. For the subordinate representation of human nature in Adam here corresponds to its primary representation in Christ. In Christ also, the man is in humanity and humanity is in the man. With one important difference: Adam is not God's Son become man, and so he cannot, like Him, be man, and at the same time be *over* all men. Adam, as the one, can represent the many; he as man can represent humanity—but only as one among others. Thus he can represent all the others only in the same way that each of them can represent him. Adam has no essential priority of status over other men. He cannot be their lord and head; he cannot determine their life and their destiny. He can anticipate their life and destiny in himself, only in so far as he is the first man among many others, only in so far as he is *primus inter pares*. The *pollō mallon* (much more) of vv. 15–17 marks this difference. Where it is taken into account, what remains of the identity between Adam and Christ is the unity of the one and the many on both sides, of his deeds and their deeds, of his condition and theirs. In this unity Christ is, like Adam, man. In this unity of the one and the many Adam is the type and likeness of Christ, although formally he differs from Christ because he is not lord and head in this unity, and materially he differs from Him, because his nature is perverted by sin. But this unity, as such, belongs not to the perversion of his nature but to its original constitution. And so Paul makes no arbitrary assertion, and he is not deceiving himself when he presupposes this unity as simply given even in Adam. He does so because he has found it given first and primarily in Christ.

Christ is not only God's Son; He is also a man who is not a sinner like Adam and all of us. He is true man in an absolute sense, and it is in His humanity that we have to recognize true human nature in the condition and character in which it was willed and created by God. To it there certainly belongs this unity of man and humanity. When we inquire about the true nature of man and seek an answer in terms of this unity, we are on firm ground, in so far as even sinful man, whom alone we know, reflects back, as far as this unity is concerned, the human nature of Christ and so has not ceased to be true man and has not ceased to show man's true nature to us.

PART V

"The Second Founder of Christianity"

The discussion of Paul in the second half of the nineteenth century was defined by the question of his place in the evolution of early Christianity. That was a distinctly post-Enlightenment question. It meant that now men were seeking to understand Christianity as one historical phenomenon among others, subject to the same laws of change as other human institutions or systems of thought. It meant also that the important role of conflict in the formation of early Christianity was being painfully rediscovered. So long as the Bible was read as a sourcebook of systematic theology, a treasury of eternally true propositions—and the post-Reformation defensive postures of Roman Catholics and Protestants alike had led by and large to a flat and rigid view of scripture—then it was hardly possible for the divergent points of view within the Bible to be recognized. The Enlightenment revolt against church institutions and dogmatic traditions assured that they would be recognized, and not only recognized but savored.

Perhaps *the* characteristic focus of modern intellectual history has been preoccupation with the processes of change. The nineteenth century produced two massive theories of evolution which were to alter man's picture of his world: on the Continent, the abstract, metaphysical dialectic of Hegel; in the English-speaking world, Darwin's empirically grounded construct of biological history. These theories were symptoms—as in turn they became also causes of further acceleration—of a widespread awareness of development and a concern for the understanding of origins and of the ways in which the process of change takes place.

In the study of early Christianity the obsessive question was how to explain the evolution of the world church—replete with metaphysical dogmas, sacramental system, and powerful hierarchy—out of the tiny band of Galilean peasants taught by Jesus. One of the most curious aspects of the post-Enlightenment critique of Christianity is the strange attraction that the figure of Jesus still exerted over the most diverse schools that were outspokenly hostile to Christianity, from the Deists to Nietzsche to the

273

Deutsche Christen. To be sure, these different critics had quite divergent pictures of what the real Jesus had been like. To some he appeared as a simple prophet or rabbi, startling the world with the charming directness and austerity of his ethical maxims. To others he might, by the directness of his talk about God and the fearlessness of his demeanor in the face of death, show that "he had denied every cleft between God and man; he *lived* this unity of God and man . . ." (Nietzsche). In any case, it was very difficult to harmonize the pictures one might reasonably draw of the historical Jesus with the *Cosmocrator* enthroned in the mosaic dome of a Byzantine basilica, or with the Second Person of the Trinity, consubstantial with the Father, of the Nicene Creed. Any one who read the gospels with a historian's eye would have to observe that Jesus had not taught any of the great ontological systems associated with the fundamental dogmas of the church. How then had these doctrines arisen?

A simple way of putting the question was, How had Greek philosophical theology replaced the teachings of Jesus? For it was evident that the Christian theologians of the second and third centuries had used the language of Greek philosophical schools to speak of God, Christ, and salvation. And a simple answer to the question was, Paul was the one who hellenized Christianity. On the face of it this answer had an immediate plausibility. As one moves in the New Testament from the synoptic gospels to Paul's letters (and the naïve reader would assume he was moving from the earlier to the later), one finds a decisive shift from Jesus' teachings about the kingdom of God to Paul's teachings about Christ. And the latter have virtually nothing to say about Jesus' life and teachings, but speak of him as a divine, pre-existent being, the Son of God, who by his death and resurrection accomplished the atonement of God with men.

Paul might be either praised or blamed for the Hellenization of Christianity, depending on one's point of view. If one thought that the essence of Christianity was the ethical teachings of Jesus, or his directly perceptible personality, then Paul might appear to have perverted that simple truth into something complex and sterile. Such a radical separation between Jesus and Paul, however, created more problems for a serious student of Christian origins than it solved, so it was not widely represented save in popular tracts. Besides, not many Christian reconstructionists were interested in a Jewish Jesus. For idealists, what was essential in Jesus had by definition to be universal, not limited to the contingencies of a particular time and place. In this discussion "Jewish" became virtually a code word for "particular," "limited," "historically conditioned," while "Greek" came to mean "universal," "rational," and "ideal." Thus for F. C. Baur, as for certain of the English Deists before him, Jesus lived and taught within the thought world of Palestinian Judaism, but his life and message implied a rational, universal religious outlook that far transcended his Jewishness. While his immediate successors, the Jerusalem apostles, obscured the universal implications of their Master by their narrow Jewishness, Paul was enabled through his conflict with the Jewish Christians to realize the universal potential of Jesus and to free his spirit from the Jewish matrix.

Of course, the picture could be stood on its head. The orientalist Paul de Lagarde, recognizing that many of the essential doctrines of Paul, notably the atonement by Jesus' death, were by no means "Greek," insisted that Paul was the *Judaizer* of Christianity, binding the universal, human religion of Jesus into the straitjacket of "rabbinic" myth. A rather similar position was adopted by Friedrich Nietzsche, particularly in his later works (note the differences between his aphorism about Paul in *The Dawn of Day* and his bitter tirade in the later *The Antichrist*, excerpted below). In the same category also are George Bernard Shaw's remarks about Paul (see below), except of course that they preserve a sense of humor and are free from the dark metaphysical and racial trappings of Teutonic anti-Paulinism.

The Baur proposals received intense criticism from students of early Christian history. Adolf von Harnack agreed that Paul had removed the Jewish "husk" from Jesus' message, but insisted that the development from Jesus to the Jerusalem church to the Gentile mission to Paul was direct and linear, not dialectical. The Hellenization of Christianity, with its fateful accretion of dogmas to be believed, *did* take place, according to Harnack, but only *after* Paul, among the Apologists of the second century.

A more fundamental attack on the Baur proposals was made by those who doubted whether Paul could be understood basically as a *theologian* at all. Was he not rather a man of deep religious experience, a mystic or devotee of the Christian sacramental cult? In that case, was it not an error to extract from his writings a system of doctrine? This counterview of Paul, which was nurtured by the new discipline of the history of religions, will be considered in Part VII. History of religions also was responsible for the gradual achievement of a much more precise, less monolithic, understanding of the varieties of Judaism and of Hellenism in the first century than had informed the nineteenth-century critics. One result was the rediscovery of Jewish and Christian apocalyptic, which had explosive effects on the critical interpretation both of the historical Jesus and of the early church. Albert Schweitzer is largely responsible for popularizing the results of the study of apocalyptic. He insisted that taking seriously Paul's debt to apocalyptic would upset not only the scheme of Baur and his "Tübingen school," but also both Harnack's simpler image of Paul and that of the mystical interpreters of the apostle (see his essay below, Part VII).

Quite a new dimension was added to the discussion by the sober exegetical study of Wilhelm Heitmüller, who showed that the Hellenization of Christianity had already taken place *before* Paul, and that Paul in fact was converted to a Hellenistic form of Christianity, complete with sacraments, cultus, and atonement doctrine. That put the entire debate in a new light, as one can readily see by examining the subsequent work of religious historians such as Wilhelm Bousset, or of New Testament scholars such as Rudolf Bultmann, particularly the plan of the latter's *New Testament Theology* (see his essay in Part VII on Paul's use of myth).

The outcome of the debate was that Paul's Jewishness *and* his Hellenism were thoroughly established. More recent detailed investigations, some of which have been as one-sided as last century's arguments, have eventually reinforced this conclusion. Moreover, the artificiality of the separation and opposition of the two has been glaringly revealed. In this connection the significance of Hellenistic Judaism in paving the way for Paul and, even before him, for the earlier Hellenistic Christian congregations, has been recognized. The study of Paul within the context of comparative religious phenomena has been fully vindicated, but not at the cost of denying the significance of Paul as a thinker. At the same time, his theology can never again be conceived of in the dogmatic categories of pre-Baur scholarship, nor of the rationalistic, idealist constructions of the Tübingen school itself. His thought was in the context of the community, not individualistic; practical, not speculative; intensely personal and existential, not abstract; and always in the service of his faith and his mission.

FERDINAND CHRISTIAN BAUR

Hebraists, Hellenists, and Catholics (1860) †

* * *

It is a proof of the strong faith of the disciples, and of the great
confidence they had already gained in the cause of Jesus, that
during the period immediately succeeding his death they neither
dispersed about the country nor agreed to meet at any more distant
spot, but made Jerusalem itself their permanent centre. Here it was
that the first Christian church was formed, and the Church of Jerusalem continued to be regarded by all Jewish believers in Jesus as
the headquarters of their religion. Recent critical investigations
show that the statements given in the Acts of the Apostles afford
but a dim and confused picture of this early community of believers, and yield little to the historian in the way of trustworthy or
consistent materials. It is not till we come to the appearance of Stephen and the persecution of which he was the occasion (Chap. vi.
and vii.) that we stand on firmer historical ground. Here there are
two things to be remarked. The charge brought against Stephen,
which is strikingly similar to that brought against Jesus at his trial,
and cannot in the latter case any more than that of Stephen have
been an entirely baseless statement on the part of the false witnesses, shows us the early beginnings of an opposition which could
only find its further development in Paulinism. The more spiritual
worship of God which Stephen opposed to the externalism of the
existing temple worship, could not fail to lead beyond Judaism. The
whole appearance of Stephen suggests that the cause he pleaded was
one which would justify us in calling him the forerunner of the
apostle Paul. It is important, however, to notice, that this opposition to Judaism to which Stephen was the first to draw public attention, seems to have existed in the Church of Jerusalem for some
time, and to have divided the church into two different parties. Stephen was a Hellenist, and it cannot be thought accidental that this
more liberal tendency appeared in one who was a Hellenist. The
fact of which he is an example, that the primitive church at Jerusalem numbered Hellenists among its members, is confirmed by the
express statement of the Acts (viii. 4, xi. 19, *sq.*) When the mem-

† From *The Church History of the
First Three Centuries*, English translation ed. by Allan Menzies (London,
1878), I, 44–66, 75–77. The translation is from the 3d German ed., 1863,
identical with the 2d, 1860. F. C. Baur
(1792–1860) was professor of theology at Tübingen and founder of the
"Tübingen School," which was long a
center of controversy.

bers of the Church fled from the persecution to which Stephen fell a martyr, and were scattered abroad throughout the regions of Judea and Samaria, not only did these fugitives carry Christianity to Samaria, to the towns of the sea-coast, and even to Cyprus and Antioch, but at Antioch some of them, men from Cyprus and Cyrene, and of course Hellenists, took the important step in advance of preaching the Gospel to the Gentiles. Antioch thus became the seat of the first church of Gentile Christians, as Jerusalem was the mother church of the Jewish Christians. It is stated in the Acts (viii. 1) that only the apostles stayed in Jerusalem at this persecution; but this is improbable. If we may judge from the occasion out of which it arose, this persecution was not aimed at the Church as a whole, but rather at the Hellenists who sympathised with Stephen in his more liberal views and his consequent hostility to Judaism. Thus the history of Stephen affords clear evidence to show that the Church of Jerusalem had all along consisted of two parties, the Hebraists and the Hellenists, who now effected a complete separation from each other. From this time forth the Church of Jerusalem consisted entirely of Hebraists. The Hellenists, however, were widely diffused even before this time; and though the more liberal tendency only found its first expression in Stephen, yet we cannot be wrong in thinking that it had been at work before, and that it was due to its influence that Hellenism was already giving birth to Gentile Christianity. It was the apostle Paul, however, in whom Gentile Christianity found in the course of these same movements, of which the proto-martyr Stephen is the centre, its true herald, and logical founder and expositor.

The history of the development of Christianity dates of course from the departure of Jesus from the world. But in Paul this history has a new beginning; from this point we are able to trace it not only in its external features, but also in its inner connection.

What the Acts tell us of the conversion of the apostle can only be regarded as the outward reflection of an inner spiritual process. The explanation of this process is to be found in the apostle's own individuality as we have it set before us in his Epistles. * * * It is true that no analysis, either psychological or dialectical, can detect the inner secret of the act in which God revealed his Son in him. Yet it may very justly be asked whether what made the transition possible can have been anything else than the great impressiveness with which the great fact of the death of Jesus came all at once to stand before his soul. From the moment of the revelation in which the Son of God was revealed in him, he lives only in contemplation of the Crucified One: he knows no other, he is crucified with him, his whole system of thought turns on this one fact. The death which was to the Jews a stumbling-block, and to the Greeks foolishness, for him contains and expresses all salvation, and that as no ideal death, but in its most obvious and material aspect as a fact, as the death on the cross from which Christianity itself is named the word, the preaching of the cross. In what other way can he have overcome his hatred and repugnance towards Christianity but by being plunged, almost against his will, in a high-wrought and intense frame of spirit, into contemplation of this death? To the Jewish imagination a crucified Messiah was the most intolerable of ideas. His mind, however, accustomed as it was to deeper thinking, came to see that even what was most repugnant to man's natural feelings might yet prove to be the most profoundly and essentially true, and so the idea ceased to be intolerable. Death, he came to see, can be transfigured into life. A Messiah who has died in the flesh cannot indeed be a *Christos kata sarka* in the sense of the Jewish national ideas. Yet all the more surely may he be discerned as one who has died to the flesh and been transfigured to a higher life and stands as a Redeemer high above all the limitations of Judaism. A death which ran so directly counter to all the facts and presuppositions of the Jewish national consciousness, could not be confined in its significance to the Jewish nation, it must have a scope far transcending the particularism of Judaism. There can be no doubt that this was the thought in which the apostle first discerned the truth of Christianity. It was certainly the thought which lay at the root of his view of the person of Christ, and from which the whole dialectical development of Pauline Christianity proceeded. Now the Christian universalism which thus became a certainty to the apostle before any other of the disciples had reached it implied from the first a much deeper breach with Judaism than we might have supposed. This is the only possible explanation of the fact, that from the time of his conversion the apostle Paul went his own independent way, and avoided intentionally and on principle all contact with the older apostles.

* * *

But the apostle takes up an attitude of so great freedom and independence not only towards the older apostles, but towards the person of Jesus himself, that one might be inclined to ask whether a view of his relation to the person of Christ can be the right one which would make the apostle Paul the originator and first exponent of that which constitutes the essence of Christianity as distinguished from Judaism. Is there not too great a distance between the founder of Christianity and one who made his first appearance altogether outside the circle of the first apostles? The difficulty is great if we are to suppose that this apostle derived no assistance from the original apostles, but did of himself what no one had done before, —introduced Christianity to its true destination as a religion for the world, and enunciated, with a full sense of its vast significance, the principle of Christian universalism. Here, however, we shall do well to attend to the two elements which we found in the person of Jesus, and to their relation to each other. First, there was the moral universal in him, the unconfined humanity, the divine exaltation, which gave his person its absolute significance. On the other side there was the cramping and narrowing influence of the Jewish national Messianic idea. The latter was the form which the person of Jesus was obliged to assume if the former element was to have a point of vantage from which to go forth into the stream of history, and to find the way on which it could pass into the general consciousness of mankind. What, then, could be more natural than that one set of his followers should hold to the national side of his appearance, and attach themselves to it so firmly as never to surmount the particularism of Judaism at all, while the other of the two elements, which in the person of Jesus were combined in a simple unity, found in another quarter a much more distinct and energetic expression than the first set of his followers ever could have given it? In this way the natural starting-point of each party is found in the life and work of the founder. The only question comes to be how the apostle Paul appears in his Epistles to be so indifferent to the historical facts of the life of Jesus. He seldom appeals to any traditions on the subject, though his apostolic activity, as well as that of the other apostles, would have been meaningless without them. He bears himself but little like a disciple who has received the doctrines and the principles which he preaches from the Master whose name he bears. But this only shows us how large and how spiritual his conception of Christianity was. The special and particular vanish for him in the contemplation of the whole. Christianity stands before him as a great historical fact which can be understood and grasped only in its unity and its immediateness as a divine revelation. The great facts of the death and resurrection of Jesus make it what it is. Around these facts his whole Christian consciousness revolves; his whole Christian consciousness is transformed into a view of the person of Jesus which stands in need of no history to elucidate it. Why should he go to eye-witnesses and ear-witnesses of Christ's life to ask what he was according to the flesh, when he has seen himself in the spirit? Why should he ask whether what he is teaching agrees with the original teaching of Jesus, and with the discourses and sayings which have been handed down from him, when in the Christ who lives and works in him he hears the voice of the Lord himself? Why should he draw from the past what the Christ who is present in him has made to be the direct utterance of his own consciousness?

* * *

As the number of converts from heathenism increased, and as the efforts of these who carried the Gospel to the Gentiles diffused it more and more widely throughout the Gentile world, the Christians of Jerusalem became alarmed. They could not look on with indifference, when they saw a Gentile Christian Church arising over-against the Church of Jerusalem in utter disregard of the ordinances and privileges of Judaism, and yet putting forth a claim to equal place and dignity with themselves. Members of the Church of Jerusalem came to Antioch, as the apostle himself tells us (Gal. ii. 1, *sq.*) He calls them false brethren, intruders, who jealously spied out the liberty that was enjoyed and claimed as a Christian right at Antioch, and made it their aim to bring the Christians there into bondage under the law. The matter appeared so important to the apostle that he felt he must himself go to Jerusalem and have the question discussed on the spot where it had arisen, and where alone it could be decided. The direct practical issue of the question which had been raised was whether or not Gentile Christians required to be circumcised. The apostle therefore took with him not only Barnabas but also Titus, an uncircumcised Gentile Christian, that there might be a case before the Church at Jerusalem, in which the strength of the resistance to the demand that had been made there might be visibly demonstrated. But who were the opponents to whom Paul and Barnabas had to offer so strenuous a resistance? Who else than the elder apostles themselves? We should have a strange conception of the Church at Jerusalem and the position the apostles occupied in it, if we thought that a question of such importance as this could arise in it, and that the apostles took no part in the discussion, the originators of the dispute being merely certain extreme Judaists, with whose assertions and demands the apostles themselves did not agree. Had such been the case, how easy would it have been to arrive at an understanding! This view is clearly contrary, not only to the nature of the case, but to the plain meaning of the apostle's own words. It has often been repeated, but it can never amount to anything more than an unwarrantable claim to set aside the original account, which bears the direct impress of the facts as they occurred, and to set above it a narrative which is inconsistent with it, and is manifestly governed by the writer's desire to give a new version of what had occurred. We need only consider the phrases which Paul selects to describe his opponents, and which are carefully designed to indicate only their own view of the position which they held. He calls them *hoi dokountes, dokountes einai ti, hoi dokountes styloi einai,* thus showing us that the older apostles themselves were the authorities for the view with which he had to contend. Then we may remember how deliberately and with how full a sense of the independence of his own position he confronted the apostle Peter himself (ii. 7, *sq.*), and lastly, what the result of the whole conference was. The three principal representatives of the Church of Jerusalem did indeed give to Paul and Barnabas the right hand of fellowship, but the agreement which was arrived at consisted simply in recognising that each party had a right to go his own way, separate from, and independent of the other. Thus there were now two Gospels, a Gospel of the circumcision and a Gospel of the uncircumcision, a mission to the Jews and a mission to the Gentiles. The two were to go on side by side, separate and independent, without crossing each other's paths. The only bond to connect the Gentile with the Jewish Christians was to be the care for the support of the poor of the parent Church. So decided an attitude of opposition did the two standpoints now assume: on the one side was the apostle Paul refusing with immovable firmness to be shaken even for a moment in any point which his principles required him to maintain, or to yield any compliance to the proposals addressed to him: on the other side were the older apostles clinging tenaciously to their Judaism.

* * *

We have seen that at the very outset of the controversy, as soon as the question of circumcision had arisen, men once and again appeared on the scene who had come from the Church at Jerusalem, and openly sought to bring about a reaction (Gal. ii. 4, 12). We meet with the same phenomenon in the Gentile Christian Churches planted by Paul. Judaists of the same stamp appeared in these churches, and made it their business to bring Pauline Christianity into discredit, and to destroy what the apostle had founded and built up as his own work, without the law and in opposition to the law, in order to rear it up again on the basis of the law. The first actual proof of this systematic opposition to the apostle Paul appears in the Epistle to the Galatians, which was occasioned by that very opposition. * * * The opponents who had taken the field against him in the Churches of Galatia were but a new detachment of the opposition with which he had had to contend before. * * * No other Epistle affords us so deep an insight into the grave significance of the rapidly widening struggle, and into the religious motives which operated on each side. The Judaists maintained it to be the absolute privilege of Judaism that only by the law and circumcision could any man be saved; while the apostle Paul set up the counter-proposition, that whoever was circumcised, Christ would profit him nothing (v. 2). According to the former it is in vain to be a Christian without being a Jew also. According to the latter it is in vain to be a Christian if, as a Christian, one chooses to be a Jew as well. And as it is impossible to be a Jew without accepting circumcision, and with circumcision the obligation to keep the whole law in all its particulars, it is evident at once how the man who takes this road must contradict himself, and be divided in his own mind. But the apostle is not content with exposing this contradiction to the Galatians, and showing them how unjustifiable and irrational the step was which they were about to take. He goes to the root of the matter, and attacks Judaism itself, showing that its being a religion based on law, far from giving it any distinction, reduces it to a subordinate and secondary place in the history of the religious development of mankind. Even within the sphere of Jewish religious history, the law is not the primary and original element. Above it stands the promise given to Abraham, which points forward to a time when the same faith which was counted to Abraham for righteousness will become the blessing of all nations. This promise can only be fulfilled when the law, whose curse passes upon all who do not continue in all things that are written in the law to do them, gives away to faith. By faith, faith that is to say in him who has redeemed us from the curse of the law, we receive that which was the object of the promise made to Abraham, namely, the spirit. * * *

Thus Judaism is nothing more than the religion of the law in contradistinction to Christianity, which is the religion of the spirit. Both its position in the world and its inner constitution declare that the function of Judaism is that of effecting a transition, of filling up an interval. The object it is there to serve is to exercise the stern severity of a watcher set to mark transgressions, and to keep the promise and the fulfilment apart, till the period which God has fixed for this event in the order of the world arrive (the *plerōma tou chronou*, Gal. iv. 4), and the promise reach its fulfilment. * * * Not only does he repudiate, as utterly unjustifiable, the demand which they had made with regard to circumcision, he denies that the law possessed that absolute right which the Jew ascribed to it. He places Judaism and Christianity together under the light of a great religio-historical contemplation, and of a view of the course of the world before the universal idea of which the particularism of Judaism must disappear. The demand of circumcision which was made upon the Gentile Christians amounted to a claim that, in submitting to that rite, they should acknowledge the absolute superiority which the Jewish nation as God's chosen people possessed over all the other nations of the world. This claim the apostle's wide and comprehensive view of history sufficiently disposed of. The cardinal point of his dialectical polemic, however, is to be found in the passage where he draws the conclusion from the previous discussion regarding the law and the promise, that all who are baptized into Christ enter at once, in that very act, into a new community, in which all the causes of division between man and man, which are to be found in the outward circumstances of life, are at once removed, so that there is no difference any longer between the Jew and the Greek, between circumcision and uncircumcision, but all may regard themselves as children of Abraham. All are one in Christ, in the same faith which manifests itself by love.

* * * Whatever may have been the result of Paul's Epistle to the Galatians, and of his controversy with his opponents in the Galatian Churches, the dispute did not end there. Not long after that Epistle was written, we meet with opponents of the apostle in a different quarter of his sphere of labour, whose attacks upon him seem to be dictated by the same motives, and to be carried on in the same spirit. There can be no doubt that the Epistle to the Galatians was written in the earlier period of the apostle's residence at Ephesus, which is to be placed in the years 54–57. The composition of our first Epistle to the *Corinthians* belongs to the latter part of his residence there. It was occasioned by news from Corinth which showed him that he had to expect a renewal of his Galatian experiences in the Corinthian Church. Judaizing teachers had made their way into this Church also, and had unsettled the faith of the apostle's converts in his Gospel. Several divisions and parties had arisen; but the main controversy about which they were ranged originated in a party which bore the name of Peter, although there can be no doubt that Peter never was at Corinth at all, and set itself in opposition to those members of the Corinthian Church who remained faithful to the principles of Pauline Christianity. The party-interests which now came to operate in various ways on the Corinthian Church arose undoubtedly out of the same great controversy which forms the subject of the Epistle to the Galatians. It is very remarkable, however, that in the two Corinthian Epistles the subjects of the law and of circumcision, which formerly occupied the forefront of the battle, have completely disappeared. A very personal question has now come to the front, a question which could not fail to be raised sooner or later, namely, the apostolic authority of Paul. What authority could he claim?

* * *

If he appealed to the inner certainty which he possessed regarding his vocation by Christ, and to his apostolic consciousness, they, on the other hand, stood on the historical ground of their actual connection with Christ. Thus principle stood opposed to principle; and only the future development of Christianity could decide which of the two principles would acquire the predominance over the other. In the meantime, the attacks made upon the person of the apostle, and on his apostolic authority, form a new and a noteworthy epoch in the controversy in which Judaism and Paulinism had now come to be engaged. The deep earnestness which the apostle throws into his contendings with these opponents is enough to show the importance they had in his eyes. We should have a very mistaken notion of them did we hold their movement to have been a mere isolated phenomenon, the undirected and arbitrary action of certain individuals who were stirred up by merely fortuitous and personal motives to create disturbance and throw obstacles in the apostle's way in his own sphere of labour. Everything combines to show that they had a great party behind them, and knew themselves to have a right to appear as the agents and emissaries of that party. Not only was the name of the apostle Peter the standard under which their efforts were carried on,—a name which showed what spirit they were of, and made their cause appear to be the common cause of all Jewish Christians. We learn from the apostle himself (2 Cor. iii. 1) that they had brought letters of recommendation with them, which left no doubt as to the party they belonged to. From whom could such letters of recommendation proceed but from men who had such a position in the mother Church, that they could count on their authority being recognised in foreign Churches too? These letters prove to us how party spirit was growing, how the two parties were being ranged in a position of antagonism to each other, how efforts were being made by each party to counteract the other locally. They also represent to us, in a new and striking way, the radical difference between the two principles which are here contending with each other. They exhibited to the Corinthians the contrast between the two conflicting principles of authority. The authority of the one party, having been outwardly communicated, was capable of being delegated by such credentials. Against this outward authority the apostle had nothing to affirm when it came to the point but his own independent self-consciousness. This is his position in the passage where he speaks of these letters of commendation of his opponents (2 Cor. iii. 1–18).

In dealing with his opponents at Corinth, he takes up, as he did in the Epistle to the Galatians, the standpoint of the higher religio-historical contemplation. Judaism and Christianity are related to each other as the old and the new *diathēkē*; the old one is antiquated and extinct, but the new one is bright and luminous. In this distinction between the two dispensations, and in the spirit as the principle of the Christian consciousness, is to be found the justification of his apostolic authority. The character of Judaism is that of a religion of concealment and restraint, the religious consciousness which belongs to it is narrow and finite, but Christianity is the opposite of this; in it the religious consciousness has opened up to perfect clearness and self-certainty, and does not need to rely on any material aids. And this is the principle of his apostolic authority too. With those who refuse to recognise him as an apostle he can use no other argument than that their religious consciousness is imperfect, that they are at a standpoint at which the veil, the symbol of Mosaism, still lies upon their Jewish consciousness, and does not allow them to perceive the fact that the end of the old religion is now come. The principle of Paulinism could not be expressed more simply and accurately than is done by the apostle in this same passage, when he sums up his argument against the old covenant and those who had gained the Christian consciousness, and yet remained standing under it, in the words (2 Cor. iii. 17): The Lord is the spirit: and the spirit is liberty. That is to say, the principle and essence of Paulinism is the emancipation of the consciousness from every authority that is external or exercised through human means, the removal of all confining barriers, the elevation of the spirit to a standpoint where everything lies revealed and open in luminous clearness to its eye, the independence and immediateness of the self-consciousness.

Thus the apostle meets the opponents of his doctrine and of his apostolic authority by demonstrating the imperfection, the narrowness, the finiteness of the religion of the Law. But to get rid altogether of that particularism which was so closely interwoven with Judaism, that national pride which led the Jew to think that because he was a Jew he was better and more highly privileged than all other men, it was necessary to attack it more directly, to lay the axe more sharply to its root. This could not be done without a profounder and more searching appeal to the moral consciousness than could be made by a discussion which after all belonged to the sphere of abstract and theoretical contemplation. It is in the Epistle to the Romans that we see the apostle proceed to this, the third and most important stage of the long and hard struggle which his principle had to support as it forced its way through all the forms of opposition it encountered. Regarded from this point of view, the Epistle to the Romans appeared in the light not merely of a compendium of Pauline dogmatics, but as a historical source of the first importance.

* * *

It is not necessary to enter in detail into the circumstances under which the apostle met his well-known fate at Jerusalem. There is one question, however, which possesses special interest, namely, who were the authors of those tumults in which the Roman military authorities had to interfere in order to rescue the apostle from the rage of his opponents? Were these tumults caused by Jews, or by Jewish Christians? They were zealots for the law, men who saw in the apostle a transgressor of the law, an apostate, a declared enemy of the national religion. But not only the Jews were zealots of this description, the Jewish Christians also shared this spirit, and carried it even further than the Jews. In their case the mission to the Gentiles had raised the question of the law into a matter of the keenest party interest. And accordingly we can discern, even in the narrative of the Acts, in which the true state of the case is as far as possible concealed, that the Jewish Christians were by no means so unconcerned in the outbreaks of hatred to which the apostle fell a victim, as is generally supposed. Protected by his Roman citizenship the apostle was removed to Rome, after two years' imprisonment at Caesarea. According to the Acts his imprisonment at Rome lasted for a further period of two years: but we are not told when or how it terminated. Even assuming the genuineness of the Epistles which profess to have been written by the apostle during his captivity at Rome, we have no certain or noteworthy information about this period. The most remarkable fact is that the termination of these two years coincides with the date of the great Neronian conflagration, and the persecution of the Christians to which it led. Nothing can be more probable, than that the apostle did not survive this fatal period.

Up to the time when the apostle disappears from the scene of the history, we have before us nothing but differences and oppositions, between which no certain way of compromise or reconciliation yet appears. It was upon that side, from which the great division had proceeded, which broke in upon the common religious consciousness, which Jews and Jewish Christians had hitherto enjoyed together, that a certain need was first felt for approximation and reconciliation between the two parties. But the advance did not meet with such a response as might have been expected from the other party. There were as yet only Jewish Christians and Gentile Christians, with divergent tendencies and interests. There was no ecclesiastical association to combine the two. Nor has history been able as yet to point to any considerable cause which can be said to have effected the filling up of the great gulf which since the events at Antioch had continued to exist between Peter and Paul, the heads of the two parties. All we can say is, that there must have been reconciling elements in the Church of Rome. This was the case before, and the influence which Paul had over this Church, both by his Epistle and by his personal residence there afterwards, must have strengthened this tendency. And how could the martyrdom with which the great apostle of the Gentiles certainly in one way or another finished his work in that city, fail to leave behind it a healing influence for the future of the Church? A legend of much significance, which however arose at a much later time, connects the brotherly unity of the two apostles with this death. This is accordingly a fixed point in the history of the further development of these relations. But the interval which elapsed between the death of the apostle Paul and that point contains many movements in many different directions, and the development of the history will conduct us to that goal by a longer road than might have been supposed.

* * *

FRIEDRICH NIETZSCHE

The First Christian (1880) †

The whole world still believes in the literary career of the "Holy Ghost," or is still influenced by the effects of this belief: when we look into our Bibles we do so for the purpose of "edifying ourselves," to find a few words of comfort for our misery, be it great or small—in short, we read ourselves into it and out of it. But who— apart from a few learned men—know that it likewise records the history of one of the most ambitious and importunate souls that ever existed, of a mind full of superstition and cunning: the history of the Apostle Paul? Nevertheless, without this singular history, without the tribulations and passions of such a mind, and of such a soul, there would have been no Christian kingdom; we should scarcely have even heard of a little Jewish sect, the founder of which died on the Cross. It is true that, if this history had been understood in time, if we had read, *really read*, the writings of St. Paul, not as the revelations of the "Holy Ghost," but with honest and independent minds, oblivious of all our personal troubles—there were no such readers for fifteen centuries—it would have been all up with Christianity long ago: so searchingly do these writings of the Jewish Pascal lay bare the origins of Christianity, just as the French Pascal let us see its destiny and how it will ultimately perish. That the ship of Christianity threw overboard no inconsid-

† From *The Dawn of Day*, Aphorism 68, tr. by J. M. Kennedy in *The Complete Works of Friedrich Nietzsche*, ed. Oscar Levy (New York, 1909–11, and reprinted), IX, 66–71. Neitzsche (1844–1900), the son of a German pastor, taught classics in Basel until forced by health problems to retire in 1879. His most provocative works were published after that, though he suffered increasing isolation and, after 1889, irreversible mental disorder.

erable part of its Jewish ballast, that it was able to sail into the
waters of the heathen and actually did do so: this is due to the history of one single man, this apostle who was so greatly troubled in
mind and so worthy of pity, but who was also very disagreeable to
himself and to others.

This man suffered from a fixed idea, or rather a fixed question, an
ever-present and ever-burning question: what was the *meaning* of
the Jewish Law? and, more especially, *the fulfilment of this Law?*
In his youth he had done his best to satisfy it, thirsting as he did
for that highest distinction which the Jew could imagine—this
people, which raised the imagination of moral loftiness to a greater
elevation than any other people, and which alone succeeded in
uniting the conception of a holy God with the idea of sin considered as an offence against this holiness. St. Paul became at once
the fanatic defender and guard-of-honour of this God and His Law.
Ceaselessly battling against and lying in wait for all transgressors
of this Law and those who presumed to doubt it, he was pitiless and
cruel towards all evildoers, whom he would fain have punished in
the most rigorous fashion possible.

Now, however, he was aware in his own person of the fact that
such a man as himself—violent, sensual, melancholy, and malicious
in his hatred—*could* not fulfil the Law; and furthermore, what
seemed strangest of all to him, he saw that his boundless craving for
power was continually provoked to break it, and that he could not
help yielding to this impulse. Was it really "the flesh" which made
him a trespasser time and again? Was it not rather, as it afterwards
occurred to him, the Law itself, which continually showed itself to
be impossible to fulfil, and seduced men into transgression with an
irresistible charm? But at that time he had not thought of this
means of escape. As he suggests here and there, he had many things
on his conscience—hatred, murder, sorcery, idolatry, debauchery,
drunkenness, and orgiastic revelry,—and to however great an extent
he tried to soothe his conscience, and, even more, his desire for
power, by the extreme fanaticism of his worship for and defence of
the Law, there were times when the thought struck him: "It is all
in vain! The anguish of the unfulfilled Law cannot be overcome."
Luther must have experienced similar feelings, when, in his cloister,
he endeavoured to become the ideal man of his imagination; and, as
Luther one day began to hate the ecclesiastical ideal, and the Pope,
and the saints, and the whole clergy, with a hatred which was all
the more deadly as he could not avow it even to himself, an analogous feeling took possession of St. Paul. The Law was the Cross on
which he felt himself crucified. How he hated it! What a grudge he
owed it! How he began to look round on all sides to find a means
for its total annihilation, that he might no longer be obliged to

fulfil it himself! And at last a liberating thought, together with a vision—which was only to be expected in the case of an epileptic like himself—flashed into his mind: to him, the stern upholder of the Law—who, in his innermost heart, was tired to death of it—there appeared on the lonely path that Christ, with the divine effulgence on His countenance, and Paul heard the words: "Why persecutest thou Me?"

What actually took place, then, was this: his mind was suddenly enlightened, and he said to himself: "It is unreasonable to persecute this Jesus Christ! Here is my means of escape, here is my complete vengeance, here and nowhere else have I the destroyer of the Law in my hands!" The sufferer from anguished pride felt himself restored to health all at once, his moral despair disappeared in the air; for morality itself was blown away, annihilated—that is to say, *fulfilled*, there on the Cross! Up to that time that ignominious death had seemed to him to be the principal argument against the "Messiahship" proclaimed by the followers of the new doctrine: but what if it were necessary for doing away with the Law? The enormous consequences of this thought, of this solution of the enigma, danced before his eyes, and he at once became the happiest of men. The destiny of the Jews, yea, of all mankind, seemed to him to be intertwined with this instantaneous flash of enlightenment: he held the thought of thoughts, the key of keys, the light of lights; history would henceforth revolve round him! For from that time forward he would be the apostle of the *annihilation of the Law!* To be dead to sin—that meant to be dead to the Law also; to be in the flesh—that meant to be under the Law! To be one with Christ—that meant to have become, like Him, the destroyer of the Law; to be dead with Him—that meant likewise to be dead to the Law. Even if it were still possible to sin, it would not at any rate be possible to sin against the Law: "I am above the Law," thinks Paul; adding, "If I were now to acknowledge the Law again and to submit to it, I should make Christ an accomplice in the sin"; for the Law was there for the purpose of producing sin and setting it in the foreground, as an emetic produces sickness. God could not have decided upon the death of Christ had it been possible to fulfill the Law without it; henceforth, not only are all sins expiated, but sin itself is abolished; henceforth the Law is dead; henceforth "the flesh" in which it dwelt is dead—or at all events dying, gradually wasting away. To live for a short time longer amid this decay!—this is the Christian's fate, until the time when, having become one with Christ, he arises with Him, sharing with Christ the divine glory, and becoming, like Christ, a "Son of God." Then Paul's exaltation was at its height, and with it the importunity of his soul—the thought of union with Christ made him lose all shame, all submission, all constraint, and his ungovernable ambition was shown to be revelling in the expectation of divine glories.

Such was the first Christian, the inventor of Christianity! before him there were only a few Jewish sectaries.

FRIEDRICH NIETZSCHE

The Jewish Dysangelist (1888) †

* * *

—I will retrace my steps, and will tell you the *genuine* history of Christianity.—The very word "Christianity" is a misunderstanding, —truth to tell, there never was more than one Christian, and he *died* on the Cross. The "gospel" *died* on the Cross. That which thenceforward was called "gospel" was the reverse of that "gospel" that Christ had lived: it was "evil tidings," a *dysangel*. It is false to the point of nonsense to see in "faith," in the faith in salvation through Christ, the distinguishing trait of the Christian: the only thing that is Christian is the Christian mode of existence, a life such as he led who died on the Cross. . . . To this day a life of this kind is still possible; for certain men, it is even necessary: genuine, primitive Christianity will be possible in all ages. . . . *Not* a faith, but a course of action, above all a course of inaction, non-interference, and a different life. . . . States of consciousness, any sort of faith, a holding of certain things for true, as every psychologist knows, are indeed of absolutely no consequence, and are only of fifth-rate importance compared with the value of the instincts: more exactly, the whole concept of intellectual causality is false. To reduce the fact of being a Christian, or of Christianity, to a holding of something for true, to a mere phenomenon of consciousness, is tantamount to denying Christianity. *In fact there have never been any Christians.* The "Christian," he who for two thousand years has been called a Christian, is merely a psychological misunderstanding of self. Looked at more closely, there ruled in him, *notwithstanding* all his faith, only instincts—and *what instincts!*—"Faith" in all ages, as for instance in the case of Luther, has always been merely a cloak, a pretext, a *screen*, behind which the instincts played their game,—a prudent form of *blindness* in regard to the dominion of *certain* instincts. . . . "Faith" I have already characterised as a piece

† From *The Antichrist, An Attempted Criticism of Christianity*, §§39-43, tr. by Anthony M. Ludovici in *The Com-* *plete Works of Friedrich Nietzsche*, ed. Oscar Levy (New York, 1909–11 and reprinted), XVI, 178–87.

of really Christian cleverness; for people have always spoken of "faith" and acted according to their instincts. . . . In the Christian's world of ideas there is nothing which even touches reality; but I have already recognised in the instinctive hatred of reality the actual motive force, the only driving power at the root of Christianity. What follows therefrom? That here, even *in psychologicis*, error is fundamental,—that is to say capable of determining the spirit of things,—that is to say, *substance*. Take one idea away from the whole, and put one realistic fact in its stead,—and the whole of Christianity tumbles into nonentity!—Surveyed from above, this strangest of all facts,—a religion not only dependent upon error, but inventive and showing signs of genius only in those errors which are dangerous and which poison life and the human heart—remains a *spectacle for gods*, for those gods who are at the same time philosophers and whom I met for instance in those celebrated dialogues on the island of Naxos. At the moment when they get rid of their *loathing* (—*and we do as well!*), they will be thankful for the spectacle the Christians have offered: the wretched little planet called Earth perhaps deserves on account of this curious case alone, a divine glance, and divine interest. . . . Let us not therefore underestimate the Christians: the Christian, false *to the point of innocence in falsity*, is far above the apes,—in regard to the Christians a certain well-known theory of Descent becomes a mere good-natured compliment.

40

—The fate of the gospel was decided at the moment of the death,—it hung on the "cross." . . . It was only death, this unexpected and ignominious death; it was only the cross which as a rule was reserved simply for the *canaille*,—only this appalling paradox which confronted the disciples with the actual riddle: *Who was that? what was that?*—The state produced by the excited and profoundly wounded feelings of these men, the suspicion that such a death might imply the *refutation* of their cause, and the terrible note of interrogation: "why precisely thus?" will be understood only too well. In this case everything *must* be necessary, everything must have meaning, a reason, the highest reason. The love of a disciple admits of no such thing as accident. Only then did the chasm yawn: "who has killed him?" "who was his natural enemy?"—this question rent the firmament like a flash of lightning. Reply: *dominant* Judaism, its ruling class. Thenceforward the disciple felt himself in revolt *against* established order; he understood Jesus, after the fact, as one in *revolt against established order*. Heretofore this warlike, this nay-saying and nay-doing feature in Christ had been lacking; nay more, he was its contradiction. The small primitive community had obviously understood *nothing* of the principal factor of all, which was the example of freedom and of superiority to every form of *resentment* which lay in this way of dying. And this shows how little they understood him altogether! At bottom Jesus could not have desired anything else by his death than to give the strongest public *example* and *proof* of his doctrine. . . . But his disciples were very far from *forgiving* this death—though if they had done so it would have been in the highest sense evangelical on their part,—neither were they prepared, with a gentle and serene calmness of heart, to *offer* themselves for a similar death. . . . Precisely the most unevangelical feeling, *revenge*, became once more ascendant. It was impossible for the cause to end with this death: "compensation" and "judgment" were required (—and forsooth, what could be more unevangelical than "compensation," "punishment," "judgment"!) The popular expectation of a Messiah once more became prominent; attention was fixed upon one historical moment: the "Kingdom of God" descends to sit in judgment upon his enemies. But this proves that everything was misunderstood: the "Kingdom of God" regarded as the last scene of the last act, as a promise! But the Gospel had clearly been the living, the fulfillment, the *reality* of this "Kingdom of God." It was precisely a death such as Christ's that was this "Kingdom of God." It was only now that all the contempt for the Pharisees and the theologians, and all bitter feelings towards them, were introduced into the character of the Master,— and by this means he himself was converted into a Pharisee and a theologian! On the other hand, the savage veneration of these completely unhinged souls could no longer endure that evangelical right of every man to be the child of God, which Jesus had taught: their revenge consisted in *elevating* Jesus in a manner devoid of all reason, and in separating him from themselves: just as, formerly, the Jews, with the view of revenging themselves on their enemies, separated themselves from their God, and placed him high above them. The Only God, and the Only Son of God:—both were products of resentment.

41

—And from this time forward an absurd problem rose into prominence: "how *could* God allow it to happen?" To this question the disordered minds of the small community found a reply which in its absurdity was literally terrifying: God gave his Son as a *sacrifice* for the forgiveness of sins. Alas! how prompt and sudden was the end of the gospel! Expiatory sacrifice for guilt, and indeed in its most repulsive and barbaric form,—the sacrifice of the *innocent* for the

sins of the guilty! What appalling Paganism!—For Jesus himself
had done away with the concept "guilt,"—he denied any gulf
between God and man, he *lived* this unity between God and man,
it was this that constituted *his* "glad tidings." . . . And he did *not*
teach it as a privilege!—Thenceforward there was gradually imported into the type of the Saviour the doctrine of the Last Judgment, and of the "second coming," the doctrine of sacrificial death,
and the doctrine of *Resurrection*, by means of which the whole concept "blessedness," the entire and only reality of the gospel, is conjured away—in favour of a state *after* death! . . . St Paul, with that
rabbinic impudence which characterises all his doings, rationalised
this conception, this prostitution of a conception, as follows: "if
Christ did not rise from the dead, our faith is vain."—And, in a
trice, the most contemptible of all unrealisable promises, the *impudent* doctrine of personal immortality, was woven out of the
gospel. . . . St Paul even preached this immortality as a reward.

4²

You now realise what it was that came to an end with the death
on the cross: a new and thoroughly original effort towards a Buddhis-
tic movement of peace, towards real and *not* merely promised *happiness on earth*. For, as I have already pointed out, this remains
the fundamental difference between the two religions of *decadence*:
Buddhism promises little but fulfils more, Christianity promises
everything but fulfils nothing.—The "glad tidings" were followed
closely by the absolutely *worst* tidings—those of St Paul. Paul is the
incarnation of a type which is the reverse of that of the Saviour; he
is the genius in hatred, in the standpoint of hatred, and in the
relentless logic of hatred. And alas what did this dysangelist not sacrifice to his hatred! Above all the Saviour himself: he nailed him to
his cross. Christ's life, his example, his doctrine and death, the
sense and the right of the gospel—not a vestige of all this was left,
once this forger, prompted by his hatred, had understood in it only
that which could serve his purpose. *Not* reality: *not* historical
truth! . . . And once more, the sacerdotal instinct of the Jew perpetrated the same great crime against history,—he simply cancelled
the yesterday, and the day before that, out of Christianity; he *con-
trived of his own accord a history of the birth of Christianity*. He
did more: he once more falsified the history of Israel, so as to make
it appear as a prologue to *his* mission: all the prophets had referred
to *his* "Saviour." . . . Later on the Church even distorted the history
of mankind so as to convert it into a prelude to Christianity. . . .
The type of the Saviour, his teaching, his life, his death, even the
sequel to his death—nothing remained untouched, nothing was left

which even remotely resembled reality. St Paul simply transferred the centre of gravity of the whole of that great life, to a place *behind* this life,—in the *lie* of the "resuscitated" Christ. At bottom, he had no possible use for the life of the Saviour,—he needed the death on the cross, *and* something more. To regard as honest a man like St Paul (a man whose home was the very headquarters of Stoical enlightenment) when he devises a proof of the continued existence of the Saviour out of a hallucination; or even to believe him when he declares that he had this hallucination, would amount to foolishness on the part of a psychologist: St Paul desired the end, consequently he also desired the means. . . . Even what he himself did not believe, was believed in by the idiots among whom he spread *his* doctrine.—What he wanted was power; with St Paul the priest again aspired to power,—he could make use only of concepts, doctrines, symbols with which masses may be tyrannised over, and with which herds are formed. What was the only part of Christianity which was subsequently borrowed by Muhamed? St Paul's invention, his expedient for priestly tyranny and to the formation of herds: the belief in immortality—*that is to say, the doctrine of the "Last Judgment."* . . .

43

When the centre of gravity of life is laid, *not* in life, but in a beyond—*in nonentity,*—life is utterly robbed of its balance. The great lie of personal immortality destroys all reason, all nature in the instincts,—everything in the instincts that is beneficent, that promotes life and that is a guarantee of the future, henceforward aroused suspicion. The very meaning of life is now construed as the effort to live in such a way that life no longer has any point. . . . Why show any public spirit? Why be grateful for one's origin and one's forebears? Why collaborate with one's fellows, and be confident? Why be concerned about the general weal or strive after it? . . . All these things are merely so many "temptations," so many deviations from the "straight path." "One thing only is necessary." . . . That everybody, as an "immortal soul," should have equal rank, that in the totality of beings, the "salvation" of each individual may lay claim to eternal importance, that insignificant bigots and three-quarter-lunatics may have the right to suppose that the laws of nature may be persistently *broken* on their account,—any such magnification of every kind of selfishness to infinity, to *insolence,* cannot be branded with sufficient contempt. And yet it is to this miserable flattery of personal vanity that Christianity owes its *triumph,*—by this means it lured all the bungled and the botched, all revolting and revolted people, all abortions, the whole of the refuse and offal of humanity, over to its side. The "salvation of the soul"—in plain English: "the world revolves around me." ... The poison of the doctrine *"equal* rights for all"—has been dispensed with the greatest thoroughness by Christianity: Christianity, prompted by the most secret recesses of bad instincts, has waged a deadly war upon all feeling of reverence and distance between man and man—that is to say, the *prerequisite* of all elevation, of every growth in culture; out of the resentment of the masses it wrought its *principal weapons* against us, against everything noble, joyful, exalted on earth, against our happiness on earth. . . . To grant "immortality" to every St Peter and St Paul, was the greatest, the most vicious outrage upon *noble* humanity that has ever been perpetrated.—And do not let us underestimate the fatal influence which, springing from Christianity, has insinuated itself even into politics! Nowadays no one has the courage of special rights, of rights of dominion, of a feeling of self-respect and of respect for his equals,—of *pathos of distance*. Our politics are diseased with this lack of courage!—The aristocratic attitude of mind has been most thoroughly undermined by the lie of the equality of souls; and if the belief in the "privilege of the greatest number" creates and will continue *to create revolutions,*—it is Christianity, let there be no doubt about it, and Christian values, which convert every revolution into blood and crime! Christianity is the revolt of all things that crawl on their bellies against everything that is lofty: the gospel of the "lowly" *lowers*. . . . .

* * *

GEORGE BERNARD SHAW

The Monstrous Imposition upon Jesus (1913) †

* * *

Paul

Suddenly a man of genius, Paul, violently anti-Christian, enters on the scene, holding the clothes of the men who are stoning Stephen. He persecutes the Christians with great vigor, a sport which he combines with the business of a tentmaker. This temperamental hatred of Jesus, whom he has never seen, is a pathological symptom

---

† From "Preface on the Prospects of Christianity" to *Androcles and the Lion* (copyright 1913, 1941 by George Bernard Shaw). Shaw's prefaces are almost as famous as his plays themselves. Born in Dubin in 1856, he died in 1950.

of that particular sort of conscience and nervous constitution which brings its victims under the tyranny of two delirious terrors: the terror of sin and the terror of death, which may be called also the terror of sex and the terror of life. Now Jesus, with his healthy conscience on his higher plane, was free from these terrors. He consorted freely with sinners, and was never concerned for a moment, as far as we know, about whether his conduct was sinful or not; so that he has forced us to accept him as the man without sin. Even if we reckon his last days as the days of his delusion, he none the less gave a fairly convincing exhibition of superiority to the fear of death. This must have both fascinated and horrified Paul, or Saul, as he was first called. The horror accounts for his fierce persecution of the Christians. The fascination accounts for the strangest of his fancies: the fancy for attaching the name of Jesus Christ to the great idea which flashed upon him on the road to Damascus, the idea that he could not only make a religion of his two terrors, but that the movement started by Jesus offered him the nucleus for his new Church. It was a monstrous idea; and the shock of it, as he afterwards declared, struck him blind for days. He heard Jesus calling to him from the clouds, "Why persecute me?" His natural hatred of the teacher for whom Sin and Death had no terrors turned into a wild personal worship of him which has the ghastliness of a beautiful thing seen in a false light.

The chronicler of the Acts of the Apostles sees nothing of the significance of this. The great danger of conversion in all ages has been that when the religion of the high mind is offered to the lower mind, the lower mind, feeling its fascination without understanding it, and being incapable of rising to it, drags it down to its level by degrading it. Years ago I said that the conversion of a savage to Christianity is the conversion of Christianity to savagery. The conversion of Paul was no conversion at all: it was Paul who converted the religion that has raised one man above sin and death into a religion that delivered millions of men so completely into their dominion that their own common nature became a horror to them, and the religious life became a denial of life. Paul had no intention of surrendering either his Judaism or his Roman citizenship to the new moral world (as Robert Owen called it) of Communism and Jesuism. Just as in our own time Karl Marx, not content to take political economy as he found it, insisted on rebuilding it from the bottom upwards in his own way, and thereby gave a new lease of life to the errors it was just outgrowing, so Paul reconstructed the old Salvationism from which Jesus had vainly tried to redeem him, and produced a fantastic theology which is still the most amazing thing of the kind known to us. Being intellectually an inveterate Roman Rationalist, always discarding the irrational real thing for the unreal but ratiocinable postulate, he began by discarding Man as he is, and substituted a postulate which he called Adam. And when he was asked, as he surely must have been in a world not wholly mad, what had become of the natural man, he replied "Adam *is* the natural man." This was confusing to simpletons, because according to tradition Adam was certainly the name of the natural man as created in the garden of Eden. It was as if a preacher of our own time had described as typically British Frankenstein's monster, and called him Smith, and somebody, on demanding what about the man in the street, had been told "Smith *is* the man in the street." The thing happens often enough; for indeed the world is full of these Adams and Smiths and men in the street and average sensual men and economic men and womanly women and what not, all of them imaginary Atlases carrying imaginary worlds on their unsubstantial shoulders.

The Eden story provided Adam with a sin: the "original sin" for which we are all damned. Baldly stated, this seems ridiculous; nevertheless it corresponds to something actually existent not only in Paul's consciousness but in our own. The original sin was not the eating of the forbidden fruit, but the consciousness of sin which the fruit produced. The moment Adam and Eve tasted the apple they found themselves ashamed of their sexual relation, which until then had seemed quite innocent to them; and there is no getting over the hard fact that this shame, or state of sin, has persisted to this day, and is one of the strongest of our instincts. Thus Paul's postulate of Adam as the natural man was pragmatically true: it worked. But the weakness of Pragmatism is that most theories will work if you put your back into making them work, provided they have some point of contact with human nature. Hedonism will pass the pragmatic test as well as Stoicism. Up to a certain point every social principle that is not absolutely idiotic works: Autocracy works in Russia and Democracy in America; Atheism works in France, Polytheism in India, Monotheism throughout Islam, and Pragmatism, or No-ism, in England. Paul's fantastic conception of the damned Adam, represented by Bunyan as a pilgrim with a great burden of sins on his back, corresponded to the fundamental condition of evolution, which is, that life, including human life, is continually evolving, and must therefore be continually ashamed of itself and its present and past. Bunyan's pilgrim wants to get rid of his bundle of sins; but he also wants to reach "yonder shining light"; and when at last his bundle falls off him into the sepulchre of Christ, his pilgrimage is still unfinished and his hardest trials still ahead of him. His conscience remains uneasy; "original sin" still torments him; and his adventure with Giant Despair, who throws him into the dungeon of Doubting Castle, from which he escapes by the use of a skeleton key, is more terrible than any he met whilst the bundle was still on his back. Thus Bunyan's allegory of human nature breaks through the Pauline theology at a hundred points. His theological allegory, The Holy War, with its troops of Election Doubters, and its cavalry of "those that rode Reformadoes," is, as a whole, absurd, impossible, and, except in passages where the artistic old Adam momentarily got the better of the Salvationist theologian, hardly readable.

Paul's theory of original sin was to some extent idiosyncratic. He tells us definitely that he finds himself quite well able to avoid the sinfulness of sex by practising celibacy; but he recognizes, rather contemptuously, that in this respect he is not as other men are, and says that they had better marry than burn, thus admitting that though marriage may lead to placing the desire to please wife or husband before the desire to please God, yet preoccupation with unsatisfied desire may be even more ungodly than preoccupation with domestic affection. This view of the case inevitably led him to insist that a wife should be rather a slave than a partner, her real function being, not to engage a man's love and loyalty, but on the contrary to release them for God by relieving the man of all preoccupation with sex just as in her capacity of housekeeper and cook she relieves his preoccupation with hunger by the simple expedient of satisfying his appetite. This slavery also justifies itself pragmatically by working effectively; but it has made Paul the eternal enemy of Woman. Incidentally it has led to many foolish surmises about Paul's personal character and circumstances, by people so enslaved by sex that a celibate appears to them a sort of monster. They forget that not only whole priesthoods, official and unofficial, from Paul to Carlyle and Ruskin, have defied the tyranny of sex, but immense numbers of ordinary citizens of both sexes have, either voluntarily or under pressure of circumstances easily surmountable, saved their energies for less primitive activities.

Howbeit, Paul succeeded in stealing the image of Christ crucified for the figure-head of his Salvationist vessel, with its Adam posing as the natural man, its doctrine of original sin, and its damnation avoidable only by faith in the sacrifice of the cross. In fact, no sooner had Jesus knocked over the dragon of superstition than Paul boldly set it on its legs again in the name of Jesus.

The Confusion of Christendom

Now it is evident that two religions having such contrary effects on mankind should not be confused as they are under a common name. There is not one word of Pauline Christianity in the characteristic utterances of Jesus. When Saul watched the clothes of the men who stoned Stephen, he was not acting upon beliefs which Paul renounced. There is no record of Christ's having ever said to any man: "Go and sin as much as you like: you can put it all on me." He said "Sin no more," and insisted that he was putting up the standard of conduct, not debasing it, and that the righteousness of the Christian must exceed that of the Scribe and Pharisee. The notion that he was shedding his blood in order that every petty cheat and adulterator and libertine might wallow in it and come out whiter than snow, cannot be imputed to him on his own authority. "I come as an infallible patent medicine for bad consciences" is not one of the sayings in the gospels. If Jesus could have been consulted on Bunyan's allegory as to that business of the burden of sin dropping from the pilgrim's back when he caught sight of the cross, we must infer from his teaching that he would have told Bunyan in forcible terms that he had never made a greater mistake in his life, and that the business of a Christ was to make self-satisfied sinners feel the burden of their sins and stop committing them instead of assuring them that they could not help it, as it was all Adam's fault, but that it did not matter as long as they were credulous and friendly about himself. Even when he believed himself to be a god, he did not regard himself as a scapegoat. He was to take away the sins of the world by good government, by justice and mercy, by setting the welfare of little children above the pride of princes, by casting all the quackeries and idolatries which now usurp and malversate the power of God into what our local authorities quaintly call the dust destructor, and by riding on the clouds of heaven in glory instead of in a thousand-guinea motor car. That was delirious, if you like; but it was the delirium of a free soul, not of a shamebound one like Paul's. There has really never been a more monstrous imposition perpetrated than the imposition of the limitations of Paul's soul upon the soul of Jesus.

The Secret of Paul's Success

Paul must soon have found that his followers had gained peace of mind and victory over death and sin at the cost of all moral responsibility; for he did his best to reintroduce it by making good conduct the test of sincere belief, and insisting that sincere belief was necessary to salvation. But as his system was rooted in the plain fact that as what he called sin includes sex and is therefore an ineradicable part of human nature (why else should Christ have had to atone for the sin of all future generations?) it was impossible for him to declare that sin, even in its wickedest extremity, could forfeit the sinner's salvation if he repented and believed. And to this day Pauline Christianity is, and owes its enormous vogue to being, a premium on sin. Its consequences have had to be held in check by the worldly-wise majority through a violently anti-Christian system of criminal law and stern morality. But of course the main restraint is human nature, which has good impulses as well as bad ones, and refrains from theft and murder and cruelty, even when it is taught that it can commit them all at the expense of Christ and go happily to heaven afterwards, simply because it does not always want to murder or rob or torture.

It is not easy to understand why the Christianity of Jesus failed completely to establish itself politically and socially, and was easily suppressed by the police and the Church, whilst Paulinism overran the whole western civilized world, which was at that time the Roman Empire, and was adopted by it as its official faith, the old avenging gods falling helplessly before the new Redeemer. It still retains, as we may see in Africa, its power of bringing to simple people a message of hope and consolation that no other religion offers. But this enchantment is produced by its spurious association with the personal charm of Jesus, and exists only for untrained minds. In the hands of a logical Frenchman like Calvin, pushing it to its utmost conclusions, and devising "institutes" for hard-headed adult Scots and literal Swiss, it becomes the most infernal of fatalisms; and the lives of civilized children are blighted by its logic whilst negro piccaninnies are rejoicing in its legends.

Paul's Qualities

Paul, however, did not get his great reputation by mere imposition and reaction. It is only in comparison with Jesus (to whom many prefer him) that he appears common and conceited. Though in The Acts he is only a vulgar revivalist, he comes out in his own epistles as a genuine poet, though by flashes only. He is no more a Christian than Jesus was a Baptist; he is a disciple of Jesus only as Jesus was a disciple of John. He does nothing that Jesus would have done, and says nothing that Jesus would have said, though much, like the famous ode to charity, that he would have admired. He is more Jewish than the Jews, more Roman than the Romans, proud both ways, full of startling confessions and self-revelations that would not surprise us if they were slipped into the pages of Nietzsche, tormented by an intellectual conscience that demanded an argued case even at the cost of sophistry, with all sorts of fine qualities and occasional illuminations, but always hopelessly in the toils of Sin, Death, and Logic, which had no power over Jesus. As we have seen, it was by introducing this bondage and terror of his into the Christian doctrine that he adapted it to the Church and State systems which Jesus transcended, and made it practicable by destroying the specifically Jesuist side of it. He would have been quite in his place in any modern Protestant State; and he, not Jesus, is the true head and founder of our Reformed Church, as Peter is of the Roman Church. The followers of Paul and Peter made Christendom, whilst the Nazarenes were wiped out.

* * *

ADOLF VON HARNACK

The Founder of Christian Civilization (1900) †

* * *

It was Paul who delivered the Christian religion from Judaism. We shall see how he did that if we consider the following points:—

It was Paul who definitely conceived the Gospel as the message of the redemption already effected and of salvation now present. He preached the crucified and risen Christ, who gave us access to God and therewith righteousness and peace.

It was he who confidently regarded the Gospel as a new force abolishing the religion of the law.

It was he who perceived that religion in its new phase pertains to the individual and therefore to all individuals; and in this conviction, and with a full consciousness of what he was doing, he carried the Gospel to the nations of the world and transferred it from Judaism to the ground occupied by Greece and Rome. Not only are Greeks and Jews to unite on the basis of the Gospel, but the Jewish dispensation itself is now at an end. That the Gospel was transplanted from the East, where in subsequent ages it was never able to thrive properly, to the West, is a fact which we owe to Paul.

It was he who placed the Gospel in the great scheme of spirit and flesh, inner and outer existence, death and life; he, born a Jew and educated a Pharisee, gave it a *language*, so that it became intelligible, not only to the Greeks but to all *men* generally, and united with the whole of the intellectual capital which had been amassed in previous ages.

These are the factors that go to make the Apostle's greatness in the history of religion. On their inner connexion I cannot here enter in any detail. But, in regard to the first of them, I may

† From *What is Christianity?* tr. by Thomas Bailey Saunders (New York, 1901). Torchbook edition, pp. 173–89. On Harnack, see above, p. 190.

remind you of the words of the most important historian of religion in our day. Wellhausen declares that "Paul's especial work was to transform the Gospel of the kingdom into the Gospel of Jesus Christ, so that the Gospel is no longer the prophecy of the coming of the kingdom, but its actual fulfilment by Jesus Christ. In his view, accordingly, redemption from something in the future has become something which has already happened and is now present. He lays far more emphasis on faith than on hope; he anticipates the sense of future bliss in the present feeling of being God's son; he vanquishes death and already leads the new life on earth. He extols the strength which is made perfect in weakness; the grace of God is sufficient for him, and he knows that no power, present or future, can take him from His love, and that all things work together for good to them that love God." What knowledge, what confidence, what strength, was necessary to tear the new religion from its mother earth and plant it in an entirely new one! Islam, originating in Arabia, has remained the Arabian religion, no matter where it may have penetrated. Buddhism has at all times been at its purest in India. But this religion, born in Palestine, and confined by its founder to Jewish ground, in only a few years after his death was severed from that connexion. Paul put it in competition with the Israelitish religion: "Christ is the end of the law." Not only did it bear being thus rooted up and transplanted, but it showed that it was meant to be thus transplanted. It gave stay and support to the Roman empire and the whole world of western civilisation. If, as Renan justly observes, anyone had told the Roman Emperor in the first century that the little Jew who had come from Antioch as a missionary was his best collaborator, and would put the empire upon a stable basis, he would have been regarded as a madman, and yet he would have spoken nothing but the truth. Paul brought new forces to the Roman empire, and laid the foundations of western and Christian civilisation. Alexander the Great's work has perished; Paul's has remained. But if we praise the man who, without being able to appeal to a single word of his master's, ventured upon the boldest enterprise, by the help of the spirit and with the letter against him, we must none the less pay the meed of honour to those personal disciples of Jesus who after a bitter internal struggle ultimately associated themselves with Paul's principles. That Peter did so we know for certain; of others we hear that they at least acknowledged their validity. It was, indeed, no insignificant circumstance that men in whose ears every word of their master's was still ringing, and in whose recollection the concrete features of his personality were still a vivid memory—that these faithful disciples should recognise a pronouncement to be true which in important points seemed to depart from the original message and portended the downfall of the religion of Israel. What was kernel here, and what was husk, history has itself showed with unmistakeable plainness, and by the shortest process. Husk were the whole of the Jewish limitations attaching to Jesus' message; husk were also such definite statements as "I am not sent but unto the lost sheep of the house of Israel." In the strength of Christ's spirit the disciples broke through these barriers. It was his personal disciples—not, as we might expect, the second or third generation, when the immediate memory of the Lord had already paled—who stood the great test. That is the most remarkable fact of the apostolic age.

Without doing violence to the inner and essential features of the Gospel—unconditional trust in God as the Father of Jesus Christ, confidence in the Lord, forgiveness of sins, certainty of eternal life, purity and brotherly fellowship—Paul transformed it into the universal religion, and laid the ground for the great Church. But whilst the original limitations fell away, new ones of necessity made their appearance; and they modified the simplicity and the power of a movement which was from within. Before concluding our survey of the apostolic age, we must direct attention to these modifications.

In the first place: the breach with the Synagogue and the founding of entirely independent religious communities had well-marked results. Whilst the idea was firmly maintained that the community of Christ, the "Church," was something suprasensible and heavenly, because it came from within, there was also a conviction that the Church took visible shape in every separate community. As a complete breach had taken place, or no connexion been established, with the ancient communion, the formation of entirely new societies was logically invested with a special significance, and excited the liveliest interest. In his sayings and parables Jesus, careless of all externals, could devote himself solely to the all-important point; but *how and in what forms* the seed would grow was not a question which occupied his mind; he had the people of Israel with their historical ordinances before him and was not thinking of external changes. But the connexion with their people was now severed, and no religious movement can remain in a *bodiless* condition. It must elaborate *forms* for a common life and common public worship. Such forms, however, cannot be improvised; some of them take shape slowly out of concrete necessities; others are derived from the environment and from existing circumstances. It was in this way that the "Gentile" communities procured themselves an organism, a body. The forms which they developed were in part independent and gradual, and in part based upon the facts with which they had to deal.

But a special measure of value always attaches to forms. By being the means by which the community is kept together, *the value of*

that to which they minister is insensibly transferred to them; or, at
least, there is always a danger of this happening. One reason for
this is that the observance of the forms can always be controlled or
enforced, as the case may be; whilst for the inner life there is no
control that cannot be evaded.

When the breach with the Jewish national communion had once
taken place, there could be no doubt about the necessity for setting
up a new community in opposition to it. The self-consciousness
and strength of the Christian movement was displayed in the creation of a Church which knew itself to be the true Israel. But the
founding of churches and "the Church" on earth brought an
entirely new interest into the field; what came from within was
joined by something that came from without; law, discipline, regulations for ritual and doctrine, were developed, and began to assert
a position by a logic of their own. The measure of value applicable
to religion itself no longer remained the only measure, and with a
hundred invisible threads religion was insensibly worked into the
net of history.

In the second place: we have already referred to the fact that it
was above all in his Christology that Paul's significance as a teacher
consisted. In his view—we see this as well by the way in which he
illuminated the death on the cross and the resurrection, as by his
equation, "the Lord is a Spirit"—the Redemption is already accomplished and salvation a present power. "God hath reconciled us to
himself through Jesus Christ"; "If any man be in Christ, he is a
new creature"; "Who shall separate us from the love of God?"
The absolute character of the Christian religion is thus made clear.
But it may also be observed in this connexion that every attempt to
formulate a theory has a logic of its own and dangers of its own.
There was one danger which the apostle himself had to combat,
that of men claiming to be redeemed without giving practical proof
of the new life. In the case of Jesus' sayings no such danger could
arise, but Paul's formulas were not similarly protected. That men
are not to rely upon "redemption," forgiveness of sin, and justification, if the hatred of sin and the imitation of Christ be lacking,
inevitably became in subsequent ages a standing theme with all earnest teachers. Who can fail to recognise that the doctrines of
"objective redemption" have been the occasion of grievous temptations in the history of the Church, and for whole generations concealed the true meaning of religion? The conception of "redemption," which cannot be inserted in Jesus' teaching in this free and
easy way at all, became a snare. No doubt it is true that Christianity is the religion of redemption; but the conception is a delicate
one, and must never be taken out of the sphere of personal experience and inner reformation.

But here we are met by a second danger closely connected with the first. If redemption is to be traced to Christ's person and work, everything would seem to depend upon a right understanding of this person together with what he accomplished. The formation of a correct theory of and about Christ threatens to assume the position of chief importance, and to pervert the majesty and simplicity of the Gospel. Here, again, the danger is of a kind such as cannot arise with Jesus' sayings. Even in John we read:—"If ye love me, keep my commandments." But with the way in which Paul defined the theory of religion, the danger can certainly arise and did arise. No long period elapsed before it was taught in the Church that the all-important thing is to know how the person of Jesus was constituted, what sort of physical nature he had, and so on. Paul himself is far removed from this position—"Whoso calleth Christ Lord speaketh by the Holy Ghost"—but the way in which he ordered his religious conceptions, as the outcome of his speculative ideas, unmistakeably exercised an influence in a wrong direction. That, however great the attraction which his way of ordering them may possess for the understanding, it is a perverse proceeding to make Christology the fundamental substance of the Gospel, is shown by Christ's teaching, which is everywhere directed to the all-important point, and summarily confronts every man with his God. This does not affect Paul's right to epitomise the Gospel in the message of Christ crucified, thus exhibiting God's power and God's wisdom, and in the love of Christ kindling the love of God. There are thousands today in whom the Christian faith is still propagated in the same manner, namely, through Christ. But to demand assent to a series of propositions about Christ's person is a different thing altogether.

There is, however, another point to be considered here. Under the influence of the Messianic dogmas, and led by the impression which Christ made, Paul became the author of the speculative idea that not only was God in Christ, but that Christ himself was possessed of a peculiar nature of a heavenly kind. With the Jews, this was not a notion that necessarily shattered the framework of the Messianic idea; but with the Greeks it inevitably set an entirely new theory in motion. Christ's *appearance* in itself, the entrance of a divine being into the world, came of necessity to rank as the chief fact, as itself *the real redemption*. Paul did not, indeed, himself look upon it in this light; for him the crucial facts are the death on the cross and the resurrection, and he regards Christ's entrance into the world from an ethical point of view and as an example for us to follow: "For our sakes he became poor"; he humbled himself and renounced the world. But this state of things could not last. The fact of redemption could not permanently occupy the second place; it was too large. But when moved into the first place it threatened the very existence of the Gospel, by drawing away men's thoughts and interests in another direction. When we look at the history of dogma, who can deny that that was what happened? * * *

In the third place: the new church possessed a sacred book, the Old Testament. Paul, although he taught that the law had become of no avail, found a means of preserving the whole of the Old Testament. What a blessing to the church this book has proved! As a book of edification, of consolation, of wisdom, of counsel, as a book of history, what an incomparable importance it has had for Christian life and apologetics! Which of the religions that Christianity encountered on Greek or Roman ground could boast of a similar book? Yet the possession of this book has not been an unqualified advantage to the church. To begin with, there are many of its pages which exhibit a religion and a morality other than Christian. No matter how resolutely people tried to spiritualize it and give it an inner meaning by construing it in some special way, their efforts did not avail to get rid of the original sense in its entirety. There was always a danger of an inferior and obsolete principle forcing its way into Christianity through the Old Testament. This, indeed, was what actually occurred. Nor was it only in individual aspects that it occurred; the whole aim was changed. Moreover, on the new ground religion was intimately connected with a political power, namely, with nationality. How if people were seduced into again seeking such a connexion, not, indeed, with Judaism, but with a new nation, and not with ancient national laws, but with something of an analogous character? And when even a Paul here and there declared Old Testament laws to be still authoritative in spite of their having undergone an allegorical transformation, how could anyone restrain his successors from also proclaiming other laws, remodelled to suit the circumstances of the time, as valid ordinances of God? This brings us to the second point. Although whatever was drawn from the Old Testament by way of authoritative precept may have been inoffensive in substance, it was a menace to Christian freedom of both kinds. It threatened the freedom which comes from within, and also the freedom to form church communities and to arrange for public worship and discipline.

* * *

When the great apostle ended his life under Nero's axe in the year 64, he could say of himself what a short time before he had written to a faithful comrade: "I have finished my course; I have kept the faith." What missionary is there, what preacher, what man entrusted with the cure of souls, who can be compared with him, whether in the greatness of the task which he accomplished, or in the holy energy with which he carried it out? He worked with the most living of all messages, and kindled a fire; he cared for his

people like a father and strove for the souls of others with all the
forces of his own; at the same time he discharged the duties of the
teacher, the schoolmaster, the organiser. When he sealed his work
by his death, the Roman empire from Antioch as far as Rome, nay,
as far as Spain, was planted with Christian communites. There
were to be found in them few that were "mighty after the flesh" or
of noble degree, and yet they were as "lights in the world," and on
them the progress of the world's history rested. They had little
"illumination," but they had acquired the faith in the living God
and in a life eternal; they knew that the value of the human soul is
infinite, and that its value is determined by relation to the invisible;
they led a life of purity and brotherly fellowship, or at least strove
after such a life. Bound together into a new people in Jesus Christ,
their head, they were filled with the high consciousness that Jews
and Greeks, Greeks and barbarians, would through them become
one, and that the last and highest stage in the history of humanity
had then been reached.

* * *

WILHELM HEITMÜLLER

Hellenistic Christianity Before Paul (1912) †

A certain peace and quiet has settled over the discussion of the
problem "Paul and Jesus." One can hardly say that the question
has been settled. Nevertheless, even where the problem has been
taken seriously, it now seems to be recognized that Paul and Jesus
belong together as religious personages, that Paul is somehow
dependent upon Jesus through the medium of the primitive community, and that the great Apostle of the Gentiles does not begin a
new series, but is a link in a chain that begins with Jesus.

Yet the very recognition of these facts raises a question that
urgently requires an answer. Assuming that Jesus influenced Paul,
assuming both phenomena belong together, how—especially in
view of the proximity by which they are joined in space and
time—can one explain the extraordinarily great differences that
undeniably exist between them? These are differences not merely
between Paul's theology and Jesus' preaching, but at many points
also between Paul's religion and the religion of Jesus. * * *

† From "Zum Problem Paulus und Jesus," *Zeitschrift für die neutesta-mentliche Wissenschaft* 13 (1912): 320–37. Heitmüller (1869–1926) was Professor of New Testament in Marburg, Bonn, and Tübingen.

I

* * * No one can contest the surprising rarity of the apostle's references to the historical Jesus. I have the impression that in theological circles people shut their eyes to this fact far too much or at least soften its impact all too much and too quickly. Arthur Drews has, as we know, again pointed it out emphatically in his "Christ-myth."[1] The deduction which he draws from it, to be sure, is simply untenable: Paulinism without the existence of a man Jesus is utterly incomprehensible. But the fact lies incontestably before us, and we must face it undiminished and unveiled: Jesus, the historical personality Jesus, does not appear in the letters as the factor that essentially determines and shapes Paulinism.

* * *

* * * "Even though we have (or, had) known Christ according to the flesh, we know (him) thus no longer" (2 Cor. 5:8). Quite decisively Paul says here that the earthly Jesus, the human personality Jesus, has no meaning whatever for his religious life, for him as one who is "in Christ" and thereby belongs to a higher reality than the earth. The whole thing upon which his opponents place so much weight and which they boast as the superiority of the earlier apostles, the knowledge of Jesus, is for Paul irrelevant. And that means that the tradition about Jesus is also irrelevant. Paul knows the exalted Lord, the "Christ according to spirit": he lives in Paul and Paul in him; by him Paul is filled. How could the earthly Jesus, the "Christ according to flesh," be important for him? * * *

This attitude of Paul toward the historical Jesus, i.e., naturally also toward the Jesus-tradition, was rooted also in the historical situation in which he found himself—or in any case sharpened by it—namely, his struggle for the rights and independence of his law-free mission. In this struggle the knowledge of the historical Jesus, by which the earlier apostles were distinguished, played a major role. Thus Paul was actually forced to oppose a high evaluation of the tradition. * * *

* * *

II

* * *

It was the apostle's sacred conviction and great pride that he had not received his gospel "from man and not through a man," but

1. *Die Christusmythe* (Jena, 1909; new ed. 1924). [*Editor*]

"through Jesus Christ and God" (Gal. 1:1). That does not affect the obvious fact that Pauline Christianity does not really stand in immediate proximity to Jesus' preaching and that it is not independent of human and historical mediation. Paul knows himself to be autonomous and yet he is at the same time dependent upon another form of Christianity. Precisely this fact is a second important element in understanding Paul's distance from Jesus.

Naturally the apostle had become acquainted with the gospel before his conversion, even if perhaps only in outline, for he had persecuted the "church of God." He had obtained impressions of the Jesus-faith and of its adherents. We must take for granted that these impressions are of decisive importance for the origin and the form of Pauline Christianity. Furthermore, even if Paul "did not confer with flesh and blood" (and according to the whole tenor of the context, this note is directed in the first instance, if not entirely, against his alleged dependence on *those* men whose authority was thrown up to him, upon whom he was said to be dependent: the earlier apostles), nevertheless he did contact a Christian congregation after his conversion, probably the one in Damascus. Gal. 1:17, 18 does not say that he spent the entire "three years" in Arabia. Even though his conversion was, as far as he was aware, an original, unprepared experience, still the more precise formation of his faith and experience could not remain untouched and independent of the Christianity that surrounded him and within which he lived. How was that Christianity constituted of which he had obtained the first and decisive impressions, and the Christianity by which he was then surrounded for a time later on?

In the debate over Paul and Jesus, it was of great importance, as has been impressively urged,[2] that Paul not be placed immediately beside Jesus, but rather beside the primitive church. It is my opinion, however, that this observation must be further developed or modified. The Christianity which Paul joins and from which he is to be understood, is not really the primitive church in the strict sense, i.e., the Christianity of the earliest Jesus-group on Jewish soil in Jerusalem and Judea, to which the immediate disciples and friends of Jesus belonged. It is rather a *form already further developed*: if one can use an expression and rightly understand it, a *Hellenistic Christianity*.

The dominant view of Paul's introduction to the new messianic sect in Jerusalem is determined by the report of Acts. According to Acts he was in Jerusalem when the first storm, occasioned by Stephen's activity, burst over the church (Acts 7:58 ff.). The future apostle to the Gentiles thus received his first impressions from the

2. Cf. Adolf Jülicher, *Paulus und Jesus* (1907).

oldest form of Christianity, the Jerusalem church. He had first persecuted it, before extending his work of desolation abroad (8:3).

In Gal. 1:22 ff. Paul says that he was personally unknown (prior
to the Apostolic Council) to the Christian congregations in Judea,
to which the Jerusalem church belonged. As long as I have known
the Letter to Galatians I have found it incomprehensible that so
little weight is commonly given to this, Paul's own statement, in
comparison with the report of Acts. If Paul had been in Jerusalem
at that time and if he had persecuted the church there (Acts 8:3),
then he could not say in Gal. 1:22 that he was personally unknown
to the "churches in Judea." Those two assertions are mutually exclusive. The tenor of the whole argument in Gal. 1:15 ff. comes to
this: Paul wants to prove here that every possibility of his contact
with, and therefore his dependence upon, the Jerusalem circles is
excluded. If he had been in Jerusalem at the time of the Stephen
incident, he would have had to defend this fact against misinterpretation. The "we" in Gal. 1:23 ("he who once persecuted us") can
no more be used to prove that Paul persecuted the Judean churches
than the "you" of 2:5 can demonstrate that the Galatian congregations already existed at the time of the Apostolic Council.

The book of Acts as such cannot claim validity against the clear
statement of Paul himself. What is more, its nature makes it easy
for us to attribute to it an error at this point. As a consequence of
an inadequate perspective and at the same time probably because
of the use of sources, the author reports *two* journeys of Paul to
Jerusalem between his conversion and the Apostolic Council, while
it is notorious from Paul's own account that there was only one.
But we must also take into account the singular viewpoint of the
author and the presentation of history that follows therefrom. The
author of Acts is convinced that the magnificent expansion of the
gospel from Jerusalem to Rome, borne by the Holy Spirit, was
achieved under the direction of Jerusalem and especially of the College of Apostles. Thus he proceeds involuntarily to show the connection also of the Gentile mission with this central authority, and
to bring its major bearer, Paul, into contact and agreement with
Jerusalem and the Twelve. One sees this intention with particular
clarity in the historically untenable depiction of the converted Paul's
first stay in Jerusalem (9:26–30; cf. Gal. 1:18, 19). From there
we can understand that the author, without adequate historical
foundation, brings Paul to Jerusalem and his conversion into causal
connection with a movement of the primitive community that was
already becoming sacrosanct. To that can be added a literary-
critical fact which has long been observed: the sentences in the Stephen report which refer to Paul (7:58–8:3) appear to be secon-
darily pasted on or patched into an existing account which originally

did not contain them. Finally we may observe that the assertion in Acts 9:1, 2; 22:5; 26:12 that Paul obtained letters from the high priest to the synagogues in Damascus, authorizing him to bring any Christians found there in bonds to Jerusalem, very probably contradicts the actual competence of the sanhedrin. Thus we need have no qualms about consigning to the realm of legend the report of the apostle's presence at the persecution of Stephen.

If that is the case, however, then the tradition no longer gives us any right or occasion to assume that Paul first became acquainted with the Christian sect in Jerusalem and persecuted the community there. We no longer have any express statement that tells where that may have taken place. We must stick to Paul himself. From his own reports we derive the certain information that he experienced his conversion near or in Damascus, probably in the midst of his activity as a persecutor. After having been in Arabia, he returned to Damascus: therefore we may conclude that at that time he was a resident of Damascus. And we may further *suppose* that he there first came into contact with the Christian sect.

What is certain and valuable, first of all, is the *negative* observation that Paul did not come to know Christianity in Jerusalem and did not receive his first decisive impressions of Christianity from the Jerusalem primitive church. And by the same token it was not the Christianity of the primitive community, let alone the immediate disciples of Jesus, who influenced the formation of his faith and theology after his conversion. Apart from the one visit to Peter, three years after his conversion, the Christian Paul consciously and intentionally kept his distance from Jerusalem and the leaders of the oldest congregations.

On the *positive* side, we learn that Paul became acquainted with the gospel on the soil of *diaspora Judaism* and therefore received the decisive impressions from a diaspora Jewish Christianity. That is of great importance. It is clear that the gospel on the soil of diaspora Judaism could and must receive a different nuance from that on specifically Jewish soil like Jerusalem. One could guess a priori what pressures, impulses, and tendencies lay hidden in diaspora Judaism and would quickly unfold when it encountered the gospel. But we can see them quite clearly and reliably in the figure of the "Hellenist," i.e., the Greek-speaking, diaspora Jew Stephen, and in the external and internal development within early Christianity that emerged from his activity. "Hellenists" first seized upon the germ of universalism that lay in Jesus' preaching; they sensed that something new, beckoning out beyond Judaism, was given with faith in Jesus as the Christ. Hellenists first consciously undertook a mission among Gentiles, probably initially among proselytes (Acts 8 and 11). Presumably a serious missionary endeavor beyond Judea began first in consequence of the Stephen uproar. Probably one may further assume that the persecution affected only the Hellenistic believers who deprecated the temple cult or the law, who then, having been driven out of Jerusalem, extended their mission also to the non-Jews. This mission movement borne by diaspora Jewish Christians will have spread as far as Damascus; by that means Paul became acquainted with Christianity, persecuted it, and received the unconscious impetus to his conversion.

The gospel first came to the Apostle to Gentiles as *Hellenistic Christianity*. By that I mean a Christianity that was carried by diaspora Jews and which already carried on a mission to the Gentiles. Hellenistic Christianity was involved in the *origin* of the Pauline faith, and Hellenistic Christianity influenced the *formation* of Paulinism. The converted Paul lived among Hellenistic Christians. Hellenistic Christianity comprised the foil and the foundation of his missionary activity. The picture that apparently emerges from the Pauline letters, as if the missionary Paul had carried on his work free-lance, entirely by his own power, is very likely false. The book of Acts at this point provides a good and necessary corrective. As others carried on a Gentile mission before Paul and alongside him (the anonymous Cypriots and Cyreneans, Acts 11:20; Barnabas; Andronicus and Junias? Rom. 16:7), so also his mission was supported by the church, at least before the Apostolic Council, which seems to have meant a turning point in his missionary style. Antioch may have furnished the principal base of operations in this period (Acts 13:1 ff.). From this matrix of his missionary work Paul naturally also drew power and stimulus for his Christianity. He not only gave; he also received.

Accordingly, if we are to solve the problem "Paul and Jesus" correctly, we must take this Hellenistic Christianity into account. Paul was separated from Jesus not only by the primitive church, but by yet a further link. The developmental series reads: Jesus—primitive church—Hellenistic Christianity—Paul. And even if the *genesis* of Pauline Christianity were to be thought of as quite independent of this Hellenistic form of primitive Christianity, it would still remain certain that the piety and theology of the missionary Paul who encounters us in the letters—written more than 14 (17?) years after his conversion—the only Paul we know—could only be understood in light of his constant contact with the Hellenistic Christianity of a congregation like Antioch, which first supported his mission and which was in part Gentile Christian.

This much is clear: if we knew this Hellenistic Christianity that was before and alongside Paul, then we would have the best key for understanding Paul. What was the nature of this Hellenistic Christianity? How did it look? Even if we could no longer identify this form of Christianity, what we have shown so far would not be without value. For from now on, in any account of Paulinism, we would have to figure in this unknown but present factor. We would always have to weigh in this x, and, at least more than previously, we would have recognized that we cannot regard Paulinism as a phenomenon conjured up out of thin air, a purely original creation. Rather we must assume a previous stage to which perhaps many things belong that appear to us now as original Pauline creations.

However, even though we are condemned here to a large measure of resignation, still we do not remain totally and absolutely helpless. To be sure we have no direct sources for this phenomenon, but some indirect and weak sources can be pointed out:

1. First the book of Acts, in the recognized good Hellenistic sources, chaps. 6, 7, 8, and 11. Here we obtain a few important hints about the Hellenistic diaspora Jewish Christianity that formed the bridge to the Gentile mission.

2. Above all, however, we must uncover in the Pauline letters themselves sources for this previous stage. That is a little-travelled, difficult, and dangerous path, but we must venture upon it.

a) We can certainly use 1 Cor. 15:1 ff. Here Paul gives the central content of his gospel and actually designates it as "received," as tradition. If the above argument is correct, if he did not become acquainted with the gospel in Jerusalem, but outside Palestine, perhaps in Damascus, then strictly speaking what he gives here is not, as is always assumed, what he received from the primitive church in the strict sense, but what he found at hand as a tradition of *Hellenistic* Christianity (see above) and took over. These are the main points of Hellenistic Christianity. To be sure, Paul expressly points to the earlier apostles in 15:11: they preach the same thing. But even though it is certainly correct that they also proclaimed Jesus' atoning death for sins and the Resurrection, yet we have every reason to doubt that the leaders of the earliest Jerusalem primitive congregation would have been satisfied to take as the core of the gospel that which Paul in 15:1 ff. calls its main points. It is not just a question of the individual statements, but above all of the position they acquired and of what things were connected or not connected with them. This passage itself, 1 Cor. 15:1 ff., suggests that Paul did not receive his tradition directly from the primitive church. Restriction to the bare scheme of death, burial, resurrection as the chief content of the gospel is not comprehensible for the church to which we owe the sayings source and the basic structure of the Markan gospel. That restriction is only explicable in a circle that was further separated from the historical reality of Jesus' life and its wealth than was the Jerusalem congregation. We become acquainted here with the chief content of the *preaching* of Hellenistic Christianity.

But elsewhere as well, apart from 1 Cor. 15:1–11, we must seek to obtain material by inference from the letters of Paul. The attempt is successful to a certain extent. I believe that we can make use of the passages in which Paul alludes to acknowledged presuppositions of his arguments and argues *e concessis*. That is, we must attempt to separate the specifically Pauline from the common Christian material.

b) In our case the letter to Romans is particularly to be considered. For it is written to a congregation that was not founded by Paul, but may have originated in a way similar to Antioch, independently of Pauline Christianity. "Hellenists" who believed in Jesus must originally have carried out the mission, winning especially proselytes. Then in time it became an essentially Gentile Christian congregation. The dominant Christianity there will have been closely related to the Hellenistic Christianity that Paul came to know and which was his starting point. We shall be able to utilize with confidence that which we can deduce from the letter about the Roman congregation's views.

c) With less confidence, only with reservations, will we use what we recognize from the remaining Pauline letters as common Christian, i.e., as the views of the respective congregations. For here we are confronted with congregations which were brought into the world by Paul (or his pupils) and which received their stamp from him: their Christianity is therefore in any case dependent upon Paul.

The more or less certain material of 1 and 2a-b produces results that can be summarized as follows:

This Hellenistic Christianity began to separate itself inwardly more and more from Judaism and to position itself freely over against Judaism, at least over against the cultus, though not yet so clearly over against observance. The first bearers of this form of Christianity were, as said above, diaspora Jews. These Jews had naturally, from the ground up, a somewhat freer attitude towards the cultic and the rigorously particularistic elements of the patriarchal religion. They were the ones most likely able to grasp the universal powers of Jesus's preaching and to break through the particularistic and national limits. Stephen recognized the religious meaninglessness of the temple and its cultus; thereby an important part of the law also collapsed. Accordingly it was only fitting that one should preach the gospel also to Gentiles—naturally without having first to lead them through Judaism; otherwise it would have been nothing out of the ordinary. Thus in any case the congregation at Antioch originated—and others like it. In Antioch Christians did not think of themselves as bound to the Jewish law. We know that from the fact that they did not observe the Jewish dietary laws (Gal. 2:12). We cannot regard that as only a consequence of

Paul's preaching; rather Paul must have found this situation already at hand. For the judgment of Pauline Christianity and of the place of Paul in the history of early Christianity it is of highest significance to note that he found at hand and proceeded from a Christianity that already conducted a Gentile mission and had actually already freed itself to a certain extent from the Jewish law and the Jewish nation.

The preaching of this Hellenistic Christianity is cited by Paul in its chief points in 1 Cor. 15:1 ff.: Christ dead for our sins, buried, risen. That scheme began already to take the place of the wealth of historical reality. That which we recognized in Paul as his conscious, fundamental position (see 1) had de facto already been prepared in this Christianity and had taken shape in his beginnings. The Christ-idea began already at this point to crowd out the historical Jesus. Christology stepped to the foreground.

Corresponding to this content of the gospel, which climaxed in the death and resurrection of Jesus Christ, was the position which was accorded to Jesus. It is subsumed in the title. "Lord." This title for Jesus Christ could be called characteristic of our Hellenistic Christianity and probably originated in it. To be sure we arrive at this conclusion not from those sources alone which were expressly mentioned above, but from the early Christian writings in general. Paul did not himself create in the place of *Christos* the designation *ho kyrios* [the Lord], which was obviously native to Gentile Christian circles and especially frequent in Paul, but found it at hand and took it over. That should be obvious even from the self-evident way in which he employs this name in his letters. Now the traditional opinion is that the primitive church already called Jesus Lord. The favorite evidence for that opinion is the *maranatha* of 1 Cor. 16:22. I cannot really convince myself of the probability of this assumption. That *maranatha* is indeed proof that in Aramaic-speaking Christian circles, from which the gospel came to Greek-speaking people, the cry or prayer "Our Lord, come" was much used, a kind of shibboleth. Thus the designation "Lord" for Jesus was common in those circles. But to surmise that the same was true for the Jerusalem primitive church would be to jump to conclusions. From 1 Cor. 16:22 can be deduced initially only that where Paul learned of the gospel, i.e., in the Christianity of diaspora Judaism, perhaps in Damascus, or where his Christian missionary base was, perhaps in Antioch, this prayer was often heard. If we take one step at a time, we can initially get no further than that. We can add that many considerations make it unlikely that in the primitive church of purely Jewish origins the designation "Lord" for Jesus would have arisen or have been common. The attitude of the basic stratum of gospel literature in relation to the name *ho kyrios* is significant. Mark never uses it of Jesus in the third person[3] (contrast Mark 16:9, 10! [Part of the spurious ending found only in late manuscripts]), nor does Matthew. Even as an address to Jesus the title *Kyrios* has no place yet in Mark; *kyrie* in the vocative serves for him only as a polite form of address. The same is true—and that is especially interesting—in the sayings—source; only in one passage, Matt. 7:21 f. (cf. Luke 6:46) can one ask whether "Lord" should be interpreted in the sacral or religious sense.[4] If that should be the case, it would be the only passage, and a quite isolated one, in this, our best source of information about the primitive community's religion. It is further to be noted (1) that, so far as I know, in the genuine Jewish literature the Messiah is never called "Lord," so that Jewish believers would not find this a natural way of naming Jesus as the Messiah; (2) that for the Jews the name "Lord" was the specific designation for God himself. On pure Jewish soil, therefore, the prerequisites for origin of the title "Lord" for Jesus were not present. All that leads to the presumption that this designation, so pregnant with consequences, must not have arisen in the primitive church. There remains then only our Hellenistic Christianity. Here the prerequisites for the development of the Messiah Jesus into the "Lord" Jesus Christ were present: the message of the Messiah Jesus, dead, exalted, imminently to come, and the fact that the name "Lord" in pagan circles was a common designation for the deity from whom one expected salvation and whose fate—that was true of some few—in violent death and in exaltation reminded one of the fate of the Messiah Jesus. Here now, at least on pagan soil, the floodgates were opened for Hellenistic–Oriental elements. The proclamation of the death and resurrection of Jesus Christ is not a product of the myth of the dying and "rising" God; nevertheless, when it reached Hellenistic soil it could and must immediately enter in pagan minds into an amalgamation with similar-sounding stories of the violent death and exaltation of gods.

By this name "Lord" Jesus was ipso facto given a divine status. With that step was linked unavoidably the cultus, divine worship in some, even if only germinal, form. Though we undoubtedly perceive in Paul the beginnings of the Christ-cult, still we know now that at this point also he was not the creator but the recipient. He had to accommodate himself to what was given; perhaps he even attenuated what was there.

Further, as a rather certain feature of this Hellenistic Christianity, a belief in sacraments has to be recognized. In the Letter to

---

3. In keeping with the evangelist's usage elsewhere, the expression *ho kyrios* in 11:3 is not to be understood in the sacral, technical sense.

4. In the material peculiar to Matthew one can think of the technical expression "Lord" in passages like 14:30; 15:22, 25; 20:30, 31; 25:37, 44.

already know baptism

Romans Paul argues (6:1 ff.) on the basis of the readers' customary view of the meaning of baptism. According to this, the Romans know baptism as a sacrament; they connect the conception of dying and new life with the act of baptism. One can hardly contest the fact that Hellenistic ways of thought have been at work here. Thus Paul did not create the singular conception of baptism present here, but received it from the Christianity which he learned and within which he lived—he is not creator but user. It will scarcely be too bold to draw implications from here also for the conception of the Lord's Supper in this pre- and extra-Pauline Hellenistic Christianity. It must have been equally a sacramental conception. And perhaps we can localize here the thought-complex of 1 Cor. 10:1 ff., 14 ff. * * * There the meal is supernatural food and supernatural drink; communion with the exalted Lord is established by bread and wine. We can assume, with appropriate reserve about certainty, that this view belonged to the pre- and extra-Pauline Hellenistic form of Christianity, upon which Paul was dependent. The influence of Hellenistic syncretism that is present in this thought-complex was therefore not first accomplished by Paul. Rather he had to accommodate himself to a sacramental concept that was essentially complete. The way in which he, for his part, works out another aspect of the Supper, corresponding more to his own conception, is shown by 1 Cor. 11:17 ff., where the meal appears primarily as the celebration of Jesus' death and its saving significance.

Finally I should like to single out as a characteristic of this movement, although with somewhat less confidence, the beginnings of Christ-mysticism. The presupposition of the conception in Rom. 6:1 ff., that the baptized person has died and has a new life, is the other notion that he has been baptized "into Christ." Thereafter the baptized person is "in Christ" (cf. Gal. 3:27). Because he is in Christ, he experiences together with Christ the latter's death and resurrection. Thus we must assume that the Christ-mysticism also was present in its initial stages, even if Paul was the first to develop it.

* * *

One could recognize still other features of the picture of the Hellenistic Christianity we have been pursuing, but I will stop here. It was my intention only to indicate the way to be travelled, not to pursue it to the end. To be sure, much of the path will remain uncertain. But that does not excuse us from the task.

It is at least certain that we cannot place Paul immediately next to the primitive church. Rather he allied himself with a form of Christianity that was already farther from Jesus and under Hellenistic influence. It is also certain that this discovery provides an important factor for understanding the distance, which in fact is very great, between Pauline Christianity and Jesus.

But not only that problem received important light from this knowledge (developed under 2 above). Paulinism appears, when placed alongside Jesus and the primitive church, to have an almost baffling originality. If the argument above is principally correct, then we see that many of the stones in the imposing structure were already quarried and hewn and were only taken over by Paul. Paul's greatness is not thereby lessened; it only becomes historically somewhat more understandable for us.

Further, dissonances and disharmonies have long been discovered in the conceptual and intellectual world of the apostle, which seemed hard to understand, because the apostle was regarded as the free creator of this world. This phenomenon becomes again more understandable, if we recognize how much Paul took over, inherited, and received as ballast.

Moreover, we can in this way know more clearly that which is specifically Pauline, the uniqueness of Paulinism. It was *not* that which Paul had in common with Hellenistic Christianity.

And finally, on this basis we understand somewhat better the peculiar phenomenon that emerges if we inquire about the effects and after-effects of Paulinism in the development of Christianity: the elements of Paulinism that were genuinely peculiar to the apostle were the ones that only later were understood and had their effect.

PART VI

Pauline Christianity and Judaism

It was inevitable, given the arguments of Galatians and Romans, that Paul would become a bone of contention wherever and whenever the separation of church from synagogue became an issue. The remarkable fact is that his name is so relatively seldom heard in the long history of controversy between Christian and Jew before the modern period. As we saw in Part III above, Paul became the center of argument when self-consciously Jewish-Christian groups fought to maintain their Jewishness within the church, or when Marcion sought to expunge all Jewishness from the gospel. Yet these were *internal* disputes within the church. In Justin Martyr's *Dialogue with Trypho the Jew* Paul is not so much as mentioned, and in the various later tracts which the church Fathers wrote "Against the Jews" Paul's doctrines play a much smaller role than one might have expected.

Paul's letters portray the same situation: the opponents he attacks are Jewish *Christians*; we hear little about arguments between him and *Jews*. We may assume, of course, that there were such arguments, since he reports that he had been flogged five times "at the hands of the Jews," three times beaten with rods, and once stoned (1 Cor. 11:25). But these are reported merely as the mishaps attendant on his missionary endeavors, in the same category as shipwreck and loss of sleep. His own attitude toward Judaism is ambivalent. Once (1 Thess. 2:14–16) he speaks so harshly of "the Jews" that one would think he regarded himself as a Jew no longer. Yet elsewhere his sense of the continuity between Israel and the Church is pervasive, and in Romans he speaks with conviction of his yearning for his fellow Jews and of his certainty that they will all ultimately be brought by God's grace into the one people of God.

In Acts the picture is quite different. There Paul himself appears as a fully observant Pharisee throughout his life, while the Jews who refuse his message are categorically read out of the People of God. Thus in Paul's letters he rejects "Judaism," in the sense of the covenanted life structured by

321

commandments, but not the Jews, while in Acts he remains true to "Judaism" but rejects the Jews.[1]

What the Jews in ancient times may have said about Paul, we do not know. The Talmud contains, in those copies that escaped the medieval Christian censors, several derogatory references to Jesus, but not a single clear allusion to Paul.[2] From medieval Judaism no description of Paul has survived comparable to the Toledot Yeshua, the legend-filled parody of Jesus' life. That is not surprising, after all, for what constituted the danger to Judaism, after the fourth century, was not any particular figure within Christian history, but Christianity as a total phenomenon, now backed by state power. Among the religious factors that contributed to Christian anti-Semitism, distinctly Pauline doctrines apparently played no major role. In the middle ages it was the "deicide" charge, nurtured by liturgy, art, and folklore, and ultimately based on the apologetic motifs in the gospel trial narratives, that was the major religious vehicle of hostility to the synagogue—not the Pauline rejection of the law.

With the Lutheran reformation the situation altered significantly, for Protestants came to see Judaism through the double spectacles of Luther's reading of Paul and Paul's reading of his Jewish-Christian opponents. Through these two distorting lenses, Judaism appeared to most Protestants identical with "narrow legalism," and Paul was identified as the one who delivered Christianity from that legalism.

The post-Renaissance infatuation with the individual "genius," together with the rise of modern historical method, led to attempts to define Paul's *distinctive* contributions to early Christianity. Thus it became possible to recognize again the thoroughly *Jewish* characteristics of Jesus and of many of the earliest traditions of Christianity, and to push the decisive transformation of Jesus' followers from a Jewish sect into a "world-religion" to a point *after* Jesus' death. With that the historical question, how that transformation came about, became acute. A simple answer was the suggestion that Paul was the innovator, which in some circles took on the further specification that Paul was the *Hellenizer* of Christianity. Further investigation showed this solution to be unsatisfactory,[3] but its very simplicity has assured its persistence as a kind of academic myth. Moreover, it had lasting influence on the conversation between Jews and Christians. It now became possible for sophisticated Jews in pluralistic environments to claim Jesus as their own, while laying at Paul's doorstep the alienation between classical Judaism and orthodox Christianity. The result, in many cases, was a significant rapprochement between liberal Jews and liberal Christians. It is noteworthy that the three Jewish authors represented on the following pages all emerged from the same German university tradition that produced, within Protestant Christianity, the debate over the relationship between Paul and Jesus (exemplified by the selections in Part V).

---

1. See Hans Windisch, *Paulus und das Judentum* (Stuttgart, 1935), pp. 11–34, and compare the essay above by Vielhauer (pp. 166–75).
2. Gerhard Kittel, "Paulus im Talmud" (in *Rabbinica* [Leipzig, 1920], pp. 1–16), has argued that the description of an apostate found in Mishnah Abot 3.11; Abot de R. Nathan, chap. 26; Sifre to Num. 15.31; b. Sanhedrin 99a; p. Pesachim 33b, is a covert description of Paul. His argument is more ingenious than convincing; the description *could* apply to Paul, but also to virtually any other apostate.
3. See the essay by Heitmüller in the previous chapter.

While these authors do not entirely agree with one another in their interpretations of Paul, they all represent to a certain extent a consensus that has been growing in this century: Paul has to be understood as a Jew and a Hellenist, and both his Jewishness and his Hellenism were transformed by his Christianity. The more we have learned about the Mediterranean world of the first century, the less useful have become the catch-all antitheses like "Jew *vs.* Greek," "Palestinian *vs.* Diaspora." The familiar game of factoring Paulinism into its specific ingredients—"Greek," "Jewish," "apocalyptic," "Gnostic"—may still serve a purpose in the interpretative task, but we are aware now that these are all abstractions which *we* impose on the data. The picture becomes more and more complicated, yet one thing remains clear: unless we understand something about Judaism, we shall never understand Paul.

MARTIN BUBER

A New Kind of Faith (1951) †

The faith, which Paul indicates in his distinction between it and the law, is not one which could have been held in the pre-Christian era. 'The righteousness of God', by which he means His declaration of man as righteous, is that which is through faith in Christ (Rom. iii. 22, Gal. ii. 16), which means faith in one who has come, died on the cross and risen.

In the matter of 'faith' against 'works', which Paul pursues, he does not therefore in fact intend a thing which might have existed before the coming of Christ. He charges Israel (Rom. ix. 31) with having pursued the 'law of righteousness' and not having attained it, because it strove after it 'not by faith but by works'. Is this to mean that ancient Israel did not fulfil the law because it did not strive to fulfil it by faith? Surely not, for it is immediately explained that they had stumbled on the stone of stumbling, and that cannot apply to the former Israel and a possible insufficiency of its faith in the future coming of the Messiah, but only to the Jews of that time, those whom Paul sought for Christ and whom he had not won for him because they did not recognize in him the promised Messiah of belief. In Isaiah's word (viii. 14), which Paul quotes here in a strange amalgamation with another (that discussed above, xxviii. 16), the 'stone of stumbling' refers to none other than God himself: the fact that His message or salvation is misunderstood and misused as a guarantee of security meant that His own word brings the people to stumbling. Paul interprets the saying as referring to Christ. 'For Christ is the end of the law, so that righteousness may come to everyone that believes.' The Jews, who refuse for themselves this faith, refuse to submit to the righteousness of God. Paul prays that they may be saved, but they do not desire it, for they have a zeal for God, but they lack the knowledge.

Again Paul refers to a sentence from the Old Testament, but this time he takes it neither from the history of the time before the law nor from the prophets, but from the 'law' itself. It is the sentence (Deut. xxx. 14): 'For the word is very nigh thee, in thy

† From *Two Types of Faith*, tr. by Norman P. Goldhawk (New York, 1951, 1961), Chapter VI and portions of Chapter XIV. Martin Buber (1878–1965), born in Vienna, taught philosophy and religion in Frankfurt until 1933. After 1938 he made his home in Israel. He is famous not only for his philosophy of religion, but also for his studies in Jewish mysticism and for his biblical translation and commentaries.

mouth and in thy heart'. 'That is', Paul continues (Rom. x. 8 ff.),
'the word of faith which we preach. For if thou confess with thy
mouth Jesus as Lord and believe in thy heart that God has raised
him from the dead, thou shalt be saved'. Paul refers to the verse of
Isaiah we have already discussed, 'he who trusts will not hasten',
but in the incorrect translation of the Septuagint, which is perplexed by the difficult text and has chosen a different version;
hence the sentence which Paul quotes has become: 'Whosoever
believeth on Him shall not be ashamed'. This is the Pauline counterpart of the Johannine reply of the apostle to Jesus, 'We have
believed and known that thou are the Holy One of God'; both
statements supplement each other as only the report of a declaration by disciples who have been apprehended by the living Jesus
and the authentic evidence of one apprehended by the dead can
supplement each other. But with that sentence from Deuteronomy,
where, as he says, (*v.* 6) 'the righteousness which is of faith'
speaks, Paul deals very curiously. In the text itself the word which
is not in heaven but in the mouth and heart means none other
than 'this commandment, which I this day command thee' (*v.* 11),
thus not a word of faith but simply the word of the 'law', of which
it is declared here that it does not come from far above man, but in
such a manner that it is felt to rise in his own heart and to force its
way from there on to his lips. But in the sentence which Paul
quotes he has omitted a word, the last word of the sentence. The
text runs: 'For the word is very nigh thee, in thy mouth and in
thy heart, *to do it*'. The word which God commands man speaks to
him in such a way that he feels it rising in his heart and forcing its
way to his lips as a word which desires to be done by him. As in
the case of the 'commandment' so Paul has also left the 'doing'
unnoticed. Elsewhere however (ii. 14 ff.) this 'doing' appears in
him precisely in conjunction with this 'in the heart': where he
speaks *of the heathen,* who 'do by nature the things of the law'
because 'the work of the law is written in their hearts'. One may
compare with this God's word in Jeremiah (xxxi. 33) that some
day the Torah of God shall be written in *Israel's* heart. Strange are
the ways of the Pauline hour and its solicitation!

'No flesh' (Rom. iii. 20, Gal. ii. 16), says Paul, becomes righteous before God by the works of the law. This thesis, of which it
has been rightly said[1] that for Paul it is 'the principle which
requires no proof and is exempted from every conflict of opinions',
means above all (Rom. iii. 28) that 'by faith alone', faith in Jesus
(*v.* 26) 'without the works of the law', the individual, heathen or
Jew, is declared righteous, so that therefore—and this is the special
concern of the apostle to the Gentiles—the Gentiles do not have

1. Lohmeyer, *Probleme paulinischer Theologie,* ZNW 28 (1929), 201.

to come through Judaism to Christ, but have their own immediate approach to him. It means further, as we have seen, that the Jews who refuse to believe in Jesus, have no prop in their possession of the law, but by their refusal reject the only possibility of being declared righteous by God. But the law did not come into the world at the same time as Jesus; how is it with the generations between the two? Unlike Paul's contemporaries, they were not faced with the question as to whether they believed in Christ; but of course they have 'believed', or rather the 'believers' amongst them have trusted God and looked for the coming of His kingship. In this 'faith' of theirs they have truly fulfilled the 'law'. As men of faith, even if, which could not be, they did not believe in the Christ who had come, they have nevertheless, so we may assume, been declared righteous like their father Abraham; did the God who justified them detach their faith from their fulfilling of the law, and heed only the former and not the latter also which was done in faith? Paul expressly says (Rom. ii. 12) that the doers of the law, its true doers in faith, were, as such, declared righteous. Or are we to understand by the futile 'works of the Law' merely a performance without faith? It is however quite obviously Paul's view that the law is not capable of being fulfilled; for he bases (Gal. iii. 10) his statement about the curse under which those are 'who are of the works of the Law' upon the alleged verse of Scripture that everyone is accursed who 'does not continue in all things which are written in the Book of the Law to do them' (the decisive word 'all things' is missing in the Masoretic Text, as stated), therefore the former are identical with the latter: nobody can in fact do everything which the law demands of him under the threat of the curse. The indivisible law which allows of no selection, the 'whole' law (Gal. v. 3), demands therefore according to Paul the impossible, without his differentiating between an external fulfilment which is possible and an impossible fulfilment in the complete intention of faith; evidently he already regards the outward fulfilment as impossible, without of course his indicating what makes it so.

Here not merely the Old Testament belief and the living faith of post-Biblical Judaism are opposed to Paul, but also the Jesus of the Sermon on the Mount, although from a different motif and with a different purpose.

* * *

The experience of suffering as innocently borne works at times in the history of faith both as a destructive factor and as an element of renewal. One can endure pain, but not the God Who sent it:

one rejects either Him or the image one has made of Him. The first case, indeterminate as it is, will not be discussed here; in the second the experience can be rectified by a greater proximity, i.e. a being drawn up, to the divine mystery, as the reality of the cloud is rectified by that of the lightning. The resulting change in the history of faith is then both stirring and constructive for succeeding generations if the experience of personal suffering was embedded in that of the suffering of a personally united community. Such was the situation with the Jewish nation from that historic moment in which its naïve trust in God was shaken. It was the time of Megiddo. At last the king, expected and proclaimed by the prophets, he who undertook to fulfil the divine commission conferred in the sacrament of anointing, sat upon the throne. In the certainty of empowerment from above, Josiah marched forth to fight against the Pharaoh for the reign of God which was about to begin, and was killed. How could this come about? In this way the new questioning of the justice of God arises, of the meaning of suffering, of the value of human effort on behalf of the right way, which surged up in the two centuries before the catastrophe, then in this itself, and then in the miseries of the Babylonian exile. Its effect has been preserved in the outcries of Jeremiah, the dialectical theologoumena of Ezekiel, the accusing speeches of 'Job', the Psalms of tormented souls and the songs of the suffering servant of God. All these records of a great spiritual process point beyond personal suffering to that of Israel. They concern the monstrous thing which has come to pass between God and Israel. So man penetrates step by step into the dark which hangs over the meaning of events, until the mystery is disclosed in the flash of light: the *zaddik*, the man justified by God, suffers for the sake of God and of His work of salvation, and God is with him in his suffering. This re-birth of trust in God has already lost its real vitality in the second kingdom, which attempted to restore it in an as it were institutional way. Centuries afterwards, during the period of suffering under the Syrians, the discovery had to be made anew. The legends of the readiness for martyrdom in the Book of Daniel, those of actual martyrdom in the Second Book of the Maccabees, above all the figure of the 'righteous one' (cf. Is. liii. 11) in the 'Wisdom of Solomon', which corresponds to that depicted by Deutero-Isaiah, the man who is called a son of God and is condemned to a disgraceful death, bear witness to this, of course in a later, derivative diction. Under the Hasmoneans the problem of suffering again recedes for a time. In the third, the Roman distress, it re-appears, but on a characteristically larger scale.

Three principal types of answer must be distinguished here.

The Hellenistic Judaism of common coinage, as we know it for instance from the statements of Josephus on his mode of thinking, an eclecticism from an attenuated Biblical tradition and a not less attenuated Stoic philosophy, is satisfied to associate God with a power of fate, which causes the suffering of the righteous. Josephus knows nothing more about the daring undertaking of Josiah and its result than to observe: 'Fate, I take for granted, drove him to it'. The philosophic Hellenism of Judaism, which strove to take seriously the contribution both of Israel and Greece and which could not take such an illusionary way, does not occupy itself with the problem; Philo does not go beyond the conception that God in the creation of the world made use of the 'powers' and that these hypostases also henceforth occupied a position between Him and men. Apocalyptics, which is influenced by Iranian dualism, and yet opposes it, approaches the problem differently. In its greatest product, the Ezra-Apocalypse, which was written at the time of the destruction of Jerusalem, but which was obviously constructed out of older ideas, there speaks the man who despairs of history, the son of an 'aged' world, who 'tries to understand the ways of the Most High'. He is acquainted with the doubtfulness of all human righteousness; Israel too is sinful and deserving of punishment. But why does God not show mercy to His chosen people, why must they suffer more than all others, why does He crush them and spare those who have trespassed more gravely? The answer is eschatological, but when all is said it is no answer, because at the End grace passes away and only judgment remains, at which nobody can any longer be a substitute for another, and 'the many who have come' must go into destruction, although God, Who loves His creation, has not desired it; from Israel too only a few (amongst them 'Ezra' himself) are saved. But the answer does not touch the fundamental question with which the questioning began. The speaker had reproached God (vii. 20 ff.) with not having influenced Israel in the hour of revelation to it, so they might receive it truly: 'But Thou didst not take the evil heart away from them, in order that Thine instruction might bring forth fruit in them.... A lasting sickness began: in the heart of the people both the instruction and the root of evil. The good disappeared and the evil remained'. But the root of evil, common to all men, grew out of 'the grain of evil seed' which 'at the beginning was sown in Adam's heart'. This question or rather complaint means that God (in that He did not take away the evil heart) preferred the freedom of man to the salvation of man, but behind it there stands the thought that He (in that He allowed the sowing to take place) put this freedom to too difficult a test. At this point 'Ezra' unmistakably goes beyond 'Job'.

He too obtains no explanation. But while for the latter the sound of the divine Voice, the actual fact of the presence and the interest of God gives a most real answer, one that is more than words, for the former, in spite of the weight and melancholy of the request, everything which happens to him from above by way of answer remains vain and without comfort.

It seems to me that Paul before his conversion had got into the circle of ideas which found its most mature expression in the Ezra-Apocalypse; in the intellectual elaboration of what happened to him on the road to Damascus, he obtained an answer to those questions, which he expressed in his epistles, particularly in the Epistle to the Romans, probably a decade or a little more before the composition of the Ezra-Apocalypse. That the influence of that circle of ideas upon him could become so strong and so fruitful is to be understood apparently by the way it worked together with the extremely personal and violent self-reflection of his last pre-Christian period, in a great tumult of soul, the memory of which has been preserved and worked up in the seventh chapter of the Epistle to the Romans (*vv.* 7–25). The view that the 'I' of these texts is a rhetorically constructed description of 'the situation of the Jew under the law' seems to me (from *v.* 24) to be unacceptable; and about his present condition as a Christian Paul could not speak in this way; yet there is this direct present tense! I can only account for it in that he uses the memory of his pre-Damascus personality in its deepest experience of itself as a pattern for an inner description of the natural man (*vv.* 7, 8b, 9a) and man under the law (*vv.* 8a, 9b, 10), so that 'I' means at the same time 'I Paul' and 'I Adam', and then 'I, a Jew of the law'. The path of the Jewish person from the natural man, as the Jew is understood to be up to the moment of the conscious taking upon himself of the 'yoke of the rule of God and the yoke of the commandments', to the man of the law is apprehended from the point of view of that former self-reflection which is moved into the powerfully illuminating light of the present existence of the Christian. As it directly comes home to his mind, the apostle cries: 'Wretched man that I am! Who will set me free from the body of this death!' and confesses at once from his present condition that he has been freed—the I which is involved in this 'Thanks be to God', which I cannot look upon as rhetorical, entirely proves to me the autobiographical background of that which precedes it. The most significant thing in the account from our point of view is the sentence: 'But I see another law in my members, which strives against the law of my reason, and takes me captive', in connexion with which it must be held fast that immediately before it Paul is speaking

about the law of God, to which he, precisely with his reason, joyfully consented. The law revealed to man by God and the 'law' set
in his members by God in creation are recognized as opposed to
one another. Here, unexpressed, but vibrating powerfully behind
the words, to that question concerning the compatibility of evil in
the sense of suffering with God's existence, is conjoined that about
the compatibility of evil in the moral sense with it; it has obviously
become the real stimulus to Paul's Gnostic view of the world. From
this point that conception of the primitive wrath of God as the
'potter' who makes and destroys vessels of wrath becomes clear to
us. Paul is not content, like the apocalyptic writers, to complain
that God has allowed it to happen, that a grain of evil seed was
implanted in man, from which guilt and punishment spring up; he
says that God, in creating man, inflicted him with a 'flesh', in
which 'nothing good dwells' (*v.* 18) and the consequence of which
is that each man does the evil which he does not will (*v.* 19). But
also in view of the revealed law of God, he, Paul, cannot tolerate
Ezra's complaint that God has not taken away the evil heart from
those who receive His revelation. For the law, which in itself is
'holy, just and good', is, he says, nevertheless so constituted that in
the unredeemed man, the non-Christian, through the commandment not to covet, arouses the desire (*v.* 7 f.), calls sin into existence and drives the soul to death (*v.* 9). Since God has given the
law precisely for such a purpose (*v.* 13) it could not be His will to
remove the evil heart from those who received it. The man who has
both, flesh and law, the still unsaved man in Israel, is 'sold under
sin' (*v.* 14). But both the creating of the flesh and the giving of
the law serve God's purpose of saving the world, like the enslave-
ment of man under the forces of fate does. Creation and revelation have taken place as they are for the sake of salvation; for
God's way to salvation leads through the 'abounding' (*v.* 20) of
human sin and through its propitiation. Paul does not pray, as Ezra
does again and again, for the mitigation of the judgment on
humanity; God's sense of justice inexorably demands the appropriate, i.e. measureless, punishment for the 'sin which is sinful beyond
measure (vii. 13). Only God Himself can effect the propitiation of
an infinite guilt, by making His Son, the Christ, take the atoning
suffering upon himself so that all who believe on Christ are saved
through him. In this way Paul laid the foundation for the doctrine,
which to be sure first arises after him and beyond his struggle, the
doctrine in which Christ is declared a Person of the Godhead: God
suffers as the Son in order to save the world, which He as the Father
created and prepared as one which needs salvation. The prophetic
idea of man who suffers for God's sake has here given way to that

of God Who suffers for the sake of man. By this the new image of God is erected, destined to give power and consolation to Christian people during a thousand years of development and a thousand years of their struggles. The problem of the meaning of unmerited suffering however is thrown back to the position of Job's friends: there is no unmerited suffering; the only difference is that now it is taught that every man is absolutely guilty and absolutely deserving of suffering, and yet, everyone can, by accepting the belief in the suffering of God, be redeemed through this suffering.

Over against this sublime religious conception, which in the fascination of its content has scarcely an equal, there stands in Pharisaic Judaism the plain effort to preserve the immediacy of the Israelite relationship to God in a changed world. For this it must guard against two ideas which had penetrated into Jewish Hellenism—the one into its popular form, the other into its philosophy as well as into its apocalyptics: the idea of a fate, which is not identical with the rule of God, and that of a mediator, different in nature from the occasional intervention of earthly and heavenly powers.

* * *

The periods of Christian history can be classified according to the degree in which they are dominated by Paulinism, by which we mean of course not just a system of thought, but a mode of seeing and being which dwells in the life itself. In this sense our era is a Pauline one to a particular degree. In the human life of our day, compared with earlier epochs, Christianity is receding, but the Pauline view and attitude is gaining the mastery in many circles outside that of Christianity. There is a Paulinism of the unredeemed, one, that is, from which the abode of grace is eliminated: like Paul man experiences the world as one given into the hands of inevitable forces, and only the manifest will to redemption from above, only Christ is missing. The Christian Paulinism of our time is a result of the same fundamental view, although it softens down or removes that aspect of the demonocracy of the world: it sees nevertheless existence divided into an unrestricted rule of wrath and a sphere of reconciliation, from which point indeed the claim for the establishment of a Christian order of life is raised clearly and energetically enough, but *de facto* the redeemed Christian soul stands over against an unredeemed world of men in lofty impotence. Neither this picture of the abyss spanned only by the halo of the saviour nor that of the same abyss covered now by nothing but impenetrable darkness is to be understood as brought about by changes in subjectivity: in order to paint them the retina of those now living must have been affected by an actual fact, by the situation now existing.

* * *

The strength of Pauline tendencies in present-day Christian theology is to be explained by the characteristic stamp of the time, just as that of earlier periods can explain that at one time the purely spiritual, the Johannine tendency was emphasized, and at another the so-called Petrine one, in which the somewhat undefined conception 'Peter' represents the unforgettable recollection of the conversations of Jesus with the disciples in Galilee. Those periods are Pauline in which the contradictions of human life, especially of man's social life, so mount up that they increasingly assume in man's consciousness of existence the character of a fate. Then the light of God appears to be darkened, and the redeemed Christian soul becomes aware, as the unredeemed soul of the Jew has continually done, of the still unredeemed concreteness of the world of men in all its horror. Then to be sure, as we know indeed from Paul too, the genuine Christian struggles for a juster order of his community, but he understands the impenetrable root of the contradiction in the view of the threatening clouds of wrath, and clings with Pauline tenacity to the abundant grace of the mediator. He indeed opposes the ever-approaching Marcionite danger, the severing not only of the Old and New Testaments, but that of creation and salvation, of Creator and Saviour, for he sees how near men are, as Kierkegaard says of the Gnosis, 'to identifying creation with the Fall', and he knows that a victory for Marcion can lead to the destruction of Christianity; but—this seems to me to be more strongly recognized again in Christendom to-day—Marcion is not to be overcome by Paul.

Even Kierkegaard, a century ago, gave expression to the fact that there is a non-Pauline outlook, that is, one superior to the stamp of the age, when he wrote in his Journal a prayer, in which he says: 'Father in heaven, it is indeed only the moment of silence in the inwardness of speaking with one another'. That to be sure is said from the point of view of personal existence ('When a man languishes in the desert, not hearing Thy voice there'), but in this respect we are not to distinguish between the situation of the person and that of man or mankind. Kierkegaard's prayer, in spite of his great belief in Christ, is not from Paul or from John, but from Jesus.

A superficial Christian, considering Kafka's problem, can easily get rid of him by treating him simply as the unredeemed Jew who does not reach after salvation. But only he who proceeds thus has now got rid of him; Kafka has remained untouched by this treatment. For the Jew, in so far as he is not detached from the origin, even the most exposed Jew like Kafka, is safe. All things happen to him, but they cannot affect him. He is not to be sure able any longer to conceal himself 'in the covert of Thy wings' (Ps. lxi. 4), for God is hiding Himself from the time in which he lives, and so from him, its most exposed son; but in the fact of God's being only hidden, which he knows, he is safe. 'Better the living dove on the roof than the half-dead, convulsively resisting sparrow in the hand.' He describes, from innermost awareness, the actual course of the world, he describes most exactly the rule of the foul devilry which fills the foreground; and on the edge of the description he scratches the sentence: 'Test yourself on humanity. It makes the doubter doubt, the man of belief believe'. His unexpressed, ever-present theme is the remoteness of the judge, the remoteness of the lord of the castle, the hiddenness, the eclipse, the darkness; and therefore he observes: 'He who believes can experience no miracle. During the day one does not see any stars'. This is the nature of the Jew's security in the dark, one which is essentially different from that of the Christian. It allows no rest, for as long as you live, you must live with the sparrow and not with the dove, who avoids your hand; but, being without illusion, it is consistent with the foreground course of the world, and so nothing can harm you. For from beyond, from the darkness of heaven the dark ray comes actively into the heart, without any appearance of immediacy. 'We were created to live in Paradise, Paradise was appointed to serve us. Our destiny has been changed; that this also happened with the appointment of Paradise is not said.' So gently and shyly anti-Paulinism speaks from the heart of this Pauline painter of the foreground-hell: Paradise is still there and it benefits us. It is there, and that means it is also here where the dark ray meets the tormented heart. Are the unredeemed in need of salvation? They suffer from the unredeemed state of the world. 'Every misery around us we too must suffer'—there it is again, the word from the shoot of Israel. The unredeemed soul refuses to give up the evidence of the unredeemed world from which it suffers, to exchange it for the soul's own salvation. It is able to refuse, for it is safe.

This is the appearance of Paulinism without Christ which at this time when God is most hidden has penetrated into Judaism, a Paulinism therefore opposed to Paul. The course of the world is depicted in more gloomy colours than ever before, and yet Emunah is proclaimed anew, with a still deepened 'in spite of all this', quite soft and shy, but unambiguous. Here, in the midst of the Pauline domain, it has taken the place of Pistis. In all its reserve, the late-born, wandering around in the darkened world, confesses in face of the suffering peoples of the world with those messengers of Deutero-Isaiah (Is. xlv. 15): 'Truly Thou art a God Who hides Himself, O God of Israel, Saviour!' So must Emunah change in a time of God's eclipse in order to persevere steadfast to God, without disowning reality. That He hides Himself does not diminish the immediacy; in the immediacy He remains the Saviour and the contradiction of existence becomes for us a theophany.

*   *   *

LEO BAECK

Paul's Romanticism (1938) †

Romanticism

If we classify types of piety in accordance with the manner in which they have historically become types of religion, then we encounter two forms above all: classical and romantic religiousness, classical and romantic religion. The distinction and opposition between these two types is exemplified especially by two phenomena of world history. One of these, to be sure, is connected with the other by its origin and hence remains determined by it within certain limits; and yet the significant dividing line separates them clearly. These two religions are Judaism and Christianity. In essential respects they confront each other as the classical religion and the romantic religion.

What is the meaning of romantic? Friedrich Schlegel has characterized the romantic book in these words: "It is one which treats sentimental material in a phantastic form." In almost exactly the same words one might also characterize romantic religion. Tense feelings supply its content, and it seeks its goals in the now mythical, now mystical visions of the imagination. Its world is the realm in which all rules are suspended; it is the world of the irregular, the extraordinary and the miraculous, that world which lies beyond all reality, the remote which transcends all things.

We can observe this disposition of the soul in relative historical proximity when we consider the German romantic of the last cen-

† From "Romantic Religion," tr. by Walter Kaufmann in *Judaism and Christianity* (Philadelphia, 1960): 189–93, 195–207, 210–17. The essay was printed in Germany in 1938 but immediately destroyed by the Gestapo. Leo Baeck (1873–1956) was a rabbi and a teacher at the famous *Lehranstalt für die Wissenschaft des Judentums* in Berlin. Imprisoned in 1943 in the concentration camp at Theresienstadt, he narrowly escaped liquidation. After the war he lived and taught in London and Cincinnati.

tury. For him, everything dissolves into feeling; everything becomes mere mood; everything becomes subjective; "thinking is only a dream of feeling." Feeling is considered valid as such; it represents the value of life which the enthusiastic disposition wants to affirm. The romantic becomes enraptured and ecstatic for the sake of ecstasy and rapture; this state becomes for him an end in itself and has its meaning within itself. His whole existence is transformed into longing—not into the longing for God, in which man, raising himself above the earth, overcomes his earthly solitude; nor into the powerful longing of the will which thirsts for deeds; but into that sweet wavelike longing which pours itself out into feelings and becomes intoxicated with itself. Suffering and grief, too, become a good to him, if only the soul is submerged in them. He revels in his agonies as much as in his raptures.

Thus something agitated and excited, something overheated or intoxicated easily enters the feelings—and not only the feelings, but the language, too. Every expression seeks to excel in this direction; voluptuousness becomes a much sought-after word. The feelings talk in terms of superlatives; everything has to be made ecstatic. Fervently, the romantic enjoys the highest delight and the deepest pain almost day after day; he enjoys the most enchanting and the most sublime; he enjoys his wounds and the streaming blood of his heart. Everything becomes for him an occasion of enraptured shuddering, even his faith, even his devotion. Thus Novalis praises his Christianity for being "truly the religion of voluptuousness."

These souls can always be so full of feeling because their abundant suffering is, for the most part, only reverie and dream; almost all of it is merely sentimental suffering. They like so much to dream; the dim distances, twilight and moonlit night, the quiet, flickering hours in which the magic flower lowers its blossoming head, represent the time for which they are wearily waiting. They love the soft, the sweet illusion, the beautiful semblance; and whereas Lessing had said to God, "Give me the wrestling for the truth," the romantics implore, "Accord me lovely illusions." They want to dream, not see; they shun the distinctness of what is clearly beheld in the light, to the very point of antipathy against fact. Disgruntled they confront reality; and in ·its stead they seek the less clear attraction of fluctuating feelings to the point of outright delight in confusion. What is within and without becomes for them a semblance and a glimmer, resounding and ringing, a mere mythical game; and the world becomes a sadly beautiful novel, an experience to be felt. As Hegel once put it: "The sense for content and substance contracts into a formless weaving of the spirit within itself."

The desire to yield to illusion, justifiable in art, here characterizes the entire relation to the world. In the deliberately sought-out
twilight of longing and dream, the border lines of poetry and life
are effaced. Reality becomes mere mood; and moods, eventually,
the only reality. Everything, thinking and poetry, knowledge and
illusion, all here and all above, flows together into a foaming poem,
into a sacred music, into a great transfiguration, an apotheosis. In
the end, the floods should close over the soul, while all and nothing
become one, as the grandson of the romantics celebrates it:

"In the sea-like rapture's billowy swell,
In the roaring waves of a drowsy smell,
In the world-breath's flowing all—
To drown—
To sink down—
Unconsciousness—
Highest bliss."

In this ecstatic abandonment, which wants so much to be seized
and embraced and would like to pass away in the roaring ocean of
the world, the distinctive character of romantic religion stands
revealed—the feminine trait that marks it. There is something passive about its piety; it feels so touchingly helpless and weary; it
wants to be seized and inspired from above, embraced by a flood of
grace which should descend upon it to consecrate it and possess
it—a will-less instrument of the wondrous ways of God. When
Schleiermacher defined religion as "the feeling of absolute dependence," he condensed this attitude into a formula.

Romanticism therefore lacks any strong ethical impulse, any will
to conquer life ethically. It has an antipathy against any practical
idea which might dominate life, demanding free, creative obedience
for its commandments and showing a clearly determined way to the
goals of action. Romanticism would like to "recover from purpose."
All law, all that legislates, all morality with its commandments is
repugnant to it; it would rather stay outside the sphere of good and
evil; the highest ideal may be anything at all, except the distinct
demands of ethical action. From all that urges and admonishes, the
romantic turns away. He wants to dream, enjoy, immerse himself,
instead of clearing his way by striving and wrestling. That which
has been and rises out of what is past occupies him far more than
what is to become and also more than what wants to become; for
the word of the future would always command. Experiences with
their many echoes and their billows stand higher in his estimation
than life with its tasks; for tasks always establish a bond with harsh
reality. And from this he is in flight. He does not want to struggle
against fate, but rather to receive it with an ardent and devout soul;

he does not want to wrestle for his blessing, but to experience it, abandoning himself, devoid of will, to what spells salvation and bliss. He wants no way of his own choosing. For the romantic the living deed is supplanted by the grace whose vessel he would be; the law of existence, by mere faith; reality, by the miracle of salvation. He wants to exist, without having an existence of his own; he wants less to live than to experience—or, to use the German, he prefers *erleben* to *leben*.

*   *   *

* * * Romanticism is not applicable merely to a particular epoch, to a mere period of history. Romanticism means much more: it designates one of the characteristic forms which have emerged again and again in the development of mankind—a certain type in which, from time immemorial, religious life in particular has manifested itself. To be sure, historical types, just like human types, never appear quite pure. Whatever exists is a mixture; nowhere does life know sharp boundaries and distinctions; it is never an equation without any remainder. There are certain romantic elements in every religion, no less than in every human soul. Every religion has its dream of faith in which appearance and reality seek to mingle; each has its own twilight valley; each knows of world-weariness and contempt for the factual. But in one religion this is merely a quiet path alongside the road, a sound which accompanies, a tone which also vibrates. In another religion it fixes the direction; it is the dominant basic chord which determines the religious melody and gives it its character. Thus, depending on whether this or a wholly different motif is the decisive one, the romantic religion distinguishes itself quite clearly from the classical. And in this sense it may be said: Judaism is the classical religion and Christianity, compared with it, the romantic religion.

Paul

Christianity accepted the inheritance of ancient—Greek and oriental—romanticism. At an early date, the traditional national religion in the Hellenic lands had been joined by a victorious intruder, probably from the north: another religion—darker, phantastic and sentimental—the Dionysian or Orphic cult of which much might be said, but certainly not: "What distinguished the Greeks? Reason and measure and clarity." It had all the traits of romanticism: the exuberance of emotion, the enthusiastic flight from reality, the longing for an experience. Holy consecrations and atonements were taught and ecstatically tasted with reeling senses. They aimed to relate man to the beyond; they aimed to make him one with the god and thus grant him redemption from primordial sin and original guilt. For this, it was said, could not be attained by mortal man with his own power, but must be a gift of grace which had to descend from hidden regions and to which a mediator and savior, a god, who once had walked on earth had shown the way. Marvelous traditions told of this and handed on the stories of the redeeming events and their mysteries, that they might be renewed again and again in the believers. Mystical music dramas, showy, phantastic presentations, seemingly removed into mysterious distances by the twilight, granted the weary, drowsy soul the beautiful dream, and the sentimental longing its fulfillment: the faith that it belonged to the elect.

In the official religion, this wish of the individual to be chosen and to stand before the god, this individual desire to be important and attain eternal life and bliss, had not found satisfaction. Now all this was offered to him by this enthusiastic religion of moods. And thus it was that this religion found its way more and more into the souls; it became the new religion which gradually decomposed the old naïve faith and the classical spirit of the Greeks, and eventually destroyed it.

Moreover, it had received further strength from all sides, wherever religious romanticism had a home: from the oriental and Egyptian mysteries, from the cults of Mithras and Adonis, of Attis and Serapis. In essentials they were all alike: they shared the sentimental attitude which seeks escape from life into living experience and turns the attention towards a phantastic and marvelous beyond. What they proclaimed, too, was at bottom always the same. It was the faith in a heavenly being that had become man, died, and been resurrected, and whose divine life a mortal could share through mysterious rites; the faith in a force of grace, entering the believer from above through a sacrament, to redeem him from the bonds of earthly guilt and earthly death and to awaken him to a new life which would mean eternal existence and blessedness. The roving yearning of a weary age was only too ready to become absorbed in these conceptions of resurrection and apotheosis, of instruments of grace and consecrations; and it even sought them out everywhere. From all lands the mysteries could flow together in mighty waves.

The tide moved along a free and wide course. The region from the Euphrates to the Atlantic Ocean had under Roman rule become the place of a matchless mixture of peoples fused into a cultural unity. Just like the ancient states, the old pagan religions, too, had more and more lost their boundaries and their former definiteness. A cosmopolitan yearning and hope gripped and united all of them. The way was prepared for a new faith without limits or boundaries. In the world-wide empire it could become the world religion and the world philosophy. Whatever it was that a human being might seek, it promised everything to everybody—mystery and knowledge, ecstasy and vision, living experience and eternity. It was everything and took the place of everything and therefore finally overcame everything. The great romantic tide thus swept over the Roman empire, and the ancient world drowned in it. Even as the old naïve poetry of the gods perished in the sentimental myth of the redeeming savior, so what was classical vanished, along with its sure sense of law and determination, and gave way to the mere feeling of a faith which was sufficient unto itself.

What is called the victory of Christianity was in reality this victory of romanticism. Before Christianity took its course, that through which it eventually became Christianity—or, to put it differently, whatever in it is non-Jewish—had already become powerful enough to be reckoned as a world faith, as a new piety which united the nations. The man with whose name this victory is connected, Paul, was, like all romantics, not so much a creator of ideas as a connector of ideas; the genius of seeing and establishing such connections was characteristic of him. He must be credited with one achievement—and this single achievement was of world-historical significance and truly something great—that he carried living Jewish ideas into the mysteries which even then commanded the allegiance of a whole world. He knew how to fuse the magic of the universal mysteries with the tradition of revelation of the secrecy-wrapt Jewish wisdom. Thus he gave the ancient romanticism a new and superior power—a power taken from Judaism. It was this blend, compounded by him, that the world of the dying Roman empire—Orient and Occident, which had become one world—accepted.

In Paul's own soul, this union in which romantic and Jewish elements were to be combined, had prevailed after a period of transition. Subjectively, this union represented the story of his struggles which became the story of his life. The images of his homeland, Asia Minor, had early revealed to him the one element, romanticism; the parental home and the years of his studies had presented him with the other, the Jewish one. Then, in the land of his people, he had found those who longingly awaited the helper and liberator of whom the prophets had spoken—some hoping that he might come, others waiting that he might return. Eventually he discovered himself among those who were thus waiting—those whose eyes were fixed on the image of their messiah, their Christ, who had died young and would return when his day came—an image similar in many of its features to that offered by his pagan homeland in its mysteries. The pagans in those days were aware of

Judaism; and Jews, too, paid attention to the thinking and seeking of paganism. Thus the promises and wisdom from here and there, from paganism and from Judaism, entered into his unrest and doubts which pulled him hither and thither, looking and listening far and wide, in his craving for the certainty of truth. He did not want merely to wait and hope; he wished it might be given him to have and to believe.

Finally he had perceived an answer. It was a victorious and liberating answer to his mind because it did not merely grant a coming, a promised, day, something yet to be, but a redemption which was fulfilled even then—as it were, a Now. This answer became for him the end which meant everything because it contained everything: both that of which the mysteries of the nations had told him and that which the proclamations of his own Jewish people had said to him. Alongside the one God before whom the gods of the pagans were to vanish, it now placed the one redeemer, the one savior before whom the saviors of the nations could sink out of sight: it placed the oneness of the savior alongside the oneness of God. Thus he experienced it: paganism, with its deepest aspirations and thoughts, was led to Judaism; and Judaism, with its revelation and truth, was bestowed on the pagans, too.

Now everything seemed to fall into place. What his Judaism had let him find in the circle of those waiting, in the proclamation of the messianic faith, as the fullment and goal of all prophecy, this faith in the final answer, in the final certainty, in him who had come and would come—all this he discovered now in the quest of the pagans; all this he perceived when he contemplated the myth which the marvelous mysteries everywhere presented to the world. And where confused strains out of the pagan world had spoken to him of the mysterious tidings of grace, in which a whole world had created for itself the satisfaction of its yearnings, his own people's faith in a messiah now permitted him to comprehend quite clearly all that had till then seemed so dark. Now he grasped it: not Attis or Adonis, not Mithras or Serapis was the name of the resurrected, the savior, who became man and had been god, but his name was Jesus Christ. And the significance of Jesus, who had become the Christ of his people, could not be that he had become king of the Jews, their king by the grace of God, their admonisher, comforter, and helper; but his life and his power signified the one, the greatest, thing, that he was the resurrected, miracle-working, redeeming God, he that had been from eternity. And for all who owned him, who had faith in him and possessed him in sacrament and mystery, the day that was promised had become today, had been fulfilled. In him Jew and pagan were the new man, the true Israel, the true present.

The last veil now seemed to Paul to have been taken from his eyes, and he saw the hitherto divided world unified. In the messianic certainty of Judaism he now recognized the goal toward which the seeking and erring of the pagans had, in the depths of truth, always aspired; and in that which the pagans had wanted but not known, he now grasped the content and the answer which was spoken, which was promised to Judaism. Judaism and paganism had now become one for him; the one world had arrived which comprehended everything, the one body and the one spirit of all life. That Jewish and pagan wisdom meant, at bottom, the same thing, was one of the ideas of the age. Now it seemed to have become the truth. Now the Jews need no longer merely wait, as the community of the expectant, for the last day, which would then in turn become the first day, when the messiah would come or come again; in a mysterious sacrament, the fulfilled time in which everything has been accomplished, the goal of the longed-for redemption, was given to them even now, given in every hour. And now the pagans really could come to know him for whom they had from time immemorial looked, the named but unknown; and now they could comprehend the mystery which had since ancient times been present among them as their precious possession. Judaism and paganism were now reconciled, brought together in romanticism, in the world of the mystery, of myth, and of sacrament.

Precisely how this net of ideas took shape in the mind of Paul, how the different threads found each other and crossed each other, which idea came first and which one it then attracted—to ask about this would merely lead to vain and useless speculation. Beginning with his childhood, Paul had been confronted both with the possession of Judaism in the parental home and with the sight of the mystery cults in his homeland. In his consciousness both had their place, and they were woven together and became one. This union which was fashioned in him then emerged out of him into the world. And it became victorious in a world which had become weary and sentimental; it became the religion for all those whose faint, anxious minds had darted hither and thither to seek strength. It represented the completion of a long development.

For what had been most essential in the ancient mysteries is preserved in this Pauline religion. It, too, believed in the romantic fate of a god which reflects the inexorable lot of man and is the content of all life. What everything represents is not a creation of God and not an eternal moral order, but a process of salvation. In a heavenly-earthly drama, in the miraculous mystery that took shape between the here and the above, the meaning of world history and of the individual human life stands revealed. There is no other word but the definite word "myth," romantic myth, to characterize this form of faith. With this, Paul left Judaism; for there was no place in it for any myth that would be more than a parable—no more for the new sentimental one than for the old naïve myths of former times. This myth was the bridge on which Paul went over to romanticism. To be sure, this man had lived within Judaism deep down in his soul; and psychically he never quite got away from it. Even after his conversion to mystery and sacrament, he only too often found himself again on the old Jewish ways of thought, as though unconsciously and involuntarily; and the manifold contradictions between his sentences derive from this above all. The Jew that he remained in spite of everything, at the bottom of his soul, again and again fought with the romantic in him, whose moods and ideas were ever present to him. But in spite of this, if we are to label him as he stands before us, the apostle of a new outlook, then we can only call him a romantic. Trait for trait we recognize in his psychic type the features that distinguish the romantic.

The Experience of Faith

Paul, too, sees everything—to use Schlegel's term—in the "phantastic form" in which the border lines of appearance and reality, of twilight and event, are lost; in which he sees images which the eye never saw and hears words which the ear never perceived; in which he can feel redeemed from this world and its harshness, from what is earthly in him and from what desires to cling to the soil of this earth. Thus he lives in the beyond which transcends all things, beyond the struggle between upward drive and gravity, beyond becoming and perishing, where only faith can reach and only miracles can take place. Therefore faith is everything to him. Faith is grace, faith is salvation, faith is life, faith is truth; faith is being, the ground and the goal, the beginning and the end; commencement and vocation meet in it. Faith is valid for faith's sake. One feels reminded of the modern slogan, *l'art pour l'art*; Pauline romanticism might be labeled correspondingly, *la foi pour la foi*.

This faith is so completely everything that down here nothing can be done for it and nothing may be done for it; all "willing or running" is nonsensical and useless. The salvation that comes through faith is in no sense earned, but wholly received; and it comes only to those for whom it was destined from the beginning. God effects it, as Luther later explained the words of Paul, "in us and without us."[1] Man is no more than the mere object of God's activity, of grace or of damnation; he does not recognize God, God merely recognizes him; he *becomes* a child of redemption or of destruc-

---

1. *in nobis et sine nobis.* Weimar edition, VI, 530 (*de capt. Babyl.*).

tion, "forced into disobedience" or raised up to salvation. He is the object of virtue and of sin—not its producer, its subject. One feels like saying: man does not live but is lived, and what remains to him is merely, to speak with Schleiermacher, "the taste of infinity," that is, the living experience; the mood and the emotional relation of one who knows himself to be wholly an object; the feeling of faith in which grace is present or the feeling of unbelief in which sin prevails.

The theory of original sin and election, which Paul formulated after the manner of the ancient mystery doctrine and then shrouded in a biblical-talmudic dress, serves only to demonstrate the completeness of that power which makes passivity—or, to say it again in the words of German romanticism, pure "helplessness" and "absolute dependence"—the lot of man. A supernatural destiny which, whether it be grace or damnation, is always a *fatum*, determines according to an inexorable law that a man should be thus or thus. He is pure object; fate alone is subject. In this way, religion becomes redemption from the will, liberation from the deed.

Later on, the Catholicism of the Middle Ages softened this conception and granted a certain amount of human participation. But Luther then returned to the purer romanticism of Paul with its motto, *sola fide*, through faith alone; "it must come from heaven and solely through grace."[2] The image which he supplies to illustrate this point is, quite in keeping with Luther's style, harsh in tone, and yet thoroughly Pauline in its meaning: *velut paralyticum*, "as one paralyzed,"[3] man should wait for salvation and faith. The heteronomy of life is thus formulated: the life of man has its law and its content only outside itself.

This faith is therefore decidedly not the expression of a conviction obtained through struggle, or of a certainty grown out of search and inquiry. Seeking and inquiring is only "wisdom of the flesh" and the manner of "philosophers and rabbis." True knowledge is not worked out by man but worked in him; man cannot clear a way toward it; only the flood of grace brings it to him and gives him the quintessence of knowledge, the totality of insight. Knowledge here is not what instructs but what redeems, and it is not gained by thinking but given in faith; it goes with the consciousness of absolute dependence. "Do not seek, for to him who has faith all is given!" This is the new principle, the axiom of romantic truth; and all wrestling and striving for knowledge has thus lost its value and, what is more, its very meaning. There is no longer any place for the approximation of truth, step for step; there is no longer any middle ground between those who see everything

---

2. Weimar edition, XXIV, 244.
3. *Ibid.*, II, 420: *oportet ergo homi-nem de suis operibus diffidere et velut paralyticum remissis manibus et pedibus gratiam operum artificem implorare.*

and those who see nothing. Grace now gives complete light where up to now only darkness held the spirit in its embrace. Grace places man at the goal, and he is the perfect, the finished man.

The conception of the finished man which appears here—truly the brain child of romanticism for which truth is only a living experience—became one of the most effective ideas in the entire Pauline doctrine. It has again and again attracted and even permanently captivated those minds who would like so much to believe in their entire possession of the truth and who long for the rest which such complete possession would afford. Since the end of the ancient world, the intellectual life of the Occident has in many ways been determined by this notion. It has established that orientation in which the answer precedes every question, and every result comes before the task, and those appear who quite simply have what is wanted and who never want to become and grow.

The philosophy appropriate to this conception of the finished man is that doctrine which considers truth as given from the outset, that scholasticism which possesses and knows the whole truth, down to its ultimate ramifications, from the start and merely needs to proclaim it or to demonstrate it *ex post facto*. Most of the thought produced by the Catholic Middle Ages shows the influence of this conception. And Luther's world of thought is completely dominated by it; for Luther clings to the rigid faith in such possession and, in that sense, to the Middle Ages.

Only the age of the Enlightenment began to push the conception back, but it really made a beginning only. For when romanticism re-awakened in the last century, the conception returned with it, and it has survived together with romanticism. It has, indeed, created what might be called racial scholasticism, with its doctrine of salvation, with its system of grace, and with its faith that this grace works through the dark abysses of the blood—this modernized *pneuma*—and gives the chosen everything, so that the finished man is once again the goal of the creation. Wherever romanticism is found, this conception appears by its side.

The much quoted *credo quia absurdum*—"I believe because it is absurd"—is nothing but the ultimate formulation which results from this conception, almost as a matter of course. What confronts the inquiring spirit and his thinking as something opposed to reason, and unacceptable, may be the truth for the finished mind of the completed man, whether he owes his completion to grace or another source. To this faith knowledge must submit. Sooner or later, every romanticism demands the *sacrificium intellectus*, the sacrifice of the intellect. Here, too, the best commentary for Paul is found in Luther's words: "In all who have faith in Christ," he says, "reason shall be killed; else faith does not govern them; for reason fights against faith."[4]

Unquestionably, the romantic certainty which Paul proclaims is derived from an original psychic experience. * * *

For the romantic, the impression, the mood, that which comes over the human being, is everything. This determines his artistic bent, too. In the Pauline, as in any romantic religion we can clearly observe it. The component of faith and revelation, of transport and ecstasy—that which is, as it were, a psychic reception of religion, a religious consecration or even seizure—is here taken for the fulfillment of religion, for ultimate truth and perfection. No religion will want to do without openness to the profound, the hidden, the secret, the miracle of revelation, the experience of faith; this is the mystery of religion, that in it which gives birth. But for all it suggests and proclaims and bestows—and often this function could be found nowhere else—it still is not all of religion or even all of religiosity, any more than it is all there is to prayer, any more than mood as such supplies content, any more than birth is equivalent to life. The romantically pious, however, finds this sufficient and considers it everything. For he is a man of lofty sentiment who is capable of feeling and knows how to pray, but often does not get beyond feeling and prayer; the type which so easily remains on the threshold to receive everything there. His whole religion is merely a receiving; and therefore he finds it always so easy to think that he has finished his task. His faith remains purely passive; it is not faith in the challenging, commanding law of God, but merely in the gift of divine grace. Activity fights for everything; passivity has everything. There demands are made; here everything is given; even the love of man which is glorified in romantic religion is merely the gift of grace which is the share of those who have faith. The only activity of the genuine romantic is self-congratulation on his state of grace.

One might characterize the Pauline religion in sharp juxtapositions: absolute dependence as opposed to the commandment, the task, of achieving freedom; leaning as opposed to self-affirmation and self-development; quietism as opposed to dynamism. There the human being is the subject; here, in romantic religion, the object. The freedom of which it likes so much to speak is merely a freedom received as a gift, the granting of salvation as a fact, not a goal to be fought for. It is the faith that does not go beyond itself, that is not the task of life; only a "thou hast" and not a "thou shalt." In classical religion, man is to become free through the commandment; in romantic religion he has become free through grace.

4. Erlangen edition, 44, 156 f.

346 · Leo Baeck

Culture and History

It is therefore no accident that peoples with a live sense of independence have turned, consciously and unconsciously, toward the paths of classical religion—increasingly so as their sense of independence grew in strength. The history of Calvinistic, Baptist piety with it affinity to the Old Testament, its "legalistic" orientation, and its ethical stress on proving oneself, shows this clearly. And it was the same story wherever the social conscience stirred; it, too, had to effect this reversion, for it, too, runs counter to romantic religion. The social conscience finds romantic religion repugnant because it is at bottom a religious egoism; all passivity is a kind of selfishness, a desire for enjoyment; in it the individual knows only himself and what God or life is to bring him, but not the commandment, not the mutual demands of men.

In the religious activity demanded by classical religion, man finds himself directed toward others; in mere religious experience, in this devotion devoid of any commandment, he seeks everything in himself. He is concerned only with himself, satisfied with himself, concentrated on himself to the point of religious vanity, of a coquettishness of faith. Thus Nietzsche, in his superlative manner, once described this type: "He is terribly preoccupied with himself; he has no time to think of others." Nothing could be more opposed to the aspirations of a social conscience than this romantic piety which always seeks only itself and its salvation.

Romantic religion is completely opposed to the whole sphere of existence with which the social conscience is concerned. Every romanticism depreciates the life devoted to work and culture, that context of life which the active human being creates for himself and in which he knows himself in relation to others. Where life disintegrates into momentary moods, as in romanticism, and where living experience alone—the instant, in other words—is recognized as essential, while everything else appears merely as "the void between the instants," work will always be counted only as something lowly, or at least as something subordinate. Mere living experience, the instant, is the contradiction of work. Hence romanticism cannot gain any clear and positive relation to work. It is not a mere poetic whim but representative of the very flesh and blood of romanticism when Friedrich Schlegel sings the praise of leisure, of romantic sloth, and "sleep is the highest degree of genius" for him. All this is nothing else than that passivity of romanticism which would rather dream than work.

This defect has become most calamitous for romantic *religion*. As soon as it entered an area of cultural activity and was to be *inside* it and not just alongside, it had to find itself divided against itself: work was depreciated and yet had to be demanded. The history of medieval Catholic ethics with all its dualism, with its distinction between earthly and heavenly vocation, with the "commandments" and "counsels" it offered, manifests this contradiction. Nor was Luther able to overcome it. To be sure, he raised the estimation of worldly work. But to begin with, he got to this point only by the way of negation, through his opposition to an idle monkhood. And as soon as he looked for a positive appreciation of work, he was unable, here, too, to get beyond the Pauline conception of absolute dependence. For him the earthly sphere of existence and work, in which man is placed after all, is a decree from above, to which man must resign himself in humility and obedience; caste and guild represent a firm barrier which must not be tampered with, because it has been erected by God. For any upward social drive Luther lacked any sense or sympathy whatever: the conception of a God-given dependency and of the subordination of social classes as a divine institution is thoroughly Lutheran. Only Calvinism—in this respect, too, returning closer to Judaism—began to recognize more clearly that there is a liberating, ethical power in worldly work and that the rights and aims of civilian occupations manifest an upward drive.

Hence romantic religion also lacks any inner compulsion to approach political and economic life in order to make it more ethical and to drive it forward. Its indifference toward any earthly upward tendency has always made it easy for romantic religion to defend submission to every earthly yoke, even to preach it. From the Pauline exhortation, "Let every soul be subject unto the higher powers," one has always and with the greatest of ease got to the point of first tolerating every despotism and of then soon consecrating it. This Pauline doctrine, too, was taken especially seriously by Luther and those who followed him. Consider the silent coldness with which the Protestant Church of Germany endured, for example, serfdom and traffic in human beings.

* * *

Many phenomena which seem to refute these assertions are merely the exceptions which confirm the rule; for they have grown on the Old Testament soil of Calvinism and Baptism. From there, too, came the Protestant social movement. The genuinely romantic Pauline faith with its heteronomy of life, with the passivity on which it is founded, can confront a culture only as an outsider without any real access to it—particularly a culture with a live social consciousness, one which finds inspiration and strength in the commandment which bids man not to stop short of cultural realization. This faith cannot as a matter of principle do justice to the tasks which the social conscience imposes on man; it can do so only *ex post facto*.

Nor are these considerations contradicted by the concept of Christian culture which has dominated so many centuries. This concept was a necessary result: for syncretism, the desire to fuse everything, is characteristic of romanticism. Romanticism wants to mean all things and hence seeks to blend all the areas of human and superhuman existence, to pull them together into a universal circle, a universal state, a universal art, a universal faith; hence, being unable to confront culture with religious tasks and goals, it always wanted to, and had to, merge faith and culture, or mistake one for the other. But quite apart from the harm done to the religious element, culture has thus always lost something of its individuality. Bereft of the commandment of freedom and of its own demanding worth, restricted within a faith which was to mean and determine everything, culture could often preserve very little of itself. Even as the relation of romantic religion to science became one in which the latter had to make the sacrifice of intellect, so the romantic union with culture gave rise to a situation in which the very task of culture, its right of development, its right to seek new possibilities, was taken away from it. In Christian culture, culture was deprived of much that belonged to it; and what prevailed under this name during the Middle Ages was—however great and wonderful—essentially an admittedly imposing ecclesiastical homogeneity, an unlimited expansion of the internal and external spheres of ecclesiastical power. All life was within the Church and its bright splendor; and only what could live there lived at all.

Only the modern age—that age which first began with the Renaissance, waned, and then re-awakened in the century of the Enlightenment—has once again restored to culture, at least in many countries, the rights which are properly its own. To be sure, it has often been claimed, even by Ranke, that the Reformation had brought this freedom about. But later, more exact research has shown this claim to be erroneous. However important Luther's work was, insofar as he destroyed the sole rule of the one universal Church over Europe, in his own thinking he still belonged clearly to the Middle Ages. He still belonged to that age, not so much because of his scholastic theology, but above all because he shared the aspiration to dominate and shape culture ecclesiastically. The culture of the Reformation, too, was nothing other than the medieval Christian one, the extensive culture of constraint; it had a smaller sphere, both in space and in content, but the same ambition. Later, when culture faced a clear and open road again, it became worldly and hence also un-Protestant, both in its genesis and its character. It was able to prevail only by fighting the Church, the Protestant Church just as much as the Catholic. It was derived not from Luther and his work but from the men and tendencies against which Luther had contended most violently. Only when the culture which he had taught began becoming a thing of the past, could the new age commence.

* * *

HANS JOACHIM SCHOEPS

Paul's Misunderstanding of the Law (1959) †

* * *

1. Christ, The End of the Law

Paul deduces from his faith that the Messiah has come in the person of Jesus the conclusion: "Christ is the end of the law" (Rom. 10: 4). The validity of the law as a divine way of salvation has finished since the resurrection of Jesus from the dead, which proves both his Messianic status and the inbreak of the last age. For "the law is binding on a person only during his life" (Rom. 7: 1). And to anyone with a knowledge of the law, this fact implies, if he is of Jewish origin, the rabbinic interpretation: "As soon as a man is dead, he is free from the obligation of the commands" (Sabb. 30a; 151b; Nidda 61b; Pes. Rabb. 51b; Jer. Kilaim IX, 3). In fact, we have here a current Jewish notion which goes back to Ps. 88:5 * * * and which had been expounded by Rabbi Simon ben Gamaliel (Sabb. 151b), who—unless a later Tannaite was meant—was certainly known to Paul as the son of his personal teacher.

The inference which Paul draws from this principle is that the man who is dead to this aeon has become free from the law (Rom. 7: 6) * * * and that in the world of the future which has already begun with the resurrection of Jesus the validity of the law has ceased. From the standpoint of rabbinic thought this inference is obvious and is already drawn by the Amora of the 4th generation, R. Joseph bar Hiyya. * * * Philo also (*Vita Adam* I, 13; also *Vita Mosis* III, 22)[1] and likewise apocalyptic writings imply the cessation of the law in the Messianic kingdom. A specially widespread opinion in rabbinic literature is that in the Messianic era the old Torah

---

† From Chapter 5 of *Paul, The Theology of the Apostle in the Light of Jewish Religious History*, tr. by Harold Knight (Philadelphia, 1961). Schoeps (b. 1909) is professor of Religion and Philosophy in Erlangen.

1. These references are apparently erroneous. Philo wrote no *Vita Adam*, and *Mos*. III. 22 (= II. 186 in modern editions) is only remotely connected with the point Schoeps is making. [*Editor*]

will cease together with the evil impulse, but that God will give a new Torah through the Messiah. Later texts too in this matter no doubt contain old traditions. And this new law not only plays a part in Matthew (5: 17–20)—it has also its place in Pauline thought, for the *nomos Christou* [law of Christ] of love (Gal. 6: 2) or the *nomos pisteōs* [law of faith] (Rom. 3: 27) in fact mean nothing else. Wherever in the early catholic period there were attempts to formulate this *nova lex Christi*, the phrases of Paul were used.

Paul's teaching about the abolition of the law is, however, falsely understood if its "Halakha" basis is ignored. To this E. Benamozegh first drew attention. My judgment is that Rom. 10: 4 is an absolutely exact inference from the standpoint of Jewish theological thought; but the rabbis did not share Paul's premiss that the Messianic age had begun with the death and resurrection of Jesus.

Moreover, pseudo-Messianic movements in later Jewish history made exactly the same "Halakha" presumption. It is reported of the followers of Sabbatai and the Frankists that believing the last age to have dawned with the coming of their Messiah, they declared the Mosaic law annulled. It is very instructive that sixteen centuries later the same circle of thought was traversed when it was attempted to explain the disaster which overtook the pseudo-Messiah, Sabbatai Sebi—this time not subjection to the cross, but apostasy—as an event necessary to salvation. In both cases it is a question of pure aeon-theology. The Messianists do not turn against the law but reject simply the further validity of the law. We have here a purely Jewish problem of saving history, not a Hellenistic one—it is something indeed quite incomprehensible to the Greeks.

Of course Paul added further pregnant reflections, retrospective considerations as to the purpose of the law and its whole meaning. Here too we can recognize common rabbinic presuppositions, although their amplification discloses the original thought of the apostle; his own personal argument with, and self-justification in face of, the law. If Paul's teaching about the law sounds so surprisingly new and non-Jewish, here again it is none the less a question of Jewish faith-ideas which have been differently and unjudaically combined and presented. As we already know, the perspective of this Jew who believed the Messiah to have come was quite different from that of his rabbinic contemporaries. And this is very largely true of Paul's teaching about the meaning and purpose of the law, as he developed it in a survey of the pre-Messianic time.

* * * There is no doubt that Judaism of the time is convinced of the general sinfulness of mankind; as also of the fact that what sinfulness is can be measured by the law and that through the law we can come to the knowledge of sin (Rom. 3: 20; 7: 7, etc.). Also

the method of putting together texts which speak of sinfulness—in Rom. 3: 9–20 Paul quotes five verses from the Psalter and one from Isaiah—is in accordance with Haggada usage. Likewise apocalypses about the evils of the latter days were frequent, especially immediately after 70; and Paul too in 2 Thess. 2: 3–12 gives such a one.

But the Pauline inference that the law, which could not prevent universal sinfulness, and on the basis of which no man could be justified by his works, is a law unto death (Rom. 8: 2–3; Gal. 3: 21) is one which no Jew could draw. He insists rather on the text: "For it is no trifle for you, but it is your life" (Deut. 32: 47). And Rabbi Aqiba added to the verse the comment so contrary to Paul: "When is it your life? When you concern yourselves about it" (Gen. R. Par. 1 on 1: 1). Or still more plainly in exposition of Lev. 18: 5 Rabbi Acha says likewise in the name of Rabbi Aqiba: "The commands were given only that man should live through them, not that man should die through them" (Tos. Sabb. 15, 17 par.). To the one who performs it the Torah is *sam hayyim* (a medicine of life); to the one who does it not, it is a *sam muth* (a poison), says Rabbi Joshua ben Levi: Yoma 72b. Paul can prove the opposite inference not from the law itself, but only from faith in Jesus Christ, the Messiah who has come. The retrospective way of thought is the real axis of his argument. Not the meaning of scripture, but Christ is the *a priori* for his judgment of the law. The fact that what is to be proved is assumed by him, springs simply from his interpretation of the post-messianic situation. From the latter there stems the retrospective judgment that law must have been *paidagōgos hēmōn eis Christon* [our custodian until Christ] (Gal. 3: 24).

2. The "Curse" of the Law

* * *

As regards the question of the law, the most interesting point lies in ch. 7, which on account of a certain anthropocentric tendency has often been regarded as autobiographical. W. G. Kümmel in particular has shown the baselessness of psychological interpretations. Ch. 7 is not autobiographical, nor even rhetorical, but is to be understood symbolically as a description of the life of all Jews, including that of Saul, just as ch. 8 describes symbolically the life of all Christians, including that of Paul—*en pneumati* [in spirit]. Hence ch. 7, as Kümmel, Bultmann, Bornkamm, Dahl, and others have pointed out, represents in the first-person form a phenomenological account of Adamic man under the law, judged from the standpoint of Christian experience. Ambrosiaster called the "I" of Rom. 7 *a causa generalis*. Beyond this the chapter is intended to describe the crisis of the legalistic attitude as experienced subjectively by Paul. Thus here the abrogation of the law is developed not from an eschatological basis but from the experience of sin. In his argument Paul goes far beyond the preaching of Jesus and the synoptic tradition, but has many rabbinic parallels.

We have already had occasion to emphasize the close connexion between the law and sin. But Paul's opinion is not only that the law incites to sin and renders guilty, thus increasing sins; he also sees the relation conversely, and shows that sin, awakened by the law (7: 8) proves the law's "unfulfillability". This not only cut the ground from beneath Jewish legal righteousness but also just as much from beneath the systems of ancient philosophy which embodied the principle that the good can be taught. The meaning of Rom. 7 is as follows: spirit and flesh, will and ability, the law of God and the law of sin, are locked in an unceasing conflict in the heart of man. The struggle, which Paul depicts in semi-mythological terms, is carried on with unequal resources, because the law of God brings into operation only man's will, whereas actual conduct is determined by the law of sin, i.e., by the fleshly nature of man (7: 14–23). This description, behind which lies a conception of sin as a daemonic power which, as it were, has taken control of man, must be regarded as a striking contribution to the rabbinic doctrine of the struggle of the *yeser hara* with the *yeser tov* [impulses to evil and good], which obviously was a favorite theme of discussion in the age of Paul.

The usual rabbinic teaching insists on an equipoise of both impulses and claims that it lies in man's free will to decide which of the two he will follow. With Rabbi Aqiba most teachers expound the idea of the absolute freedom of the human will (Aboth 3: 15) and teach that by the practice of the law man can free himself from sin (e.g., Qiddushin 81a). Man's inherent tendency to sin, which was implanted in him at birth with the *yeser hara*, is compensated by the Torah, which was adapted to the whole will and nature of man. There are, however, pessimistic opinions which register a predominance of the evil impulse. Thus in the Tannaite R. Eliezer ben Hyrcanus, who lived at the close of the 1st century, hence not much later than Paul, we have a rabbinic exponent of the Pauline doctrine of the general sinfulness of mankind. In Sanh. 101a it is reported that Rabbi Eliezer emphasized to his pupils his favourite text, which was always on his lips, Eccl. 7: 20: "Surely there is not a righteous man on earth who does good and never sins." In Arakhin 17a he expressly declares that even the patriarchs would not have been able to stand before strict justice, which, moreover, Justin also (*Dial.* 95) gives as a

Jewish opinion. And from a somewhat obscure report about a "minim" controversy in which Rabbi Eliezer was involved may be recognized his opinion which as *divre shel minut* was perhaps taken from Jesus, to the effect that its sinful origin adheres to the object and what springs from the unclean never loses its uncleanness (cf. Tos. Hullin, 2: 24; Aboda Zara 17a varied in Midr. Eccl. 10: 8).

Other voices are raised which go farther and understand the *yeser hara* as an independently effective cosmic power, not merely as an impulse to evil but as an evil impulse conceived on almost daemonological lines, almost as an alien god dwelling in the body of man. Quite in Paul's style, the picture is drawn of man lusting for what the law forbids (Jer. Yoma 6: 4) and the lustfulness is daily renewed and daily nourished (Sukka 52a). If the evil impulse was initially only a guest in the habitation of a human life, later it gains mastery as the * * * master of the house (Gen. Rabba Par. 22 on 4: 7). From this it is only a step to regarding the evil impulse as innate. In this connexion we adduce that the Midrash Rabba Par. 34: 10 on Gen. 8: 21 * * * ("from his youth") explains with regard to the origin of the evil impulse: "as soon as man leaves his mother's womb". The Rabbi says even that the *yeser hara* arises before birth in man. Further, it is stressed that the good impulse is only born in man after the evil has gained control (M. Teh. 9: 2); the latter is in man as soon as he is taken from the womb (*ibid.*), the former is added only when he attains the age of thirteen years (M. Eccl. 9: 14–15; similarly 4: 14). This implies that the *yeser hara* is more powerful than the *yeser ha-tob*, that it will always conquer all good impulses in any critical situation. Such meditations come very near to Pauline ideas.

The position is similar with regard to apocalyptic writings such as IV Ezra, the testimony of which is important for the New Testament period and often as typical as the expressions of rabbinic literature. In their judgment on the corruption of mankind, including the Jews, the apocalyptists often go quite as far as Paul in that they note man's inability to keep the law "on account of the law of sin in his members".

* * *

All these voices which always express the same truth, often very movingly—prayer texts coming at least from the 2nd century (cf. Yoma 87b) should be added—allow it to be clearly enough recognized that Paul's doctrine of sin was not unusual but indeed typical of his time. This is confirmed likewise by the Qumran literature, in particular the psalms. More problematic are only the special turns which Paul has given to this doctrine of sin, and the consequences drawn from it.

Thus the peculiarity of Paul's idea of sin has often been seen in the identification of [flesh] (as contrasted with [spirit]) with [sin], and in this regard he falls decisively outside the framework of rabbinic thought. But this opinion cannot be accepted without further question. According to a doctrine of Rabbi Ishmael, the body of man springs from a place that is sinful (Lev. Rabba Par. 4 chapter 4, 1). Or take the explanation of the Midrash Num. Rabba Par. 13 chapter 7, 12 on Gen. 8:21: "Woe to the dough of which the baker himself says that it is bad" (Doubl. Pes. R. Kah. IX, 157 ff.; R. Hiyya in Midr. Teh. 103:14; Gen. Rabba Par. 34, 8:21). And the opinion of Rabbi Alexandrai (Am. 2nd gen.) given in Berakhoth 17a is concerned with nothing else than the conflict between the will and the power to perform which is occasioned by the sinful flesh: "Lord of the worlds, it is open and known to Thee that it is our will to do Thy will, and that we are prevented from doing so by nothing other than the leaven in the dough" (i.e., the evil impulse in man's body). It is, however, typical of Jewish piety that Rabbi Alexandrai continues: "May it be Thy pleasure that we return to fulfil the commands of Thy will with all our hearts." Paul, on the other hand, is concerned to abide by the conflcit he has observed and to understand it not as an exception but as the rule and norm (Rom 7:21: * * *) in order to show conclusively the powerlessness of the law. For any other solution apart from faith in Jesus Christ he excludes from the start.

Here in fact we come upon a real opposition, because the Pauline doctrine must be deemed erroneous from the standpoint of Biblical theology. Judaism has always held fast to the tenet that man was created to do the will of God, as it is presented in the Torah (Rabbi Jochanan b. Zakkai in Pirqe Aboth 2,9). The right fulfilment of the law, of course, always implies the creaturely situation of the fear of God * * * which the doing of the law ever renews. But Paul does not seem to know this idea of the fear of God; the terms theosebia and eusebia, which are but a pale Greek equivalent, are completely lacking in Paul. Without reference to such ideas Paul has simply understood the law as a sum of prescriptions and has played off the fact of sin as offence against the commands. But the power of sin was never able to dissipate the faith of the Jewish teachers in the "fulfillability" of the law. Paul, however, arrived at the fundamental conviction that man is basically incapable of doing the will of God. We see here a singular maiming of the will—even of the will to recognition—in the apostle, who apparently does not know the power which resides in tshuvah [repentance] which according to Jewish belief of all ages is able to break the mastery of sin. That the somewhat analogous idea of metanoia in Greek plays hardly any part in the thought of the apostle has often struck New Testament critics. Unlike Jesus and the prophets, Paul did not summon to repentance; he set little value on man's freedom of decision and discounted the fact that he is able to turn again to God. The reason for this is simply that *metanoia* by its relation to the death and resurrection of Jesus was wholly subsumed in *pistis* [faith]. The advent of the Messiah signified the great revolution of all things; faith in Him made the conversion of the individual soul unnecessary.

* * *

5. Faith and Works

Paul's struggle against the Jewish law was the necessary consequence of his presuppositions. The dualism which so strongly characterizes Pauline thought: flesh-spirit, sin-righteousness, etc., is now well known to us from Qumran writings too. But Pauline dualism is eschatological in structure, and in the last analysis is based on his fundamental dualistic position: the aeon of the law—the aeon of Christ.

It was for this reason that Paul had to do battle with the law regarded as a principle of salvation. For in the interim period between the resurrection and the parousia in which Paul believed himself to be living and teaching, the old authority of the law could not subsist alongside the new authority of the Messiah who had come in the flesh. Otherwise Christ would have died in vain (Gal. 2:21). His conflict with the Jewish-Christian thesis that the death of Christ, while admittedly an atonement for the sin and guilt incurred by transgressions of the law, upheld in fact the ancient status of the law, was carried out not from the standpoint of a Gentile Christian antinomism but rather as the natural result of his Messianological convictions. This Messianic dogmatism induced him to assemble all those features of the law which indicated that it would be cancelled in the Messianic age. Every criterion suggesting that the law was inadequate for salvation was emphasized in order to [dispense] with the old covenant for intrinsic reasons, and to make the sun of the new covenant shine the more brightly. If then the Mosaic law whose validity was limited temporarily could be shown to be no longer the divinely appointed way of salvation, if Christ as the end of the law and the content of the new covenant could be shown to have taken its place, then the legal principle of life through obedience to the Torah could be replaced by the new principle of life through faith in Christ.

The characteristic fixation of the apostle's mind on the Old Testament is shown in that he cannot develop his principle otherwise than as he finds it proved in the Torah itself. And not only does he find it proved, but he thinks he is able to show that it is the true meaning of the Torah. His proof is conducted by his pointing to the figure of Abraham, venerable to every Jew as his ancestor, and through whose merits in fact the world subsists (Gen. Rabba Par. 35, etc.). In particular, in Judaic Hellenism the glorification of Abraham as the pattern of steadfastness in faith was somewhat paraded as being adapted to the needs of Gentiles whom it was desired to convert. * * * According to Philo, Abraham embodied faith as the [queen of the virtues] (*De Abr.* II, 39): "To free oneself completely from all earthly goods, and to believe in God alone, is the mark of a high and heavenly spirit, unfettered by earthly ties" (*Quis rerum div. heres* 93). Paul shared this opinion of Philo, only he went far beyond Philo's idea of faith as fidelity to the law. The centre of gravity in Paul's argument is that righteousness can be attained apart from the law and as a pure gift of grace, just as was promised to Abraham. For faith was reckoned to him as righteousness when he was still in an uncircumcised state (Gen. 16:6); the question of circumcision arises with regard to him two chapters later. The confident trust in the promise which is older than the law, was in itself already sufficient for the attainment of righteousness. Hence, deduces Paul, true righteousness springs from faith and not from the law (Rom. 5:20). "For we hold that a man is justified by faith apart from works of law" (Rom. 3:28).

But this new tearing asunder of polarities, this absolute opposition between faith, on the one hand, and the law, on the other, quite contrary to the continuous meaning of the Biblical narrative, has always been unintelligible to the Jewish thinker. None the less, the categories in which Paul thinks and argues are thoroughly rabbinic. Thus Midr. Teh. 27:13 and 94:17 (Doubl. Gen. Rabba Par. 74 on Gen. 31:42) conceptually distinguishes a merit or a righteousness flowing from faith * * * in the terms of Ps. 27:13, from righteousness when he was still in an uncircumcised state (Gen. Ps. 119: 32. But here the two kinds of righteousness or merit are set alongside each other, and not played off against each other. There is no occasion for such an attitude unless it is desired to prove the priority and superiority of faith over against the law. And it is precisely this which Paul wishes to do.

* * *

6. Paul's Fundamental Misapprehension

We have now clarified the most important points in Paul's doctrine of the law, which is closely connected both with anthropology (the experience of sin) and with soteriology (faith, works, justification). At particular junctures we have also tried to explain Jewish teachings, in order to establish whether and in what way Paul deviates from them or surpasses them. In this essay we have noted the complete absence of certain basic ideas of Judaism, such as *Yirath Adonai, Teshubhah* and freedom over against the evil impulse. But the real problem lying behind all this has not yet been systematically treated: the problem whether Paul really did justice to the faith of his fathers, or whether the problematics with which he was concerned did not in fact obscure this faith from his vision. Did Paul rightly understand the law as the saving principle of the old covenant?

I think that we must answer this question in the negative, for in my opinion Paul succumbed to a characteristic distortion of vision which had its antecedents in the spiritual outlook of Judaic Hellenism. Paul did not perceive, and for various reasons was perhaps unable to perceive, that in the Biblical view the law is integral to the convenant; in modern terms was the constitutive act by which the Sinai covenant was ratified, the basic ordinance which God laid down for His "house of Israel". In the first place it was given in order to bind the Israelite people to its covenant God as His peculiar possession * * * The maintenance of this ordinance, the proving of this constitutive act, is required of every member of the people in order that the covenant might be really embodied in Israelite life at all times and in all places. *Dowsbles*

Now when Paul speaks of the Jewish *nomos* he implies a twofold curtailment, which was obviously customary in the Diaspora: in the first place he has reduced the Torah, which means for the Jews both law and teaching, to the ethical (and ritual) law; secondly, he has wrested and isolated the law from the controlling context of God's covenant with Israel. We will, of course, grant that in consequence of the post-Biblical inadequacy of normative doctrine even in the schools of Palestine, there hardly existed clear ideas about the relation of Torah and Berith, and it was scarcely realized that what Paul calls *nomos*, i.e., *holos ho nomos*, represented in fact the instrument of the Berith, the organ and foundation of the covenant. In order to be able to appreciate the falsity of the sharp antithesis, *the law and Christ*, we must first consider the truth about this relation of law and covenant, then the ominous reduction of it in Hellenistic Judaism (dependent on the LXX) to which Paul by his origins belongs. Hence the point is a failure to appreciate the *berith* as the basis of the fulfilling of the law—a failure which was part of Paul's fateful inheritance.

* * *

Accordingly, the covenant and the law stand in a clear relation with each other. Firstly, as regards the form of the covenant: Israel is the people of the covenant, and its partner is God as the King of the Israelite people. As Max Weber and Martin Buber have luminously shown, the *foedus iniquum*, which represents merely the idea of an alliance between God and one nation of the earth, has become by God's free election will and grace on Sinai a *foedus aequum*. As a theopolitical event the Sinaitic *berith* is a sacral legal act of reciprocity, in the contraction of which both partners stand on one platform and speak on equal terms, recognizing each other (Deut. 26: 17–18). This expresses fairly pregnantly what is to be understood by the election of Israel.

The content of the covenant is God's commission to Israel in the royal proclamation from Sinai to embody the sovereignty of God on earth: "You shall be my own possession among all peoples; for all the earth is mine, and you shall be to me a kingdom of priests and a holy nation" (Ex. 19: 5–6). The entire pre-exilic history of Israel may be regarded as an attempt to realize the covenantal constitution on the soil of Palestine and to embody it in a theocracy. This constitutent act of the Sinaitic covenant is the ordinance which God lays down for His own house of Israel. It is expressed in the form of law and statutes intended to bind the people of Israel as a *'am sgullah* [special people] to its covenant God. This is in particular the deuteronomic conception, which connects law and covenant very closely. The people maintain the covenant inasmuch as they observe the laws. And the reciprocal character of the covenantal partnership comes to expression in Deuteronomy by the fact that God's blessing and curse are made dependent on the attitude of the people, its maintenance or otherwise of the laws (Deut. 28: 1 ff., 15 ff.). Strict adherence to the covenantal constitution is required of every member of the people so that the covenant may be effectively realized; the salvation of the individual depends on this. "You shall therefore keep my statutes and my ordinances, by doing which a man shall live" (Lev. 18: 5), i.e., he will stand in the living divine fellowship of salvation and holiness.

It is important for us to note that the binding character of the *berith* obviously consists in this, that man stands under oath to observe the law. Hence the law is the constituent act of the covenant, which, as a manifestation of God's election-grace to the man who is faithful, produces sanctification. For the law's requirements of holiness (Lev. 19: 2) flows from the binding relationship with the holy God who requires man to reflect His holiness. The prophets speak very aptly of Israel's transgression of the law when they say that it has broken the eternal covenant (Is. 24: 5). For the classic consciousness of ancient Israel the law was the basic act constituting the covenant, a constitutional act effected by God and as such regarded as unchangeable and irrevocable. Admittedly these are modern ideas of law, which are not directly reflected in the Bible, but they correspond approximately to the visibly growing situation in the evolution of Israel.

Hence we see that covenant in the Old Testament has the character both of history and of revelation. The covenant is concluded so that the people might be and remain God's people. It serves to maintain the laws of God, just as the laws serve to maintain God's covenant which they are intended to illuminate. The members of the covenant (*confoederati*) stand under the guidance of God and are obliged to render obedience. There exists a genuine relationship of contract—expressed in a Roman legal formula, a *mutua obligatio*—which is indissoluble and unredeemable. In this covenantal league of Israel with God, religious and juridical aspects are so closely linked as to be identifiable.

Early post-canonical writings, such as the Book of Jubilees, dating probably from the third century B.C., clearly subordinate, in this important sense, law to covenant, the latter as the promulgation of Moses embracing all the statutes. *Berith* becomes an epitome of the ordinances of the covenant to which Moses committed the people—a timeless quantity. In Hebrew, both Biblical and post-Biblical, it retains the character of reciprocity, so that not only on the part of God has there been an inviolable declaration of the divine will, but man too has been bound by certain decrees, and committed by certain duties and rights. Hence the Israelite *berith* has not only the significance of an order of grace, of divine institution, but also that of a covenantal charter, the determination of statutes and laws to govern the life of the Israelite people. The Mekhilta Ex. 20: 6 invoking Deut. 28: 9 establishes the point: "By covenant is meant nothing other than the Torah." In other words, the Torah is the body of the *berith*; in its 248 commands and its 365 prohibitions according to rabbinic enumeration, the *berith* is embodied as a manifestation of the divine will; the "ethical schematization of faith in God", as Joh. Hempel expresses it, was carried out in Israel with the help of ideas of law and right.

The Greek translation, however, *diathēkē*, used almost exclusively in the LXX for *berith*, shows a shift of emphasis which has often struck the attention of critics (Riggenbach, Lohmeyer, Behm, etc). The voluntary pact involving mutual obligations has become an authoritative legal disposition rather like a testamentary decision familiar to Greek civil law, from which the profane use of the term derives.

* * *

The LXX translation on account of its broad and free character has had, theologically, serious consequences. For, as early as Philo, God's covenant with the patriarchs and the people of Israel—which was the result of an agreement between two parties—was transformed into a one-sided declaration of the divine will in the sense of testament (a symbol of grace) or else in the sense of revelation of the divine nature (thus *De Mut. Nom.* 53; *De Som.* II, 223 ff. on Gen. 6: 18).

Philo is the first of a long series of writers for whom it may be shown that the use of the LXX alongside of or in place of the original text has led to a distortion of the classical Jewish teaching. The whole of the literature of Judaic Hellenism consequently discloses a rationalization or spiritualization of the laws of the Torah such as in either case deviates from Jewish faith-ideas.

Now Paul, as W. Bauer rightly observes, is entirely dependent on LXX usage, and understands *diathēkē* as a one-sided declaration of the will of God, an arrangement which God has made and authorized. Behind this lies the thought that God drew up a testament in our favour, in consequence of which we were entitled to expect an inheritance (* * * Gal. 3: 18; 4: 1 ff., etc.). Paul goes so far as to describe believers as the "heirs of God and fellow heirs with Christ" (Rom. 8: 17). If we disregard the distorted picture in Gal. 3: 15 ff., where Paul uses *diathēkē* in the sense of testament according to Hellenistic law, and tries to illustrate a saving event by a figure drawn from the sphere of civil law, he uses the term more in the sense of a divinely authorized arrangement. When in 2 Cor. 3: 14 he speaks of the *palaia* [old] *diathēkē*, which is superseded in Christ, *diathēkē* becomes for him a sort of collection of ancient statutes identified with the *nomos*, while the *kainē* [new] *diathēkē* is equated with justification which includes the forgiveness of sins. *Palaia* and *kainē diathēkē* become for Paul the antithesis between Judaism and Christianity, and indicate the stark contrast between the religion of the law and the religion of grace. Because Paul had lost all understanding of the character of the Hebraic *berith* as a partnership involving mutual obligations, he failed to grasp the inner meaning of the Mosaic law, namely, that it is an instrument by which the covenant is realized. Hence the Pauline theology of law and justification begins with the fateful misunderstanding in consequence of which he tears asunder covenant and law, and then represents Christ as the end of the law.

* * *

PART VII

Paul and Religious Experience

Inevitably the episode in Paul's career that provokes instant fascination is his conversion. The fact that he never describes it and that he alludes to it only in passing can easily be overlooked, since the reports in Acts more than make up for his reticence. The transition from Pharisaic zealot, persecuting the Jesus sect, to fanatic missionary of that sect, combatting continued observance of the law, was obviously cataclysmic. "Paul belongs to that rare class of men whose lives, by a single event, are cut clean in two. . . . He becomes another man, and lives thenceforward in the consciousness that he is another man . . ."[1] Those figures in the history of Christendom who have themselves experienced a bifurcation of life, whether in becoming Christians or in coming to a new and total awareness of the meaning of Christianity, have naturally found in Paul a prototype. It is not surprising that Augustine, who gave to Western Christianity the first classic of "spiritual autobiography" in his *Confessions*, or that Luther, in his agonies to find peace before the awful justice of God, should find illumination from Paul's experience. It is also not surprising that they should have read their own experiences into Paul's bare allusions.

Paul becomes the exemplar of the "twice-born man." This is true in all those movements within Christianity for which the central issue is how the individual moves from disbelief to faith: in missionary movements, particularly the modern ones that stressed individual conversion rather than Christianization of communities; pietist movements, seeking to leaven dry and rationalistic orthodoxies; "revival" movements and "awakenings" on the American frontier. These movements are particularly fond of one chapter in Paul's writings, Romans 7, which they treat as the autobiographical "testimony" of a convert, such as one might hear in the course of a revival meeting. Typical, in thought if not in prose, is this statement by James S. Stewart, a Scottish preacher and writer:

1. Wilhelm Wrede, *Paul* (tr. by Edward Lummis; London, 1907), p. 6.

361

Of Romans 7 and 8 it is surely true to say that nowhere in the literature of personal confession could a nobler fulfilment be found of the
Psalmist's injunction, "Let the redeemed of the Lord say so, whom
He hath redeemed from the hand of the enemy." *Let the redeemed
say so*—and Paul, by disclosing the wretchedness and misery in which
Christ had found him, and the glory and romance into which Christ
had ushered him, is bearing his witness to bowed and burdened spirits
everywhere: "This, by God's grace, happened to me, and this, under
God, can happen to you." In the service of Christ and of humanity,
the man has opened his very heart, and written in his very blood, and
taken us into the shame and glory of his secret soul; and for this the
world stands for ever in his debt.[2]

Romans 7 is part of Paul's discussion of the Jewish law. Read as the
"confession" of a convert, it tended to focus the understanding of conversion upon the problem of moral failure. That is, in the subtle interaction
between Paul and his conversionist interpreters, conversion comes to be
defined as release from guilt, and guilt comes to be understood more and
more in subjective terms. Paul's almost mythical scheme of the history of
salvation, in which the law had its special function in the history of Israel
"until Christ came" (Gal. 3–4), is transposed into an account of *each
individual's* progress toward conversion. The function of the law in this
progress is precisely to awaken guilt, to produce that despair of one's own
powers that is the reverse side and the negative prerequisite for accepting
God's grace. That, of course, was precisely the aspect of Christianity that
Nietzsche and George Bernard Shaw found so loathsome. But Søren Kierkegaard, whose encomium on the joys of guilt is reprinted below, made it
the touchstone of his explorations of human existence, which were to have
such profound effects on twentieth-century European self-consciousness. It
was Kierkegaard who focused the attention of modern theologians on that
other Pauline statement, "Whatever does not proceed from faith is sin"
(Rom. 14:23), and who taught us that the opposite of faith is *despair*,
which manifests itself in hidden or open anxiety.

Some of the interpreters of Paul who have emphasized his experience, as
opposed to his thought, have done so in reaction to the tendency of theologians to force Paul's variegated writings into a system. Very frequently
such systems not only flattened out differences within the Pauline literature, but also tended to make Paul into a two-dimensional figure in the history of ideas, disregarding his historical setting. The Tübingen School (see
Part V above) was a magisterial attempt to overcome the hiatus between
history and thought, but it failed ultimately because its own picture of
early Christian development was colored by a rationalistic understanding of
history. Those who reacted against such rational schemas pointed out that
in living religious communities the basis for the community's existence is
not ordinarily *ideas* held in common so much as common *experiences*
shared by the adherents. Theology, it was argued, is the product of a
second stage of development, which always *follows* the creative period of
actual religious experience. Paul, for these interpreters, was not to be seen

2. *A Man in Christ* (London, 1935), pp. 102f.

as a great theologian, but as a profoundly religious personage, whose primary concerns were with the religious, not the intellectual, life of the communities he founded. Paul was thus transferred from a chapter in the history of ideas to a chapter in the history of religions.

The new interest in Paul as a *homo religiosus* coincided with the rise around the turn of the century of the academic discipline known in Europe as "the history of religions" and in English-speaking countries as "comparative religion."[3] It sought to locate Paul (and other early Christian phenomena) within the complex developments of old and new religious groups in the Greco-Roman world. It observed that some of Paul's language had certain parallels with the language of the mystery cults, and the sacramental practice in his churches seemed analogous to rituals of the mysteries. Some of Paul's language, too, seemed similar to that used by contemplative mystics in diverse religious movements. Moreover, Paul does describe one mystical experience of an extraordinary sort in 2 Cor. 12. Presumably wider knowledge of mystical and cultic phenomena in Paul's time and cultural milieu would add greatly to the possibility of understanding Paul aright. A number of fortunate archaeological and literary discoveries contributed to the search; naturally there were enthusiasts for each new "find" who tended to interpret Paul exclusively in terms of their own latest discovery. One of the most important discoveries, and one which has been expanded by repeated new additions down to the present, was of caches of papyrus documents contemporary with earliest Christianity, which had been preserved in the arid sands of Egypt. Many of these documents were simply commercial and private papers illustrating ordinary life in the first centuries, including a great number of private letters. The latter were seized upon by Adolf Deissmann to show that Paul had not written theological treatises, but simple, occasional letters. He ought therefore to be understood not as a theologian, but as a representative of popular piety. Equally important was the recovery, somewhat earlier, of a number of Jewish and early Christian *apocalypses*, a genre of books that spoke in cryptic or mythical images of the end of the present world and the coming of the messianic age or the kingdom of God. (Canonical examples of the genre are the book of Daniel and the New Testament Apocalypse or Revelation of John.) Among the enthusiasts who sought to interpret Paul primarily within the framework of apocalyptic ideology was Albert Schweitzer. Excerpts from Deissmann's and Schweitzer's books on Paul are included below.

The one-sidedness of much of the early history-of-religions interpretation of Paul naturally provoked a new reaction. A small but enormously influential book by Wilhelm Wrede, published in 1904, insisted that neither the religious experience of Paul nor his thought should be emphasized at the expense of the other:

> . . . The two cannot be separated. *The religion of the apostle is theological through and through: his theology is his religion.* The idea that we can find in him a cold doctrine, to be grasped by the understanding, a doctrine which soars more or less beyond the reach of

---

3. In American universities today the European terminology has become dominant.

mere piety, is false; and equally false is the idea that the piety of Paul can be described without mention of those *thoughts* in which he had apprehended Christ, his death and his resurrection.[4]

Two important essays by Martin Dibelius, one of which is excerpted below,[5] undertook a careful investigation of the "mystical" passages in Paul in comparison with a great variety of Hellenistic material.

Probably the most influential—and controversial—recent attempt to make a unified statement of Paul's experience and thought is the existential interpretation by Rudolf Bultmann. In a programmatic lecture in 1941, he called for the "demythologizing of the New Testament," urging that in the modern world it was necessary to complete the process of radical reinterpretation of myth which Paul and John had begun. The excerpts below indicate how central to the whole program is Bultmann's interpretation of Paul.

Krister Stendahl's essay not only provides a fine survey of Western interpretations of Paul, but challenges them all, "theological" and "religious" alike, as a cumulative distortion of the historic personage.

4. Wrede, *op. cit.*, p. 76.
5. The other: "Glaube und Mystik bei Paulus," in *Botschaft und Geschichte*, II (Tübingen, 1956): 94–116.

SØREN KIERKEGAARD

The Joy in the Thought that in Relation to God a Man Always Suffers as Being Guilty (1847) †

* * *

Guilty?—Not guilty? This is the serious question in legal procedure; the same question on the part of self-concern is even more
serious, for if the authorities penetrate even into the most secret
recesses of the house in order to arrest the guilty, self-concern
forces its way in even deeper after guilt than does any judge, into
the heart's most secret chamber, where only God is judge.

As long as the judge is human, and the relation is between man
and man, we shall indeed all agree that to be innocent is the only
thing desirable, that innocence is the refuge which no human injustice or lack of appreciation can capture or demolish; that innocence
is the purity which not even violation can injure, the invulnerabil-
ity which not even death can wound mortally. And yet it does not
work quite in this way, and it really works so only as long as the
essential tension of the relationship is a relation between two; for
precisely in the most sincere and tenderest relationship of love
between man and man, the highest desire of love may be to be in
the wrong, aye, to be the one guilty. Humanly we speak of
unhappy love as the hardest suffering, but in unhappy love this is
again the hardest, the most painful, when the object of love is such
that it essentially cannot be loved, which, however, the lover in his
inmost heart still desires as the only thing. That is, if the object of
love can essentially still be the object, and only the possession is
denied, then the unhappy love is less unhappy, less painful; then
possession is indeed denied, but the object is not lost; on the contrary it possesses all the essential perfection which happily satisfies
the demand of love.

* * *

But if a man has a relationship to God, and the question there is

† From *The Gospel of Suffering*, tr. by
David F. Swenson and Lillian Marvin
Swenson (Minneapolis, 1948). Hardly
known outside Denmark before 1900,
Søren Kierkegaard (1813–55) has had
immeasurable influence not only on
theology, but also on philosophy and
literature in this century. This "edifying discourse" is actually based on
Luke 23:41, but the portion excerpted
here reads almost like a meditation on
Rom. 1–8.

about being right or wrong: I wonder whether any man has ever really been able even to think this horrible thing, that in relation to God there could be any question of an unhappy love, because God could not become its object! For not because God through seventy years, if such it was, makes a man's life harder than any man's has ever been, not because He guides him so that he understands nothing, nothing at all of this dark saying: not for this reason is God either lost or lost to him. But if the least thing happened, which might, or which might even merely seem to be able to prove that God was not love: aye, then would everything be lost, then would God be lost, for if God is not love, and if He is not love in everything, then God simply does not exist. Oh, my hearer, if you have experienced the hardest moment of a human life, when everything went black before your soul, as if there were no love in heaven, or as if that which is in heaven is really not love; when it was to you as if there was a choice you should make, the horrible choice between being in the wrong and winning God, or between being in the right and losing God—is it not true that you then found the happiness of heaven in choosing the former, or rather in the fact that it still was not a choice, that, on the contrary, it was heaven's eternal demand upon you, its demand upon your soul, that there must be absolutely no doubt about God being love! Alas, while many wonder vaguely whether God is really love, when it would truly be better if they would inflame the love in themselves merely by the dreadful thought that God was not love; would inflame and kindle the love, for if God is love, then He is also love in everything; love in that which you can understand, and love in that which you cannot understand, love in the dark saying that lasts a day, and in the dark saying that lasts seventy years. Alas, whereas many call themselves Christian, and yet perhaps live as in the uncertain with respect to whether God really is love, then it would truly be better to enkindle the love merely by the thought of the horror of paganism: that He who holds the destiny of everything and all your destinies in His hand, that He is equivocal, that His love is not a fatherly embrace but an ensnaring trap, that His hidden Being is not eternal clarity but concealment, that the deepest ground of His being is not love but the cunning, which one cannot understand. For it is not indeed required that one should be able to understand the plan of God's love, but certainly one must be able to believe, and believing understand that He is love. It is not terrible that you should fail to understand God's plan, if He is still eternal love; but it is terrible if you could not understand it because He is cunning.

If, on the other hand, according to the presupposition of the discourse, it is true that in relation to God a man is not only always in the wrong, but is always guilty, so that consequently when he suffers he suffers as guilty: then can no doubt in yourself (if you yourself will not sin anew) and no occurrence outside yourself (if you will not yourself sin anew by taking offense) supplant the joy.

The joy is: that now and at every moment, and at every future moment, it is eternally true that nothing has happened or can ever happen, even if the most distressingly conceived horror of the most morbid imagination were to become reality, nothing which can shake the belief that God is love; and the joy is, that if a man will not understand this by the good, then the guilt will help him to understand it. *If a man in relation to God always suffers as being guilty, then at every moment, whatever happens, he is assured that God is love; or rather, then he is at every moment prevented from entering into doubt, because the consciousness of guilt focusses the attention upon itself.*

Most men doubtless have a conception, sometimes a vivid conception, at particular moments a sincere feeling, that God is love; and yet there are perhaps many who live in such a way that it is obscure to them, as if, if this or that horror came upon them, at which they particularly shudder, then they must renounce faith, give up God, lose Him. But is there anything more indefensible than to live in this way: to exhaust the highest passion in a half-dormant condition between doubt and confidence, so that one never catches sight of the cunning enemy who sucks the blood from one's inmost parts, so that one never comes to shudder over this condition, thinking that one is not in despair—because one is slumbering in despair! Alas, God is not the one who loses something thereby; but he, the sleeper, he, who truly sins by sleeping, he loses everything, loses that without which life means really nothing.

* * *

If it were now possible that a man might even merely appear to be justified in giving up his belief that God is love, then must he *first* be unconditionally pure and entirely without guilt, not only, humanly speaking, in this or that, but entirely without guilt as over against God; for it is only through this presupposition that doubt can gain a foothold; without it doubt is not only deprived of a stronghold, is not only built upon the sand, but it is built above an abyss. And *next*, that must happen which is not consistent with the idea that God is love. But no man would be able to endure this horror; only once was it endured by Him who was the Holy One, by Him who was without guilt *before* God. And that is why we should always speak with fear and trembling, and preferably with the silence of worship, about the suffering of Christ, because human thought as little as human language is able to describe or clearly to suspect the depth of this horror; that is why a man should speak with cautious humility, or keep humbly silent about how Christ suffered, so that one may not be led into temptation by the ungodly thirst to explore the mysteries of God, which even the pagan conception punished with an eternally burning thirst. That is why a man should especially guard himself in these times, when in so many ways they wish to frighten the life of faith, as if believing it were to apprehend it, as if one could not believe fearlessly and believe unto salvation, because one cannot impudently apprehend it. Only Christ was without guilt *before God*, and precisely for that reason He must suffer the superhuman suffering, must be led to the limit of justly distrusting, as it were, whether God was indeed love, when He cried: "My God, my God, why hast thou forsaken me?" But it was different with the thief of whom we speak. Whereas the Savior of the world groans, "My God, my God, why hast thou forsaken me," words which our church's greatest, but also its most orthodox, preacher, words which Luther, precisely because of his orthodoxy, scarcely dared to preach from: then the thief at the Savior's side, like a true preacher, preaches first and foremost for his own edification, on the godly thought: "I suffer as being guilty."

* * *

He is the true preacher of repentance; for the camel's-hair shirt is indeed a tight-fitting garment, but crucifixion is still an even more constrained position. And certainly, to dwell in the desert is a humble evaluation of life, but to be crucified is still the hardest thing in life; and the fact of saying: "Repent *ye*," is still not so excellent a sermon of repentance as to say, "I suffer as being guilty"; and the fact of saying about one's self, "I am a prophet," is still not so arousing as to say: "I am a sinner who suffers as being guilty." The thief is preaching to himself, and to the other thief, and to all those present, and he says, "You are all sinners; only He who hangs between us is without guilt before God; He suffers innocently." "For," says this exalted preacher of repentance, "in the world it is usually the custom for one thief to walk between two so-called righteous men, but this custom and this righteousness is imagination: here we see the truth indeed: that the only righteous man, the only one, is crucified between two thieves. Lo, that is why the Scripture says: 'He was reckoned with the transgressors';—not, however, because we two are thieves, and, humanly speaking, sinners above all others. No, take me down, hang whomsoever you will of those present in my place, He, the Holy One, is still, like those crucified with Him, numbered among the transgressors. Moreover, as soon as He, the Holy One, is classed with the race, He is numbered with the transgressors. Or I wonder if any man, aye, even if he were, humanly speaking, innocently persecuted, condemned and crucified, I wonder if at the side of the crucified Savior he would dare to say: 'I suffer innocently!' " This is a Christian sermon of repentance, which reminds even the martyr that *before God* he suffers as being guilty. It is a Christian sermon of repentance, for the Jews still adhere to the idea that there are holy men who can preach repentance; who teach that by striving one becomes holy enough to preach repentance. In Christianity, on the contrary, an *actual* sinner preaches repentance, and even those, humanly speaking, holy men, must agree that the preacher of repentance is an actual sinner, who does not say: "Woe to you," when he begins, but he says: "God be merciful to me a poor sinner, I suffer as being guilty."

And yet, the penitent thief is no preacher of repentance, his sermon is not a sermon of repentance. If it were, then it would not have anything to do with the subject of the present discourse: the joy in the thought that in relation to God a man always suffers as guilty. But it is just from this thought that the thief preaches alleviation and comfort to himself. This is the edifying, the instructive point concerning this thief, that at the moment of his most ignominious death, he still had depth and humility enough to understand the fact of suffering guiltily as an alleviation, in comparison with the painful death suffered on the cross which stands in the middle. The penitent thief finds, in comparison with this suffering, relief and comfort in the thought that he suffers as being guilty. And why? Because then the suffering does not wholly come into contact with the concerned question of anxious doubt as to whether God is love. The thief is then no preacher of repentance except in so far as the joyful message of the Gospel is always that: he proclaims the joy which is painful and humiliating only to the proud. Thus when in paganism a man suffered wrong at the hands of another, was persecuted for the sake of the good, was condemned to death for the sake of the good: alas, then he became self-important, and said in relation to God: "I suffer innocently," and proudly believed that it was easier—to be in the right. But at the side of Christ such a one learns that there is but One who suffers innocently before God, and this humbles him. In paganism, because a man was in the right in one respect toward men, or if this is too weak, oh, well, because a man was in the right in everything as over against men, he also wished to carry this over into his relationship with God, and be in the right as over against God—with respect to whom a man is always in the wrong in everything; the pagan was proud and blind enough not to be able to apprehend this horror; he boasted proudly of his "splendid vices" as if they were virtues.

* * *

For what is it the doubt about God's love wishes? It wishes to reverse the relationship; it wishes to sit calm and secure, judging and reflecting on whether God is indeed love; it wishes to make Him the defendant, make Him into the one from whom something is exacted. But God's love is never to be found in this way; accursed of God will the endeavor of doubt be to God, because it begins with audacity. On the contrary, it is the eternal happiness of faith, that God is love. It does not thereby follow that faith understands how God's plan for a man is love. This exactly constitutes the conflict of faith—to believe without being able to understand. And so when the struggle of faith begins, when doubts arise, or when "doubt with many wild thoughts storms against faith": then the consciousness of guilt enters as a relief, as the final strengthening. One might think that this consciousness were a hostile power, but no, it wishes precisely to help faith, to help the believer by teaching him not to doubt about God, but about himself. Instead of the mendacity about thinking through the doubt, which is precisely doubt's most dangerous invention, the consciousness of guilt thunders its: "Halt!" and faith leads safely back, safely, because there would be no conflict if God was love. For as the Scriptures say that God has laid all things under sin, so every mouth shall be stopped, so this humbling but also saving thought stays the lips of doubt. When the thousand questions of doubt wish to tempt faith, and make it appear as if God could not answer, then the consciousness of guilt teaches the believer that it is he who cannot answer one to a thousand: ergo, God is love. If you do not understand the absolute authority of this conclusion, then faith understands it. If you do not understand the joy in the thought that it is everlastingly assured that God is love: then faith understands it. It understands that it is an illusion to believe it possible to penetrate the doubt, but that it is blessed that it is made impossible to doubt. If it is terrible for a son to be in the right as against his father; if it is an edifying thought that a son is always in the wrong as against his father: oh, then it is also a blessing that it is impossible to doubt that God is love. Let only the half-hearted praise of God's love be silent, the true exculpation is this: I always suffer as guilty—so certain is it in all eternity that God is love.

*   *   *

If, according to the assumption of the discourse, it is true that a man in relation to God always suffers as guilty, *then this constitutes the joy: that the fault consequently lies in the man, that, as a result of this, there must constantly be something to do, there must be tasks, and yet also human tasks,* and along with the tasks the hope that everything can and will become better, when he becomes better, more industrious, more prayerful, more obedient, more humble, more devoted, more sincere in his love, more ardent in spirit.

Is this not joyful? For if it is true that courage justly says: "Where danger is, there am I too"; or turns it about and says: "Where I am, there is also danger"; and if it is true that the loving sympathy rightly says: "It is even harder to sit by and have nothing to do, than to be the sufferer," then it is also true that where there is a task there is hope. But if a man always suffers as guilty in relation to God, then is there always a task and always hope.

*   *   *

Aye, when there is nothing to do, when not even the suffering itself is the task, then there *is* hopelessness, and then there is an appalling leisure from labor for slowly perishing in hopelessness. As long as there is a task, as long as there is something renounced, so long a man is not hopelessly abandoned; as long as there remains a task, so long there is a way to shorten the time, for work and exertion shorten the time. But when there is nothing to do, when there is no task, but only the deep mockery of deceit in refusing the task; then is there hopelessness, and then is the time mortally long.

Consequently, only when there is nothing at all to do, and the one who says this *would be* without guilt *before God*—for if he is guilty, then there is always something to do; only when there is nothing to do, and this is understood as meaning that there is no task: then there is hopelessness. That is if someone says that there is nothing to do, then it by no means follows from that that there is no task, for patience can indeed be the task; but if there is no task, and the sufferer *was* without guilt *before God*, then, and only then, is there hopelessness. If therefore a sufferer could be in the right as over against God, if it were possible that the fault could lie in God, aye, then would there be hopelessness and the horror of hopelessness, then would there be no task. For the tasks of faith and hope and love and patience and humility and obedience, in short all human tasks, rest in the eternal certainty, wherein they have confidence and assurance that God is love. If this were ever to happen to a man with respect to God that the fault lay in God, then there would be no task; if this were ever to happen to a single man, then there would be no tasks for the whole race. It would be not only in this particular case that there was no task; no, if God had showed but a single time that He was not love, in the least thing or the greatest, if He had left a sufferer without a task: then there is no longer a task for any man, since it is nonsense and vanity and the evil and painful vexation of spirit to believe, and self-contradiction to labor, and an agony to live. Life issues from the heart, and if a man has been injured therein, then there is for him, through his own fault, no longer a task except the busy pain of sin and emptiness. But from the heart of God issues all life, life in the tasks. If it is true that the creature must die when God takes its spirit back; then it is also true that if God for a single moment denied His love, then are all tasks dead and made into nothing, and hopelessness is the only thing which exists.

Alas, most men sometimes feel and themselves admit that in this or that particular the fault lay in them; and yet perhaps the malicious thought dwells in the secret heart of many that it might happen, that it perhaps would happen, and God would be responsible for the fact that a man was lost. And so people live on in this way, busily occupied with everything else; they do not think that they are in despair, they never come to shudder over this condition, because no light has power to pierce this gloom; moreover, this is not even dimly desired, because the inner darkness has an uncomfortable suspicion that it would become a clarity hard to understand—the demand which God has upon a man's soul; a clarity hard to understand, that there is always a task. But still if only the one is mortal who is dead, I wonder if the living, when death is his lullaby, is not exactly called and is a mortal: and in the same way, if the one is not also desperate, who did not even come to despair because he simply did not notice that he was in despair! Or if a merchant in making up his reckoning discovers that he is ruined—and despairs, is he in greater despair than the merchant who vaguely knows that things are bad, but hopes to get out of it sometime in the future? Is it more despairing to despair over the truth than not to dare face the truth? And every man in whose heart dwells that malicious thought of God, he is in despair; that one can in the spiritual sense, as it were, see in him; for in relation to God he is not like the one who casts down his eyes in the consciousness of his own guilt and of what he owes to God, nor is he like one who humbly lifts his confident glance to God; no, he scowls.

Truly, to get the gloom expelled would be better than scowling; to come to shudder at the thought of this horror, the horror which really belongs to paganism, that God could not, or would not, give a man confidence. For an idol can neither make a man into nothing, nor make him sensible of the nothing he is—for that the idol is too weak; nor can an idol give a man confidence—he is not strong enough for that; therefore we may say that the idol itself taught the pagan to scowl. Even the wisest pagan who ever lived, however much wiser he was in other respects than the humblest believer, has still in comparison with that believer a gloom in his heart, because in the final analysis the pagan could not become eternally certain and clear whether the fault lay in him, or whether it were not possibly the rare case, when the fault lay with God; whether hopelessness were not a condition in which a man may be without guilt, because God is Himself responsible through leaving the man without a task. And one can make excuses for the pagan for this being the case, because his god is himself gloomy.

But the God of the Christian is clarity; therefore every man is without excuse, and without any excuse. But if you take away all the excuses, aye, if you take away that engendering gloomy dullness which breeds excuses, then there is no melancholy; and if you take away all excuses; then is a man without any excuse, and always without excuse. But if before God he is never pure and is always without excuse, then he is always guilty, even when he suffers. But if he always suffers as one who is guilty, then it is eternally certain that God is love, and therefore it is a cause for rejoicing that there are always tasks, and always something to do.

Is not this a cause for rejoicing? "What," perhaps someone asks, "that a man in relation to God always suffers as one who is guilty?" Aye, if this is rightly understood to mean that it is eternally certain that God is love, and that there is always a task. Lo, doubt wishes in all comfort with shameless audacity to force itself into the nature of God, and prove that God is love. But in all eternity it will never succeed with the proof, because the beginning is a presumption. And after all, what really is doubt other than that grumbling obscurity; what is it except the source of all excuses and the *excuse* which reverses the relationship—and doubts about God? But if that is so, if it is right for a man to doubt concerning God's love, then is the man indeed excusable. If, on the contrary, the fact of doubting God's love is presumptuous, then is the man without excuse, accused, guilty, always engaged in the task; this is the law, but there is joy as well: that there is also always the task. If doubt is present in the beginning, then is God lost long before the end, and the man is freed from always having the task, but also always freed from having the consolation that there is always the task. But if the consciousness of guilt is the beginning, then the beginning of doubt is made impossible, and then it is joyful that there is always the task.

* * *

ADOLF DEISSMANN

The Christ-Mystic (1925) †

What happened at Damascus ought not to be isolated, but it should be regarded as the basal mystical experience of the religious genius to whom also in later life extraordinary and even ecstatic experiences were vouchsafed. All that can be called Paul's Christ-mysticism is the reaction to this initial experience. Damascus is perhaps the clearest example of an initial impulse to reacting mysticism, a mystical initiation arising from a divine initiative.

The conversion of the persecutor into a follower and of the Pharisee Apostle into the Apostle of Christ was a sudden one. Yet it was no magic transformation, but had its psychological preparation both negative and positive.

Negative in the experiences through which the soul of the young Pharisee had gone in its passionate hunger for righteousness under the yoke of the law; in the letters of the convert decades later we still hear the echo of his sighs at that time: the terrible discovery[1] had come to him as a curse, that even for the most earnest conscience, in fact especially for the most earnest conscience, it was impossible really to keep the whole law.

The positive preparation for the conversion came, on the one hand, through the prophetic inwardness of the Old Revelation which had influenced Paul even as a Jew; on the other hand, through a relatively close touch with the genuine tradition of Jesus and with the effects wrought by Him in the characters of the confessors whom Paul persecuted. I do not regard it as probable that the young zealot ever was personally acquainted with the earthly Jesus, although weighty voices have again declared recently in

† From *Paul, A Study in Social and Religious History*, tr. by William E. Wilson (2d, rev. ed., New York, 1926), portions of Chaps. V, VI, VIII. Deissmann (1866–1937) was Professor of New Testament in Heidelberg and Berlin.
1. Gal. iii. 10, and many sad words in Romans.

favour of this hypothesis.[2] But it is most certainly probable that the Pharisee was acquainted with his opponent through His words and the influence He continued to exert on His disciples.

So the lightning of Damascus strikes no empty space but finds deep in the soul of the persecutor plenty of inflammable material. We see the flame blaze upwards and after a generation we can still feel that the glow then kindled has lost none of its power in the man grown old: Christ is in Paul, Paul in Christ.

* * *

We have not merely recognised the secret of Paul's spiritual life but also described it with sacred Pauline formulae when we use the two phrases:

Christ in Paul,[3] Paul in Christ.[4]

It is no doubt generally admitted that Paul's religious experience was Christo-centric; but how differently people view that Christo-centric Christianity of Paul! Often Christo-centric has been identified with Christo-logical. But Paul's religion is Christo-centric in a much deeper and more realistic sense. It is not first of all the product of a number of convictions and elevated doctrines about Christ; it is 'fellowship' with Christ,[5] Christ-intimacy.[6] Paul lives 'in' Christ, 'in' the living and present spiritual Christ, who is about him on all sides, who fills him,[7] who speaks to him,[8] and speaks in and through him.[9] Christ is for Paul not a person of the past, with whom he can only come into contact by meditating on the words that have been handed from him, not a 'historical' personage, but a reality and power of the present, an 'energy,'[1] whose life-giving powers are daily expressing themselves in him,[2] and to whom, since that day at Damascus, he has felt a personal-cult dependence.

The difference between these two conceptions of Paul's Christo-centric religion can be well expressed in Greek by contrasting *Christologos* and *Christophoros*. Certainly Paul was also a

2. The phrase in 2 Cor. v. 16 is to be understood otherwise; if '*we have known Christ after the flesh*' * * * refers to personal acquaintance with the earthly Jesus, then the conclusion '*now we know him so no more*' is a triviality.
3. Gal. ii. 20, etc.
4. Numerous passages.
5. 1 Cor. i. 9; x. 16; Phil. iii. 10. The inimitably vivid expression is *koinōnia*.
6. [German, 'Christ-Innigkeit'—W.E.W.] With the coining of this expression '*Christ-Innigkeit*' I hope to render a service to those who in carrying on

Christian work at the present day want to speak about Paul's Christ-mysticism without using a word so productive of misunderstanding as '*Christusmystik.*' In using this term '*Christ-Innigkeit*' I am consciously linking on to the ancient usage of *innic* and *innikeit* in the German mysticism of the Middle Ages * * *
7. Gal. ii. 20.
8. 2 Cor. xii. 9.
9. 2 Cor. xiii. 3.
1. Phil. iii. 21; Col. i. 29; Eph. i. 19.
2. 2 Cor. xii. 9; Phil. iii. 10; 1 Cor. i. 24; v. 4. * * *

Christological thinker, but above all and in everything (even in his 'Christology') he was a *Christ-bearer*.

We must first of all try to understand the Christ of the Apostle. Usually the attempt is made under the title 'The Christology of the Apostle Paul.' But it is more accurate because more in accord with historical sense to inquire about the 'Christophory' or 'Christolatry' of the Apostle, or, if that sounds too strange, about his 'knowledge of Christ,' about his 'experiences of Christ' or his 'revelations of Christ.' Any tendency to petrify the original fellowship with Christ pulsating with life into a doctrine about Christ is mischievous.

We ask what Christ did Paul know, experience, carry with him into the world and bring into the depths of the souls of his churches? The answer can only be: it was the spiritual, living Christ.

This certainty of Christ, nevertheless, has different tendencies. In each case indeed the living, risen Christ stands at the centre, but two chief, opposing tendencies can be distinguished.

On the one hand, Christ to the Apostle is the Son of God 'highly exalted'[3] to the Father, who dwells in Heaven above 'at the right hand'[4] of God in glory, and 'is coming' soon to earth as Judge.

This assurance about Christ which has strong Jewish tendencies, being especially influenced by Psalm cx., might be called in doctrinaire phrase the assurance of the transcendence of Christ. In more Pauline phrase, and therefore historically more correctly, it is called the assurance of the 'highly exalted' Christ. That word 'highly exalted' is indeed especially Pauline, and though in later days it gave very strong stimulus to dogma, it was originally not a word artificially formed for dogmatic use, but a simple popular expression of the assurance about Christ that sprang out of the cult.

Even more characteristically Pauline is the other; it exhibits more the Hellenistic-mystical tendency of the experience of Christ: the living Christ is the Pneuma. As Pneuma, as Spirit the living Christ is not far off, above clouds and stars, but near, present on our poor earth he dwells and rules in His own. Here again, there is no lack of suggestion in this direction in the Septuagint, and Paul himself created the significant formulae:

The Lord is the Spirit,[5]
The last Adam became a life-giving Spirit,[6]
He that is joined to the Lord is one Spirit.[7]

3. Phil. ii. 9, * * *
4. (Following Ps. cx. 1), Col. iii. 1; Eph. i. 20; Rom. viii. 34.
5. 2 Cor. iii. 17, * * *
6. 1 Cor. xv. 45, * * *
7. 1 Cor. vi. 17, * * *

and others like them. Perhaps even more important than such symbolical phrases is the fact, that in a number of places Paul makes precisely similar statements of Christ and of the Spirit. This is specially to be noted in the parallel use of the mystical formulae 'in Christ' and 'in the (Holy) Spirit.' The formula 'in the Spirit,' which occurs in Paul's writings only nineteen times, is in almost all these places connected with the same specifically Pauline fundamental ideas which elsewhere he connects with the formula 'in Christ': faith, righteousness, being justified, being in, standing, rejoicing and joy, free gift, love, peace, sanctified, sealed, circumcised and circumcision, testifying, speaking, being filled, *one* body, the temple of God,—all this is seen and experienced by the Christian who is 'in Christ,' but also by him who is 'in the Spirit'; that means as a matter of fact 'in Christ who is the Spirit.' Therefore also the technical expressions 'fellowship of the Son of God' and 'fellowship of the Spirit' are parallel in Paul's use. For it always refers to the same experience whether Paul says that Christ lives in him, or that the Spirit dwells in us, and whether he speaks of Christ making intercession for us with the Father, or of the Spirit who helps us in prayer.

This Christ-experience of the Apostle might be called in doctrinaire phrase the experience of the immanence of Christ; it is more Pauline and therefore also historically more correct to speak of the experience of the Spirit-Christ.

This certainty of the nearness of Christ occurs far more frequently in Paul's writings than the thought of the distant Christ 'highly exalted' in Heaven.

Christ in me

—that is indeed a confession poured forth from the depths of the soul, the confession of an assurance which illuminates and holds under its sway the remotest recesses of the ego. Corresponding to this assurance is the other:

I in Christ.

Christ is Spirit; therefore He can live in Paul and Paul in Him. Just as the air of life, which we breathe, is 'in' us and fills us, and yet we at the same time live in this air and breathe it, so it is also with the Christ-intimacy of the Apostle Paul: Christ in him, he in Christ.

This primitive Pauline watch-word 'in Christ' is meant vividly and mystically, as is the corresponding phrase 'Christ in me.' The formula 'in Christ' (or 'in the Lord') occurs 164 times in Paul's writings: it is really the characteristic expression of his Christianity. Much misunderstood by exegetes, rationalised, applied to the 'historical' Jesus in isolation, and thereby weakened, often simply ignored, this formula—so closely connected in meaning with the phrase 'in the Spirit'—must be conceived as the peculiarly Pauline expression of the most intimate possible fellowship of the Christian with the living spiritual Christ. That it is used by Paul with differing shades of meaning is true: there are, for example, places where it is already used in a really formal sense. And it may reasonably be assumed that the Christ-intimacy of the Apostle itself had also its differing degrees of elevation. After the mountain peak of Damascus there followed the normal life in Christ moving upon a less exalted plane of personal experience, then in the rare times of trouble and consecration it rose again to a passionately intensified communion of prayer with the Saviour.

Related to this, if not identical with it, is the similarly misunderstood formula 'through Christ,' which also in far the greater number of cases is to be referred to the spiritual Christ.

It may now be asked What was Paul's conception of the spiritual Christ? The answer depends upon the way in which the Spirit, as Paul uses the term, is defined. Here it seems best to start with the sharp contrast always made between *pneuma*, spirit, and *sarx*, flesh. *Pneuma*, at any rate, is something not *sarkic*, not earthly, not material. True, the Spirit-Christ has a *soma*, a body, but a spiritual body,[8] that is a heavenly body,[9] a body consisting of divine effulgence.[1] Sharp, philosophically pointed definition of the concept of 'spiritual' is happily absent from Paul's writings. The Apostle remains popular, and in ancient style, vivid in his formulation. He probably thought of some light, ethereal form of existence, such as he doubtless attributed to God. But there is no binding definition. We have the greatest possible latitude if we desire to transplant the Apostle's ideas of Christ into our religious thinking. To Paul the Spirit, God, the living Christ is a reality, the reality of all realities; therefore he does not puzzle about definitions. The Spirit that is living in Paul searches all things, even the deep things of God[2] but it brings to light no definition of God. Religious definitions are always attempts at salvage, but Paul had not suffered shipwreck over the problem of Christ's person.

If Paul had attempted a definition, he would have defined like a man of the ancient world, in a manner more realistic, more massive, more concrete perhaps than a speculative thinker of our own times, but certainly not in ordinary materialistic terms. The Spirit has nothing of the fleshly, nothing of the earthly; it is divine, heavenly, eternal, holy, living, and life-giving—these are all predicates which Paul applies to it or could apply, and they can all also be applied to the spiritual Christ.

8. 1 Cor. xv. 45 f.
9. 1 Cor. xv. 47 ff.
1. Phil. iii. 21.
2. 1 Cor. ii. 10.

But here there is a point that must not be overlooked. The Spirit-Christ of Paul is no feeble, indistinct image set up by the phantasy-producing power of religious imagination, which evaporates into a boundless, empty cloudland; on the contrary, He has his hold on concrete reality at the cross. He is, and remains, the crucified.[3] That is to say, mystical communion with the Spirit-Christ transforms all that we call the 'historical' Christ, all that found its climax on Golgotha, all that had been entrusted to the Apostle as tradition about Jesus, into a present reality. It is here that the mystical dependence of the cult religion shows itself particularly clearly. The basis of facts in the past, which, when regarded only as material for christological formulations, may easily become wooden and thus impossible to assimilate,—this, as it is made a present reality by the mystical power of the cult, receives again its flow of sap. Thereby also the Christ-mystic is protected from the danger that threatens him of becoming a 'reed shaken by the wind' and 'a man clothed in soft raiment'—the danger that the straying of 'believing thoughts into the broad fields of eternity'[4] may lead to nothing better than vague, stumbling wandering.

These great certainties, too, it must be confessed, were not 'defined' by Paul. What he introduced into Christ-mysticism was not definitions, but a rich treasure of technical phrases, which express often in popular pictorial language the spiritual communion between Christ and His own. The not unimportant problem of setting forth in order this technical vocabulary of Paul, a few details of which we have sketched, has not yet been solved in all its bearings, and can be mentioned here only as an object of research. He who desires to solve it must be at home in the atmosphere and language of the mysticism both of the East and the West.

The question, What according to Paul brings about the communion with Christ? is answered by the hints which we have given about Paul's conversion. It is God Who brings about the communion with Christ. He has the initiative at the mystic initiation. Not that every Christian experiences anything like the occurrence at Damascus, but everyone who possesses the living Christ, or the Spirit, has received Him from God, or has been 'apprehended' by Christ Himself. Those passages are numerous in which God is celebrated as giver of the Spirit.

The assertion that according to Paul baptism is the means of access to Christ, I hold to be incorrect. There are passages which, taken in isolation, can be made to prove it, nevertheless it is, I think, more correct to say, that baptism does not bring about communion with Christ, but seals it. In Paul's own case, at all events,

3. * * * Gal. iii. 1; 1 Cor. i. 23; ii. 2.
4. * * * The quotation is from the opening lines of the well-known hymn of Johann Gottfried Hermann (†1791).

baptism was not the deciding factor, but the Christophany at Damascus, and not baptism but preaching the gospel was in his view the purpose of his apostleship. Also the Lord's Supper is not for him the real cause of communion with Christ, but an expression of that communion. It is a peculiarly intimate contact with the Lord. The Lord's Supper does not bring about the communion, it only brings it into prominence. Neither baptism nor the Lord's Supper is regarded as of magical effect. The decisive factor in each case is God's grace. The Pauline Christian can say with Paul,

> By the grace of God I am what I am.

Powerful and original as the spiritual experience of Christ was with Paul, there were not lacking other stimuli, which influenced him, derived most directly, I think, from the Septuagint religion. The Greek Old Testament has, and here we must recognise an important Hellenisation of the original, a great number of prominent passages in which the formulae 'in God' or 'in the Lord' are used in a mystical sense. The words of the prophet:[5]

> Yet I will rejoice in the Lord

sounds like the prelude of the Pauline Jubilate:[6]

> Rejoice in the Lord.

The formula 'in God' which is especially frequent in the Septuagint Psalms is a great favourite with Paul[7] and is closely connected with the formula 'in Christ.'[8] The confession in the speech on Mar's Hill,[9]

> In Him (God) we live and move and have our being,

comes from the pre-Christian Jewish mysticism of Paul which had been inspired by the Septuagint, but Paul did not understand this being-in-God in a neo-platonic sense such as is presented to us in the works of Dionysius the Areopagite. The watchword 'in Christ,' inspired by the Damascus experience, seems to be a more vivid substitute for the sacred formula 'in God.' But it only seems to be so. In reality the wider mystic circle 'in Christ' lies like a concentric circle containing the older circle, as though protecting it and inviting to that holy of holies 'in God,' which from now onwards appears really accessible[1] 'through Christ' and 'in Christ.'

To speak of Hellenistic influence is surely justifiable here, when we remember the importance in Greek mysticism of those inspired people who were filled with their God and given power by their God. Placed in the great context of mysticism in general, Paul's

---

5. LXX., Hab. iii. 18, * * *
6. Phil. iii. 1; iv. 4, * * *
7. 1 Thess. ii. 2; Col. iii. 3; Eph. iii. 9; Rom. ii. 17.

8. 1 Thess. i. 1; 2 Thess. i. 1.
9. Acts xvii. 28, * * *
1. Eph. ii. 18; iii. 12; Rom. v. 2 * * *

religion gains the stamp which indicates its true place in the history of religion. It is Christ-mysticism.

* * *

There is a double bifurcation of the types of mysticism according as they are judged by their origin or by their results, and this leads on to a great multitude of blendings and combinations in which widely differing forms are often found in union.

First, when we investigate the question of origins, we see that 'great dividing' line in the history of religion, which we noted in the case of the cult, also drawn through the history of mysticism. The decisive matter is the initiative: who is it that gives (or gave in the first instance) the impulse to the mystical movement of the soul? There is acting mysticism and re-acting mysticism, *anabatic* and *catabatic* mysticism. Man approaches God, or God approaches man. Mysticism of performance or mysticism of grace! Striving mysticism and mysticism of the divine gift.

Secondly the aim of mysticism is either *unio* or *communio*; either oneness with God, or fellowship with God; either loss of the human personality in God or sanctification of the personality through the presence of God; either transformation into the deity, or conformation of the human towards the divine; either participation in the deity or prostration before the deity. In fact ego-centric mysticism or Theo-centric mysticism! Mysticism of aesthetic intoxication or mysticism of ethical enthusiasm! Mysticism that denies personality, or mysticism that affirms personality!

I make no attempt to set forth in detail those blendings and combinations of the different types, nor to describe even for example the reaction mysticism which has lost its original nature and become reduced to the pure acting type, or the acting *unio*-mysticism, or the peculiar form of *communio*-mysticism which develops into *unio*-mysticism. Only I must obviously explain one thing, namely how I classify Paul, the mystic.

Paul is a reacting mystic and a *communio*-mystic. He was even as a Jew a fellowship mystic, but an acting mystic at any rate as regards his longings, only it would seem that through his action he did not reach real communion with God. He felt the fact that he remained far off from God to be the bankruptcy of 'works,' the tragedy of this can still be felt as we read the letters he wrote as a Christian. It was Damascus that transformed his acting mysticism into the reacting mysticism and the soul shaken and thrown open to creative energy by that impact from that time onwards had its firm support 'in Christ': In communion with Christ he found communion with God; Christ-intimacy was experience and confirmation of God-intimacy. He was not deified nor was he transformed into spirit by this communion, nor did he become Christ. He was not like some who at a later day imagined themselves Christ, though they were only possessors of a second-hand Christology and were further removed from Christ than was Paul. But he was transformed by God, he became spiritual and he was one whom Christ possessed[2] and a Christ-bearer.

Paul himself was conscious of the difference between acting and reacting mysticism. His conflict with the 'spirituals' at Corinth[3] is the protest of reacting mysticism against the ecstatic chaos caused by the mysticism of intoxicated enjoyment developing into unrestrained action. But he had also conquered in the same battle within his own breast, when the old mystical activism had whispered to him its words of temptation, *eritis sicut Deus*—'ye shall be as God.' No doubt it was out of such a struggle that that wonderful paradox was born:

I—yet not I

which repeatedly flashes out of the lines of his letters.[4]

A generation ago, in my student days, a heavy hand stretched out from the side of the dogmatists and banished mysticism, which was forced into one narrow pattern, from the German lecture-rooms. The study of Paul suffered, along with other things, from this anathema. The few scholars who then emphasised the mystical element in Paul could have appealed to teachers greater than Albrecht Ritschl. Luther and Calvin had a sympathetic understanding of the Apostle's Christ-mysticism, and going further back we find the real Paul alive in the ancient Church, especially in the Greek Fathers. But the greatest monument of the most genuine understanding of Paul's mysticism is the gospel and epistles of John. Their Logos-Christ is the Spirit-Christ, once more made incarnate for the congregation of the saints in a time of fierce conflict, by the evangelist who was inspired in equal degree by the earthly Jesus, by Paul and by the Spirit-Christ.

This also supplies the answer to the question, How did Paul influence later thought? The witty saying that in the second century only *one* man understood Paul (Marcion) and he misunderstood him, only has truth in it, if the enquiry as to Paul's influence is confined to his 'doctrine,' perhaps indeed to the 'doctrine of Justification.' But if enquiry be made about Christ-mysticism, the traces of the Apostle's influence are clear, and shine through from the most ancient times down to our own day, being seen not least clearly in the two Catholic Churches.

2. Gal. iii. 29; v. 24; 1 Cor. i. 12; iii. 23; xv. 23; 2 Cor. x. 7. ∗ ∗ ∗
3. 1 Cor. xii–xiv.
4. 1 Cor. xv. 10 (cf. also vii. 10); Gal. ii. 20.

There can be no doubt that Paul became influential in the world's history precisely through his Christ-mysticism. The spiritual Christ was able to do what a dogmatic Messiah could not have done. The dogmatic Messiah of the Jews is fettered to the country of his origin. The spiritual Christ could move from place to place. Coming from the East, He could become at home in the West, and in defiance of changing centuries He could spread out His arms over every generation.

The Spirit bloweth where it listeth.[5]

Paul would certainly not have had this influence on the great scale, if the fires of the mystical elements in him had consumed the ethical. On the contrary, the ethos in his case stood the test of fire. The Pauline Christ-intimacy is no magic transformation, and it is no intoxication of ecstatic enthusiasts who are left as yawning sluggards when the transport is over. Paul himself subordinated ecstasy to ethos.[6] Thus we may rightly and fittingly apply to him the conception of 'voluntary' mysticism, which has lately come into vogue, understanding thereby 'the inner coming of the spiritual life-energy which directs us in the depths of our own being.'[7] Christ-mysticism is in him rather a glowing fire than a flickering flame. He who was 'apprehended' by Christ speaks with deep humility:[8]

Not that I have already obtained [Him].

But he also makes the heroic confession:[9]

I can do all things in Him that strengtheneth me.

Similarly, too, the gifts of the Spirit set the saints of Paul's churches mighty tasks: they who had 'put on Christ,'[1] were daily to put Him on anew,[2] and 'in' this Christ only that faith is of value whose energy is proved by love.[3]

Let us look back for a moment! Christ the Living, exalted with the Father, but by God's Grace as Spirit in Paul and Paul in Him—that is the Apostle Paul's assurance of Christ and experience of Christ. According to the doctrinaire view 'Paulinism' contains at this point an 'antinomy' through the 'dualism' of the transcendence and immanence of Christ. But in fact we see here two moods of Paul's piety, which could exist side by side in his great soul. They no more represent an internal contradiction than do the mutually intertwined experiences of the transcendent and the immanent God which every believer knows. Rather it is the polar contrast of these two moods that gives the inner life of the Apostle its prophetic tension.

5. John iii. 8.
6. 1 Cor. xiii. 1–3.
7. R. Seeberg, *Die Lehre Luthers* (*Lehrbuch der Dogmengeschichte*, iv., 12/3), Leipzig, 1917, p. 310. * * *

8. Phil. iii. 12 ff., * * *
9. Phil. iv. 13, * *
1. Gal. iii. 27.
2. Rom. xiii. 14.
3. Gal. v. 6, * * *

This tension finds its release in an abundance of detailed assurances, experiences, and confessions.

* * *

With the assurance of Damascus 'Christ in me' and the assurance of equal content 'I in Christ,' an inexhaustible religious 'energy' was concentrated in the deep, and to religious impulses extremely sensitive, soul of the convert. In every direction Paul now radiated the 'power of Christ' that ruled in him, gave out the 'riches of Christ,' the 'blessing of Christ,' and the 'fulness of Christ' which had come to him.

To designate this abundant 'power of Christ,' which flowed through him and took effect from him, Paul used a well-known technical religious word, the Greek term *pistis*, which we are accustomed to translate 'faith.'

Though one of the most frequently considered Pauline 'conceptions,' the faith of the Apostle can perhaps be more precisely formulated than it usually is. Generally faith as used by Paul is defined as believing 'on' Christ, and thus the frequent genitival construction the 'faith of Christ Jesus,'[4] and the prepositional constructions 'faith in Christ Jesus,'[5] and 'to believe in Christ Jesus,'[6] are identified with belief 'on' Christ.

I believe that this proceeding obliterates a characteristic Pauline feature on one of the most important points. Faith is in Paul's usage faith 'in' Christ, that is to say, faith is something which is accomplished in union of life with the spiritual Christ. That is the meaning of those passages in which Paul connects the preposition 'in' with the words 'faith,' 'believer,' 'believe,' and also of the passages in which the genitival construction appears.

It is not yet generally recognised that Paul uses the genitive 'of Jesus Christ' in a wholly peculiar manner. We have numerous passages in Paul in which the usual rough classification of 'subjective genitive' or 'objective genitive' is insufficient. Later Greek (and Latin) has also in addition to these a genitival use, sometimes rather remarkable, which is to some extent the result of the survival of an older type. So, too, in Paul, it would be possible to establish the use of a special type of genitive, which might be called the 'genitive of fellowship' or the 'mystical genitive,' because it indicates mystical fellowship with Christ. 'Of Jesus Christ' is here in the main identical with 'in Christ.'

'The faith of Christ Jesus' is 'faith in Christ,' the faith which the Christian has in fellowship with Christ.

4. * * * Gal. ii. 16, 20; iii. 22; Eph. iii. 12; Phil. iii. 9; Rom. iii. 22, 26.
5. * * * Gal. iii. 26; v. 6; Col. i. 4; ii. 5 (* * *); Eph. i. 15; 1 Tim. i. 14; iii. 13; 2 Tim. i. 13; iii. 15.
6. * * * Gal. ii. 16; Phil. i. 29 (Eph. i. 13). Cf. 'the faithful in Christ' [lit. believers], * * * Eph. i. 1; Col. i. 2.

Numerous other religious root ideas are similarly bound up with the mystical genitive. Alongside 'faith of Christ' we find in Paul the 'love of Christ,' the 'hope of Christ,' the 'peace of Christ,' the 'meekness and gentleness of Christ,' the 'tender mercies of Christ,' the 'patience of Christ,' the 'obedience of Christ,' the "truth of Christ,' the 'fear of Christ,' the 'circumcision of Christ,' the 'sufferings of Christ, the 'afflictions of Christ,' and other similar technical expressions. Throughout it is understood that these special experiences or assurances of the soul in the Christian come about through the mystic-spiritual fellowship with Christ.

So too 'the faith of Christ' is faith which is alive in fellowship with the spiritual Christ, and it is faith 'on' God, in its content identical with the faith which Abraham had in the sacred past, an unconditional reliance upon the living God in spite of all temptations to doubt. This faith of Abraham, heroic by its 'nevertheless,' which afterwards was made impossible by the law, has in Christ again become possible and real for us. 'Separated from Christ,' Paul says in one place, we are 'without God in the world'; in union with Christ we have boldness to approach God.

The faith of Paul is then the union with God which is established in fellowship with Christ. It is, like that of Abraham, an unshakable confidence in the grace of God. God-intimacy in Christ Jesus, God-intimacy of those who are Christ-intimates, that is Paul's faith.

The unshakableness, which often makes faith appear as something paradoxical, is just as important as the other characteristic, that faith as Paul uses the term is not a conviction reached by reason, but something practical, an inner personal dependence, an attitude of the personality, and inner bearing. Thus Paul's conception of faith is to be transferred out of the sphere of dogma into that of mysticism and cult religion. 'Faith or consciousness of faith and mysticism belong together.'[7]

And now we must try to recognise this 'faith of Christ 'of the Apostle as the centre of energy, from which the many separate confessions concerning salvation of Christ radiate. We must seek to understand the rich variety of Pauline experience and testimony about salvation which finds expression in the confessions in Paul's letters as refractions of the one beam of light, 'faith of Christ.'

Here, in my opinion, lies the most important problem of the study of Paul, as far as that is concerned with Paul's inner self. The solution of the problem lies in the recognition that the Pauline testimonies concerning salvation are psychically synonymous.

In the older study of Paul it was generally the custom first to isolate the so-called 'concepts' of justification, redemption, reconcili-

7. This profound sentence of Schaeder   applied to Paul. * * *
(*Geistproblem*, p. 118) can rightly be

ation, forgiveness, and so forth, and then from these isolated and thereby theologically stiffened 'concepts' to reconstruct the 'system' of 'Paulinism.' Paulinism so constructed appeared according to one theologian as a triangle, according to another as a square or a hexagon, and occasionally it looked like the side view of a staircase—in any case it was very geometrical and conventional. In our conception of it also there are straight lines, but they do not form closed geometrical figures, rather like rays of light, unlimited and immeasurable, they stream in all directions from the central point, the light of the experience of Christ.

* * *

Finally there is one characteristically Pauline conviction, little regarded by the doctrinaire students who are more interested in the theories of Primitive Christianity than in its psychic forces, namely, the conviction of being in Christ raised especially above *suffering*. Paul has here given form to one of the profoundest conceptions that we owe to him: since he suffers in Christ, his sufferings are to him the 'sufferings of Christ,' or the 'afflictions of Christ.' It is not the old Paul who suffers, but the new Paul, who is a member of the Body of Christ, and who therefore mystically experiences all that that Body experienced and experiences; he 'suffers with Christ,' is 'crucified with Christ,' 'has died with Christ,' 'been buried,' 'raised up,' and 'lives with Christ,' Thus suffering is no anomaly in Paul's life, but as the 'sufferings of Christ' a normal part of his state as a Christian; and a certain fixed measure of 'afflictions of Christ' must according to God's plan be 'filled up' by Paul.[8]

In this Pauline passion-mysticism it is easy to recognise what I have called the undogmatic element in Paul. Dogmatic exegesis, which tortures itself over the problem of interpreting such passages and takes away from them their original simplicity by introducing into them an artificially forced '*as it were*,' cannot express in theological terms the intimacy of this mystical contemplation of the passion. But under the cross of Jesus a suffering man will be able even to-day to experience for himself the depth of meaning and the comfort implied by Paul's 'sufferings of Christ.' Similarly the ancient Christians were able easily to understand the mystical meaning of the several stages of baptism to the death, burial and resurrection with Christ, because having been baptised as adults, they had an indelibly vivid recollection of the ceremony performed upon them by immersion. It is by no means easy for us, brought up in the practice of infant baptism, to realise this vividness. The usages and sentiments attached to other cults of their environment

8. Col. i. 24, * * *

may have rendered the mystical interpretation of their sacrament easier. But that thorough investigation of the Pauline passion-mysticism which is so urgently needed must give the whole problem its right place not only in the general history of religion, but also in the world-wide history of that Christian piety which centres upon the passion, a subject which cannot yet be properly comprehended by any of us, but whose memorials in written word and drama, in music and pictures often give us a wonderfully sympathetic interpretation of Paul's profoundest meaning.

ALBERT SCHWEITZER

Eschatological Mystic (1930) †

When we say that Paul is a mystic, what do we mean by mysticism?

We are always in presence of mysticism when we find a human being looking upon the division between earthly and super-earthly, temporal and eternal, as transcended, and feeling himself, while still externally amid the earthly and temporal, to belong to the super-earthly and eternal.

Mysticism may be either primitive or developed. Primitive mysticism has not yet risen to a conception of the universal, and is still confined to naïve views of earthly and super-earthly, temporal and eternal. The entry into the super-earthly and eternal takes place by means of a 'mystery', a magical act. By means of this the participant enters into communion with a divine being in such a way that he shares the latter's supernatural mode of existence. This view of a union with the divinity, brought about by efficacious ceremonies, is found even in quite primitive religions. The most fundamental significance of the sacrificial feast is, no doubt, that by his meal the partaker becomes in some way one with the divinity.

In a more developed form magical mysticism is found in the oriental and Greek mystery-religions at the beginning of our era. In the cults of Attis, Osiris, and Mithras, as well as in the Eleusinian Mysteries in their later more profound form, the believer attains, by means of an initiation, union with the divinity, and thereby becomes a partaker in the immortality for which he yearns. Though these sacraments he ceases to be a natural man and is born again into a higher state of being.

† From *The Mysticism of Paul the Apostle* (New York, 1931 and reprinted), tr. by William Montgomery, portions of Chaps. I and XIV. Albert Schweitzer (1875–1965) was equally famous for his theological, philosophical, and musical accomplishments, and for his decision to become a missionary doctor in Lambarene, West Africa.

But when the conception of the universal is reached and a man reflects upon his relation to the totality of being and to Being in itself, the resultant mysticism becomes widened, deepened, and purified. The entrance into the super-earthly and eternal then takes place through an act of thinking. In this act the conscious personality raises itself above that illusion of the senses which makes him regard himself as in bondage in the present life to the earthly and temporal. It attains the power to distinguish between appearance and reality and is able to conceive the material as a mode of manifestation of the Spiritual. It has sight of the Eternal in the Transient. Recognising the unity of all things in God, in Being as such, it passes beyond the unquiet flux of becoming and disintegrating into the peace of timeless being, and is conscious of itself as being in God, and in every moment eternal.

This intellectual mysticism is a common possession of humanity. Whenever thought makes the ultimate effort to conceive the relation of the personality to the universal, this mysticism comes into existence. It is found among the Brahmans and in Buddha, in Platonism, in Stoicism, in Spinoza, Schopenhauer, and Hegel.

Even into Christianity, naïvely dualistic as it is, distinguishing strictly between the present and the future, the here and the hereafter, this mysticism penetrates. Not indeed unopposed; but whenever in the great thinkers or under the influence of great movements of thought Christianity endeavours to attain to clarity regarding the relation of God and the world, it cannot help opening the door to mysticism. Mysticism finds expression in the Hellenistic theology of Ignatius and the Johannine Gospel, in the writings of Augustine and in those attributed to Dionysius the Areopagite; it is found in Hugo of St. Victor and other scholastics, in Francis of Assisi, in Meister Eckart, in Suso, in Tauler and the other fathers of the German theological mysticism; it speaks in the language of Jakob Boehme and other mystical heretics of Protestantism; there is mysticism in the hymns of Tersteegen, Angelus Silesius, and Novalis; and in the writings of Schleiermacher mysticism seeks to express itself in the language of the Church.

The type of intellectual mysticism differs according to place and time. Among the Brahmans and in Buddhism it is found in its most abstract form. The mystic thinks of his existence under the pure indifferentiated conception of being, and sinks himself therein. Jakob Boehme is the herald of an imaginative mysticism. In the Christian mysticism of Meister Eckart and his followers the conception is of being in the living God, as is also the case with the mysticism of Hindu pietism, which endeavours to get beyond the cold Brahmanic mysticism. Whatever colouring it may take on, however, what intellectual mysticism is concerned with is Being in its ultimate reality.

Of what precise kind then is the mysticism of Paul?

It occupies a unique position between primitive and intellectual mysticism. The religious conceptions of the Apostle stand high above those of primitive mysticism. This being so, it might have been expected that his mysticism would have to do with the unity of man with God as the ultimate ground of being. But this is not the case. Paul never speaks of being one with God or being in God. He does indeed assert the divine sonship of believers. But, strangely enough, he does not conceive of sonship to God as an immediate mystical relation to God, but as mediated and effected by means of the mystical union with Christ.

Thus, higher and lower mysticism here interpenetrate. In Paul there is no God-mysticism; only a Christ-mysticism by means of which man comes into relation to God. The fundamental thought of Pauline mysticism runs thus: I am in Christ; in Him I know myself as a being who is raised above this sensuous, sinful, and transient world and already belongs to the transcendent; in Him I am assured of resurrection; in Him I am a Child of God.

Another distinctive characteristic of this mysticism is that being in Christ is conceived as a having died and risen again with Him, in consequence of which the participant has been freed from sin and from the Law, possesses the Spirit of Christ, and is assured of resurrection.

This 'being-in-Christ' is the prime enigma of the Pauline teaching: once grasped it gives the clue to the whole.

* * *

One thing which made it easy to overlook the absence of God-mysticism in Paul is the fact that, according to the Acts of the Apostles, Paul did in his speech on the Areopagus in Athens proclaim a mysticism of being-in-God. The absence of statements about being in God in the Paul of the Letters is accordingly regarded as something accidental and without significance, since after all the Paul of Acts expressly says of God "in Him we live and move and have our being" (Acts xvii. 28). On the strength of this passage from Acts Adolf Deissmann, for example, thinks himself justified in assuming in Paul a mysticism of being-in-God which has its roots in pre-Christian Jewish thought. This forms an inner core to which the Christ-mysticism which arose out of the experience on the road to Damascus forms an outer envelope.

But was the Areopagus utterance really Paul's? There are weighty objections to this assumption, which make it probable that the speech to the Athenians is to be ascribed solely to the writer of the Acts. It was of course the general practice of the historians of antiquity to compose speeches such as seemed to them appropriate to a particular person and occasion, and represent them as spoken by the person in question. This custom the author of the Acts had no scruples in adopting. His purpose was to exhibit a Paul at Athens who to the Greeks had become a Greek.

* * *

In the Stoic view the world is thought of as static and unaltering. The world is Nature, which remains constantly in the same relationship to the world-spirit pervading it and pervaded by it. For Paul, however, the world is not Nature but a supernatural historical process which has for its stages the forthgoing of the world from God, its alienation from Him, and its return to Him.

This dramatic view of world history is also in its own way a kind of mysticism, a mysticism which can assert that all things are *from* God and *through* God and *unto* God. But what it can never assert is that all things are *in* God. This is for it simply not the case so long as there is a sensible, material world, and a sensible world history. It is only when the End comes, when time gives place to eternity and all things return to God, that they can be said to be in God.

Since Paul lives in the conceptions of the dramatic world-view characteristic of the late Jewish Eschatology, he is by consequence bound to the logic of that view. He concludes the hymn to God at the end of the 11th chapter of Romans with the declaration "For *from* Him and *through* Him and *unto* Him are all things" (Rom. xi. 36); but he cannot take a step further and add that all things are *in* God.

* * *

According to the Eschatological view the elect man shares the fate of the world. Therefore, so long as the world has not returned to God, he also cannot be in God.

That Paul does not think of Sonship to God as being-in-God depends ultimately on the fact that this sonship is for him, as it also was for Jesus, a thing of the future. Not until the coming of the Messianic Kingdom will men be Children of God. Before that, they are those who have the assurance of having been called to this sonship and are therefore, by anticipation, denominated Children of God.

Being-in-God is for Paul impossible so long as the angelic beings still possess some kind of power over man. Once Christ has, in the progress of the Messianic Kingdom, overcome them and has destroyed death as the last enemy, He will Himself give back His now unneeded power to God "in order that God may be all in all" (1 Cor. xv. 26–28). Then only will there be a being-in-God.

Paul does thus recognise a God-mysticism; but it is not in being contemporaneously with the Christ-mysticism. The presuppositions of his world-view make it impossible that they should co-exist, or that one should necessitate the other. They are chronologically successive, Christ-mysticism holding the field until God-mysticism becomes possible.

The peculiarity that the mysticism of Paul is only a mysticism of being-in-Christ, and not also a mysticism of being-in-God, has thus its foundation in the fact that it originally had its place in an eschatological world-view.

*   *   *

The Sacraments are similarly conditioned. They do not directly communicate eternal life, as is the case with the Greek mystery-religions, but a participation in a world-condition which is still in preparation. The Sacrament is related to the Cosmic event. This view finds expression in the fact that for Paul the Sacraments are ephemeral institutions. In the Hellenistic mystery-religions it is of the essence of the sacrament that it reaches back into the mysterious past of the world, and is efficacious for all times and all generations of mankind. For Paul it is far otherwise. His Sacraments have their beginning in the death of Jesus—that is, in the immediate present—and continue until His return in glory—that is, into the immediate future. It is only for this span of time that they exist. Before, they were impossible; after, they will be unnecessary. They were created *ad hoc* for a particular class of men of a particular generation, the elect of that generation "upon whom the ends of the world are come" (1 Cor. x. 11).

As temporary *ad hoc* institutions they have their counterpart in the sacraments of the Israelites on their way from Egypt to Canaan; these also were valid for one generation and with reference to a benefit expected in the near future.

The character of Paul's sacramental views is clearly indicated by the fact that he can regard as sacraments events experienced once or a few times only, and by a great multitude of men, such as the passing through the Red Sea, or the wanderings beneath the Cloud, the feeding with Manna, and the drinking of the water from the Rock.

The fact, to which for him mysticism and sacraments alike go back, is the dying and rising again of Christ, which took place in the immediate past. This fact is a cosmic event. In the death of Jesus begins the cessation of the natural world, and in His resurrection the dawning of the supernatural world. This cosmic event translates itself in the created being, man, as a dying and rising again.

Paul's mysticism is then historico-cosmic where that of the Hellenistic religions is mythical. The difference is fundamental. Mythical mysticism is orientated towards the remote beginnings of the world, historico-cosmic mysticism towards the times of the end. In mythical mysticism an event lying in the past acquires universal significance and efficacy, by being repeated in symbol, and in a sense re-experienced, by a person who makes a conscious effort to that end. The myth is brought down into the present. In the mysticism of Paul, on the other hand, the whole happening is objective. World-transforming forces, which are manifested for the first time in the dying and rising again of Jesus, began thenceforward to show their efficacy in a certain definite category of mankind. The only necessary condition is to belong to the Elect and to be subjected through Baptism to the working of these forces.

The mysticism of the mystery-religions is individualistic; that of Paul collectivistic; the former has an active character, the latter has something peculiarly passive about it.

In the Hellenistic mysteries the initiate acquires immortality, entering into possession of it on his death. Pauline mysticism is concerned with the passing away and restoration of the world, and the fate of the Elect amid these events. It does not even assume that all will die, but expects that many of them will live to see the end of the world while still in their mortal bodies, and will enter, transformed, into the glory to which they have become entitled through the being-in-Christ.

The fact that it occurs in connection with the expectation of the end of the world, and is founded upon cosmic events, gives its distinctive character to the Pauline mysticism. It is in vain that literary artifice has been applied to give to the expectation of death in the Hellenistic mysticism some faint suggestions of the expectation of the end of the world, in order to bring the Hellenistic sacramental mysticism into closer touch with the Pauline.

In advocacy of its expectation of the end of the world Pauline mysticism is something absolutely unique. There is no mysticism, whether earlier, contemporary, or later, which comes into comparison with it.

*   *   *

Wherein consists, in the ultimate analysis, the specific character of the Pauline Mysticism?

The fact of being thought out by the aid of the conceptual apparatus of the eschatological world-view constitutes only its outward character, not its inner. This inner character is determined by the fact that Paul has thought out his conception of redemption through Christ within the sphere of belief in the Kingdom of God. In Paul's mysticism the death of Jesus has its significance for believers, not in itself, but as the event in which the realisation of the Kingdom of God begins. For him, believers are redeemed by entering already, through the union with Christ, by means of a mystical dying and rising again with Him during the continuance of the natural world-era into a supernatural state of existence, this state being that which they are to possess in the Kingdom of God. Through Christ we are removed out of this world and transferred into the state of existence proper to the Kingdom of God, notwithstanding the fact that it has not yet appeared. This is the fundamental idea of the concept of redemption, which Paul worked out by the aid of the thought-forms of the eschatological world-view.

Since the transformation of the world into the Kingdom of God begins for Paul with the death of Christ, the Primitive-Christian belief which looked to a redemption only to be realised in the future is changed into the belief in a redemption which is already present, even though it is only to be completely realised in the future. A faith of the present arises within the faith of the future. Paul connects the expectation of the Kingdom and of the redemption to be realised in it with the coming and the death of Jesus, in such a way that belief in redemption and in the Coming of the Kingdom becomes independent of whether the Kingdom comes quickly or is delayed. Without giving up eschatology, he already stands above it.

* * *

The great weakness of all doctrines of redemption since the Primitive Christian is that they represent a man as wholly concerned with his own individual redemption, and not equally with the coming of the Kingdom of God. The one thing needful is that we should work for the establishment of a Christianity, which does not permit those who allow their lives to be determined by Christ to be "of little faith" in regard to the future of the world. However much circumstances may suggest to them this want of faith, Christianity must compel them to realise that to be a Christian means to be possessed and dominated by a hope of the Kingdom of God, and a will to work for it, which bids defiance to external reality. Until this comes about Christianity will stand before the world like a wood in the barrenness of winter.

A change has come over our belief in the Kingdom of God. We no longer look for a transformation of the natural circumstances of the world; we take the continuance of the evil and suffering, which belong to the nature of things, as something appointed by God for us to bear. Our hope of the Kingdom is directed to the essential and spiritual meaning of it, and we believe in that as a miracle wrought by the Spirit in making men obedient to the will of God.

But we must cherish in our hearts this belief in the coming of the Kingdom through the miracle of the Spirit with the same ardour with which the Primitive Christianity cherished its hope of the translation of the world into the supernatural condition. Christianity cannot get away from the fact that God has laid upon it the task of spiritualising its faith. Our concern must be to see that the strength of our faith is not impaired by this transformation. It is time for our Christianity to examine itself and see whether we really still have faith in the Kingdom of God, or whether we merely retain it as a matter of traditional phraseology. There is a deep sense in which we may apply to the theological preoccupations of our day the saying of Jesus, "Seek ye first the Kingdom of God and His righteousness, and all these things shall be added unto you."

But whenever Christian faith attempts the task of bringing the significance of the appearance of Jesus and the nature of the redemption brought by Him into living relation with belief in the Kingdom of God, it finds Paul before him as the pioneer of such a Christianity. In his words there speaks the voice of a Primitive Christianity which will never pass away.

Great has been the work as a reforming influence which Paul, by his doctrine of justification by faith alone, has accomplished in opposition to the spirit of work-righteousness in Christianity. Still greater will be the work which he will do when his mystical doctrine of being redeemed into the Kingdom of God, through union with Christ, begins to bring quietly to bear upon us the power which lies within it.

* * *

The experience which Paul sets before us as the gateway to the eternal is the dying and rising again with Christ. What deep significance lies in the fact that he does not speak of the method of the new life's beginning as a rebirth! He seems deliberately to pass by this term, already coined in the language which he spoke and wrote, and lying ready to his hand. He does so because it is impossible to fit it into the eschatological doctrine of redemption. If the Elect who belong to the Kingdom of God are already in the resurrection state of existence, their redemption, conceived of as anticipatory participation in the Kingdom while still in their natural being, must consist in their undergoing, through the union with Christ, a hidden dying and rising again, by which they become new men raised above the world and their own natural being, and are translated into the state of existence proper to the Kingdom of God. This conception of redemption, with its naturalistic realism, due to its embodiment in the thought-forms of the eschatological world-view, at the same time carries within it an intensely spiritual realism. Whereas the idea of rebirth remains a metaphor, imported into primitive Christian beliefs out of another world of thought, the conception of dying and rising again with Christ was born out of Christianity itself, and becomes for every man who seeks new life in Christ a truth continually renewed, at once primitive and permanent.

Paul powerfully urges men, by the self-revelations in which he lays bare his inner life to them, to embark upon an experience like his own. From the point of view of a later fully formulated theology his doctrine is incorrectly stated. He has not been sufficiently careful to express himself in such a way as to exclude the misunderstanding that a man, through union with Jesus Christ, redeems himself—to exclude it, that is, with the decisiveness which a later religious thought, having lost its hold on simplicity, might consider desirable. It is the prerogative of the mystic to think truth in its living vigour, unconcerned about formal correctitude.

Paul's mystical doctrine of redemption has not been taken up into Church dogma. It has preferred to adopt the concept of the sacrificial death of Jesus, basing itself on the formulation of this thought which it has received in the Pauline doctrine of justification by faith. Mysticism can never become dogma. But, on the other hand, dogma can never remain living without a surrounding aura of mysticism. Therefore Paul's mystical doctrine of redemption is for us a precious possession, without which we cannot form the right conception either of Christianity or of our individual state as Christians. It is truth which a man who has been taken possession of by Christ urges his brethren to verify in experience.

* * *

MARTIN DIBELIUS

Mystic and Prophet (1941) †

* * *

A decade and a half before the [First] World War, students of antiquity rediscovered the significance of Hellenistic mysticism. It

† From "Paulus und die Mystik," first published in *Eine Heilige Kirche* 22 (1941), rp. in *Botschaft und Geschichte* (Tübingen, 1956): II, 134–59, and in *Das Paulusbild in der neueren Deutschen Forschung*, ed. K. H. Rengstorf (Darmstadt, 1964): 447–74.

Martin Dibelius (1883–1947) was a pioneer in form criticism and style criticism of the New Testament, as well as in detailed use of comparative religious materials for interpreting early Christian history.

was established that in Greek philosophy and in the Roman philos·ophy dependent on it, there was a turn to religion. At that time, with dubious justification perhaps, this turn was said to be the work of the last great philospher of the Greek tongue, the Stoic Posidon·ius. The shift manifests itself in the notion that the philosophizing man is elevated, in his vision of the All, beyond the human realm, and that the soul, thought of as a divine, fiery breath, achieves con·tact with the divine world which is its home. Elevation of the soul to union with God, made possible by its natural relationship to God—that is the goal of philosophical mysticism. While this research was going on, scholarly interest also turned to the mystery religions, especially those oriental cults which had been Hellenized, the cults of Isis, Attis, Adonis, and Mithras. In these it seemed that the initiate (*mystēs*) gained union with the god by means of sacred actions—by baths, like the blood-baptism of the Taurobolium, by sacred meals, by marriage and adoption rites. It may be that the scholars, in the understandable enthusiasm of discovery, overesti·mated much of the evidence; nevertheless it is indisputable that the *mystēs* became, through certain initiatory rites, a higher being—like the deity or even a new incarnation of him.

Classicists and theologians have sought to demonstrate a connec·tion between the apostle Paul and this mysticism. They had in mind more than just the prehistory of certain theological ideas of the apostle, which seemed to stem neither from primitive Chris·tianity nor from Palestinian Judaism. Rather they wanted to use this approach in order to free the interpretation of Paul's theology from a certain one-sidedness imposed on it by the ecclesiastical tra·dition (since the Reformation) and by theological systematizing (especially since Albrecht Ritschl). They wanted to see in the apostle not the theological teacher of the justification of sinners, but also and perhaps even essentially the *homo religiosus*, who felt himself to be transformed and who now preached the transforma·tion of mankind for the coming world-transformation. This under·standing of Paul on the basis of mysticism and the mysteries, as represented by such men as Reitzenstein, Deissmann, and Bousset, was then attacked by Dialectical Theology. Thus again a theologi·cal interest was really decisive. The Dialectical Theologians thought the mystical interpretation of Paul perverse, because it seemed to bring the apostle suspiciously close to that which these theologians regarded as the original sin of theology: the illusion that God and world, God and man could ever be viewed together, indeed even merged into one.

That explains why today the theme "Paul and Mysticism" is accorded only the most limited validity among theologians. Some wish to avoid using the word "mysticism" at all in connection with

Paul. Others add modifiers, speaking of "reactive" mysticism[1] or "objective" mysticism, of "faith-mysticism," of "formative" (as opposed to "de-forming") mysticism, and finally of "eschatological" mysticism.[2]

This is not the place to explore the right and wrong of these mediating designations. Rather we have to ask whether relationships do exist between Paul and the streams of Hellenistic mysticism that were present in his environment, and what meaning they had for the apostle's Christianity and for his preaching.

I

We must have one thing clear from the outset. If we employ the distinction, introduced by Söderblom and Heiler, between prophetic and mystical types of piety within the higher religions, then Paul's place is easily determined: He is a representative of the *prophetic*, not the *mystical* type of piety.

The difference between the two types is most readily grasped when one observes the source of the religious person's power. The mystic denies the world for himself, denies his own self insofar as it can be separated from God, and denies for himself the abyss that separates God and world. For him the separation between temporal and eternal worlds no longer exists. Whether he himself enters into the higher world or whether God comes to him and unites with him—in either case the power of the mystic derives from the overcoming of that abyss and from the complete or nearly complete union with God. But the religious man of the prophetic type lives in the consciousness of the opposition between God and man. The power of his religiosity comes from the experience that God has bridged that abyss in a revelation, of whatever kind. But man responds to this divine self-disclosure by turning to him in obedience, faith, and also through the formation of life or world. Man perceives that he is on earth and God in heaven, but he also perceives himself as bound and obligated to this distant God. The question of the basis of this bond and the goal of this obligation is answered differently in the particular religions.

It is easy to show that Paul receives the essential power of his religion in the consciousness of the separation of God and man, not from their union.

* * *

It is an indisputable fact that mysticism has no place in Paul's thoughts about sin and forgiveness, God's righteousness and atone-

1. Adolf Deissmann * * * [See above, pp. 374–87.—*Editor*]

2. Albert Schweitzer * * * [See above, pp. 387–95.—*Editor*]

ment, faith, the cross of Christ, resurrection of the Christians, and judgment. The believing man remains on earth; in the mission of Christ God announces to him forgiveness, ·i.e., atonement. But even afterward God and man remain separate; God still hails him before his judgment, only that judgment loses its terrors for man because Christ is his defender. These trains of thought are typical of Paul. They include his rejection of Judaism and the freedom of Gentile Christians from the Law, and they form the basis of his preaching and his missionary activity. Therefore it is clear that *the type of piety to which Paul belongs is the prophetic, not the mystical.*

II

Neither is the theology of Paul a mystical theology. In his theology Paul does not aim at new perceptions of God and the world, from which a system could then be erected, but seeks the intellectual justification of perceptions that have forced themselves upon him. Forced themselves upon him: through his conversion, which he understands as being overpowered by God. As a Jew he had found the proclamation of the gallows-Messiah blasphemous; he had regarded the claim to salvation by Galilean fishermen and tax-farmers—from the Pharisaic standpoint a group estranged from God—as wickedness. Now, by a violent conversion, he had been forced over to the side of these men, required to accept that preaching of the gallows-Messiah. For the Pharisee, with his scribal training, this new standpoint raised questions of whose seriousness Jesus' disciples were still oblivious. The primary question was this: how could one hold together the thought of the righteous God of the Law with the unrighteousness of the cross, with the paradox of the reconciliation message, with the unworthiness (from the standpoint of the Law) of the Christian group? * * * Thus Paul's theology had to become a *theodicy*, to justify in the eyes of men this puzzling God and his paradoxical behavior. What aroused Paul's questioning was not the hiddenness and inaccessibility of God, but just the fact that he had revealed himself, though in a quite unanticipated manner that made havoc of all the presuppositions of Jewish thought. Theology now had the task of forming new presuppositions. Therefore it is historical theology, thinking through God's plan in the history of salvation and in eschatology. It concerns itself with the meaning of the Jewish people and its Law, with God's aim for world and mankind. Theology that is thus preoccupied with salvation history is not a mystical theology.

But it is only a question of the presuppositions of salvation. They have to be deduced from the given reality of salvation. For salvation has appeared in Christ—it needs only to be proclaimed, not excogitated. For that reason the questions from which Paul's theology emerges are not anxious or despairing questions. The certainty of salvation does not depend upon answers to them. * * * He lives from the certainty that in Christ God actually drew near to him and remains with him continually.

And it is here that those statements of the apostle that resemble the statements of mysticism in form or content have their place. When Paul ventures to speak of his connection with the divine world, he chooses *words or images of mysticism*.

It is characteristic of Paul that he obtains the most mystical—and therefore the most Hellenistic—statements of this kind from a midrash on an Old Testament passage. * * * The apostle reaches the climax in 2 Cor. 3:18: But we (we Christians) all see (or: reflect) with unveiled faces the "glory" of the Lord and thus are ourselves transformed into the same images as he (namely, into bearers of the divine "glory"), to ever increasing "glory," for this comes to us from the Lord of the Spirit (and therefore we are certain of that freedom, the absence of any veil interposed between us and God).

We see the divine "glory" and by this vision are transformed into bearers of this glory: that is the conception of the form of mysticism that was cultivated in the Hellenistic mysteries, but also outside the cult. Thus Lucius, according to Apuleius, *Metamorphoses* XI. 23, 24, became an incarnation of the sun god in the Isis mystery, after he had seen Sol in radiant light and the gods of the upper and lower worlds. Similarly, but more subjectively and mystically, the initiates of Hermes are counseled to observe the image of God with the "eyes of the heart" in order to find the way to the higher world (*Corpus Hermeticum* 4:11). And the same initiates are assured that the divine, if it illuminates their spirit and soul, will transform them into the divine substance (10:6). Paul himself, probably thinking of his conversion, confesses that the God who once created the light has also caused a light to shine in him, consisting of the "gnosis" of the "glory" of God in the face of Christ (2 Cor. 4:6). Remembering that for Paul *gnosis*, applied to superterrestrial things, does not mean rational knowledge but irrational subjective awareness, one may interpret thus: the glory of God, which Paul saw shining in Christ's face, created in him a "bright radiance" that increased more and more—vision produces transformation! That is conceived as a real event, yet not as a procedure enacted in the cultus, as in the mysteries, but as an event that had occurred in Paul's personal history. What we meet here is a typical phenomenon of Pauline mysticism: history in the place of cultus (also in the place of myth) as the place of the mystical experience. However, there is no doubt that the conception is modelled after the cultic experience of the mysteries.

The reader is thrown into the midst of this experience also by this sentence: "All of you who are baptized into Christ are clothed with Christ" (Gal. 3:27). Just before that it is said, quite unmystically, "You are all sons of God in Christ Jesus through faith." If the statement about "clothing" is supposed to prove this sonship, then it has to be connected with the kinship with God that is brought about in *baptism*. Then one has to think not so much of the heavenly garment that redeems the primeval man, as of the donning of the robes of the deities in the mysteries (Apuleius, *Metamorphoses* XI. 24), which deifies the initiate. And this new nature invalidates all differences which belong to the old sphere of life: neither Jew nor Greek, neither slave nor free, neither male nor female, but all are one "in Christ Jesus." Obviously that is for Paul already a fixed circle of thought, for in Col. 3:10 he moves in the same way from the putting on of the new man to the unity of Greek and Jew, circumcised and uncircumcised, etc. But the process that is alluded to in Colossians is not baptism, but ethical transformation—the passage belongs to the admonitions of the so-called *parenesis*. Here, then, the allusion to the new garment that conveys divine power is meant only figuratively, an irrational metaphor for a rational process. * * *

By still another allusion baptism is connected with mystery piety: in the familiar passage Rom. 6:4 it is conceived as a repetition of the burial of Christ. Immersion in water is compared with interment. But the meaning and aim of the comparison in this case as well is to elucidate the following condition: Christian life, as a new existence, resembles the new life of the resurrected one. The comparison itself, without any doubt, rests on the practice in many mysteries of having the initiate experience some form of the mythical fate of the god. When one receives the initiation of Osiris or of Attis, one rises from the dead (either in this world or in the beyond) as that god. The Christian parallel Rom. 6:4 is not quite the same. First, it does not deal with a myth, but with a matter of history, and in this history the death of Christ occurs on the cross—but baptism does not portray crucifixion! Not until the Gnosticism of the Odes of Solomon (27 and 42) do Christians dare to form a sacrament in analogy to crucifixion: the extension of the hands in prayer counts as "his sign," by which one dedicates himself to the Lord, and "the extension of my hands is the extended wood." But baptism is a water bath—and Christ was not drowned! Hence, in order to find an analogy between the passion narrative—as an "etiological cult-myth"—and baptism, Jesus' burial had to be used instead of his death. But it was not Paul who took that step. Others before him must have presented this interpretation, for he can presuppose it in the Roman church which he had neither founded nor taught. Indeed, perhaps it was only through this cultic connection that Christ's burial became a salvation event and was added to the creed. * * *

It is hardly possible for a genuinely mystical tone to arise in the comparison of baptism with the burial, which was not original with Paul and whose meaning is not deification of the believer, but overcoming of the power of sin. Still more is that the case with Paul's *mysticism of suffering*. The suffering of the Son of God on the shameful cross, the most terrible offense to Paul as a Jew, was affirmed by Paul the Christian as an event willed by God and necessary for salvation. Now when he himself had to endure suffering—and occasions for that were not lacking—the thought was bound to occur to him that the suffering made him more like Christ. It is true that at first he regarded the suffering of chronic illness which plagued him, probably with occasional convulsions, as an unendurable burden, perhaps also as a limitation of his work, and he "prayed three times to the Lord" (2 Cor. 12:8) that this "angel of Satan" should leave him. But Christ granted him an answer, a revelation whose content, but not its form, Paul tells to the Corinthians: "My grace is sufficient for you, for divine power comes to perfection only in weakness." Now he made the discovery which so many Christian mystics have made: precisely when the vessel is weak, wretched, and fragile, power must all the more certainly appear as a miracle from God. Thus he could confidently take not only illness but all the sufferings which he had to endure on his apostolic journeys as signs of Christ, even as an ever increasing permeation of his whole humanity by Christ. * * *

This context also explains Col. 1:24: he rejoices in his sufferings because with them he fulfills in his body the measure of "Christ's afflictions," for the good of the "body of Christ," the church. That may be said in the sense of representation: I suffer in Christ's stead. But it can also have an eschatological meaning: until his return Christ, i.e., his earthly body, is fated for a definite measure of suffering, and the apostle helps to bear it. In any case, suffering in this passage is not a burden which Paul takes upon himself in Christ's service, but a crown that confers on him honor and consecration, and which makes him ever more like Christ. Here the mystical tone is palpable; it is also perceptible where Paul, without mentioning Christ at all, emphasizes insatiably his life's distress and dangers, the mortality of his existence, as in 1 Cor. 4:9–13.

But what kind of "mysticism" is that? Here the "mystic" is not made by cultic initiations into a godlike being, as in the mysteries. Here the believer does not by lonely contemplation lose himself in the image of his God until the god appears to the visionary or fills the passionate lover with the consciousness of his sweet presence, as in contemplative mysticism. The place of initiation and contemplation is taken in Paul by the apostle's itinerant life with its struggles and sufferings. Real historical life is the arena where the likeness with Christ can be won, just as Christ himself is not a mythical but a historical figure.

"In any and all circumstances I have been initiated," says Phil. 4:12, "into plenty and hunger, abundance and want—I can do everything through him who gives me strength!" It is true: the mystic initiation is provided by the apostolic life, which becomes more and more a Christ-life, transcending everything earthly, a life that possesses joy and honor, but also norm and judgment, only as a Christ-existence, as a resurrection life. Paul designates this new existence as life "in Christ."

III

Here we have the formula which has occasionally been regarded as the essential mark of Paul's Christ-mysticism, the formula "in Christ (Jesus)." Adolf Deissmann understood it quite generally as a designation of place, and therefore as a proper mystical formula.[3] Johannes Weiss narrowed this thesis by classifying the usage, actually quite diverse, of the formula.[4] Albert Schweitzer explained it as a secondary derivative from the notion of dying and rising with Christ.[5] Down to the most recent time, the debate over the formula's meaning has not come to rest. We shall do well to begin by determining the usages that lie at the greatest distance from each other, since they are most easily recognizable.

The word group "Christian," "to be Christian," "Christianity" was not yet available for Paul. As a substitute he often uses, especially in connection with proper names, the formula "in Christ" or "in the Lord." * * * Paul is quite serious in his consciousness that these expressions point to a new state of existence, but since he can evidently apply the formula to the Christianity of every member of the community, it is perfectly clear that it lacks any mystical tone. "Christ" is the community. Insofar as this community mani-

3. Adolf Deissmann, *Die neutesta-mentliche Formel 'in Christo Jesus,'* 1892.
4. Johannes Weiss, *Theol. Studien und Kritiken*, 1896, pp. 1–33, and *Urchristentum*, p. 359, n. 2 (ET: *Earliest Christianity*, [1937], 1959, pp. 46 ff., n. 22.)
5. Albert Schweitzer, *Die Mystik des Apostels Paulus*, 1930, pp. 122–29 (ET: pp. 122–30).

fests his body, every member is "in Christ." Perhaps whoever first coined the formula did connect it with a collective mysticism— every Christian is in the body of Christ, hence mysteriously united with Christ. But anyone who uses the formula the way Paul does will scarcely conjure up this picture. And when the apostle admonishes a church with the "meekness and gentleness of Christ" (2 Cor. 10:1), or longs for another one "with the emotion of Christ" (Phil. 1:8), what he is doing is to remove the secular character of certain attributes or affects and to transpose them to a new, higher plane. It is very doubtful that he really forms the conception that in some measure not he but the Christ dwelling in him possesses these attributes or emotions.

On the opposite side stand a few statements in which "in Christ" resounds with the full pathos of the miraculous new existence. The most important, because it is the most fundamental of these statements, is 2 Cor. 5:17: "If anyone is in Christ, he is a new creation." Paul has just denied all human relationships. This radicalism grew out of the thought that with Christ "all" died and from hence, in the new life, no longer had their own lives at their disposal, but must belong to him who died for them. "Nam cum coeperis deae servire, tunc magis senties fructum tuae libertatis" ("For once you have begun to serve the Goddess, you will all the more enjoy the fruit of your liberation"), says the priest of the Isis mysteries to Lucius in Apuleius (*Metamorphoses* XI. 15). This notion that the redeeming deity rules the new life is thus not foreign to mysticism. And Paul expresses this rule in 2 Cor. 5:14 by the words, "The love of Christ governs us." Love is thus the ruling principle for Christians. The saying mentioned above, Phil. 4:12, also belongs in this context: "I can do everything through him who gives me strength." It is clear that Paul liked to express himself in the manner of mystical piety in order to present the miracle of the new life, the state of being actually permeated by the power of Christ. The expressions are too radical, their content too comprehensive, to permit the opinion that Paul is only using mystical formulas. He must have experienced the meaning of permeation by divine power and (redeemed) humanity.

He can also express this union with the word "spirit." To be sure, "spirit" is for him the sign of the new aeon in the midst of the old world, a sign common to all Christians, and this universal possession of spirit can naturally not be understood as "mystical" (in the sense of mystical temperament). Yet there are a few statements which probably do show traces of personal experience that can be called mystical. * * * [1 Cor. 6:16 f.; Rom. 8:15] * * *

Occasionally the resurrection life is connected closely with this conception. We have already spoken of the mysticism of suffering. To it belongs the certainty that, "as Christ was raised by the glory of the Father, so ought we also to walk in new life" (Rom. 6:4). This life is usually applied to the new ethical life (as here and Col. 3:1), or to the resurrection of deceased Christians (1 Cor. 15:12 ff.; 1 Thess. 4:14). But there is also a resurrection life, a new creation, an existence in the spirit already in the present. This last is meant when Paul wants "to gain Christ and be found in him" (Phil. 3:8, 9), and perhaps there is even an allusion here to mystical formulas (and mystical experiences). That is the case if the former expression, "gain," refers to the immanence of Christ's power, its dwelling in us, and the second ("be found") to coherence, being in Christ. Coherence and immanence were merged in the well-known mystical response, "I in you, you in me." But then immediately this new existence is expressed thus (Phil. 3:10): "to know (not in a rational sense, so perhaps in English we should say 'become aware of') the power of his resurrection and to share his sufferings." By placing the resurrection first, he shows that he does not mean earthly suffering and eschatological resurrection, but the power of the new mystical Christ-life, from which—in tribulation—the community of suffering proceeds. First one must have received the Resurrected into oneself in order to be able to realize the Crucified in one's own life. Only then follows the glimpse of the eschatological resurrection: "That if possible I may attain the resurrection from the dead."

* * *

Paul spoke of [the] "immanence" of Christ only rarely. The best-known passage, Gal. 2:20, * * * brings the tension of the Christian existence—its belonging to two worlds—to clearest expression. "I am crucified with Christ; now it is no longer I who live, but Christ lives in me. The life which I now (still) have in the flesh, I live by faith in the Son of God, who loved me and gave himself for me." A statement of the suffering-mysticism supports the fact that the place of his human life has been taken by another life. That new life is then depicted so absolutely that it seems hardly to leave any room for the human life. Yet surprisingly the human life recurs: "The life which I now still have in the flesh . . ." In one moment Christ is so fully in the believer that the abyss between God and man is not mentioned at all—but then Christ is in heaven and the connection between him and man is faith. Mystical piety, which bears Christ within the self, and prophetic piety, which extends faith on high, across the abyss, to Christ, stand side-by-side! And this side-by-side is what constitutes Paul's Christianity.

IV

* * *

Paul has personal experience of areas which are closely related to mysticism, but which precisely for that reason are inaccessible to many members of the Christian community. He is acquainted with *gnosis*, visions, ecstasy. But as definite as is his assurance that he participates in these, his endeavor is equally clear to avoid making these phenomena of an intimate religious life normative for Christian faith.

He speaks of *gnosis* in the irrational sense of becoming aware of divine power and divine wisdom, when he contrasts the active verb "know" with its passive: "Then I shall know as I am known" (1 Cor. 13:12). The object of the active "knowing" and the subject implied by the passive "to be known" is Christ. Gal. 4:9 describes the conversion of former Gentiles: "Now you know God—rather, you are known by God." Also Phil. 3:12 is probably to be interpreted in terms of this *gnosis*: "Not that I have already grasped (him) or am already perfected but I strive onward that I may grasp (him), as I have already been grasped by Christ Jesus." Here again one should supply as object of the active verb "grasp" the personal object, Christ, corresponding to the passive construction. That is the style of mystical theology. * * * Yet, however "Gnostic" these expressions may sound in Paul, he shows his churches a quite different path in the discussion of *gnosis* and love, 1 Cor. 8:1–3. "We know that we all have knowledge," he says. "Knowledge puffs up, but love builds up. If any one imagines that he knows something, he does not yet know as he ought to know. But if one loves God, one is known by him." Love, which proves itself here by quite practical concern for the "weak" brothers, is more than *gnosis*, which produces only pride. The aristocratic claim of all *gnosis* to be closer to God than are the others, is shattered by the command to love these others. The egoism of mysticism has to recede before the altruism of the gospel.

* * *

An extraordinary picture! The apostle himself confesses full participation in this mystical-Gnostic piety which claims to establish a secret union with the divine world. Yet he deprecates this piety of the few for the sake of the divine message that is accessible to all. He knows mysticism, but he is no mystic. He knows the individual experience of Gnostic wisdom, but he values the "foolishness of the gospel" higher. The same picture is presented by his attitude towards *ecstasy*, which was cultivated in Corinth particularly in the form of enthusiastic, inarticulate "speaking in tongues." Paul declares, "I thank God that I speak in tongues more than you all" (1 Cor. 14:18). "But," he adds immediately, "in the assembly of the congregation I would rather speak five intelligible words to instruct others than ten thousand words in a tongue." He does not forbid the ecstatic utterances, but he demands concern for those to whom they give nothing. And this is not an occasional concern, but a basic one. "If I could speak in tongues of men and of angels, and had no love, I would be a resounding piece of brass or a clanging cymbal." Paul directs to this "way above all ways" (1 Cor. 12:31) all those who strive after union between man and God, above all the mystics. Glossolalia belongs to the things that "will cease," but love "never ceases" (1 Cor. 13:8). Ecstasy and *gnosis* are only imperfect possibilities for pressing from time into eternity. They are "piecework," but love, reflection of God's love for us, is a bit of eternity in the midst of time. Here Paul censures, if not mystical emotion, at least mystical technique in the realm of human means. But he accords to love, insofar as it is not just a humane ideal but an emanation of God's love, the rank of a revelation of God. And that from a man who himself knows and again and again experiences what mystical piety, the ecstatic penetration of the heavenly realm, could give.

This man also knows of *visions*. And, while visions are not foreign to the prophetic piety, the mysterious experiences of which Paul speaks in 2 Cor. 12:2–4 may be placed in the same context with the ecstatic phenomena of glossolalia. Paul himself does seem to be more aware of the special grace present in occurrences of this kind than he was in the case of glossolalia. But neither here where he mentions them nor elsewhere in his letters does he make any real use of it. "I went up by a revelation," says Gal. 2:2—but who knows wherein this communication of the divine will consisted? In any case Paul avoids with almost painful care giving play to the egocentric self-consciousness of the mystic, anywhere or anytime. If one must boast, he will boast of his troubles. For only in the distress of weakness and illness does he experience the full power of God (2 Cor. 12: 9).

The results of this examination of individual passages are confirmed when we consider the whole of Paul's completely or half-mystical statements and compare them with that which we otherwise call mysticism in the history of religions. The mysticism of Paul exhibits the characteristics of mysticism only in limited degree. There are four particularities of mysticism—not uniformly encountered elsewhere, but still frequently observable—that one misses in Paul.

1. Paul's mystical statements relate only to Christ, in whom God

made himself known humanly, never to God. The immediacy, the boldness, with which mysticism dares occasionally to penetrate even to the throne of God, is not to be found in the Pauline letters known to us. And this is likely no accident, for we think we know the reason for this reserve. It is the best heritage of Old Testament piety that manifests itself in the apostle's reticence before the eternal God. * * * There is *no God-mysticism* in Paul, because man cannot unite with God, but only with him who has revealed God within humanity.

2. But something is missing even from this Christ-mysticism: the *mysticism of identity*. Christ lives in me, I can do all things in him—that Paul can say, but not: I am Christ and he is I. To make this clear by an example: Paul might perhaps pray to Christ as did the Isis initiate (Apuleius, *Metamorphoses* XI. 25), "I will always keep thy divine appearance in remembrance, and close the imagination of thy most holy godhead within my breast."[6] But he could not speak the way the Hermes initiate did (Pap. London, p. 117, no. 122.36): "You are I, and I am you. Your name is mine and mine is yours; for I am your image." Even in this case genuine Israelite abhorrence of any impudent familiarity with God is normative in Paul; it keeps the apostle at a decent distance from his Lord.

3. Paul's mysticism thus also lacks the final goal of every mysticism of identity, *deification*. A single time Paul's description comes close to that which in mysticism is called deification. In 2 Cor. 3:18—the passage that in general exhibits an especially mystical tone—he speaks of the transformation of the Christian by contemplation. But he avoids the use of the word deification, nor does he presuppose the occurrence in Christians. Obviously both word and matter are for him pagan.

4. Even in the statements in which we think we discern a mystical tone, we perceive no sensual lingering in the union with Christ. There is no *fruitio dei*, no enjoyment of God, in Paul. Even in the apostle's relationship to Christ everything is directed toward the end. Therefore there is no rest, only tension. Only in a limited sense is there a having; there is very essentially a consciousness of not having and a longing for fulfillment.

But that points us toward a broader context, in which still another limitation of Paul's mystical piety emerges. Paul's faith rests upon *history*, the real, known, datable revelation of God in Christ. And this segment of history has its prehistory, which on the one hand leads from promise to fulfillment, on the other includes man's sins, the proof that they cannot be overcome by the Law, the need for redemption as well as the fact of impenitence. And this history points beyond itself to the end and the messianic

6. The Adlington-Gaselee translation (Loeb Classical Library). [*Editor*]

"advent" of the Christ; it is goal-directed salvation-history. The mystical event, where Paul alludes to it, does not have as its foundation a myth which is imparted to the initiate as a lore of salvation, secret if possible. Rather it is founded upon a historical event of recent occurrence, experienced by yet-living eye-witnesses. And the mission, the journeys of the apostle, the afflictions and sufferings that are destined for him and for the Christians in general—all these are part of that history. While in other mysticism the mystics experience the mystery of union with their god only in contemplation, in adoring absorption, in cultic celebration—the Christians experience it in everyday reality.

* * *

What distinguishes Paul's religion most deeply from the Hellenistic mysticism known to us is this: the Christian enters either by believing or by mystical experience into an objective event, which is grasped in its facticity and which moves toward the imminently awaited end. That excludes the possibility that the Christian could already experience in mysticism the perfection of his existence. He knows that perfection lies ever in the future. Over every mystical experience of the present stands the sentence, "Not as if I had already grasped him or were already perfected, but I strive onward that I may grasp him" (Phil. 3: 12). But because it is an objective event, which occurs in the world as well as in the individual Christian, the apostle does not need to wait with questioning anxiety for the future, but is certain of it. The decisive event, the dawn of the new world in the resurrection of Christ, has already happened. Therefore the reality of the new life exists for the Christians, whether they appropriate it by faith or in mystical contemplation.

* * *

A further problem must * * * remain unsolved * * *. That is the question whether the mystical experiences, especially the trances and visions, were dependent upon the apostle's ill health—the "thorn in the flesh" (2 Cor. 12: 7). It is tempting to posit a psychosomatic connection here—but it is equally tempting to exaggerate it by reducing the experiences into a pathological condition. The consciously limited importance accorded those experiences shows at least that the apostle was master of any disorders in his psychological life. Anyone who can write about glossolalia the way Paul does in 1 Cor. 14, anyone who makes so little of extraordinary conditions as he does in 2 Cor. 12: 1–6, anyone who praises love as the most certain bond between man and God (1 Cor. 13) is no psychopath nor the helpless victim of illness.

We have made a great number of observations about Paul's religion. The unity in this variety can be seen in this fact: Paul, the first radical Christian, was always concerned to assure himself and his readers of the break with the old life and the reality of the new. When the new life is perceived as a possession, then the apostle can depict it with the colors of mystical piety. But when the new life is taken to be the sign and pledge of the coming fulfillment, then the Christian lives by faith and not by sight. The Spirit is mostly thought of as a guarantee of what is to come, but its mention can also express the bliss of possession. "In Christ" in its proper sense designates the mystical union with the Lord, but it also designates membership in the waiting community. The Christian's location between the times is grasped in having and in not-having—and despite all changes in conceptuality and phenomena of the religious life, this double-sidedness has remained the mark characteristic of the Christian faith to the present day.

RUDOLF BULTMANN

Paul's Demythologizing and Ours (1941) †

* * *

The mythology of the New Testament is in essence that of Jewish apocalyptic and the Gnostic redemption myths. A common feature of them both is their basic dualism, according to which the present world and its human inhabitants are under the control of daemonic, satanic powers, and stand in need of redemption. Man cannot achieve this redemption by his own efforts; it must come as a gift through a divine intervention. Both types of mythology speak of such an intervention: Jewish apocalyptic of an imminent world crisis in which this present aeon will be brought to an end and the new aeon ushered in by the coming of the Messiah, and Gnosticism of a Son of God sent down from the realm of light, entering into this world in the guise of a man, and by his fate and teaching delivering the elect and opening up the way for their return to the heavenly home.

The meaning of these two types of mythology lies once more not in their imagery with its apparent objectivity but in the understanding of human existence which both are trying to express. In

† From "New Testament and Mythology," in *Kerygma and Myth*, ed. Hans Werner Bartsch, tr. Reginald H. Fuller (London, 2d ed., 1964), pp. 1–44. The essay was first published in 1941. Rudolf Karl Bultmann (b. 1884), Professor of New Testament in Giessen, 1920, and Marburg, from 1921 until his retirement, has been the most influential New Testament scholar of Europe in this century.

other words, they need to be interpreted existentially. A good example of such treatment is to be found in Hans Jonas's book on Gnosticism.[1]

Our task is to produce an existentialist interpretation of the dualistic mythology of the New Testament along similar lines. When,
for instance, we read of daemonic powers ruling the world and
holding mankind in bondage, does the understanding of human
existence which underlies such language offer a solution to the
riddle of human life which will be acceptable even to the non-
mythological mind of to-day? Of course we must not take this to
imply that the New Testament presents us with an anthropology
like that which modern science can give us. It cannot be proved by
logic or demonstrated by an appeal to factual evidence. Scientific
anthropologies always take for granted a definite understanding of
existence, which is invariably the consequence of a deliberate decision of the scientist, whether he makes it consciously or not. And
that is why we have to discover whether the New Testament offers
man an understanding of himself which will challenge him to a
genuine existential decision.

Demythologizing in Outline

A. THE CHRISTIAN INTERPRETATION OF BEING

1. *Human Existence apart from Faith*

What does the New Testament mean when it talks of the
"world", of "this world" * * * or of "this aeon" * * *? In speaking
thus, the New Testament is in agreement with the Gnostics, for
they too speak of "this world", and of the princes, prince, or god of
this world; and moreover they both regard man as the slave of the
world and its powers. But there is one significant difference. In the
New Testament one of these powers is conspicuously absent—viz.,
matter, the physical, sensual part of man's constitution. Never does
the New Testament complain that the soul of man, his authentic
self, is imprisoned in a material body: never does it complain of the
power of sensuality over the spirit. That is why it never doubts the
responsibility of man for his sin. God is always the Creator of the
world, including human life in the body. He is also the Judge
before whom man must give account. The part played by Satan as
the Lord of this world must therefore be limited in a peculiar way,
or else, if he is the lord or god of world, "this world" must stand in
a peculiar dialectical relation to the world as the creation of God.

1. *Gnosis und spätantiker Geist*. I. *Die mythologische Gnosis*, 1934. [Rev. ed., 1964. See the simplified and shortened version. *The Gnostic Religion* (Boston, 1963).]

"This world" is the world of corruption and death. Clearly, it was not so when it left the hands of the Creator, for it was only in consequence of the fall of Adam that death entered into the world (Rom. 5. 12). Hence it is sin, rather than matter as such, which is the cause of corruption and death. The Gnostic conception of the soul as a pure, celestial element imprisoned by some tragic fate in a material body is entirely absent. Death is the wages of sin (Rom. 6. 23; cf. 1 Cor. 15. 56). True, St Paul seems to agree with the Gnostics as regards the effects which he ascribes to the fall of Adam as the ancestor of the human race. But it is clear that he later returns to the idea of individual responsibility when he says that since Adam death came to all men "for that all sinned" (Rom. 5. 12), a statement which stands in formal contradiction to the Adam theory. Perhaps he means to say that with Adam death became possible rather than inevitable. However that may be, there is another idea which St Paul is constantly repeating and which is equally incompatible with the Adam theory, and that is the theory that sin, including death, is derived from the flesh (*sarx*, Rom. 8. 13; Gal. 6. 8, etc.). But what does he mean by "flesh"? Not the bodily or physical side of human nature, but the sphere of visible, concrete, tangible, and measurable reality, which as such is also the sphere of corruption and death. When a man chooses to live entirely in and for this sphere, or, as St Paul puts it, when he "lives after the flesh", it assumes the shape of a "power". There are indeed many different ways of living after the flesh. There is the crude life of sensual pleasure and there is the refined way of basing one's life on the pride of achievement, on the "works of the law" as St Paul would say. But these distinctions are ultimately immaterial. For "flesh" embraces not only the material things of life, but all human creation and achievement pursued for the sake of some tangible reward, such as for example the fulfilling of the law (Gal. 3. 3). It includes every passive quality, and every advantage a man can have, in the sphere of visible, tangible reality (Phil. 3. 4ff.).

St Paul sees that the life of man is weighed down by anxiety (* * * 1 Cor. 7. 32ff.). Every man focuses his anxiety upon some particular object. The natural man focuses it upon security, and in proportion to his opportunities and his success in the visible sphere he places his "confidence" in the "flesh" (Phil. 3. 3f.), and the consciousness of security finds its expression in "glorying" * * *.

Such a pursuit is, however, incongruous with man's real situation, for the fact is that he is not secure at all. Indeed, this is the way in which he loses his true life and becomes the slave of that very sphere which he had hoped to master, and which he hoped would give him security. Whereas hitherto he might have enjoyed the world as God's creation, it has now become "this world", the world in revolt against God. This is the way in which the "powers" which dominate human life come into being, and as such they acquire the character of mythical entities. Since the visible and tangible sphere is essentially transitory, the man who bases his life on it becomes the prisoner and slave of corruption. An illustration of this may be seen in the way our attempts to secure visible security for ourselves bring us into collision with others; we can seek security for ourselves only at their expense. Thus on the one hand we get envy, anger, jealousy, and the like, and on the other compromise, bargainings, and adjustments of conflicting interests. This creates an all-pervasive atmosphere which controls all our judgements; we all pay homage to it and take it for granted. Thus man becomes the slave of anxiety (Rom. 8. 15). Everybody tries to hold fast to his own life and property because he has a secret feeling that it is all slipping away from him.

THE LIFE OF FAITH

The authentic life, on the other hand, would be a life based on unseen, intangible realities. Such a life means the abandonment of all self-contrived security. This is what the New Testament means by "life after the Spirit" or "life in faith".

For this life we must have faith in *the grace of God*. It means faith that the unseen, intangible reality actually confronts us as love, opening up our future and signifying not death but life.

The grace of God means *the forgiveness of sin*, and brings deliverance from the bondage of the past. The old quest for visible security, the hankering after tangible realities, and the clinging to transitory objects, is sin, for by it we shut out invisible reality from our lives and refuse God's future which comes to us as a gift. But once we open our hearts to the grace of God, our sins are forgiven; we are released from the past. This is what is meant by "faith": to open ourselves freely to the future. But at the same time faith involves obedience, for faith means turning our backs on self and abandoning all security. It means giving up every attempt to carve out a niche in life for ourselves, surrendering all our self-confidence, and resolving to trust in God alone, in the God who raises the dead (2 Cor. 1. 9) and who calls the things that are not into being (Rom. 4. 17). It means radical self-commitment to God in the expectation that everything will come from him and nothing from ourselves. Such a life spells deliverance from all worldly, tangible objects, leading to complete detachment from the world and thus to freedom.

This detachment from the world is something quite different

from asceticism. It means preserving a distance from the world and dealing with it in a spirit of "as if not" (*hōs mē*, 1 Cor. 7. 29–31). The believer is lord of all things (1 Cor. 3. 21–3). He enjoys that power (*exousia*) of which the Gnostic boasts, but with the proviso: "All things are lawful for me, but I will not be brought under the power of any" (1 Cor. 6. 12; cf. 10. 23f.). The believer may "rejoice with them that do rejoice, and weep with them that weep" (Rom. 12. 15), but he is no longer in bondage to anything in the world (1 Cor. 7. 17–24). Everything in the world has become indifferent and unimportant. "For though I was free from all men, I brought myself under bondage to all" (1 Cor. 9. 19–23). "I know how to be abased, and I know also how to abound in everything, and in all things I have learned the secret both to be filled and to be hungry, both to abound and to be in want" (Phil. 4. 12). The world has been crucified to him, and he to the world (Gal. 6. 14). Moreover, the power of his new life is manifested even in weakness, suffering, and death (2 Cor. 4. 7–11; 12. 9f.). Just when he realizes that he is nothing in himself, he can have and be all things through God (2 Cor. 12. 9f.; 6. 8–10).

Now, this is eschatological existence; it means being a "new creature" (2 Cor. 5. 17). The eschatology of Jewish apocalyptic and of Gnosticism has been emancipated from its accompanying mythology, in so far as the age of salvation has already dawned for the believer and the life of the future has become a present reality. The fourth gospel carries this process to a logical conclusion by completely eliminating every trace of apocalyptic eschatology. The last judgement is no longer an imminent cosmic event, for it is already taking place in the coming of Jesus and in his summons to believe (John 3. 19; 9. 39; 12. 31). The believer has life here and now, and has passed already from death into life (5. 24, etc.). Outwardly everything remains as before, but inwardly his relation to the world has been radically changed. The world has no further claim on him, for faith is the victory which overcometh the world (1 John 5. 4).

The eschatology of Gnosticism is similarly transcended. It is not that the believer is given a new nature (*physis*) or that his pre-existent nature is emancipated, or that his soul is assured of a journey to heaven. The new life in faith is not an assured possession or endowment, which could lead only to libertinism. Nor is it a possession to be guarded with care and vigilance, which could lead only to asceticism. Life in faith is not a possession at all. It cannot be exclusively expressed in indicative terms; it needs an imperative to complete it. In other words, the decision of faith is never final; it needs constant renewal in every fresh situation. Our freedom does not excuse us from the demand under which we all stand as men, for it is freedom for obedience (Rom. 6. 11ff.). To believe means not to have apprehended but to have been apprehended. It means always to be travelling along the road between the "already" and the "not yet", always to be pursuing a goal.

For Gnosticism redemption is a cosmic process in which the redeemed are privileged to participate here and now. Although essentially transcendent, faith must be reduced to an immanent possession. Its outward signs are freedom (*eleutheria*), power (*exousia*), pneumatic phenomena, and above all ecstasy. In the last resort the New Testament knows no phenomena in which transcendent realities become immanent possessions. True, St Paul is familiar with ecstasy (2 Cor. 5. 13; 12. 1ff.). But he refuses to accept it as a proof of the possession of the Spirit. The New Testament never speaks of the training of the soul in mystical experience or of ecstasy as the culmination of the Christian life. Not psychic phenomena but faith is the hallmark of that life.

Certainly St Paul shares the popular belief of his day that the Spirit manifests itself in miracles, and he attributes abnormal psychic phenomena to its agency. But the enthusiasm of the Corinthians for such things brought home to him their questionable character. So he insists that the gifts of the Spirit must be judged according to their value for "edification", and in so doing he transcends the popular view of the Spirit as an agency that operates like any other natural force. True, he regards the Spirit as a mysterious entity dwelling in man and guaranteeing his resurrection. (Rom. 8. 11). He can even speak of the Spirit as if it were a kind of supernatural material (1 Cor. 15. 44ff.). Yet in the last resort he clearly means by "Spirit" the possibility of a new life which is opened up by faith. The Spirit does not work like a supernatural force, nor is it the permanent possession of the believer. It is the possibility of a new life which must be appropriated by a deliberate resolve. Hence St Paul's paradoxical injunction: "If we live by the Spirit, by the Spirit also let us walk." (Gal. 5. 25). "Being led by the Spirit" (Rom. 8. 14) is not an automatic process of nature, but the fulfilment of an imperative: "live after the Spirit, not after the flesh". Imperative and indicative are inseparable. The possession of the Spirit never renders decision superfluous. "I say, Walk by the Spirit and ye shall not fulfil the lust of the flesh" (Gal. 5. 16). Thus the concept "Spirit" has been emancipated from mythology.

The Pauline catalogue of the fruits of the Spirit ("love, joy, peace, long-suffering, kindness, goodness, faithfulness, temperance", Gal. 5. 22) shows how faith, by detaching man from the world, makes him capable of fellowship in community. Now that he is delivered from anxiety and from the frustration which comes from clinging to the tangible realities of the visible world, man is free to enjoy fellowship with others. Hence faith is described as "working through love" (Gal. 5. 6). And this means being a new creature (cf. Gal. 5. 6 with 6. 15).

1. *Christian Self-Understanding without Christ?*

We have now suggested an existentialist unmythological interpretation of the Christian understanding of Being. But is this interpretation true to the New Testament? We seem to have overlooked one important point, which is that in the New Testament faith is always *faith in Christ*. Faith, in the strict sense of the word, was only there at a certain moment in history. It had to be *revealed*; it *came* (Gal. 3. 23, 25). This might of course be taken as part of the story of man's spiritual evolution. But the New Testament means more than that. It claims that faith only became possible at a definite point in history in consequence of an *event*—viz., the event of Christ. Faith in the sense of obedient self-commitment and inward detachment from the world is only possible when it is faith in Jesus Christ.

Here indeed is the crux of the matter—have we here a remnant of mythology which still requires restatement? In fact it comes to this: can we have a Christian understanding of Being without Christ?

* * *

The point at issue is how we understand the fall. Even the philosophers are agreed about the fact of it. But they think that all man needs is to be shown his plight, and that then he will be able to escape from it. In other words, the corruption resulting from the fall does not extend to the core of the human personality. The New Testament, on the other hand, regards the fall as total.

How then, if the fall be total, can man be aware of his plight? He certainly is aware of it, as the philosophers themselves testify. How can man be aware that his fall is total and that it extends to the very core of his personality? As a matter of fact, it is the other way round: it is only because man is a fallen being, only because he knows he is not what he really ought to be and what he would like to be, that he can be aware of his plight. That awareness of his authentic nature is essential to human life, and without it man would not be man. But his authentic nature is not an endowment of creation or a possession at his own disposal. The philosophers would agree thus far, for they also know that man's authentic nature has to be apprehended by a deliberate resolve. But they think that all man needs is to be told about his authentic nature.

This nature is what he never realizes, but what at every moment he is capable of realizing—you can because you ought. But the philosophers are confusing a theoretical possibility with an actual one. For, as the New Testament sees it, man has lost that actual possibility, and even his awareness of his authentic manhood is perverted, as is shown by his deluded belief that it is a possession he can command at will.

* * *

This means, in the language of the New Testament, that man is a sinner. The self-assertion of which we have spoken is identical with sin. Sin is self-assertion, self-glorying, for "No flesh should glory before God. . . . He that glorieth, let him glory in the Lord" (1 Cor. 1.29, 31; 2 Cor. 10.17). Is that no more than an unnecessary mythologizing of an ontological proposition? Can man as he is perceive that self-assertion involves guilt, and that he is personally responsible to God for it? Is sin a mythological concept or not? The answer will depend on what we make of St Paul's words to the Corinthians: "What hast thou that thou didst not receive? but if thou didst receive it, why dost thou glory, as if thou hadst not received it?" (1 Cor. 4.7). Does this apply to all men alike, or only to Christians? This much at any rate is clear: self-assertion is guilt only if it can be understood as ingratitude. If the radical self-assertion which makes it impossible for man to achieve the authentic life of self-commitment is identical with sin, it must obviously be possible for man to understand his existence altogether as a gift of God. But it is just this radical self-assertion which makes such an understanding impossible. For self-assertion deludes man into thinking that his existence is a prize within his own grasp. How blind man is to his plight is illustrated by that pessimism which regards life as a burden thrust on man against his will, or by the way men talk about the "right to live" or by the way they expect their fair share of good fortune. Man's radical self-assertion then blinds him to the fact of sin, and this is the clearest proof that he is a fallen being. Hence it is no good telling man that he is a sinner. He will only dismiss it as mythology. But it does not follow that he is right.

To talk of sin ceases to be mere mythology when the love of God meets man as a power which embraces and sustains him even in his fallen, self-assertive state. Such a love treats man as if he were other than he is. By so doing, love frees man from himself as he is.

For as a result of his self-assertion man is a totally fallen being. He is capable of knowing that his authentic life consists in self-commitment, but is incapable of realizing it because however hard he tries he still remains what he is, self-assertive man. So in practice authentic life becomes possible only when man is delivered from himself. It is the claim of the New Testament that this is exactly what happened. This is precisely the meaning of that which was wrought in Christ. At the very point where man can do nothing, God steps in and acts—indeed he has acted already—on man's behalf.

St Paul is endeavouring to express this when he speaks of the expiation of sin, or of "righteousness" created as a gift of God rather than as a human achievement. Through Christ, God has reconciled the world to himself, not reckoning to it its trespasses (2 Cor. 5. 19). God made Christ to be sin for us, that we through him might stand before God as righteous (2 Cor. 5. 21). For everyone who believes, his past life is dead and done with. He is a new creature, and as such he faces each new moment. In short, he has become a free man.

It is quite clear from this that forgiveness of sins is not a juridical concept. It does not mean the remission of punishment. If that were so, man's plight would be as bad as ever. Rather, forgiveness conveys freedom from sin, which hitherto had held man in bondage. But this freedom is not a static quality: it is freedom *to obey*. The indicative implies an imperative. Love is the fulfilment of the law, and therefore the forgiveness of God delivers man from himself and makes him free to devote his life to the service of others (Rom. 13. 8–10; Gal. 5. 14).

Thus eschatological existence has become possible. God has *acted*, and the world—"this world"—has come to an end. *Man himself has been made new*. "If any man is in Christ, he is a new creature: the old things are passed away; behold, they are become new" (2 Cor. 5. 17). * * *

The event of Jesus Christ is therefore the revelation of the love of God. It makes a man free from himself and free to be himself, free to live a life of self-commitment in faith and love. But faith in this sense of the word is possible only where it takes the form of faith in the love of God. Yet such faith is still a subtle form of self-assertion so long as the love of God is merely a piece of wishful thinking. It is only an abstract idea so long as God has not revealed his love. That is why faith for the Christian means faith in Christ, for it is faith in the love of God revealed in Christ. Only those who are loved are capable of loving.

* * *

The classic statement of this self-commitment of God, which is the ground of our own self-commitment, is to be found in Rom.

8. 32 "God spared not his Son, but delivered him up for us; how shall he not also with him freely give us all things?" Compare the Johannine text: "God so loved the world, that he gave his only-begotten Son, that whosoever believeth in him should not perish, but have eternal life" (John 3. 16). There are also similar texts which speak of Jesus' giving up himself for us: ". . . who gave himself for our sins, that he might deliver us out of this present evil world" (Gal. 1. 4); "I have been crucified with Christ; yet I live; and yet no longer I, but Christ liveth in me: and the life which I live in the flesh I live in faith, the faith which is in the Son of God, who loved me and gave himself up for me" (Gal. 2. 19f.).

Here then is the crucial distinction between the New Testament and existentialism, between the Christian faith and the natural understanding of Being. The New Testament speaks and faith knows of an act of God through which man becomes capable of self-commitment, capable of faith and love, of his authentic life.

* * *

(A) THE DEMYTHOLOGIZING OF THE EVENT OF JESUS CHRIST

Now, it is beyond question that the New Testament presents the event of Jesus Christ in mythical terms. The problem is whether that is the only possible presentation. Or does the New Testament itself demand a restatement of the event of Jesus Christ in non-mythological terms?

* * *

In the end the crux of the matter lies in the cross and resurrection.

(B) THE CROSS

Is the cross, understood as the event of redemption, exclusively mythical in character, or can it retain its value for salvation without forfeiting its character as history?

* * *

In its redemptive aspect the cross of Christ is no mere mythical event, but a historic (*geschichtlich*) fact originating in the historical (*historisch*) event which is the crucifixion of Jesus. The abiding significance of the cross is that it is the judgement of the world, the judgement and the deliverance of man. So far as this is so, Christ is crucified "for us", not in the sense of any theory of sacrifice or satisfaction. This interpretation of the cross as a permanent fact rather than a mythological event does far more justice to the redemptive significance of the event of the past than any of the traditional interpretations. In the last resort mythological language is only a medium for conveying the significance of the historical (*historisch*) event. The historical (*historisch*) event of the cross has, in the significance peculiar to it, created a new historic (*geschichtlich*) situation. The preaching of the cross as the event of redemption challenges all who hear it to appropriate this significance for themselves, to be willing to be crucified with Christ.

But, it will be asked, is this significance to be discerned in the actual event of past history? Can it, so to speak, be read off from that event? Or does the cross bear this significance because it is the cross of *Christ*? In other words, must we first be convinced of the significance of Christ and believe in him in order to discern the real meaning of the cross? If we are to perceive the real meaning of the cross, must we understand it as the cross of Jesus as a figure of past history? Must we go back to the Jesus of history?

As far as the first preachers of the gospel are concerned this will certainly be the case. For them the cross was the cross of him with whom they had lived in personal intercourse. The cross was an experience of their own lives. It presented them with a question and it disclosed to them its meaning. But for us this personal connection cannot be reproduced. For us the cross cannot disclose its own meaning: it is an event of the past. We can never recover it as an event in our own lives. All we know of it is derived from historical report. But the New Testament does not proclaim Jesus Christ in this way. The meaning of the cross is not disclosed from the life of Jesus as a figure of past history, a life which needs to be reproduced by historical research. On the contrary, Jesus is not proclaimed merely as the crucified; he is also risen from the dead. The cross and the resurrection form an inseparable unity.

(c) THE RESURRECTION

But what of the resurrection? Is it not a mythical event pure and simple? Obviously it is not an event of past history with a self-evident meaning. Can the resurrection narratives and every other mention of the resurrection in the New Testament be understood simply as an attempt to convey the meaning of the cross? Does the New Testament, in asserting that Jesus is risen fom the dead, mean that his death is not just an ordinary human death, but the judgement and salvation of the world, depriving death of its power? Does it not express this truth in the affirmation that the Crucified was not holden of death, but rose from the dead?

Yes indeed: the cross and the resurrection form a single, indivisible cosmic event. "He was delivered up for our trespasses, and was raised for our justification" (Rom. 4. 25). The cross is not an isolated event, as though it were the end of Jesus, which needed the resurrection subsequently to reverse it. When he suffered death, Jesus was already the Son of God, and his death by itself was the victory over the power of death. St John brings this out most clearly by describing the passion of Jesus as the "hour" in which he is glorified, and by the double meaning he gives to the phrase "lifted up", applying it both to the cross and to Christ's exaltation into glory.

Cross and resurrection form a single, indivisible cosmic event which brings judgement to the world and opens up for men the possibility of authentic life. But if that be so, the resurrection cannot be a miraculous proof capable of demonstration and sufficient to convince the sceptic that the cross really has the cosmic and eschatological significance ascribed to it.

* * *

Yes indeed: the resurrection of Jesus cannot be a miraculous proof by which the sceptic might be compelled to believe in Christ. The difficulty is not simply the incredibility of a mythical event like the resuscitation of a dead person—for that is what the resurrection means, as is shown by the fact that the risen Lord is apprehended by the physical senses. Nor is it merely the impossibility of establishing the objective historicity of the resurrection no matter how many witnesses are cited, as though once it was established it might be believed beyond all question and faith might have its unimpeachable guarantee. No; the real difficulty is that the resurrection is itself an article of faith, and you cannot establish one article of faith by invoking another. You cannot prove the redemptive efficacy of the cross by invoking the resurrection. For the resurrection is an article of faith because it is far more than the resuscitation of a corpse—it is the eschatological event. And so it cannot be a miraculous proof. For, quite apart from its credibility, the bare miracle tells us nothing about the eschatological fact of the destruction of death. Moreover, such a miracle is not otherwise unknown to mythology.

It is however abundantly clear that the New Testament is interested in the resurrection of Christ simply and solely because it is the eschatological event *par excellence*. By it Christ abolished death and brought life and immortality to light (2 Tim. 1. 10). This explains why St Paul borrows Gnostic language to clarify the meaning of the resurrection. As in the death of Jesus all have died (2

Cor. 5. 14f.), so through his resurrection all have been raised from the dead, though naturally this event is spread over a long period of time (1 Cor. 15. 21f.). But St Paul does not only say: "In Christ shall all be made alive"; he can also speak of rising again with Christ in the present tense, just as he speaks of our dying with him. Through the sacrament of baptism Christians participate not only in the death of Christ but also in his resurrection. It is not simply that we *shall* walk with him in newness of life and be united with him in his resurrection (Rom. 6. 4f.); we are doing so already here and now. "Even so reckon ye yourselves to be dead indeed unto sin, but alive unto God in Jesus Christ" (Rom. 6. 11).

Once again, in everyday life the Christians participate not only in the death of Christ but also in his resurrection. In this resurrection-life they enjoy a freedom, albeit a struggling freedom, from sin (Rom. 6. 11ff.). They are able to "cast off the works of darkness", so that the approaching day when the darkness shall vanish is already experienced here and now. "Let us walk honestly as in the day" (Rom. 13. 12f.): "we are not of the night, nor of the darkness. . . . Let us, since we are of the day, be sober . . ." (1 Thess. 5. 5–8). St Paul seeks to share not only the sufferings of Christ but also "the power of his resurrection" (Phil. 3. 10). So he bears about in his body the dying of Jesus, "that the life also of Jesus may be manifested in our body" (2 Cor. 4. 10f.). Similarly, when the Corinthians demand a proof of his apostolic authority, he solemnly warns them: "Christ is not weak, but is powerful in you: for he was crucified in weakness, yet he liveth in the power of God. For we also are weak in him, but we shall live with him through the power of God toward you" (2 Cor. 13. 3f.).

In this way the resurrection is not a mythological event adduced in order to prove the saving efficacy of the cross, but an article of faith just as much as the meaning of the cross itself. Indeed, *faith in the resurrection is really the same thing as faith in the saving efficacy of the cross*, faith in the cross as the cross of Christ. Hence you cannot first believe in Christ and then in the strength of that faith believe in the cross. To believe in Christ means to believe in the cross as the cross of Christ. The saving efficacy of the cross is not derived from the fact that it is the cross of Christ: it is the cross of Christ because it has this saving efficacy. Without that efficacy it is the tragic end of a great man.

* * *

The real Easter faith is faith in the word of preaching which brings illumination. If the event of Easter Day is in any sense an historical event additional to the event of the cross, it is nothing else than the rise of faith in the risen Lord, since it was this faith which led to the apostolic preaching. The resurrection itself is not an event of past history. All that historical criticism can establish is the fact that the first disciples came to believe in the resurrection. The historian can perhaps to some extent account for that faith from the personal intimacy which the disciples had enjoyed with Jesus during his earthly life, and so reduce the resurrection appearances to a series of subjective visions. But the historical problem is not of interest to Christian belief in the resurrection. For the historical event of the rise of the Easter faith means for us what it meant for the first disciples—namely, the self-attestation of the risen Lord, the act of God in which the redemptive event of the cross is completed.

* * *

KRISTER STENDAHL

The Apostle Paul and the Introspective Conscience of the West (1963) †

In the history of Western Christianity—and hence, to a large extent, in the history of Western culture—the Apostle Paul has been hailed as a hero of the introspective conscience. Here was the man who grappled with the problem "I do not do the good I want, but the evil I do not want to do is what I do ..." (Rom. 7:19). His insights as to a solution of this dilemma have recently been more or less identified, for example, with what Jung referred to as the Individuation Process;[1] but this is only a contemporary twist to the traditional Western way of reading the Pauline letters as documents of human consciousness.

Twenty-five years ago Henry J. Cadbury wrote a stimulating study, "The Peril of Modernizing Jesus" (1937). That book and that very title is a good summary of one of the most important insights of biblical studies in the 20th century. It has ramifications far beyond the field of theology and biblical exegesis. It questions the often tacit presupposition that man remains basically the same through the ages. There is little point in affirming or denying such a presupposition in general terms—much would depend on what

† A paper delivered at the Annual Meeting of the American Psychological Association, September 3, 1961; published in the *Harvard Theological Review* 56 (1963): 199–215. An earlier version appeared in Swedish in *Svensk Exegetisk Årsbok* 25 (1960): 62–77. Krister Stendahl is Dean and John Lord O'Brian Professor of Divinity at Harvard Divinity School.
1. D. Cox, *Jung and St. Paul: A Study of the Doctrine of Justification by Faith and Its Relation to the Concept of Individuation* (1959). * * *

the foggy word "basically" could mean. But both the historian and the theologian, both the psychologist and the average reader of the Bible, are well advised to assess how this hypothesis of contemporaneity affects their thinking, and their interpretation of ancient writings.

This problem becomes acute when one tries to picture the function and the manifestation of introspection in the life and writings of the Apostle Paul. It is the more acute since it is exactly at this point that Western interpreters have found the common denominator between Paul and the experiences of man, since Paul's statements about "justification by faith" have been hailed as the answer to the problem which faces the ruthlessly honest man in his practice of introspection. Especially in Protestant Christianity—which, however, at this point has its roots in Augustine and in the piety of the Middle Ages—the Pauline awareness of sin has been interpreted in the light of Luther's struggle with his conscience. But it is exactly at that point that we can discern the most drastic difference between Luther and Paul, between the 16th and the 1st century, and, perhaps, between Eastern and Western Christianity.

A fresh look at the Pauline writings themselves shows that Paul was equipped with what in our eyes must be called a rather "robust" conscience. In Phil. 3 Paul speaks most fully about his life before his Christian calling, and there is no indication that he had had any difficulty in fulfilling the Law. On the contrary, he can say that he had been "flawless" as to the righteousness required by the Law (v.6). His encounter with Jesus Christ—at Damascus, according to Acts 9:1–9—has not changed this fact. It was not to him a restoration of a plagued conscience; when he says that he now forgets what is behind him (Phil. 3:13), he does not think about the shortcomings in his obedience to the Law, but about his glorious achievements as a righteous Jew, achievements which he nevertheless now has learned to consider as "refuse" in the light of his faith in Jesus as the Messiah.

The impossibility of keeping the whole Law is a decisive point in Paul's argumentation in Rom. 2:17–3:20 (cf. 2:1ff.); and also in Gal. 3:10–12 this impossibility is the background for Paul's arguments in favor of a salvation which is open to both Jews and Gentiles in Christ. These and similar Pauline statements have led many interpreters to accuse Paul of misunderstanding or deliberately distorting the Jewish view of Law and Salvation. It is pointed out that for the Jew the Law did not require a static or pedantic perfectionism but supposed a covenant relationship in which there was room for forgiveness and repentance and where God applied the Measure of Grace. Hence Paul should have been wrong in ruling out the Law on the basis that Israel could not achieve the perfect obedience which the Law required. What is forgotten in such a critique of Paul—which is conditioned by the later Western problem of a conscience troubled by the demands of the Law—is that these statements about the impossibility of fulfilling the Law stand side by side with the one just mentioned: "I was blameless as to righteousness—of the Law, that is" (Phil. 3:6). So Paul speaks about his subjective conscience—in full accordance with his Jewish training. But Rom. 2–3 deals with something very different. The actual transgressions in Israel—as a people, not in each and every individual—show that the Jews are not better than the Gentiles, in spite of circumcision and the proud possession of the Law. The "advantage" of the Jews is that they have been entrusted with the Words of God and this advantage cannot be revoked by their disobedience (Rom. 3:1ff.), but for the rest they have no edge on salvation. The Law has not helped. They stand before God as guilty as the Gentiles, and even more so (2:9). All this is said in the light of the new avenue of salvation, which has been opened in Christ, an avenue which is equally open to Jews and Gentiles, since it is not based on the Law, in which the very distinction between the two rests. In such a situation, says Paul, the old covenant, even with its provision for forgiveness and grace, is not a valid alternative any more. The only *metanoia* (repentance/conversion) and the only grace which counts is the one now available in Messiah Jesus. Once this has been seen, it appears that Paul's references to the impossibility of fulfilling the Law is part of a theological and theoretical scriptural argument about the relation between Jews and Gentiles. Judging from Paul's own writings, there is no indication that he had "experienced it in his own conscience" during his time as a Pharisee. It is also striking to note that Paul never urges Jews to find in Christ the answer to the anguish of a plagued conscience.

If that is the case regarding *Paul the Pharisee*, it is, as we shall see, even more important to note that we look in vain for any evidence that *Paul the Christian* has suffered under the burden of conscience concerning personal shortcomings which he would label "sins." The famous formula "simul justus et peccator"—at the same time righteous and sinner—as a description of the status of the Christian may have some foundation in the Pauline writings, but this formula cannot be substantiated as the center of Paul's conscious attitude toward his personal sins. Apparently, Paul did not have the type of introspective conscience which such a formula seems to presuppose. This is probably one of the reasons why "forgiveness" is the term for salvation which is used least of all in the Pauline writings.

It is most helpful to compare these observations concerning Paul with the great hero of what has been called "Pauline Christianity," i.e., with Martin Luther. In him we find the problem of late medieval piety and theology. Luther's inner struggles presuppose the developed system of Penance and Indulgence, and it is significant that his famous 95 theses take their point of departure from the problem of forgiveness of sins as seen within the framework of Penance: "When our Lord and Master Jesus Christ said: 'Repent (*penitentiam agite*) . . . ,' he wanted the whole life of the faithful to be a repentance (or penance)."

When the period of the European mission had come to an end, the theological and practical center of Penance shifted from Baptism, administered once and for all, to the ever repeated Mass, and already this subtle change in the architecture of the Christian life contributed to a more acute introspection. The manuals for self-examination among the Irish monks and missionaries became a treasured legacy in wide circles of Western Christianity. The Black Death may have been significant in the development of the climate of faith and life. Penetrating self-examination reached a hitherto unknown intensity. For those who took this practice seriously—and they were more numerous than many Protestants are accustomed to think—the pressure was great. It is as one of those—and for them—that Luther carries out his mission as a great pioneer. It is in response to *their* question, "How can I find a gracious God?" that Paul's words about a justification in Christ by faith, and without the works of the Law, appears as the liberating and saving answer. Luther's unrelenting honesty, even to the gates of hell (cf. especially his *De servo arbitrio*, "On the Bondage of the Will"), his refusal to accept the wise and sound consolation from his spiritual directors, these make him into a Christopher Columbus in the world of faith, who finds new and good land on the other side of what was thought to be the abyss.

In these matters Luther was a truly Augustinian monk, since Augustine may well have been one of the first to express the dilemma of the introspective conscience. It has always been a puzzling fact that Paul meant so relatively little for the thinking of the Church during the first 350 years of its history. To be sure, he is honored and quoted but—in the theological perspective of the West—it seems that Paul's great insight into justification by faith was forgotten. It is, however, with Augustine that we find an interpretation of Paul which makes use of what to us is the deeper layer in the thought of the great Apostle. A decisive reason for this state of affairs may well have been that up to the time of Augustine the Church was by and large under the impression that Paul dealt with those issues with which he actually deals: 1) What happens to the Law (the Torah, the actual Law of Moses, not the principle of legalism) when the Messiah has come?—2) What are the rami-

[handwritten margin note top: Paul concerned not with individual conscience but concrete historical fact of gentile world]

fications of the Messiah's arrival for the relation between Jews and Gentiles? For Paul had not arrived at his view of the Law by testing and pondering its effect upon his conscience; it was his grappling with the question about the place of the Gentiles in the Church and in the plan of God, with the problem Jews/Gentiles or Jewish Christians/Gentile Christians, which had driven him to that interpretation of the Law which was to become his in a unique way. These observations agree well with the manner in which both Paul himself and the Acts of the Apostles describe his "conversion" as a call to become the Apostle to and of the Gentiles. This was the task for which he—in the manner of the prophets of old—had been earmarked by God from his mother's womb (Gal. 1:15, cf. Acts 9:15). There is not—as we usually think—first a conversion, and then a call to apostleship; there is only the call to the work among the Gentiles. Hence, it is quite natural that at least one of the centers of gravity in Paul's thought should be how to define the place for Gentiles in the Church, according to the plan of God. Rom. 9—11 is not an appendix to chs. 1–8, but the climax of the letter.

This problem was, however, not a live one after the end of the first century, when Christianity for all practical purposes had a non-Jewish constituency. Yet it was not until Augustine that the Pauline thought about the Law and Justification was applied in a consistent and grand style to a more general and timeless human problem. In that connection we remember that Augustine has often been called "the first modern man." While this is an obvious generalization, it may contain a fair amount of truth. His *Confessiones* are the first great document in the history of the introspective conscience. The Augustinian line leads into the Middle Ages and reaches its climax in the penitential struggle of an Augustinian monk, Martin Luther, and in his interpretation of Paul.

Judging at least from a superficial survey of the preaching of the Churches of the East from olden times to the present, it is striking how their homiletical tradition is either one of doxology or meditative mysticism or exhortation—but it does not deal with the plagued conscience in the way in which one came to do so in the Western Churches.

The problem we are trying to isolate could be expressed in hermeneutical terms somewhat like this: The Reformers' interpretation of Paul rests on an analogism when Pauline statements about Faith and Works, Law and Gospel, Jews and Gentiles are read in the framework of late medieval piety. The Law, the Torah, with its specific requirements of circumcision and food restrictions becomes a general principle of "legalism" in religious matters. Where Paul was concerned about the possibility for Gentiles to be included in the messianic community, his statements are now read as answers to the quest for assurance about man's salvation out of a common human predicament.

This shift in the frame of reference affects the interpretation at many points. A good illustration can be seen in what Luther calls the Second Use of the Law, i.e., its function as a Tutor or Schoolmaster unto Christ. The crucial passage for this understanding of the Law is Gal. 3:24, a passage which the King James Version—in unconscious accord with Western tradition—renders: "Wherefore the law was our schoolmaster (R.V. and A.S.V.: tutor) to bring us unto Christ," but which the Revised Standard Version translates more adequately: "So that the law was our custodian until Christ came." In his extensive argument for the possibility of Gentiles becoming Christians without circumcision etc., Paul states that the Law had not come in until 430 years after the promise to Abraham, and that it was meant to have validity only up to the time of the Messiah (Gal. 3:15–22). Hence, its function was to serve as a Custodian for the Jews until that time. Once the Messiah had come, and once the faith in Him—not "faith" as a general religious attitude—was available as the decisive ground for salvation, the Law had done its duty as a custodian for the Jews, or as a waiting room with strong locks (vv. 22f.). Hence, it is clear that Paul's problem is how to explain why there is no reason to impose the Law on the Gentiles, who now, in God's good Messianic time, have become partakers in the fulfillment of the promises to Abraham (v. 29).

In the common interpretation of Western Christianity, the matter looks very different. One could even say that Paul's argument has been reversed into saying the opposite to his original intention. Now the Law is the Tutor *unto* Christ. Nobody can attain a true faith in Christ unless his self-righteousness has been crushed by the Law. The function of the Second Use of the Law is to make man see his desperate need for a Savior. In such an interpretation, we note how Paul's distinction between Jews and Gentiles is gone. "*Our* Tutor/Custodian" is now a statement applied to man in general, not "our" in the sense of "I, Paul, and my fellow Jews." Furthermore, the Law is not any more the Law of Moses which requires circumcision etc., and which has become obsolete when faith in the Messiah is a live option—it is the moral imperative as such, in the form of the will of God. And finally, Paul's argument that the Gentiles must not, and should not come to Christ *via* the Law, i.e., *via* circumcision etc., has turned into a statement according to which all men must come to Christ with consciences properly convicted by the Law and its insatiable requirements for righteousness. So drastic is the reinterpretation once the original framework of "Jews and Gentiles" is lost, and the Western problems of conscience become its unchallenged and self-evident substitute.

Thus, the radical difference between a Paul and a Luther at this one point has considerable ramification for the reading of the actual texts. And the line of Luther appears to be the obvious one. This is true not only among those who find themselves more or less dogmatically bound by the confessions of the Reformation. It is equally true about the average student of "all the great books" in a College course, or the agnostic Westerner in general. It is also true in serious New Testament exegesis. Thus, R. Bultmann—in spite of his great familiarity with the history of religions in early Christian times—finds the nucleus of Pauline thought in the problem of "boasting," i.e., in man's need to be utterly convicted in his conscience. Paul's self-understanding in these matters is the existential, and hence, ever valid center of Pauline theology. Such an interpretation is an even more drastic translation and an even more far-reaching generalization of the original Pauline material than that found in the Reformers. But it is worth noting that it is achieved in the prolongation of the same line. This is more obvious since Bultmann makes, candidly and openly, the statement that his existential hermeneutic rests on the presupposition that man is essentially the same through the ages, and that this continuity in the human self-consciousness is the common denominator between the New Testament and any age of human history. This presupposition is stated with the force of an a priori truth.

What in Bultmann rests on a clearly stated hermeneutic principle plays, however, its subtle and distorting role in historians who do not give account of their presuppositions but work within an unquestioned Western framework. P. Volz, in his comprehensive study of Jewish eschatology, uses man's knowledge of his individual salvation in its relation to a troubled conscience as one of the "trenches" in his reconstruction of the Jewish background to the New Testament. But when it comes to the crucial question and he wants to find a passage which would substantiate that this was a conscious problem in those generations of Judaism, he can find only one example in the whole Rabbinic literature which perhaps could illustrate an attitude of a troubled conscience (bBer. 28b).

To be sure, no one could ever deny that *hamartia*, "sin," is a crucial word in Paul's terminology, especially in his epistle to the Romans. Rom. 1–3 sets out to show that all—both Jews and Gentiles—have sinned and fallen short of the Glory of God (3:19, cf. v. 23). Rom. 3:21–8:39 demonstrates how and in what sense this tragic fact is changed by the arrival of the Messiah.

It is much harder to gage how Paul subjectively experienced the power of sin in his life and, more specifically, how and in what sense he was conscious of actual sins. One point is clear. The Sin with capital S in Paul's past was that he had persecuted the Church of God. This climax of his dedicated obedience to his Jewish faith (Gal. 1:13, Phil. 3:6) was the shameful deed which made him the least worthy of apostleship (1 Cor. 15:9). This motif, which is elaborated dramatically by the author of the Acts of the Apostles (chs. 9, 22 and 26), is well grounded in Paul's own epistles. Similarly, when 1 Timothy states on Paul's account that "Christ Jesus came into the world to save sinners, of whom I am number one" (1:15), this is not an expression of contrition in the present tense, but refers to how Paul in his ignorance had been a blaspheming and violent persecutor, before God in his mercy and grace had revealed to him his true Messiah and made Paul an Apostle and a prototype of sinners' salvation (1:12–16).

Nevertheless, Paul knew that he had made up for this terrible Sin of persecuting the Church, as he says in so many words in 1 Cor. 15:10: ". . . his grace toward me was not in vain; on the contrary, I worked harder than any of them—though it was not I, but the grace of God which is with me."

Thus his call to Apostleship has the same pattern as the more thematic statement that Christ died for us godless ones, while we were yet sinners (Rom. 5:6–11). We note how that statement is only the subsidiary conditional clause in an argument *e majore ad minus*: If now God was so good and powerful that he could justify weak and sinful and rebellious men, how much easier must it not be for him to give in due time the ultimate salvation to those whom he already has justified. Hence, the words about the sinful, the weak and the rebellious have not present-tense meaning, but refer to the past, which is gloriously and gracefully blotted out, as was Paul's enmity to Jesus Christ and his Church.

What then about Paul's consciousness of sins after his conversion? His letters indicate with great clarity that he did not hold to the view that man was free from sin after baptism. His pastoral admonitions show that he had much patience with the sins and weaknesses of Christians. But does he ever intimate that he is aware of any sins of his own which would trouble his conscience? It is actually easier to find statements to the contrary. The tone in Acts 23:1, "Brethren, I have lived before God in all good conscience up to this day" (cf. 24:16), prevails also throughout his letters. Even if we take due note of the fact that the major part of Paul's correspondence contains an apology for his Apostolic ministry—hence it is the antipode to Augustine's Confessions from the point of view of form—the conspicuous absence of reference to an actual consciousness of being a sinner is surprising. To be sure,

Paul is aware of a struggle with his "body" (1 Cor. 9:27), but we note that the tone is one of confidence, not of a plagued conscience.

In Rom. 9:1 and 2 Cor. 1:12 he witnesses to his good conscience. This tone reaches its highest pitch in 2 Cor. 5:10f.: "For we must all appear before the judgment seat of Christ so that each one may receive the retribution for what he has done while in his body, either good or evil. Aware, therefore, of the fear of the Lord, we try to persuade men, but to God it is clear [what we are]; and I hope that it is clear also to your conscience." Here, with the day of reckoning before his eyes, Paul says that the Lord has approved of him, and he hopes that the Corinthians shall have an equally positive impression of him, and of his success in pleasing the Lord (5:9). This robust conscience is not shaken but strengthened by his awareness of a final judgment which has not come yet. And when he writes about the tensions between himself and Apollos and other teachers, he states that "I have nothing on my conscience" (1 Cor. 4:4; N.E.B.—literally "I know nothing with me"; the verb is of the same stem as the word for conscience); to be sure, he adds that this does not settle the case, since "the Lord is my judge," but it is clear from the context that Paul is in little doubt about the final verdict. His warning against a premature verdict is not a plea out of humility or fear, but a plea to the Corinthians not to be too rash in a negative evaluation of Paul.

Thus, we look in vain for a statement in which Paul would speak about himself as an actual sinner. When he speaks about his conscience, he witnesses to his good conscience before men and God. On the other hand, Paul often speaks about his *weakness*, not only ironically as in 2 Cor. 11:21f. In 2 Cor. 12 we find the proudly humble words, "But He said to me: 'My grace is sufficient to you, for the power is fulfilled in weakness.' I will the more gladly boast of my weakness, that the power of Christ may rest upon me. For the sake of Christ, then, I am content with weaknesses, insults, hardships, persecutions, and calamities; for when I am weak, then I am strong" (vv. 9–10). The weakness which Paul here refers to is clearly without any relation to his sin of his conscience. The "thorn in the flesh" (v. 7) was presumably some physical handicap—some have guessed at epilepsy—which interfered with his effectiveness and, what was more important, with his apostolic authority, as we can see from Gal. 4:13, cf. 1 Cor. 11:30. Sickness was seen as a sign of insufficient spiritual endowment. But there is no indication that Paul ever thought of this and other "weaknesses" as sins for which he was responsible. They were caused by the Enemy or the enemies. His weakness became for him an important facet in his identification with the work of Christ, who had been "crucified in weakness" (2 Cor. 13:4; cf. also 4:10 and Col. 1:24).—In the passage from Rom. 5, mentioned above, we find the only use of the word "weak" as a synonym to "sinner," but there these words helped to describe primarily the power of justification as a past act (and the New English Bible consequently renders it by "powerless"). This is the more clear since the third synonym is "enemy" (v. 10), and points to Paul's past when he had been the enemy of Christ.

Yet there is one Pauline text which the reader must have wondered why we have left unconsidered, especially since it is the passage we mentioned in the beginning as the proof text for Paul's deep insights into the human predicament: "I do not do the good I want, but the evil I do not want to do is what I do" (Rom. 7: 19). What could witness more directly to a deep and sensitive introspective conscience? While much attention has been given to the question whether Paul here speaks about a pre-Christian or Christian experience of his, or about man in general, little attention has been drawn to the fact that Paul here is involved in an argument about the Law; he is not primarily concerned about man's or his own cloven ego or predicament. The diatribe style of the chapter helps us to see what Paul is doing. In vv. 7–12 he works out an answer to the semi-rhetorical question: "Is the Law sin?" The answer reads: "Thus the Law is holy, just, and good." This leads to the equally rhetorical question: "Is it then this good (Law) which brought death to me?", and the answer is summarized in v. 25b: "So then, I myself serve the Law of God with my mind, but with my flesh I serve the Law of Sin" (i.e., the Law "weakened by sin" [8:3] leads to death, just as a medicine which is good in itself can cause death in a patient whose organism [flesh] cannot take it).

Such an analysis of the formal structure of Rom. 7 shows that Paul is here involved in an interpretation of the Law, a defense for the holiness and goodness of the Law. In vv. 13–25 he carries out this defense by making a distinction between the Law as such and the Sin (and the Flesh) which has to assume the whole responsibility for the fatal outcome. It is most striking that the "I", the *ego*, is not simply identified with Sin and Flesh. The observation that "I do not do the good I want, but the evil I do not want to do is what I do" does not lead directly over to the exclamation: "Wretched man that I am . . .!", but, on the contrary, to the statement, "Now if I do what I do not want, *then it is not I who do it*, but the sin which dwells in me." The argument is one of acquittal of the ego, not one of utter contrition. Such a line of thought would be impossible if Paul's intention were to describe man's predicament. In Rom. 1–3 the human impasse has been argued, and here every possible excuse has been carefully ruled out. In Rom. 7 the issue is rather to show how in some sense "I gladly agree with the Law of God as far as my inner man is concerned" (v. 22); or, as in v. 25, "I serve the Law of God."

All this makes sense only if the anthropological references in Rom. 7 are seen as means for a very special argument about the holiness and goodness of the Law. The possibility of a distinction between the good Law and the bad Sin is based on the rather trivial observation that every man knows that there is a difference between what he ought to do and what he does. This distinction makes it possible for Paul to blame Sin and Flesh, and to rescue the Law as a good gift of God. "If I now do what I do not want, I agree with the Law [and recognize] that it is good" (v. 16). That is all, but that is what should be proven.

Unfortunately—or fortunately—Paul happened to express this supporting argument so well that what to him and his contemporaries was a common sense observation appeared to later interpreters to be a most penetrating insight into the nature of man and into the nature of sin. This could happen easily once the problem about the nature and intention of God's Law was not any more as relevant a problem in the sense in which Paul grappled with it. The question about the Law became the incidental framework around the golden truth of Pauline anthropology. This is what happens when one approaches Paul with the Western question of an introspective conscience. This Western interpretation reaches its climax when it appears that even, or especially, the will of man is the center of depravation. And yet, in Rom. 7 Paul had said about that will: "The will (to do the good) is there . . ." (v. 18).

What we have called the Western interpretation has left its mark even in the field of textual reconstruction in this chapter in Romans. In Moffatt's translation of the New Testament the climax of the whole argument about the Law (v. 25b, see above) is placed before the words "wretched man that I am . . ." Such a rearrangement—without any basis in the manuscripts—wants to make this exclamation the dramatic climax of the whole chapter, so that it is quite clear to the reader that Paul here gives the answer to the great problem of human existence. But by such arrangements the structure of Paul's argumentation is destroyed. What was a digression is elevated to the main factor. It should not be denied that Paul is deeply aware of the precarious situation of man in this world, where even the holy Law of God does not help—it actually leads to death. Hence his outburst. But there is no indication that this awareness is related to a subjective conscience struggle. If that were the case, he would have spoken of the "body of sin," but he says "body of death" (v. 25; cf. 1 Cor. 15:56). What dominates this chapter is a theological concern and the awareness that there is a positive solution available here and now by the Holy Spirit about which he speaks in ch. 8. We should not read a trembling and introspective conscience into a text which is so anxious to put the blame on Sin, and that in such a way that not only the Law but the will and mind of man are declared good and are found to be on the side of God.

We may have wasted too much time in trying to demonstrate a fact well known in human history—and especially in the history of religions: that sayings which originally meant one thing later on were interpreted to mean something else, something which was felt to be more relevant to human conditions of later times.

And yet, if our analysis is on the whole correct, it points to a major question in the history of mankind. We should venture to suggest that the West for centuries has wrongly surmised that the biblical writers were grappling with problems which no doubt are ours, but which never entered their consciousness.

For the historian this is of great significance. It could of course always be argued that these ancients unconsciously were up against the same problems as we are—man being the same through the ages. But the historian is rightly anxious to stress the value of having an adequate picture of what these people actually thought that they were saying. He will always be suspicious of any "moderniz-ing," whether it be for apologetic, doctrinal, or psychological pur-poses.

The theologian would be quite willing to accept and appreciate the obvious deepening of religious and human insight which has taken place in Western thought, and which reached a theological climax with Luther—and a secular climax with Freud. He could per-haps argue that this Western interpretation and transformation of Pauline thought is a valid and glorious process of theological devel-opment. He could even claim that such a development was fostered by elements implicit in the New Testament, and especially in Paul.

The framework of "Sacred History" which we have found to be that of Pauline Theology (cf. our comments on Gal. 3:24 above) opens up a new perspective for systematic theology and practical theology. The Pauline *ephapax* ("once for all", Rom. 6:10) cannot be translated fully and only into something repeated in the life of every individual believer. For Gentiles the Law is *not* the Schoolmaster who leads to Christ; or it is that only by analogy and a secondary one at that. We find ourselves in the new situation where the faith in the Messiah Jesus gives us the right to be called Children of God (1 Jn. 3:1). By way of analogy, one could of course say that in some sense every man has a "legalistic Jew" in his heart. But that *is* an analogy, and should not be smuggled into the texts as their primary or explicit meaning in Paul. If that is done, something happens to the joy and humility of Gentile Christianity.

Thus, the theologian would note that the Pauline original should not be identified with such interpretations. He would try to find ways by which the church—also in the West—could do more justice to other elements of the Pauline original than those catering to the problems raised by introspection. He would be suspicious of a teaching and a preaching which pretended that the only door into the church was that of evermore introspective awareness of sin and guilt. For it appears that the Apostle Paul was a rather good Christian, and yet he seems to have had little such awareness. We note how the bibilical original functions as a critique of inherited presuppositions and an incentive to new thought. Few things are more liberating and creative in modern theology than a clear distinction between the "original" and the "translation" in any age, our own included.

EPILOGUE

The Christian Proteus

WAYNE A. MEEKS

The significance of Paul for the development of European and American religious traditions can hardly be overestimated, however difficult it may be to describe the precise nature of his influence. Sydney Ahlstrom, the historian of American religion, has said:

> Just as the European philosophical tradition, in Whitehead's famous phrase, consists of a series of footnotes to Plato, so Christian theology is a series of footnotes to St. Paul, and back of him stretches still another series of rabbinic footnotes on the Law and the Prophets of Israel.[1]

That is not an overstatement, but it must be qualified by the reminder that footnotes can express many things: rejection, for instance, or utter bafflement, as well as agreement and expansion. Harnack was more judicious when he suggested, "One might write a history of dogma as a history of the Pauline *reactions* in the Church, and in doing so would touch on all the *turning points* of the history."[2] The history of Paulinism, as we have noted earlier, contains a peculiar ambivalence. The "most holy apostle" of the sacred traditions is at the same time, again and again, "the apostle of the heretics." There is singular irony in the fact that the great system builders of Christian doctrine quarried their choicest propositions from Paul's letters, only to have later generations discover that they had thus built time-bombs into the structure that would, in a moment of crisis, bring the whole tower of syllogisms crashing down. Paul has become the foe of all authoritative systems,

---

1. Sydney E. Ahlstrom, *Theology in America* (Indianapolis, 1967), p. 23.
2. Adolf von Harnack, *History of Dogma*, tr. by Neil Buchanan (Boston, 1902) I, 136 (italics added).

although he himself—and that is the strange part—was not a revolutionary in any sense of the word. "Paulinism has proved to be a ferment in the history of dogma, a basis it has never been."[3]

The ferment of Paulinism has become visible anew in a number of recent developments: the idea of a secular Christianity, the attempt to "demythologize" the New Testament, the contextual approach to ethics, the dialogue between Christians and Jews.

The "secular theology" which became very popular in the 1960's has its roots in a radical Paulinism, as a reader of the very early Karl Barth[4] will learn. Dietrich Bonhoeffer, the German martyr whose letters from a Gestapo prison became a manifesto for this movement, made the connection explicit:

> The Pauline question whether *peritōme* [circumcision] is the prerequisite for justification means today, in my opinion, whether religion is the prerequisite for salvation. Freedom from *peritomē* is also freedom from religion.[5]

Rudolf Bultmann's proposal for "demythologizing" the New Testament[6] also emerged from wartime Germany. In order to make plain to modern man both the gift offered and the radical decision required by the gospel, he urged, the mythical statements of the New Testament must be translated into existential categories. To justify this enterprise, Bultmann appealed to Paul (and John), who, he maintained, had already begun the process of demythologizing the myths of Gnosticism and of apocalyptic. Bultmann saw himself as carrying on Paul's project more consistently than Paul himself was able to do.

Attempts to restate the basis for Christian morality in terms neither legal nor idealistic resulted in a series of proposals labelled "contextual" and "situational" ethics. This development is unthinkable apart from Paulinism. Readers of Hans von Soden's article (above, pp. 257–68) will see how direct is the connection between the contextual ethic and the contemporary understanding of Paul.[7]

In the serious conversation between Jews and Christians which has begun since the Nazi holocaust and has developed, though in fits and starts, nevertheless into an extremely hopeful and candid

3. *Ibid.*
4. See above, pp. 250–57.
5. *Widerstand und Ergebung*, ed. Eberhard Bethge (Munich, 1956, pp. 180 f.; ET, *Letters and Papers from Prison*, New York, 1967, p. 154).
6. Above, pp. 409–22; further, *Jesus Christ and Mythology* (New York, 1958).
7. I am thinking of works like H. Richard Niebuhr, *The Responsible Self* (New York, 1963), Paul Lehmann,

Ethics in a Christian Context (New York, 1963), Joseph Fletcher, *Situation Ethics: The New Morality* (Philadelphia, 1966), Gordon Kaufmann, *The Context of Decision* (Nashville, 1961), and, in important respects, also Bernhard Häring, C.SS.R., *The Law of Christ* (Westminster, Md., 1963). See also J. M. Gustafson, "Context versus Principles: A Misplaced Debate in Christian Ethics," in *Harv. Theol. Rev.* 58 (1965): 171–202.

dialogue, the name of Paul frequently stands at the center of discussion. We have observed the irony implicit in historic attitudes toward Paul's Jewishness. Jews have often regarded Paul as a traitor, the first of the long line of Christian anti-Semites, while the professional anti-Semites have rejected Paul as altogether too Jewish. In recent years, however, several of the most penetrating studies of Paul have been written by Jewish scholars. Some Jews are discovering that, if they wish to understand what was going on in first-century Judaism, one of the authors they must read is Paul, while Christians are finding that, if they want to understand Paul, they must learn about Judaism.

In the face of such continued interest in Paulinism, the multiple pictures of Paul and his influence represented by the excerpts in this volume constitute a difficult problem. The history of European and American thought is crowded with a discouraging variety of interpretations of Paul. The variety is in fact so great and of such polar tendencies that one may reasonably doubt whether an accurate and consistent judgment of the apostle is possible. "Relevance" has been purchased again and again at the cost of fidelity to history. Moreover, the fault has not lain solely in wilful distortion, nor even altogether in the paucity of information or the failure of imagination or the excess of imagination where information is wanting. There is no figure in the first generation of Christianity about whom we know so much as about Paul—and precisely at the points where he reveals most about himself we are most puzzled. The polar tendencies of the interpretations of Paul are finally significant because there is something polar in Paul himself.

> For though I am free from all men, I have made myself a slave to all, that I might win the more. To the Jews I became as a Jew, in order to win Jews; to those under the law I became as one under the law—though not being myself under the law— that I might win those under the law. To those outside the law I became as one outside the law—not being without law toward God but under the law of Christ—that I might win those outside the law. To the weak I became weak, that I might win the weak. I have become all things to all men, that I might by all means save some. I do it all for the sake of the gospel . . . .[8]

This rather rhetorical statement is more than an admission of tactical disguises. The conditions that Paul lists are not superficial customs that the missionary could adopt in order to gain a better hearing with a given cultural group. Rather, each goes to the heart of that group's understanding of its very existence. For the Jewish

8. I Cor. 9:19–23. My interpretation of this passage is indebted to G. Bornkamm, "The Missionary Stance of Paul in I Corinthians 9 and in Acts," in *Studies in Luke-Acts*, ed. L. E. Keck and J. L. Martyn (Nashville, 1966), pp. 194–207.

Christians in Galatia, to be "under the law" was a prerequisite for salvation; for the Corinthian spirituals, to be free from the law was the sign of one's resurrection. "The weak" was Paul's term for those whose consciences were still torn by anxieties over religious taboos, and who tried to impose their own scrupulosity on the liberty of the strong-minded. In each case Paul vigorously opposed the condition named, when it had been made a requirement for spiritual perfection. Yet here he tells us that he could himself adopt each of these conditions (though the "as" is not to be overlooked) when that served his purpose to gain adherents to the Christian affirmation.

Clearly then, Paul's adaptation to the positions of the contending parties did not involve his capitulation to them. Rather, when he became "as one under the law," it was only in order to insist to those under the law that Christ had replaced the law as the way to reconciliation with God. When he became "as a lawless one," it was to insist that "we must all still stand before the tribunal of Christ." The Paul who was "all things to all men" was the same man who could shout down the compromising Peter at Antioch (Gal. 2:11–14) and hurl anathemas at angels and men who might dare to deviate from "his gospel" (Gal. 1:8 f.). Polemics were just as important in Paul's missionary and pastoral methods as were apologetics. He veered from one side to another not only in order to approach different audiences, but in order to *resist* different points of view that he rejected.

Consequently any one who wishes to understand Paul must recognize the large part his opponents played in shaping his literary bequest. We never see pure Pauline thought being developed at leisure by its own inner logic; rather we see Paul always thinking under pressure, usually in the heat of immediate controversy. And it would be an illusion to suppose that the "real" Paul could be filtered out of this disconcerting ebb and flow by the proper logical analysis or psychoanalytic theory. The real Paul is to be found precisely in the dialectic of his apparent inconsistencies. Paul is the Christian Proteus.

Homer's Proteus was a *daimon* of the sea who could assume any form he chose. When Menelaos and his men seized him, hoping to learn from the Old Man the way of escape to their distant homeland,

> First he turned into a great bearded lion,
> and then to a serpent, then to a leopard, then to a
> great boar,
> and he turned into fluid water, to a tree with towering
> branches . . .[9]

9. *The Odyssey of Homer*, tr. by Richmond Lattimore (New York, 1967), iv, 456.

Only when the captors had clung undaunted to the many-formed *daimon*, compelling him to resume again his human shape, did he answer their questions—and then not until *he* had questioned *them*.

Other ages have seen single shapes of Paul; our generation recognizes Proteus in him. Yet in this recognition also there is irony and a further warning. Our generation sees the protean qualities of Paul because we are ourselves "protean men," as Robert Jay Lifton has said.[1] The plasticity of contemporary man is capable of a certain resonance with ambiguities heretofore undetected in men of other ages. There are things about Paul's age that bear comparison with our own. Naturally we must beware of stretching a typology into a cultural umbrella, and especially of modernizing the things in ancient culture that seem to us familiar. Paul was subjected to no electronic media, to name only the most obvious difference. Yet the imperial wars and the Roman road system did create a political and technical environment in which the experience of many people became almost unbearably manifold in both potential and threat. Syncretism meant, in personal terms, the flooding into consciousness of possibilities, of symbols, of allegiances. Men became experimenters, searchers, spiritual wanderers. The fact that we have so much trouble squeezing Paul into the neat categories of "rabbi," "diaspora Jew," "Hellenist," and the like shows how much he belonged to that fluid world.

But the *daimon* we have seized begins to question us. Has our sophisticated eclecticism spared us the distortion imposed on Paul by previous generations of searchers? Can we ever say confidently that we "know" such a historic personage? The montage of the shapes Paul has assumed in the hands of those who have sought to hold him forces the question upon us, and we must not seek to elude it. At the same time, however, it is a question that should press us into caution, not despair. The historian needs modesty; some things we shall not know, ever. But there are some things we do know. There has been some progress in scholarship. Some of the interpretations of Paul which we have surveyed in this book have become impossible. Some of the plaguing questions have either been answered with a fitting degree of assurance, or have been shown to be improperly put. Historical scholarship has had modest success in holding fast to the Christian Proteus, so that Paul speaks to a number of questions with clarity.

Was Paul a Jew or a Hellenist? Certainly the answer to this question is "both." Paul is much more Jewish than last century's scholarship believed. But Judaism in Paul's time turns out to have

1. "Protean Man," in *History and* (New York, 1970), pp. 316–31. *Human Survival* by Robert Jay Lifton

been much more "Hellenistic" and more variegated than had been supposed. Paul had been a Pharisee, and there are many aspects of his thought and method that are recognizably kin to the Pharisaism we know through the later Talmudic and midrashic sources. Nevertheless, it cannot be explicated simply by searching out "parallels" from rabbinic literature—or from apocalypses, or from the Dead Sea Scrolls. The same is true from the other side. Paul certainly belonged to a hellenized diaspora Judaism, and there are many passages in his letters than can be illuminated by comparison with his older contemporary Philo of Alexandria, or with the earlier Greek Jewish compositions like the Wisdom of Solomon. And even beyond the circle of Jewish Hellenism, there are passages from pagan writers, preachers, and religious propagandists that shed light on Paul's language and imagery. But "parallelomania" (to use Samuel Sandmel's term) is not appropriate in the use of Greek sources any more than of Hebrew and Aramaic ones.

Perhaps the most significant discovery about Paul in this century's scholarship has been the recognition of his Christian precedents. Paul cannot be called the "second founder of Christianity," as Wrede named him less than seventy years ago. Christianity in the "Pauline" form—with sacraments, cultic worship of Jesus as Lord, Gentile members, and the doctrines of pre-existence and atoning death of the Christ—had already been "founded" before Paul became first its persecutor and then its missionary. Heitmüller's demonstration of this point (above, pp. 308–19) will continue to be corrected in detail, but it will not be reversed.[2] By the same token, Paul cannot be called the "hellenizer of Christianity," a term which in any case more obscures than illuminates the complexity of early Christian evolution.

Was Paul a theologian, an activist, or a mystic? No one of these captures the "essence" of Paul, though the first two more than the last are descriptive. He was in fact all three together, and that mixture is not without parallel. Again, comparison with Philo is instructive, for Philo also longed after and occasionally achieved a mystic vision not unlike that reported by Paul in 2 Cor. 12, but found himself constantly required to give his energies rather to practical affairs and to writing. His form of activism was more aristocratic than Paul's, and so was his literary effort; Philo thought of himself as a philosopher, a *sophos*, while Paul disdained the Hellenistic wisdom in both its intellectual and occult forms. Philo, on the other hand, as literateur and a man of obvious civic prestige, who could risk his career and his life as an envoy to the mad emperor Caligula, would doubtless have found Paul's kind of mission vulgar.

---

2. His results have been confirmed by the independent investigation of A. M.   Hunter, *Paul and his Predecessors* (rev. ed., London, 1961).

Nevertheless, both were Jews of deep religious sensitivity, whose lives, immersed in a syncretist world, combined thought, action, and contemplation.

If we ask which of the three modes of life dominated Paul's time and strength, there can be no question but that he would have to be called the missionary first and foremost. But if we ask about the impact of his career on the lasting forms of Christianity, it is equally clear that it was his thought that was important. That his ideas now seem less original and isolated in early Christianity than they did a generation ago does not diminish the significance of those elements that were genuinely unique and prolific. It can also be said with some confidence that all attempts to make "mysticism" the center of Pauline Christianity have failed. Categories which have seemed to many readers "mystical," such as the pregnant phrase "in Christ," turn out to have largely social and cultic significance. And as we have learned to evaluate carefully the polemical situations of Paul's letters, we find that many of his concerns are specifically anti-mystical, addressed to dangers he saw in certain forms of early Christian spiritualism.

Did Paul radically excise law from the Christian life? This has proved to be a much more difficult question on which to gain a consensus, but perhaps that is as much because of the reluctance of theologians to accept the implications of an affirmative answer as because of the inherent ambiguities in Paul's statements. It is true, as a number of recent scholars have argued, that Paul's direct statements about the law and justification by grace are found only in a few places in his letters; they are the principal themes only of Galatians and Romans. Nevertheless, those statements are more radical than the church has ever, except in rare moments of some crisis, been willing to admit. And, while they certainly do not represent the whole of Paul's thought, perhaps not even the precise center, still if we ask about what is most characteristic of Paulinism, the answer must lie in this topic. On the other hand, this rejection of the law as legally binding within the Christian community by no means implies a rejection of the Jewish scriptures and traditions as revelatory. What it does mean is a *krisis*—a crisis and judgment—of that tradition at a particular point, but a point at which every human tradition, every "experience," every certainty, every ground of boasting, meets its *krisis*. The point, of course, is Paul's insistence that the crucifixion and resurrection of God's Messiah was the ultimate revelation in weakness of God's power. "Judaism" is utterly relativized: "Neither circumcision counts for anything, nor uncircumcision, but a new creation" (Gal. 6:15). Yet even as Judaism's ultimacy is undercut, its penultimate value and validity is affirmed (Rom. 9–11). The same is true of the whole "world"—of human community, of the state, of marriage, of sex, of money, of ascetic discipline, of wisdom, custom, reason, nature, and conscience (1 Cor. *passim!*)—and therefore also of "Christianity" itself, which cannot claim over against Judaism that *it* is the ultimate (1 Cor. 15:25; cf. Rom. 11 :11–36).

Did Paul see God's grace as the solution to man's troubled conscience? Not at all. Krister Stendahl's essay (above, pp. 422–34) on the introspective conscience has with splendid acerbity and clarity articulated a consensus that had been quietly forming for a generation: Paul was not a Lutheran pietist nor an American revivalist. Paul did not reduce the gospel to the forgiveness of sins, let alone to the assuaging of guilt feelings. If he had, it would have been nothing new in the Judaism of his youth; he needed no crucified Christ to obtain assurance of God's merciful response to the repentance of his covenanted people. (It is a measure of the extent to which the distortion of Paulinism has also distorted Christian apperception of Judaism that the teachings about repentance, forgiveness, and the love of God which appear throughout rabbinic sources were virtually unknown to most Christians until a generation ago). Neither did Paul use the law as a means of showing men's inability to obey and thus to evoke guilt and repentance for "conversion." There is no evidence that he used the law at all in his missionary preaching—that was the work rather of his opponents in Galatia and Corinth.

Could there be a consistent Pauline ethic? Here too it is true that Paulinism has been ferment rather than foundation. No one will ever succeed in constructing a systematic ethic on the basis of Paul's writings. Perhaps, indeed, Paul's chief value in the ethical realm lies precisely in showing up the dangers of systems. It is dangerous to generalize from Paul's immediate historic situation, his ad hoc admonitions, and his use of culturally conditioned moral catchwords; nevertheless we may risk stating a thesis that tries to sum up the direction of Paul's ethical concern.

There is a self-defeating tendency built into man's pursuit of his ultimate good. Even the most noble striving after ethical perfection contains the seeds of division—between group and group, man and man, and within the self. That this divisiveness may ordinarily be quite unrecognized does not diminish the objective plight of man against himself. Healing of the human fracture, or, to use language depending on a different kind of myth, becoming human finally cannot be accomplished by *more* striving, but only by receiving: by grace. Nietzsche correctly recognized in Paul, despite the latter's attack on the law, the enemy of the will to power. The aggressive willfulness of the Western moral tradition has always found Paul's doctrine of grace either embarrassing or incredible. Radical grace has seemed to require of man a response too passive, too feminine; Western man has been compulsively phallic in his morality, even in his asceticism. But in this metaphorical realm, too, Paul's Christianity is one in which "there is no more male and female." He is the activist who nevertheless knows that "you have nothing that you have not received." He uses the image of the inheritance which a son receives as pure gift, but also the metaphor of the athlete who strives unremittingly after "the prize."

Those who inquire after a Pauline ethic are generally asking at least two questions: (1) Does Paul's understanding of grace afford a *basis* for ethical motivation? (2) Does Paul provide viable *norms* by which to determine the sort of ethical action that is appropriate? In answer to the first, at least one thing can be said clearly: The basis for ethical motivation is God's love for man, which precedes and relativizes every "good" thing which man may be and do. The objection that has been raised endlessly through the history of Western thought, that this notion of grace removes the ultimate sanction for goodness by separating the threat of damnation and the promise of salvation from the framework of reward and punishment, depends upon a hopelessly superficial view of human motivation. Whatever else may be said about Paul's ethics, it is an ethics of response. Those modern moral theologians, such as H. Richard Niebuhr and Bernhard Häring, who have described ethical decision-making as response of the self to the prior action of God, within the community bound by conscious faith, sacrament, and tradition to that divine action, in and toward the world of God's making, may certainly claim St. Paul as their patron.

The question of norms, How can I know what I ought to do? is much less likely to receive a clear and helpful answer from Paul. One of the intriguing things about his responses to practical ethical dilemmas in his congregations is the diversity of norms and guides that he employs. He appeals to catechetical rules of thumb—some with a long history in popular Greek morality—to "nature"; to the practical harmony and "building up" of the congregation; to his own life-style, depicted as analogous to the death and resurrection of Christ; to a rather general notion of "freedom." But one thing he never does: he never uses "the law," either the Torah of Moses or any Hellenistic substitute for it, to lay down regulations for the Christian community. What stands behind every Pauline admonition—and they are many and manifold!—is the requirement that the Christian be "transformed by the renewal of your mind" in order to "test what is the will of God."

This does not mean that a Pauline ethic would be one of subjective individualism. That kind of "new morality" was already condemned by Paul in his correspondence with the Corinthians. The point becomes clearer if Paul is compared with those of his contemporaries whose ethics sound superficially most like his: the Roman Stoics. Both Paul and the Stoics recommend and practice essentially conventional behavior while in principle relativizing the whole ordinary basis for that behavior. Both demand a constant, practiced "testing" of the immediate situation, in order to discover what is the "fitting" response to the ultimate reality that is only indirectly visible in that situation. But for Paul that ultimate reality is not discovered by rational analysis of "what depends upon yourself" (Epictetus). Rather it is determined by the complex of symbols clustering around one central event, the crucifixion and resurrection of God's Messiah. And the significance of that event is not discerned in the sage's heroic detachment from all things not under his inner control, any more than it is found in the mystic's transport. Rather, it has to be learned within the life of the community formed by that event through memory, faith, and hope, a community which Paul will not permit to segregate itself from "the world." Therefore not the untroubled conscience but the free action of love is the hallmark of his ethics.

Not least among the things which we learn from the attempt to lay hold on the protean apostle is that earliest Christianity was itself a polymorphous movement, often taking shape only in the forge of conflict. In our present century, when the future of Christianity and its relationship to Western culture have become almost as uncertain and paradoxical as they were before Constantine, a more accurate understanding of that crucial and complex first period of expansion may provide useful insight into our own cultural flux. If so, the study of Paul and his context will have a central place. He embodies some elements which are peculiarly expressive of the Christian center: the dialectic character of his fundamental assertions; his waging of controversy for the sake of peace; his affirmation of the world in the name of what transcends and relativizes it; his speaking harsh truth for the sake of love; his exercise of severe discipline for the protection of freedom; his insistence that the power of God is experienced and transmitted only in weakness. One of his "peristasis-catalogues" could stand as the superscription over the history of the Christian movement at its best:

> But we have this treasure in earthen vessels, to show that the transcendent power belongs to God and not to us. We are afflicted in every way, but not crushed; perplexed, but not driven to despair; persecuted, but not forsaken; struck down, but not destroyed; always carrying in the body the death of Jesus, so that the life of Jesus may also be manifested in our bodies.
>
> (2 Cor. 4:7–10)

Selected Bibliography

This is intended as a working bibliography for undergraduate students. It is therefore very brief and limited to works in English, except for section I, which will guide the advanced student into a broader range of scholarly literature. Works which have been excerpted above are not included here. Titles available in paperback editions are starred.

I. BIBLIOGRAPHY AND REVIEW OF RESEARCH

Metzger, Bruce M., *Index to Periodical Literature on the Apostle Paul* (Grand Rapids, 1960). Articles through 1957.

Mattill, A. J., Jr., and M. B., *A Classified Bibliography of Literature on the Acts of the Apostles* (Grand Rapids, 1966), pp. 237- 57, 305–21. Books as well as periodical articles, through 1961.

*Schweitzer, Albert, *Paul and His Interpreters* (New York, 1964). Orginally published in 1911; traces Pauline studies from the seventeenth to the beginning of the twentieth centuries.

*Ellis, E. Earle, *Paul and His Recent Interpreters* (Grand Rapids, 1961). Limited selection of topics and scholars.

Rigaux, Beda, *The Letters of St. Paul: Modern Studies*, tr. by S. Yonick (Chicago, 1968). Excellent survey.

Bultmann, Rudolf, "Zur Geschichte der Paulus-Forschung," *Theologische Rundschau*, n.s. 1 (1929): 26–59; "Neueste Paulusforschung," *ibid.*, 6 (1934): 229–46, 8 (1936): 1–22.

Coppens, Joseph, "L'état présent des études paulinniennes," in *Ephemerides theologicae lovanienses* 32 (1956): 363–72.

Kepler, Thomas S. (ed.), *Contemporary Thinking About Paul, An Anthology* (Nashville, 1950). A useful collection representing scholarship between the World Wars.

II. LIFE AND CULTURAL SETTING

*Beare, Frank W., *St. Paul and His Letters* (Nashville, 1962, 1971).

*Bultmann, Rudolf, "Paul," in *Existence and Faith*, ed. Schubert M. Ogden (New York, 1960), pp. 111–46. A fine summary, originally for an encyclopedia.

Dibelius, Martin, *Paul*, ed. and completed by W. G. Kümmel (Philadelphia, 1953).

Hatch, W. H. P., "The History of the Early Church. II. The Life of Paul," *The Interpreter's Bible*, ed. G. A. Buttrick, *et al.* (Nashville, 1951), VII, 187–99.

Hunter, A. M., *Paul and His Predecessors* (London, rev. ed., 1961). On Paul's use of earlier Christian traditions.

Knox, John, *Chapters in a Life of Paul* (Nashville, 1950). A novel approach to the question of chronology and unconventional questions about Paul's ethical thought.

Knox, Wilfred L., *St. Paul and the Church of Jerusalem* (Cambridge, 1925) and *St. Paul and the Church of the Gentiles* (Cambridge, 1939). Dated, but containing a wealth of detailed observations and insight.

Nock, Arthur Darby, *St. Paul* (New York, 1939). Still valuable; a brief introduction by an outstanding student of Hellenistic religions.

Ramsey, Sir William M., *St. Paul the Traveller and the Roman Citizen* (London, 1895; numerous reprints). Obviously out of date at many points, but there has been no recent work of this scope.

*Sandmel, Samuel, *The Genius of Paul: A Study in History* (New York, 1958, 1970). From a Jewish perspective.

Unnik, W. C. van, *Tarsus or Jerusalem? The City of Paul's Youth* (London, 1962).

III. PAUL'S THOUGHT

Bornkamm, Günther, *Paul*, tr. by D. M. G. Stalker (New York, 1971).
*Bultmann, Rudolf, *Theology of the New Testament* (New York, 1951), I, 185–352. Perhaps the outstanding study of Paul's theology in last generation; dominated by Bultmann's consistent existential interpretation.
Cerfaux, Lucien, *Christ in the Theology of St. Paul* (New York, 1959) and *The Church in the Theology of St. Paul* (New York, 1959).
*Fitzmyer, Joseph A., S.J., *Pauline Theology: A Brief Sketch* (Englewood Cliffs, N.J., 1967). Also part of the *Jerome Bible Commentary*.
Fridrichsen, Anton J., *The Apostle and His Message* (Uppsala, 1947).
Munck, Johannes, *Paul and the Salvation of Mankind* (London, 1959, Richmond, Va., 1960). In opposition to Bultmann and his school; from the perspective of "salvation-history."
Whiteley, D. E. H., *The Theology of St. Paul* (Philadelphia, 1964).

IV. RELATION TO JUDAISM

Baeck, Leo, "The Faith of Paul," in *Judaism and Christianity* (Philadelphia, 1960), pp. 139–68. A much more positive assessment of Paul than in Baeck's "Romantic Religion" excerpted above.
*Davies, W. D., *Paul and Rabbinic Judaism* (London, 1948, 1965). A very detailed attempt to explain Paul's thought from parallels in rabbinic literature.
Ellis, E. Earle, *Paul's Use of the Old Testament* (Edinburgh and Grand Rapids, 1957).
Klausner, Joseph, *From Jesus to Paul* (London, 1944).
Montefiore, Claude, *Judaism and St. Paul* (London, 1914).
Sandmel, Samuel (see above under II.)

V. ETHICS

*Enslin, Morton S., *The Ethics of Paul* (New York, 1930; Nashville, 1962).
Furnish, Victor Paul, *Theology and Ethics in Paul* (Nashville, 1968).
Schnackenburg, Rudolf, *The Moral Teaching of the New Testament* (Freiburg, London, New York, 1964), pp. 261–306.

VI. STYLE, LANGUAGE, AND FORM OF THE LETTERS

Dibelius, Martin, *A Fresh Approach to the New Testament and Early Christian Literature* (New York, 1936), pp. 137–85, 217–34.
Funk, Robert W., *Language, Hermeneutic, and Word of God* (New York, 1966), pp. 224–74. An important review of research on Pauline style.
Schubert, Paul, *Form and Function of the Pauline Thanksgivings* (Berlin, 1939). A classic analysis of style; technical. For a more general review of the field, see his "Form and Function of the Pauline Letters," *The Journal of Religion* 19 (1939): 365–77.

VII. INDIVIDUAL LETTERS

Good commentaries in English are rare. Probably the most generally reliable of the recent series are *The Harper's* (in England: *Black's*) *New Testament Commentaries*. On a smaller scale, the *Jerome Bible Commentary* maintains a high standard of scholarship. The *New International Commentary* presents detailed comment from a conservative Protestant perspective. Of older series, the *Interpreter's Bible*, the *Moffatt New Testament Commentary*, and the very technical *International Critical Commentary* are often useful. The new *Hermeneia* series (Philadelphia, 1971 ff.) promises to be particularly fine.

An "Introduction to the New Testament" is an indispensable reference tool. Good ones are in print by several authors, including: Paul Feine—Johannes Behm–W. G. Kümmel (Nashville, 1966); *Alfred Wikenhauser (New York, 1963); A. Robert and A. Feuillet (New York, 1965). The shorter, more theological introduction by Willi Marxsen (Philadelphia and Oxford, 1968) is also useful.

VIII. INFLUENCE AND EARLY INTERPRETATION

Barnett, A. E., *Paul Becomes a Literary Influence* (Chicago, 1941).
Barth, Markus, "The Challenge of the Apostle Paul," in *Journal of Ecumenical Studies* 1 (1964): 58–81.
Chadwick, Henry, *The Enigma of Paul* (London, 1969).
Lake, Kirsopp, *Paul: His Heritage and His Legacy* (New York and Oxford, 1934).

Index